Networking Windows NT 4.0

Workstation and Server

John D. Ruley

David Methvin

Tom Henderson

Martin Heller

WILEY COMPUTER PUBLISHING

John Wiley & Sons, Inc.

New York • Chichester • Weinheim • Brisbane • Singapore • Toronto

This book is dedicated to the authors' fathers:
David D. Dix, Arthur H. Germain, Jr., William T. Hall, Aaron Heller, Richard L. Henderson, Arthur G. Methvin, Charles B. Powell, Arnold Sloman, and, *MSgt. Joseph A. Ruley, USAF (R.I.P.).*

Executive Publisher: Katherine Schowalter
Editor: Marjorie Spencer
Managing Editor: Brian Snapp
Text Design & Composition: Benchmark Productions, Inc.

Designations used by companies to distinguish their products are often claimed as trademarks. In all instances where John Wiley & Sons, Inc., is aware of a claim, the product names appear in initial capital or ALL CAPITAL LETTERS. Readers, however, should contact the appropriate companies for more complete information regarding trademarks and registration.

This text is printed on acid-free paper.

This publication is designed to provide accurate and authoritative information in regard to the subject matter covered. It is sold with the understanding that the publisher is not engaged in rendering legal, accounting, or other professional service. If legal advice or other expert assistance is required, the services of a competent professional person should be sought.

Library of Congress Cataloging-in-Publication Data:
Ruley, John D., 1958-
  Networking Windows NT 4.0 : Workstation and Server / John D. Ruley
[with] Martin Heller, David Methvin, Thomas Henderson.
    p. cm.
  Rev. ed. of: Networking Windows NT 3.51. 2nd ed. c1995.
  Includes bibliographical references.
  ISBN 0-471-17502-1 (paper : alk. paper)
  1. Operating systems (Computers)   2. Microsoft Windows NT.
3. Computer networks.   I. Ruley, John D., 1958-   Networking
Windows NT 3.51.   II. Title.
QA76.76.063R853   1996
005.4'4769--dc21   96-46445
                                                        CIP

Printed in the United States of America
10 9 8 7 6 5 4 3 2 1

Contents

Acknowledgments

Any project of this magnitude involves the assistance of many people—and this book is no exception. While we can't hope to create an all-inclusive list, these are some of the people who contributed. We hope that those who don't find their names here won't be too offended—there were so many that it's hard to remember them all. But some we managed not to forget include:

Mike Abrash, Sheila Ambrose, Bob Aronds, Kate Bolton, M.D. (now Mrs. John D. Ruley), Tammy Boyd, Diane Cerra, Rick Furnival, Jean Goddin, Doug Hamilton, Dave Hart, Lee Hart, Johnny Haskins, Phil Holden, Erin Holland, Jake Kirchner, Tom Johnston, Catherine Merten, Liz Misch, Mike Nash, Carole Parrot-Joppe, Matt Ragen, Ruth Rizzuto, Blanche M. Ruley (R.I.P.), Brad Silverberg, Linda Stephenson, Brad Swigert, David Thacher, Jerry Wilkinson, Doug Wills, Stephen Wolf.

Special thanks to: Fred Langa, vice president and editorial director, CMP Media; and Mike Elgan, editor of *WINDOWS Magazine*—who made *WINDOWS* lab resources available for us to use while working on all three editions this book, and to Scott Wolf, vice president and group publisher, and Claire O'Hare, *WINDOWS Magazine*'s publisher. Many thanks also to the folks at John Wiley & Sons, including: Marjorie Spencer, our editor; Margaret Hendrey, Marjorie's assistant; Frank Grazioli and Brian Snapp, who managed the book's production and put in long hours matching up copy edits and author input.

Very special thanks to Katherine Schowalter, our executive publisher at John Wiley & Sons, who supported us when a matter of editorial controversy arose with Microsoft. It's good to know we're backed by people who believe in (and live by) freedom of the press!

We all want to thank our families for putting up with the time we spent bringing this project together—lots of late nights writing. Finally, we want to acknowledge the entire Windows NT development team, especially Dave Cutler, Lou Perazzoli, Mark Lucovsky and others who must remain nameless. You've given us so much to write about!

About the Authors

Martin Heller, Ph.D. is the author of several best-selling books on Windows programming and writes the Programming Windows column for *WINDOWS Magazine*. Martin is responsible for Appendix 1, which tells programmers all they need to know to write network-aware Windows NT programs.

Tom Henderson is vice president of engineering for Unitel, Inc., and is director of its subsidiary, Beach Labs. Tom, who is the Enterprise Administrator columnist for *Windows Magazine*, is a prolific writer with more than 500 magazine articles and seven books to his credit. In the third edition of *Networking Windows NT 4.0*, Tom assumed primary responsibility for Chapter 10 (on Netware), and helped rewrite Chapter 8 (on enterprise networking).

David Methvin is an Executive Editor at *WINDOWS Magazine*. Dave's been an editor at *PC Tech Journal* and at *PC Week*, and has installed several large networks as a consultant. In this edition, Dave was responsible for Chapters 7 (NT and the Internet) and 9 (Microsoft connectivity), and Appendix 3 (legacy support).

John Ruley is senior technology editor and Windows NT columnist at *WINDOWS Magazine*. John is principal author of *Networking Windows NT*—which, among other things, means that he's ultimately responsible for the technical accuracy of this book, and assumes the blame for any and all errors, omissions and goof-ups. Aside from overall supervision and editing in this edition John wrote Chapters 1–6, 11 and 12, and Appendices 2 and 4–6. He also co-wrote Chapter 8.

Dave Dix, Arthur Germain, Eric Hall, Jim Powell and Jeff Sloman—all of whom helped write earlier editions—weren't involved with this one. We missed them.

Preface

A funny thing happened on the way to writing the third edition of *Networking Windows NT 4.0*—the Web arrived, and in a big way.

In our first and second editions, we covered the TCP/IP protocol quite extensively (and still do—in Chapter 6), but the Internet was mentioned only in passing, and we made few (if any) references to HTTP:, the Web, or URLs.

As the old saying goes, the times they are a-changing. In the last 18 months use of the Web has exploded, and Microsoft has jumped into the resulting new market with both feet. You can see the results in our completely new Chapter 7, and in extensive references to internet resources in all chapters. NT is now *really* Internet-ready, and so are we!

Aside from the Internet, you'll find that we've updated every chapter and appendix in the book to bring them up to date for NT 4.0. That includes the artwork—most of which had to be completely redone, as NT 4.0 sports a new (Windows 95 style) look. Similarly, all of our step-by-step instructions have been updated to account for changes in the way NT 4.0 operates, and we've added extensive material on new NT 4.0 features on each Chapter.

Connections

Advanced PCs and workstations are rarely used alone. They're nearly always *connected* to a server, a mainframe host, or other workstations. So the *connections* between Windows NT systems and the outside world is the theme of this book.

Networking Windows NT is organized as 12 chapters and six appendices. We have attempted to make each chapter stand alone. Feel free to browse through the book and pick an interesting topic with confidence that it will be completely exposed in the chapter you are reading. You may find, if you start in the middle of the book, that you'll wish you'd read some of the earlier chapters. But we will refer you in the right direction and you can always make use of the index, which we have attempted to make as comprehensive as possible.

While Networking Windows NT is designed for browsing, it's also possible to lay out an ordered study program that may be useful to particular individuals. Some suggestions follow.

Those unfamiliar with either Windows NT or networking, should start at the beginning and read Chapters 1 through 4. Pick one of Chapters 6, 9, 10, or 11—as appropriate—if (like most people) you're going to work in an environment that has more than just Windows NT machines. For example, if you are in a Netware environment, read Chapter 10. If you are in a TCP/IP environment, read Chapter 6. Look through Appendices 3 and 4, and read Chapters 8 and 12. If you're interested in the Internet (and who isn't these days?) read Chapter 7, too.

If you are familiar with Windows NT but not with networks, then skim Chapter 1, skip to Chapter 3, and read Appendix 4. Again, pick from Chapters 6, 9, 10 and 11 as appropriate (but definitely read Chapter 6 and Chapter 8 if you're going to work in an enterprise environment). Finally, read Chapter 12 and any of the Appendix material that appears to be useful. As above, add Chapter 7 for Internet coverage.

If you are a support professional, you'll want to read all of the above *and* Chapters 2 and 5.

If you are familiar with networks in a Netware or TCP/IP environment, but not familiar with Windows NT, then read Chapters 1 through 4, 7 and 8, Appendix 3, and pick from Chapters 6, 9, 10 and 11 as appropriate. Skim Chapter 12 (or read it if you like). Again, if you're a support professional, read Chapters 2 and 5 as well.

Programmers should read Chapters 1, 7, and 11, then Appendix 1. Refer back to appropriate chapters when you run into a concept that doesn't seem to make sense. Just go to the index, look up the desired entry, turn to its corresponding page, and read all about it.

Management Information Systems people and decision makers—those trying to decide where Windows NT fits into a heterogeneous network environment—should read Chapters 1, 3, 6, 7, and 8, then pick from 9, 10, or 11 to match the particular system you have (you may need to read them all if you run a complex network). You should then read Chapter 12 and Appendix 5. That's a pretty comprehensive set, so if you're in a hurry, a short form that may be useful is to read Chapters 1, 3, 7, 8, and 12, and refer to other information as necessary.

Getting the Most from Networking Windows NT 4.0

Direct your attention particularly to the "After reading this chapter you should understand..." section at the beginning of each chapter. We've included this specifically to help you decide whether a particular chapter is interesting enough to invest your time reading and to help you get the most out of the chapter. We encourage you to read the statement, read the chapter, go back and read the statement again, and as you go through the bullet-points, and if you see something that you don't remember or don't understand, you should probably look through that part of the chapter again.

We've also included a "For More Information" section at the end of each chapter. This section includes reference materials—magazine articles, books, etc. If you find that a particular topic has not been covered sufficiently, take a look through the list at the end of the chapter, and see if one of the other references covers the material you're looking for. We've included a comprehensive index and we encourage everyone to use it. In the third edition, we've made extensive use of Internet references (mainly Web URLs) which you will find in chapter text, footnotes, and/or at the end of a chapter.

Finally, we encourage everyone who reads this book to experiment yourself. By that we mean to apply what you've learned in a real environment. We realize that many people are likely to read this book for information without having access to a Windows NT system, and that's fine. It's our fondest hope that the book will be helpful to people in that situation who need to make decisions about what equipment to purchase, what version of the system to purchase, or whether Windows NT fits their situation at all.

We've also designed this book to be a useful reference for people who are doing real-world work on Windows NT networks. If you fit that description, we cannot emphasize enough that all the fine writing we can do—all the graphs and charts we can design—all the further reference reading we recommend to you can't do as good a job as the learning reinforcement that comes by actually getting your hands dirty and trying things out for yourself. Many people are uncomfortable experimenting with networked computers (especially servers). That's unfortunate because networked computers are not fundamentally much more difficult to deal with than individual PCs. If you're expecting to maintain a Windows NT system and fix it when something goes wrong, you'd better get some experience manipulating it when it is working correctly!

We can't emphasize this enough: *Get out on the net, and try things yourself!* That's the best way to learn.

The Chapters Networking Windows NT is organized as a set of more or less independent chapters, each of which attempts to cover a particular topic in some depth.

Chapter 1, *An Operating System Designed to Connect,* is an overall introduction to Windows NT and to basic networking concepts. It includes a detailed discussion of the differences between a Windows NT Workstation and a Server (in this edition, including Microsoft's new *ten inbound connection license limitation on NT Workstation*), as well as concepts like portability, scalability, virtual memory, network redirection, and administrative domains.

Chapter 2, *Preparing to Connect,* covers installation and set-up of Windows NT systems, including both Workstations and Servers. It includes a discussion of how to conduct a *network needs analysis* for your organization, how to select the right hardware for your Windows NT system, and all three Windows NT installation mechanisms: CD-ROM, over-the-network, and unattended. Troubleshooting information guides you in solving problems as they arise. This chapter has been completely revised to track Microsoft's revision to NT setup.

Chapter 3, *Administrative Connections,* covers Windows NT administration issues for LANs. It includes the duties of the *network administrator*, the tools used for NT net administration (in this edition, including the new NT 4.0 *policy editor* and administrative aspects of the NT 4.0 desktop, in addition to familiar tools like User Manager, Disk Administrator, Performance Monitor, Backup, Event Viewer, the NET command-line interface, and batch files), covers user profiles and log-in scripts, and discusses in detail the differences between Windows NT *workgroups* and Windows NT Server *domains.*

Chapter 4, *Using NT Networking Features*—completely revised in the third edition to take into account NT 4.0's new *Windows Explorer* desktop—covers the use of Windows NT's built-in networking features; including shared file access, shared printer access, shared clipboards, and network utilities. It also provides an introduction to the command-line NET interface that can be used to write batch files in Windows NT.

Chapter 5, *Keeping Connected,* remains one of *Networking Windows NT 4.0*'s strongest chapters. In addition to detailed coverage of NT maintenance and troubleshooting tools—including Performance Monitor, Event Viewer, the configuration Registry Editor, NT Diagnostics, and (new for NT 4.0) Network Monitor (which we fondly think of as *NT Server's wire-tap*), we have many pages of troubleshooting information in this chapter. (These pages are shaded for easy reference.) We also cover how to get technical support.

Chapter 6, *Connecting to the World with TCP/IP*, covers NT support for Internet-standard TCP/IP as a routable protocol for Windows NT on LANs, WANs, and the Internet itself. It's an essential precursor to Chapters 7 and 8. Windows NT's built-in TCP/IP utilities and TCP/IP routing capability are also discussed in detail.

Chapter 7, *NT and the Internet,* is completely new for the third edition. It covers the new Internet Information Server (IIS) included with NT Server 4.0, and its close cousin, Peer Web Server (PWS) included with NT Workstation 4.0. IIS/PWS features including Web, FTP, and Gopher servers are covered in detail, as are related topics, including how to get connected to the Internet, and Internet security. This chapter includes extensive references (mainly Web URLs) to related information and add-on products from Microsoft and third parties.

Chapter 8, *Enterprise Connections,* covers enterprise-wide network issues, including Windows NT Server domain administration, wide-area networking (including both Microsoft's *Remote Access Services*—and the new *Dial-Up Networking* interface for NT 4.0—as well as third-party alternatives), electronic mail (including detailed instructions for upgrading the *workgroup-level* Windows Messaging bundled with NT 4.0 to Microsoft's Exchange Server for multi-postoffice connectivity), WANs, Macintosh support, and enterprise management (including coverage of Microsoft's Systems Management Server and third-party products).

Chapter 9, *Microsoft Connections,* covers interoperability with LAN Manager, Window for Workgroups, Windows 95, and other networks based on the Server Message Block (SMB) protocol used by Microsoft. Detailed instructions are included for upgrading LAN Manager networks to Windows NT Server, as are instructions on interoperating in mixed LAN Manager/NT/Windows for Workgroups/Windows 95 environments.

Chapter 10, *Novell Connections: Windows NT and NetWare,* covers interoperation with Novell Netware, including Novell's Netware Client for Windows NT, Microsoft's NWLink protocol and NetWare related services including CSNW, GSNW, FPNW and DSMN, Novell's netware client and services for NT, and the "back door" NFS/FTP method of NetWare access pioneered at *WINDOWS Magazine*. Updates for the third edition include NetWare 4.0 NDS support using both Microsoft and Novell components.

Chapter 11, *Other Connections*, covers using Windows NT with other networks, including IBM LAN Server/Warp Server and Systems Network Architecture, UNIX NFS and X/Windows, DEC Pathworks, and Banyan VINES.

Chapter 12, *Client Server, Distributed Computing, and the Future of Windows NT,* discusses client/server issues, including the use of Windows NT as a *network application server,* distributed processing, and explores the future of network computing and how Windows NT fits into it. For the third edition, we have completely revised this chapter to bring it up to date, covering Microsoft's approach to using Client-Server computing on the Internet and providing a preview of Cairo's underlying services (including DCOM, OLE-DS and DFS).

Appendices Appendix 1 is a succinct and yet (we seriously hope), complete introduction to the network application programming interfaces (APIs) of Windows NT. For the third edition, it's been revised to add new APIs (many Internet-related).We hope that this appendix, used in conjunction with the rest of this book, will serve as a good introduction and give a programmer some idea of where to begin.

Appendix 2 covers drivers, low-level protocols, and other definitional issues that cause a great deal of confusion, even among those experienced with networking.

Appendix 3 covers compatibility issues. Windows NT is capable not only of running Win32 programs designed for it, but also Windows 3.x programs, OS/2 1.x programs, and many DOS programs as well as POSIX programs. This appendix discusses the issues involving compatibility for each of these systems, gives some guidance on what will and will not work, and (specifically in the case of DOS and OS/2) describes how to customize the various subsystems to your best advantage. It has been completely revised to bring it up to date for NT 4.0.

Appendix 4 covers the Windows NT Resource Kits.

Appendix 5 covers the new classes of systems on which Windows NT runs. Unique among modern desktop operating systems, Windows NT was designed to be platform independent, and it is capable of exploiting very radically different processor designs. We discuss the DEC Alpha, MIPS R4xxx, and Motorola Power-PC 6xx RISC CPUs, as well as machines constructed using symmetric multiprocessor (SMP) architectures. Among other things, we discuss how to tell whether using such an architecture is justified, given the power available in high-end single processor systems using Intel's Pentium and Pentium Pro processors.

Appendix 6 covers the theory behind preventative maintenance, which is the foundation for the maintenance and troubleshooting information we provide in Chapter 5. Unique among all the other chapters and appendices, it has not been revised since Chapter 1 (an oldie but a goodie!)

Late-breaking Developments

As with the first and second editions, writing a book on such a broad (and rapidly changing) topic turned out to be a real challenge. Every chapter required major updating, and as always, we've found it difficult to keep our coverage ahead of the NT development team.

Those coming to this book from the first and second editions will find changes throughout the text—as described above. Even with all that work, we're still struggling to keep pace with the drastic rate at which this topic changes. Since the manuscript went to press, Microsoft has:

- released a single-volume NT Workstation 4.0 Resource Kit *that includes low-level file system tools*, and a three-volume NT Server 4.0 Resource Kit,

- delivered the first NT 4.0 Service Pack (and reliable sources tell us more than one is coming), featuring, among other things, fax support for NT Workstation (and Server), and IIS 3.0 (for NT Server). The latter features support for embedding scripts (using Visual Basic, Java, Perl or REXX) *directly into web pages*. IIS 4.0 (code-named *K2*) is rumored to be on the way as well,

- introduced a new series of Internet products, code-named *Normandy*, including News (NNTP), Chat (IRC), Mail (SMTP/POP3), Personalization, Membership, and Merchandising servers. Think of Normandy as "shrink-wrapping MSN (or CompuServe)" and you'll get the idea,

- previewed NT 5.0 (*Cairo*) features, including Kerberos security, a true hierarchical directory, and distributed file systems,

- previewed *Active Server Frameworks*, a technology that may simplify the development of true distributed enterprise client-server applications by at least an order of magnitude, and

- terminated development of new versions of NT for the Mips R4x00 RISC architecture.

Keeping up with these developments is a full-time job, but *don't panic*! We've come up with a way to help you stay informed.

Electronic Update to
Networking Windows NT

In the second edition, we introduced the idea of an *Electronic Updates to Networking Windows NT*—at the time, this was a simple text file you could download from several popular information services. That idea worked well, but we're going one better: for this book, our electronic update is a Web page: http://www.winmag.com/netnt.

We will update the information on that site periodically as developments warrant, and we expect the first update to be posted by the time you read this.

Foreword

to the First Edition

Today's network professionals deal with change every working day. Corporate mainframe applications of the seventies are being *downsized* to local area network (LAN)-based client/server application suites, while departmental single-user PC applications of the eighties are *upsized* into multiuser online solutions. As a result, the simple local area networks of yesterday are rapidly becoming business-critical, enterprise-wide, *electronic highways.* Can this rapid evolution in information systems technology succeed? Can the distributed client/server networks of today provide the same level of reliability that yesterday's centralized mainframe systems delivered? Ultimately, will this next generation of computing systems improve our own personal productivity—and thus make a *real* contribution to your company's bottom line?

Microsoft clearly feels that the answer to all three of these questions is *yes*—and with the release of their most complex operating system to date, Windows NT, they've bet their corporate future on delivering this promise. For you and me, as networking professionals, this means we will soon be asked (or in my case, have already been asked) to take the client/server *promises* of Windows NT and create a business *reality.* That's no small challenge, considering the complexity of today's enterprise networks and the mission-critical, moment-by-moment role they play in today's corporate world.

Are you nervous? Take heart: In *Networking Windows NT* you will find something no business-critical network of today can afford to be without, a business-critical *attitude.* It's an attitude that comes from years of experience in dealing with the day-to-day issues involved in the support of business-critical information systems. With the publication of this book, John Ruley and his associates at *WINDOWS Magazine* and *Network Computing* have done something I find unique: They've truly understood what George Santayana meant in 1905, when he wrote:

"Progress, far from consisting in change, depends on retentiveness... Those who cannot remember the past are condemned to repeat it."[1]

This is not just another book describing the marvels contained within the first operating system that doesn't treat the network as an add-on. *Networking Windows NT* shows you how to not only make it work but *keep it working*, day-in, day-out, and month-after-month. The book covers the full spectrum of what you need to know—and do—as we move from the host-centric world of raw data to the information-centric world of distributed objects.

Networking Windows NT takes you step by step from simple NT-based LANs all the way to optimized enterprise-wide electronic networks that communicate with everyone and everything. First it covers the fundamentals of an operating system designed around the client/server model (Chapter 1, "An Operating System Designed to Connect"), then what you will need to do today (Chapter 2, "Preparing to Connect"), what you will need to do tomorrow (Chapter 3, "Administrative Connections"),and what you will need to do to link your back-end, the server, to your front-end, your clients (Chapter 4, "Using NT Networking Features").

---

1   *Life of Reason*, Volume 1, Chapter 10.3

Now the fun really begins; keeping your Windows NT network running so smoothly and flawlessly that you'll reach that loftiest goal of any networking professional, managing the network *invisibly*. Chapter 5 ("Keeping Connected") along with its associated appendix (Appendix 6: "Maintenance Theory") were my two favorite sections. Within this chapter and appendix you will learn now to *proactively* put the sophisticated administrative tools included with Windows NT to work—not only keeping your network at its peak of performance but also ensuring that you get *mission-critical* reliability. I've used this information myself at Chevron Canada's data center—and I can assure you the advice given is *well* worthwhile.

The hard lessons learned during the days of the mainframes and minicomputers are retold in the context of Windows NT. The advice is fundamental and pragmatic, something one would expect when learning about troubleshooting computer systems. Appendix 6 also explains *precisely* why following a program of preventative maintenance is so important. Yet, like the rest of the book, it has been written with a humorous style that delivers a refreshing feeling of confidence and long-term optimism. It's obvious that the authors really enjoy what they're writing about, and you will find this grain of enthusiasm throughout the book. Where else would you find the Configuration Registry included with Windows NT compared to a nuclear reactor?

As your Windows NT Advanced Server network grows it will expand beyond the comfortable confines of your data center. In Chapter 7 (*Enterprise Connections*) you'll find information on file replication, Wide Area Networking and remote network access. No doubt you will also start bumping into different operating environments such as the world of UNIX (Chapter 6, "UNIX Connections"), other network operating systems such as NetWare (Chapter 9, "Novell Connections"), and a veritable host of hosts, the legacy systems (Chapter 10, "Other Connections").

Finally, what about the future (Chapter 11, "Connecting to the Future")? Some feel we are about to enter the true second generation of information systems—an electronic environment that creates a fully distributed world of objects and (as a result) blurs the lines between information and the systems that process it. An environment that delivers something more than just raw data or static information, tomorrow's distributed systems will deliver real-time *knowledge* to the new tenants at the top of the information systems model: you and me. The final chapter of Networking Windows NT examines the precursors of this next generation of operating systems, both already in alpha form, *Chicago* (Windows 4.0) and *Cairo* (Windows NT 4.0). As we approach the twenty-first century, what you and I do today as networking professionals will be a cornerstone of this technological revolution. *We* are the *invisible facilitators of change* in today's businesses—and I honestly believe that what we do today and tomorrow can make a valuable and essential contribution to the quality of life on this planet.

It's something worth doing well.

—*Doug Farmer*
Lead—Network Operations
Chevron Canada Ltd.
Vancouver, BC
November 1993

Foreword

to the Third Edition

Everyone's heard of Windows NT, but few can claim to know it as well as John Ruley, or as well as you'll know it when you finish this book. Here's why:

John has tracked NT since it was an Alpha prototype back in 1991. Originally designed as the follow-up to OS/2 (then still a joint project of IBM and Microsoft), the early OS/2 contained some core elements that carry over into today's matured product.

Over the years, John has followed NT's evolution every step of the way. He's written about NT extensively in *WINDOWS Magazine* columns, sections, features and reviews, and (of course) in the very successful first edition of this book, published in 1994. In *all* his work, John brings you a deep insider's knowledge of not just how things work, but why, and what it means in the real world.

That last part is key. As you'll see when you read this book, John's knowledge isn't merely theoretical or simply based on what others have told him. John lives with NT every day. He's run it for years as the primary OS on his servers, workstations, and even on his portables. John has more hands-on experience running NT in a variety of settings than almost anyone else I know outside of Microsoft. But unlike a Microsoft employee, John is independent and calls his own shots. He has no NT axe to grind and no NT agenda to support. He knows what NT can do, but also what it can't do. He knows what's good about NT, and what's not so good. He knows the strengths, but he's also had to learn ways around the weaknesses.

The distillation of that experience is in your hands. In a dozen tightly focused, wonderfully rich chapters, John will walk you through NT from top to bottom. Starting with an excellent overview of what NT is and what makes it tick (Chapter 1), John will guide you through the process of getting ready to install your new OS (Chapter 2), setting up and managing NT's system administration features (Chapter 3), and understanding NT's networking features (Chapter 4).

Many books stop there, but John's real-life experience means you can dig much deeper. Chapter 5 shows you how to unlock the full potential of NT through performance tuning, registry maintenance, and other system-level tweaking. Chapters 6, 7, and 8 explore NT's native strengths with TCP/IP, lingua franca of intranets and the Internet, and goes into fresh, full detail on how and where NT can fit into the World Wide Web and its private corporate cousins, intranets. (This is one of the most heavily updated sections of the book, with *tons* of new information added since the first version.)

Chapters 9 and 10 complement each other with a full exploration of how NT interoperates with Microsoft and Novell-based networks. And while that by itself covers a huge slice of the networking pie, Chapter 11 discusses all the other major players—UNIX, IBM, Digital, Banyan, and even Lantastic. No matter what you're trying to connect NT to, or to NT, *this book will help.*

Finally, Chapter 12 looks ahead to what's next in NT evolution—including Cairo—so you won't be caught short by unexpected developments. Finally, a beefy series of six appendices rounds out this extraordinarily complete package.

Whether you're looking for some specific piece of NT information to help solve an immediate problem, or you're looking for comprehensive coverage of the entire topic of networking Windows NT, you'll find it right in your hands, in practical, readable, hype-free form.

When you've finished the book, you can join John online for a free (and free-ranging!) discussion of the topics you'll find here. I'm very pleased to tell you that the *Windows Magazine* Web site is the official host of the this book's Web site: come visit http://www.winmag.com/netnt/.

—Fred Langa

VP/Editorial Director

Windows Magazine/CMP PC Group

An Operating System Designed to Connect

Windows NT Networking: A Technical Overview

After reading this chapter, you will understand the basic features of Windows NT 4.0, especially those related to networking. You will also understand the basic concepts to be used in the rest of the book, including:

- Core operating system concepts, including the microkernel, client/server architecture, portability, object model, layered device drivers, and installable file systems
- Networks and network-related features, including network redirectors
- Key differences between Windows NT Workstation, which is suitable for use as a network client, and Windows NT Server
- The critical relationship between NT Server and the Internet
- Deciding between NT Server client-access licensing and concurrent connection licensing

Windows NT 4.0 is a whole new ball game in several respects, not least because it shares an updated user interface with Windows 95. Although the basic networking features of the operating system have not changed much—with the exception of Internet-related features (so extensive in the third edition that we've devoted an all-new Chapter 7 to them)—quite a few new features have been added. Among them are a new, more capable form of remote network access (the client component of which is now called Dial Up Networking, as in Windows 95), a new Netware 4.*x*-compatible redirector that supports Novell Directory Service[1] (NDS) trees and NetWare log-in scripts, Microsoft's Internet Explorer 2.0 multimedia-enhanced Web browser, the long-overdue "Exchange" e-mail client, hardware profile support (which allows laptop users to have at-home and on-the-road boot configurations with different video display and network settings), and enhanced metafile-based printer spooling (which improves response at the client by farming most of the rendering out to the print server).

Also new for NT 4.0 are a Windows 95-compatible System Policy editor, Network OLE (now called Distributed COM), and DirectX I/O support that lets NT users run Windows 95-compatible multimedia and game software. NT Server 4.0 also gains the Multi-Protocol Router (MPR) feature introduced with Service Pack[2] 2 for NT Server 3.51. New administration tools in NT Server 4.0 include Administrative Wizards, an enhanced Windows NT Diagnostics tool, and Network Monitor (a software "sniffer" previously provided only with Microsoft's Systems Management Server). The old User Profile Editor from NT Server 3.*x* is replaced by a new System Policy Editor that's compatible with both NT and Windows 95 and a Web-based administration tool that makes the features of the NT administrative tools suite available through any Web browser (a secure one, we hope!)

NT Server 4.0 continues to provide all the major features of NT Server 3.51, including in-the-box native support for Microsoft's legacy NetBEUI protocol, NetWare-compatible IPX, and Internet-standard TCP/IP; basic file and printer

1   Formerly NetWare Directory Service—perhaps the name change portends an attempt by Novell to support NDS on more than NetWare?

2   Microsoft uses Service Packs as a way to distribute bug fixes and minor upgrades between full revisions of the operating system. NT 3.51 went through no fewer than four of these before NT 4.0 was introduced. As the third edition went to press, rumor had it that the first NT 4.0 service pack would be out by the end of 1996. Information on the latest service pack may be found at http://www.microsoft.com/support. Pick Windows NT from the GO! List and search the resulting page for the words Service Pack.

sharing are standard, as are NetWare gateway support, remote access support for up to 256 simultaneous users (provided that sufficient hardware and licenses are available), multi-domain administration, directory replication, support for DOS, Windows 3.*x*, Windows 95, NT Workstation, OS/2 and Macintosh clients, on-the-fly IP address allocation using DHCP, and on-the-fly Internet name assignment using WINS.

Irrespective of the version, Windows NT is uniquely well suited to a wide variety of networking applications. To understand why, we must examine a number of features of the basic operating system design. The first and most pervasive of these is Windows NT's *client/server* architecture.

Scalability and the Client/Server Architecture

"Windows NT is not a microkernel operating system ... it's more accurate to call NT a client/server operating system."—David Cutler, Windows NT Professional Developer's Conference, Seattle 1995.

In the first edition of this book, we called this section "Scalability and the Microkernel Architecture" because the available references made much of NT's use of a microkernel design. Since then it's become clear that NT isn't a pure[3] microkernel operating system (though it *does* employ a microkernel internally—read on), so we've changed the section head, and the text that follows, to reflect how NT has developed.

Conventional PC operating systems like DOS, Novell NetWare version 3.*x*,[4] and Microsoft's new Windows 95 are not *secure, scalable,* or *portable*. That is, they can all be hacked with fairly easily, they cannot exploit more than one central processing unit (CPU), and they cannot be executed natively on RISC processors. These limitations make such operating systems suitable only for small-scale (single-user desktop, departmental LAN) operations.

Windows NT was designed to eliminate these limits. To this end, it employs a client/server architecture, in which no application program is permitted direct access to the hardware or to protected portions of the operating system. All such access is mediated by the NT *Executive,*which performs the requested access on the application's behalf.

---

3 In a pure microkernel operating system, like Carnegie-Mellon's Mach, only the microkernel itself operates in privileged (ring 0) mode. The rest of the operating system and applications operate at ring 3. Windows NT modifies this model by placing device drivers and privileged subsystems (i.e., most of the operating system code) at ring 0, which improves performance. Applications, however, still run at ring 3. Perhaps it would be most fair to call NT a "modified microkernel design."

4 NetWare 4.1 is in many respects comparable to Windows NT Server.

All operating systems have a *kernel,* which is the minimum set of functions that must be kept in memory. In the DOS operating system, the kernel consists largely of the basic input/output system (BIOS[5]), the basic disk operating system (BDOS[6]), and a number of essential glue functions that bring these pieces together. The other parts of DOS, which are not necessary all the time, are stored on disk and loaded into memory only when needed. As illustrated in Figure 1.1, when you type DIR on a DOS machine, you're actually employing an external component: the COMMAND.COM file typically found in the root of the C drive. COMMAND.COM provides DOS with its user interface. It monitors the keyboard, looking for certain combinations of characters—of which DIR is one—interprets this as a request for a directory, and issues the necessary BIOS commands to retrieve the directory information. Another set of BIOS commands is then called to display the directory on screen. The BIOS calls for retrieving the directory information, in turn, access the equivalent BDOS functions to access the disk drives and retrieve that information from the disk. Because both BIOS and

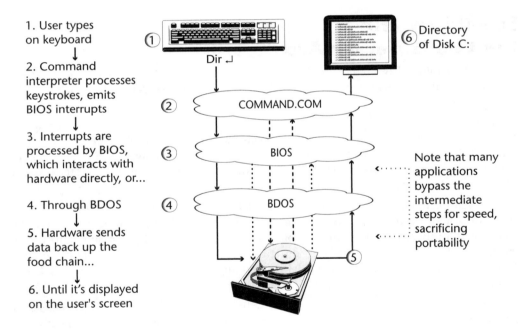

FIGURE 1.1 Classical OS operation. In conventional operating systems both applications and operating system components interact directly with low-level device drivers and the hardware, limiting portability and security.

---

5 We're referring here to the BIOS component of the operating system (implemented as the IO.SYS file in DOS systems), not the ROM BIOS.

6 Actually, this is now an obsolete term. It originated with Control Program for Microcomputers (CP/M), the first OS for PCs. We find the CP/M terminology more descriptive, and DOS began as a CP/M clone anyway.

BDOS functions are used by almost all DOS programs, they are kept resident in memory and thus are part of the DOS kernel.

In Windows NT neither the equivalent of the BIOS (the Hardware Abstraction Layer or HAL) nor the equivalent of the BDOS (one of the many installable file systems) is a part of the kernel (though they both execute in kernel mode and are therefore part of what is generally known as the NT Executive). At the core of the executive lies the *microkernel*, which comprises only those services that are absolutely required to remain in memory at all times. The microkernel in Windows NT is therefore designed to be as small as possible. It functions much as a traffic light functions, directing the flow of information between various parts of the system.

When you type DIR on an NT system, your keystrokes are intercepted by CMD.EXE, which provides a text-based user interface, monitors the keystrokes, and determines what you've typed. CMD.EXE interfaces to a layer analogous to the BIOS layer, in this case, a subsection of the WIN32 Application Programming Interface (API). However, no application program in Windows NT is ever permitted to communicate directly with the HAL or any device drivers. As noted earlier, all such interactions occur with the Windows NT executive.

The microkernel takes the requests issued by the application program, validates those requests according to a security object model, and if it finds the request valid, issues those requests on the applications program's behalf. The requests may pass to a transitional layer such as some form of API. This may be implemented as a dynamic-link library, for example, so that it's loaded into the system only when it's required. The library will wish to issue commands in much the same way the BIOS issues commands to the BDOS in DOS, but, again, this is not permitted in Windows NT. Instead, requests are issued through the microkernel, and if the microkernel determines that those requests are reasonable, it issues those requests on the subsystem's behalf.

This mechanism is called a Client/Server approach: any subsystem that "services" other subsystems is a server, and any program requesting those services is a client. All Windows NT functions are handled through server processes. Servers can function as clients, although they do not necessarily have to. All interactions between clients and servers are controlled by the microkernel. In addition to providing the basics for the security approach that will be discussed later, this approach has one tremendous benefit: it makes it possible for Windows NT to employ a very small, tight microkernel. The microkernel is so small that on a multiprocessor implementation, one copy is executed on *each* CPU, providing Windows NT with truly *symmetric* multiprocessing (each CPU can handle tasks in exactly the same manner as any other processor).

Very few operating systems behave this way. The principal ones that do are the Carnegie-Mellon *Mach* variant of the UNIX operating system, Sequent Computer Systems' *Dynix,* and Sun's *Solaris*. Virtually all other multiprocessor operating systems are asymmetric in some manner, meaning that each processor can do certain things, but in general, only one processor can execute the operating system microkernel. By breaking down this barrier, Windows NT provides tremendous flexibility and scalability. Up to *30* processors may be employed in custom versions of Windows NT,[7] providing computing power that was, until

---

7 Out of the box, Windows NT Workstation supports one or two CPUs, and Windows NT Server supports up to four. Supporting more processors requires a customized HAL, which is provided by the hardware manufacturer. Upgrading a single-CPU system to the multi-CPU version requires the use of an NT resource kit utility. See Appendix 4.

recently, available only in mainframe-class systems. The implications for network servers are revolutionary: there is, for all intents and purposes, no upper limit on the power of a Windows NT-based network server.[8]

There is a price to pay for the scalability, security, and flexibility that the client/server architecture confers. When a DOS application calls a kernel-mode function, only one kernel-mode transition is required. All other processing occurs in the kernel, until the requested information (if any) is ready to be returned to the application. In contrast, NT requires *one kernel-mode call for each interaction between subsystems,* as illustrated in Figure 1.2. Every time a Windows NT application calls through the API layer, there must be a transition.

To save time and speed up common operations, the Windows NT Executive (the microkernel and associated subsystems) is designed to make kernel-mode access as efficient as possible, but there is some overhead involved. In practice, extensive laboratory testing at *WINDOWS Magazine* has indicated that the overhead is negligible, and in NT 4.0 Microsoft has addressed the one significant area in which the client/server design imposed a significant performance penalty by converting two major components of the NT video subsystem into kernel-mode drivers. The result is a major improvement in video performance, as illustrated in Figure 1.3.[9]

Portable Design Windows NT provides a second major innovation: it's designed to be independent of any particular hardware, breaking a tradition that began with IBM's introduction of the first PC[10] in 1981. Beginning with the PC the world of desktop computing underwent a dramatic change. Prior to that time a variety of operating systems vendors had competed along with a variety of hardware systems vendors. Many desktop computers were completely proprietary, combining a unique operating system with unique hardware, but a majority of pre-PC desktop computers used one implementation or another of the CP/M operating system. CP/M could be made to work efficiently on a variety of different computers by making changes to its BIOS layer (which described the behavior of the hardware to the operating system and vice versa). Programmers, instead of writing code for specific pieces of hardware, such as the disk controller, would execute BIOS functions that would access the disk controllers for them. The advantage of this approach was that it made programs *portable.* Instead of writing a whole new word processor for each CP/M computer, the programmer could write just one CP/M-compatible program, and it would run on any of them. The only disadvantage was that BIOS-based programs tended to be slower than those optimized for a particular system.

---

8   Actually, there *are* effective limits on performance because of non-linear scaling and system-wide bottlenecks when applications are run on a multiprocessor. See Appendix 5 for more details.

9   Despite the fears of many ill-informed observers, moving the two components in question (the Win32 and User32 subsystems) into the kernel has little or no effect on stability. It does, however, mean that NT 4.0 is incompatible with older video drivers.

10   In this context, we use "PC" to mean IBM-compatible personal computer.

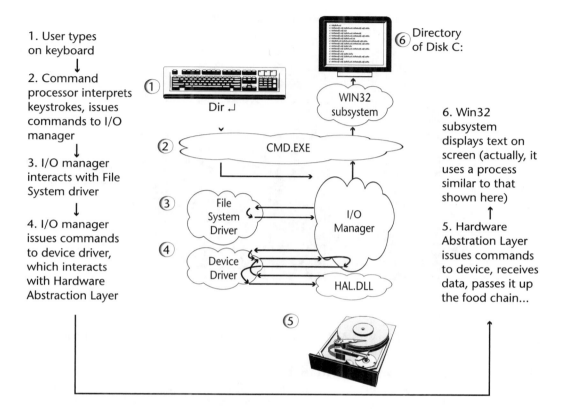

1. User types on keyboard

2. Command processor interprets keystrokes, issues commands to I/O manager

3. I/O manager interacts with File System driver

4. I/O manager issues commands to device driver, which interacts with Hardware Abstraction Layer

6. Win32 subsystem displays text on screen (actually, it uses a process similar to that shown here)

5. Hardware Abstration Layer issues commands to device, receives data, passes it up the food chain...

FIGURE 1.2 Microkernel operation. Windows NT employs a modified microkernel architecture—applications cannot access low-level drivers or hardware services without the intervention of the operating system. Hardware dependencies are isolated in the drivers (and the Hardware Abstraction Layer), ensuring portability. Security is provided when the application and operating system interact.

The IBM PC killed this concept stone dead. Because the PC provided a standard hardware design, programmers could bypass BIOS and access the low-level hardware directly, gaining significantly in performance. The hardware was standardized, so programs would still run on "PC-clones" from many vendors. In effect, by providing a uniform standard for the design of desktop hardware, IBM inadvertently created the world in which commodity pricing would be introduced. Cloners soon came into play, and now it's possible to buy IBM PC-compatible computers from almost anyone, except IBM.[11]

---

11   That is, PC compatibles, which IBM stopped making in 1987.

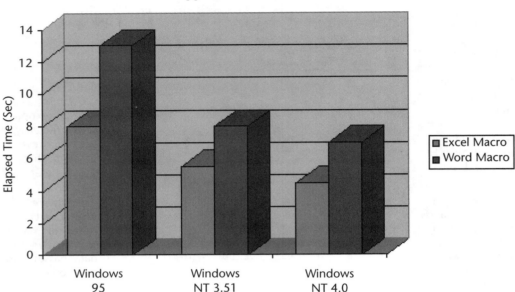

Office 95 Application Performance

NOTE: All tests on P6-200 with 32 MB RAM. Shorter elapsed time = better performance.

FIGURE 1.3 Application performance. NT 4.0 is capable of providing performance about 10% better than that for NT 3.51 and significantly better than for Windows 95 when operated on high-end systems (in this case a 200MHz Pentium Pro with 32MB RAM).

Windows NT attempts to reverse this history, by reverting to the concept of the CP/M BIOS. In Windows NT the equivalent to BIOS is the Hardware Abstraction Layer (HAL). To make Windows NT available on a particular architecture, the manufacturer must write a machine-specific HAL, provide a Microsoft-compatible C compiler, and then obtain the Windows NT sources from Microsoft and recompile them to the architecture. Most vendors will try tuning the operating system specifically for their hardware. By writing parts of the NT microkernel in machine language that best fits their specific architecture, they can hope to achieve speed gains, but they can do that as time permits. The point is that it's relatively easy to make NT work on virtually *any* type of machine without staying PC compatible.

At this writing, NT 4.0 operates on at least four different CPU architectures: Intel *x*86, MIPS R4*x*00, Digital Alpha AXP 21*xxx*, and Motorola Power PC 60*x*. Before it became public, Windows NT also operated on the Intel i860 (this was the first architecture on which NT became operational), and versions of Windows NT have been created experimentally for HP's PA-RISC architecture, Intergraph's Clipper, and Sun's SPARC-2. It probably will be made available on more architectures over time.

Why So Many Architectures? Although the Intel x86 series microprocessors have been extraordinarily successful (with an installed base exceeding 100,000,000 as of this writing), they do not represent the upper limit of computer performance in the 1990s. There are performance limitations in the Intel designs because, like the PCs in which they execute, successive generations of Intel CPUs have been forced to carry forward design limitations to stay compatible with their predecessors. An entirely different kind of processor design, Reduced Instruction Set Computer (RISC), has for many years been popular in high-end UNIX workstations. However, although these workstations have been theoretically capable of much higher performance than their Intel counterparts, it has not been possible to run conventional DOS- and Windows-based applications programs on them.

Making Windows NT portable to RISC systems makes it possible to bring the richness and depth of applications support we have in the DOS and Windows world onto these advanced (some would say exotic) architectures. The implication to a computer user, and particularly to a network user, is that for the first time there is someplace to go when the current top-of-the-line Intel CPU isn't fast enough. As of this writing the fastest Intel processor is the Pentium Pro (or P6) chip. In its current top-of-the-line 200MHz incarnation it's capable of achieving over 400 million instructions per second (MIPS) and is a very high-performance processor by any standard. However, it's capable of less than half the floating point performance of a top-of-the-line 466MHz Digital Alpha CPU. For those running a floating-point-intensive application like Computer Aided Design (CAD) or Computer Aided Engineering (CAE), there was, until now, no place else to go: changing to another CPU meant changing all your software.

With Windows NT the game has fundamentally changed. If you are unsatisfied with the performance of a Pentium Pro-based workstation for CAD work, you can carry it to any of the other architectures mentioned and possibly achieve substantially better performance.

From a networking point of view, the implication of making Windows NT portable to different architectures is astounding flexibility. NT runs on many different platforms, yet behaves nearly identically on all of them. It's possible for a Window NT network to consist of a symmetric multiprocessor functioning as a server and an arbitrary combination of single-processor or even multiple-processor workstation machines, some using Intel CPUs and some RISC. You can put together the precise hardware required to do a particular job while providing a consistent user interface, uniform networking protocols, and generally identical behavior throughout the system.

Of course, all of this flexibility comes at a price—portability has three negative implications. For any architecture other than Intel x86, there is a significant performance hit when one is executing "legacy" applications—DOS, 16-bit Windows, 32-bit Intel (ie: Windows 95) and OS/2 programs. These applications weren't designed to run on RISC processors, and the steps NT must take to execute them involve a substantial execution overhead (see Appendix 5 for details).

Applications also need to be compiled for the specific platform on which they will be executed. Even programs written directly for Windows NT, using the 32-bit Windows (WIN32) API, have to be compiled specifically for the processor on which they will be executed. You cannot take an Intel version of a Windows NT application and expect to run it on a RISC platform,[12]

---

[12]   As the third edition of this book went to press, Microsoft began to preview a technology that *can* execute Intel 32-bit programs (ie: Windows 95 applications) on RISC systems—see *32-bit Intel Applications on Any RISC: WX86*, in Appendix 5.

nor can you take a version of a Windows NT application developed on one RISC platform and run it on another.

For example, Intergraph Corporation uses Windows NT as the operating system for its Intel Pentium- (and Pentium Pro-) based workstations for Computer Aided Design and Computer Aided Engineering (CAD/CAE) applications. However, Intergraph is also interested in the Motorola Power PC and DEC Alpha architectures. Intergraph has therefore compiled versions of its CAD/CAE programs for both Alpha and Power PC CPUs but not for the MIPS R4000/4400 architecture. This need for architecture-specific applications can be a critical problem for network administrators faced with decisions about which specific hardware to acquire. The fact that Windows NT is portable does not necessarily mean that Windows NT applications are. Worse, this situation extends to some parts of the network services—for instance, a RISC-based print server with Intel clients must provide Intel-compatible printer drivers.

Finally, there is an overhead associated with Windows NT's portable design. The bulk of Windows NT is written in C, which makes it portable. Design a C compiler for a particular environment, design a HAL for that environment, recompile the Windows NT sources, and you have a version of Windows NT for the new environment. Unfortunately, C code is not optimized for a variety of performance-intensive tasks. In NT 3.1, this shortcoming resulted in some performance compromises that were eliminated by better optimization—and in some cases, rewriting critical code in assembly language—for NT versions from 3.5 on.

Object Model and the Security Subsystem

The subject of object-orientation is one of the most pervasive and controversial in modern computer science. The idea of object orientation is to deal abstractly with data, code, and instructions as an object, without being concerned about whether the object referred to is a data file, text, a picture, a program, or something else. The concept is not uniformly seen as effective. Fortunately, Windows NT does not claim to be an object-oriented operating system. It does, however, employ the concept of objects to a high degree in one subsystem: the security subsystem.

Security is an important point in Windows NT. Microsoft is positioning the security features of Windows NT as a major advantage in commercial applications such as banking. Although there is undoubtedly some truth to its claim, it's also interesting to speculate. Helen Custer's excellent book, *Inside Windows NT*, makes it clear that the genesis of the concept that would lead to Windows NT began in 1988, at the very height of the Reagan/Bush defense buildup. Could it be that Windows NT is something of a Cold War operating system? It's certain Windows NT was designed with the needs of the United States government and the defense industry in mind, because Windows NT is unique among desktop operating systems in having been designed to be certifiable at the federal government's C2 and B security levels.[13]

To understand the implications of security requirements for an operating system, let's consider a hypothetical example. Suppose that you're an employee of the Central Intelligence

---

13 See "Trusted Network Interpretation," a Publication of National Computer Security Conference (NCSC), tel: (202) 783-3238.

Agency and are cleared for Top Secret information. You work with an employee who is cleared only for Secret information. As a Top Secret cleared employee you have the clearance necessary to see any of the documents that are used by the Secret cleared employee. The reverse, however, is not true. Suppose further that you have a need periodically to print documents. Clearly, Top Secret documents cannot be printed on just any laser printer anywhere in the building. Your Top Secret documents can be printed only on a Top Secret paper laser printer (probably located behind armed guards, a vault door, and with whatever other security requirements the CIA may feel a need to enforce). The documents from the Secret cleared employee can be printed on your Top Secret printer (although the Secret cleared employee may have some difficulty getting past the armed guards and through the vault door to retrieve documents). However, if you attempt to print a document on a printer "owned" by that Secret cleared employee, whether or not your document prints will depend upon whether the document itself is cleared Secret or Top Secret.

If you found the previous paragraph confusing, we have made our point!

The issue of security is extremely complex. To provide a truly "secure" operating system, every file and every device in the system must have an *owner*. A security access level, in this case Secret or Top Secret, is associated with each of those files and devices. The designers of Windows NT were very aware of this requirement, and they decided that this was the one place where objects made sense.

Windows NT provides an object-based security model. A security object can represent any resource in the system—files, devices, processes, programs, users—and a security object is associated with it. A security object carries information about what the object is permitted or not permitted to do. These permissions are carried forward with the security objects associated with system resources, and a more or less sophisticated sense of inheritance will determine what is and is not permitted to be done with any such resource. Server processes that provide secure access employ a technique called *impersonation:* the process takes on the security identifier (SID) of its client and performs operations in the client's security context. All of this is transparent to both programmers and end users, and (provided the security system is properly configured) interferes minimally with normal system operations.

The situation isn't really quite as complex as it seems because a computer security system designed to deal with Secret and Top Secret information would have to be certifiable to the government's B security level. Windows NT is not secured at that level (because it would be all but unusable to mere civilians). In such a system all resources are totally secured by default, and it's necessary to take specific steps to apply permissions to them so that they can be used by the general public.

Windows NT enforces a less restrictive standard called C2 that is not certifiable for the handling of Secret information. It's certifiable for the handling of Confidential information, and it's well suited to banks and other facilities requiring a degree of security without making their systems virtually unusable as a side effect. The security system is theoretically capable of being upgraded to the B standard. Moreover, the security system is implemented as a privileged subsystem (a concept that we will examine shortly), and it can be replaced by another security system if desired. As of this writing, Microsoft has begun to publicly discuss its intent to replace the entire security system with the Kerberos distributed security system (implemented by the Massachusetts Institute of Technology) in a future version[14] of Windows NT.

What Does Security Mean to You? The implications of NT security are most significant for file servers. Windows NT's provision of a relatively sophisticated security system, including the concepts of file ownership and specific access permissions granted on a per-file or per-directory basis, makes it possible to completely isolate each user's files from other users of the system. This separation is clearly of vital importance in a high-security environment and may be equally important to companies that carry vital information on their networks. The corporate nightmare in the 1990s is to have one's accounting files hacked by a sixteen-year-old with a modem who has recently seen the movie *War Games*. If such a sixteen-year-old kid hacks a Windows NT server, *assuming security has been properly set up*, his opportunity to do mischief will be significantly restricted. Whether the system is therefore hacker-proof is an open question (and a somewhat controversial one).

In principle, what one human being can invent in a piece of software another human being can, if sufficiently determined, sabotage. No matter how sophisticated Windows NT security may be, any Windows NT system that's physically accessible (a programmer can walk up to it and access the keyboard, screen, and disk drive) is vulnerable. If you want your server to be protected, you must lock it up. It's also worth noting that the most sophisticated system of passwords, user accounts, and security access rights in the world is worthless if it's not used. If you create a Windows NT server and provide total access to all files for everyone in the system, you're vulnerable. NT's sophisticated security system is meaningless because you have turned it off.

Windows NT systems also provide a powerful remote access service designed to make it possible to log into those systems remotely through use of a modem. Windows NT security systems are impressive, but there is always a risk in connecting a system to a modem. The security procedures must be enacted with great rigor.

Finally, does the provision of such security have drawbacks? As with scalability and portability, the need for security objects to be checked as they are passed from subsystem to subsystem implies a certain amount of overhead in the system. Interestingly, however, such security capabilities have in the past been built into many kinds of software. Network databases, such as Oracle, typically incorporate private security authentication layers in their OS/2 and UNIX incarnations. Windows NT versions may dispense with that layer,[15] improving performance and simplifying administration.

Privileged Subsystems

The client/server design of Windows NT involves a certain amount of overhead. Whenever one process, such as an application program, communicates with another process, the Executive is

---

14 Code-named *"Windows NT Cairo"* and expected to be available in 1997 or early 1998.

15 In practice, both Microsoft and Oracle have retained proprietary security in their NT databases for compatibility with other versions but have provided for use of NT's built-in security as well. See Chapter 12 for details.

involved. But there are components of the system that require higher operating performance than is possible in such an arrangement. There are also components of the system requiring access to system resources not generally made available to applications programs. These subsystems are referred to as *privileged subsystems*, and they run with essentially the same privileges as built-in components of the Windows NT system. Privileged subsystems are important to us because one obvious place where the concept of a privileged subsystem applies is in the networking interface.

If Windows NT's client/server approach were carried to its limit in all components of the networking interface, one could quite reasonably expect that network performance in Windows NT would be poor by comparison with that for less-protected operating systems. This, however, is not the case. Major components of the networking system are implemented as privileged subsystems communicating between and among themselves with privilege levels comparable to those used by the NT Executive itself.

There is another area where privileged subsystems are employed, and it's critical in understanding NT's place in the network world on desktops. That area is in providing "programmable personalities."

Traditionally, each operating system has had a clearly defined (and unique) user interface. For example, the CP/M operating system had a user interface characterized by a certain set of user commands, and this was paralleled by an application programming interface containing certain possibilities. The DOS operating system includes a similar but more sophisticated user interface and a similar but more sophisticated programming interface. The OS/2 operating system has a still more sophisticated user interface (major components of which are implemented graphically) and a still more sophisticated application programming interface.

This proliferation of user and programming interfaces eventually tends to become an overwhelming burden for an operating system to carry. Operating systems such as OS/2 have had to make a terrible choice between carrying the overhead of compatibility to earlier systems (such as DOS) and seeing their market share sharply reduced. Windows NT, by contrast, exploits the concepts of privileged subsystems and the client/server architecture to provide completely replaceable personalities. In effect, Windows NT can take on the characteristics of 16-bit Windows, DOS, 32-bit Windows, OS/2, or POSIX. From the point of view of the programmer and from the point of view of an applications program, it is *exactly the same* as 16-bit Windows, DOS, 32-bit Windows, OS/2, or POSIX. To the user it does appear a bit different.

Standard User Interface Although there was early discussion of providing interchangeable user interfaces so that those familiar with OS/2 would see an OS/2 Presentation Manager interface while those familiar with Windows would see a Windows-like user interface, Microsoft has wisely decided to standardize on a user interface governed by the 32-bit Windows (Win32) subsystem. Application programs functioning within any of the subsystems can share this user interface, as illustrated in Figure 1.4. Standardizing on the Windows user interface confers tremendous advantages upon Windows NT, for both end users and system managers. It's not necessary to develop and acquire a completely new base of software when one moves to a Windows NT system. "Well-behaved"[16] DOS, Windows, and OS/2 1.x applications will run

---

16   See Appendix 3 for a definition of well-behaved in this context.

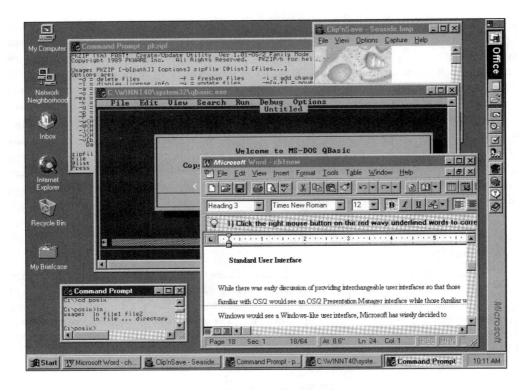

FIGURE 1.4 NT 4.0 with DOS, OS/2, POSIX, Win16, and Win32 apps. The Windows Explorer user interface (used by both NT 4.0 and Windows 95) provides an integrated desktop metaphor for applications designed for 32-bit Windows, 16-bit Windows, DOS, OS/2 (16-bit character mode only), and POSIX. All are shown here.

correctly in the Windows NT environment. Well-behaved UNIX applications can be recompiled using NT's POSIX compatibility libraries and will become native POSIX applications in the Windows NT environment.

Let's look at an example: A company that has standardized on SQL Server as its corporate database and has its employees use the DOS version of Word Perfect along with Windows Excel to get work done should be able to move to Windows NT without changing any of its software. SQL Server is an application that's implemented on OS/2, UNIX, and NT. The OS/2 version of SQL Server can be executed directly under Windows NT (on Intel platforms). Windows NT also incorporates TCP/IP compatible (UNIX-style) networking so that if a UNIX-based SQL Server implementation is employed, it can be left in place, and Windows NT will use it.[17] On the other hand, if it's preferable to move directly to Windows NT, a native version of SQL Server is available.

---

17 See Chapter 6 for details of Windows NT's UNIX-compatible TCP/IP networking features.

Similarly, WordPerfect for DOS and Excel for (16-bit) Windows will execute directly under Windows NT (although it may be desirable to acquire native 32-bit/native versions of these applications because they will give better performance). If the company uses a specialized application, it will probably run in one of NT's emulation subsystems (assuming the application was developed for DOS, Windows, or OS/2). If the applications was developed for the UNIX environment (where portability is normally accomplished at the source code level), and if it's a well-behaved basic character-mode UNIX application, it should be possible to recompile it for Windows NT's POSIX implementation. For that matter, if it's a graphic application, it could be possible to use it in conjunction with one of the third-party "X/Server" utilities for Windows NT (see Chapter 11).

Of course there are limitations to this approach. One is reminded of the old saw "Jack of all trades, master of none." That's not true of Windows NT. It's a master of one trade, and that trade is 32-bit Windows. With respect to the other subsystems, it has greater or lesser limitations, depending on the particular subsystem. With respect to the DOS subsystem in particular, a significant problem introduced by Windows NT security architecture prevents low-level access to hardware. Applications such as backup applications and utility programs that expect direct access to hardware such as the hard disk controller will not work under Windows NT. Windows applications that take liberties with the Windows interface, employ undocumented system calls, attempt direct hardware access, or employ private device drivers (scanner applications and the like) will not work.

The OS/2 support is at the OS/2 1.3 level, which is unfortunate because Windows NT was introduced in parallel with IBM's introduction of its second major revision of the OS/2 2.x system, and NT's built-in OS/2 support is character-mode only.[18] This is sufficient for carrying forward server-based applications such as SQL Server, but it's insufficient for carrying forward much of anything else. The POSIX implementation suffers similar limitations to the OS/2 implementation and, of course, requires that development effort in that application be recompiled. All of this is typical of the UNIX world as a whole.

The idea that bringing Windows NT into an organization will allow the existing software base to be carried forward without *any* change is probably naive. However, Microsoft has made great strides in improving matters since NT 3.1. In Chapter 10, we explain how NT is able to masquerade as a native client on NetWare 3.x and 4.x LANs and (with appropriate add-on software) can even appear to be a NetWare 3.x *server*. Thus, although the notion of a chameleon-like ability to change user interfaces hasn't panned out in practice, something similar has happened at the network interface level.

Access to the World Outside: I/O

No operating system exists in isolation. People buy an operating system to run application software, and they do so in the expectation that it will work with a wide range of hardware. Windows NT therefore provides a very rich device-independent model for I/O services that

---

18   An add-on package available for NT 3.51 provides an OS/2 Presentation Manager interface. See Appendix 3 for details. Microsoft is working on a version for NT 4.0, but no release date is available as of this writing (August 1996).

takes critical advantage of a concept called a *multi-layered device driver*. In DOS and other conventional operating systems device drivers are generally *monolithic*, which means they provide a large and complex set of services that will be understood by an intermediate layer of the operating system. In DOS this intermediate layer is the Basic Disk Operating System (BDOS). The device driver then communicates directly with the hardware, so when BDOS commands are issued, the driver provides the necessary hardware interface. BDOS commands are relatively high-level functions. They do things like open a file, read a byte from a file, and close a file. The physical actions needed to fill these requests are hidden (or *encapsulated*) within the driver.

This model works, but it has some severe problems. Consider that there may be more than one type of file system. If the driver has been designed to respond to the Open File command, it will, given a filename, go to a directory structure, find the file, and carry out the operations necessary to open it (this assumes the device driver knows the file system format to be used). Now in DOS this is no problem because there is only one file format to worry about, the File Allocation Table (FAT) format, so DOS device drivers assume that this is the format they'll see on the disk.

Windows NT, as we will see in the next section, is designed to use a variety of file system formats. So it's not safe for a device driver to make any assumptions about the underlying format. To get around this problem, NT uses a *multi-layer* device driver approach in combination with a new operating system layer called the *I/O manager*. Application programs (and intermediate levels of the operating system) do not communicate directly with the device drivers. They communicate with the I/O manager, which in turn communicates with the device drivers on their behalf.

Let's consider how this communication works when an application program needs to access files on an NTFS (New Technology File System) partition. The application program issues a request to open a file. The request travels to an underlying operating system layer, perhaps the Win32 API layer. The Win32 API layer then issues an NT internal command, requesting the NT executive to open a file. The NT executive passes this request to the I/O manager and the I/O manager communicates this request to a file system driver—specifically, the NTFS file system driver. The NTFS file system driver responds by issuing the NTFS specific hardware level requests. It says, "I want the information from track x sector y," which will be the location of the first tier of the directory structure, and based upon that, it issues C commands to get information from other locations on the disk. I/O manager then relays these requests to a hardware device driver, which knows that it's receiving specific requests related to getting very simple information from the device. It knows nothing about the file system. Notice that this process will work exactly the same if the NTFS driver is replaced by a FAT driver, a UNIX file system driver, a Macintosh file system driver, a CD ROM driver, or any other driver.

Of course, some overhead is involved with the I/O manager passing requests for information back and forth. For simple devices such as serial ports and parallel ports Windows NT provides a single-layer device driver approach in which the I/O manager can communicate with the device driver and the device driver will return information directly. But for more complicated devices, and particularly for hard disks, tape drives, and other devices that depend on a file system (or other logical arrangement of data), a multi-layered approach is superior.

Asynchronous I/O, Synchronization, and Power-Failure Recovery Three additional device driver features are unique to Windows NT. The first is that virtually all low-level I/O operations are asynchronous. Rather than issue a request for information from a file and wait until the request is filled, in Windows NT, you issue the request for information to the file and then go on and do something else. When the information from the file is ready, you're notified.

This characteristic is masked at the programmer API level and neither programmers nor users need ever see it (programmers *do* have the option to explicitly use it through a mechanism called *overlapped I/O*). If you type DIR at an NT command prompt, it will behave in much the same way as typing DIR on a DOS system. Underneath the user interface, however, very different things are going on. Windows NT is a *preemptive multitasking system*, which may be running many tasks at the same time, so it's vital that the operating system not waste time waiting for a request to be filled if it can be doing something else. The various layers in the operating system use the preemptive multitasking and multithreading characteristics of NT to enable themselves to get more work done in the same time.

Rather than waiting for a hard disk to spin up or waiting on a request to read a directory, Windows NT continues with other tasks and deals with the directory request only when data becomes available. This feature also plays a role in NT's scalability. From our discussion of the client/server design and its application to symmetric multiprocessors you will remember that multiple instances of the Windows NT microkernel execute on all CPUs simultaneously. This means that it's theoretically possible for all the CPUs in a system to attempt simultaneous device driver access, causing contention. To avoid this problem, device drivers, like other components of the NT Executive, make use of synchronization objects (in particular, semaphores and spin locks). The precise details of how this is done are outside the scope of this chapter. Suffice it to say that although it's possible for multiple instances of a device driver or other critical code to execute on multiple processors, they are designed in such a way that only one of those drivers at a time will have access to any critical shared resource. Just as with the asynchronous I/O, this is automatic and invisible to end users.

The final unique feature of Windows NT device drivers is provision for power failure recovery. Windows NT is designed as, among other things, a platform for mission-critical applications such as SQL Server (an Enterprise database). If a corporation has implemented its entire accounting system on SQL Server, it's absolutely critical that the system on which SQL Server is running be protected from power failure; or if a power failure occurs, it's vital that there be a graceful path to recovery. Otherwise, the entire accounting system could be corrupted, and a corrupt accounting system can cost a company millions of dollars.

Windows NT provides protection against this nightmare on several levels, the most important of which are the uninterruptible power supply (UPS) service and certain sophisticated features of the NTFS file system (both of which we discuss later). There is also provision for protection from power failure *even at the device driver level*. In a power failure, even if it is very brief, the precise operating state of hardware devices becomes unstable. A disk drive, for example, which has a memory buffer for Direct Memory Access (DMA) data transfer, may be loaded with corrupt data during a power failure. Attempting to access that data will yield garbage—or worse, if that data gets written to disk, it may damage the application requesting it.

The classic way to deal with power failure in an operating system is to force a "cold" (power-switch) boot, lock everything out, and restart all operations from the power-off state. That takes a long time, and itself is dangerous because there may have been I/O requests outstanding. The classic example is a power failure while one is writing a disk file. Typically the disk file data is lost. Windows NT attempts to protect against loss by designing warm boot code into the device drivers. In other words, there is a known good state for device drivers short of the power-off state. In a power failure situation the operating system will notify all device drivers that a power failure has occurred. The device drivers then set themselves to their known good states and continue with the I/O operations that were outstanding when the power failed. If this capability works—and we've seen it demonstrated—a power glitch on a Windows NT system need have no effect other than the brief period of time that the machine was turned off. Operations pick themselves up where they were and carry on transparently.

File Systems Traditionally, operating systems are associated with a particular file structure that's used by that operating system for mass storage devices such as hard disks. Thus, we speak of a UNIX file system (i-nodes), a DOS file system (FAT), and a Macintosh File System (resource and data forks). Although there is a native NT file system (NTFS), uniquely among modern operating systems (with the possible exception of OS/2 from which some of these capabilities were inherited) Windows NT is designed to be independent of the file system on which it operates. This capability enforces some severe requirements on Windows NT's I/O system design and device drivers, as was discussed in the last section. But it provides a very high degree of flexibility in Windows NT implementations.

By default, Windows NT supports two file systems for hard disks: the familiar File Allocation Table (FAT) system that's standard for DOS and NTFS, which is designed to exploit Windows NT's security and fault-tolerance features. Unlike past versions, NT 4.0 provides no support for OS/2's High Performance File System (HPFS). Microsoft recommends converting HPFS partitions to NTFS partitions. Windows NT also supports a CD-ROM file system, eliminating the need for the Microsoft CD Extensions (MSCDEX) patch to the DOS file system that's required by all CD-ROM drives used with DOS machines. Windows NT Server also supports the Macintosh file system. Finally, *network services are treated as file systems in Windows NT.* Windows NT comes with LAN Manager network services that are, in effect, a file system that exists over a network. If you add Novell NetWare support you add NetWare network services— yet another file system that spans a network.

Windows NT is capable of running all these file systems simultaneously. By far the most important is NTFS. NTFS is designed as a file system for building anything from a desktop computer to a mainframe-class enterprise server. It's designed to perform well with very large disk volumes (up to 2^{64} bits!), a situation that is difficult for the FAT system. These are features it shares with OS/2's HPFS system. But Microsoft learned some things from its experience with HPFS design and development.

In contrast to HPFS, NTFS provides a unique data-logging capability that enables Windows NT to restore the state of the file system in power failure or other disk error situations, and to do so very quickly. HPFS system has a similar capability, but it uses an HPFS version of the DOS *chkdsk* function, and in large volumes it can literally take *hours* to execute. Like HPFS, NTFS provides support for long filenames.[19] You can refer to a file called 1993 Quarterly Accounts and use that name for it rather than calling it something cryptic like 93QTR.ACT. However, the use of long filenames creates compatibility problems for legacy applications. Windows NT eliminates this problem by providing automatic conversion of filenames to standard DOS style 8.3 names for DOS and Windows 16-bit applications. Thus, if you named your file 1993 Quarterly Accounts while using a 32-bit Windows application, when you go back and look for the file from a 16-bit Windows application or DOS application you will see 1993QU~1.[20]

Finally, beginning with NT version 3.51, NTFS supports compression as an attribute, allowing the end user or administrator to provide file compression on a per-file and per-directory basis. The compression is efficient, giving roughly a 50% reduction in space on most text files, 40% on executables, and potentially much higher compression on sparse data files such as databases. The performance impact of compression appears to be minimal, no doubt because of NT's combination of dynamic disk caching (data is decompressed on entry to the cache) and asynchronous I/O (which allows compression to take place in parallel with reading the next block of data from the disk). The combination of efficient compression and a minimal performance impact with an inherently reliable design is unique to NTFS and makes it the first compressed file system suited to use on servers as well as desktop systems.

File System Features for Programmers Besides supporting multiple installable file systems, Windows NT provides a couple of unique features that ensure high performance. The first of these is an entirely new capability called *memory-mapped files*. Windows NT is a *Virtual Memory* operating system—it allows for arbitrarily large memory objects to be dealt with (if the object is too large to fit in physical memory, only part is stored in memory while the rest resides on disk). Memory-mapped files exploit this capability by allowing a programmer to open a file of arbitrary size and treat it as a single contiguous array of memory locations. A 100MB file can be opened and treated as an array in a system with only 12MB of memory. Of course, at any one time 12MB or less (probably substantially less) of file data is physically present in memory, and the rest is "paged" out to the disk. When the program requests data that's not currently stored in memory, the Virtual Memory System automatically gets it from the file. But it does so very efficiently, and it completely masks this operation from the programmer.

This memory-mapped files feature could revolutionize disk-based programs (like database applications) once programmers understand how to use it. Writing applications in which large amounts of file data are manipulated in a computer is something of an art form.[21] You must find a way to load the right data into memory at the right time and manipulate it there for speed, then unload it and load in new data. Windows NT changes this process to one of manipulating disk-based data as you would any other array of bytes. Although the entire file is never actually present in memory at any one time, Windows NT masks the deception. The programming implications of this, and other Windows NT features, is explored in Appendix 1.

---

19 In NT version 3.5 (and later), a similar capability exists for the FAT file system as well.

20 Further details on the New Technology File System and on setting up file systems in general are in Chapter 2.

21 See Appendix 1 for helpful hints on NT network programming.

Preemptive Multitasking

Computers spend much of their time doing absolutely nothing. Consider what happens when you type DIR on a DOS machine. In between your typing of the letters D, I, and R the CPU sits idle. You cannot possibly type fast enough to keep it busy. When you finish typing DIR and press the Enter key, the CPU very quickly decides that you wanted a disk directory, issues the necessary commands, and issues instructions to the hard disk controller. It then waits while the hard disk controller gets the information, and while it waits it can accomplish no useful work.

Because of *preemptive multitasking*, this situation is very different under Windows NT. A component of the operating system called the *Task Scheduler* switches a variety of processes into or out of the CPU(s), either according to a set time schedule or based on the existence of some high-priority event, such as an interrupt. To understand how this works in practice, let's consider the very same process of typing DIR but this time on a Windows NT machine. It's all but certain that when you type DIR, that won't be the only thing you are doing with the NT machine. You will probably have a variety of other windows open, and several programs running. Yet you won't have to wait any longer for the system to respond after you type DIR than you would on the DOS machine (in fact, you may not even have to wait as long!).

The *foreground* process (the one running in the foreground window on the machine's display) in Windows NT gets a substantially higher priority than background processes, and *real-time* I/O (such as keyboard input) has the highest priority in the system. Therefore, whenever you strike a key, the CPU will drop what it's doing to handle the keystroke, but in the intervening time between the keystrokes (when a DOS system would be idle) the Task Scheduler will switch among the other processes running in the system. Even if you're running only the window into which you're typing DIR, the Task Scheduler will still switch time between your processes and the processes of the Windows NT Executive. These include the processes that provide networking capability, and here we see one of the first and most important of Windows NT's advantages. Instead of being an afterthought as they are with Novell NetWare's NetX Shell and DOS, networking functions are built into Windows NT, and the preemptive multitasking model makes for a far more effective networking implementation.

Now, suppose you finish typing DIR and press the Enter key. Just as in DOS, the Windows NT command interpreter determines that DIR is a command to receive a directory. It then issues the necessary commands through the NT Executive to the I/O Manager, which in turn calls the installable file system for whichever file system you're using on the relevant drive. This in turn sends a series of requests for specific information to the I/O Manager, which passes those requests on to a low-level hard disk driver, which gets the information from the hard disk. Now, this is a reasonably efficient process and happens very quickly—up to the point that the hard disk becomes involved. But the operating times of hard disks are measured in milliseconds whereas the operating times of microprocessors occur in nanoseconds. Compared with a modern microprocessor, a hard disk is an extraordinarily slow device.

Rather than waiting while it receives the information from the hard disk, the Task Scheduler continues to switch other processes in and out of the CPU. When the data on the hard disk becomes available, this will interrupt other processes because I/O has a very high priority, and information from the hard disk will be passed "up the food chain" to the process that requested it. This process of having I/O and other work accomplished simultaneously is called *asynchronous I/O*. Because of asynchronous I/O, preemptive multitasking systems such as Windows NT can be substantially faster on I/O-intensive tasks than are single-thread-of-execution systems such as DOS. Best of all, because Windows NT's built-in disk cache manager is itself multithreaded, the benefits of asynchronous I/O are available to *all* applications that access disks—whether or not they are themselves multithreaded.[22]

Multithreading The discussion about preemptive multitasking to this point could apply equally to a variety of other systems, particularly UNIX systems (which also run a preemptively switched, multitasking operating system kernel). Windows NT shares with OS/2 a substantial extension to this concept called *multithreading*. A thread is a low-overhead process that can be switched by the Task Scheduler (just like any other process), but it does not carry with it the overhead of starting up, ending, and managing its own resources. It inherits these from its parent process. A process may have many threads.

Consider a database application. If it's written in a traditional single-threaded manner, Windows NT will benefit from asynchronous I/O (through disk caching, if nothing else) but the application will not. The application cannot continue to process input for a new database record until the last record has been added—it hangs up while writing to the disk (and the user's eyes glaze at the sight of that hated Windows hourglass cursor). Windows NT can use this time to get other tasks done, but that's not terribly helpful to your end user.

However, if the database application is multithreaded, as a Windows NT application should be—you might be able to get other work done within the application while it's filling that request. Instead of hanging up, the application could accept input for the next record *at the very same time that the last record is being added* (see Figure 1.5). The extra productivity you achieve this way is, to abuse an accounting term, "found money" that was otherwise going to waste (because you are paying for that end-user's time regardless).

A properly written Windows NT database will *never* show that hourglass cursor. Instead, Windows NT provides a combination hourglass cursor and arrow pointer to show you that work is going on, but you can get other things done at the same time. Specifically, what should happen when you enter another record into the database is that one thread will start writing the last record to the disk, while the thread in which you're entering the data remains active. Asynchronous I/O now applies to the human part of the I/O equation as well as to the computer's part.

Multithreading on an SMP: Parallel Processing On multiprocessing systems, Windows NT gains an additional advantage—*each thread in a program can execute on its own CPU, speeding up the application.* As we discussed in the section on client/server design, Windows NT can simultaneously execute as many copies of the microkernel as there are processors in the system. Each copy of the microkernel is in fact a thread of the Windows NT Executive, which is (obviously) multithreaded.

---

22 Automatic disk caching *does* have its limitations. Applications that perform continuous disk I/O (databases, for instance) can sometimes achieve better performance if they bypass NT's cache and access the disk directly.

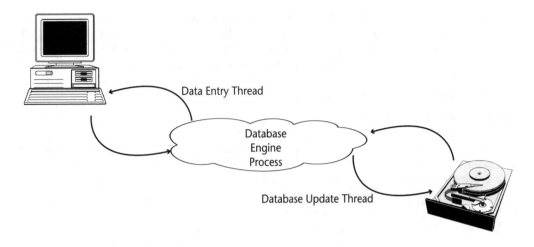

Data Entry Thread

Database Engine Process

Database Update Thread

FIGURE 1.5 Multithread database insert. Use of multithreading can significantly improve productivity in applications like database inserts, because the operator need not wait for one insert to complete before beginning another.

There are other multiprocessor operating systems—in particular, various forms of UNIX[23]. Typically, these systems employ the processors to execute separate processes or programs. Thus, for instance, a database application may be executing in one processor, and another application in another processor, and so on. Because each process can execute in its own processor, each executes faster and the system as a whole is faster. But no single process executes faster than it would if it were executing by itself.

Multithreaded processes in Windows NT can actually gain a speed benefit from executing on a multiprocessor. In our example (the database with records being entered), the thread for adding the record to the database could not only continue to execute in parallel with the execution of the thread that's taking the data from the user, it could execute in separate processors at the same time. Now, in point of fact, the advantage from multiprocessor execution of this specific example would be small. Both disk-based file I/O (the major limiting factor in updating the database) and human interface I/O (waiting for the user to enter a keystroke) are very slow processes. There is plenty of idle time between the user's keystrokes, and while the hard disk spins, Windows NT's asynchronous I/O capabilities can take advantage of it even on a single processor. But consider a database *search*.

As we discussed in the section on file I/O, Windows NT can provide impressive database capabilities using memory-mapped files. Programmers can, in effect, load the entire file into memory

---

23 Novell and IBM introduced multiprocessor-enabled versions of NetWare and OS/2, respectively, late in 1995. Both support SMP-multithreading in somewhat the same way NT does, though because SMP capability was added to them rather than designed in, how well they will exploit additional processors is an open question.

(or at least *act* as if they have loaded the entire file into memory), and then search it as they would search any memory array. In a multiprocessor implementation, one could have several threads of execution searching on that array simultaneously. If each of those threads has its own CPU, this could substantially increase the speed of the database search, as illustrated in Figure 1.6.

This approach has its limitations—specifically, in the example above (a multiprocessor database search), contention will occur when two CPUs attempt to access the same memory address. If the programmer's job has been done right, this will be minimized; but it can't be completely eliminated, and contention will slow down the system substantially. Similarly, multithreaded tasks that compete for single shared resources such as the hard disk, network cards, or the video screen will cause contention, and performance will deteriorate.[24] But for a wide variety of applications, especially server applications, parallel processing is very, very important.

Consider the operation of a large server on a large network. It may be servicing requests from dozens, even hundreds, of users simultaneously. In a typical file and print server situation, most of what it's doing is I/O and, as in the earlier example, a single CPU machine will have no trouble keeping up with other information requests in its free time between filling I/O requests. The major problem is keeping all the requests straight (100 people can try to open files at the same time, but the hard disk can handle them only one at a time).

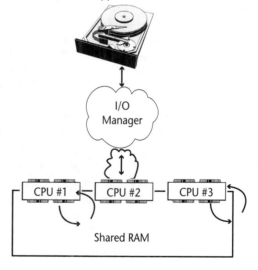

FIGURE 1.6 MP contention on file server. By dividing a computation-intensive task such as a database search into multiple *threads of execution*, an NT 4.0 application can achieve significant performance gains when run on Symmetric Multi-Processor (SMP) hardware.

24   See Appendix 5 for a more complete discussion of the contention problem on SMP systems.

The situation is different, however, if we begin to consider client/server applications, of which modern databases are a primary example. These applications tend to be *compute intensive* at the server. Queries on the database are received as requests from a client computer. The actual query is conducted at the server. If 5 or 10 people are attempting to perform database queries at the same time, you not only have an *I/O* problem (getting the data into memory from disk), you also have a compute problem (searching the data in memory). At this point, NT's multiprocessor support becomes a tremendous advantage. By providing additional CPU resources, it can fulfill those requests. This is the key to understanding that Windows NT is more—far more—than a simple operating system for desktop computers. Windows NT is the ideal operating system for computers that until recently we would think of as being in the mainframe class.

Memory Management In contrast to more conventional operating systems, Windows NT runs a near-mainframe-class memory management subsystem that employs demand-paged virtual memory. In this scheme programs are presented with a contiguous (flat) address space, up to 2GB in size,[25] although there will generally not be that much memory in the system. In fact, what's present in the system may not be contiguous at all.

Within the contiguous address space, memory is organized as 4KB pages.[26] Pages can be freely moved between memory and a hard disk at the command of the *memory manager subsystem*. The memory manager does this through a mechanism called a *page fault*. Whenever a program attempts to access memory that's not physically present in the machine, a page fault is generated. The NT Executive then takes over and loads in the requested memory. It also unloads the least recently used memory pages from the system to make room for the memory that's being loaded in. This process is automatic and (under all but the most extreme conditions) completely transparent, and it means that programs can behave as though they have nearly unlimited memory space, when they are in fact limited to memory physically present in the machine. When Windows NT runs out of memory (in the sense that programs are asking for more memory than the machine has), response slows down because the memory manager must periodically swap pages between memory and the hard disk.

This is particularly important for server-based applications in which, as the number of users grows, eventually the physical memory in the machine is insufficient. NT's major competitor, Novell NetWare 3.*x*, does not run a virtual memory system, and (as we've personal experience and scars to prove) when you add enough users and enough load to a system without adding memory, eventually the system begins to crash regularly. This should not happen with the Windows NT system because the virtual memory subsystem can take advantage of disk space.

---

25 It is technically possible for NT's memory manager to support a 64-bit address space, which would allow it to access 2^{64} bits. Applications would have to be rewritten to exploit such a large memory space.

26 This is true on Intel- and Mips-based systems, for reasons that Helen Custer explains well in *Inside Windows NT*. Systems based on Digital's Alpha CPU use an 8KB page size, and it's possible that other processors will use different page sizes as NT becomes available on additional architectures.

(If you run out of *both* physical memory and disk space, you may very well hit a situation in which the memory manager does run out of available resources.[27])

Besides managing virtual memory, the memory manager provides *memory protection*, preventing one application from manipulating memory within another application's address space. If memory protection was not provided, it would be possible for a rogue program to take actions that would result in other programs crashing or becoming unstable (much like a computer virus). To prevent this, the Memory Manager checks the *page boundaries* of the application's memory space. When an application attempts to address memory outside its page boundary, a page fault will occur and the memory manager will attempt to load in the missing memory page. If it determines that the page does not belong to the application, the memory manager raises a *protection exception*, which can be caught by an exception handler in the thread requesting the page or by a debugger. As a last resort, the Executive could shut down the offending application (making a note of this in an audit file, if the system is so configured), giving the user a Dr. Watson popup as an error indication.

There are times when it's desirable to have two applications share memory, so the memory management system must provide a way around the memory protection. It does so with Windows NT's *memory-mapped files* mechanism, the same mechanism that can be used for high-speed access to disk file data (by treating the file as a memory array).

The system can allocate memory as part of a *named shared memory object*, which can be opened by name by another process that will be given a *handle*[28] on the object. Once that handle has been made available, other applications can access it, as long as they have the necessary permissions from the security object manager. Synchronization objects are provided so that even on a multiprocessor system, two applications will not access the same memory location at the same time. Windows NT also provides a wide range of client/server mechanisms other than shared memory for the interaction of programs.

Shared memory brings up the final issue of memory management with Windows NT—security. Windows NT registers handles to named shared memory objects in the security object manager, which verifies whether programs requesting access to those objects have the privileges necessary to access it.

The implications of the memory management subsystem for network applications provide a substantially more reliable base upon which to run applications, particularly client/server applications. The memory mapping scheme frees Windows NT from concerns about what happens when the physical memory becomes inadequate, provides an automatic mechanism for the protection of applications from interference with one another, and provides an effective mechanism for single servers to perform multiple tasks. It also provides a powerful base upon which to build sophisticated client/server applications, and it does so with great attention to security. That combination is quite effective.

---

27 Fortunately, NT has a graceful way to handle even this case, as discussed in the section on memory management in Chapter 5.

28 *Handles* are identifiers used to manipulate objects, including files, memory locations, devices, and the like.

Built-in Networking

As we've seen, every subsystem in Windows NT has been designed with connectivity and networking in mind. This is true of other operating systems as well, particularly OS/2 (in which much of the same low-level infrastructure we have discussed here is provided). But Windows NT goes a step further: it provides built-in networking features that go beyond anything packaged with any other operating system. The NEXTstep operating system comes close, but even it doesn't quite match what is provided with Windows NT.

When Windows NT 3.1 was introduced, it brought with it networking that was widely described as a "superset of Windows for Workgroups peer networking"—that is, peer-level file- and printer-sharing. An unlimited number of simultaneous connections was supported, irrespective of whether the base NT 3.1 product or the more sophisticated NT Advanced Server (NTAS) 3.1 was used (though only the latter provided the tools required to effectively manage large multi-server networks). As a result, the first edition of this book contained a long discussion of when and why to use NTAS instead of NT (among other things, we recommended using NT as a file server on most smaller LANs).

Beginning with Windows NT 3.5, Microsoft changed the rules. The base product, now renamed *Windows NT Workstation,* supports a maximum of 10 simultaneous in-bound connections for file- and printer-sharing.[29] This renders it unusable as a server on all but the smallest LANs. NTAS, renamed *Windows NT Server*, continues to support an unlimited number of users and supports basic NT-style *workgroups* as well as multi-server *domains*. As a result, we now recommend using only NT Server where a file and print server is required.[30]

Windows NT Workstation

Adding "Workstation" to the low-end product's name marks two significant changes: the introduction of real workstation features in NT and a much clearer distinction between a workstation (or advanced desktop) system and a server.

To compete with UNIX as a workstation platform, Microsoft added OpenGL graphics to Windows NT. OpenGL provides really fast 3D rendering with shading, textures, and light source

---

29 The resulting *10*-connection limit has not been popular with Windows NT users or with members of the NT development team (though statements by Dave Cutler to the effect that there's no difference in the NT Server and Workstation Code are a mite excessive). What NT Workstation gives up in its connection limit is more than made up for desktop users by its desktop-optimized memory tuning and by incorporation of true workstation features like OpenGL 3D graphics (the latter is available on NT Server as well).

30 With NT 4.0 Microsoft changed the rules again. Beta versions of NT 4.0 Workstation had the same "10-connection limit" as NT 3.5 and 3.51 Workstation, but the first release candidate extended the limit to low-level Internet protocol (IP) connections, rendering NT 4.0 Workstation useless as an Internet server platform. Microsoft bowed to pressure from users and third-party vendors and removed this software-enforced limit from the shipping version—however, the NT 4.0 Workstation license agreement restricts *all* use of the system for more than 10 network users.

position handled automatically. Unlike the original NT base product, in which OpenGL support was available only as an add-on from Intergraph Corp,[31] from version 3.5 on Windows NT Workstation has OpenGL support built-in at the kernel level. As a result, as long as fast graphics hardware is available, it really *can* compete with UNIX workstations in performance and typically does so for a much lower cost.

Moreover, as hardware accelerators for OpenGL appear (Intergraph sells several models for use with its systems, and more are coming from other manufacturers), Windows NT Workstations will provide performance equal to (or better than!) that of the most highly optimized UNIX workstations (for examples of NT's penetration in the heretofore UNIX-dominated Workstation realm, see Chapter 11).

Aside from providing high-performance 3D graphics, Microsoft took several other steps to optimize NT Workstation as a desktop platform. In particular, NT Workstation's memory footprint was reduced significantly. Several steps that were taken to do this—such as reducing the overhead in NT's object storage and using a different optimization when compiling the NT kernel—also benefit NT Server. However, one obvious step could have been taken to further shrink the operating system: removing all network server functionality from the Workstation version.

Microsoft chose not to do this. Workstations aren't servers, but they're often *used* as servers, particularly in UNIX environments where X/Windows distributed applications are run across a range of machines. After considerable debate, Microsoft decided to keep file-and-print server functionality in NT Workstation, but limited it to a maximum of 10 concurrent connections.

What about people who used Windows NT 3.1 as a server in small networks? In the first edition of *Networking Windows NT* we flatly recommended that people running a simple single-server LAN buy NT 3.1 rather than NTAS, because it was cheaper and easier to install. Did the 10-connection limit leave those users out in the cold? No. Microsoft wisely provided an alternative for users upgrading from the Windows NT 3.1 base product. Those using NT mainly as a desktop environment could upgrade to NT Workstation for $99. Those using it as a server could upgrade to Windows NT Server for $149, including licenses for 20 client connections (about which we'll learn more shortly), which brings us to the other version of Windows NT.[32]

---

31   This company originated the RISC-based UNIX graphical desktop workstation in 1984 and has now converted its product line to Windows NT on Intel-based systems. Intergraph sells several such systems, along with a vast range of technical workstation software and UNIX compatibility tools for NT. The company is located in Huntsville, Alabama, and can be contacted at (608) 273-6585.

32   As this is written, Microsoft has announced plans for a new upgrade to NT 4.0 Server for NT 3.51 Workstation users who have been using the workstation product as an Internet server (Web and/or FTP) platform. Exactly what the terms of this upgrade may be is uncertain; however—assuming that its cost is reasonable—we highly recommend that users investigate it, if only to avoid getting caught in whatever future steps Microsoft may take to enforce its new interpretation of the NT Workstation "10-connection limit."

Windows NT Server

Just as workstations aren't optimized for file-and-printer sharing, server products aren't ideal for high-performance desktop applications. Because NT Server isn't expected to be used as a workstation, it doesn't have to make compromises, so for instance, it doesn't automatically load DOS/Windows VDM support (as NT Workstation does, to improve 16-bit application startup speed). NT Server also has a different lazy write algorithm on its disk cache, stores its file-and-printer sharing code in non-pageable memory, allocates more threads to system services, and provides additional performance tuning options (see Chapter 5), all of which improve its server performance

The NT Server console can still be used as an application platform, so the option to use Windows NT as a non-dedicated server on small networks is preserved, but such a system won't deliver the performance of an NT workstation.[33]

In short, if you want to run NT as a server, get NT Server, not NT Workstation.

Windows NT Server Networking Windows NT Server provides a more sophisticated variant of the networking features that are built into Windows NT Workstation. It delivers domain-wide administration capability, which is important because the one great limitation of the built-in peer networking in Windows NT Workstation is that each system has to maintain its own database of user accounts. If you want to share files from your machine with everybody in the office, you simply open the Windows Explorer, right-click on the directory you want to share, click Sharing, and you will see a Properties dialog box with a button for file permissions. Select *everyone* as having *full access,* and you are done.

The trouble with that approach is it really does mean *everyone.*[34] Everyone sitting on a Windows NT, Windows 95, Windows for Workgroups, or LAN Manager-compatible system connected to yours will see every file in the shared directory. If that directory is the accounting database, you probably did not want to select everyone and full access rights. If you want to select limited access rights, just to provide access to one person for example, you must create a user account for that person on your computer using User Manager (see Chapter 3 for details). Once you've created an account for that person, you can select *everyone* as having *no access* rights but then override that by assigning full access rights to the boss.[35]

---

33 You can compensate to a large extent by adding RAM. Eight to 16MB more than would otherwise be used in a server configuration will generally limit swapping and give desktop performance that's almost indistinguishable from that of an NT Workstation. It's also possible to force a server to pre-load WOW with a registry setting, though this will be a waste of RAM unless 16-bit applications are being run. See Chapter 5 for details.

34 That is, if the built-in *guest* account is enabled (on NT Servers it's disabled by default to prevent exactly this sort of security problem). With *guest* disabled, giving "everyone" full access means that all users with valid accounts are authorized to access the resource in question.

35 Actually, this is redundant; if you omit everyone/no access you get the same result.

There are variants on the full-access and no-access privileges. One is to provide *read only* access rights. This is a powerful capability that goes well beyond the security features provided with most peer-to-peer networking systems. The one problem with it is that you have to set the access rights on your computer, as other individuals must on their computers, because there is no central administration and no provision for a global user account that would apply to all the systems. This lack of centralized management could prove to be a substantial burden if 50 different people need access to your system and all of them require separate access rights, some for accounting and some for your tape drive to perform backup operations and others for another type of access. The system is technically capable of supporting that many users, but you as an individual Windows NT user probably are not.

By providing *domain-wide* administration, Windows NT Server gets around this problem. In an administrative domain the user has an account that applies on all servers in the domain. This is a far better approach to dealing with the kind of 50 users/50 different access rights scenario just described.

Windows NT Server also has more sophisticated versions of some of the basic Windows NT services. For instance, the remote access service that allows a single user to dial into to any Windows NT system is upgraded to a multi-user remote access service that allows many users to dial into a Windows NT Server domain. The Windows NT Server also provides access capabilities to Macintosh computers.

The resulting combination of features—Domain administration, Macintosh file system support, multi-user RAS—along with the extremely powerful basic Windows NT feature set makes it possible to construct very complex (and powerful) *enterprise networks* using Windows NT (see Figure 1.7). The following sections briefly examine each of these features (for more details, see Chapter 8).

Domain Administration Windows NT Workstation *can* function as a file server and does so any time you use the Windows Explorer to share a directory. It can also share printers, and in principle it can share other devices, so it is a server and a very powerful one. It does, however, have two serious limitations. First, as noted earlier, it's limited to 10 simultaneous inbound file and printer connections, so it's a usable server only on very small networks (and, beginning with version 4.0, it's limited to supporting a maximum of 10 network users for all types of services). Second, the user accounts created for a Windows NT Workstation extend only to that particular machine (an approach called *Workgroup Security*). Suppose you have a network with two file servers, one of which is used for accounting information and the other for sales information. Obviously, sales representatives have accounts on only the sales computer and accountants have accounts on only the accounting computer. But what about a corporate manager who has an urgent need for access to both? In a basic Windows NT Workgroup the only way to provide such access is to give that manager two accounts, one for each server. Now the manager can have the same account name and password on both servers, making life simpler. But life becomes complicated for a system administrator asked to maintain such a system because anytime passwords are changed or accounts are changed, the administrator must change the account database information individually on each server on the network.

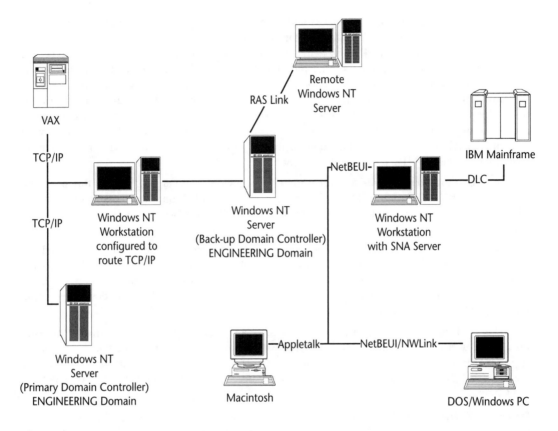

FIGURE 1.7 Enterprise network diagram. NT 4.0's built-in networking functions include Microsoft NetBEUI protocol for local workstations and servers, routable TCP/IP protocol for the enterprise, Remote Access Services (RAS) for connecting remote machines over telephone, X.25, and ISDN lines, NetWare-compatible NWLink IPX protocol for application servers, and (NT Server *only*) Appletalk and Macintosh File System support. An add-on product (SNA Server for Windows NT) exploits the built-in Data Link Control (DLC) protocol to provide connectivity to IBM mainframes. Not shown is an array of built-in printer support functions that include print pooling, network printer support, and (NT Server *only*) built-in PostScript printer emulation.

Worse, because Windows NT Workstation is not designed to be administered remotely, the system administrator must go to each individual server to perform these changes in the account database. This is the basic technical limitation of Windows NT Workstation-based networking: *It cannot be centrally administered.*

Windows NT Server changes this situation by introducing the concept of *domain-based security*. A domain is an arbitrary group of Windows NT Servers. At least one of these servers, however, will be designated as a domain controller. Domain controllers maintain a central user account database that applies to all servers within the domain. The effect is dramatic from the point of view of a system administrator, and it is even convenient from the standpoint of end users. Each end user needs only a single account, which can provide privileges as required by any server within the domain. Indeed, because of the unique Windows NT Server feature called *inter-domain trust,* it is possible for a single user account to have privileges spanning many domains. This concept, one of the most powerful that Windows NT Server has introduced, is called a *Single Enterprise Logon*, which we will return to in Chapter 8.

Administrative User Profiles Just having the ability to create domain-wide user accounts is a big advantage, of course. But Windows NT Server goes further by allowing administrators to define *user profiles* and *system policies* that span all servers on the network. The user profile determines which servers a user can access, which workstations he may log in from, what time(s) of day he may log in. It even allows an administrator to determine which folders are displayed by the Windows Explorer. This capability, used alone or in conjunction with Windows NT's powerful log-in scripts, allows tremendous administrative control, making Windows NT Server (with Domain Security enabled) your best choice for all but the most limited Windows NT installations.

In NT 4.0 this powerful capability is extended to NT and Windows 95-based clients with a universal System Policy Editor that supports both. See Chapter 3 for more details.

Directory Replication Another feature the Windows NT Server adds is the ability to replicate directory tree structures from one server to another. This is useful on large networks to allow users to get logged in and access network-wide services without having to wait for a response from a particular server, and it can be a boon to administrators who need to provide copies of material (such as corporate standard documents) that changes regularly.

NT Server's built-in replication is, however, limited to servers within a domain and to servers that operate as domain controllers. A more flexible form of replication is available through the software distribution feature of Microsoft's Systems Management Server (SMS) add-on product. See Chapter 8 for details.

Fault Tolerance Though modern off-the-shelf PC hardware is acceptable for a broad range of applications including basic network servers up to the departmental level, when you consider enterprise services for mission-critical applications, situations in which file servers simply must not go down, support for fault-tolerant hardware becomes essential. Windows NT Server approaches fault tolerance by providing redundancy at the weakest points of PC hardware and software—mass data storage, generally in the hard disk. Windows NT Server achieves this redundancy through the transaction-logging features of NTFS, ensuring that short of a hardware failure, the disk *structure* (but not necessarily the data) can be recovered, either alone or in conjunction with conventional redundant data storage techniques: mirrored disk partitions, disk duplexing, and RAID5 mass storage.

NTFS—A Recoverable File System NT provides a file system that's designed to be proof against anything short of a head crash. Along with its other features (per-file security, long filenames, support for large media, etc.) NTFS is a *recoverable* file system. Operations on an NTFS disk are treated as transactions, and are logged, redundantly, in a special log file. On boot-up, the NTFS driver examines this log file, determines if any transactions are incomplete, and "rolls back" incomplete transactions from the disk.[36] This practice ensures that after boot-up, an NTFS device will always be in a known state, but it does *not* ensure that the data will be written to disk. When a transaction is rolled back, any data associated with it is lost. To ensure data integrity, it's necessary to use one of NT's data redundancy techniques.

Mirroring The easiest of these concepts to understand is partition mirroring. In a mirrored disk environment Windows NT Server maintains two images of the data for a particular disk. It does this on two separate disk partitions coupled to a single controller. The first drive, called the primary partition, receives data just as it otherwise would. The second partition, called the mirror, receives a back-up copy of the primary's data. Windows NT Server then performs a comparison to verify that the data written to the two partitions matches. If it does, Windows NT Server assumes that the data is correct. If the data does not match, Windows NT Server can consult parity information to determine which set of data is correct. The result is a mirrored disk drive, and it is about as reliable as you can get, short of duplicating the disk controllers altogether.

Duplex Drives Duplex drives provide a level of redundancy beyond that of the mirrored disk drives, and they do so in the simplest possible way. Two physical disks and two disk controllers are used. Windows NT Server writes all information twice using the two different controllers. Again, a comparison is done every time disk information is read, and this process can exact a significant performance impact because two separate disk controllers must be accessed over and above the overhead of accessing the two drives. But it does provide an additional degree of redundancy in case of extreme failure conditions. Both drive duplexing and disk mirroring are covered in Chapter 3.

Stripe Sets and RAID5 Traditional methods of achieving redundancy in mass storage, such as drive duplexing and disk mirroring, exact a performance penalty on servers that use them. The operating system simply must do more work because data has to be written twice. In parallel with and to a certain extent competing with this method has been a move to a new technology for creating very large disk spaces. This technology is called RAID, which stands for Redundant Array of Inexpensive Disks. The concept is very simple. Instead of buying a single 100GB disk drive, why not buy ten 10GB disk drives and drive them all in parallel? You achieve a number of advantages this way.

Small-volume drives are often cheaper. Although economy can be lost when you initially buy many small drives (a 100GB disk pack built on RAID principles is likely to cost more than a single 100GB disk drive), there is one overwhelming advantage: the hardware is redundant. A failure in one of the disk drives can lose, at most, one-tenth of the overall data. And the replacement cost of one small disk drive will be much less than the cost of replacing a 100GB drive. It is a very attractive proposition. It has one other great advantage: vastly increased performance.

---

36 If you think this terminology sounds more like that for a database than a file system, you're paying attention—and you'll find the much-ballyhooed *Object File System (OFS)* of Windows NT *Cairo* that much easier to understand!

When a RAID drive is accessed, data is striped across all the disks. That is, parts of a sector are written on drive one, parts on drive two, parts on drive three, and so forth. In a RAID5 drive, parity information is written to one of the disks to validate data. That parity information is vital because the one great problem with a RAID drive is recovery from disk errors. Requiring data to be written simultaneously on 10 disk drives means that 10 times the hardware is involved, making failures 10 times as likely. So in a RAID environment, reliability and performance trade off.

RAID5 combines the advantages of performance and data redundancy. The redundancy in this case does come with a price. In a mirrored or duplexed disk drive situation, recovering from a disk failure is simple—just remove and replace the disk mirror or the duplex disk drive at fault and copy the data from the intact partition or disk drive. (Simply disabling the mirroring on a mirrored partition or reverting from drive duplexing to a single drive will also let you continue to operate, but you risk losing all data because redundancy is gone.) In any case, restoring data is a very quick process.

In a RAID5 drive, data restoration is a slower process because the data must be reconstructed from the parity information. However, because parity information represents total redundancy across all drives connected, short of simultaneous failure on two drives, RAID5 data is completely redundant. This redundancy combines the ultimate in protection with very, very high disk performance, the penalties being expensive hardware and slow restoration of redundant data if a write error occurs. Because of the requirement to drive many hard disks in parallel, RAID5 support is usually achieved with a high-speed SCSI disk controller and multiple SCSI hard disks. Windows NT Server can provide RAID5 support with from three to nine disk drives or partitions.

Clustering The holy grail of fault tolerance is the "cluster", in which several physically separate servers are grouped together in a single logical unit. Clusters come in two general types: in "fail-over" (also called "hot-standby") clusters a failure in the primary server will cause it to fail and its place to be taken by the standby server. In a true distributed cluster, two or more physical servers operate constantly—as client requests come in, they're serviced by whichever server is least heavily loaded. The latter approach has a major advantage over the simpler type: you get a performance benefit by running additional hardware.

At this writing, NT doesn't come with any built-in cluster support;[37] but add-on support is available from several third parties. See Chapter 8 for details.

Remote Access Services Like Macintosh file system support, Remote Access Services (RAS) is a built-in feature of both Windows NT Workstation and Server. Remote Access Services amounts to a technique for providing dial-in access (through modems and phone lines

---

37 Microsoft is working on a clustering technology code-named "Wolfpack," which should be available shortly after this book is published. Initially, it will be a simple fail-over cluster; eventually it's supposed to be generalized to a distributed approach. If past experience with Microsoft's beta-on-the-Internet approach is any guide, you can expect to see a "WolfPack Beta" item on http://www.microsoft.com/ntserver not long after the third edition of this book goes to press.

or special-purpose X.25 and ISDN interfaces) that, aside from the reduced data rate, is not visibly different from logging directly into the server over a normal network connection. RAS is well suited to copying small data files, such as text files. It is ill suited to remote execution of networked programs or to transmission of a large data file such as Postscript bitmaps or the like.

In NT 4.0, Microsoft renamed the client-side component of RAS dial-up networking for consistency with Windows 95. The new version was also modified to use standard universal modem (Unimodem) drivers, which are also used by the Telephone Dialer accessory and the Hyperterminal application. Among other things, Unimodem vastly improves NT 4.0's support for Integrated Services Digital Networking (ISDN) devices. NT 4.0 Dial Up Networking also provides client-side support for PPTP.

A single-user RAS implementation is provided in Windows NT Workstation, and Microsoft has similar software available for DOS, Windows 3.*x,* and Windows 95 clients. Windows NT Server provides a more sophisticated version, capable of supporting up to 256 remote workstations at each server.[38] Further details on Remote Access Services (and other forms of Wide-Area Networking) may be found in Chapter 8.

Macintosh File System Support As mentioned earlier, Macintosh support has been a feature available for LAN Manager since version 2.1, but it has always been an extra-cost item. Windows NT Server includes Macintosh file system support at no additional cost. That's significant because the Macintosh does represent a significant proportion of the installed base of networking personal computers and because bridging requirements in connecting Macintosh computers into conventional networks have generally been high. Windows NT Server exploits NTFS to provide Macintosh clients with what amounts to a native file space, while making that space available to DOS, Windows, OS/2, and Windows NT clients at the same time. For more details, see Chapter 8.

Other NT Server Features Beginning with version 3.5, Microsoft enhanced NT Server to include a range of new features. Chief among these were a completely rewritten TCP/IP stack featuring Dynamic Host Configuration Protocol (DHCP), Windows Internet Name Service (WINS), and UNIX-compatible line printer support (see Chapter 6 for details on TCP/IP) followed by a range of TCP/IP-compatible Internet services in the NT 3.5 Resource Kit (see Appendix 4 for Resource Kit information). NT Server 4.0 extends this Internet support to a sophisticated Internet Information Server, which is covered (along with other Internet-related topics) in Chapter 7.

NT Server 3.5 also gained migration tools for NetWare and a Gateway Server for NetWare service. This was followed by full NetWare 3.12-compatible server emulation, called File and Print services for NetWare (FPNW), made available as an add-on for NT Server 3.51 and 4.0 (see Chapter 10 for details on NetWare support).

Do You Need Windows NT Server?

Windows NT Server's many advanced features make it sound like an extremely attractive package, and indeed it is. But there is a price to be paid for all these features—literally. As of this writing,

---

38 In NT Server 3.5 and later versions NTAS 3.1 supported only 64 simultaneous RAS users, and RAS in 3.1 was generally much less capable.

Windows NT Workstation is "estimated retail priced" (Microsoft no longer publishes "list" prices) at $319. That price buys one NT Workstation capable of supporting up to 10 clients for file and print services. The equivalent price for NT Server, currently $619, includes *no* client licenses. Those are extra and start at about $30 each. This split model, in which there are two license fees—one per server and another per client—is a concept Microsoft refers to as an "information access" license.

"Information Access" Licensing In NT 3.1, Microsoft took a very bullish position on licensing: it was per server, period. NTAS 3.1 had a list price of $2,995. Users never paid that much, because Microsoft introduced it at a "promotional price" of $1,495, which never went up. As part of the promotion it gave the client software away free, downloadable from CompuServe or by ftp from Microsoft's FTP site. That was a great deal, especially compared with NetWare, which is traditionally licensed to a certain number of users per server.

With the introduction of Windows NT Server 3.5, Microsoft moved to an "information access license" as described above. For NT Server 3.5, the "estimated retail prices" on introduction were approximately $619 per server and $30 per client.

This model *seems* similar, at first glance, to the traditional up-to-a-given-number-of-clients licensing scheme used by Novell for NetWare and by Microsoft in earlier networking products. It isn't. In that model, if you have 100 users and two servers, you need to buy two 100-user licenses. If you add a server, you need to add it with a 100-client license. In the "information access" model, you buy two server licenses and 100 client licenses. Because the client licenses authorize access to any number of servers, adding a server doesn't require adding client licenses.

This model is a bit complicated to understand at first but is actually a bargain for many network administrators. To date, Microsoft has priced its licenses so competitively that in a worst-case scenario wherein you have just one server and thousands of clients, the price is substantially less than that for any competitor. In more realistic scenarios, with a lower client-to-server ratio, the "information access" scheme provides lower average cost because the server licenses are priced competitively as well.

The one problem with "information access" licensing is the need to have a client license, which would render NT useless as a disconnected operating system for Internet use. Microsoft has recognized this, initially excepting FTP Internet access from the client licensing requirements. With NT 3.51, a "concurrent connections" license option was added, in which the server may be licensed for a given maximum number of concurrent connections, with the client requiring no license for server access. This allows you, for example, to buy a 20-user license to a given server and make it available to hundreds of users, provided no more than 20 are logged in at any given time. The decision to use concurrent licensing as opposed to per-client information access licensing is made at the time the server is installed and is covered in more detail in Chapter 2.

Regardless of the license option you choose, NT Server requires one license for each connected user. That requirement differentiates it from NT Workstation, which requires no client license but is limited to a maximum of 10 concurrent connections at a time.

Choosing Between NT Server and NT Workstation Obviously, it's a lot less expensive to use NT Workstation than NT Server if you can. To help make the decision, here's a list of the features NT Server includes that NT Workstation lacks:

- Support for use by more than 10 concurrent network users

- Single-user accounts that span multiple servers

- Administrative user profiles

- Directory replication

- Fault-tolerant disk support

- Macintosh file system support

- Multi-user remote access service

- Advanced TCP/IP support (DHCP, WINS, etc.)

- Advanced NetWare support (GSNW, Migration Tool, FPNW-compatible)

- Support for upgrading LAN Manager 2.*x* user accounts

- Integrated Internet (Web, FTP, and Gopher) services, licensed for unlimited access (NT Workstation provides a less capable version licensed only for 10 simultaneous connections, as explained below.)

If you need any of the above features, you have no choice—Windows NT Server is your operating system. Windows NT Server is also important because it's the platform for Microsoft's *Back Office* server suite.

Microsoft Back Office There is a larger element to all this. Microsoft is applying the NT Server "information access" license scheme to its entire server-based product line: SQL Server, SNA Server, Systems Management Server, and NT-based versions of MS Mail (and its successor, Exchange Server). All carry "information access" licenses and are available bundled in a suite called "Microsoft Back Office."

Before the Back Office announcement, Microsoft had at least four different models in place for client licensing of server-based software: NTAS 3.1 was licensed per server with unlimited clients, SQL Server had a NetWare-style per-client license, SNA Server was licensed per connection, and MS-Mail had separate per-server and per-client prices (rather like the new "information access" model). This approach was something of a nightmare for both Microsoft and network managers.

Under the new policy, there's a much simpler approach: if a client needs access to file-and-print services from NT Servers, you buy the appropriate license. If the same client needs SQL Server access, that's another license, and so on. Note that these are per-client licenses, independent of which server (or how many) the client is accessing. And, as with NT Server, there aren't any hard-coded limits you have to beat. When you add your 201st user, you need to buy your 201st client kit, not a new box of server software.

Of course, just as with NT Server, not all users are happy with information access licensing, so Microsoft also offers "concurrent connection" licensing for most Back Office products.[39]

---

39 Systems Management Server is currently restricted to per-user licensing.

This is particularly important for products like SNA Server, in which you might well have a single server with hundreds (even thousands) of clients. If you can live with only a limited number of those clients having simultaneous access to the server, a concurrent connection license will be substantially cheaper.

Aside from a common licensing model, all applications in the Back Office bundle share a common Windows NT-based architecture, user interface, and administrative options, including common support for unattended installation using SMS' software distribution feature. The applications are available either separately or as a unified suite that includes all the component applications. Microsoft has also introduced a "designed for Back Office" logo program, which denotes third-party applications that support the same range of common features.

Back Office is bundled by several server manufacturers, among them AT&T GIS and Motorola, on high-end NT Server systems. Whether the economics of selling several software products in a single package will prove as compelling on servers as on desktop systems remains to be seen.

Microsoft's license terms, pricing, and upgrade policy for Back Office products changed considerably during the first three editions of this book and appears to be changing again as this is written. Rather than present a table of prices that will probably be obsolete by the time you read this, we recommend that you browse http://www.microsoft.com/BackOffice (check the How to Buy link) or call Microsoft sales at (800) 426-9400 for current terms and restrictions.

System Requirements In addition to the higher price for Windows NT Server, bear in mind that the system requirements for the Windows NT Server exceed those of Windows NT Workstation. See Chapter 2 for detailed information.

NT Server Limitations NT Server does have some limitations when operated in extremely large installations. Although a limited directory replication service is built into the product, it replicates only user accounts and selected read-only data, such as log-in scripts. Scalability is currently limited to a maximum of 16 CPUs per server (though demonstration systems have been built with more), and in real applications a practical limit is currently nearer six to eight CPUs. There is also currently no built-in support for clustering, and in any case, NT lacks the kind of per-user charge-back accounting and quota enforcement software that's essential in "glasshouse" operations.[40] In 1995, David Cutler (the ex-Digital software architect who designed NT), said that NT Server wouldn't be ready to operate as a full-scale mainframe replacement for "two years or so." Although some might disagree (National Westminster Bank, for one, is moving to NT as a standard platform corporation-wide), we're inclined to agree with his assessment.

Other Networks The built-in networking features of Windows NT are quite sophisticated, but they have one basic problem. They are proprietary to Microsoft, and therefore, although they will interact beautifully with other Microsoft systems, they aren't designed to interoperate with Novell NetWare or other third-party networks. Microsoft has, however, provided a mechanism that makes it relatively easy to provide additional networking services in Windows NT. This capability depends, first of all, on the layered device driver model and the treatment of networks

---

40   Third parties are working on some of these problems. See Chapter 8 for details.

as a file system that we described earlier. It also depends on two new levels of interface that are built into Windows NT at the device driver level, the *Network Device Interface Specification* (NDIS), which is the way that network device drivers for Windows NT are built, and above that, the *Transport Driver Interface* (TDI), which provides a direct link among all redirectors or network file systems and the network transport drivers.

A network provider who wishes to provide a redirector for Windows NT needs only to write an installable file system to provide services on that network and a transport driver for the type of networking protocol that's in use (such as IPX/SPX on NetWare, or NBF for NT's native Microsoft networking, or TCP/IP on UNIX systems[41]). There is no need to write drivers for the specific network cards because NDIS can provide this. It's necessary only to write the other components. There is an option to write conventional monolithic network card drivers, and some network manufacturers have done so. In particular, early versions of Novell's NetWare Client director for NT required *Open Datalink Interface* (ODI) drivers.

By doing this, Novell bypassed the various layers of the NT subsystem below the redirector. Instead of the redirector behaving like a file system, communicating with the I/O manager, then communicating with a transport driver through the transport driver interface and in turn, to a network card via NDIS in the NetWare system, the NetWare redirector is communicating directly with the ODI subsystem, which is communicating with an ODI driver. There are some theoretical advantages to this monolithic approach. First, it's faster. The overhead involved in the multi-layered interface used by the Windows NT native networking is eliminated. There are reports that the ODI-based Windows NT redirector is significantly faster than the built-in NT networking on the same network hardware. It's also true that this kind of approach simplifies matters for a company like Novell that has a lot of internal expertise built up in a system like ODI and can leverage this to quickly provide services for systems like Windows NT if they move the entire system over.

Unfortunately, this created a situation in which Windows NT users who required NetWare support would have to deal with two completely different types of network drivers. Because Novell persisted in using this non-standard approach, Microsoft introduced its own Client Services for NetWare (CSNW) for NT Workstations, Gateway Services for NetWare (GSNW), and NetWare migration tool for NT Servers, and File and Print services for NetWare (FPNW). All are described in Chapter 10.

TCP/IP Services In addition to the native LAN Manager-compatible networking built into Windows NT, a second kind of networking is built in: TCP/IP services of the type used by UNIX systems. The terminology gets a little complicated because one can refer to a couple of different things when one refers to TCP/IP. On one hand, TCP/IP is a transport, and there is a TCP/IP transport driver that is fully compatible with the built-in networking system. If you wish, you can run TCP/IP networking instead of NetBEUI-based networking, and if you're running a large network, you'll want to. See Chapter 6 and Appendix 2 for details.

UNIX systems also use TCP/IP, but most do not use the LAN Manager Universal Naming Convention (UNC) interfaces that are used by Windows NT nor the NetBIOS protocols on which they're based. So simply installing the TCP/IP transport to Windows NT will not immediately give you connectivity to UNIX systems. What will give you connectivity to UNIX systems are

---

41   See Appendix 2 for details on protocols and device drivers.

the low-level TCP/IP utilities (ping.exe, ftp.exe, etc.), which provide essentially native UNIX-style TCP/IP services. Windows NT lacks a Network File System (NFS) redirector and other facilities that would make this a complete end-to-end system (though such products are available from third parties—see Chapter 11). NT Server 3.5 augmented these basic features with some exciting new ones, as mentioned above, and the NT 3.5 resource kit added a variety of Internet tools, including World Wide Web, gopher, WAIS, and DNS servers. By the time NT Server 3.51 came out, Internet mania was beginning to take hold in a serious way, and Microsoft decided to address it, initially by providing Internet Information Server (IIS) as an add-on and then by integrating Internet features directly into NT 4.0.

IIS—along with its various competitors—was a breakthrough category of products for NT Server. Until shrink-wrapped NT-based Webservers became available, most Webmasters ran UNIX-based servers. With the availability of Microsoft's IIS, Netscape's Commerce Server, and O'Reilly's WebSite (among others) it became possible to set up an NT-based Internet server much more simply and cheaply than a UNIX-based one.

NT 4.0 and the Internet Windows NT 4.0 is Microsoft's first major product release since the Internet became the holy grail of networking. As a result, the new version incorporates many Internet-related features, including the following:

- IIS for NT Server, and a compatible *Peer Web Server* (PWS) in NT Workstation *Point-to-Point Tunneling Protocol* (PPTP), which allows you to use the Internet as a virtual private network

- Firewall-like *packet filtering* for each network adapter (NT 4.0's TCP/IP driver can filter packets to limit them to specific port numbers, source addresses, or destination addresses.)

- Microsoft's *Internet Explorer 2.0* client-side Web browser

- *Dynamic DNS support* in NT 4.0 Server

Beyond the Internet features bundled into NT 4.0, Microsoft has discussed general plans for several additional Internet-related products but, as of this writing, has yet to announce pricing, availability, or in some cases even the final product names. "Tripoli" is the code name for an efficient search engine add-on to IIS and PWS, "Catapult" is the code name for an NT-hosted proxy server, and "Normandy" is the code name for a scalable high-capacity server technology originally built for the Microsoft Network (MSN). Normandy provides mail, news, chat, document search, user customization, and on-line shopping features (as this was written, CompuServe had just announced plans to deploy Normandy technology).

The level of Internet support built into NT 4.0 is so significant that in this edition of *Networking Windows NT* we've devoted all of Chapter 7 to it, in addition to our basic coverage of TCP/IP in Chapter 6.

Conclusion

The basic system features of Windows NT have been developed with connectivity in mind. From a client/server design that supports symmetric multiprocessing for very large servers to built-in networking and a file system designed to support very large volumes, virtually every element of Windows NT incorporates some feature that makes networking easier. Truly, this is an operating system *designed* to connect, as the explosive growth of NT support on the Internet over the last 18 months proves!

For More Information

Cringely, Robert X. (1992), *Accidental Empires.* New York: Harper Business (a division of Harper Collins), ISBN: 0-88730-621-7. Biting but generally accurate history of the personal computer industry. The NT coverage here is limited (the book was published before NT 3.1 shipped), but the history leading up to its release—as a Windows operating system rather than an advanced version of OS/2—is excellent, as is Cringely's brilliant yet simple explanation of such esoteric topics as why computers change so quickly (Moore's Law). If you read only one of the additional books referenced in this work, read this one!

Custer, Helen (1993), *Inside Windows NT.* Redmond, WA: Microsoft Corp., ISBN: 1-55615-481-X. Outstanding (and detailed) general coverage of the Windows NT architecture. Chapter 6 (on NT's networking features) is especially valuable.

Custer, Helen (1995), *Inside the Windows NT File System.* Redmond, WA: Microsoft Corp., ISBN: 1-55615-660-X. Thin but necessary volume that adds vital file system information to the original *Inside Windows NT.* Custer is one of the original Digital refugees whom Dave Cutler took with him to Microsoft, and her work in documenting the system as it's being developed has been a vital factor in its success.

Microsoft Staff (1993–1996), *Windows NT Resource Kit, Volumes 1–6.* Redmond, WA: Microsoft Corp. Detailed coverage of all aspects of Windows NT operation. An essential reference for all Windows NT system administrators. Volume 2 ("Windows NT Networking Guide") is particularly useful, containing information available nowhere else, including in this book (though *some* things are better covered here!).

Zachary, G. Pascal (1994), *Showstopper!.* New York: The Free Press (a division of Macmillan, Inc.), ISBN: 0-02-9535671-7. An insightful, often hilarious, history of NT development, written by a Wall Street Journal reporter. Occasionally inaccurate (one of the principal characters covered in the book calls it "about two-thirds right") but well worth reading for the flavor of how and why NT became what it is and why its future is certain to be as unpredictable as its past.

Preparing to Connect

Windows NT Installation

When you have finished reading this chapter, you should understand:

- ⇨ How to conduct a network needs analysis
- ⇨ How to select and organize components for a Windows NT Network
- ⇨ The Windows NT installation process
- ⇨ How to install Windows NT over a network
- ⇨ Supporting NT on portable systems (including the use of NT 4.0 Hardware Profiles)
- ⇨ The most common installation problems and how to work around them

> You should feel comfortable installing and configuring Windows NT
> Workstations and stand-alone servers. You should *not* feel "comfortable" about
> assuming responsibility for the network planning on your own, but you should
> understand how to *become* comfortable with your particular network needs.

Before you purchase Windows NT and install it, you must first create a plan for your network. You should think of this plan as a network blueprint which, like an architect's blueprint for a building, must contain the information necessary to create a sturdy structure for many people to use on a regular basis.

The plan will be based on the data that you provide through a network needs analysis for your particular business. The needs analysis is really a series of questions that you answer to provide yourself with the information you'll require to create your network plan and set up your server. A network needs analysis checklist appears below. Use this as a guide when creating your network.

Your network blueprint will provide for more than just information about users; you'll also need to include information about the type of users and the work they'll be doing, the amount of storage space they'll require, and their hours of operation. This information will help you plan for the type of hardware that you'll need and the amount of RAM and server storage, in addition to the reliability of the equipment you'll use for your server and network.

Conducting a Network Needs Analysis

Network Needs Analysis Checklist

- Goal statement

- Number of initial users

- Maximum number of expected users

- Type of work to be conducted

- Application requirements

- Estimated minimum storage requirements

- Hours of operation

- Building power

- Type of office space

- Uninterruptible power supply (UPS) required

- Level of reliability required

- Level of security required

Let's begin by looking at what you intend to do with your network and server in the first place. To start, you should be able to define your network's goal in a few sentences. Your goal needn't be complex, but it should be concrete and specific. For instance, "a way for my users all over the building to store their data," is not only vague, but, if it were truly all you wanted in a network, you'd be wasting a lot of time installing such a powerful network operating system as Windows NT Server, when all you really wanted was some common data storage.

Your goal statement should be specific to your particular business requirements, such as:

> *Goal: A method for the twelve-person accounting department to store and share billing and payable information, including a system of electronic mail and shared printers for printing checks, invoices, and correspondence, considering the demonstrated 20% annual increase in this department's staffing.*

This goal is concrete and finite; it defines the purpose of the network and server and outlines the specific required network functions. This plan also includes the department's future needs.

While conducting your network needs analysis, you should plan for expansion and flexibility. Planning for the definite contingencies is often difficult, and planning for the future may seem impossible; but you do have certain facts to assist you. For example, you can look at the department's historic growth rate and the amount of work you will be performing. You also should consider the cyclical nature of the department and business. In other words, you should be aware of when your peak work cycles occur. All of this information is important when creating your plan.

From this information, you can begin to assess your network's requirements. While you conduct your network needs analysis, it's also important to include comments from your users. If you refer again to the network needs analysis checklist, you'll see the general nature of the questions to ask.

This planning stage is the relatively simple part of creating your plan, asking and answering questions; however, people often skip this step entirely. Sometimes they forget to include users or plans for future growth. Either mistake will create a problem later when the network has been purchased and installed. Better to spend a couple of days planning now than to spend many weeks later on debating the need to purchase more hard disk storage. Enough lecture; don't neglect your plan.

Planning the Physical Layout

Once you have collected the needed information, you can begin to blueprint your physical network. The physical location of all the cabling and equipment necessary for your network should be drafted on a layer over the building blueprint. When planning the physical layout, be as accurate as possible so that the correct amount of cabling will be purchased and network connections will be convenient for each workstation.

Blueprinting your network in a logical order (e.g., from the server out to the desktops and peripherals) will help you take into account all needed hardware. Blueprinting will also highlight any problem areas that you need to consider while having cabling installed.

Server Location and Power Concerns The server must be located where it will be immediately accessible to the network administrator and inaccessible to daily office traffic. A well-ventilated storage closet that can be locked would serve the purpose. If your building is not air-conditioned, you may elect to purchase and install an air-conditioner for your server closet. You need to be sure that the server receives power from a different electrical circuit than the air-conditioner.

Speaking of power, you *must* have an uninterruptible power supply (UPS) for your server. Power failures are especially common during the summer months, when severe electrical storms and heavy electrical usage for air-conditioning combine to create an atmosphere conducive to brownouts or blackouts. An unexpected power failure can wreak disaster on an unprotected server.

Uninterruptible power supplies vary in their power ratings and features, but all sources provide the same basic functionality. A UPS is a DC battery source that sits between your server (or workstation) and your building's AC power and uses building power to sustain its charge, usually enough power to keep your server running through a proper shutdown cycle. Windows NT Server's built-in UPS device management monitors the power to your server and, in case of power failure, uses the UPS battery power to automatically, and gracefully, shut down server operations.

The Windows NT UPS Control Panel option lets you configure your server to work with UPS data received via one of the serial ports. When it receives data indicating that the UPS has activated, an automated shutdown procedure executes. You can specify that a custom command file run prior to shutting down the system if your server has special requirements. Chapter 3 will give you more details about the UPS services for Windows NT.

Hub Location   As you plan your network hardware, working your way out from the server, you encounter a box called a *Hub* or *LAN Concentrator*. A hub provides a method to connect all of your workstations, servers, and peripherals.

Let's look at one type of topology: 10 Mbps Ethernet over UTP (unshielded twisted pair), or 10BaseT. The 10BaseT cabling connects your desktop systems in a star configuration to a hub, which can handle as few as four and, theoretically, as many as 1,024 devices. However, most stackable hubs contain 12 or 24 ports and are then connected to other hubs, via 10Base2 cabling or proprietary connectors, so you can expand your network. Larger hubs employ a chasis with a single backplane into which multiple cards containing Ethernet ports and other standards are mounted. Ethernet has a practical limit of 1,024 devices, including servers, that you can connect in this fashion. Don't try to exceed it! Plan for subnets, a series of smaller networks within your LAN connected via bridges or routers.

Typically, 10BaseT hubs are located in the telephone service closets where the wiring can be punched down onto a block and then wired to the hub. Your hub should be mounted in a rack for stability and placed in a ventilated area. It should also be protected by a UPS, unless it has some type of on-board power management. Again, the location of these devices should be away from high-traffic areas in a place that can be locked.

Hardware Requirements and Considerations

Chapter 1 provided an overview of the advanced features and functionality of Windows NT. Before installing Windows NT on every workstation in an enterprise, it's wise to step back and evaluate just who does and who does not need NT.

Do You Really Need Windows NT on Your Workstations? The most important consideration is the hardware that you will need to run NT. Workstations need a minimum of 12MB,[1] and servers need a minimum of 16MB. Note the word *minimum*. Systems that will make heavy use of multitasking or act as special-purpose servers will require more capacity (as you will see in the next section). Further, if you are running on the Intel platform, do not consider NT unless you are running on 486 machines. On older or lower-end machines with smaller amounts of memory, use Windows for Workgroups or Windows 95. However, you also need to evaluate which features you will use, and those you might use, before making your decision.

For example, if you are working in a secure environment such as a financial institution, NT's file sharing security, file access audit trails, and C2 security features might justify a move to NT. If security is not a high priority, a suitable workstation solution may be Windows for Workgroups (or Windows 95), because such systems can easily be connected as clients to a Windows NT server.

Furthermore, not all Windows applications can run under Windows NT. Applications that directly access hardware (such as some backup programs) cannot be run in NT because that behavior violates NT's security model.

Another consideration when making the jump to NT is the availability of drivers for your current hardware. NT Driver support for peripherals is limited and developers have noted that writing drivers is much more difficult under NT. Thus, you may wish to consider which drivers are available and match them to your current hardware devices to ensure that you can in fact run your applications.

Considering those caveats, if you've decided certain people need to run Windows NT on their desktops, then here are the system requirements:

Windows NT Hardware Requirements Here's a consolidated list of requirements and recommendations that will allow you to select and configure an appropriate computer for operation as either a Windows NT Workstation or server. The recommended configurations are based on personal experience and information published by Microsoft.[2] We absolutely recommend that you consult the current published Windows NT specifications for further information.

The particular system configuration that you will use will be some combination of a central processor unit, RAM (including CPU cache RAM), hard disk capacity (or other mass storage space), backup device, CD-ROM, floppy disk, network card, and printer. There are also a variety of special devices such as modems, multiport cards, and X.25 cards that may be appropriate in certain special circumstances.

---

1   As of this writing (August, 1996). However, memory requirements change over time. Consult Microsoft's current Windows NT Workstation Evaluation Guide for up-to-date information.

2   Configurations change regularly. The best sources we've been able to find for up-to-date information are the Planning, Migration & Deployment links on the NT Workstation (http://www.microsoft .com/ntworkstation) and NT Server (http://www.microsoft.com/ntserver) pages of Microsoft's Web site.

CPU The basic Windows NT 4.0 processor requirement published by Microsoft is a 33MHz 486 or better, Intel-compatible CPU, or an ARC[3] system-compliant Reduced Instruction Set Computing (RISC) computer (MIPS R4000 or better). We recommend that if you are investigating the purchase of a RISC system (such as one of the DEC Alpha or Motorola Power PC systems) you should consult with the manufacturer for current specifications.

As a practical matter, although NT 4.0 really will run on a 486 CPU (previous versions supported 386DX CPUs as well), we recommend at least a Pentium, or if you can afford it, a Pentium Pro. The small additional cost is more than compensated for by the performance, even on stand-alone client systems.

Most Pentium-based and all Pentium Pro-based systems come with 256KB of cache RAM. Although Microsoft has published no specifications on the subject, experiments conducted by *WINDOWS Magazine*[4] indicate that providing 256K or more of cache RAM will provide a nearly linear performance gain as the cache RAM is increased. Intel 486-series processors have an 8KB on-chip cache, and the Pentium processor has a 16KB on-chip cache. Neither processor even begins to approach the kind of cache sizes that give a real benefit in Windows NT; they are too small by a factor of ten![5] Providing 32K of cache RAM will improve matters, 64K will improve it even more, 128K provides an enormous improvement, and providing 256KB seems to be approximately the point at which the benefit tops out. Increasing from that amount to 512KB or even a megabyte will still provide an incremental improvement, but the percent improvement probably will not be worth the additional cost, where workstations are concerned.[6]

An exception to this situation might occur with technical workstations that are principally intended for compute-intensive tasks such as Computer-Aided Design, (CAD) and Computer-Aided Engineering (CAE), advanced graphics such as animation and rendering, or scientific computation. Such tasks are generally performed by RISC workstations. In such situations, increasing to 512KB or even one megabyte of cache can provide a substantial benefit; that's why we recommend that all RISC workstations be equipped with at least 512KB external cache, preferably a megabyte if it is available.

Memory Windows NT is a memory hog by DOS standards. NT requires a minimum, according to Microsoft, of 12MB RAM. However, based on experience in this and other configurations, we recommend that *all* Windows NT Workstations have a minimum of 16MB RAM. On systems

---

3   Advanced Resource Computer (ARC) part of the Advanced Computing Environment (ACE) initiative sponsored by Microsoft, MIPS, and others.

4   See "Enterprise Windows" in the August 1994 issue.

5   Intel's Pentium Pro (P6) CPU, however, has 256KB of cache on chip, perhaps a reflection of Microsoft's cooperation in its design!

6   Servers can and will benefit from even larger caches. Compaq's latest servers have a 3-tier memory architecture, and Compaq can equip such machines with 2MB of cache. Digital is using a similar approach with the most recent AXP servers, and employing such a cache allows a 200MHz AlphaServer 1000 to actually outperform a 275MHz AlphaStation 400. See the Windows NT 3.5 review in *WINDOWS Magazine's* January and February 1994 issues, and the discussion of RAM Cache in Appendix 5 for details.

that will be heavily multitasked, or that will run any NT Services (including the Peer Web Server bundled with NT 4.0 Workstation), we recommend 24MB. The small additional cost of the RAM more than pays off in improved performance.

These requirements seem excessive to people accustomed to DOS-based systems that would require only a megabyte or two, but for Windows NT, strange as it may seem, 12 or 16 megabytes is just a starting point. That is significant because, as many users are beginning to find out, 16 megabytes or more in a DOS/Windows environment may present a practical upper limit. Although it is possible to expand the memory in many current systems to 32 megabytes, DOS and Widows have fundamental limits that cannot be expanded simply by adding more memory.

A good example is Windows 3.1 system resources: 128K, no more, no less, of system space reserved for two system memory heaps that contain common resource information used by Windows applications. If you run many applications at one time and exhaust that 128K of resource space, your system will crash. Whether the system has 16MB of memory, 32MB of memory, or 100MB of memory will not matter. The system will crash. Windows NT, on the other hand, has no fundamental upper limits.[7] Beyond the basic 16MB recommendation, various Windows NT options may require additional memory.

Print Server Memory Requirements If a Windows NT Server will be used to provide shared print services to other Windows NT Workstations, it will need an additional four or more megabytes of storage space to efficiently process remote print requests. This memory is needed because Windows NT employs a powerful new concept in that you need not install the print device driver for a particular printer on all workstations. Instead, when a Windows NT Workstation initiates a PRINT command, it will open up a dialog with the print server and transmit the low-level graphics commands to the print server, which will then perform the print formatting itself. This process is easier to administer, but it does mean that the print server has to carry out a significant portion of all print operations itself. To avoid a significant performance hit, the additional memory is required in print servers. Based on examination of Microsoft documentation, it appears that 4MB of memory will be sufficient to support up to about six printers. If more printers are to be supported in a print pool, it may be necessary to add memory.

Windows NT Server Memory Requirements Windows NT Server requires a minimum of 16MB RAM, plus additional memory depending on whether you've installed any optional services. The fault-tolerance driver requires approximately 2MB additional memory (consult the Microsoft documentation or your hardware supplier for details). If, in addition to fault tolerance, you employ RAID level 5 support (stripe sets with parity), you'll need an additional 4MB of memory to support the overhead involved (three times the regular memory requirement for disk writes to provide necessary parity-computation space). Employing Windows NT Server's multi-user Remote Access Services or Macintosh file system support will also require additional memory (again, consult the latest Microsoft documentation for minimum requirements). Our own experience with operation of Windows NT Server on 32MB RISC-based and Intel-

---

7   The practical limit set by the 32-bit address range employed by Windows NT is 4GB of system memory. Moreover, Microsoft has announced that future versions of NT will support a limited form of 64-bit addressing to support systems with over 4GB of physical RAM.

based platforms has been completely satisfactory; we believe this will be sufficient for most small network file-and-printer sharing applications. Small sites running as both file-and-print and Web servers should probably start with 48MB, departmental servers need at least 64MB, and larger network servers will require more memory.

If you intend to run additional server-based applications (the various Microsoft Back Office modules, database servers, etc.), you'll need additional RAM. Because the published minimum for all NT Server versions to date is 16MB, you can determine the amount of additional memory required by subtracting 16MB from the application manufacturer's recommended minimum configuration. For example, Microsoft recommends 24MB as the minimum configuration for the Systems Management Server (SMS) component of Back Office. Subtraction yields 8MB, so add 8MB to the above numbers to come up with a working minimum for an NT Server running SMS.

Running *all* the components of Microsoft Back Office on a single server (not a very good idea, for reasons explained in Chapter 8) would require at least 64MB RAM and around 500MB of hard disk. In that case, you should use a Pentium Pro or RISC processor.

Hard Disk Space The official Microsoft requirement for Window NT 4.0 Workstation is currently 114MB of hard disk space, of which at least 20MB will be used for a paging file. For NT Server, the requirement is 147MB. Now you begin to reach one of the most complex parts of the overall Windows NT equation because that paging file can grow, and the efficiency of the paging file will be higher if its initial size is set near to the size it will eventually expand to. This is something that can only be found by experiment, and it is discussed in more detail in Chapter 5.

We recommend a minimum 500MB hard disk for Windows NT Workstations. Note that we say *workstations*, and it's important to be very clear about this distinction. If you are running Windows NT stations that are connected to a network, *and* if these stations get all of their applications support over the network and store little or nothing locally, you can work with a smaller hard disk. If you wish to use any local applications, need local storage space, or wish to operate the Windows NT system as a stand-alone workstation, then we think that the disk should be at least 500MB. Server requirements, of course, are higher, and you must provide additional space for the user files, and undoubtedly, over time, for a growing paging file.

A 1GB hard disk represents a practical minimum for a small-to-medium size server. You should add approximately 100MB for each user who will be logged in to the system, more if you make little use of server resources in your configuration. In general, if the workstations are constrained in hard disk space, you will need more server hard disk space, or vice versa.

Besides the basic storage space requirements, another consideration should be borne in mind when selecting a hard disk for a Windows NT system: the disk controller. Windows NT's preemptive multitasking, as discussed in Chapter 1, provides for a very powerful feature to improve performance: asynchronous I/O. To recap, the central processor can initiate an I/O request, for instance a request to read information from a disk file, and continue to work on other tasks while it waits for the hard disk controller to inform it that the request is complete. However, this process only applies if a hard disk controller is used, which will allow the central processor to continue to perform its work.

Very inexpensive, low-end IDE and other ST-506 interface hard disk controllers don't support this mode of operation; the CPU will have to perform the actual transfer of information into the controller, and while it's doing that, it cannot do anything else. (Such systems are particularly ill-behaved when used with NTFS compression on NT 3.51 or later.) Therefore, performance of both Windows NT Workstations and Servers will be significantly enhanced if you select a better type of disk controller such as SCSI.

For servers, if either disk-striping or RAID level 5 (disk striping with parity) support is desired, the only practical choice is a SCSI disk controller as only SCSI supports chaining of more than two or three disk drives. As a practical matter, for server operations with large hard disks, we consider SCSI the only practical choice.[8] Choices for workstations vary depending on the expense. For high-performance workstations, we recommend that SCSI be considered closely, especially given Windows NT's preference for SCSI-based CD-ROMs and tape drives (discussed later in this section). In servers, best performance will be achieved using intelligent disk controllers, which can carry out operations independently of the system's CPU.[9] Investigate the Windows NT hardware compatibility list (HCL), and talk to the systems' manufacturer about the specific configurations that are available. You probably won't want to risk selecting a hard disk controller or *any* component not listed on the NT HCL unless you have actually seen the component demonstrated with a non-Beta driver. Otherwise, you are asking for trouble.

Bus Architectures As you may imagine from the foregoing discussion of CPU, memory, and hard disk capacities required for Windows NT, the system bus architecture becomes extremely significant with Windows NT, especially in a high-performance configuration. There are currently three popular bus architectures, each with its own advantages and disadvantages. Here's a brief discussion of each architecture.

ISA Bus The most popular of today's bus architectures remains the Industry Standard Architecture (ISA) bus—that is, the original IBM AT bus as updated by today's cloners (curiously enough, not generally available from IBM!). The ISA bus in today's incarnation is a 16-bit bus architecture generally operating at a bus data rate of 8MHz. Memory is generally not available on the bus but instead is connected locally to the CPU; it will operate at significantly higher speeds, typically 25MHz. There may or may not be a *local bus* connection between the CPU and the video card operating at higher speeds. If this connection is available, you should investigate one, particularly on workstations because it can provide a significant performance enhancement.

The major advantage of the ISA bus architecture is cost. ISA bus machines are the popular "PC clones" that have made modern business computers a commodity. The major disadvantage is that ISA combines a 16-bit bus bandwidth and an 8MHz data rate, yielding a functional maximum throughput of 16MB per second. Modern CPUs operate at 32-bit data widths and hundreds of MHz, producing overall throughput of about 16 times the ISA bus throughput or higher! As you might imagine, this limit can present something of a performance bottleneck, definitely for high-performance servers or for diskless workstations that are transmitting most of their information over the network. No matter how fast your network interface card is, you can't access it any faster than the bus rate. Therefore, we recommend an ISA bus for use only for the smallest Windows NT

---

8   This text was written before the advent of ESDI, and we *still* consider SCSI to be the way to go.

9   However, beware of older intelligent controllers, which employ low-speed CPUs. If the disk controller is served by a 4MHz 186, you can bank on it being a bottleneck!

server installations. It may make sense in low-cost workstations, but it should never be used where high performance is required.

A new development in ISA is the "Plug-and-Play" ISA specification jointly developed by Intel, Compaq, Microsoft, and others. The Plug-and-Play specification provides for software control of peripheral configuration but does nothing to improve ISA's limited bandwidth. Moreover, at this time NT doesn't support Plug-and-Play (though future versions probably will), so there is little advantage in purchasing plug-and-play hardware for Windows NT.

Local Buses: VESA and PCI The bandwidth limits of ISA have led many peripheral card manu-facturers, especially video card makers, to seek a compatible alternative. They've found it in the concept of *local bus*, which basically extends the high-speed parallel bus used by RAM on the computer's motherboard to peripheral devices. Early local bus implementations were propri-etary, varying among manufacturers, and in some cases between models in a single product line. Such buses should be avoided for obvious reasons.

The need to standardize on a nonproprietary local bus architecture for video cards drove the Video Electronic Standards Association (VESA) to define the VL-Bus (VESA Local) standard. VL-Bus provides a relatively high-speed 32-bit connection, initially optimized for 25MHz machines and currently extended to support 33MHz.

VL-Bus is fine as far as it goes, but it has two problems. First, it is restricted in bandwidth (though that bandwidth is at least 6 times higher than the basic ISA bus!). Second, it is tied to the Intel x86 architecture. Intel developed a competing standard, Peripheral Connect Interchange (PCI), that eliminates those limits, and, as of this writing, PCI seems to be emerg-ing as the new industry standard for high-speed peripherals.

As always, when considering VL-Bus versus PCI for NT, it is *essential* to consult the cur-rent NT hardware compatibility list. Make sure the system you are considering is supported, and make sure the peripherals you require are available for that system's bus. If the system is new, demand a demonstration running shrink-wrapped NT—not a customized beta version—and ask for a list of compatible peripherals.

EISA Bus The Extended Industry Standard Architecture (EISA) bus was developed by a con-sortium of PC-clone manufacturers led by Compaq. EISA is functionally a 32-bit extension of the 16-bit ISA bus architecture. It has two great advantages, the first of which is that by doubling the number of bits, it effectively doubles the system throughput. EISA also provides features that allow *bus-mastering* of certain devices. That is, a hard disk controller or network interface card (or other peripheral) can effectively replace the CPU for some operations and operate independently of the CPU. This is a decided advantage, especially in servers where the bottleneck introduced by shoving data across the bus and waiting for it to be processed by a peripheral can be significant. A further advantage is compatibility: 32-bit EISA bus systems will accept 8- or 16-bit ISA bus cards, although the introduction of such cards will introduce a significant performance hit into the system and, therefore, should be avoided.

The major disadvantage of EISA bus systems is cost, both for the system itself and for the peripheral cards. In competition with the VL and PCI variants of Local Bus, high cost has led to a decline in the availability of EISA systems and peripherals.

MCA Bus The Micro Channel Architecture (MCA) used in IBM's Personal System/2 (PS/2) line of PCs was IBM's answer to the EISA bus development and an attempt to replace the ISA bus that IBM originated with the AT computer. MCA is a from-the-ground-up redesign of the computer bus with many advantages. The principal ones are significantly higher system bus data rate (25MHz) as well as provisions for bus mastering and for burst data transmission at high speeds. The MCA bus is a good choice for both workstations and servers, but it also has great limitations: cost and availability of components. At this writing, MCA is available only in a limited range of PS/2 systems from IBM, and it is likely that those systems will be discontinued in the not-too-distant future. We regretfully do not recommend the purchase of new MCA-based systems (a pity, because in many ways, MCA was a superior architecture, and we suspect that when a true successor to ISA and Local Bus emerges, it will bear more than a passing resemblance to MCA in its fundamental design).

Other Choices Several other bus options are available, especially in the more exotic computers, such as the Symmetric Multi-Processor (SMP) and RISC machines discussed in Appendix 5. A variety of approaches have been used, including multiple parallel memory bus architectures and proprietary local bus architectures, among others. If you are considering any computer using such a proprietary bus architecture, you should examine two aspects carefully: the availability of peripherals on this bus architecture, and support for an auxiliary bus (such as MCA, EISA, or PCI) for peripheral interface cards. Be very, very careful when you look at the system configuration. As with using ISA bus interface cards in an EISA bus computer, any EISA, MCA, or PCI bus cards in a proprietary bus computer will affect performance.

How noticeable that performance impact is will depend on the devices in use. A tape drive, for example, or CD-ROM drive, might slow performance *while you are using that device*. On the other hand, in a network server, if the network interface card is sitting on the EISA bus, every time a network request is transmitted, the system has to operate at the lower bus speeds. This configuration can have a significant impact, and it should be investigated closely.

Backup Every Windows NT server *requires* a backup device. This requirement is not an option. Can you configure a Windows NT Server without a backup device? Yes, and you will pay for that choice.

Windows NT has a simple backup program built into it, which is discussed in more detail in Chapter 3. The system's basic limitation is that it supports only tape-drive devices with SCSI interfaces and a limited range of other tape drives (such as QIC-40, -80, and in NT 4.0, QIC-3010 compatibles, and 4mm DAT drives). Therefore, to use NT's built-in backup, you'll need a compatible tape device from the Windows NT hardware-compatibility list. A wide range of NT-compatible tape drives are available; consult the latest Windows NT HCL.

In larger networks, NT's built-in backup is really inadequate. If you have to maintain backup data for a network of any size, we recommend investigating *Backup Alternatives* in Chapter 3.

UPS As with the backup device, a UPS is *mandatory* on all Windows NT Servers (and advantageous on workstations). Windows NT includes a *UPS Service* that can be used with a compatible UPS, *provided it is equipped with a serial port that can be used to signal power/fail conditions*.

In selecting a UPS for NT, it's important to consider three factors:

1. The switching time for the UPS to resume power after AC failure, which should be 4 milliseconds or less (ideally, zero).

2. Serial-port signalling, so that the NT UPS service can be notified that a failure has occurred.

3. Capacity. UPSs are typically rated for capacity using two measures: peak power output in Volt-Ampheres (VA or Watts) and a duration in minutes. You'll need a UPS with a peak power output sufficient for your complete system, and a duration long enough to complete critical tasks and shutdown gracefully. This varies from installation to installation, of course. A small departmental server can probably get by with 500 VA peak output and a ten-minute duration. The PD (Primary Domain Controller) of a large site, however, may need considerably more capacity.

Today's UPSs offer a wide range of optional features beyond those required for NT compatibility. Among these are SNMP support, hot-swappable batteries, and significant monitoring and management capability.[10] The latter feature, of course, will help on an NT network only if it is NT compatible, or at least Windows compatible. Don't pay extra for NetWare-based management software if your UPS will be used only with NT!

Windows NT's UPS service depends on signalling through a serial port using a compatible cable. Table 2.1 presents a list of manufacturers who provide NT-compatible UPS devices.[11] The specifics of setting up the UPS service are covered in detail in Chapter 3.

CD-ROM As with backup, CD-ROM capability should be considered essential for all Windows NT servers, and it is highly desirable for workstations. Beginning with NT 4.0, Microsoft ceased distributing Windows NT on floppy disks (the last floppy-based installation consisted of about 24 diskettes, not an installation that anyone would want to undertake lightly) and stopped supporting the use of floppy diskettes during setup. Thus, NT 4.0 *requires* either a local CD-ROM or access to one over a network connection.

Placing the CD-ROM on the server and sharing it over the network will permit you to conduct efficient over-the-network installation, and other network shared-CD operations. Therefore, a CD-ROM should be considered a necessity on Windows NT servers, not an option.

As with tape drives, the major limitation here is that Windows NT supports a limited range of CD-ROM controllers, mostly controllers based on SCSI. So, again, you're going to need a controller and CD-ROM from the Windows NT hardware-compatibility list. As you may imagine, given that SCSI is the best-supported controller type for both CD-ROM and tape backup,

SCSI makes sense as the primary transport mechanism for your hard disks as well. SCSI allows you to have just one disk controller for the entire system. Because SCSI also supports use of the various disk array options supported by Windows NT Server, we recommend SCSI as the stan-

---

10 The February 15, 1996 issue of *Network Computing* magazine has an excellent review of high-end UPS hardware.

11 This list is based on information from Microsoft's *Windows NT Hardware Compatibility List,* and is up-to-date as of August 3, 1996. Consult the current NT hardware compatibility list for up-to-date information.

Table 2.1 NT-compatible UPS Suppliers

Company	Address	Telephone
American Power Conversion	**http:www.apcc.com** 132 Fairgrounds Rd., West Kingston, RI 02892	(800) 800-4272 (401) 782-2515
Best Power Technologies	**http:www.bestpower.com** P.O. Box 280, Necedah, WI 54646	(800) 356-5794 (608) 565-7200

dard disk controller type for all NT server installations. The number of NT-compatible CD-ROM suppliers is far too high for a table. Consult the latest Windows NT hardware-compatibility list.

Floppy Disks Floppyless operation of Windows NT is certainly possible; however, should the system's registry ever become corrupted, you will find employing the standard Windows NT Emergency Diskette approach inconvenient. The maintenance team will first have to open up the workstation and physically connect a floppy disk to boot the recovery diskette.

For fully secure operations, a better choice may be physically locking the floppy disk drive, or using the FLOPLOCK application supplied with the Windows NT Resource Kit. Providing one 3.5-inch, 1.44-megabyte capacity floppy diskette on each workstation will save a great deal of trouble.

Miscellaneous Devices The use of Windows NT Remote Access Services (RAS) to provide Wide Area Networking connections between isolated Windows NT machines and the network requires compatible modems at both ends. For efficiency, the server requires an X.25, ISDN, or multiport card. We discuss these requirements further in Chapter 8. Likewise, Chapter 8 is also the place to look for information on the necessary hardware to support the Macintosh file system, which may require either an AppleTalk card installed in the server or preferably, for performance reasons, an Ethernet card in the server coupled to EtherTalk hardware on the Macintosh machines. The selection of appropriate UPS hardware is discussed elsewhere in this chapter. Remember that the first place to look when considering the selection of a particular hardware device is the current Windows NT hardware-compatibility list.

Portables After talking about 16+ megabyte RAM and 500MB hard-disk requirements, to even consider running Windows NT on a portable PC may seem ridiculous. Yet, it can be done, and it has some interesting advantages, which may explain why at least four major manufacturers are expected to be shipping notebook systems with NT preloaded by the end of 1996.

Configuring a portable is most conveniently done with a Xircom Pocket LAN adapter (or other device, such as a PCMCIA network card) to give the portable access to a shared CD-ROM for an over-the-network installation using the WINNT.EXE file.

The most significant problem with this kind of installation is NT failing to detect your network card. If that happens, your best bet is to skip the network installation (you can try to conduct the installation, but with no network adapter set up, you'll probably crash NT when you shut it down). One alternative is to install the MS Loopback adapter (which is a dummy), finish the rest of the NT install, then boot back to DOS. Once back in DOS (with access to whatever network WINNT.EXE was started from), you can copy all of the NT 4.0 installation files from the CD's \x86 directory; they take up less than 80MB. You may also want to copy the CD's \drvlib\netcard\x86 directory, which contains additional drivers for less common cards—it's only another 30MB.

In any case, after the files are copied, reboot to NT, and select Control Panel from the Start menu's Settings folder. Then double-click the Network icon in the Control Panel. You can then install the network card manually.

You can save time and trouble when installing and configuring a Windows NT portable system by installing RAS on the first pass. This process will allow you, using a null-modem serial cable connection (or a compatible modem), to communicate with the server computer. This option is an effective alternative to installing from floppy disks. Given a RAS connection and access to a phone line or null-modem cable, updating drivers and the like from the CD-ROM at the central site is always possible, of course.

Hardware Profiles With NT 4.0, Microsoft introduced a new feature of special interest to portable users: *Hardware Profiles*. This extends the multiple boot menu entries that NT has always offered to a two-stage approach: The top level allows you to select an operating system to boot, but at the second level (at the same point in execution as the "last known good" option; see Chapter 5 for an explanation), you can specify a particular hardware configuration to run.

This capability—which is potentially useful to anyone who routinely uses a system in more than one configuration. It is especially valuable to portable users because most portable computers routinely operate in *docked* (connected to a network, printer, external keyboard and monitor, etc.) and *undocked* (stand-alone) configurations.

Given that setting up a portable is most conveniently done over the LAN as stated above, you get the docked configuration by default. To create an additional (undocked) configuration:

1. Open the System Properties dialog (shown in Figure 2.1) by right-clicking on My Computer, and selecting Properties (or by selecting System from Control Panel).

2. Select the Hardware Profiles tab.

3. By default the only entry in the list will be Original Configuration (Current). Press the Copy... button. The Copy Profile dialog will appear. Type "Undocked Configuration" in the To: field, and press the OK button.

4. You will now have two entries in the list. Make sure Undocked Configuration is selected and click the Properties button. The Undocked Configuration Properties dialog (see Figure 2.2) will appear. Check the This is a portable computer box, and select The computer is undocked.

5. Click the tab, and check the Network-disabled hardware profile box.

6. Click the OK button to exit Undocked Configuration Properties.

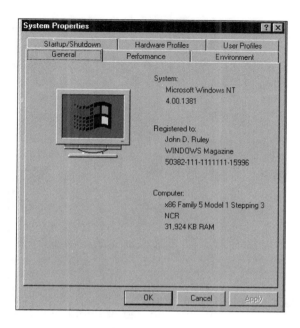

FIGURE 2.1 System properties. The System Properties dialog provides a single point of access for control over a variety of NT features, including hardware profiles.

7. The Multiple Hardware Profiles options will now be enabled on the System Properties dialog. By default, the system will wait 30 seconds for you to select a configuration, then execute the first one if no selection is made. You can change this to a shorter time (or make it wait indefinitely). You can also change the default to be the Undocked configuration, using the ↑ and ↓ buttons to the right of the list.

You can now shut down and restart NT in either of two modes: docked, with your network operational, and undocked with no networking. You can further customize the system using Control Panel Services, which allows you to selectively disable services not required in the undocked configuration (select a service you're interested in, click the H/W Profiles button, select Undocked Configuration and press the Disable button).

Hardware Profiles are not a panacea. NT still lacks the Plug-and-Play and Power Management features that make Windows 95 so much easier to live with on portables. If you must run NT on a portable, however, hardware profiles can help.

Printers The printing situation in Windows NT is good news indeed. Windows NT supports most printers that are supported by Windows 95 and also, using the built-in DLC (Dynamic Link Control) driver, supports network printers such as the Laser Jet IIIsi. The latter printers can be extremely convenient since they can be plugged into the network at any convenient location without requiring a direct physical connection to the print server.

All Windows NT machines can function as print servers (though NT Workstations are limited to a maximum of 10 simultaneous connections, to support more users an NT Server is

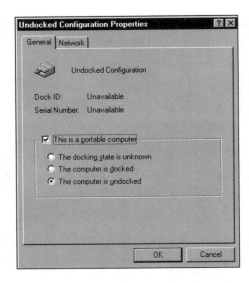

FIGURE 2.2 Configuration properties. This Dialog allows you to identify a particular hardware profile configuration as docked or undocked. The Network tab also allows you to disable all network features, if desired.

required). You need not dedicate a machine to this task, nor do you necessarily need to connect all the printers to the file server. In general, you have as wide a choice of printers as you could ask for. Selecting a printer will largely be a matter of speed, reliability, and cost. For desktop publishing and other graphics work, PostScript printers remain advantageous because of the tremendous infrastructure of PostScript-compatible software. For most other applications, any laser printer that supports True Type will provide a perfectly acceptable result.

One issue that does bear some consideration is the implication of mixing RISC and x86 type computers in a Windows NT network. The over-the-network printer-driver approach used by Windows NT has the great advantage that each workstation does not have to have its own print driver. That approach does have the slight disadvantage that the print server has to store any needed types of printer drivers. Therefore, if you're network includes x86-based workstations, MIPS R4000-based workstations, and DEC Alpha AXP workstations, your print will require all three types of print drivers.

This installation is not difficult to do. On the print server, bring up the Properties dialog for the printer in question, select the *Sharing* tab (see Figure 2.3), and pick the required drivers from the list. The Windows NT Print Spooler[12] will determine on-the-fly whether the request is coming from a RISC workstation as opposed to an x86 system and will employ the proper print driver at that time.

The simultaneous use of multiple print-driver types on a high-capacity print server does not require additional memory. As noted earlier, 4MB of memory is generally considered sufficient

---

12 Implemented as a separate service in NT versions from 3.5 on.

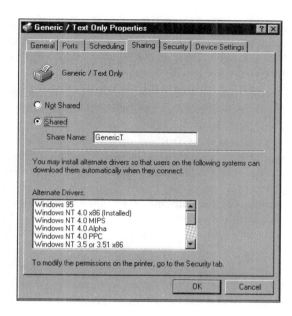

FIGURE 2.3 Printer properties. This dialog allows you to designate alternate print drivers, so that all clients can print remotely on the print server without requiring a local print driver.

for a Windows NT print server that services up to six printers. NT print servers, however, only execute native print-driver code. Non-native driver code is transported over the network to the printing station and executed there.

Beginning with version 3.5, NT Server also supports a UNIX-compatible Line Printer Daemon (LPD) service for plain-text and postscript printing on TCP/IP networks. See Chapter 6 for further information on the LPD service.

Limitations Note that Windows NT cannot be run on all systems. Specifically excluded are those that use the DoubleSpace compression algorithm from DOS 6, as well as competing products, such as Stacker (Stac Electronics) or SuperStor (AddStor). This limitation is a pity, because the disk-space requirements for Windows NT are such that it could undoubtedly benefit from a compatible compressor.[13] We hope that some third party will fill this need in the near future.

Compression *can* be used with the NTFS file system, as described later in this chapter and in Chapter 4.

Hardware The major problem with hardware support on Windows NT occurs when you want to upgrade existing equipment to run Windows NT. You will discover every piece of proprietary or otherwise incompatible hardware in your inventory. A useful first step is to examine

---

13   Indeed, usually reliable sources tell us that a DoubleSpace/DriveSpace-compatible compressed file system for NT *does* exist, and may be shipped with future versions.

the hardware requirements section earlier in this chapter because that discussion will provide a good working understanding of possible pitfalls. You should also make a point of checking to see that the hardware in question is listed in the Windows NT HCL.[14] In the meantime, here are a few other situations that we *know* will cause problems.

CD-ROMs A variety of manufacturers (notably Creative Labs in the Sound Blaster series of add-on cards) have produced multimedia upgrade kits in which a sound board is provided with a proprietary CD-ROM interface. Generally, this is a partial SCSI interface. Windows NT is not compatible with such boards, and the CD-ROM drives associated with them will not work *unless* a compatible device driver is provided, as, indeed, is included in the *Windows NT Device Library*.[15] Unfortunately, only a limited range of such devices is supported. Thus, for example, some Creative Labs and Mitsumi multimedia kits and CD-ROMs are supported, but other generally equivalent kits may not be. An alternative to allow reuse of this hardware within a Windows NT network is to install those boards into systems that will run Windows 95. The drives can then be shared over the network. You cannot, however, install and use such unsupported CD-ROM drives using Windows NT Workstations or servers.

Tape Drives Make sure that any tape device you purchase for use with NT is on the HCL, or that the manufacturer provides an appropriate driver. As mentioned earlier, most SCSI-interface drives will work, as will QIC-40 and -80 compatibles. QIC-3010 drives will *not* work.

Motherboards This limitation can be one of the most serious with Windows NT. Any organization embarking on a Windows NT pilot project (more so, on a wholesale conversion to Windows NT from Windows 3.*x*) should examine this carefully. Some motherboards can be upgraded only to 16MB. Some—in particular, earlier 486 motherboards from Dell—will operate more slowly if more than 16MB is introduced. Another major concern is the availability of cache RAM, because many early 486 motherboards not only didn't ship with cache RAM but made no provision for adding it. Additionally, Windows NT does not reach its full performance capability until significant amounts of cache RAM are introduced into the system. The only way to deal with this situation is to inspect the manufacturer's information for the motherboards for each computer in the organization.

Obviously, when buying new equipment, avoid any system that has such problems. Make sure that the system is expandable to at least 32MB of RAM (64MB for servers), and that the system will accommodate at least 256KB of on-chip SRAM cache. You can save yourself much time and trouble as you investigate the potential for upgrades within your organization if you check Microsoft's Knowledge Base[16] to see which motherboards have been reported as having

---

14   Which is found in the SUPPORT directory of the NT distribution CD, and is available online from Microsoft's Web site (http://www.microsoft.com)—check the NT Workstation and NT Server product information pages.

15   Which may be found in the DRVLIB directory on the NT distribution CD, or on the monthly TechNet CD; the latter is liable to be more up-to-date.

16   Available on Microsoft's Website at http://www.microsoft.com/support (look for a button or link labeled "Knowlege Base"). This database contains up-to-date technical notes on Windows NT issues, including installation. A periodic search of this area, using the keywords "Windows NT" and "motherboard," will provide you with a wealth of valuable information—and may save you from making a serious mistake.

problems with Windows NT. Finally, a useful reference that will save time by identifying problem-free systems is the current Windows NT HCL.

Planning Your Installation

Before you install Windows NT, you must make several decisions and gather information. In this section, we'll look at information that you need to acquire before you begin.

File Systems The primary decision you need to make involves the file system to use. Windows NT 3.1 introduced NTFS (New Technology File System), which has now seen several revisions. If you select NTFS, filenames can be 256 characters long,[17] Windows NT can fully recover in the case of problems (you no longer have to run CHKDSK), and auditing and security features found in Windows NT can be enabled. In addition, beginning with version 3.51, file compression is available. On the other hand, if you want compatibility with existing operating systems (DOS, Windows 95, etc.) then file allocation table (FAT) will be your only choice.

Security Only NTFS drives can be made secure according to the C2 security specifications. You can create access-control lists locally and remotely with NTFS, but only remotely for other file systems. Auditing on NTFS drives can monitor which users access which files. Furthermore, you can set a variety of file permissions on NTFS drives, such as restricting which users may rename files or directories. In comparison, files and directories on FAT drives may be shared or not shared, but you cannot restrict a user to read-only access as you could if the file were located on an NTFS drive.

Access by DOS Applications During installation, you can also select the dual-boot option, which allows you to select the operating system that you want to use, either the one originally installed or Windows NT. You cannot convert your C: (boot) drive to an NTFS drive if you still plan to use the original operating system (such as MS-DOS), because it will not be able to boot from an NTFS drive. Furthermore, if you choose to install NT on a drive other than your boot drive, such as the D: drive, and select the NTFS file system for that drive, the drive and all its files will be invisible when DOS is loaded.

Filenames Both NTFS and (NT versions 3.5 and after) FAT allow you to create filenames with up to 256 characters, including spaces but excluding special characters (such as question or quotation marks, forward and backward slashes, less-than and greater-than symbols, etc.). The file extension is separated from the filename by a period (.). To maintain DOS compatibility, NT also creates a DOS-compatible filename. The algorithm for this takes the first nonblank eight characters for the filename. If a duplicate name results, NT uses the last character in the filename as a numeric serial number, incrementing the number until a unique filename is created. For example:

```
C:\long directory name>dir /x
 Volume in drive C is PANTHER
 Volume Serial Number is D4F4-CDAF
```

---

17 Beginning with NT version 3.5, DOS-compatible FAT partitions also support long filenames, which are compatible with the long filenames used by Windows 95.

```
Directory of C:\long directory name

08/27/96   08:41p      <DIR>                                 .
08/27/96   08:41p      <DIR>                                 ..
08/18/96   07:17p                102,912 CHAPTE~1.DOC     Chapter 10--New
Version.DOC
04/07/95   04:34a                 24,064 CHAPTE~2.DOC     Chapter 10--Old
Version.DOC
              4 File(s)           126,976 bytes
                              94,038,016 bytes free
```

Thus, though you can mix both short and long names on the same system (and most important, support legacy clients with short names from an NT Server), you will need to be prepared to handle converted *filenames*.

OS/2 HPFS File System Microsoft has eliminated support for HPFS partitions in NT 4.0 and recommends converting from HPFS to NTFS.

Apple Macintosh File System and POSIX Support Windows NT Server supports a Macintosh-accessible directory format on NTFS partitions. You'll find this subject covered in more detail in Chapter 8; for now, you should be aware that you'll need at least one NTFS partition on an NT Server if you intend to support Macintosh computers on your network. Similarly, NTFS is required if you expect to use NT's POSIX subsystem with applications that expect a UNIX-style file structure.

Network Information Before you begin to install Windows NT, you also need to have network information and settings.

You must know the name of your computer and the name of the workgroup or domain the computer will be part of. If the computer is already part of a Windows for Workgroups group, you may use the same name.

You must also know the type of network adapter card installed, the card's interrupt number (IRQ), and its base address. Although the installation program will attempt to automatically sense these settings, if the derived settings are incorrect, knowing the information beforehand is advantageous.

You can install NT without network settings, then add or change the settings through the Control Panel's Network icon. However, setting up the network when the system starts is much simpler. In particular, systems being added to a Windows NT Server domain cannot be logged in and used as domain members until a network card has been installed and configured—which makes this as good a time as any to address the issue of Domains-*vs*-Workgroups.

Domains and Workgroups All new NT users, and many NT network administrators, are confused by the distinction between Workgroups and Domains. In a nutshell, some people want to run centrally managed NT networks, and other people want to run NT systems on a stand-alone basis. If you are running an NT network, you should put your machines in a *domain*. A domain is an administrative unit with centralized user-account information stored on a Primary Domain Controller (PDC). The account information may then be replicated by Backup Domain Controllers (BDCs). When a user logs in to an NT system (either a Workstation or Server), the log-on request is validated by whatever DC is available. If none is available, the user may be logged in locally using account information cached on the particular workstation or server he or she is logging on to.

The advantage of a Domain setup is that *all* NT systems in a domain are managed as a single unit. Domain-wide user accounts and policies (created using User Manager for Domains from the NT Server's Administrative Tools group; see Chapter 3 for details) apply to *all* servers and workstations in the domain, not just to one machine. This concept can even be extended to multiple domains using inter-domain trust relationships, covered in Chapter 8. Thus, when using NT servers in a large organization, organizing them into domains is clearly the preferred approach.

The alternative to centralized domains is *Workgroup* security in which each individual NT system, whether a Workstation or Server, must maintain its own set of user accounts. This arrangement is far from optimal in any but the smallest LANs, and we only recommend it for stand-alone NT systems. On such systems, there is no benefit to the overhead of making the isolated server a DC, so set it up with workgroup security. Finally, groups of NT Workstations operating without any NT Servers cannot be a domain, because only NT Servers can be operated as Domain Controllers (hint: in such a situation, you should have at least one NT Server!). In all other cases, set up a domain.

Why use so much space discussing this issue in a chapter on installation? Because on NT servers, the decision to support either Domain or Workgroup security *must* be made when the system is installed (on Workstations, you can change the security model at will).

Network Protocols By default, NT 3.1 was installed with the Microsoft-standard NetBEUI (NetBIOS Extended User Interface) protocol. Beginning with NT 3.5, this changed. NT Servers now install with TCP/IP as the base protocol, and NT Workstations (and Servers, for that matter) that are installed in a NetWare-compatible environment get Microsoft's NWLink IPX/SPX protocol by default. All three base protocols can be selected for installation, and add-in protocols are available from third parties (see Chapter 11 for details). This entire subject is very complex, and we will not attempt to cover it in detail here; see Appendix 2 for detailed information on Windows NT protocols and drivers, and Chapters 6, 7, and 8 about using TCP/IP for internetworking. Chapter 9 contains information on interoperating with other Microsoft network products, Chapter 10 has information about using Windows NT with Novell NetWare, and in Chapter 11 we discuss using Windows NT with other types of networks.

If that list seems like too much reading, stick to installing the default protocol(s) selected by NT's Express installation option on the first pass and add another protocol later if your situation requires it.

Printer Information Unlike Windows 3.1 and Windows for Workgroups, you need only install a printer driver on the server machine in Windows NT; you do not have to define a printer on any computer that does not have a printer directly attached. In NT 4.0, you change the printer configuration using the Printers folder, not the Control Panel, and you can add a printer at a later time. If you want to install a printer during the NT installation process, you need to know the printer's make and model as well as the communications port (LPT1, etc.) used.

Passwords You will need to know the name of the user you want assigned to this copy of Windows NT, and you will be asked for a password. You can press the Enter key to bypass setting up a password, though this defeats a major security feature. Passwords are case sensitive, and they can be changed. An administrator can also force the expiration of passwords at regular intervals, such as every 30 days (see Chapter 3 for more information).

Installation Overview

The installation of Windows NT occurs in two phases. The first phase is a text-based application, asking you for the basic parameters and settings NT needs. In the second phase, the installation process turns graphical as Windows NT copies additional files and actually sets up and displays new Start menu folders.

The installation process also varies by your responses to the questions asked by the setup program. As all machines and environments vary, we cannot offer one foolproof description to all users.

As with most Microsoft application setup programs, two installation options are available at the outset. The first, Express Setup, makes most of the decisions for you, and substitutes defaults (such as the destination directory name) for you. If you select Custom setup, you will have more control over the exact installation details. Because of the complex nature of Windows NT, novice users will probably prefer, and I recommend, the Express Setup option.

The Installation Process By far the easiest way to install Windows NT is by using a CD-ROM drive that is directly attached to the computer. However, other methods also allow NT to be installed if you do not have a CD-ROM drive, and they will be described here. You should allow at least 30 minutes for a Windows NT installation, a period that varies according to the hard disk and CD-ROM speed, and whether problems arise during the installation process.

Floppy-based Installation Microsoft eliminated support for floppy-disk-based installation in NT 4.0, and in all honesty, if you're going to install NT, you should have a CD-ROM (or access to one).

CD-ROM Installation NT comes with three (3) setup floppies and a CD. Boot the first diskette, and you will be prompted to insert the others when appropriate. If you lose the diskettes, you can still do an over-the-network-style installation using WINNT32.EXE, which has an option to create the floppies (which it does in a separate thread while continuing to copy files from the CD to your hard disk). Alternatively, you can use the /B option (see below) to eliminate the need for the setup floppies altogether. Make no mistake, however: You need to make and keep at least one set of those Install disks.

Without the first (boot) diskette, you cannot use an NT emergency diskette, and being able to use the emergency diskette can be a lifesaver.[18]

---

18 One of the authors once accidentally deleted a registry key on an NT system. The system had been installed using a floppyless installation, and no emergency disk—which would have allowed the damage to be repaired—was available. The only solution was to completely reinstall NT—in the process a complete NTFS partition (and about a month's work) was lost. Having a backup copy of the registry might have prevented this—especially if the boot partition is FAT-formatted, and is compatible with DOS-based disk tools. Don't let this happen to you!—JDR

Over-the-Network Installation On machines that lack a CD-ROM, the easiest way to install NT is over the network. On machines where NT is already running, use WINNT32.EXE, which has the following command-line options:

```
Winnt32

Performs an installation or upgrade of Windows NT 4.00.
winnt32 [/s:sourcepath] [/i:inf_file] [
/t:drive_letter] [/x] [/b] [/ox] [/u[:
script] [/r:directory] [/e:command]

Parameters

/s:sourcepath
Specifies the location of the Windows NT files.
/i:inf_file
Specifies the filename (no path) of the setup information file. The default
is DOSNET.INF.
/t:drive_letter
Forces Setup to place temporary files on the specified drive.
/x
Prevents Setup from creating Setup boot floppies. Use this when you already
     have Setup boot floppies (from your administrator, for example).
/b
Causes the boot files to be loaded on the system's hard drive rather than
on floppy disks, so that floppy disks do not need to be loaded or removed
by the user.
/ox
Specifies that Setup create boot floppies for CD-ROM installation.
/u
Upgrades your previous version of Windows NT in unattended mode. All user
settings are taken from the previous installation, requiring no user inter-
vention during Setup.

/u:script
Similar to previous, but provides a script file for user settings rather
than using the settings from the previous installation.
/r:directory
Installs an additional directory within the directory tree where the
Windows NT files are installed. Use additional /r switches to install addi-
tional directories.
/e:command
Instructs Setup to execute a specific command after installation is
complete.
```

Just running WINNT32 (from the command line, or the Start menu) will start the process. WINN32 will prompt for the source files' location (the \i386 directory of the installation CD, for intel systems; \mips, \alpha etc. for RISC systems). Otherwise, it's pretty much like running the CD-based install locally. One nice option is the /B switch, which eliminates creation of the boot floppys and the emergency disk. However, as mentioned earlier, you won't know how badly you want that emergency disk until you *really* need it.

Of course, WINNT32 is only useful if NT is already installed.[19] What about installing NT over-the-network on DOS- or Windows 95-based systems? You'll need a network connection to the shared directory on the CD which could be the client software provided with NT server, for instance, or a NetWare redirector running against FPNW or GSNW on an NT server. Once that's done, run WINNT.EXE, which is basically a 16-bit version of WINNT32. Like its 32-bit sibling, WINNT.EXE has several options:

```
D:\I386>winnt /?
Installs Windows NT.

WINNT [/S[:]sourcepath] [/T[:]tempdrive] [/I[:]inffile]
      [/O[X]] [/X | [/F] [/C]] [/B] [/U[:scriptfile]]
      [/R[X]:directory] [/E:command]

/S[:]sourcepath
        Specifies the source location of Windows NT files.
        Must be a full path of the form x:\[path] or
        \\server\share[\path].
        The default is the current directory.
/T[:]tempdrive
        Specifies a drive to contain temporary setup files.
        If not specified, Setup will attempt to locate a drive for you.
/I[:]inffile
        Specifies the filename (no path) of the setup information file.
        The default is DOSNET.INF.
/OX     Create boot floppies for CD-ROM installation.
/X      Do not create the Setup boot floppies.
/F      Do not verify files as they are copied to the Setup boot floppies.
/C      Skip free-space check on the Setup boot floppies you provide.
/B      Floppyless operation (requires /s).
/U      Unattended operation and optional script file (requires /s).
/R      Specifies optional directory to be installed.
/RX     Specifies optional directory to be copied.
/E      Specifies command to be executed at the end of GUI setup.

To get help one screen at a time, use WINNT /? | MORE
```

Most of these options are the same as those in WINNT32; but WINNT.EXE adds a /O option to create just the boot disks, plus options regarding free space. The latter options are necessary because WINNT.EXE copies the NT setup files onto the target system's hard disk, then boots into NT to run the rest of setup. A fair amount of disk space (about 100 MB) must be available for it to run.

With appropriate use of the options, WINNT setup can be extremely powerful. For example, a typical command line that would carry out a complete installation over the network (assuming that the Windows NT installation CD-ROM is shared as disk-d of \\mips-lab-server) would be:

---

19   It doesn't support Windows 95 or OS/2.

```
WINNT /s:\\mips-lab-server\disk-d\i386 /t:c /i:\\mips-lab-server\install\dosnet.inf /x /f /c
```

This command line will carry out a complete installation using the files in the i386 directory of the CD device on MIPS lab server, with temporary file storage on the local C: drive, getting the DOSNET.INF file from the install share on MIPS lab server. It will not create, verify, or perform free-space checks on a boot floppy (which would assume that you are carrying a boot floppy with you). This process is probably the fastest way to do an installation for small- to medium-sized networks. For larger networks, you should see the later section on computer profile setup

Hints, Tips, and Tricks Early in the installation process, NT Setup will check to see if you have enough free disk space on any partition to complete installation. The space required is substantial: around 150MB for a complete NT Server installation. Additionally, this space cannot be part of a mirror, stripe set, or volume set. If your system has an existing NT directory tree on it, setup has an option to overwrite existing NT installations or to reformat partitions to gain the space necessary to complete setup.

Note: These are one-shot operations; there is no way to recover the data thus lost.

If you are upgrading to NT from Windows 3.*x*, don't try to run WINNT.EXE from a Program Manager or File Manager File/Run dialog; it fails with "Setup cannot run in a 386 Enhanced Mode Windows MS-DOS Command Prompt. Exit Windows and run Setup again." Do as the prompt says: Exit to DOS, and run it from there. This seems a bit silly (you have to run the Windows NT installation program from DOS?!), but is apparently necessary because of the way WINNT.EXE forces a reboot halfway through the setup process. Windows 95, fortunately, doesn't have this problem.

One more thing: if you install NT on a system that already has Windows 3.*x* on it, you'll be given the option to install NT in the existing Windows directory. *Accept that option!* It automatically migrates all of your installed Windows applications for you, which is a great time-saver.

Updating Your Current Windows Installation The NT installation program will look for an existing Windows or Windows NT installation and offer to update the version of Windows. If you select this option, NT will maintain your Start menu folders and other settings. However, if you use the Dual Boot option, you will be unable to run NT from DOS, for example. Thus, if you are evaluating NT, installing NT as a separate directory until your evaluation is complete is probably wise, then re-install over your Windows 3.1 or Windows for Workgroups program.

Step-by-Step Windows NT Installation

Though every environment is different, here is the typical sequence of events that occur during installation.

Installing Locally from the Distribution CD If you're installing locally, insert the NT distribution CD-ROM into your system. If you're running NT 4.0, Windows 95, or any other system that supports CD autoplay, a Windows NT CD-ROM window will be displayed (Figure 2.4). You can click the Windows NT Setup icon to begin setup.

FIGURE 2.4 Windows NT CD-ROM. Windows NT 4.0 Setup uses the CD Autoplay feature to display this window automatically in NT 4.0 (or higher) when the distribution disc is inserted in a properly configured CD-ROM drive.

If your system doesn't support autoplay, you'll need to use the special boot diskettes supplied with NT (or created using WINNT.EXE; see above). Simply insert the NT boot diskette in your floppy drive and reboot the computer.

1. Setup will begin by asking for the location of the Windows NT files (Figure 2.5). They will normally be in the I386 directory (on Intel systems) of the NT CD-ROM. Verify that the correct directory is selected, and hit Enter.

2. NT Setup will copy files to your hard disk. Once files are copied, NT Setup will advise you to restart your system to continue with the next phase of setup. Do so.

3. After the normal boot process, your computer will enter character-mode Windows NT Setup and will present a short Welcome to Setup menu:

Windows NT Workstation Setup

```
============================
Welcome to Setup
The Setup program for the Microsoft(R) Windows NT(TM) operating system
version 4.0 prepares Windows NT to run on your computer.
```

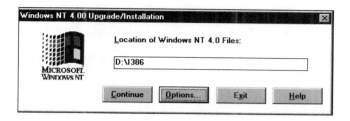

FIGURE 2.5 NT Upgrade/Installation dialog. This dialog is used to specify the directory from which NT Setup loads files.

```
To learn more about Windows NT Setup before continuing, press F1.
To set up Windows NT now, press ENTER.
To repair a damaged Windows NT version 4.0 installation, press R.
To quit Setup without installing Windows NT, press F3.
```

4. If this is your first experience with NT Setup, press F1 for a brief explanation of the options. Otherwise, press Enter.

5. Setup will attempt to detect mass storage devices (e.g., disk controllers). Inspect the resulting list. If it doesn't reflect one or more controllers that you know you have, press the S key. You'll then have an opportunity to specify the controller in question (this requires a floppy disk with special drivers provided by your controller's manufacturer).

   Note: This list will not include your standard AT-type hard disk controller, which is detected automatically.

6. Once all mass storage devices have been detected or specified, press Enter. Setup will display the NT license agreement. You will need to read the entire agreement and then indicate that you agree to abide by the agreement terms to continue with setup.

   Note: Read the agreement carefully. Microsoft has changed the text in NT 4.0. Among other things, Microsoft now restricts the use of NT Workstation as a server for any type of connectivity (including Web, FTP, X, etc.) to a maximum of ten inbound connections.

7. On first-time installations, NT Setup displays a list of hardware and software components that it has detected, including the system type, video display, keyboard, and pointing device. Make any necessary corrections, then select "The above list matches my computer" and press Enter to continue with setup.

8. Setup will search your hard disk for an existing version of NT and offer to perform an upgrade. It's usually best to accept that option; your only other alternative is to install a

completely fresh copy of NT in a separate directory. Doing so will not preserve any existing network, printer, or video drivers and will require reinstalling any applications.

9. If no previous version of NT is detected (or if you choose to install a fresh copy) NT Setup will display a list of available partitions. Select a suitable partition from that list.

10. If you are installing NT on a DOS or Windows 95 system, you will be offered the opportunity to convert the partition to the NTFS file format. Because there is no way to convert a partition back to FAT format once it has been converted to NTFS, *we do not recommend accepting this option unless you have no plans to ever use this computer with another operating system* (you can always convert the partition to NTFS later).

11. On first-time installations, NT Setup suggests a directory tree in which to install the NT system files: normally the WINNT directory. You can change the directory's name, but we don't recommend this.

12. NT Setup will offer to examine your hard disk(s) for corruption, a potentially lengthy process. If you have the time, accept this option because it may save trouble later.

13. NT Setup then copies the NT System files onto your hard disk into the partition and directory selected previously (or the existing directory, if you're upgrading from a previous installation).

14. When all files are copied, NT Setup initializes the files, and advises you that "This portion of Setup has completed successfully." Press Enter to restart your computer.

15. Your computer will reboot, NT itself will start, and you will enter the graphical phase of NT Setup. More files will be copied. Eventually, the Windows NT Setup Wizard will appear (Figure 2.6), which will guide you through the remaining phases of NT Setup. Press the Next button.

16. If you are conducting a first-time installation, you will be offered a number of setup options. For most purposes, "Typical" is the best choice (others are "Portable," "Compact," and "Custom"—they're self explanatory). Select the option that suits your needs, and click the Next button. You will also be asked to enter your name and organization. Type them in on the form presented, and click the Next button

17. If you are conducting a first-time installation, you will be asked to enter a computer name. It must be unique to your network.

18. On NT Server systems, you will be asked whether the computer will be used as a Primary or Backup Domain Controller (PDC/BDC) or stand-alone server. You will also be prompted for the name of the domain or workgroup in which the server will participate.

    Note: Setting up a machine as BDC requires that it be able to communicate with the domain's PDC. If the PDC is down, you may have to promote a BDC to PDC status.

19. If this is a first-time installation, you will be asked to enter a password for use with the built-in administrator account. The password must be easy to remember. Enter it in both the Password and Confirm Password field on the form, then click the Next button.

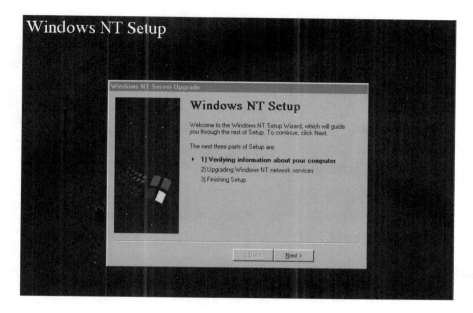

FIGURE 2.6 NT Setup Wizard. The Setup Wizard guides you through the remainder of the NT installation process.

20. You will be offered the opportunity to create an Emergency Repair Disk (Figure 2.7). *We highly recommend that you accept this option*, as it will make recovery possible in situations where NT will otherwise be unable to start. (Note that taking full advantage of this feature requires that you have the NT boot diskettes available; they can be created using the /OX option of the WINNT or WINNT32 command, as described earlier.) Click the Next button.

21. You will be offered the option to install various NT Components. In most circumstances, the default components are fine, though you may want to inspect the options. For example, the Portable installation does not install Microsoft Exchange or any of the Games by default. Click the Next button to continue with setup.

22. In a first-time installation, you will be asked whether the computer will participate in a network and whether it will do so over a LAN or by modem. Select the appropriate option, and click the Next button.

23. In a first-time installation, you will be offered the option to either have NT Setup autodetect your network card or you can select detect manually from a list. Autodetection is usually the best option, though it will not work with all cards. Once your network card is detected or specified, click the Next button.

24. In a first-time installation, NT Setup asks you to select which network protocols should be installed. The default options will include TCP/IP for the Internet, IPX/SPX for NetWare LANs, and NetBEUI for Microsoft (LAN Manager, Windows for Workgroups)

FIGURE 2.7 Emergency disk. NT Setup gives you the opportunity to create an emergency disk that can be used to recover from serious system crashes.

LANs. There is also a Select from List button that will provide some additional options, including AppleTalk, DLC, and PPTP. Once the proper protocols are selected, click the Next button.

25. NT Setup will next offer to install or upgrade preselected NT networking components. If you are upgrading an existing installation, the system will upgrade existing components for you automatically, preserving settings (you can add new features later using Settings, then Control Panel, then Networks). On first-time installations, the components selected in the previous steps will be installed. In either case, click the Next button.

26. On first-time installations, a variety of pop-up dialogs will appear, asking (for example) whether or not to use DHCP to automatically assign the system's IP address (if DHCP is available on your LAN, answer Yes); the number of Virtual Private Networks to be supported by PPTP (the default is 1); the Modem or other device you wish to use with NT Remote Access (as with network interface cards, modems can be autodetected or selected from a list—the latter option is convenient if the modem isn't physically installed at the NT setup time); and the COM port it should be installed on, etc.

27. If this is a first-time installation, NT setup will attempt to start the network. It will ask you to verify the computer name and to designate whether it is a member of a domain or workgroup. If it's a member of a domain, you will be presented with an option to create a computer account for the system on the domain controller—this is required if the computer has not previously been attached to the domain. A domain administrator account name and password are required. Fill in the form and click the Next button.

28. NT Setup will announce that it is "almost finished with setup." Click the Finish button. On first-time setups, some additional pop-up dialogs will appear, asking you to specify your time zone, verify the display settings, etc.

29. If you accepted the option to create an Emergency Repair Disk (see step 20 above), you are now asked to insert a diskette in your floppy drive. NT Setup then formats it and creates the necessary files.

30. Setup prompts you to restart your computer (Figure 2.8). When you do, your computer will restart with NT 4.0 loaded.

Upgrading Windows 95 Systems Initially, Microsoft planned to offer a one-shot upgrade to NT 4.0 from Windows 95; they were unable to make this work reliably, however, so it was not delivered in the NT 4.0 release. As a result, the best alternative for a Windows 95 upgrade is to install NT in a new directory that is separate from the directory tree (normally WINDOWS) used by Windows 95. Note that this will be a completely separate installation; it will not inherit any Windows 95 settings, including but not limited to network, video, and printer drivers. Application installations will also not be preserved.

Once NT is installed, booting between Windows 95 and NT using the NT multiboot menu is possible. Once all applications have been installed and tested under NT, the BOOT.INI file can be edited to remove the Windows 95 boot option, and the entire Windows 95 directory tree can be deleted.

If insufficient disk space is available to support both Windows 95 and NT installations, the best approach is to create a DOS 7 (Windows 95 character-mode) boot disk, then boot the system from that disk and delete the entire Windows 95 directory structure. Then install NT. Again, note that no settings will be preserved, and all applications will have to be reinstalled.

Upgrading Earlier Versions of Windows Oddly enough, the upgrade situation is significantly better for Windows 3.x users. When NT Setup detects the presence of an existing

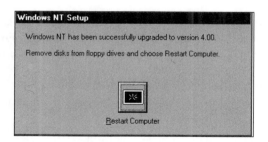

FIGURE 2.8 Restart. When complete, NT 4.0 Setup prompts you to restart your computer.

WINDOWS directory, it will offer to install NT in that directory. This installation is safe and has the desirable side effect of preserving Win16 application settings because NT does not modify files in the existing WINDOWS\SYSTEM directory structure—it simply adds a new WINDOWS\SYSTEM32 directory and installs its own system files there. It will also automatically transport Win16 .INI files into the NT registry.

It's a pity that this upgrade wasn't preserved for Windows 95 systems.

Installation on RISC Computers

RISC-based installation is similar to that of Intel-based systems, with some minor differences early in the process. The following instructions are representative. Details for specific configurations may vary. See the hardware manufacturer's specifications for details.

Step-by-Step RISC Installation

> *Note: If NT is already installed on the machine, and you're only attempting a version upgrade, use WINNT32.EXE described earlier.*

1. NT may require a particular processor-stepping or firmware upgrade; consult the Windows NT installation guide and SETUP.TXT provided in the \mips, \alpha, or \ppc directory, as appropriate, of your installation CD. If necessary, contact your hardware manufacturer to upgrade the CPU hardware and/or system firmware. In particular, all versions of NT on MIPS R4x00 systems require R4000 version 2.0 or later, and Digital Alpha systems require upgrading to the latest firmware version.

2. If necessary, configure the system for "little-endian" mode. If it displays the ARC boot loader when you start or cold-boot the system, then it's already configured for little-endian mode. If not, you must get the boot floppy that came with the machine, insert it in the floppy disk drive, reboot the computer, and when the boot floppy executes and asks you if want to configure a Windows NT PROM, answer Yes. It will then make the necessary changes in the system's Programmable Read Only Memory and on a reboot the system will display an ARC boot loader prompt with several options, the most important of which, from our point of view, is "run a program."

3. If necessary, format a system partition. RISC systems require a system partition to hold the OSLOADER.EXE and HAL.DLL files. This partition must be a FAT partition, even if you don't want to store anything else that way and you want to run a fully configured system using NTFS. In the latter case, the system partition need be no larger than 2MB. Alternatively, you can make that partition the size of the hard disk and use it as the single drive partition for the system, or you can do any variation in between that suits your particular needs.

   In general, using a small-system partition just for those files and formatting the rest of the disk as NTFS will be beneficial. There's little advantage to providing a FAT partition on RISC-based systems because they are incapable of running DOS anyway. In any case, to partition the disk, select RUN A PROGRAM from the ARC boot loader menu and enter:

```
SCSI()CDROM(0–7 as appropriate)fdisk()\mips\arcinst.exe
```

This will run the ARC system-installation program and ask if you would like to create a partition. Answer Yes, and you can create a system partition of any size, minimum of 2MB, to store the necessary files.

4. Start setup. Again, from the ARC boot loader, select Run A Program and then enter the path name:

```
SCSI()CD-ROM(0-7)fdisk()\setupldr.
```

This line will start the setup loader that performs the same function as the boot sector on the Windows NT CD-ROM boot disk for x86 based systems. This in turn will start the Windows NT setup program from the CD-ROM, and the installation will proceed exactly as it proceeds for CD-ROM installation on x86-based computers.

Customizing NT Setup

For departmental network installations where a large number of machines with a common configuration have to be set up for Windows NT, Microsoft has provided a series of options that allow you to extensively customize NT setup. These options (which are fully documented in the *Windows NT 4.0 Deployment Guide*, included with the NT 4.0 Resource Kit)[20] include:

- Unattended Installation (/U)

- Uniqueness Database Files

- Custom Directories

- SYSDIFF.EXE

All of these options depend on copying the contents of the NT distribution CD-ROM to a shared network directory (called the *distribution sharepoint*) on a server and adding additional files. Installation is then carried out over the network using either the WINNT.EXE or WINNT32.EXE applications described earlier.

Unattended Installation Unattended Installation is accomplished using a *response file*, which contains the detailed information such as the time zone, display and network settings that a user would interactively provide in the usual installation process. You create the response file using any standard text editor (an example file, UNATTEND.TXT, may be found on the NT 4.0 distribution CD, in the \i386, \alpha, or \ppc directory, depending on the version you're using). Once the response file has been created, you invoke it by adding the /U:*response file* option to the WINNT.EXE or WINNT32.EXE command line. Details of the response file format are beyond the scope of this chapter (see Microsoft's *Windows NT 4.0 Deployment Guide* for more information).

Uniqueness Database Files Uniqueness Database Files, or UDFs, extend the response file concept to include multiple options. Sections in the response file are marked with a Uniqueness

---

20 The options documented in this edition—particularly the SYSDIFF utility—differ from those available in earlier versions of NT. They appear to have superseded the little-used Computer Profile Setup (CPS) from the NT 3.*x* Resource Kit.

ID. If that ID is specified in the WINNT.EXE or WINNT32.EXE command line (via the syntax /UDF:*ID*) sections with the corresponding ID from $UNIQUE$.UDF will replace the corresponding response file sections. If you prefer, you can specify a different filename on the command line: /UDF:*ID, filename*. As with the response file format, details are beyond the scope of this chapter; see the *Deployment Guide*.

Custom Directories You can add custom drivers and components—even entire applications—to the Windows NT Setup process by creating a OEM directory on your distribution sharepoint and placing the necessary files in appropriate subdirectories of OEM. You can include hardware drivers, system files, network components, or even a complete application directory. Consult the *Deployment Guide* for more information.

SYSDIFF.EXE The foregoing options are sufficient to handle custom setup of NT itself, but for the ultimate level of customization, you may need a way to install not only the operating system, but selected applications. Such options are offered by the new SYSDIFF utility, which is included in both the NT 4.0 resource kit, and in the OEM software distribution kit (ODK).

Sysdiff has a simple command syntax:

sysdiff /snap *SnapshotFile*

sysdiff /diff *SnapshotFile DifferenceFile*

sysdiff /apply *DifferenceFile*

sysdiff /inf *DifferenceFile OEMroot*

(All sysdiff commands can also accept /log *LogFile* to enable error logging.)

Sysdiff essentially operates in this way: you set up an example system, called the *reference system*, using the methods described above, and take a *snapshot* of the reference system configuration (directories, registry entries, etc.) with the /snap command. Then install your applications and run sysdiff again, this time with the /diff command. Sysdiff then provides you with a *difference file* that shows everything that changed between the two snapshots. That difference file can be applied to subsequent custom setup scripts, or to systems already running NT, using the /apply command. Alternatively, you can use the /inf command to generate additional inf file scripts for use in a custom setup.

For more information on the sysdiff command and unattended/custom setup, see Microsoft's *Windows NT 4.0 Deployment Guide* in the NT 4.0 Resource Kit.

Required Files

For Intel-based systems, the installation program adds BOOT.INI, NTLDR (NT Loader), and NTDETECT.COM to the boot drive's root directory. If you selected the dual-boot option (among operating systems at boot time), you will also have a BOOTSECT.DOS file in the boot drive's root directory, which is used to boot the previous operating system.

RISC-based systems will also find HAL.DLL and OSLOADER.EXE loaded to the \OS\NT directory of the boot drive.

The above files are all *required* for NT. If any one of them is missing, NT cannot be loaded.

Of course, the files in the /WINNT or /WINDOWS/SYSTEM32 directories (depending on whether you've installed Windows NT from scratch or added it in an installation to an existing Windows system) are also required.

> *Note: When upgrading from one version of Windows NT to the next, you must examine the documentation that comes with the new version to determine whether it is necessary to remove the previous installation before carrying out the new installation. Do not assume that simply installing the new one over the old one will necessarily give you a working installation. If you have any doubts on the matter backing the old installation off onto a tape drive, deleting it, deleting all files, and starting the new installation all over fresh may very well be better.*

Starting Windows NT

After the installation process is completed, the installation program will ask you to boot the system. The Boot Loader program appears and asks you to select the operating system you want to use. Windows NT will be listed first, and your previous operating system will be listed next. Press Enter. The Windows NT log-on dialog then appears and asks you to press *CTRL+ALT+DEL* to begin NT. You'll be prompted for a case-sensitive password.

Installation Troubleshooting

Typically, installation problems encountered with Windows NT fall into one of two categories: those in which the system successfully boots but doesn't operate properly, and those in which the system refuses to boot.

The first category is by far the simpler. If the system boots and Windows NT starts, but other things don't seem to work properly for you, log in using the administrator account, run the Event Manager, and examine the system Event Log. The odds are good that this will show error messages referring to specific devices. For example, if you are coming up but failing to log on to the network, you are quite likely to see an Event Log with a series of network error messages indicating that your driver has failed to bind. This generally indicates that either the wrong network card driver has been used or the settings on the network card do not match the settings provided to the network in the control panel's Network applet.

If the system fails to boot, the situation is generally more complex and either indicates that the system as configured is incompatible with Windows NT or that inappropriate information has been provided to Windows NT during setup. The following list includes some of the most common errors. No such list can be all inclusive. We recommend that you examine the release notes for your version of Windows NT as well as this list. If you are unable to resolve the problem using the release notes, the Windows NT manuals, and this list, consult the hardware manuals that came with your system. Finally, you may wish to call the system vendor or Microsoft for more assistance.

Common Installation Errors

RAM If the setup program indicates that memory is insufficient to load the system when you know, in fact, that there is enough memory to load the system, then the odds are quite good that the system configuration has not been reset since the memory was upgraded, particularly with EISA and MCA systems. It can also happen with certain ISA systems. Run the system configuration utility supplied by your hardware manufacturer. If you are attempting to install Windows NT on a system that lacks sufficient memory (12MB) to run the graphical install program that comes with the Windows NT CD-ROM, you may be able to accomplish an installation using the WINNT.EXE MS-DOS based CD installation. However, note that Windows NT in its present configuration, though it will run in 8MB, will not run acceptably on less than 12MB. This requirement is why Microsoft does not recommend this configuration. If, regardless of these facts, you decide to do an installation in an 8MB system, consult the section earlier in this chapter on over-the-network installation using WINNT.EXE.

If the BIOS is unable to recognize RAM above 16MB, (a problem known to happen on some ISA-bus computers, including early-model Dell 486 systems, among others), then you must upgrade the BIOS on the particular system. Contact your hardware manufacturer for further information.

If you have *any* memory parity errors, Windows NT will refuse to run. If you encounter this problem, your best approach, unfortunately, is to try swapping RAM chips or SIMMs until the system starts, at which point you throw away the offending RAM chip or SIMM because it has a hard error on it and is useless. This error is not a bug in Windows NT—you've had a hardware error all along. If you have had unpredictable system crashes that you have been attributing to Windows, it is entirely likely that after changing the offending RAM chip you will find that your 16-bit DOS and Windows system has become more reliable.

Finally, you should disable any "shadow RAM" on the system; it has no effect on Windows NT because the BIOS is never employed in Windows NT after the initial system start. Whatever memory is used for shadowing, either the BIOS or video BIOS is not available to the system and is therefore completely wasted when Windows NT is running. In case of memory checksum errors, try swapping the RAM chips. The error number is F002 Parity error. Windows NT is extremely sensitive to system RAM and will not operate at all in situations where other operating systems may permit the systems to run in a crippled mode.

Network Interface Card (NIC) The most common NIC problems are related to the I/O address, interrupt (IRQ), and jumper settings. Interrupt conflicts are likely to cause the system to crash with an error number 0X000000A, IRQ expected to be less than or equal. Windows NT is extremely sensitive to interrupts, and it will fail to load in situations that would be perfectly tolerable in the same hardware for DOS or Windows 3.1. In particular, Windows NT will not allow two hardware devices to share the same interrupt.

This problem is typically found in systems where a network interface card or other device has been configured to use IRQ 3, which is also typically used by COM2. In such a situation, you must disable COM2, using the CMOS setup built into your machine, the manufacturer's utility programs, or by physically removing the COM2 port card. Alternatively (and much more easily), you may wish to consider using a different IRQ setting on your network card. Similar problems can be seen with I/O address and card jumper settings, either in a situation where the I/O address duplicates an I/O address for another device or where the jumper settings on the card do not match the settings that were provided to Windows NT during the installation.

These problems will usually allow the system to boot, in which case you will observe the problems in the Event Manager. The best solution then is to shut down Windows NT, turn the system off, remove the card that is suspected to be the problem, inspect the jumper settings and inspect the hardware documentation that came with the card to see which settings, in fact, are set. A number of cards that are supposed to be software configurable may not work properly with Windows NT with a software setting for which the cards have never been programmed, and it may be necessary to run a DOS-based configuration utility to reconfigure the card, and then run Windows NT.

One helpful approach is to examine the Adapter Card Help (NTCARD*xx*.HLP) file supplied with the Windows NT Resource Kit. This file provides a complete description of NT-compatible network cards, including on-line diagrams showing the jumper settings, relating these to the IRQ, and jumper addresses. This examination can be an enormous time saver in debugging network card problems. Note that other common IRQ conflicts include COM2, as described earlier, and blind printer ports. Again, Windows NT absolutely will *not* permit you to share interrupts.

If the system is starting and the Event Manager indicates that there are no hardware errors in the driver, check to make sure that there is no duplicate computer name on your network and also to make sure that the computer name is different from the workgroup or domain name that has been set on your system. The workgroup name cannot be the same as the computer name, or you'll get no network connection.

Note also that Windows NT setup only autodetects NICs supported by drivers located in one of the main setup directories (i386, MIPS, Alpha, PPC) of the distribution CD-ROM. Additional NIC drivers are found in the DRVLIB directory, but they require manual installation (as will any third-party drivers).

Video If a video card refuses to operate at the specified video resolution, you may want to check and ensure that the video card has sufficient video RAM for the specification. Also check to see that any hardware switch settings on the card match the settings that were provided to Windows NT installation. Normally, if Windows NT cannot otherwise determine how to control the video card, it will default to VGA, 640x480x16 color VGA, which works with most modern video cards. In general, on a system where the video has been set to an incorrect resolution, you can solve the problem by using the Emergency Repair Disk.

Unfortunately, there is one major exception. The JZSETUP program used on MIPS and other RISC systems has a series of settings allowing you to set a variety of video resolutions. On early MIPS R4000 workstations with fixed-frequency monitors, setting any of these resolutions other than the system default produces a totally screwed-up video display. The only solution to this appears to be complete reprogramming of the system PROM on the R4000 systems. Should this happen to you, call MIPS technical support. You won't believe what they tell you to do, but, amazingly enough, it *will* work.[21]

Certain specific video cards can create problems when used with NT; examples have included S3 video cards that have an address conflict with other peripherals, Weitek-based video cards that are not compatible with Microsoft's Weitek driver, and incompatibilities with a wide range of older Diamond and ATI cards (the latter can be handled using NT's 8514/a compatible driver). Consult your Windows NT release notes for up-to-date information.

---

21   Do we know something? Yes. Do we believe it? Well, we take the Fifth on that...

Although using NT 3.1 video drivers in NT 3.5 and 3.51 was possible, Microsoft recommended against it for performance reasons. NT 4.0 uses a completely different video model, as explained in Chapter 1, and cannot use earlier video drivers at all.

CD-ROM If Windows NT loads from the CD but fails to recognize the CD-ROM after the graphical install has started, or if Windows NT goes through the installation correctly but refuses to recognize the CD-ROM after installation is complete, check to see if the SCSI ID has been set to 0 or something else. If so, check to see if the system's configuration is such that 0 and 1 are reserved for hard disk addresses, in which case you may wish to set another CD-ROM ID. Most CD-ROMs will come from the factory configured for ID = 6. If Windows NT fails to detect this, try setting it to 0 or 1.

You may also have to determine that your CD-ROM is terminated—that in the chain of SCSI devices, the last device connected has a termination plug attached or has a termination switch thrown. Consult your hardware manufacturer's specifications for details. In addition, on some SCSI controllers, you must check to see that the bit interrupt is specified. Some controllers have a "no interrupt" specification that is incompatible with Windows NT.

Finally, on systems with more than one CD drive, Windows NT should be installed from the one that has first priority (the lowest SCSI ID number, typically 0).

Boot Failure First check to make sure that there is enough space on the boot device for the paging file. A minimum of 20MB is required, and it may be larger depending on what you specify during the installation. Windows NT will not start if the paging file cannot be created. Make sure that BOOT.INI points to the correct path. BOOT.INI is a hidden file that is normally in the root directory of the boot device. You can unhide this using the DOS attrib command and then examine the file, which is in text format. It will list the path using ARC-system-style addressing. You will need to check to make sure that the path it is pointing to indeed exists on your system.

Multiple Operating Systems In a multiple operating system environment such as DOS-OS/2 - Windows NT, NT should always be the *last* operating system installed on the system. The reason for this is that some operating system boot loaders, such as OS/2 multiboot, will interfere with the operation of the Windows NT Boot Manager. The Windows NT Boot Manager, on the other hand, will generally permit other boot options to be executed. From the Windows NT Boot Manager menu, select the option for *previous operating system* on drive C, and the system will reboot. You will then be presented with the Boot Manager subsystem that had previously been installed. This process is known to work with the OS/2 Boot Manager approach, for example, and it provides a high degree of compatibility and flexibility in multiple boot situations such as those used by system developers.

For dual-boot between NT and Windows 95, it's safe to install NT first, but then install Windows 95 from the distribution CD's SETUP program.

> *Note: If you install from a boot floppy, the Windows 95 boot program will overwrite NT's boot sector, and you'll have a major problem.*

Hard Disk Controller If the system is unable to recognize your hard disk after installation, it is entirely possible that the disk is not recognized by the BIOS, which makes it impossible for the AT loader to determine that it's there and functioning. In that case, you will have to manually edit the BOOT.INI file and replace the path name with the fully qualified ARC name path. The Resource Kit provides a special tool (NTDETECT.COM) that may help diagnose this sort of problem; see Appendix 4 for details.

In some cases, NT can fail to recognize a second drive in a two-disk EIDE setup. The EIDE adapter is incorrectly recognized as a generic ATAPI controller by NT setup, which automatically loads the ATAPI.SYS driver. To correct the problem, disable ATAPI.SYS, and load the appropriate EIDE driver.

The 1,024-Cylinder Limit Prior to version 3.51, Windows NT used the BIOS to determine the hard disk geometry on AT compatible disk controllers. In some cases, this information is limited to 10 bits and the cylinders larger than 1,024 cannot be addressed. You may be able to use part of the disk by setting a custom configuration employing only the first 1,024 cylinders. Or, you may be able to use an approach called "head doubling" in which you state that the hard disk has 10 times the number of heads physically present and half the number of cylinders. The geometry table information in the hard disk controller translates this to the drive's actual physical dimensions. Finally, you may need a BIOS upgrade or a different hard disk controller.

From NT 3.51 on, NT supports Integrated Drive Electonics (IDE) and Enhanced IDE (EIDE) drives with more than 1,024 cylinders by providing support for Ontrack Corporation's Disk Manager program. Disk Manager is supplied with most high-capacity IDE and EIDE drives. It provides a customized boot sector and (in DOS) remaps the disk BIOS so that the additional cylinders are recognized. NT cannot create the required boot sector, but it *can* recognize such a sector once it's created. To do so, use the Disk Manager boot disk, and follow instructions to create the boot sector. Then install Windows NT.

Pentium Floating-Point Bug Early Pentium[22] processors contained an error in floating-point division logic that could produce incorrect results in certain circumstances. Versions of Windows NT from 3.51 on automatically detect this error during setup and offer to correct it for you. Applying automatic correction has a small performance impact but assures that floating-point division will always produce correct results. If you wish, you can check and modify these settings using the PENTNT command-line function after setup is complete:

```
C:\>pentnt /?
Reports on whether local computer exhibits Intel(tm) Pentium
Floating Point Division Error

pentnt [-?] [-H] [-h] [-C] [-c] [-F] [-f] [-O] [-o]

        Run without arguments this program will tell you if the
        system exhibits the Pentium floating point division error
        and whether floating point emulation is forced and whether floating
        point hardware is disabled.

    -?  Print this help message
    -h
```

---

22   Mainly the original 60Mhz and 66MHz versions.

```
    -H

    -c  Turn on conditional emulation. This means that floating
    -C  point emulation will be forced on if and only if
        the system detects the Pentium floating point division
        error at boot. Reboot required before this takes effect.
        This is what should generally be used.

    -f  Turn on forced emulation.  This means that floating
    -F  point hardware is disabled and floating point emulation
        will always be forced on, regardless of whether the system
        exhibits the Pentium division error. Useful for testing
        software emulators and for working around floating point
        hardware defects unknown to the OS. Reboot required before
        this takes effect.

    -o  Turn off forced emulation. Reenables floating point hardware
    -O  if present. Reboot required before this takes effect.

The Floating Point Division error that this program addresses only
occurs on certain Intel Pentium processors. It only affects floating
point operations. The problem is described in detail in a white paper
available from Intel. If you are doing critical work with programs that
perform floating point division and certain related functions that
use the same hardware (including remainder and transcendtal functions),
you may wish to use this program to force emulation.
```

Common Error Messages

- *Error 0x0000000A—IRQ expected to be less than or equal*. This indicates an interrupt conflict. See the sections on network interface card, COM port, and other interrupt conflicts earlier in this section.

- *Error 0x00000067 or 0x00000069—Initialization error*. This generally indicates a problem with the hard disk controller. On AT controllers, try running at a lower DMA transfer rate. This generally will require a jumper switch change. On SCSI systems, verify that the SCSI chain is terminated. On any system, check the IRQ, check for memory address conflicts, and check to see that the NTDETECT.COM file is in the root of the boot device. Absence of other NT files can also cause error 69, and if you find that a significant group of files is missing from the hard disk, a sector error on the hard disk may be the cause. You will need to clean up the hard disk using a DOS-based disk-maintenance utility, such as the Norton Disk Doctor, and reinstall Windows NT from scratch, unfortunately.

- *System Error F002*. This message generally indicates a hardware problem, typically parity error on the RAM. It could also indicate a hardware problem machine check exception with math coprocessor. It might conceivably be caused by a machine check exception on a Pentium-based system indicating an overheat. It may also be caused by hardware problems with the accessory cards. You will need to use the hardware diagnostics supplied by your system's manufacturer. If you formatted an NTFS partition on the system, you will have to use the DOS fdisk utility to deactivate the partition, reassign it, and reformat it as a FAT partition. An alternative way to do this is to use the Windows NT setup program, select Custom Setup, refuse the setup suggested path, select the NTFS partition, select P to delete the partition, then recreate the partition as a FAT partition and either continue on with the Windows NT setup or exit. Use the DOS fdisk and format commands to replace the partition with a DOS-recognized FAT partition.

Error 0000001E. This error indicates something is wrong in the file system. You'll need to run CHKDSK or a DOS-based utility such as Norton Disk Doctor.[23]

- *Couldn't Find NTLDR.* This message indicates that the NT bootstrap (NTLDR) is missing from the root directory of the boot device. You can copy it directly from the CD-ROM's \I386 (or \mips, \alpha, \ppc) directory; or use EXPAND.EXE to uncompress NTLDR.$ from setup diskette #2.

Uninstalling Windows NT

Should you wish to completely remove NT from your Intel-based system and return to a DOS-based system, it's possible using the following steps.

1. Shutdown and restart the system—and boot DOS (if you installed NT on a DOS system, this process will probably be an option on system startup; if not, use a boot floppy).

2. From DOS, create a boot diskette using the *format /s* command, and copy CONFIG.SYS and AUTOEXEC.BAT on it.

3. Delete the entire WINNT35, WINNT, or WINDOWS\SYSTEM32 directory—whichever was used (it depends on whether NT was installed fresh, over NT 3.1, or into an existing DOS/Windows setup)—and all subdirectories from the boot partition on the target system's hard disk. (This is most easily done using Windows Explorer.)

4. Delete the following files from the root of the boot drive:

   pagefile.sys

   boot.ini

   ntldr

   ntdetect.com

   bootsect.dos

   Some of these files are hidden; use the DOS *attrib* command to unhide them. BOOTSECT.DOS will only exist if the system was set up to dual-boot between NT and DOS.

---

23 The latter approach, obviously, works only on DOS-compatible FAT partitions. On NTFS this error indicates a major problem. As of this writing (July 1996) no low-level disk tools for NT are commercially available. However, there are shareware disk editors available, which—along with an NT-formatted boot diskette—can be a lifesaver. See the *Disk Maintenance* section of Chapter 5 for details.

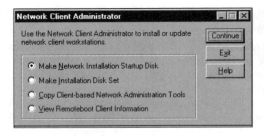

FIGURE 2.9 Network client administrator. NT Server includes this application, which is used by administrators to create client installation disks, copy client-based administration tools, and control the remoteboot service for diskless workstations.

At this point, attempting to boot your machine will give the error message "BOOT: Couldn't find NTLDR please insert another disk." To get around this, take the boot floppy you made earlier, and do a SYS to your boot disk (typically *sys c:*) to transfer DOS and make the hard disk bootable.

Additional Notes for Servers NT Server versions from 3.5 on contain some additional installation tools that may be useful once the operating system itself is installed. One of the nicest tools is the Network Client Administrator. This is a complete, NT-based program that makes setup disk sets for Microsoft's NT-compatible DOS, Windows, and OS/2 clients (see Figure 2.9). It can also make an update disk with new network support for WFWG clients. Using this tool with the over-the-network WINNT.EXE can just about automate installing NT Workstation on desktops. The tool will build a DOS client disk, install it on the target system, connect to the shared CD, and run WINNT to complete the installation.

Windows-based NT administration tools (finally!) are included so that it's no longer necessary to have an NT Workstation on your desk if you want to remotely manage an NT Server. Those tools are in the \clients\srvtools\windows directory of the CD—just connect to it over the network, and run the SETUP.EXE in that directory.

NT Servers also have the Dynamic Host Configuration Protocol (DHCP) and Windows Internet Name Service (WINS) services. These functions make administering TCP/IP-based networks much easier (see Chapter 6) than with earlier versions. NT Servers also have a remoteboot service that lets you support DOS and Windows on diskless workstations and there are other powerful features like Microsoft's Migration Tool for NetWare (see Chapter 10).

Conclusion

You've learned how to carry out a Network Needs Analysis, how to select appropriate hardware for your needs, where to situate that hardware, and how to install and configure Windows NT on it. The next step is to establish the user-accounts database, security policies, and access rights that will make the network useful to your end users. These topics will be covered in Chapter 3.

For More Information

Microsoft Staff (1995), *Windows NT Server Concepts and Planning Guide.* Redmond WA: Microsoft Corp. This guide, which comes with complete Server systems (or you can get them in a Windows NT Server documentation kit), is invaluable. It's the best place to start (other than right here, of course!). The complete NT Server kit (or documentation kit) also provides an informative video that helps in understanding concepts like Domains *vs.* Workgroups, primary domain controller, etc. If you do nothing else before installing an NT Server, at least skip the guide and watch the video. They make things much less confusing for the first-time NT user!

Microsoft Staff (1995), *Windows NT System Guide.* Redmond, WA: Microsoft Corp. This guide contains all the specifics you'll need to get set up.

Microsoft Staff (1995), *Windows NT Resource Kit, Volumes 1-4.* Redmond, WA: Microsoft Corp. Volume 1 includes setup information, and the Computer Profile Setup (CPS) is especially helpful.

Microsoft Staff (monthly), *TechNet CD.* Redmond, WA: Microsoft Product Support Services (PSS). TechNet is a monthly publication on CD-ROM containing a digest of topics from the Microsoft Knowledge Base, the Net News publication, Resource Kits, and other information. It's available from Microsoft sales; a one-year subscription (12 CDs) costs $295 and is worth every penny.

Microsoft Staff, *Books Online.* Redmond, WA: Microsoft Product Support Services (PSS). Books Online is a feature of the Windows NT distribution CD. It essentially duplicates the printed documentation in online .HLP format, and may be found in the \SUPPORT\BOOKS directory of both Workstation and Server CDs.

Microsoft Staff, *Windows NT Workstation Evaluation Guide (version 3.5).* Redmond, WA: Microsoft Product Support Services (PSS). The evaluation guides are floppy diskettes containing a wealth of information on NT Workstation and NT Server. They're available for download from Microsoft's Internet site (ftp.microsoft.com) and, for a nominal fee, from Microsoft Sales (800) 426-9400.

Administrative Connections

Administering Windows NT Networks

When you have read this chapter, you will understand the basic concepts of system administration, user accounts and system security including:

⇨ Why and how to create administrative user groups

⇨ How to create and manage user accounts

⇨ How to assign user permissions

⇨ Formatting and management of disk volumes (including spanned volumes)

⇨ Administrative management using the built-in Performance Monitor, Event Viewer, System Policy Editor, and Distributed COM Configuration tools

⇨ Creating and managing network print queues

You should feel comfortable carrying out the basic tasks of system administration on a Windows NT network and be prepared to set up and use a small single-workgroup (or single-domain) network on your own.

System Management and the Network Administrator

All Windows NT systems are servers, and administrative tasks have to be carried out on them. As a secure operating system, Windows NT requires all users—even local users logged in on the system console—to have a valid user account and password. The user's account, in turn, will determine what *user rights* and *resource access permissions* the user will have, in effect controlling what the user is allowed to do. Setting up, maintaining, and controlling the accounts is the job of the Network Administrator: you.

The Network Administrator

The *Network Administrator's* role is part systems technician, part shop foreman, part traffic cop—and more. The Network Administrator's responsibility is to provide access to the server and networked services on the LAN that is always available and—this is very important—*invisible* to the users.

An always-available network is easy to understand, if not easy to provide. The server and networked services on the LAN must be ready for users whenever they need to work. Of course, hardware will need to come down for maintenance, and software must be upgraded, but the network administrator's job is to manage these activities around users' peak production periods. You want to *plan* for maintenance, rather than fight fires as they occur.

Providing a network that is *invisible* to the users is more difficult. Users must have access to the server and peripherals, like printers and network modems, without having to know how they are provided. In the movie *Running Scared,*[1] two policemen ask their vehicle maintenance officer for a fast, powerful, and invisible car. He gives them a cab. This type of car is perfect: the car is quick, the engine powerful and in Chicago, nothing is more invisible than another yellow cab.

Your network should be much like that cab. The network should be quick; users' workstations should be configured to have access to the facilities they need without having to search through endless directories. It should be powerful; users must be able to print and store files on the server with confidence that their printouts will be processed quickly and their data will be backed up daily. Most of all, however, using the network should be familiar. Users should work on the network the way they do on their own systems. Understanding the few network facilities they use should be as easy as pointing and clicking.

Windows NT 4.0 lends a hand to the network administrator to achieve these goals. Because Windows NT 4.0 is based on the familiar look and feel of Windows 95, your users will be in

---

1   Metro-Goldwyn-Meyer, 1986.

familiar territory when they log in to your server and access data from it. Configuring and managing the users' systems to do so are the network administrator's responsibilities.

Many items go into a properly configured network to ensure that it is both available and invisible.

The first factor is network reliability, which takes into account server performance monitoring, the system's fault tolerance, UPSs, and proper backup and recovery systems. Windows NT Server provides you with many of the required tools. For example, using the Performance Monitor provides a quick overview of the server's current performance; it even sets up particular items that you want to view plotted as charts. You can also set alerts to warn you when various thresholds are exceeded.

The second aspect is user management, which includes installation and configuration of desktop equipment, creation and maintenance of user accounts and account groups, monitoring the desktop systems' performance, user training, providing user backups, and properly preparing and anticipating for user growth. It also means providing for an automated method of user and group creation via templates. This function will help you to save time and avoid making simple errors when granting access permissions.

The third ingredient is establishment of procedures. Once procedures for providing both network reliability and user management are in place, providing a stable and usable network environment becomes easier. Setting up or terminating user accounts, performing daily backups, and maintaining printers should all become documented and repeatable procedures.

Performing a function one day without the ability to duplicate the steps may work well once, but it's not at all useful. You need to have documentation to provide a full-time network. Who knows? You may find yourself on the phone trying to explain to a user how to retrieve a file from a backup tape. The process is a lot easier if he or she has a document to refer to, for both of you, rather than trying to communicate a series of dialog boxes and steps in the correct order.

The fourth component is planning for the future. This area includes many items. A properly planned network allows the Network Administrator to easily add additional users and additional storage to the server. Don't assume the job is over when you have provided your group with the network they requested. If you've done a great job, your users will expect *more* from you. More nodes, more user directory space, more remote connectivity. The list is never-ending. The circumstances are actually simple: your users have needs and desires, related to your network, that will help them be more productive. Your task is also simple: you must be prepared to fulfill their requests.

The fifth factor, and perhaps most important aspect of all, is proper documentation. Network documentation is often considered an oxymoron, but its usefulness can't be overstated. Documenting every stage of your LAN for future reference is imperative. *Network Computing* magazine lists six excellent suggestions for network documentation that you can follow *now* to avoid future headaches:[2]

Cross reference users with node addresses. This process is especially useful if you are assigning IP (internet protocol) addresses to your users. Otherwise, put together a list showing your users' logins with their computer names.

---

2 Mike Franks, "Documenting Your Network (When You Don't Have Time)." *Network Computing*, August 1992, pp. 128-130.

Network diagrams are worth 1000 words. You can get as fancy as you have time and patience for here. The essential items in your diagram are the approximate locations of:

- shared network resources (servers, concentrators, printers, network faxes, etc.)

- desktop PCs

- basic cabling

- bridges

- routers

- WAN (wide area network) services to which your network is connected

This diagram should be documented as fully as possible to include items like disk capacities and amount of installed RAM for your servers and desktop systems, user names and titles, user phone numbers and modem numbers if applicable, and network interface card (NIC) machine access code (MAC) addresses for servers and desktop systems. In addition, include each node's concentrator patch number next to the node location. This step will help solve many of the endless mysteries usually associated with the phone-wiring closet.

Document user and security information. Your list should contain the groups that each user belongs to, including global and local groups. Any special access should be noted here.

Document software on servers. When you install software document the title, version, and publisher; give a description, show the directory location, and list the groups and users who have access to this software. Also, add a few lines that include the serial number, the disks' physical location, and the technical support phone number for the product.

Document software information online. Take this documentation process a few steps further and organize all of the information into a simple database. This step will help you to locate that single needed item in an emergency. In fact, if you create your network diagram using your computer, you should be able to incorporate it into your database as well. That way, you can also compile all of your physical location data with your user information in one place.

Document network policies and procedures online. With proper planning, the database you created in the previous step can contain all of the information you need to run your network, including policies and procedures.

One last thought: make *hard copies* of all of your documentation, place a copy with your server, and distribute the copies to the appropriate IT departments. That way, the documentation's available even if power is not.

The Network Administrator's Responsibilities The network administrator has a series of responsibilities that fall into nine categories. You can think of those categories as a pyramid. The bottom-most responsibilities consume most of the network administrator's time, but are continuous activities, spread out over time. The top-most tasks are not as frequent, but can consume an entire day in one shot.

Network Administrator's Pyramid of Responsibilities

Putting out fires

Training users

User account management

Group account management

User desktop configuration and maintenance

Backups, performance monitoring, network security

Server and network hardware and software maintenance

Backup and recovery

Disaster planning

Growth planning

For example, growth planning requires listening to users and anticipating their future network and server requirements. Realistically, this planning occurs all the time; as the network administrator, you are constantly planning for future network growth. Windows NT Server provides you with many ways to monitor performance, and it's your job to put these fiunctions together and draw conclusions about them that will assist you when making future hardware and software acquisitions.

Putting out fires, on the other hand, is a shorter, more concentrated task that has immediate consequences. When a fire occurs, such as a failed NIC in your server, you aren't just storing away data for later use. You are going into action *now!* You'll have to down your server, replace the card, bring the server back up, test the new card, and make the server available to users. If you've built your server with proper fault tolerance and fail-safes in mind, and if your budget permits, you may have a backup server on standby. In that case, you may only have to migrate users to the new server and replace the other when your users have met their deadlines.

The pyramid's items are daily, weekly, and monthly tasks. For an established network, most of the work that you do can be planned along these lines, though such guidelines are not strict requirements. New user creation, for example, might occur only twice a year in our original accounting department example. When new user account creation is necessary, however, it becomes an urgent item, but we'll leave it under the monthly tasks due to its infrequency.

Whether the network administrator is you or someone you hire, here are a few guidelines that you can refer to when managing your server and LAN.

Daily Tasks

- *Check Error Logs*. All error logs should be checked for new entries, including those from *both* the Windows NT Event Manager and Performance Monitor (discussed later in this chapter). All warnings should be followed up; see Chapter 5 for troubleshooting and performance tuning information.

- *Check Help Desk E-Mail*. Read and prioritize user help requests.

- *Check Volume Free Space*. Look for anomalous disk space loss and potential space shortages. You may want to consider automating this process using Performance Monitor *alerts*, a procedure that is covered later in this chapter.

- *Perform Daily Backups* (if used). If you are performing daily backups (and you must back up either daily or weekly or both), and are having the backup performed automatically (using the scheduler service with NT's built-in backup or a third-party product), remember to check that a new tape, or the correct tape, is ready in your tape drive. If necessary, periodically check and tension the tape-drive mechanism.

- *Confirm Overnight Backups* (if made). If daily backups are performed overnight, ensure that they were successful. You can do this either by running a full verify pass or by retrieving a sample set of files (in the latter case, don't always try to retrieve the same set of files). Remove and store the tapes. *Do not* store your only set of backup tapes in the same room as your only server; doing so *risks losing all of your data* in a single event, such as a fire.

Weekly Tasks

- *Clear Errant Temporary Files*. Remove dead temporary files from user and mail directories. (You may wish to automate this task using the Windows NT *at* script command covered at the end of this chapter.)

- *Create And Distribute User Space Lists*. Look for excessive disk-space use, and distribute memos to responsible users requesting that they either delete or archive the files.

- *Check Mail System Status*. Look for excessive mail message archiving, such as dead backup files and other temp files that should be deleted.

- *Perform Week-End Backups* (if used). If you are performing weekly backups (and you must back up either daily or weekly or both), remember to check that a new tape, or the correct tape, is ready in your tape drive. Periodically, check the tape drive mechanism. Be sure to confirm the backup, as specified in *Daily Tasks* above.

Monthly Tasks

- *Archive And Delete Dead Files*. Check files for activity and delete or archive files that have not had any activity for more than a month.

- *Perform Disaster Drill.* During off time (yes, I know, "Ha ha, very funny"), perform disaster drills to test your disaster recovery plan and backup strategy. This test is *very* important and can mean the difference between being able to recover from a problem during peak periods and not being able to recover at all.

- *Perform Month-End (or Cycle-End) Backups* (if used). These are different from both daily and weekly backups and should be performed for use as an archive if your data is cyclical in nature. For example, you might perform backups in the middle of every other month if that is when your production cycle ends. The data that you archive will contain the final report from each of your cycles. This data should be archived off-site as a disaster recovery tool.

Creating Groups and Users The name of this section is "Creating Groups and Users," rather than the other way around, for a reason. As you discovered while conducting your network needs assessment (in Chapter 2), it is possible to collect your users into groups who share the same access and security requirements. For example, you may have a directory that contains network applications. Not all of the users in your network will require access to all of these subdirectories containing applications. The directory containing a CAD/CAM application should only be accessed by the engineers who use the program. Everyone on the network probably requires access to a word processing application. You should build groups according to access requirements.

Domains and Workgroups Before exploring the details of user account and group management, we need to understand the concepts of *domains* and *workgroups*. In a Windows NT network, a workgroup is a collection of computers that are grouped together for convenience when users browse network services. The network administrator designates a workgroup for each Windows NT system, and this name appears to other systems on the local area network.

A workgroup's major limitation is that each server in the workgroup must maintain its own database of user accounts independently of other workgroup servers. This requirement means that users who need to access more than one server will require separate accounts on each server, a situation that can quickly become an administrative nightmare on a large network.

Windows NT Server expands this capability with the concept of an administrative domain. Like workgroups, domains appear in the browse list, and they group servers and workstations together logically. However, domains reduce redundancy by maintaining a single account database that applies to all servers in a domain. All account information is maintained in a single database on the *primary domain controller* (PDC). Other servers that are configured as domain controllers[3] (DCs) on the network (which can include Windows NT Servers and LAN Manager 2.0 or higher servers) maintain a copy of this central database. Changes in that database are updated every five minutes (a process called *replication* that will be covered in more detail in Chapter 8). Any server can validate a log-on request.

The great advantage of a domain over a workgroup is that users need only one account to access any network system. Indeed, through a process called *inter-domain trust* (see Chapter 8 for details) this approach can be applied between domains, so that a user with an account in one domain can access servers in other domains.

---

3   Unlike NTAS 3.1, NT Server from version 3.5 on does not have to be installed as a DC—it can be installed as a stand-alone server that acts like NT Workstation where user accounts are concerned.

As a practical matter, however, you need not worry too much about the division between Workgroups and Domains: if your network includes a Windows NT Server, you are using Domains. If not (even if you are joining a Windows NT Workstation to an existing LAN Manager Domain), you have a Workgroup. In situations where the difference between workgroups and domains is more than just semantics, we will point it out. For now, just assume that the Workgroup is a lightweight Domain, and you'll get the gist of the difference.

You should choose your domain (or workgroup) name to reflect its primary function. TIM1 is not a good choice for the accounting department, even if the vice president of accounting is named Tim. ACCT_DEPT is a better choice. That name helps users understand which department this server belongs to and takes into account the possibility of growth to ACCT_DEPT_2. Another possibility, which may make sense in very large networks, is the use of geographical domain names. Indeed, Microsoft uses this approach, as you will see in Chapter 8.

Working with Groups The processes of creating and managing user accounts and account groups are basically the same, whether you are operating a stand-alone Windows NT server for a workgroup, or an enterprise-wide multiserver network. Allowing one user to belong to more than one group is perfectly fine; in fact, that flexibility is essential to planning your network. Windows NT Server provides for the creation of two types of groups.

Local Groups are groups of users and global groups that have access to servers from their own domain. *Global Groups* (NT Server only) are groups of users that have access to servers and workstations from their own domain or other domains that "trust" their home domain.

Predefined groups in the basic Windows NT product include Administrators, Users, Power Users, Backup Operators, and Guests. Windows NT Server adds Domain Admins, Domain Users, Account Operators, Print Operators, Server Operators, and Replicator, and it eliminates the Power Users group. Some of these groups, as you can see from their names, involve special functions and rights that you may assign to particular users. Not every one of these groups is a stand-alone group. Some of them are, by default, members of other groups.

Administrative Tools

Both Windows NT Workstation and Server provide a set of tools for system management. All tools are found in the Start menu's Administrative Tools folder. The *User Manager* application is used to create and modify both local and global groups. Once it creates these groups, you can use Windows Explorer to grant directory permissions to these groups' members. The *Performance Monitor* application provides a way to track the performance of NT services and applications, and the Windows NT *Event Viewer* is used to examine the system's log files. Windows NT also includes a simple built-in *Backup* application. We will also cover Windows NT Server's *Licensing* application.

Windows NT Server provides more sophisticated versions of these tools for domain management, including *User Manager for Domains, Server Manager,* and *System Policy Editor*.[4]

---

4   As well as a completely new Web-based administration tool for use in conjunction with Microsoft's Internet Information Server (IIS) built-in Webserver product. See Chapter 7 for information on IIS, and Chapter 8 for preliminary information on the Web-based administration tool (in beta as this was written).

Because these functions are used primarily in larger networks, we cover them in Chapter 8. NT Server also provides a set of client-based administration tools that run on NT Workstations, Windows for Workgroups, or Windows 95 systems, which are also covered in Chapter 8.

User Manager The User Manager application helps you add, change, and delete accounts for individuals and groups. It also sets the server (or domain) security and audit policies.

Individual users are assigned a user type that corresponds to security levels. For example, users who are in the Administrators group may perform all User Manager tasks, and have the most control over a network. Users who are part of the Users group can create groups, then modify or delete them, and can give user account memberships in the groups created.

> *Note: When you modify the user account database on a server—whether you add a user, remove one, or assign permissions—take an extra minute and use the Repair Disk utility (covered in Chapter 5) to update your emergency diskette. Otherwise, those changes will not be reflected if you ever have to restore the accounts after a crash!*

To start User Manager, click on the icon in the Start menu's Administrative Tools folder, or select Start, Run and type MUSRMGR.EXE in the Command Line text box and click on OK. The main window of User Manager is shown in Figure 3.1.

To exit User Manager, select User, Exit.

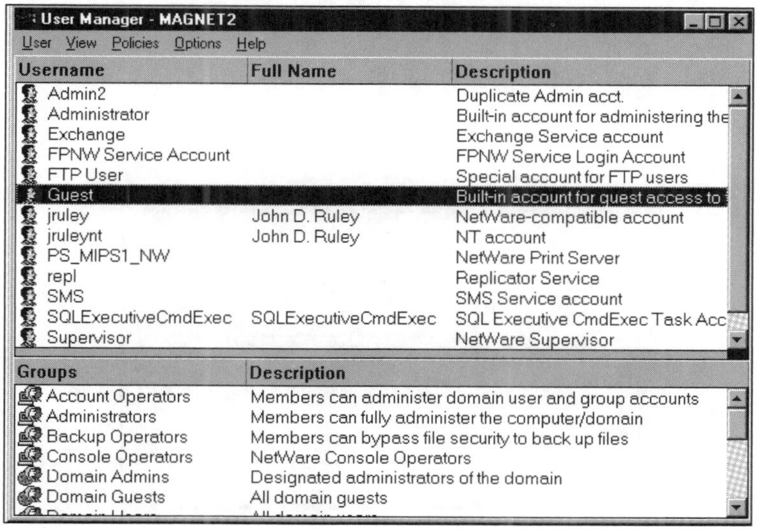

FIGURE 3.1 User manager. The Windows NT User Manager, or the NT Server User Manager for Domains shown here, is the primary administrative tool for controlling user accounts, groups, access permissions, and user rights.

Adding a Group You can create your own local groups (Domain Administrators in Windows NT Server Domains can also create Global Groups). To do so:

1. Select the user accounts you want added to a group, or select a user group so that no user accounts are selected. Choose User, New Local Group. The Local Group Properties dialog box shown in Figure 3.2 appears.

2. Type in the name of the group and its description at the top of the New Local Group dialog box.

3. If you want to see the complete names of the users you chose in the first step, click on Show Full Names.

4. Select Add to add members to the group. Click on OK when all users are added.

5. Select OK to exit the dialog box.

Deleting a Group If you want to delete a local group, select the group from the User Manager window. Select User, Delete. If User Manager displays a confirmation message, click on OK. Click on Yes to delete the group.

Adding a User Account A user account is a collection of information about a user, including rights and membership in groups. Several user accounts come predefined within Windows NT, and are arranged in a hierarchy by default.

To add a user account to the system:

1. Select User then New User. The dialog box shown in Figure 3.3 is displayed.

2. Enter the user name in the Username box. User names must be unique, cannot exceed 20 characters, and cannot contain any characters except:

   " / \ ; : [ ] < > | = + , * ?

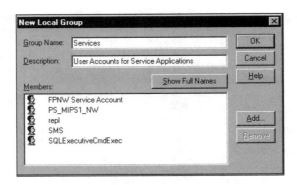

FIGURE 3.2 New local group. Administration of NT networks can be greatly simplified by exploiting the Local and Global groups. Assigning access permissions and user rights to Groups automatically allocates the same permissions and rights to users within the Group.

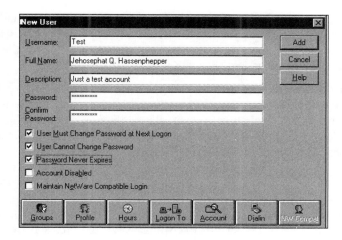

FIGURE 3.3 New user. You add a new user to your network using the New User dialog from the NT User Manager.

3. You can optionally enter the full name (first, middle initial, and last name) of the user in the Full Name box.

4. Optionally enter a text description in the Description box.

5. Enter the same password in the Password and Confirm Password text boxes. Passwords must not exceed 14 characters and are case sensitive.

6. To require a user to enter a new password when he or she logs on for the next session, check the User Must Change Password At Next Logon check box. If selected, be sure the User Cannot Change Password check box is not checked.

7. If you want to prevent the user from changing the password you assign, check the User Cannot Change Password check box.

8. To override the Maximum Password Age in the Account policy setup (see Managing Security Policies below), check the Password Never Expires box.

9. Select Account Disabled to temporarily disable an account, a useful option for setting up multiple users in advance of their use of the system. (Users can be activated individually when they actually join the workgroup.)

10. To administer a group or profile, select the option from the bottom of the dialog box and fill in the information as necessary.

11. Click on OK.

Note that sometimes it is actually faster to copy an existing user account and make changes as necessary. To copy a user account, select the user name from the list in the User Manager window, then choose User, then Copy. The Copy Of dialog box requests information similar to that asked for new users. Complete it, and click on OK.

Changing User Accounts When a user forgets his or her password, or when conditions change in your organization, you may need to change information about a user account. To change the information in a single-user account, choose the user account from the list in User Manager, then select User, Properties (alternatively, double-click on the user account name). Make the necessary corrections.

You can change more than one account simultaneously in a similar fashion. Select the user accounts from the list in User Manager by clicking on each one, then select User, Properties. If the users you selected share a common description, the description is displayed in the Description text box. You can enter a new description or edit the description if you wish. Next, set the Users Cannot Change Password, Passwords Never Expire, and Accounts Disabled check boxes as needed, and select the Groups or Profile options if desired. Finally, select OK.

You can also rename, disable, and delete user accounts. This capability brings up an important point: user account references are stored by Security Information Descriptor (SID), *not* by name in permissions and group memberships. Thus, renaming an account leaves permissions and group membership intact; but deleting an account and creating a new one requires all permissions and group assignments to be rebuilt from scratch. Similarly, disabling an account and re-enabling it later leaves permissions and group memberships intact, saving time and effort over deleting an account and then creating a new one.

To rename a user account:

1. Select the user account.

2. Select User, Rename.

3. In the Change To text box enter the new user name. The same naming conventions used for creating new accounts are in effect here.

4. Click on OK.

To remove one or more user accounts:

1. Select the user account(s) from the User Manager window.

2. Select User, Delete.

3. If you are asked to confirm the delete, click on OK.

4. Select Yes to delete the account name displayed in the dialog box. Select Yes to All to delete all user accounts (if multiple accounts were selected in step 1).

An alternative to deleting accounts is inactivating them. Such inactivation keeps the underlying user information, but temporarily disables their user account. To disable an account:

1. Select the user account.

2. Select User, Properties.

3. Check the Account Disabled box, and click on OK.

Connecting Users to Groups Once you have established user(s) and group(s), you need to attach (connect) a user to a group. Maintaining user and group connections is simple. To perform the update:

1. Select the user, then click on the Groups button at the bottom of the dialog box. The Group Membership dialog box, shown in Figure 3.4, is displayed.

2. The groups to which the selected user belongs are displayed in the Member of list box. The groups to which the user is excluded (does not belong) are displayed in the Not member of list box.

3. To add a user to a group, select one or more groups from the Not member of list, then click on Add.

4. To remove a selected user from one or more groups, select the group(s) from the Member of list, then click on Remove.

5. Select OK to exit the dialog box.

Adding, changing, and removing multiple users simultaneously is very similar. To do so:

1. Select the user accounts from the User Manager window.

2. Select User, Properties.

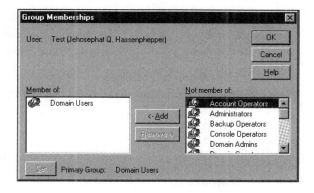

FIGURE 3.4 Groups. Once the user is added, designate the groups to which he or she belongs; by doing so, you automatically assign all necessary access privileges and rights.

3. Click on Groups.

4. The groups to which all users belong (the common groups) are displayed in the All Are Members Of list box. The groups to which one or more members may be a part is shown in the Not All Are Members Of list box.

5. To add all selected users to one or more groups, select the group(s) from the Not All Are Members Of list, then click on Add.

6. To remove all users from one or more groups, select the group(s) from the All Are Members Of list, then click on Remove.

7. Select OK to exit the dialog box.

Managing Security Policies

User Manager allows you to define and configure policies that control user rights, how events are audited, and the method of password use.

Setting Account Policies To manage the way passwords are used:

1. Select the User Account.

2. Select Policy, Account. The Policy/Account dialog box shown in Figure 3.5 appears.

3. Select the required password policy or policies. Select a maximum password period (up to 999 days), minimum password age (up to 999 days minimum), minimum password length, and password history options.

4. Click on OK.

Setting Audit Policies To manage the events that are added to the audit log:

1. Select Policy/Audit.

2. To turn off all auditing, click on Do Not Audit. To audit one or more events, select Audit These Events, then select the event you want to audit. Check whether you want to log a successful event, a failed event, or both.

3. To stop Windows NT when the audit log is full, check the Halt System when Security Event Log is Full check box.

4. Select OK.

The following table describes the events that can be audited and what they mean.

Events	Triggers
File and Object Access	Access a directory, printer, or file set for auditing (see Windows Explorer for details)
Logon and Logoff	Log into or log off a computer system or connect to a network

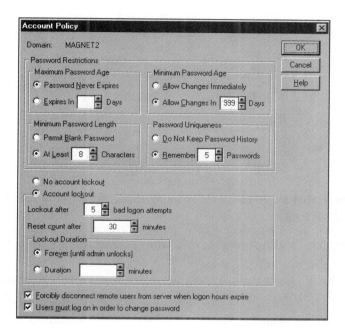

FIGURE 3.5 Policy/account. You can enforce an appropriate security policy on your NT network by setting appropriate policy settings on your system or Domain. NT Server adds a capability to force disconnection of users who operate outside their designated log-on periods.

Events	Triggers
Process Tracking	This covers a wide variety of events, including starting a program
Restart, Shutdown, and System	Restart or shutdown a computer, or trigger an event that impacts the security log or security of the system
Security Policy Changes	Changes to rights of users or to audit policies
Use of User Rights	Using a user right
User and Group Management	Add, modify, or delete a user account or group account; rename, disable, or enable a user account; or change a password

Setting User Rights To manage the authorization for a task:

1. Select Policy, User Rights. The User Rights Policy dialog box shown in Figure 3.6 appears.

2. Select the right from the Right pulldown list box. The users and groups granted the right are listed in the Grant To box. To display the advanced user rights, check the Show

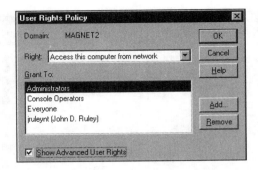

FIGURE 3.6 User rights. Security is further assured by allowing the administrator to selectively assign user rights to particular groups of NT users. This process assures that only users who have a need to carry out sensitive operations (such as account maintenance, backup and restoration, or shutting down the system) can do so.

Advanced User Rights at the bottom of the dialog box. Rights are detailed below. For a more detailed explanation, see the User Manager chapter of the *Windows NT System Guide*.

3. To remove a user or group from the list of the right, select it and click on Remove.

4. To add a user or group to the list, select Add. Complete the Add Users And Groups dialog box, and click on OK.

5. Select OK.

User Right	Permissions Granted
Access this computer from network	Connect to the computer (via a network)
Back up files and directories	Permission to back up files and directories, this overrides file and directory permissions
Bypass traverse checking	An advanced right allows user to change directories and move through a tree regardless of any existing directory permissions
Change the system time	Set internal clock of the computer
Force shutdown from a remote system	Shuts down (and optionally restarts) Windows NT. This right isn't used by any of the administration tools supplied with NT, but is employed by *Systems Management Server* (SMS), and some third-party tools.[5]

---

5   Including a public-domain *shutdown* command-line application, available for download from the Windows NT section of Compuserve's WinShare forum.

User Right	**Permissions Granted**
Log on as a service	Register with the system as a service (used for Replicator local group's Replicator service)
Log on locally	Log on to the computer using the active computer's keyboard
Manage auditing and security log	Specify the events and file access that can be audited; furthermore, this right permits a user to view and clear a security log
Restore files and directories	Permission to restore files and directories; note that this right overrides file and directory permissions
Shut down the system	Shut down Windows NT
Take ownership of files and other objects	Assume ownership of files and directories

In our earlier example, we looked at two groups, one that needed access to the CAD/CAM application and another that needed access to the word processing application. Using the Windows Explorer, you can highlight the needed directory, right click to get a context menu, select Properties from that menu and the Security tab from the resulting Properties dialog. Then click the Permissions button. In the Directory Permissions dialog box you can allow particular access to the selected directory. First, you highlight a group or user, then choose Special Directory Access from the Type of Access pulldown menu. You'll open the Special Directory Access dialog box, where you can grant either full control or choose a combination of six permissions.

Managing Profiles

Windows NT optionally stores a profile as part of a user's account information. The profile associates a log-on script name and the home directory with a particular user account. This can speed up the login process or help you as an administrator control the login process of your users.

To set a profile for a user account:

1. When adding, copying, or changing a user account, select the Profile button at the bottom of the dialog box.

2. Optionally enter the logon script in the Logon Script Name box.

3. If you want to use a local path as the home directory, enter the local directory in the Local Path text box. Use %username% to substitute the username for a subdirectory name.

4. To use a network directory as the home directory, click on Connect. Enter a drive letter (or select one from the pulldown list), then enter the network path in the To text box.

5. Select OK.

Monitoring Performance

As we noted earlier in our discussion of the Network Administrator's responsibilities, day-to-day performance monitoring is critical. Windows NT provides a powerful set of tools for this that includes Performance Monitor and Event Viewer.

Performance Monitor

The Performance Monitor utility of Windows NT lets you observe the performance of your current system, viewing information as charts or reports. You can also create charts and log files, and set warnings about system activity levels. Although Performance Monitor provides data on the current performance, it does not offer suggestions for improving performance.

You can create up to four simultaneous views, one each for charts, alerts, logs, and reports. Each of these views can be customized, and each view's settings can be saved and recalled for future sessions. Setting and working with each of the views is quite similar. You can save the performance statistics from any of the views and use the data at a later time.

To start Performance Monitor, select its icon from the Start menu's Administrative Tools folder. To exit the utility, select File, Exit.

Views There are four views in Performance Monitor.

- *Chart View* allows you to display information graphically, which helps you spot system problems immediately. A sample chart view is displayed in Figure 3.7.

- *Alert View* provides information about events that exceed user-defined limits. You can monitor more than one condition at a time. When an event occurs, Windows NT can run a program to take corrective or preventive action or alert you to the existence of the condition.

- *Log View* sends key information to a separate disk file for later analysis.

- *Report View* displays a simple report of event values you select to display.

To switch between alert, chart, log, and report view, select View, then select:

- *Alert* to move to alert view. Shortcut: press Ctrl+A.

- *Chart* to move to chart view. Shortcut: press Ctrl+C.

- *Log* to move to log view. Shortcut: press Ctrl+L.

- *Report* to move to log view. Shortcut: press Ctrl+R.

  To clear a view, select Edit, Clear Display.

Working with Performance Monitor The toolbar at the top of the Performance Monitor is shared by the four views. The buttons are all used in essentially the same way, but the information changed within each view is different. For example, to remove a element from a display, select the event being monitored, then select Edit, Delete, or click the Delete button from the toolbar.

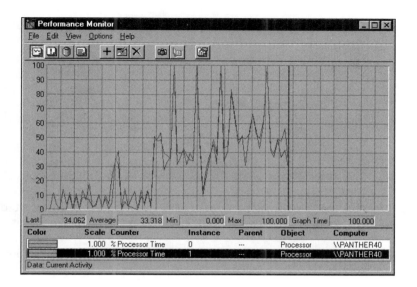

FIGURE 3.7 Performance monitor chart. The NT Performance Monitor application provides a powerful capability to monitor system operations. You can observe system performance and display it graphically, set alerts when variable limits are exceeded, and log data to a file for later analysis or historical use.

On the toolbar, the plus sign button lets you add items to be monitored (charted, logged, reported, and so on). The next button (a pencil eraser moving across a screen) lets you edit values of parameters already set. The third button (an x) is used by all views to delete an element from the monitor.

The next button on the toolbar, a camera, is used to tell Windows NT to take measurements immediately. This is the Update Now button. You can also select Options, Update Now to update the display. To change the method of updating the display, select Options, then choose either periodic or manual updating. If you select periodic updating, enter a value for the frequency for periodic updates in the Interval text box. Finally, click on OK.

The button with the open-book picture on it tells Windows NT to place a bookmark at the current measurement. The last button on the toolbar provides quick access to the monitor's options.

Specific instructions for each view are provided below.

Alert View To add items to be monitored to the alert view, switch to the alert view, then:

1. Select Edit, Add To Alert or select the Add To Alert button from the toolbar. The Add to Alert dialog box, shown in Figure 3.8, appears.

2. Select an object type from the Object pulldown list.

3. The Counter list box changes to display the elements of the selected object type that can be measured. Select one or more items from this list. (To read more about a counter, select

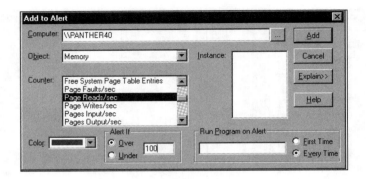

FIGURE 3.8 Performance Monitor Alert/ADD. Setting alerts on selected performance variables can give an early warning of system problems or security issues.

Explain. Performance Monitor displays a text box that provides more information about the selected counter.)

4. Select an instance if this is appropriate to the object type you have selected.

5. The Color box is automatically updated with the next available color. To change the color, choose one from the pulldown list.

6. Enter the alert condition in the Alert If box. Enter a value that sets the minimum or maximum condition that will trigger an alert.

7. Windows NT can run a program when the alert condition is detected. To trigger this, type the full path name to the program in the Run Program on Alert text box. Select First Time to run the program once, or select Every Time to run the program each time the condition is detected.

8. Select Add.

9. Repeat steps 2 through 8 until all alert conditions have been added, then click on Done.

10. To save these settings, select File, Save Alert Settings. To create a new settings file, select File, Save Alert Settings As. Enter a file name, then select OK.

To change any alert conditions:

1. Double-click the element in the legend, select Edit, Edit Alert Entry, or select the Edit Alert Entry button from the toolbar.

2. Change the desired values: color, Alert If, and/or Run Program on Alert.

3. Click on OK.

Changing Alert Notifications To change how an alert notifies you of when a condition is detected:

1. Select Options, then, Alert or select the Alert button from the toolbar.

2. Select a notification option. Windows NT can switch to the alert view when the condition is met. To set this property, select Switch to Alert View.

3. Select Send Network Message to notify you of a condition. Enter a computer name (do not include backslashes in the name) to be sent the notice in the Net Name box. Both Switch to Alert View and Send Network Message options may be selected at the same time.

4. Select the Update Time option: choose either Manual Update or Periodic Update. If you select Periodic Update, enter the time interval in the Interval text box. If you select Manual Update, select Update Now to check for alert conditions.

5. Click on OK.

Chart View To add items to a chart view, switch to this view, then:

1. Select Edit, Add To Chart or click on the Add To Chart button from the toolbar.

2. Select an object type from the Object pulldown list.

3. The Counter list box changes to display the elements of the selected object type that can be measured. Select one or more items from this list.

4. Select an instance if appropriate to the object type you have selected.

5. The Color box is automatically updated with the next available color. To override the selection, choose a color from the pulldown list. Likewise select a line scale, width, and style.

6. Select Add.

7. Repeat steps 2 through 6 until all items have been added. Select Done.

8. To save these settings, select File, Save Chart Settings. To create a new settings file, select File, Save Chart Settings As. Enter a file name, then select OK.

To change a chart's characteristics:

1. Select Options, Chart or click on the Options button from the toolbar.

2. Select the option you want to display from the Chart options dialog box.

3. Update the values desired, then click on OK.

Changing Items in a Chart To change the options of an item in the chart:

1. Select the element you want to change from the legend.

2. Double-click on the element, select Edit, Edit Chart Line, or click on the Edit Chart Line button from the toolbar.

3. Make your selection of color, scale, width, or style, then click on OK.

Log View The log file lets you record information on specific objects, then view these events later. The log file keeps an informational record and sends this information to a separate disk file for analysis by other programs. In addition, log files can be used as input to the other views, which can then display the values captured in the log file.

To select which events are recorded in a log file, switch to Log View, then:

1. Select File, Open and enter the name of the file (log setting files have the extension .PML). To create a new log file, select File, New Log Settings.

2. Select Edit, Add To Log or click on the Add To Log button from the toolbar to add items to an existing log file. The Add to Log dialog box, shown in Figure 3.9, appears.

3. Select the type of object you want to add to the log from the Objects box, then click on Add. Repeat this step until all items are added.

4. Click on Done.

To change how events are recorded in the log file:

1. Select Options, Log or click on the Options button from the toolbar.

2. Enter the name of the log file in the Log File text box.

3. Enter the new values as appropriate.

4. Click on OK to record the options but not start the logging process. Otherwise, select Start Log to begin immediate logging of the selected events.

5. To stop logging events to the log file, select Options, Log and select Stop Log.

Sub-Log Files You can create a log file that contains only *some* of the information of a full log file, thus allowing you to analyze a limited number of events using a smaller file.

To create a smaller log file, a process called relogging a log file:

1. Select Log View.

2. Select Options, Data From.

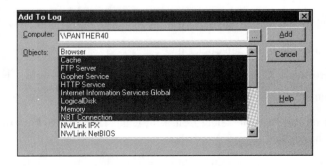

FIGURE 3.9 Performance Monitor Log/ADD. Writing data to a permanent log file allows you to analyze it off line and retain it for maintenance histories and auditing.

3. Enter the name of the full log file.

4. Select Edit, Add To Log (to select which objects should be relogged), Edit, Delete From Log (to prevent an object from being relogged), and/or Edit, Time Window (to change the starting and stopping time points of the selected activity).

5. Select Options, Log and type the name of the new log file. Select a new log interval, if desired, then select Start Logging.

Bookmarks in a Log File Bookmarks, available in all views, are probably most useful in a log file. Bookmarks allow you to find key locations within the file; bookmarks are free-form text you can place anywhere within the log. Bookmarks are useful for noting the beginning and ending points of a log file when the file is used as input to a Chart, Alert, or Report view.

To add a bookmark to a log file:

1. Select Options, Bookmark or click on the Bookmark button from the toolbar (the icon that looks like an open book).

2. Type the text of your bookmark in the Bookmark Comment text box.

3. Click on Add.

Viewing the Contents of Log Files in Other Views To use the log file as input to Alert, Chart, and Report views:

1. Switch to the view you want to use.

2. Select Options, Data From.

3. In the Data Values Displayed From box, select Log File.

4. Enter the log file name, and select OK.

Use the options within the view to limit what events are displayed. Unless otherwise specified, an Alert, Chart, or Report view will use the entire log file. To limit the analysis to specific beginning or ending points, select the view you want to use, then follow steps similar to those below, which explain how to control the values within a specified starting and stopping point.

1. Select Edit, Time Window.

2. Drag the beginning or ending point of the time-frame to a new location. As you move it, the dialog box displays the new time.

3. To use a bookmark as a starting or ending point, select the bookmark, then select Set As Start (to use the bookmark as the beginning point for analysis), or select Set As Stop (to use the bookmark as the end point).

4. Click on OK.

Use the Edit menu and other editing tools for each of the appropriate views to analyze data from the log file. The steps are identical to those used for analyzing live performance data.

Report View To add items to a report view:

1. Select Edit, Add To Report or click on the Add To Report button from the toolbar.

2. Select an object type from the Object pulldown list.

3. The Counter list box changes to display the elements of the selected object type that can be measured. Select one or more items from this list.

4. Select an instance if appropriate to the object type you have selected.

5. Select Add.

6. Repeat steps 2 through 5 until all items have been added, then click on Done.

7. To save these settings, select File, Save Report Settings. To create a new report file, select File, Save Report Settings As. Enter a file name, then select OK.

The most common change you will make to a report is to change the frequency with which it is updated. To change the frequency, select Options, Report or click on the Options button from the toolbar. Select Manual Update or Periodic Update from the Update Time section. Note that if you select Periodic Update, you *must* enter a time interval in the Interval text box. Click on OK.

Reusing Settings In each view you can save the events being monitored (and critical values, if any). These settings are created using the File, Save or File, Save As settings.

To use one of these settings for future monitoring:

1. Select the view you want to use.

2. Select File, Open.

3. Select the existing activity file. Alert files use the .PMA file extension; Chart files use .PMC; Log files use .PML; and Report files use .PMR. You can select a workspace file (.PMW) which contains settings for all four views.

4. You may change any settings at this point and use File, Save to update the settings if you wish, or use File, Save As to create another settings file.

Analyzing Performance Data To export performance data for analysis by another program, such as a spreadsheet:

1. Select the view whose data you want to export.

2. Select File, Export.

3. Select either the tab or the comma delimited format for separating data in fields in a record, according to the format your analysis tool can import.

4. Enter the full path name of the export file.

5. Click on OK.

Event Viewer

An event is any significant occurrence in the computer system or from an application that requires notification of a user, either using a pop-up alert message or by writing a message to a log file for later review by an administrator. Windows NT makes a record of these events in an event log.

There are three types of event logs:

- The *System Log* tracks events triggered by the Windows NT system components, such as when a component doesn't load during startup. Another common message in the System Log is a power fluctuation involving the Uninterruptible Power Supply (UPS). A sample system log appears in Figure 3.10.

- The *Security Log* tracks *audit* events triggered by security violations, such as illegal logons to the system or unauthorized file opens.

- The *Application Log* tracks events that are written by an application program. These vary by the application.

You specify the type of events that are logged to the Security Log by selecting the Audit option from the Policies menu in User Manager (see User Manager for details). You can control the file and directory events logged in a Windows Explorer folder by clicking the Auditing button on the Security tab of the folder's Properties menu.

The event log shows the following information:

Computer   The name of the computer on which the event occurred

Category   A classification of the event, this varies by the event source

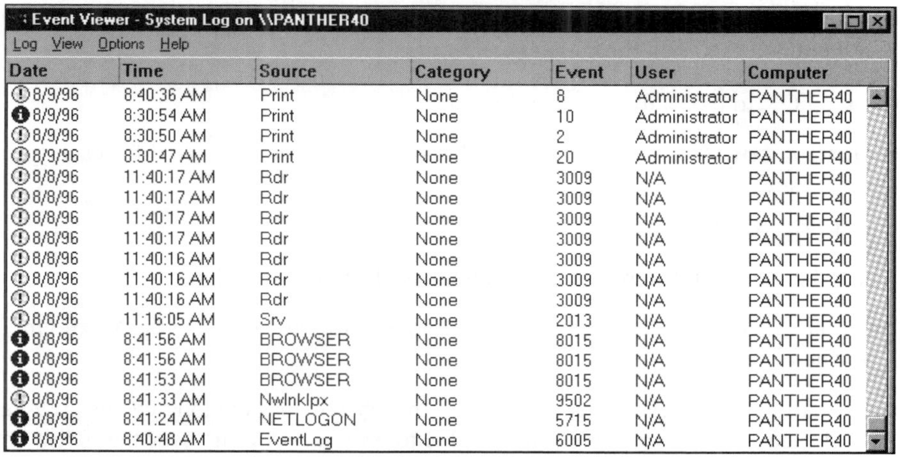

Date	Time	Source	Category	Event	User	Computer
⚠8/9/96	8:40:36 AM	Print	None	8	Administrator	PANTHER40
ⓘ8/9/96	8:30:54 AM	Print	None	10	Administrator	PANTHER40
⚠8/9/96	8:30:50 AM	Print	None	2	Administrator	PANTHER40
⚠8/9/96	8:30:47 AM	Print	None	20	Administrator	PANTHER40
⚠8/8/96	11:40:17 AM	Rdr	None	3009	N/A	PANTHER40
⚠8/8/96	11:40:17 AM	Rdr	None	3009	N/A	PANTHER40
⚠8/8/96	11:40:17 AM	Rdr	None	3009	N/A	PANTHER40
⚠8/8/96	11:40:17 AM	Rdr	None	3009	N/A	PANTHER40
⚠8/8/96	11:40:16 AM	Rdr	None	3009	N/A	PANTHER40
⚠8/8/96	11:40:16 AM	Rdr	None	3009	N/A	PANTHER40
⚠8/8/96	11:40:16 AM	Rdr	None	3009	N/A	PANTHER40
⚠8/8/96	11:16:05 AM	Srv	None	2013	N/A	PANTHER40
ⓘ8/8/96	8:41:56 AM	BROWSER	None	8015	N/A	PANTHER40
ⓘ8/8/96	8:41:56 AM	BROWSER	None	8015	N/A	PANTHER40
ⓘ8/8/96	8:41:53 AM	BROWSER	None	8015	N/A	PANTHER40
ⓘ8/8/96	8:41:33 AM	Nwlnklpx	None	9502	N/A	PANTHER40
ⓘ8/8/96	8:41:24 AM	NETLOGON	None	5715	N/A	PANTHER40
ⓘ8/8/96	8:40:48 AM	EventLog	None	6005	N/A	PANTHER40

FIGURE 3.10 System log. NT provides automatic logging of significant system events, including errors.

Date   Date of the event

Event ID   A unique number that identifies the event

Source   The application or system resource that triggered the event

Time   Time of the event

Type   Windows NT classifies the event as: error, warning, information, success audit, or failure audit

User   The username that was logged onto the computer when the event occurred. If this column contains N/A, the event triggering the log record did not capture the username (as may be the case with application programs).

To open the log file for viewing, select the Event Viewer application in the Start menu's Administrative Tools folder.

Viewing a Log File To select which log file you want to view, select Log from the main menu. Select System, Security, or Application to display the type of log file you want to view.

By default, the event log displayed when you start Event Viewer is that of your own computer. Administrators can view events for another computer. To select another computer, Select Log, Select Computer. Type the name of the computer in the Computername text box or select one from the list provided. Click on OK.

In addition to the date, time, source, type, category, event ID, user, and computername of each event, you can also view a description and the binary data logged by the event, usually created by an application.

To view detailed information about an event:

1. Double-click the event in the event list, or select the event and select View, Detail.

2. Click on Next to move to the next event in the sorted event order. Click on Previous to move to the previous event in the sorted event order.

3. Click on OK to return to the event log list.

Managing a Log File You can change the amount of space allocated for each type of log and settings for event retention. To do this:

1. Select Log, Settings.

2. Select the log file from the Change Settings for Log pulldown list.

3. Enter the maximum space (in number of kilobytes) for the log file in the Maximum log size box. The default is 512K.

4. Select an Event Retention Period option to specify how or how long events are retained in the log. Select Overwrite Events as Needed to write new events over the oldest entries in the log (Generally this option should be used for all logs to prevent lost recent events at the expense of uninteresting older events). If you select Keep Events, you must select the number of days to retain events in the log. If you select Never Overwrite Events (preferable for secure servers, especially for the security log, where evidence of hacking will be most

likely to appear), you must clear the log manually. An option also exists to force a system halt when the security log is full, which may be of interest to users in secure environments.

5. As an alternative to steps 3 and 4, select Default and all settings will be restored to the system-defined default.

6. Click on OK.

To erase the log file and begin with a new, empty file, select the type of log file you want to clear. Select Log, Clear All Events. You are asked if you want to save the current log file. Select Yes and you will see the Save As dialog box. Enter the file name and click on OK.

Managing Events You can display only a desired type of event (called filtering), search for a specific event, or sort the list of events.

Filtering Events The log file records all events according to other settings in the Windows NT system, but you can view only the desired events by setting a filter.

To view a subset of the events in the event log:

1. Select View, Filter Events. The Filter dialog box is shown in Figure 3.11.

2. In the Filter dialog box enter the options you want. Events that meet these specifications will be displayed. A complete description of events can be found in the Event Viewer chapter of the Windows NT System Guide.

3. Click on OK.

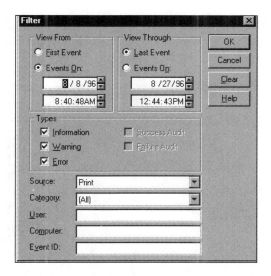

FIGURE 3.11 Filter dialog. Inspection of a complex log file can be greatly simplified by filtering, selecting only the events you're immediately interested in.

To remove the filters, select View, All Events.

Searching for Events To locate specific events, use the Find feature of Event Log. To search for a specific event or range of events:

1. Select View, Find. The Find dialog box shown in Figure 3.12 appears.

2. Select the options you want to use in the search in the Find dialog box. Select the direction (Up or Down) to search from the current event forward (Down) or backward to the beginning of the log (Up). Other options are detailed in the Event Viewer chapter of the *Windows NT System Guide*. (Most are self-explanatory.) If multiple Types are selected, the search will look for any event that meets any of the criteria.

3. Select Find Next to find the event that meets your criteria.

4. Press F3 to find the next event using the same criteria.

Sorting Events To sort the order of events in the log file, select View, Newest First to see the most recent events at the top of the list, or select View, Oldest First to see the oldest events at the top of the list.

Archiving a Log File As log files grow, you may wish to save the event log to another file. You may also wish to perform this function as part of regular maintenance, such as every week or once each month. Archiving a log file is also useful if you want to export the data to another application, such as a database or spreadsheet, for further analysis.

When you archive a log file, the complete contents are archived, and the filter options are ignored. The archived file does retain the sort order based on the selected export-file format.

You can archive a log file in one of three file formats:

• The standard log file format allows you to use the Event Viewer to view the contents of the archived file. The events' sort order is ignored.

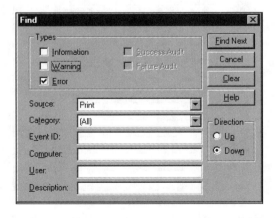

FIGURE 3.12 Find dialog. Beyond filtering, a straight search capability is provided—giving you the tools to get the information you need from the log quickly.

- In an ASCII text file format, the sorted order of the events is used. The binary data associated with an event is not included in the new file.

- A comma-delimited format may also be selected. Comma-delimited format is used most often when you are exporting the data to a database or spreadsheet. As with ASCII text files, the sorted order of the events is used, but binary data associated with an event is not included in the new file.

To archive a log file:

1. Select Log, Save As.

2. Select the file format you want from the Save File As Type list.

3. Enter the file name in the File Name text box. If you select the standard log file format, the file extension assigned is .EVT. The file extension .TXT is used for text and comma-delimited files.

4. Click on OK.

To view an archived log file (for log files using the standard log file format) with the Event Viewer:

1. Select Log, Open.

2. Enter the log file name in the File Name box or select it from the list of existing files.

3. Click on OK.

4. Select the type of log file you want (Application, Security, or System) in the Open File Type box, then click on OK.

Managing Disks

Disk Administrator

Windows NT's Disk Administrator program provides tools for managing disks, allowing you to create partitions on hard disks, create volumes and stripe sets, read status information (such as partition size), and assign partitions to drive letters.

To start Disk Administrator, select the Disk Administrator icon from the Administrative Tools folder in the Start menu, or select Start, Run, and enter WINDISK on the Command line. The main Disk Administrator dialog box is shown in Figure 3.13.

Once you have requested changes to your disk partitions, then quit Disk Administrator normally, Disk Administrator will remind you of your request and note which changes cannot be reversed. At this point, you can change your mind and cancel the changes. In many cases, you may also want to notify all users of your changes, because some modifications, such as deleting partitions, may directly impact system users.

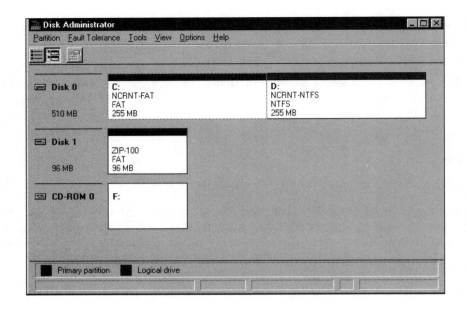

FIGURE 3.13 Disk Administrator. The NT Disk Administrator program provides a graphical view of disk partitions, along with central location of all disk management/maintenance functions.

Assigning Drive Letters In many computer systems, adding a new hard drive disrupts the order of existing drive letter assignments. In Windows NT, Disk Administrator allows you to statically assign drive letters so that this disruption does not happen. Once assigned, drive letters are maintained when another drive is added to the system.

To assign a drive letter:

1. Select the partition or logical drive you want to assign to a letter.

2. Select Tools, Drive Letter.

3. The Assign Drive Letter dialog box appears. Select the assignment option you want.

4. Click on OK.

Drive letters for CD-ROM drives may be set with the Tools, CD-ROM Drive Letters... command.

Primary and Extended Partitions A primary partition is a subdivision of a physical disk; up to four primary partitions can be created per disk. A primary partition cannot be subdivided. In x86 systems, the primary partition of your C: drive is the partition from which you boot the system. Only one of the four primary partitions can be designated an extended partition (as explained below).

In contrast, an extended partition is created from free space on your hard disk and can be subpartitioned into logical drives.

To create a primary partition on a hard disk:

1. Select the free space area on a disk.

2. Select Partition, Create.

3. The Create Primary Partition dialog box displays the minimum and maximum size for the partition. It also displays a text box labeled Create partition of size, in which you should enter the new partition size.

4. Click on OK.

On Intel x86-based computers, the system partition that contains the hardware-specific files needed for booting must be marked as active. In contrast, RISC-based computers do not use such markings but are controlled by a configuration program supplied by the computer manufacturer.

To mark a partition as active for x86-based computers, select the partition that contains the necessary startup files. Select Partition, Mark Active, then click on OK.

An *extended partition* can be set up and used to create multiple logical drives, or as part of a volume set.

To create an extended partition:

1. Select the free space area on a disk.

2. Select Partition, Create Extended.

3. The Create Extended Partition dialog box displays the minimum and maximum size for the partition, and displays a text box named Create partition of size. Enter the appropriate size, then click on OK.

To create logical drives within an extended partition, select the space in the extended partition, select Partition, Create, enter the size of the logical drive in the Create Logical Drive dialog box, and click on OK.

To delete a partition, volume, or logical drive:

1. Select the partition, volume, or logical drive you want to remove.

2. Select Partition, Delete.

3. Select Yes to confirm your delete request.

Formatting Partitions Once a partition has been created, it must be formatted for use. This process may be done using the format command-line function, or using the Tools, Format.... command. Note that beginning with NT 3.51, no support is provided for formatting partitions with OS/2-compatible HPFS format, though NT continues to recognize such partitions (they must be formatted from OS/2). OS/2 subsystem users may want to investigate NTFS, which appears to be HPFS so far as OS/2 applications running on NT are concerned.

Volume Sets A volume set is a method for allocating free space on several partitions as though the resulting set was a single partition itself. All space in the first area of a volume set is filled before space in the second area is filled; all space in the second area is used before space is used from the third area, and so on, until all areas (up to a maximum of 32) are used.

Free space from partitions can be of unequal size, and several areas can be on the same drive, in contrast to a stripe set, in which all areas must be on different drives. Volume sets also help you allocate the I/O across drives in an effort to improve overall system performance.

To create a volume set:

1. Select two or more areas of free space (up to 32 areas can be selected). Select the first area, then press and hold the Ctrl key as you select the remaining area(s).

2. Select Partition, Create Volume Set.

3. Enter the size of the volume you want to create. If the size you enter is less than the total space of the selected free space, Disk Administrator attempts to divide the total space by the number of areas and allocate the same amount of space from all areas to the volume set.

4. Click on OK.

To delete a volume set, select the volume set. Select Partition, Delete. Click on Yes to confirm your delete request. All data is deleted from the selected areas.

Extending Volumes and Volume Sets If you are using NTFS volumes or volume sets, you can expand their size by using current free space. Doing so automatically logs you off the system and then formats the new area, a process that does not affect your existing data. Note that you cannot extend a volume if it is part of a stripe or mirror set.

To extend a volume or a volume set:

1. Select the existing volume or volume set.

2. Select one or more free space areas.

3. Select Partition, Extend Volume Set.

4. Enter the size of the new volume set that will be the result of combining the existing and new space.

5. Click on OK.

Stripe Sets A stripe set is similar to a volume set. A key difference is that Windows NT fills one stripe of the first area, then one stripe of the second area, and so on, until one stripe from each area is filled. Windows NT then proceeds to fill the second stripe on the first area, the second stripe on the second area, and so on.

Each area of a stripe set must be on a different disk. Furthermore, Disk Administrator creates stripe sets with areas of uniform size.

To create a stripe set:

1. Select two or more areas of free space (up to 32 areas can be selected). Select the first area, then press and hold the Ctrl key as you select the remaining area(s).

2. Select Partition, Create Stripe Set.

3. Enter the size of the stripe set you want to create. Disk Administrator divides this number by the total number of areas and allocates this uniform space from each selected area.

4. Click on OK.

To delete a stripe set:

1. Select the stripe set.

2. Select Partition, Delete.

3. Select Yes to confirm your delete request. All data is deleted from the selected areas.

Disk Configuration Information You can save, restore, and search for information such as the assigned drive letters, stripe sets, and so on, using the Disk Administrator's configuration settings. This function is particularly useful when installing a new copy of NT on a previously configured machine. This information is also stored on the Windows NT *emergency repair disk* (although, if you only create the emergency disk during system setup, and never update it, the information on the disk may be out of date; see the *Making and Updating Boot and Emergency Repair Diskettes* section of Chapter 5).

To save the current configuration settings, select Partition, Configuration. Note that changes to the configuration made during the current session are not saved. To save the changes, you must log off and log back in to the system.

To save the settings, select Configuration, Save, and place a floppy disk into the A: or B: drive. Click OK, and Disk Administrator will write the information to the diskette.

To restore the disk configuration information, select Partition, Configuration. Select Configuration, Restore, then insert the floppy containing the configuration information into the A: or B: drive, and click on OK.

To search disk configuration information:

1. Select Partition, Configuration.

2. Select Configuration, Search.

3. Click OK to acknowledge the warning message.

   Warning: The search procedure erases your current disk configuration information, as well as any changes made during the session.

4. Windows NT searches for other installations. When it finds one or more, it displays them in a list. Select the installation you want, then select OK.

Backup

The Windows NT Backup program lets you copy data from your hard disk (or across the network, provided a local disk letter has been assigned) to a tape cassette, protecting you from loss from accidental erasure, hardware failure, or damage resulting from power interruptions. Backup uses a graphical environment that is similar to the Windows Explorer; you can select which files are backed up or restored by clicking on files, directories, and/or drive letters.

Backup can work with FAT, HPFS, and NTFS file systems. You can backup files from different drives and select from several of backup techniques. For example you can back up only those files that have changed since the previous backup.

To start Backup, double-click on the Backup icon in the Administrative Tools folder, or select Start, Run and type NTBACKUP in the Command Line text box.

Selecting Files to Back Up

You can select all files on a drive, all files in a directory, or individual files. The technique is similar to the method used for selecting files in Windows Explorer. The major difference is that in Windows Explorer you select files by highlighting them. In Backup a check box is used for selecting files.

To select files to back up:

1. Select the Drives window and double-click on the disk drive icon or letter of the drive that contains the files you want to back up. The Backup program opens a window for the selected drive, as illustrated in Figure 3.14.

2. To select all files, choose Select, Check. You can also select all files by clicking on the Check button on the toolbar, or check the box for the drive from the Drives window.

3. To select a single file, select the box positioned before the file you want to select.

FIGURE 3.14 Backup program. NT includes built-in support for tape backup, a necessity for servers and highly desirable on high-performance workstations.

4. To select multiple files, press *and hold* the Ctrl key, then select each file. When all files are selected, release the Ctrl key.

5. To select a range of files that are listed contiguously, select the first file, then press *and hold* the Shift key and select the last file in the range. Choose Select, Check to select each file's check box. Alternatively, select the Check button on the toolbar.

Backing Up Files to Tape The backup process uses three pieces of information: the files you want to back up; the type of backup you want (full, only changed files, etc.); and optionally a description of the backup, which is useful for identifying the right backup when files must be restored.

Backup graphically shows its progress and prompts you when it is time to insert tape cartridges.

To back up files:

1. Select the files (see above), then click on Backup. The Backup Information dialog box appears.

2. Enter a description of the tape in the Tape Name text box, to a maximum of 31 characters.

3. Select Append to add the backup to the end of an existing tape set, or select Replace to erase the information already on the tape and replace it with the current backup. If you select Replace, Backup asks you to confirm your request.

4. To protect the tape contents from unauthorized use, check the Restrict Access To Owner Or Administrator box. Only the tape's owner or administrator with Backup rights can read, write, or erase the tape. If you restrict access, the file will have to be restored using the same user account that created the tape originally.

5. To add a verification step to the backup (to compare the original with the copy on tape), check the Verify After Backup box.

6. To add the Registry files to the tape backup, select the Backup Registry check box.

7. Select the type of backup you want (see Table 3.1).

8. Select an option that describes how you want to log the backup session. Choose Summary Only to log the major events (loading a tape, for example). Choose Full Detail to list all operational details, including the full path name of the files backed up. Select Don't Log if you don't want information added to a log file.

9. Click on OK. The Backup Status dialog box appears and shows the activities as they occur. The dialog box also displays the number of directories, files, bytes being backed up, the elapsed time, and the number of files it could not back up because of security considerations.

10. If the backup requires more than one tape, you will be prompted to insert a new tape when appropriate.

11. To stop a backup operation at any time, click on Abort.

Table 3.1 Types of Backup

Backup Type	What Backup Will Do
Normal	Back up selected files; files are marked as backed up (the archive bit is turned off)
Copy	Back up selected files, but files will not be marked as backed up (the archive bit is unchanged)
Incremental	Back up selected files modified since the last backup (the archive bit is on); files are marked as backed up (the archive bit is turned off)
Differential	Identical to incremental, but files are not marked as backed up (the archive bit is unchanged)
Daily Copy	Back up files that have been modified on the current date; files are not marked as backed up (the archive bit is unchanged)

Restoring Files from Tape The restore operation is the converse of the backup operation. You can restore all files on a tape or just selected files.

To restore files:

1. Insert the tape into the tape drive unit and click on the Tapes icon.

2. Backup displays the tape information on the left side of the Tapes window. It shows the drive backed up, the backup type, and the date and time of the backup. Select the tape containing the file(s) you want to restore: Double-click the tape's icon, select Operations, Catalog, or click on the Catalog button in the toolbar.

3. Backup displays a list of the backup sets in the Tapes window. A question mark is displayed with each icon, meaning the catalog (list of files) has not yet been read from the tape's directory. Select the backup set you want: Double-click on the backup set's icon, select Operations, Catalog, or click on the Catalog button in the toolbar.

4. The program displays the list of directories and files in a hierarchy in the Tape File Selection window. To restore all files, select the check box for the tape and select Select, Check or click on the Check button in the toolbar.

5. To restore an individual file, select the file's check box.

6. To restore multiple files that are not listed contiguously, press and hold the Ctrl key while you select each file.

7. To restore multiple files listed contiguously, press and hold the Shift key and select the first and last files. Choose Select, Check or click on the Check button in the toolbar.

8. Click on Restore. Restore may ask you to enter the drive to which you want to restore the file(s).

9. To force Restore to compare the data on the tape with the data restored to the hard drive, check the Verify After Restore box.

10. Select the log option you want. Choose Summary Only to log the major events (such as loading a tape or completing a backup). Choose Full Detail to list all operations and the fully qualified (path and filename) of all restored files. Choose Don't Log to bypass writing information to a log file.

11. To restore the Registry files, select the Restore Local Registry check box.

12. Click on OK to start the restoration. If the program needs additional tapes, you will be asked to insert a tape when necessary.

13. You may be asked to confirm replacing an existing file that has been modified since the backup with a file on the backup tape. Answer Yes to replace the file and No to restore the next selected file.

14. To stop the restore operation at any time, select Abort.

Tape Maintenance

Erasing a Tape There are two types of tape erasure. The Quick Erase method erases only the tape header, which contains information about the name of the tape, and the Backup process considers the tape empty and rewrites over all of it. The process is usually very short (typically under one minute). However, the files backed up to the tape remain on the tape. A Secure Erase overwrites the entire tape, and hence may be a very long process.

To erase a tape, insert the tape into the tape drive unit, then select Operations, Erase Tape or click on the Erase Tape button in the toolbar. Select Quick Erase or Secure Erase, and click on Continue to begin the tape erasure.

Retensioning Tapes Older backup devices used tapes that required periodic retensioning to reduce slippage and improve reliability. The retensioning process fast forwards the tape to the end of the reel, then rewinds it.

To retension a tape, insert the tape in the tape drive unit and select Operations, Retension Tape, or click on the Retension Tape button in the toolbar.

Newer tape devices don't require retensioning, in which case the Retension Tape item will be disabled.

Backup Alternatives Microsoft is to be commended for including Backup with all NT systems, but in all honesty NT backup has some fairly severe limitations, the worst of which (in our opinion) include: (1) no support for backup from one server's hard disk to another, (2) no support for dynamically connecting and disconnecting network drives during a backup operation, and (3) a very limited selection of supported backup devices.[6] It also limits you to backing up devices that

---

6   In the process of updating this chapter for the third edition, we were delighted to discover that the range of devices has been extended to include the more modern QIC-3010 type along with the older QIC-40/80 devices.

have been assigned drive letters (it has no support for NT-standard UNC names), is not multi-threaded, and does not support compression. In effect, NT Backup is good only for backing up the local machine to tape, (you can get around this by writing your own backup script—see the section on Scripts at the end of this chapter for details). Quite simply, the built-in backup is inadequate for serious network-wide use. Fortunately, alternatives are now available (see Table 3.2).

Most of these solutions use NT's standard tape API and drivers, so check the NT hardware compatibility list before buying tape-backup hardware (you may also need to check with the backup software vendors—in particular, Cheyanne's ARCserver uses nonstandard drivers). In general, you should buy a tape device with a capacity equal to (or for growth, greater than) the total hard disk capacity of your system. Some of the third-party batch languages covered later in this chapter offer UNIX-style *tar* and *cpio* backup as well, which may be useful for those running NT in a mixed environment with UNIX systems.

Uninterruptible Power Supply (UPS)

An uninterruptible power supply (UPS) is a battery-powered power supply that maintains power to a computer when the main power source is interrupted, such as during power failures. The UPS allows for the safe shutdown of the system until the main power source is restored (rationale for using UPS and factors for selecting an appropriate one are covered in Chapter 2).

Windows NT allows you to configure the UPS and manage how it works with the operating system.

The main UPS window is shown in Figure 3.15.

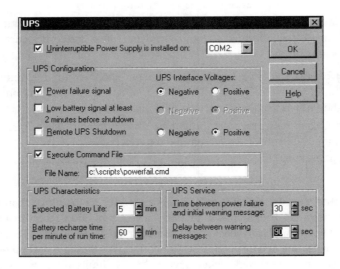

FIGURE 3.15 Main UPS window. Built-in support for Uninterruptable Power Supply (UPS) assures that NT systems need never experience a total power failure without the opportunity to execute a controlled system shut-down procedure.

Table 3.2 Third-party Backup Applications for NT

Product	Company	Address	Telephone	Notes
ARCserve for Windows NT **http://www.cheyenne.com**	Cheyanne Software	3 Expressway Plaza, Roslyn Hts., NY 11577	(800) 243-9462 (516) 484-5110	NT version of popular cross-platform backup. Tape format is identical across platforms.
Backup Exec **http://www .smg.seagatesoftware.com**	Seagate Software	37 Skyline Dr. Lake Mary, FL 32746	(800) 327-2232 (407) 262-8000	Enhanced backup from the maker of NT's built-in backup. Tapes are format-compatible with built-in NT backup. Storage Director Visual Storage Manager
Octopus **http://www.wunbelt.co.uk**	Sunbelt Software Distribution Inc.	Suite 415, Bay Drive, Largo FL 34640	(800) 636-6787 (813) 586-6363	Server-resilient client-server backup and storage management
SM-arch **http://www.moguls.com**	Software Moguls	12301 White Water Suite 160 Minnetonka, MN 55343	(612) 932-6738	Enterprise Backup, utilizing single-point catalog. Ported from UNIX.

Setting Up a UPS

To establish the software connection between a UPS and Windows NT, select the Control Panel icon from Start, Settings. Click on the UPS icon, then check the Uninterruptible Power Supply installed on box. Choose the port from the pulldown list box, then click on OK.

After set up, you need to specify how the UPS will interact with Windows NT once it is triggered. Select the UPS icon from the control panel. Then:

1. Check the Power failure signal box if the UPS is capable of sending a message to Windows NT when it detects a problem. Select the Negative or Positive interface voltage value according to your UPS hardware instructions (this varies by make and model).

2. If you checked the Power failure signal box in step 1, enter the value in the UPS Characteristics box. The Expected Battery Life values can range from 2 to 720 (2 is the default). The setting is used in messages to notify you of the time remaining. The Battery recharge time per minute of run time values range from 1 to 250 minutes (100 is the default).

3. Check the Low battery signal at least 2 minutes before shutdown box if your UPS can send a message when it detects a low battery. Select the Negative or Positive interface voltage value according to your UPS hardware instructions.

4. Check the Remote UPS Shutdown box if your UPS can respond to a signal to shut itself off. Select the Negative or Positive interface voltage value according to your UPS hardware instructions.

5. Enter the number of seconds between the moment a power failure is recognized and the display of a warning message. Enter the value in the UPS Service area in the text box labeled Time between power failure and initial warning message. Valid values are between 0 and 120 seconds; the default is 5 seconds.

6. Enter the number of seconds between warning messages in the Delay between warning messages box. Valid values are between 5 and 300 seconds; the default value is 120 seconds (2 minutes).

7. Click on OK.

Once the settings have been established, you can test your UPS's ability to recover your system. To test the system, disconnect the power from the UPS to simulate a failure. Windows NT displays a warning or alert message, and the battery will begin to run down (you may want to allow this to continue the first time, so that you can get a feel for exactly how long the system can stay up.) When the UPS battery reaches its low level, the system will begin its shutdown. At this point, reconnect power to the UPS. Use the Event Viewer to see that all actions were properly recorded and that none caused an error.

Services

Many server-side programs act as service routines, running in the background and providing support for other applications. On Windows NT such applications are called *services*, and they are handled differently from other applications. An NT service typically has no user interface of its own. Instead, it is controlled through NT's Service Control Manager, which is exposed through the Services applet in the NT Control Panel (see Figure 3.16).

This interface allows services to be started and stopped, allows their startup mode to be configured (whether they're started automatically on system boot, or manually), and to be started using a different account than the one currently logged in. In general, services are installed and preconfigured by Windows NT setup (or the installation routine used to install the service). From time to time, however, administrative intervention may be required (for example, it may be necessary to stop NT's RAS if you need to use a RAS-configured device for other purposes).

Starting and Stopping Services

To start or stop a Windows NT Service, select the Control Panel icon from Start, Settings. Click on the Services icon, and choose the service you want to stop or start from the list. You can then click the Start or Stop button, as required (note that in general, any user may start a service, but administrative privilege is required to stop a service).

Pausing and Continuing Services Many services offer the additional option of being paused and continued. This option offers an advantage: the service remains in memory and can continue without having to be reloaded. On the other hand, depending on how the service is set up, any service-controlled resources may not be released when the service is paused. Click on the Services icon, and choose the service you want to stop or start from the list. You can then click the Pause or Continue button, as required (note that in general, any user may start a service, but administrative privilege is required to stop a service).

If you're logged in on an account with administrative permissions, you can control a services startup parameters, in particular, the user account the service initially logs in under. That can be important for certain services, such as Microsoft's SMS, which require a special user account.

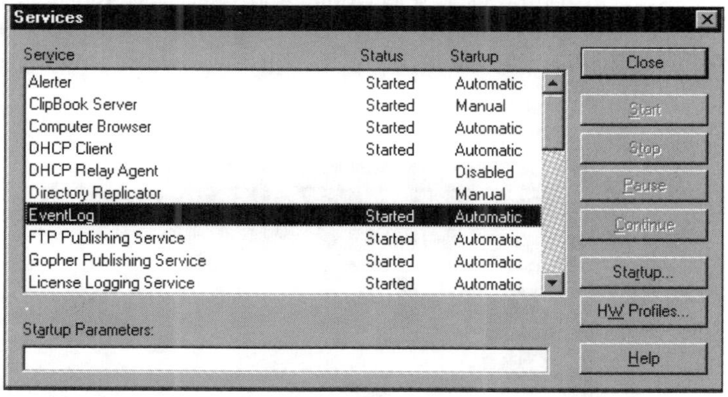

Service	Status	Startup	
Alerter	Started	Automatic	
ClipBook Server	Started	Manual	
Computer Browser	Started	Automatic	
DHCP Client	Started	Automatic	
DHCP Relay Agent		Disabled	
Directory Replicator		Manual	
EventLog	Started	Automatic	
FTP Publishing Service	Started	Automatic	
Gopher Publishing Service	Started	Automatic	
License Logging Service	Started	Automatic	

Buttons: Close, Start, Stop, Pause, Continue, Startup..., HW Profiles..., Help

Startup Parameters:

FIGURE 3.16 Services. NT provides a class of applications called *services* that run as background processes. They are controlled through the Services icon in the NT Control Panel.

> *Note:* *If you change the password on such an account, you may have to reinstall the associated service! At a minimum, you will need to bring up the service's startup dialog box in the Services applet and type in the new password.*

You can also configure a service to permit desktop interaction, which can be useful for debugging services, and it may be necessary for certain services. (Internally, services are basically old-fashioned command-line programs with a thin layer of additional code that interacts with NT's Service Control Manager; see Appendix 1 for details.) NT's scheduler service, for example, *must* have permission to interact with the desktop if it is to be used with Windows (16- or 32-bit) software such as NT Backup, because the Win32 and Win16 subsystems interact with the desktop by definition.

System Policy Editor

Beginning with NT 4.0, a Windows 95-compatible System Policy Editor is added to the NT Server administrative tools. This tool, illustrated in Figure 3.17, allows an administrator to specify which computers a particular user is authorized to use, which programs the user can run, and whether the user is permitted to make configuration changes, among other things.

System Policies are stored in policy files, which carry a .POL extension. The .POL file contains entries that are automatically added to the system Registry whenever a user logs on. Policy files contains separate entries for each authorized user and one set of common entries for all guests.

> *Note:* *The policy file format used by Windows 95 differs from that used by Windows NT. While the NT Policy Editor can deal with both, attempting to use a Windows 95 .POL file on an NT system—or vice versa—will fail.*

To use the Policy Editor, select Start, Menu, Programs, Accessories, System Tools, System Policy Editor. Once the editor starts, select FILE, NEW. By default, you will see two icons in the program's main window: Default User and Default Computer.

To add policies for a specific user, select Edit, Add User. The Add User dialog appears (Figure 3.18). You can type in the name directly, or press the Browse button and pick an existing user from the resulting list. Each user you select will now have an icon in the editor, representing the policy for that user.

FIGURE 3.17 System policy editor.

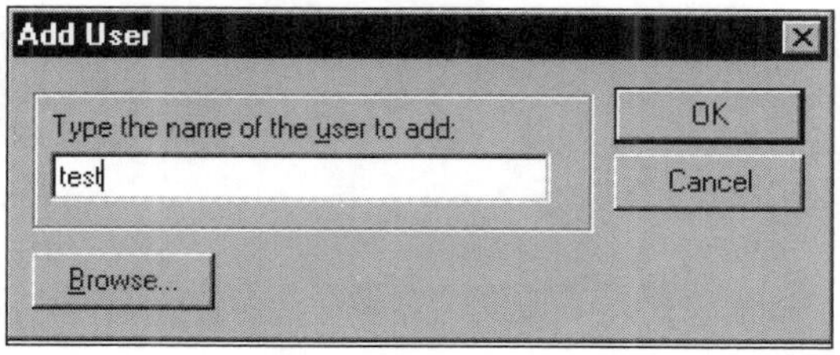

FIGURE 3.18 Add user. Users are added to the Policy Editor with this dialog.

The policy created for new users, by default, permits a user to perform all tasks and actions, so edit the policy thus created. To do so, double-click on the user's icon. You will see a Properties dialog (Figure 3.19) containing a list of available policy categories. Clicking on any category will expand it to list subcategories (if any) and settings available to restrict the user. For example, clicking the Control Panel category yields a Display sub-category, and below that a Restrict Display setting.

By default, the Restrict Display setting is gray (restrictions not set). Click it once to check it, and a list of Settings appears (see Figure 3.20). You can check boxes to Deny access to the

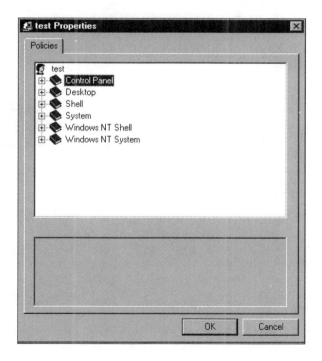

FIGURE 3.19 User policies. Policies for a particular user are set using this dialog.

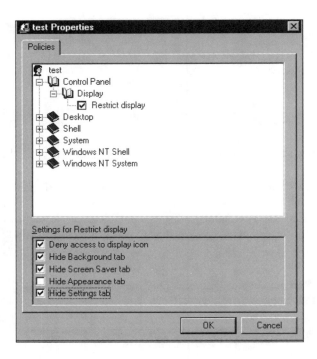

FIGURE 3.20 Settings. Settings for a particular policy are controlled with this dialog.

Display icon in Control Panel, and to Hide the Background, Screen Saver, Appearance; and Settings tabs. You can clear all such settings by un-checking the Restrict Display setting. The same approach can be used to modify all other restrictions available through the Policy Editor—including those on particular computers or administrative user groups, rather than just single users.

When you've set all the restrictions you wish for a user, computer, or group, click the OK button to close the *Properties* dialog. The restrictions you've set will come into effect the next time the user logs in.

Once you've created all the policies you need, save the policy file with Select File, Save As. A file selector window will appear, into which you can type the name of your policy file (normally, a .POL extension is used). To enforce the resulting policy on all computers in a domain, name it NTconfig..POL, and save it in the *netlogon* directory of the primary domain controller (ie: \\pdc\netlogon).

You can also edit the Default Computer and Default User icons themselves. If you do so, any restrictions you set will apply to all users and computers in the domain (provided replication is properly set up; see Chapter 7 for details).

For more information on the System Policy Editor, see Chapter 3 of the *Windows NT Server 4.0 Concepts and Planning Guide*.

Administrative Wizards

NT 4.0 Server also adds a new set of Administrative Wizards, illustrated in Figure 3.21, that provide semiautomatic step-by-step assistance in performing common administrative tasks:

- adding user accounts

- managing administrative groups

- controlling file/folder access

- adding print drivers

- adding and removing programs

- installing modems

- creating network client installation disk sets

- managing license compliance

The basic idea is sound, but in our opinion the Wizards don't go nearly far enough to be of much use to any but a complete novice. No wizard is provided, for example, to change a user's

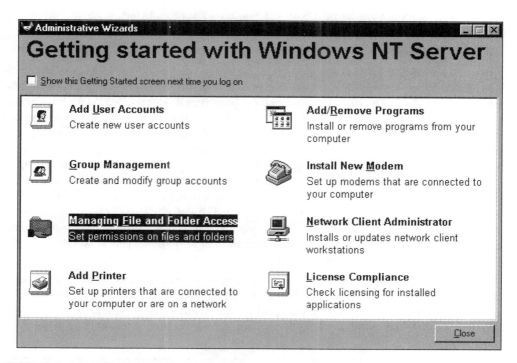

FIGURE 3.21 Administrative Wizards. NT Server 4.0 offers a simplified Wizards interface for the most common administrative tasks.

account name or to move a user account from one domain to another, two apparently simple procedures that drive NT administrators to distraction (each requires deleting an existing account and creating a new one). Let's hope that this situation will improve in future releases.

Distributed Common Object Model Configuration

One of NT 4.0's most interesting new features is the Distributed Common Object Model (DCOM), an extension of Microsoft's Object Linking and Embedding (OLE) to allow transparent operation across the LAN (this function differs from Remote Procedure Calls (RPCs), which require applications to be written specially for network-wide operation). Applications written to the COM/OLE interface can operate transparently across anything from the local network to the Internet—in theory.

In practice, DCOM is currently quite limited in scope (so limited that we've been unable to devise a working example for illustrative purposes).[7] Still, administrators should be aware of DCOM, as it is the centerpiece for Microsoft's eventual plans to make NT itself both object-oriented and Internet-friendly (see Chapter 12).

In NT 4.0, all DCOM administration is handled through the DCOM Configuration utility (DCOMCNFG.EXE), shown in Figure 3.22.

This utility does not appear on any of the Windows Explorer menus, even the administration menus. The DCOM Configuration utility must be launched from the command line.

DCOM Configuration has the following tabs:

Default Properties: This tab sets properties that will be used by default for all DCOM applications (though the properties in question may be overridden by setting properties for a specific application; see below). The most important of these properties is whether DCOM itself is enabled on the computer (it is by default), and if it is, the level of authentication and impersonation to be used. These are important from a security perspective; the default level of authentication, *connect*, employs a secure challenge/response only when establishing the initial connection between client and server. Other authentication options range from *none*, which seems self-explanatory, up to *packet privacy*, which encrypts all data being transferred between the client and server. The *impersonation* settings control whether and how the server impersonates the client user's identity (see Chapter 1 for a general discussion of impersonation). The default setting, *Identity*, permits the server to validate the client user's identity but does not require that the server fully impersonate the client user. A check box on the Default Properties tab also allows you to specify reference tracking for additional security, causing the DCOM server to track each application separately.

Default Security: This tab provides a series of *Permissions* buttons that may be used to control who can or cannot access, launch, or configure DCOM applications that do not provide their own security settings. The default settings generally allow Administrators, the System, and interactively logged-in users to launch applications. Only administrators are permitted to configure them.

---

7   See Appendix 1 for an explanation of COM and DCOM from the programmer's point of view.

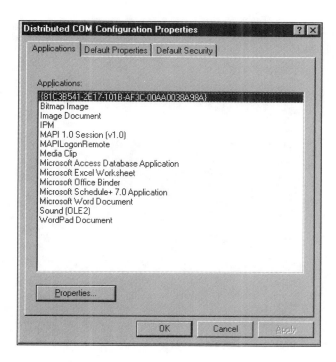

FIGURE 3.22 DCOM configuration. Settings for Distributed Common Object Model (DCOM)-enabled applications are controlled using this dialog.

Applications: This tab shows a list of the applications that are registered with DCOM. Clicking on an application from the list selects it; making it possible to manipulate the application's properties, by clicking on the Properties button, which in turn brings up a Document Properties dialog (see Figure 3.23) for the application you selected. The Document Properties dialog has four tabs: General, Location, Security, and Identity.

The *General* tab identifies the Application's name, type, and the tab gives a local path name to the associated .EXE file. The path is not editable (there is nothing to set) and really serves only as an information source to the administrator.

The *Location* tab specifies where the application is to execute. Options include running the application wherever the data is being loaded from (useful if a large file must be loaded), running the application locally (the default setting), or running the application on a specific, DCOM-equipped computer. A *browse* button allows locating an appropriate Domain/Computer combination for the latter option. Unlike other option check-boxes in DCOMCNFG, these are cumulative: you may check them all, in which case DCOM will first attempt to run the app where the data is located, then try to run it locally, and finally launch from the specified server if all else fails.

The *Security* tab provides exactly the same settings as the top-level Default Security tab, but with the addition of Use Default or Use Custom radio buttons on each setting. This function

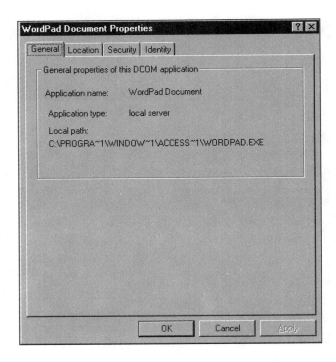

FIGURE 3.23 Document properties. Settings for the DCOM-aware application associated with a particular document type are controlled using this dialog.

allows you to standardize security settings for most applications and make special settings for special cases. By default, most applications are set to use Default Access and Launch permissions, but have custom Configuration settings.

The *Identity* tab controls which user DCOM impersonates when launching and interacting with the application. Choices include the Interactive user (whoever is logged in on the local console; if nobody is logged in locally, this call will fail), Launching user (whoever started the app that made the DCOM request), or a specific user whose name and password have been typed in. The last option can be used to create a special user account for specific processes, with the properties for that account tuned to the needs of the application in question. Finally, if the application in question is installed as a system service, the System account can be specified, with the same limitations as when it is used for the service (mainly, no access to network resources).

Batch Files and Logon Scripts

Microsoft's documentation is strikingly silent on the topic of logon scripts; indeed, at one point in the original NT 3.1 documents, there was a statement to the effect that scripts are obsolete, replaced by User Profiles.

Hogwash!

Logon scripts are as valuable—and necessary—on NT as they are on any other network operating system. Although NT *reduces* the need for logon scripts by maintaining a list of permanent network connections (designated as such in the Windows Explorer, see Chapter 4) and automatically reinstating them, scripts are nonetheless necessary to assign a home directory, carry out tasks automatically on log-in, or to reinstate network connections when multiple user names and passwords are employed.

Scripts are fundamental tools in any client/server networking environment. They are what an administrator uses to ensure that users will see a particular configuration when they log in. They're also the key to fully exploiting some of NT's features, especially if you run an NT server unattended. You can set a log-in script to be executed automatically when a user logs in to a Windows NT server (using NT's User Manager, select the account you want to set a script for, then select Properties, click the Profile button, and you can type in a script file name).

NT Scripts: Basic Syntax

To begin with, NT gives you pretty much all the command-line capabilities available in either DOS or OS/2 1.x (it lacks the OS/2 2.x built-in REXX command language). Typical command-line functions like *copy* and *move* are supported, as is the use of command-line parameters. For instance, to implement the unix *mv* and *cp* command syntax[8] instead of NT's DOS-style *copy* and *move*, the following scripts would work. For cp.bat:[9]

```
copy %1 %2
```

As in DOS, the %1 and %2 will be replaced by the first and second arguments that you type on the command line. When the user types "cp test1.txt test2.txt," test1.txt replaces %1 and test2.txt replaces %2, so the following executes: copy test1.txt test2.txt. Similarly, we can create an mv.bat file:

```
move %1 %2
```

That command works the same way. As in DOS or OS/2, NT provides conditional statements. The *if* statement determines if an error has happened, checks existence of a file or directory, or compares strings for instance. For example:

```
if "%2"=="" goto usage
if exist %2 goto fail
copy %1 %2
goto done
:fail
```

---

8   UNIX mavens will no doubt observe that these implementations are exceedingly primitive—among other things, providing no support for multiple command-line arguments. Serious users of UNIX-style commands should check out the Hamilton C-shell, MKS toolkit and Toolbuster—all covered in Table 3.3—or the POSIX tools included in the NT resource kit (see Appendix 4).

9   While NT itself accepts either the .BAT or .CMD extension for command scripts, DOS and Windows-based clients expect the .BAT extension, while OS/2 clients expect .CMD—in a mixed environment, it may be necessary to provide both, and to use the %OS% environment variable to determine which is used.

```
echo ERROR-%2 exists!
goto done
:usage
echo usage:  cp  fromfile  tofile
:done
```

Now if the user attempts to copy one file over another using *cp*, it will print an error message, and fail. To override that, we can add a third parameter:

```
if "%2"=="" goto usage
if "%3" == "FORCE" goto doit
if exist %2 goto fail
:doit
copy %1 %2
goto done
:fail
echo ERROR--%2 exists!
goto done
:usage
echo usage:  cp  fromfile  tofile  [ FORCE ]
echo (use FORCE to overwrite an existing file)
:done
```

The user can now override the error message for an overwrite by using FORCE as the third parameter on the command line.

Built-in Commands

You can get a list of the built-in commands that CMD.EXE understands by typing *help* at the command prompt:

```
C:\WINNT40\system32>help
```

For more information on a specific command, type HELP command-name.

```
ASSOC      Displays or modifies file extension associations.
AT         Schedules commands and programs to run on a computer.
ATTRIB     Displays or changes file attributes.
BREAK      Sets or clears extended CTRL+C checking.
CACLS      Displays or modifies access control lists (ACLs) of files.
CALL       Calls one batch program from another.
CD         Displays the name of or changes the current directory.
CHCP       Displays or sets the active code page number.
CHDIR      Displays the name of or changes the current directory.
CHKDSK     Checks a disk and displays a status report.
CLS        Clears the screen.
CMD        Starts a new instance of the Windows NT command interpreter.
COLOR      Sets the default console foreground and background colors.
COMP       Compares the contents of two files or sets of files.
COMPACT    Displays or alters the compression of files on NTFS partitions.
CONVERT    Converts FAT volumes to NTFS. You cannot convert the current drive.
COPY       Copies one or more files to another location.
DATE       Displays or sets the date.
```

DEL	Deletes one or more files.
DIR	Displays a list of files and subdirectories in a directory.
DISKCOMP	Compares the contents of two floppy disks.
DISKCOPY	Copies the contents of one floppy disk to another.
DOSKEY	Edits command lines, recalls Windows NT commands, and creates macros.
ECHO	Displays messages, or turns command echoing on or off.
ENDLOCAL	Ends localization of environment changes in a batch file.
ERASE	Deletes one or more files.
EXIT	Quits the CMD.EXE program (command interpreter).
FC	Compares two files or sets of files, and displays the differences between them.
FIND	Searches for a text string in a file or files.
FINDSTR	Searches for strings in files.
FOR	Runs a specified command for each file in a set of files.
FORMAT	Formats a disk for use with Windows NT.
FTYPE	Displays or modifies file types used in file extension associations.
GOTO	Directs the Windows NT command interpreter to a labeled line in a batch program.
GRAFTABL	Enables Windows NT to display an extended character set in graphics mode.
HELP	Provides Help information for Windows NT commands.
IF	Performs conditional processing in batch programs.
KEYB	Configures a keyboard for a specific language.
LABEL	Creates, changes, or deletes the volume label of a disk.
MD	Creates a directory.
MKDIR	Creates a directory.
MODE	Configures a system device.
MORE	Displays output one screen at a time.
MOVE	Moves one or more files from one directory to another directory on the same drive.
PATH	Displays or sets a search path for executable files.
PAUSE	Suspends processing of a batch file and displays a message.
POPD	Restores the previous value of the current directory saved by PUSHD.
PRINT	Prints a text file.
PROMPT	Changes the Windows NT command prompt.
PUSHD	Saves the current directory then changes it.
RD	Removes a directory.
RECOVER	Recovers readable information from a bad or defective disk.
REM	Records comments (remarks) in batch files or CONFIG.SYS.
REN	Renames a file or files.
RENAME	Renames a file or files.
REPLACE	Replaces files.
RESTORE	Restores files that were backed up by using the BACKUP command.
RMDIR	Removes a directory.
SET	Displays, sets, or removes Windows NT environment variables.
SETLOCAL	Begins localization of environment changes in a batch file.
SHIFT	Shifts the position of replaceable parameters in batch files.
SORT	Sorts input.
START	Starts a separate window to run a specified program or command.
SUBST	Associates a path with a drive letter.
TIME	Displays or sets the system time.
TITLE	Sets the window title for a CMD.EXE session.
TREE	Graphically displays the directory structure of a drive or path.
TYPE	Displays the contents of a text file.
VER	Displays the Windows NT version.

```
VERIFY    Tells Windows NT whether to verify that your files are written
          correctly to a disk.
VOL       Displays a disk volume label and serial number.
XCOPY     Copies files and directory trees.
```

Most of these commands are not specifically network-related, and therefore we will not cover them in detail here. Most of the commands accept standard /? syntax to request help, for example:

```
C:\WINNT40\system32>xcopy /?
Copies files and directory trees.
XCOPY source [destination] [/A | /M] [/D[:date]] [/P] [/S [/E]] [/V] [/W]
             [/C] [/I] [/Q] [/F] [/L] [/H] [/R] [/T] [/U]
             [/K] [/N] [/Z]
source       Specifies the file(s) to copy.
destination  Specifies the location and/or name of new files.
/A           Copies files with the archive attribute set, doesn't change
             the attribute.
/M           Copies files with the archive attribute set, turns off the
             archive attribute.
/D:m-d-y     Copies files changed on or after the specified date.
             If no date is given, copies only those files whose source
             time is newer than the destination time.
/P           Prompts you before creating each destination file.
/S           Copies directories and subdirectories except empty ones.
/E           Copies directories and subdirectories, including empty ones.
             Same as /S /E. May be used to modify /T.
/V           Verifies each new file.
/W           Prompts you to press a key before copying.
/C           Continues copying even if errors occur.
/I           If destination does not exist and copying more than one
             file, assumes that destination must be a directory.
/Q           Does not display file names while copying.
/F           Displays full source and destination file names while
             copying.
/L           Displays files that would be copied.
/H           Copies hidden and system files also.
/R           Overwrites read-only files.
/T           Creates directory structure, but does not copy files. Does
             not include empty directories or subdirectories. /T /E
             includes empty directories and
             subdirectories.
/U           Copies only files that already exist in destination.
/K           Copies attributes. Normal Xcopy will reset read-only
             attributes.
/N           Copies using the generated short names.
/Z           Copies networked files in restartable mode.
```

For administrators, the most important of the commands are not in the list above. They are the commands provided by the *Net* command-line interface, described next.

Administrative Net Commands

Although most administrative functions in Windows NT are performed using one or the other of the graphical applications—User Manager, Server Manager, etc—discussed elsewhere in this chapter, a very powerful set of command-line functions for administrative control are essentially an extension of the basic net commands discussed at the end of Chapter 4. In this section we will discuss these commands and explore how they can be of considerable administrative use because they can be employed in batch files and logon scripts. The basic NET commands for control of file sharing, printer sharing, attaching two shared directories, and the like are discussed at the end of Chapter 4. In addition to those commands, there is a set of commands that are intended for administrative use only. By using these commands in a batch file or logon script, you can generally accomplish all the same tasks that would otherwise be performed in User Manager, Server Manager, etc.

When Windows NT 3.1 was in beta, there was much dispute over how "new" NT really is; many people pointed out that it was originally planned as OS/2 3.0. NT's kernel design really *is* new; but most of the networking functionality is actually a ported (and improved) version of Microsoft LAN Manager. For script writers, this difference means that most LAN Manager commands work in Windows NT. The most important of these are the NET commands and the AT command scheduler.

To get a list of *NET* commands, just type NET at a command prompt:

```
    The syntax of this command is:


NET [ ACCOUNTS | COMPUTER | CONFIG | CONTINUE | FILE | GROUP | HELP |
      HELPMSG | LOCALGROUP | NAME | PAUSE | PRINT | SEND | SESSION |
      SHARE | START | STATISTICS | STOP | TIME | USE | USER | VIEW ]
```

To get a better explanation of any command, type NET HELP followed by the command name. For instance, NET HELP VIEW gives:

```
The syntax of this command is:
NET VIEW [\\computername | /DOMAIN[:domainname]] [/NETWORK:networkname]
```

We present a complete list of the Windows NT NET commands below:

Setting System-wide Security Policy: *Net Accounts* This command may be used to control the account policies for single servers or for all servers within a domain, if a domain administrator (NT Server domains only) uses the command. The syntax of the command is net accounts followed by any of several command switches. Issued by itself, the command displays the current account policy for the server in which it is activated:

```
C:\users\default>net accounts
Force user logoff how long after time expires:      Never
Minimum password age (days):                        0
Maximum password age (days):                        42
```

```
Minimum password length:                        0
Length of password history maintained:          None
Machine role:                                   WORKSTATION
The command completed successfully.
```

Alternatively, through the use of the */domain* switch, it will display the domain-wide policy set by the PDC. All major factors of the server account policy may be directly controlled using the following switches:

/force logoff: This command controls whether a user will be forcibly logged off of a system when his account password has expired or when his allowed time on the system is exceeded. The default value is *no* which will not force a logoff. The alternative is to set a time in minutes. For example, the command *net accounted/force logoff: 10* will give a user ten minutes in which to change his account password if he logs in with an expired account or will give him ten minutes after notification that he has exceeded his permitted time on the system in which to finish up his business.

/minpwlen: Minimum password length. This command sets the minimum length for passwords for the server. Permitted values are in the range zero to 14 characters where a value of zero will permit users to have a blank password. By default, Windows NT Server requires a six-character minimum password length.

> *Note: The entire NT security system depends upon proper use of passwords. Setting /minpwlen:0 is functionally equivalent to disabling the majority of the Windows NT security system.*

/maxpwage: Maximum password age. This command is similar in function to the force logoff function. It determines the maximum age of a password before the user will be required to change passwords. Legal values are a range of days from one to slightly over 40,000 or the keyword UNLIMITED, which allows passwords to be used indefinitely.

> *Note: Again, the Windows NT security system depends upon effective use of passwords. Setting an unlimited password makes it technically possible, though perhaps not feasible, for passwords to be hacked. It is better to force passwords to be changed on a regular basis. For example, once a month would be /maxpwage:30.*

/minpwage: Minimum password age. Functionally the opposite of the */maxpwage* command, */minpwage* could set the minimum number of days that must pass before a user is permitted to change his or her password. This one may seem like a ridiculous setting. After all, why not provide a minpwage of zero days, which is the default, and allow people to change the password at will? The reason for setting a minimum password age is to foil intruders who temporarily change the password and then try to change it back, and to enforce the *password history* mechanism by preventing users from using a program to cycle through however many passwords are kept in the history in quick succession, then change back to the original. Legal values are in the range of zero to slightly over 40,000. The default, again, is zero days.

/uniquepw: unique password. This command requires the user's password to be unique through a specified number of changes ranging from zero through 8. Thus, for instance, setting uniquepw:2 will require that a user's password be unique through the last two passwords. That is, he cannot repeat an earlier password until he has used at least two new ones. This will pre-

vent users from repeatedly entering the same password and thus functionally defeating the use of the */maxpwage* command.

/domain: The domain switch. Use of the */domain* switch in conjunction with any of the other net accounts commands will make the command refer to the entire domain rather than just to the server on which it is executed. You have to have domain administrative permissions and be logged in to a Windows NT Server Domain to use this command. The command will be remote-executed on the PDC and will then affect domain-wide account policies. not merely single server account policies. For example, *net accounts /minpwage:2 /domain* will set a domain-wide account policy requiring a minimum password age of two days.

> *Note: This parameter only has an effect if it is executed from a Windows NT computer that is a member of a Windows NT Server domain but is not functioning as a Domain Controller. The /domain switch has no effect if it is executed on a Domain Controller.*

/sync: User account database synchronization. This switch, usable only on a Windows NT Domain Controller, forces an update on the user accounts database to synchronize database information across the domain. It may only be used by a domain administrator and then only on a Domain Controller. It cannot be executed remotely.

Adding Computers to a Domain: *Net Computer* (NT Server Only) This command can be used to add computers to a domain database and is the primary command that needs to be executed by domain administrators to add new computers to an NT Server domain. The command syntax is *net computer \\name of computer to add* followed by either a */add* or */del* switch. The */add* switch adds the computer to the domain. The */del* switch deletes it. This command can be executed only on a Domain Controller. It cannot be executed remotely. Functionally the command determines which computers will be affected by domain-wide updates. You can accomplish the same effect as this command using the network settings section of the Windows NT control panel. By selecting the change button adjacent to the domain name, you are presented with a selector with a member of a workgroup or domain and create computer accounts in domain. By creating a computer account in the domain you are functionally performing the same thing as a *net computer \\computername /add*. You can also add computers to (and remove them from) a domain using Windows NT Server Manager, (covered in Chapter 8).

Viewing the System Configuration: *Net Config* This command displays information related to the operation of the server and workstation services. The command has two variants:

```
net config server
```

displays the following information:

```
C:\users\default>net config server
Server Name                        \\JOHNR-NT486-66
Server Comment

Software version                   Windows NT 3.10
Server is active on                Nbf_ODINSUP02 (00001b48d2aa)

Server hidden                      No
Max Logged On Users                Unlimited
Max. open files per session        256
```

```
Idle session time (min)              15
The command completed successfully.
```

Or:

```
net config workstation
```

which displays the following information:

```
C:\users\default>net config workstation
Computername                      \\JOHNR-NT486-66
Username                          jruleynt

Workstation active on             Nbf_ODINSUP02 (00001B48D2AA)
Software version                  Windows NT 3.10

Workstation domain                MAGNET2
Logon domain                      MAGNET2

COM Open Timeout (sec)            3600
COM Send Count (byte)             16
COM Send Timeout (msec)           250
The command completed successfully.
```

This command may be useful, for example, in running a periodic automatic maintenance report to a central logging facility. See the example later in this section.

Controlling Services: Net Start, Net Stop, Net Pause, and Net Continue All of these commands are used to control the various services that are built into Windows NT. These services include:

- the alerter service

- the computer browser service

- the directory replicator service

- the event log

- the rpc locator

- messaging

- net logon

- rpc subsystem

- schedule subsystem

- the server service

- the UPS service

- the workstation service

In other words, it includes the very same services that one controls from the services applet in the Windows NT Control Panel.

The syntax of the commands is NET START. By itself, the Net Start command will list all of the services that are started in the system. NET START SERVICE will start the service in question. For example, NET START CLIPBOOK starts the *clipbook* service. NET STOP SERVICE will stop a particular service. The service may then be restarted using the *Net Start* command. NET PAUSE service will temporarily suspend a service or resource. This command can only be used with the netlogon, schedule, server, or workstation services. The suspension amounts to putting the service on hold. That is, it will not accept new requests until this command is overridden by a NET RESUME command; of course, NET RESUME undoes what was done with the NET PAUSE. Despite what is printed in the *Windows NT System Guide*, at least in the Beta version, NET PAUSE does not appear to have any effect when used in association with printers or shared directories.

Controlling User Groups: *NET GROUP, NET LOCALGROUP* These commands allow you to add and remove user account groups from a Windows NT server or Windows NT domain. User groups are among the most basic fundamental features of the Windows NT administrative account system and are covered earlier in this chapter. (See the section on the Windows NT User Manager.) The NET GROUP and NET LOCALGROUP commands allow you to add or delete user groups from the accounts system. The NET LOCALGROUP command affects the local Windows NT server on which it is executed. *Net localgroup group-name/add* adds a group to the account database. *Net localgroup group-name /delete* removes the group. The */domain* switch causes this function to be executed domain-wide (it must be executed by a domain administrator). The command is actually executed on the primary DC. The net group command may only be executed on a Windows NT Server and sets domain-wide groups. Again, *net group group-name/add* adds the group, and *net group group-name/delete* deletes an entire group.

Note that the */domain* switch from the NET LOCALGROUP command has no effect when it is executed on a Windows NT Server because Windows NT Servers by default carry out their operations on the primary DC. However, you should not make the mistake of thinking that a NET LOCALGROUP and a NET GROUP command are the same when executed on a Windows NT Server. NT Servers maintain separate domain groups and local groups. Domain groups are user groups that are employed for domain administration and apply to all machines within the domain, whereas local groups apply to individual machines whether they are NT Server machines or standard Windows NT machines. You can also add or delete individual users from groups and local groups using the NET GROUP and NET LOCALGROUP commands. For example, the command:

```
net group "Domain Admins" jruleynt /add
```

adds the account jruleynt to the group of Domain Admins for a Windows NT Server domain. The command

```
net localgroup administrators fred /delete
```

deletes the user account fred from the local group of administrators on a local Windows NT server. If you do not specify the user name, the NET GROUP and NET LOCALGROUP commands will list the groups or the members of a particular group. For example, the command

```
net localgroup
```

without other arguments will list the groups within the Windows NT account database:

```
C:\users\default>net localgroup

Aliases for \\JOHNR-NT486-66


-------------------------------------------------------------------------
*Administrators              *Backup Operators          *Guests
*Power Users                 *Replicator                *Users
The command completed successfully.
```

Then typing

```
net localgroup administrators
```

will list the user accounts that are members of the administrators group:

```
C:\users\default>net localgroup administrators
Aliasname        administrators
Comment          Members can fully administer the system

Members

-------------------------------------------------------------------------
Administrator            MAGNET2\Domain Admins
The command completed successfully.
```

Individual user accounts can be added, deleted, or controlled using the NET USER command covered later in this section.

> *Note: Although the net group and net localgroup commands will allow you to add or delete administrative groups both for individual servers and for NT Server domains, you cannot control permissions, the user rights granted to groups, or for that matter individual users using the command line. User rights can only be issued from the Windows NT User Manager (from the User Rights item of the Policies menu) and then only by a Windows NT administrator or domain administrator (where domain accounts are concerned). The absence of any capability to set permissions from the command line does present a limitation from the standpoint of writing batch files, for example, to create a mass migration of accounts. This restriction is unfortunate, but it apparently was considered a security feature by the Windows NT designers. Therefore, you can create the accounts, and you can create the groups in a batch file, but you have to go to the User Manager to set the permissions manually.*

Controlling Who Gets Messages: *NET NAME* As described in Chapter 4, Windows NT provides a reasonably powerful system for the issuing of system-wide messages through the NET SEND command. Normally NET SEND can be used either with individual computer names, with individual account names, or through the */broadcast* or */domain* switch it can send messages that will be received by all computers on a segment or by all computers within a domain. It can sometimes be desirable, however, to send a message alias, i.e., a name of convenience that can be used to identify a particular user or a particular computer without using the actual computer name or the actual user name. This can be accomplished by using the NET NAME command. The syntax of the NET NAME command is:

```
net name alias /add
```

to add the name, or

```
net name alias /delete
```

to delete the name. If neither the */add* or */delete* switch is used, an */add* switch is assumed—thus the command *net name boss* is functionally equivalent to

```
net name boss/add.
```

This command must be issued at a particular workstation. You can do it conveniently as part of a logon script and it can be useful if you use long, descriptive computer names. Instead, you can issue a short name or a more friendly name. For instance, as opposed to sending a command to the jruleynt account, you could send a message to John, assuming that NET NAME John has been executed on the same workstation as jruleynt is logged into. This process may seem rather pointless, but a certain degree of informality is often useful. An administrative message addressed to John will appear to be much more personal than an administrative message delivered to jruleynt, for instance. Note that message aliases must be unique. You cannot add net name John on two workstations in the same network.

Checking Performance: *Net Statistics* This command provides a concise report of system information for either the server or workstation service. It can be used as part of an automatic maintenance reporting system; see the example later in this section. The command has two forms:

```
net statistics server
```

displays statistics for the server service, e.g.:

```
Server Statistics for \\JOHNR-NT486-66
Statistics since 07/30/93 03:20pm
Sessions accepted            1
Sessions timed-out           1
Sessions errored-out         1

Kilobytes sent               262
Kilobytes received           722

Mean response time (msec)    25

System errors                0
Permission violations        0
Password violations          0

Files accessed               136
Comm devices accessed        0
Print jobs spooled           0

Times buffers exhausted

  Big buffers                0
  Request buffers            0

The command completed successfully.
```

and:

```
net statistics workstation
```

displays statistics for the workstation service, e.g.:

```
Workstation Statistics for \\JOHNR-NT486-66
Statistics since 07/30/93 03:20pm
   Bytes received                             50734
   Server Message Blocks (SMBs) received      429
   Bytes transmitted                          58320
   Server Message Blocks (SMBs) transmitted   429
   Read operations                            0
   Write operations                           8
   Raw reads denied                           0
   Raw writes denied                          0

   Network errors                             0
   Connections made                           13
   Reconnections made                         1
   Server disconnects                         9

   Sessions started                           17
   Hung sessions                              0
   Failed sessions                            0
   Failed operations                          429
   Use count                                  20
   Failed use count                           0

The command completed successfully.
```

Note that any Windows NT system with file-sharing enabled will have both. The server service is necessary to provide browsing functionality to a Windows NT's system, so even though the system is not in fact used as a server, do not assume that no server service is running. The command NET STATISTICS by itself simply lists the services for which statistics may be requested, that is *server* and *workstation:*

```
net statistics
Statistics are available for the following running services:

Server                    Workstation
The command completed successfully.
```

Controlling User Accounts: *Net User* This command allows user accounts to be added or deleted on a Windows NT server or domain server. It also allows control of certain account features including a text comment, a descriptive comment, country code, expiration date, home directory, etc. as described later. As with the NET GROUP and the NET LOCALGROUP commands you can add users and assign users to existing groups. However, you cannot control other than by group assignment, you cannot control the permissions assigned to a user account from the command line. This has to be done in the Windows NT User Manager. The syntax of the NET USER command is:

```
net user user-name password (or asterisk)
```

and one or more switches. User-name is the name of the user account to add, delete, modify, or view. Password, if present, will assign or change the password for the user account. It must satisfy the minimum length set with the */minpwlen* option in the NET ACCOUNTS command. The asterisk character, if used, will produce a prompt for a password rather than putting the password in manually. This can be used if one wishes to set up a batch file requiring new passwords to be entered, for example, and one wishes to avoid the inherent security breach that would be represented by having the clear text password present in the file.

The */domain* switch will cause the operations employed in the net user command to be carried out on the primary DC in a Windows NT Server domain. As with other places where a domain switch is used, this has no effect if it is executed on a Domain Controller, because by default DCs carry out all operations on the PDC. On a Windows NT Workstation, or an NT Server that is not configured as a DC, NET USER commands issued without the */domain* switch only affects the local machine. Also, the */domain* switch can be used only by a domain administrator (or account operator).

The */add* switch will add a user account to the database. The */delete* switch eliminates a user account from the database. A variety of options may be added following the */add* switch. These include */active:* which takes the arguments *yes* or *no*. This command will activate or deactivate the account. If the account is not active, the user cannot access the server using the account; however, unlike the */delete* switch, this does not remove the account from the database. This can be useful if a user has intermittent access to a server.

You can use the */active:no* to prevent the user from having access until some formal action is taken.

The */comment:* switch followed by a text message with a maximum length of 48 characters will provide a descriptive comment about the user account. You should enclose the comment text in quotation marks. For example:

```
net user jruley /add /comment:"John D Ruley's account"
```

The */countrycode:* switch, which takes a number as an argument, will user the operating system country code specified by that number to set the user's help and error messages. The default is country code:0, which uses whatever the default country code is for the Windows NT server in question. This command can be useful in an international system where users who will expect to see different languages may be logging in to the system. You can custom configure with this logon system the language base that should be employed once the user logs in. Unfortunately, this setting will affect only help and error messages. It will not affect the primary Windows NT language set at the workstation. This setting has to be controlled manually.

/expires: is a command that takes a date or the keyword *never*. This command will determine when the account expires, for example:

```
net user jim /add /expires:12/25/93
```

will create a jim account expiring on Christmas Day. The keyword *never* will create an account that never expires.

/fullname: followed by a string in quotes sets a user's full name. For example:

```
net user jim/add/fullname:"James M. Ruley"
```

sets my brother's full name in association with the jim account.

/homedir: followed by a path name will set the path to a user's home directory (the default directory set during a remote logon). Note that the path must already have been created—so when writing a batch file that creates and sets home directories for one or more users, you must create the directories first before using */homedir* to set them.

/homedirreq: followed by a *yes* or *no* specifies whether a home directory is required. If so this should be used in association with a */homedir* switch to set the directory.

/passwordchg: followed by a *yes* or a *no* specifies whether the user can change his or her own password. Saying */passwordchg:no* will require administrative change in a password and can be used in systems where for certain reasons users are not trusted to set their own passwords.

/passwordreq: followed by a *yes* or a *no* specifies whether a user account must have a password.

/profilepath: followed by a path sets a path for the user's logon profile. This profile is functionally equivalent to the logon profile information that is set using the User Manager.

/scriptpath: followed by a path name sets the location of a user's logon script. Again, functionally it is the same as that set in the User Manager.

/times: followed by either a time or the keyword *all* sets the hours during which the user is permitted to log on. The times are formatted as day-day,day-day,time-time,time-time where time is limited to one-hour increments. The days may be spelled out or abbreviated. Hours can be twelve or twenty-four hour notation. For example:

```
net user jim /times:monday-friday,8 a.m.-5 p.m.
```

will set the jim account with the permission to log in on weekdays during normal working hours. Attempts to log in at other times or on other days will fail.

/usercomment: followed by a text string lets the administrator add or change the user comment for the account; the comment being displayed is a text message that is displayed when the user logs in.

The */workstations:* command followed by computer names lists the workstations that the user is permitted to log in on. If this string is absent, the user is assumed to be able to log in from any workstation.

You should note by this time that the NET USER command provides a considerable—not to say enormous—degree of administrative control. You can determine the time of day a user can logon, you can determine which days the user can logon, you can force the location of a home directory, force the execution of a logon script, present information to the user on logon, and determine which machines he is permitted to logon from. As described in Chapter 1, Windows NT is a fully secure operating system. Your opportunity to effectively use this security is largely controlled by NET ACCOUNTS, NET USER, and their equivalents in the Windows NT User Manager.

If I forgot to mention it, NET USER typed by itself simply provides a list of the user names defined for a particular system:

```
User accounts for \\JOHNR-NT486-66

--------------------------------------------------------------------------------
Administrator              Guest       Jim     Fred   Jruley         Jruleynt
The command completed successfully.
```

An interesting intellectual exercise would be to consider what it would take to write an application that would first issue a NET USER command, then parse the results identifying each user and carrying out some operation on each user in sequence. But I digress...

Viewing, Controlling, and Unlocking Shared Files: *Net File* When shared files are open on a Windows NT system, you can view a list of which files are in use, to see specifics on the use of the file (that is, who has the file open, whether it is locked, and what permissions are in use), and if necessary eliminate sharing on the file using the NET FILE command. The syntax:

```
net file
```

prints a list of which shared file names are in use, whether they are locked, who has them, and what the file ID is:

```
C:\users\default>net file

ID         Path                                  Username           # Locks

--------------------------------------------------------------------------------
43         d:\netnt\uuencode                     administrator            0
The command completed successfully.
```

Net File followed by an ID number prints a more specific display for the particular file:

```
C:\users\default>net file 43
File ID        43
Username       administrator
Locks          0
Path           d:\netnt\uuencode
Permissions    XA
The command completed successfully.
```

net file ID number /close will close the file, terminating the share. This step can be useful in two situations. Obviously one situation is if there is unauthorized use of a file, although in that circumstance, it would probably make the most sense to kick the user off the system rather than simply disconnecting the file. Also, certain applications, particularly 16-bit applications, may not do a proper job of cleaning up after themselves. A file may be opened at the beginning of an application session and not closed when the application shuts down. If this happens the user will then attempt to reconnect to the file but not be permitted to do so. He or she will receive a message indicating a sharing violation or indicating that the file is otherwise in use. In this circumstance, you may find it useful to issue a NET FILE, view the list of files, probably identify the file in question, then issue a

```
net file ID number /close
```

to close the file, disable sharing, and permit the user to use the file again. Unfortunately, there is no such thing as NET CLOSE ALL, which could be useful in some emergency situations. If you wish to eliminate a user completely from a system, force them off, you can use the NET SESSION command that is described next.

Controlling Logon Sessions: *Net Session* The net session command lists or disconnects logon sessions connected to the server. Issued by itself the NET SESSION command presents a list of the computers that are logged into the server:

```
C:\users\default>net session

Computer                    User name          Client Type    Opens Idle time
--------------------------------------------------------------------------------
\\MIPS-LAB-SERVER         administrator          NT             1      00:30:28
The command completed successfully.
```

Issuing the command:

```
net session \\computer name
```

for a particular computer lists statistical information about the session, including which users are operating in the session and which shares are open:

```
C:\users\default>net session \\mips-lab-server
Username         administrator
Computer         MIPS-LAB-SERVER
Guest logon      No
Client type      NT
Sess time        23:43:28
Idle time        00:31:24

Sharename        Type      # Opens
-----------------------------------------
disk-d           Disk      1
The command completed successfully.
```

The */delete* parameter will force the session to logoff and will disconnect the session. For example, *net session\\mips-lab-server /delete* will disconnect mips lab server from the current session and terminate all connections. This command should be used only as a last resort and is functionally equivalent to employing the disconnect button from the *users session* dialog in the server portion of the control panel.

Time Synchronization: *Net Time* One problem that often occurs in networking is ensuring that all workstations within a domain have their system clocks synchronized. Lack of such synchronization can, for example, cause substantial problems in carrying out a distributed backup in the event that some random event such as a change to daylight saving time or hard reset on a computer has inadvertently changed the system clock. A particular machine may then carry out a backup at an unwarranted time. You can use the NET TIME command to provide synchronization between computers and the network. The command

```
net time
```

with no arguments will print the time determined by the currently defined time server in the network, if any. In addition:

```
net time \\computer name
```

will print the time on the selected computer. The command:

```
net time /domain
```

will print the time on the current primary domain server.

```
net time /domain: domain name
```

will print that time for any specified domain server that is on the network. Any variation on this command can be followed by the keyword */set,* which will set the time at the machine on which the net time command is executed to match the time on the machine from which the time was requested. Thus, for example:

```
net time/domain/set
```

will synchronize the workstation by setting the local workstation time to be the same as the time of the DC. This command should normally be executed as part of a logon script.

Scheduling Commands for Execution: *AT*

Up to now, we have been concerned with commands within the NET series that are specific to Windows NT networking. To understand how commands can be executed at a specified time, we now need to understand the AT command, which is a unique feature of the Windows NT Batch command set. The *AT* command allows you to schedule commands for execution at a particular time. It also allows you to schedule these commands for execution on remote computers. It is a very powerful command for use by system administrators. The command has the following syntax:

```
at \\computer-name time "command-string"
```

where *\\computer-name* refers to the computer at which the command is to be executed. If this portion is omitted, then the command is assumed to refer to the local computer. Time refers to the time for execution and may be used in conjunction with the flags */every:* which may be followed by a date of the week or month or with the */next*: which will run the command the next occurrence of the day. So, for example, the command */every:Monday* will cause the command to be executed the set time every Monday. The command */next Monday* will cause the command to be executed on the next Monday.

The command-string in quotes is a string that will be executed on the machine in question. For example, the command:

```
at \\mips-lab-server 10:28a.m. "net send jruleynt the time is 10:28"
```

will at the time 10:28 execute a NET SEND command, sending to jruleynt the message that the time is 10:28. This command requires the schedule service to be started (net start schedule) on the machine on which it is to be executed. Just typing AT on a machine will list any at jobs which are currently scheduled and their ID numbers. The */delete* keyword will delete a particular ID number or if no ID number is set will delete all jobs on the specified computer. For example:

```
        at \\mips-lab-server
```

will print

```
        C:\users\default>at
Status  ID   Day              Time            Command Line
------------------------------------------------------------------------
        0    Tomorrow         10:30AM     net send ADMINISTRATOR It's 10:30!
```

The command

```
at \\mips-lab-server 0 /delete
```

will delete this job. The command

```
at \\mips-lab-server /delete
```

without any ID number will delete all jobs. The command string can include any valid Windows NT command, including start commands, to cause a separate process to start or even batch commands. Thus it is possible using the AT command to schedule remote execution of processes such as backups, administrative maintenance reports, or whatever, and to have them occur at a specified time on a specified date repetitively. This capability is in addition to Windows NT's basic capability to support logon scripts.

As an example, to backup really critical information to a central directory one server can be very helpful. You can do this backup for any number of other servers/workstations with a simple combination of NET USE and XCOPY:

```
net use z: \\ncr_nt\disk-c
xcopy z:\data c:\backup\ncr_nt /d /v
net use z: /DELETE
```

will copy files from the *data* directory on \\ncr_nt to the c:\backup\ncr_nt directory, copying only files that have been updated since the last backup (that's what the */d* switch is for), and verifying that the copies are good (the */v* switch). You could repeat this process for other systems using similar commands, and then just run NT's tape backup on the local c:\backup directory, backing up all the systems at once.

Obviously, having a log for something as critical as this process would be nice. That log-creation can be handled by redirecting the console output from XCOPY to a file:

```
xcopy z:\data c:\backup\ncr_nt /d /v >BACKUP.LOG
```

But what do you do with the file once you've got it? Here's what: *run*, don't walk, to your system, and download Martin Heller's MAILFILE command-line e-mail utility (MAILFILE.ZIP) from one of *WINDOWS* Magazine's software libraries.[10] That process allows you to send the log off via e-mail:

---

10 Available from the software download areas of the WinMag forum on Compuserve, WinMag on America On-Line, or www.winmag.com.

```
mailfile BACKUP.LOG to ADMINISTRATOR
```

will send the log as an MS-Mail message. The same approach lets you run a daily status report:

```
net statistics >net.log
mailfile NET.LOG to ADMINISTRATOR
```

To have this done automatically at noon five days a week:

```
AT 12:00pm EVERY monday tuesday wednesday thursday friday REPORT.CMD
```

The NT Resource Kit includes a graphical interface to the scheduler service that gives you an alternative to the AT command—Windows AT (WINAT.EXE)—that does everything the AT command-line interface does, but does it in a Window; which makes it a bit easier to see what's happening, as illustrated in Figure 3.24.

From its second edition on, the Resource Kit also includes a universal service (SRVANY) application that allows any NT program, including scripts, to be treated as NT services. This capability has several advantages and should be considered for mission-critical scripts. See Appendix 4 for more information.

Environment Variables Windows NT provides a powerful capability to simplify administrative script creation through *environment variables*. These are character strings that can be referred to by name in a logon script or using NT's set command. Typing *set* at the command line with no arguments gives a list of the current environment variables:

```
set
COMPUTERNAME=COMPAQ-LTE
ComSpec=C:\WINDOWS\system32\cmd.exe
HOMEDRIVE=C:
HOMEPATH=\users\default
OS=Windows_NT
Os2LibPath=C:\WINDOWS\system32\os2\dll;
Path=C:\WINDOWS\system32;C:\WINDOWS;C:\;C:\DOS;C:\MOUSE
```

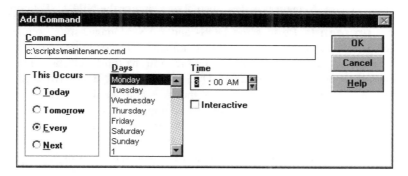

FIGURE 3.24 Command scheduler. WINAT.EXE from Microsoft's NT Resource Kit provides a graphical interface to the scheduler service, as an alternative to the AT command-line program.

```
PROCESSOR_ARCHITECTURE=x86
PROCESSOR_LEVEL=4
PROMPT=$P$G
SystemRoot=C:\WINDOWS
SystemDrive=C:
TEMP=C:\temp
tmp=C:\temp
USERDOMAIN=MAGNET2
USERNAME=jruleynt
windir=C:\WINDOWS
```

As you can see, there's a wealth of information here. To use these variables in logon scripts, enclose them with the % character. For instance:

```
%username%
```

would evaluate to *jruleynt* in this case. In the examples at the end of this section, we will see how to exploit environment variables; among other things, we will be dynamically assigning a local printer depending on which workstation a user logs into.

Setting Environment Variables Environment variables can be locally set using NT's Set command. For instance:

```
set homepath=\
set
COMPUTERNAME=COMPAQ-LTE
ComSpec=C:\WINDOWS\system32\cmd.exe
HOMEDRIVE=C:
HOMEPATH=\
...
```

However, such local settings apply *only* to a particular command-line session (and child sessions). If you start another session, you will still find homepath set to *users\default*.

You can *permanently* set some (but by no means all) environment variables with the *user profile* portion of NT User Manager, as described above, and/or the NET USER command.

NT-Specific Commands Besides the DOS- and LAN Manager-style commands, some commands are specific to Windows NT. These commands are documented in the Command Reference section of Windows NT Help (the Help icon in the top-level Start menu). The sections on "What's New or Different from MS-DOS and "What's New or Different from LAN Manager" provide lists with details. Some of the new commands are rather esoteric; the IPXROUTE command used for routing on NetWare-compatible LANs for instance. Others are quite useful; the START command, for instance, will start a program running in a separate session from the one where the command line is executing. The PUSHD and POPD commands change the current directory and then get back to where you started from.

Some commands are not documented in the NT Command Reference; in particular, a command-line option to dial out using NT RAS that is ideal for making economical use of Wide-Area Network (WAN) links. RAS is implemented as a service, so it can be controlled using NET START and NET STOP. Dialing the phone is accomplished using the undocumented RASDIAL command (type RASDIAL /? on the command line for a very limited amount of documentation). As an example, if you've upgraded your system to have a full MS-Mail postoffice (see Chapter 8), and want to perform transfer messages in the middle of the night, you might want to use RAS.CMD:

```
net start remoteaccess
rasdial mail_server
net use w: \\mail_server\MAILDATA
m:external.exe -A -Ww
net use w: /DELETE
rasdial mail_server /DISCONNECT
net stop remoteaccess
```

where EXTERNAL.EXE is the Microsoft Message Transfer Agent (MTA) that is used to transfer data between postoffices (discussed in Chapter 8). The script starts the remote access service, creates a temporary connection to the other mail server's MAILDATA directory, runs the MTA over that temporary connection, then disconnects and shuts down.

To have this command run five days a week at midnight:

```
AT 12:00am /EVERY: monday tuesday wednesday thursday friday RAS.CMD
```

Fortunately, the days may be abbreviated as follows:

```
AT 12:00am /EVERY: m,tu,w,th,f RAS.CMD
```

You can also execute NT's built-in backup software from the command line—and thus from a script, using the NTBACKUP command (documented in the Helpfile for the NT Backup application: run Backup from the Administrative Tools group, execute the SEARCH FOR HELP ON... command from the Help menu, and type in "batch"). This process can be combined with the NET USE command to get around Backup's inability to handle dynamic drive assignments by assigning a drive before running Backup:

```
NET USE X: \\mips-lab-server\vb
NTBACKUP backup X:   /A
NET USE X: /DELETE
NET USE X: \\ncr-nt\disk-c
NTBACKUP backup X: /A
```

This script will back up first the vb directory on \\mips-lab-server, and then the disk-c directory on \\ncr-nt and appending them to the existing tape (via the /A switch on *ntbackup*). Data must be restored using the graphical interface; *ntbackup* does not provide a command-line restoration capability.

Finally, some very powerful (even dangerous) command-line programs are included in the NT Resource Kit (described in Appendix 4). Probably the most useful of these is CHOICE.EXE from the Resource Kit, which enables you to create interactive scripts, ones where the batch file can ask for the user's input. This capability is key to writing real (if simple) programs using scripts. For instance, our unix-style "safe" copy script can now ask the user whether or not to overwrite a file:

```
if exist %2
goto ask_user
do_copy:
copy %1 %2
exit
ask_user:
choice /c:yn File exists, overwrite it
if ERRORLEVEL 1 goto do_copy
```

If the user types cp this that, and that exists;, a prompt is displayed:

```
File exists, overwrite it [Y,N]?
```

If the user hits a 'y,' the file will be overwritten. If not, the command aborts.

The most powerful—and dangerous—of the additional tools is REGINI.EXE, which is included in the \SUPPORT directory of all NT CD-ROMs, as well as in the Resource Kit. This tool is a command-line interface to the configuration registry, and allows registry settings to be changed from the command line. Like the registry editor, REGINI.EXE is powerful because it lets you change almost anything. Also, like the registry editor, it's dangerous. Use it with care!

Examples[11]

Example 1 Automatic server maintenance report

```
report.cmd
REM This is a 3 time-per-week maintenance report
REM
REM First, get to the \temp directory:
c:
cd \temp
REM
REM delete any old stuff:
REM
del a b c d
REM
REM run NET CONFIG and NET STATISTICS, piping output to files:
REM
net config server >a
net statistics server >b
net config workstation >c
net statistics workstation >d
```

---

11   An outstanding article on client OS-independant scripting for NT Servers written by Richard Furnival may be found in the Enterprise Windows section of the February 1996 *WINDOWS Magazine*.

```
REM
REM copy the results to the administrator's system:
REM
copy a+b+c+d R:\reports\system1\reptnew.txt
REM
REM It is the administrator's responsibility to see that REPTNEW.TXT is
REM copied or otherwise taken care of before the next night,
REM so that it won't be overwritten--he can run another scheduled
REM process to do this--or transfer the file using e-mail, as described
below
```

To cause this script to be executed nightly, it is only necessary:

- That the administrator place it in the path on each server

- Issue the following AT command for each server

```
at  \\server_name 3:00am /each:monday,wednesday,friday "report.cmd"
```

(Obviously, the file should be edited slightly for each system, with the copy placing the file in reports\system2 for the second system). To have this report mailed to the administrator, rather than copied would be very nice. This process is technically feasible; see Example 6 below.

Example 2 Workstation logon script As mentioned at the start of this section, Microsoft's NT documentation could easily lead you to believe that logon scripts are obsolete. Nothing could be further from the truth. Here's a script that performs the following functions:

- Sets a message alias for the current user.

- Synchronizes system time with the PDC *(this is essential for use of scheduled commands across multiple systems).*

- Starts the Schedular service (this could be done automatically using the NT control panel).

- Announces the logon to other users in the domain.

- Assigns a network drive letter.

Note that all this is done without hard-coding a user name. This process allows the same login script to be used by all users (or at least many users) on a given server; and *that* capability greatly simplifies maintenance. For example, the assignment of the M: drive in the following example allows an administrator to move the mail directories to another drive (or server), and by making the change in *one* logon script, all users will be automatically connected to the proper server and drive.

```
logon.cmd
REM
REM Add a message alias for the user (we use the user's name--by default
REM the only name stored is the computername):
REM
net name %username% /ADD
REM
```

```
REM Synchronize time with the domain server
REM
net time /DOMAIN /SET
REM
REM Start the Schedule service (so remote at... commands will work)
REM
net start schedule       .
REM
REM Announce the log-in to the domain
REM
net send /DOMAIN:%userdomain% %username% is logged in
REM
REM Set M: to the mail directory (doing this in a logon
REM script makes it maintainable)...
REM
net use M: \\win1\msmail\maildata
```

Example 3 Converting a List of NetWare Users into Windows NT Accounts
In the first edition of *Networking Windows NT*, we talked about how this might be done. Since then, Microsoft has provided a Migration Tool for NetWare Servers with NT Server, which does a far better job than any script. So, the example has been deleted from this chapter, and we recommend using the Migration Tool instead. You'll find more on it in Chapter 10.

Example 4 Wandering Users An NT administrator with a real-world problem suggested this example; the administrator runs an NT-based network at a major hospital. His users are the hospital's doctors, nurses, and support staff. The problem: doctors and nurses do not always access the same computer. When a patient is brought to the emergency room, for instance, his or her doctor may need to access the patient's chart from a computer in the ER. The patient may then be moved to intensive care, and the doctor follows the patient, needing to logon from there. The doctor may then need to logon from his or her office, and... you get the picture.

NT's profiles certainly help in this situation. Using them, the doctor can be given his or her personal preference of desktop, folders, shortcuts, etc., and a home directory can be forced on a particular server. "But how," the administrator asked, "can the doctor's default *printer* be handled? When the doctor's in the ER, printing to a printer in the physician's lounge isn't very helpful."

The answer: a logon script, and nothing else. There is no way to assign location-dependent printer connections from a user profile or Print Manager! A logon script, however, makes the problem easy to solve: first, the location the doctor logs in from can be determined using the %computername% environment variable, and based on that, an appropriate printer can be assigned via the NET USE command:

```
If %computername%==\\ER_NT net use lpt1: \\ER_Laserjet
If %computername%==\\ICU_NT net use lpt1: \\ICU_Laserjet
...
```

Of course, in Print Manager, the default printer is just LPT1:, and an appropriate print driver has been installed for that port. The one limitation of this approach is that all the printers have to be identical, or at least compatible with a single standard print driver.

The same approach can be used to maximize efficiency in large networks by assigning the user's home directory to an appropriate local server. Data integrity can be assured using the replication service (see Chapter 8) to replicate data from a single location to all servers in the domain.

Example 5 Weekly Backup The Windows NT Backup application can be controlled through the AT command schedule and a command script, as described above. To execute a daily backup on the server, start the scheduler service, and type:

```
AT 10:00pm /EVERY mo,t,we,th,f,sa,su backup.cmd
```

This will cause the BACKUP.CMD script to be executed every night at 10:00. Because *AT* also supports specifying the computer that you want the command to be run on, you can use the same approach to command remote backups on other systems:

```
AT \\mips-lab-server 2:00am /EVERY m,w,f backup.cmd
```

will cause a three-day-per-week execution of BACKUP.CMD on \\mips-lab-server.

To back up multiple machines on the network, a temporary drive connection can be established and backup executed on that temporary drive, as discussed earlier. A better approach, however, may be to do a *multistage backup*, in which critical information is regularly copied to a central directory on one server, and then backed up from there. This backup can be accomplished with a combination of *net use* and *xcopy*:

```
net use z: \\ncr_nt\disk-c
xcopy z:\data c:\backup\ncr_nt /d /v
net use z: /DELETE
```

This command will copy files from the \data directory on \\ncr_nt to the c:\backup\ncr_nt directory, copying only files that have been updated since the last backup (that is what the */d* switch is for), and verifying that the copies are good (the */v* switch). You could repeat this process for other systems using similar commands, and *then* run NT's tape backup on the local c:\backup directory—backing up all the systems at once.

Obviously, it would be nice to have a log for something as critical as this. That can be handled by redirecting the console output from XCOPY to a file:

```
xcopy z:\data c:\backup\ncr_nt /d /v >BACKUP.LOG
```

Also, as with Example 1, it is then possible to transfer the file via e-mail, as described below.

Example 6 E-mail and Scripts Microsoft's myopia about use of the command-line generally—and scripts in particular—is especially obvious when you realize (1) that NT provides e-mail as a basic feature, but (2) no command-line interface to mail is provided. That is ridiculous, as Examples 1 and 5 make clear. What *should* happen at the end of those scripts is that the log files should be e-mailed to an administrator. That way you have a log, and tracking information available to you whenever and wherever you need it.

To fill this gap, download Martin Heller's MAILFILE command-line e-mail utility from *WINDOWS* Magazine listings.[12] This command will allow you to send the logs off via e-mail:

---

12   MAILFILE.ZIP from any of the download locations specified in the *Electronic Update* section of the Introduction.

```
mailfile BACKUP.LOG to ADMINISTRATOR
```

The same approach can be used with the three-time-per-week status report in Example 1:

```
mailfile REPTNEW.TXT to ADMINISTRATOR
delete REPTNEW.TXT
```

Example 7 SMS Logon Script Curiously enough, despite Microsoft's tendency to ignore the command line and scripts in the NT documentation, the single most extreme example of NT batch file complexity we've seen (by far!) is the logon script used by Microsoft's own Systems Management Server (SMS) application. The script is far too long to reproduce here (even if Microsoft would permit us to do so), but it is discussed in Chapter 8, as is Microsoft's use of its TEST application to extend the concept of command scripts to graphical applications.

Extending NT Scripts with a Command Language As the examples above show, NT's built-in batch language is actually a good bit more powerful than most people think, but in some situations, it is inadequate. Some people also cringe at the idea of using a direct descendant of the DOS (and OS/2) batch language for enterprise applications.

For those who want a more powerful (or simply a more elegant) solution, several alternatives are shown in Table 3.3.

Summing up NT Scripts The ultimate future of scripting in NT doubtless is OLE2 automation and a universal command language, as outlined in Chapter 12. In the meantime, creative use of NT's built-in batch language and environment variables (augmented, if you like, with a third-party script language) provides a very useful alternative.

NT Administration: Still Not Perfect

Although the enhancements provided since NT debuted (not to mention SMS!) have greatly improved NT's manageability, NT Server suffers from at least three serious limitations in comparison to other network operating systems: changing drivers still generally requires a reboot; there is still no per-user accounting; and there is no way to set per-user resource quotas.

Such limitations are serious, especially at large sites. If you've spent the money to buy fault-tolerant hardware that supports hot-swapped hard disks and tape drives, it is a bit much to be forced to reboot every time you install a new driver (especially so for printers, a problem that wa solved with the introduction of the print spooler service in NT 3.5). SCSI devices and network protocols ought to be handled the same way. If you are supporting users from many organizations, the lack of a way to track how much time each has spent online can make cross-departmental charging all but impossible, and the lack of quotas makes NT all but unusable in educational institutions. If the system permits students to fill a hard disk, you can count on them to do so.

Still, all network operating systems have some problems, and I would rather worry about these issues than have to deal with server crashes when one more user is added than the

Table 3.3 Third-party Batch Languages for NT[13]

Product	Company	Address	Telephone	Notes
VLC **http://www.tiac.net/bbc**	Boston Business Computing	13 Branch St. Methuen, MA 01844	(508) 725-3222	Emulates Digital's VMS command language
OpenNT **http://www.softtway.com**	Softway Stystems	185 Berry St, Suite 5514 San Francisco, CA 94107	(800) 438-8649 (415) 896-0708	Posix.2 extenstions to NT Posix.1 subsystem
Perl5 **http://www.hip.com**	Hip Communications Inc.	#350-1122 Mainland Vancouver, BC, Canada V6B-5L1	(604) 606-4600	Perl language for NT (often used with Webservers)
Personal Rexx **http://www.quercus-sys.com**	Quercus Systems	P.O. Box 2157 Saratoga, CA 95070	(800) 440-5944 (408) 867-7399	REXX for Windows NT (common in OS/2 environments)
SLnet **http://www.seattlelab.com**	Seattle Labs	9606 N.E. 18th St. Bothell, WA 98011	(206) 402-6003	Multi-user telnet with common NT command shell
4DOS for Windows NT **http://www.jpsoft.com**	JP Software, Inc.	P.O. Box 1470, E. Arlington, MA 02174	(800) 368-8777	Improved command-line interpreter with batch processing
Batch Services for Windows NT **http://www.intergraph.com**	Intergraph Corp.	Huntsville, AL 35894	(800) 345-4856	Priority-based, network-wide scheduling of non-interactive jobs. Resubmits jobs automatically if the network is down
Hamilton C-Shell	Hamilton Labs	21 Shadow Oak Dr. Sudbury, MA 01776-3165	(508) 440-8307	Multithreaded NT port of OS/2-based UNIX shell toolkit (primarily useful for programmers). Includes both TAR and CPIO

Table 3.3 (Continued)

Product	Company	Address	Telephone	Notes
MKS Toolkit http://www.mks.com	Mortice Kern Sysystems, Inc.	185 Columbia St. W. Waterloo, ON, Canada N2L-5Z5	(800) 265-2797 (519) 884-2251	UNIX-style toolkit (primarily useful for programmers). Includes UNIX-compatible Tape Archive (TAR)
Queue Manager http://www.sunbelt.co.uk /aqmnt.htm	Argent Software	49 Main St., Torrington, CT 06790	(203) 489-5553	Job queueing and scheduling with workload support
Systems Management Server MS-TEST http://www.microsoft.com	Microsoft Corp.	One Microsoft Way, Redmond, WA 98052	(800) 426-9400 (206) 882-8080	MS-Test is a graphical scripting tool originally written for use in regression testing. (SMS is covered in Chapter 8.)
VX/DCL http://www.sector7.com	Sector 7 USA, Inc.	2802 W. 50th St, Austin, TX 78731	(512) 451-3961	NT implemention of VAX print and batch queue manager with DCL support
WinBatch http://www.windoware.com	Wilson WindowWare Inc.	2701 California Ave SW, Suite 212 Seattle, WA 98116	(800) 762-8383 (206) 938-1740	Advanced batch services for Windows applications—can send keystrokes to graphical apps. Supports DDE and OLE

13 This table presents selected, commercially available, batch/command language enhancements available for NT as of this writing (August 1996). A much wider range of products is available, including many excellent shareware products. To get a current list, browse the Advanced Search option of http://altavista.digital.com, and search for '(batch or command) near (language or shell) near "Windows NT".'

server's memory supports, as still happens on one of today's most popular NOSes. Moreover, every one of these limitations is an opportunity for an ambitious third-party developer. Let's hope some of them get the message!

Conclusion

In this chapter, you've learned what the responsibilities of the Network Administrator are, how to create user accounts and account groups, how to assign user permissions, how to monitor performance and log events, and how to write command scripts. You should be ready to get your users online, and in Chapter 4 we will look at how users can exploit the networking features of Windows NT.

For More Information

Microsoft Staff (1996), *Windows NT Server Concepts and Planning Guide.* Redmond, WA: Microsoft Corp. Included with NT Server (full version) and the NT documentation kit. Electronic version in NT Server CD Books Online. Excellent overall coverage of Windows NT concepts from the administrator's point of view.

Microsoft Staff (1996), *Windows NT System Guide.* Redmond, WA: Microsoft Corp. Included with NT Workstation. Basic information on administrative tools, including User Manager, Performance Monitor, etc. Note that the similar *Windows NT Server System Guide* adds information for the domain-management tools, including User Manager for Domains, Server Manager, etc.

Microsoft Staff (1996), *Windows NT Resource Kit.* Redmond, WA: Microsoft Corp. Volumes 2 and 3 are especially helpful.

Using NT Networking Features

After reading this chapter, you will understand the basic networking features that are built into (or included with) Windows NT. You will also understand how to do the following:

- ➪ Share resources (including folders and printers) with other network users
- ➪ Use shared resources

You will be introduced to the utility programs that are bundled with Windows NT, including the NT 4.0 Desktop, Windows Messaging (electronic mail), Chat, the Printers folder, ClipBook, and the NET Command-Line interface. You should feel comfortable performing basic network operations like sharing files and devices, using mail, and sending messages after reading this chapter.

The Windows Explorer

Prior to version 4.0, Windows NT used a somewhat enhanced variant of the familiar Windows 3.x File Manager application to handle all file operations, including sharing files on the network and accessing shared files over the network. These file operations were separated from manipulating programs through use of the Program Manager application. In NT 4.0, this approach was fundamentally changed. All file operations. including those involving programs, are handled through the Windows Explorer.

Along with providing both program and file management functions, the Windows Explorer is now the Shell application for NT, providing a standard desktop with a Start Menu and several icons (Figure 4.1). Because this menu is the primary interface for using the system, we begin with a brief tour of the Explorer desktop and then focus on the specific features of the desktop that have networking implications. (Readers who have access to an NT 4.0 machine may wish to follow along on-screen, and those unfamiliar with the new user interface might find it helpful to press the Start button and select the Help item.)

NT 4.0 Desktop—A Brief Tour

Looking at the desktop in its default configuration, we can see a Start menu (by default, at the bottom of the screen) and several icons (by default, on the left side of the screen). In the NT 4.0 desktop, all of these menus and icons are *objects*; that is, they all have properties associated with them, and they can all be manipulated in a more or less consistent way.

Shortcuts The most pervasive concept in the NT 4.0 user interface is that of a shortcut, which is an icon or menu item that represents a document or program. Shortcuts do not need to be located in the same folder as the program or document to which they point. In fact, a single document or program can have multiple shortcuts pointing to it. When you look at the NT 4.0 desktop, practically everything you see is actually a shortcut!

Start Menu Let's begin with the Start menu at the bottom of the display. It combines a multilevel command menu (see Figure 4.2), which the user accesses by left-clicking on the Start button, with a *taskbar* containing buttons that represent the programs currently in use. Switching from one program to another is as easy as clicking that program's button. On the right end of the taskbar may be a system clock display, and this space can also be used for status information. (Both NT 4.0 dial-up networking and the exchange e-mail client will use the tray in this way if you so desire.)

FIGURE 4.1 NT 4.0 desktop.

Figure 4.2 shows a multilevel menu. Some items have an ➤ on their right edge, indicating that a submenu (or folder) is associated with that item. Moving the mouse over the ➤ or pressing the right arrow key on your keyboard causes the contents of the folder to be displayed.

The main folders in the Start menu structure are:

- Programs: shortcuts to programs (and folders containing more shortcuts)

- Documents: shortcuts to documents (files opened by programs)

- Settings: shortcuts to the control panel and printers folders and to a settings dialog for the taskbar

- Find: shortcuts to utility programs that help find files or folders on your machine and other computers on the LAN

- Help: a shortcut to the Windows NT helpfiles

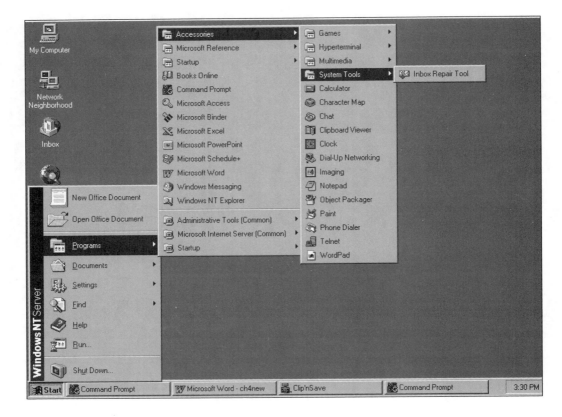

FIGURE 4.2 Start menu.

- Run... : a shortcut to a dialog box from which you can run programs

- Shut Down... : a shortcut to the dialog from which you shut down, restart, or log off Windows NT

Exploring the Desktop's Icons

In addition to the shortcuts in the Start menu, a number of shortcuts are in permanent view on the desktop itself (if you're following along on screen, you might want to double-click each in turn as we discuss it). These include:

- *My Computer*: A sort of "master" shortcut that gives you access to all aspects of your system, including both local and network disk drives and printers and system folders

- *Network Neighborhood*: A folder that contains shortcuts to all the computers in your workgroup or domain, as well as an Entire Network shortcut that gives you access to other domains and workgroups

- *Recycle Bin*: A folder into which Explorer places files when you delete them

  Note: *The Recycle Bin is used only by Windows Explorer. It provides no protection against files deleted from the command line.*

- *Briefcase*: For users who operate both desktop and notebook computers, a special folder that automatically synchronizes files copied into or out of the briefcase replacing any older copy of a file with the most recent version

Depending on what options you have installed, you may see shortcuts to other features (such as Internet Explorer, which is Microsoft's Web browser, the Inbox for Microsoft's Windows Messaging system, and a browser for the Microsoft Network on the desktop as well).

Views To this point, we've spoken about only double-clicking on a shortcut to open it, but other operations can be carried out on shortcuts. In particular, as objects, shortcuts have properties. Right-clicking on any shortcut will bring up a *context menu* (for example, see Figure 4.3) from which a number of operations can be performed. Perhaps the most interesting such operation for folder shortcuts is Explore, which will bring up an enhanced, Explorer view of the folder.

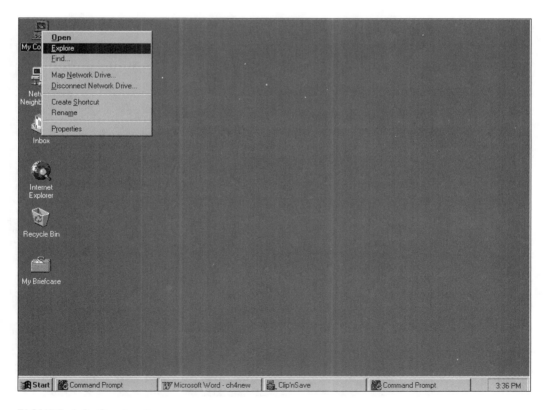

FIGURE 4.3 Context menu.

Exploring a folder gives you a two-pane view of its contents (see Figure 4.4), with a tree for all objects in the system on the left and the contents of the current folder on the right. This setup is reminiscent of the File Manager on the older NT 3.*x* user interface. At the top of the Explorer is a toolbar with iconic buttons for common operations, such as connect to or disconnect from a network drive, cut and paste, undo, and delete. (All the toolbar buttons have tooltips enabled—just move the mouse pointer over the button, and a label will appear.)

Aside from providing a more convenient way of looking at the contents of folders, Explorer view sometimes shows things that are hidden in the standard Open view. For example, exploring My Computer using the left pane's hierarchic view allows you to browse not only its contents, but also the Network Neighborhood and Recycle Bin.

Both the Open and Explorer views have a range of options associated with them (see View/Options), including whether to hide or show system files and file extensions, and whether to show compressed filenames in an alternate color. And, if you prefer a more Explorer-like view, you can modify Open to have a toolbar and status bar (see the top of the View menu) and to browse in a single window rather then opening a separate one for each folder you click (using View/Folder).

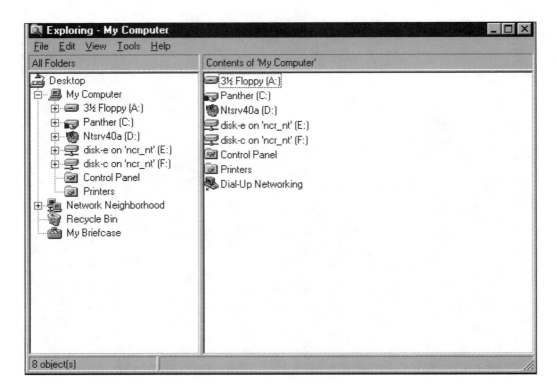

FIGURE 4.4 Explorer view.

Properties In addition to Opening and Exploring shortcuts, you can inspect their properties by right-clicking on a shortcut and then selecting Properties from the context menu. A Properties dialog will appear, containing settings specific to the shortcut you've clicked on. For the top-level shortcuts on the desktop, the Properties are:

- *My Computer*: Properties for the system itself, including Startup/Shutdown behavior, Hardware Profile, and User Profile settings (see Chapter 3 for details), Environment variables, and (if you have administrative privileges) foreground application performance and virtual memory settings. You can reach these same settings from the Control Panel's System item.

- *Network Neighborhood*: Properties for your network configuration, including your computer's name, the domain or workgroup you're logged in to, the services and protocols that are loaded, settings for your network adapter, and the *bindings* between protocols and services. You will need to be logged in as an administrator to change these settings, which can also be reached from the Control Panel's Networks item.

- *Recycle Bin*: Settings for the recycle bin on your computer allowing you to determine whether to use a single setting globally or a separate one for each disk, the maximum size the recycle bin's contents can reach, whether to actually copy files into the recycle bin or just delete them, and whether to confirm before permanently deleting files.

- *Briefcase*: Settings specific to the briefcase folder, including attributes, whether the briefcase is shared, and what security permissions are applied to it.

The same basic approach applies to any object in the system; right-click to see a context menu, and select Properties to see the settings for the object. For example, right-clicking on the taskbar and selecting properties produces a properties dialog with taskbar and Start menu settings (see Figure 4.5).

Now that we've had an overview of the Explorer, let's focus on some specific functions of interest to network users.

Exploring the Network

The key entry point for use of network resources in NT 4.0 is, of course, the Network Neighborhood folder on the desktop. This folder provides a simple graphical interface for easy browsing (either double-click to open or right-click and then select explore) to find network shared folders and printers. It also provides administrative users with an entry point to network settings (right-click, then select Properties from the context menu). Other network applications that the NT user may encounter include the Windows Messaging Inbox, Chat, the Printers folder, ClipBook, and the NET Command-Line interface. We will examine common tasks for each in turn.

Note that all of the tasks discussed here require specific user rights (granted or restricted with User Manager and/or the System Policy Editor—see Chapter 3 for details). By default,

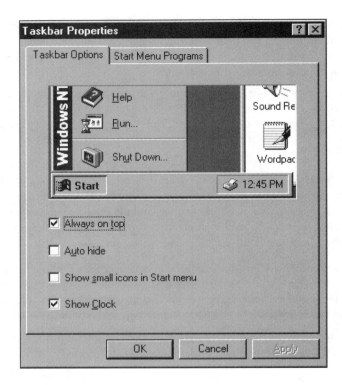

FIGURE 4.5 Taskbar properties.

users have the rights for most common operations. We identify cases in which special rights or an administrative login are required.

Sharing a Folder

To share a folder, simply browse My Computer until you find the folder you want to share, then click on the folder to select it and select File/Sharing... A properties page for the folder will appear (see Figure 4.6) with the Not Shared radio button selected by default. Select the Shared As: radio button to share the folder. You will need to fill in the share name (by default, it will be the same as the name of the folder).

Optionally, you may type in a comment and limit the number of users permitted to use the shared folder at any one time. You can also set permissions on the folder, as discussed in more detail below.

When you've filled in the fields, click the Apply button, and the share will be created. A New Share button will then appear, permitting you to create another share of the folder under another name. When you've created all the shares you require, click the OK button to exit the Properties dialog.

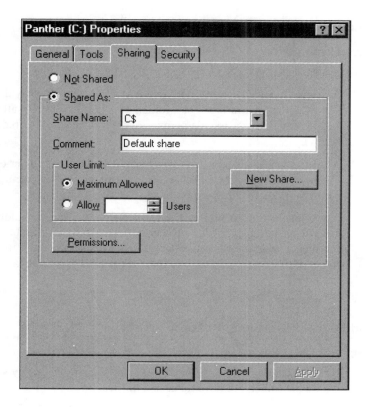

FIGURE 4.6 File/sharing properties.

Setting Folder and File Permissions

You can control who has access to your files and folders (or directories), as well as the extent of that access, using what Windows NT calls permissions (you must be an Administrator or Power User to manage permissions on shared directories). You can limit access on any *shared folder*, but you can restrict access only to *files* that use the Windows NT file system (NTFS).

Windows NT's set of standard permissions can be set for both files and folders.

Both shared folders and local folders on NTFS drives support the range of permissions listed in Table 4.1

Local folders on NTFS drives support some additional permissions shown in Table 4.2.

Permissions on a shared NTFS directory are cumulative with those set for sharing over the network (for users connecting over the LAN). If the permission is less extensive on the directory, the directory's permission takes precedence.

Permissions for files are listed in Table 4.3.

Table 4.1 Permissions for Folders

Access Right	Explanation
No Access	None.
Read	All rights from List permission. In addition, user can display the name of the owner and permissions of a folder. This permission also allows the same Read permissions as for file permissions for all files in the folder (see below).
Change	All rights from Add and Read. User can also delete the folder or any subfolders below the selected folder. This permission allows the same Change permissions as for file permissions for all files in the folder.
Full Control	All rights from Add and Read and Change permissions. In addition, users can change permissions for a folder or delete subfolders and the files in it (no matter what their permissions). Users can also take ownership of the folder. Full Control allows the same Full Access permissions as for file permissions.

Table 4.2 Additional Permissions for Local Folders

Access Right	Explanation
List	Display a folder's files and attributes. Users can move to any subfolder within the folder, but have no access to files.
Add	Same as List, plus the ability to add files to the folder.
Add and Read	All rights from Read permissions. In addition, the user can create subfolders, add files to the folder, and change the attributes of a folder.

Table 4.3 Permissions for Files

Access Right	Explanation
Standard permission	Access allowed
No Access	None.
Read	Display the file's data; view the file's attributes.
Change	In addition to Read activities, users can launch program files, change the file's attributes, and display the name of the file's owner and the permissions assigned to the file.
Full Access	In addition to the Read and Change activities, users can change or append data to the file.

To set permissions on a folder or disk drive:

1. Browse for the folder (or drive) in My Computer. Select it, and right-click to bring up its context menu. Select Properties to bring up the Properties dialog, select the Sharing tab (for shared folders) or the Security tab (for local security on NTFS devices), and click the Permissions button. A Permissions dialog box will appear (see Figure 4.7).

2. On an NTFS device, the changes you make may or may not affect subfolders and files, depending on the setting of the Replace Permissions on Subfolders and Replace Permissions on Existing Files check boxes.

3. You can change permissions, add new user permissions, or delete existing permissions as follows.

   a. To change a permission, select the name of the user group or the individual user whose permission you want to change. Select the permission type from the Type of Access pull-down list. Then click on OK.

   b. To add a user permission, click the Add... button. The Add Users and Groups dialog box appears (see Figure 4.8). Select the name(s) of the users or user groups you want to add and click the Add... button. The name(s) are added to the Add Names box. When all users have been added, click on OK.

   c. To delete a user permission, select the user, then click on Remove.

4. When you finish setting permissions, click OK to close the Permissions dialog box.

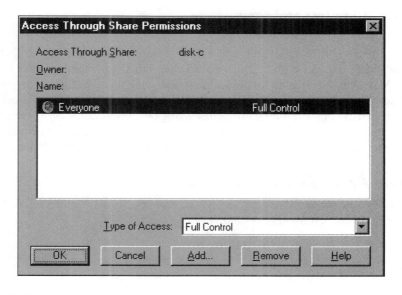

FIGURE 4.7   Share permissions.

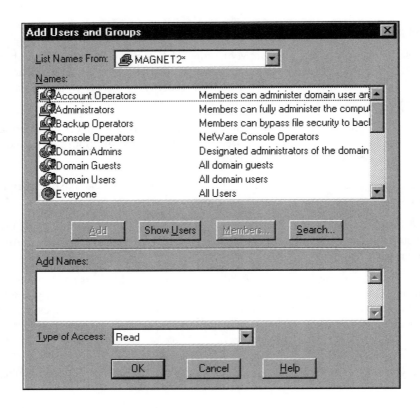

FIGURE 4.8 Add users and groups.

Setting file permissions is similar to setting folder permissions. By default, the File Permissions dialog box shows the permissions that are inherited from the folder in which it is contained. Managing file permissions is almost identical to managing folder permissions. Instead of selecting a folder, select one or more files, right-click to bring up the context menu, and select Properties. In the resulting properties dialog box, select the Security tab and click the Permissions button. The Permissions dialog will appear. Select the user(s) you want to remove or change, or click on the Add... button to grant user(s) permission to the selected file(s).

Special Access Permissions

If the standard permissions are not sufficient to limit access to files or directories, you can use a set of special access permissions as follows:

D   Delete

O   Take Ownership

P   Change Permissions

R   Read

W   Write

X   Execute

To set a *special access* permission:

1. Browse for the folder (or drive) in My Computer. Select it, and right-click to bring up its context menu. Select Properties to bring up the Properties dialog box, select the Sharing tab (for shared folders) or the Security tab (for local security on NTFS devices), and click the Permissions button. A Permissions dialog box will appear.

2. Select the user or user group to whom you want to grant special access. Select Special Access from the Type of Access drop-down list. The Special Access dialog will appear (Figure 4.9).

3. Select the check boxes for the access(es) you want to grant. Then click on OK to close the Special Access dialog box.

4. Click on OK to return to close the Permissions dialog.

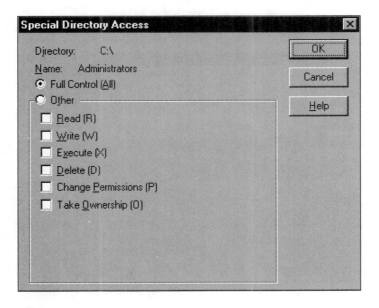

FIGURE 4.9 Special access.

Stop Sharing a Folder

When it is no longer necessary to share a folder, browse for it in My Computer, select File/Properties (or right-click on it and select Properties from the context menu), and select the Sharing tab. If multiple shares are open, select the appropriate one (using the Share Name drop-down list box), and click the Remove Share button. You can terminate all sharing of the folder by selecting the Not Shared radio button at the top of the dialog box. Click the Apply button to terminate your share(s), and click the OK button to close the Properties dialog box.

Auditing Files

Auditing provides a view of the users or user groups using your files or directories. The volume containing the file(s) must be an NT File System volume (NTFS volume).

To audit a file or directory:

1. Browse for the folder (or drive) in My Computer. Select it, and right-click to bring up its context menu. Select Properties to bring up the Properties dialog box, and select the Security tab and click the Auditing button. The File Auditing dialog box shown in Figure 4.10 appears.

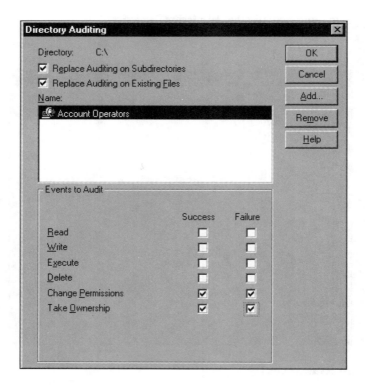

FIGURE 4.10 File auditing.

2. Set the Replace Auditing on Existing Files and/or Replace Auditing on Existing Subdirectories check-boxes if you want to audit existing files and/or directories. Leave the box empty (unchecked) if you want to audit only new files and subdirectories.

3. Click the Add... button. The Add Users and Groups dialog box appears. Select the user(s) or user group(s) you want to audit, and click Add to add them.

4. Choose the events you want to audit. A check in the corresponding box means that NTFS will audit the event; an empty box means it will not audit the event. You can audit the following actions for either (or both) success or failure:

   • Read

   • Write

   • Execute

   • Delete

   • Change permissions

   • Take ownership

5. Click on OK to close the Directory Auditing dialog box, and click OK again to exit Properties.

Ownership of Files

When you create a file or directory, you are its designated creator/owner. You, therefore, can grant permission to other users so that they can act as owner and, in turn, set permissions. When you grant another permission to take ownership of a file or directory, and that user takes ownership, you give up ownership of the file or folder in question.

If you are using an NTFS device, you must have adequate permission to take ownership.

To take ownership of one or more files or folders, browse for the appropriate icon(s) in My Computer and select them. Right-click to bring up the Permissions dialog box and select Properties. A Properties dialog box appears. Select the Security tab and click the Ownership button. The Owner dialog box appears (see Figure 4.11). Click the Take Ownership button. If multiple files or directories were selected, Windows NT asks if you want to take ownership of all selected items. Click Yes.

Controlling Compression

Beginning with version 3.51, Windows NT provides file compression on NTFS partitions. To compress a file, group of files, directory, or an entire disk, simply select the file(s), directory(ies), or disk(s) in question, right-click, and then select Properties from the context menu. The resulting Properties dialog box will have a Compressed check-box on its General tab. Check that box to compress your file(s), and un-check it to uncompress them.

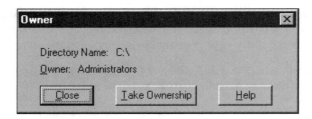

FIGURE 4.11 Owner.

If you've selected multiple files, Windows NT will ask if you want to compress all of them, and if you answer yes, compression will proceed automatically (uncompression works in exactly the same manner).

If you compress a directory and decline when asked if you want to compress files in the directory, the directory is marked for compression while existing files remain in their uncompressed form. Files will still be compressed automatically when copied or moved to the directory. Similarly, you can mark a compressed directory as Uncompressed without decompressing the files it contains.

Alternatively, you can control compression using the *compact* command-line function.

```
C:\>compact /?
Displays or alters the compression of files on NTFS partitions.

COMPACT [/C | /U] [/S[:dir]] [/A] [/I] [/F] [/Q] [filename [...]]

    /C        Compresses the specified files. Directories will be marked
              so that files added afterward will be compressed.
    /U        Uncompresses the specified files. Directories will be marked
              so that files added afterward will not be compressed.
    /S        Performs the specified operation on files in the given
              directory and all subdirectories. Default "dir" is the
              current directory.
    /A        Displays files with the hidden or system attributes. These
              files are omitted by default.
    /I        Continues performing the specified operation even after errors
              have occurred. By default, COMPACT stops when an error is
              encountered.
    /F        Forces the compress operation on all specified files, even
              those which are already compressed. Already-compressed files
              are skipped by default.
    /Q        Reports only the most essential information.
    filename  Specifies a pattern, file, or directory.

Used without parameters, COMPACT displays the compression state of
the current directory and any files it contains. You may use multiple
filenames and wildcards.  You must put spaces between multiple
parameters.
```

Running compact on a typical directory yields the following results:

```
C:\users\default>compact

Listing C:\users\default\
New files added to this directory will be compressed.

   404160 :    402944 = 1.0 to 1 C 05nav96.exe
      278 :       278 = 1.0 to 1 C jruley.htm
   481078 :     78848 = 6.1 to 1 C nt2.bmp
      231 :       231 = 1.0 to 1 C sql.bat
      211 :       211 = 1.0 to 1 C test.sql
     6623 :      5632 = 1.2 to 1 C urgent.TXT
        0 :         0 = 1.0 to 1 C WGPO

Of 7 files within 1 directories
7 are compressed and 0 are not compressed.
892,581 total bytes of data are stored in 488,144 bytes.
The compression ratio is 1.8 to 1.
```

Files are automatically decompressed when they are accessed over the network, so compression is completely transparent to client applications; however, you cannot assume that files copied to a partition will be compressed automatically unless you've marked the partition itself for compression.

Browsing the Network for Shared Folders

To use a shared folder from another system on the LAN, first browse for it using Network Neighborhood (remember that double-clicking will open an object in single-pane view; you can right-click on the object and Explore to get the two-pane view).

Once you find the folder you want, you have several options. You can simply double-click on the folder to open it and manipulate its contents directly, in which case it will act like any other folder on your system. You can press Ctrl+Click on the folder to make a shortcut, which you can drag to the desktop, making it easier to access the folder. Or you can map the folder to a network drive.

Mapping a Shared Folder to a Drive Letter Drive mapping is a holdover from DOS, where it was usually necessary to assign a drive letter to a shared folder so that programs—which knew nothing about the network—could deal with them. Drive mapping frequently isn't necessary in NT, but can be convenient, in part because mapped folders appear as "virtual disk drives" in My Computer. To map a shared folder to a drive letter, click once to select it, then right-click to bring up its context menu, and select Map Network Drive… A Map Network Drive dialog box will appear (see Figure 4.12). You will need to assign a drive letter to the share (by default, the system will pick the first unused letter). Optionally, you can choose to fill in the Connect As field with a username different from the one under which you are currently logged in. This option can be convenient if you log into multiple networks with different usernames

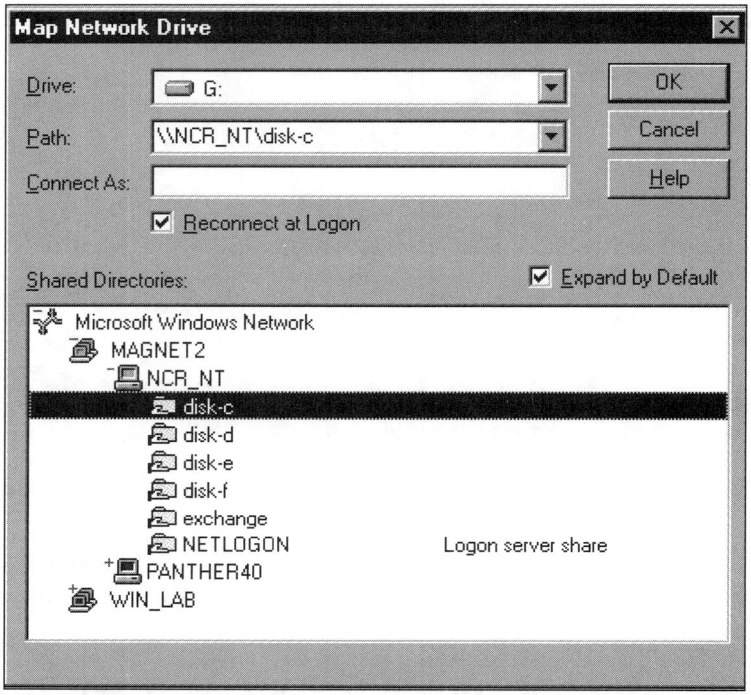

FIGURE 4.12 Map network drive.

and passwords (a mixed NT-NetWare LAN, for example). Indeed, in such situations mapping a shared folder to a drive letter may be the only way to use it at all!

You can also choose whether to check the Reconnect at Logon box (it is checked by default). If you do, the drive mapping will be reestablished automatically whenever you log in.

If you browse with Explorer view or have the Toolbar enabled in Open view (check the View/Toolbar menu item), you can also map shared files by clicking the Map Network Drive toolbar button (second from the left on the toolbar). Clicking that button produces a somewhat larger Map Network Drive dialog box, with an associated browsable list of Shared Folders. This view will be more familiar to users of NT 3.*x,* with which a very similar dialog was presented from File Manager. It's also more convenient to use if multiple drive mappings need to be established at one time.

Finally, it's also possible to map shared folders from the command line (see the Net Use command later in this chapter).

Terminating a Drive Mapping When you no longer need to use a particular mapped drive, you can disconnect from it. To do so, browse the mapped drive in My Computer, right-click to bring up its context menu, and select Disconnect. You may need to refresh your view (either select View/Refresh or press the F5 key) before the drive icon disappears.

Network Settings

To inspect (and if you have administrative permissions, change) settings for your computer's network card driver(s), protocol(s), network services, and bindings, select Start/Settings/Control Panel and open the Network icon by double-clicking on it (or you can right-click the Network Neighborhood icon and select Properties from the resulting context menu). The Network dialog appears (Figure 4.13). From the tabs on this dialog you can control virtually all network settings for your computer.

The Network Settings tabs are:

- *Identification*: The computer's identifying name and the name of the workgroup or domain to which it belongs (see Chapter 2 for details)

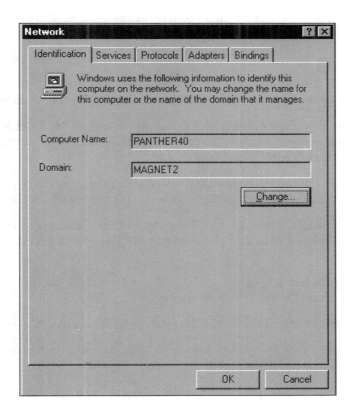

FIGURE 4.13 Network settings.

- *Services*: The various network software components, discussed in Chapters 1 (overview), 6 (TCP/IP), 8 (Remote Access / Dial-up Networking), and 10 (NetWare-Related)

- *Protocols*: The network protocols loaded on the system, discussed further in Chapters 6 (TCP/IP), 9 (NetBEUI), 10 (IPX), and Appendix 2

- *Adapters*: Drivers for your network card(s)

- *Bindings*: The links between and among the various network software components and the underlying hardware. We discuss disabling certain bindings to enhance Internet security in Chapter 7.

Other Settings

The Control Panel also contains several other items of interest to the network user. A few are of special interest:

- *Dial-Up Monitor*: Settings for a convenient set of simulated modem lights that are of real value when NT's dial-up networking feature is used (covered in Chapter 8)

- *Internet*: Settings for Microsoft's Internet Explorer (and compatible browsers) (covered in Chapter 7)

- *Licensing (NT Server only)*: License mode and settings (covered in Chapters 1 and 2)

- *Mail and Microsoft Mail Post Office*: Settings for the built-in Microsoft Messaging client and associated workgroup postoffice (covered below) or for Microsoft Exchange (covered in Chapter 8) if installed

- *Modems*: Universal Modem (unimodem) driver settings, used by the Hyperterminal application, and by dial-up networking /Remote Access (covered in Chapter 8)

- *Monitoring Agent*: A feature new to NT 4.0 and a valuable troubleshooting aid, providing password and network card descriptions used by NT's built-in network monitor (covered in Chapter 5)

- *ODBC*: Open Database Connectivity (ODBC) driver settings, used to connect database clients to server applications (covered in Chapter 12)

- *Printers*: Windows NT printer drivers and print queue management (covered below)

- *Server*: Information on file sharing, replication settings, shared devices in use, and administrative alerts (covered in Chapter 3)

- *Services*: Settings for invisible service applications that run in the background (covered in Chapter 3)

- *System*: Settings for your computer, including foreground application performance, virtual memory paging, environment variables, startup, recovery, hardware, and user profiles (covered in Chapters 3 and 5)

- *Tape Devices*: Drivers and settings for any tape backup devices in the system (covered in Chapter 2)

- *Telephony*: Standard telephony API (TAPI) driver settings used by the same programs as described for the Modem icon above

- *UPS*: Settings for an uninterruptible power supply, if in use (covered in Chapter 2)

Electronic Mail

Windows NT includes Windows Messaging, an electronic mail application that lets you send and receive messages to and from other users on your network. In addition to text messages, you can send files as attachments. You can save messages in a folder, delete them, or forward them to others.

The version of Windows Messaging bundled into Windows NT is sufficient for a single-server workgroup, but lacks advanced capabilities that would make it useful for electronic mail in a large organization. Microsoft offers an upgrade to this package called Exchange, which we discuss in Chapter 8. Most procedures described here apply equally to either version.

Windows Messaging uses *Postoffices*, collections of users, and a storage location on hard disk for messages. Incoming messages appear in the Inbox, though messages can be moved to other folders for better organization. Each incoming message includes the sender's name, a subject, and the date and time the message was received. An icon to the left of each Inbox message provides information about the message: an exclamation point indicates a high-priority message; a paper clip indicates there is an attachment to the message.

To Start Windows Messaging double-click the Inbox icon on the desktop. You may exit the Windows Messaging application in one of two ways. Because Windows Messaging may be in use by other applications, such as Microsoft's Schedule Plus, you may log out of the current session but keep the Windows Messaging application running (so that you can send meeting requests in Schedule+ via Windows Messaging) or exit Windows Messaging and terminate the application completely. To keep Windows Messaging running, select File/Exit. To quit Windows Messaging and stop the application, select File/Exit and Log Off.

Setting Up a Postoffice

When you create a new Postoffice, you are added as the administrator for the account. In this role, you may add or delete users as well as change their passwords.

To create a new Postoffice and an administrator account, double-click the Microsoft Mail Postoffice icon in the Control Panel. The Microsoft Mail Workgroup Postoffice Admin dialog box appears (see Figure 4.14). Select Create a new Workgroup Postoffice and click the Next button.

Enter the path to a disk or directory for storing messages and user files for the Postoffice in the Postoffice Location field (it isn't necessary to make up a new directory name because Windows Messaging will create a name for you). This path can be on a local hard disk, but is more usually set up on a network server. To select a network server, choose the Browse... button

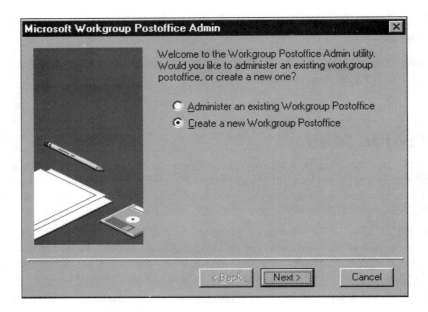

FIGURE 4.14 Postoffice Admin.

and find the appropriate network server and shared directory name, then click on OK. (You can create a Postoffice on a NetWare server if you grant full trustee rights to the NetWare directory in which the Postoffice is being created.) When you've filled in the Postoffice Location field, click the Next button. Windows Messaging will ask you to confirm the directory you just selected. Click the Next button again.

Windows Messaging will now ask you for the administration details, using the dialog box shown in Figure 4.15. An explanation of the administration data is shown in Table 4.4. After you enter the details, click on OK. Mail will advise you that it has created the workgroup postoffice, and it will remind you that the postoffice directory needs to be shared.

Once you've added a Postoffice, the next step is to add users. To add a user to a Postoffice, double-click the Microsoft Mail Postoffice icon in Control Panel. When the Microsoft Workgroup Postoffice Admin dialog box appears, select Administer an Existing Workgroup Postoffice, then click the Next button. Enter the Postoffice location (the default location will be filled in for you), and click the Next button. Then fill in the Mailbox and Password you entered when you created the postoffice, and click Next. The Postoffice Manager dialog will appear (see Figure 4.16).

Choose Add User... and enter the new user's information as listed in Table 4.4. Finally, click on Close.

To remove users from a Postoffice, select their names from the list and click the Remove User button. Select Yes to confirm your request, then click on Close.

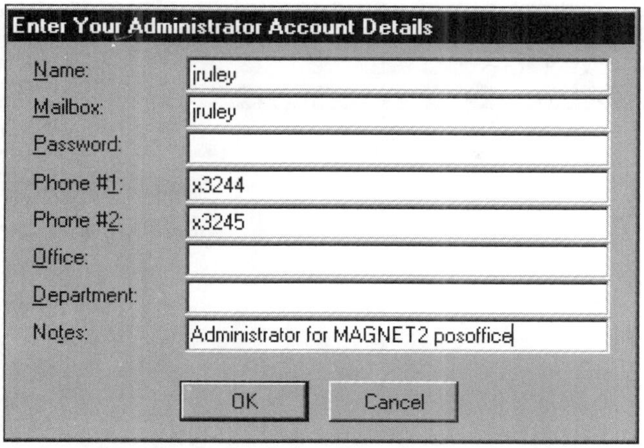

FIGURE 4.15 Administrator account details.

Table 4.4 User Information Needed by Windows Messaging

Information	Explanation
Name	Enter your full name (typically in first name, last name order).
Mailbox	The abbreviation for your mailbox must be unique (such as the first letter of your first name and your complete last name) and no more than 10 characters long. You will use it to log on to the mail system when you want to perform administrative duties. The name is *not* case sensitive. Enter letters or numbers only.
Password	To password protect access to your mailbox, enter a password of no more than eight characters, using letters and numbers only.

The following information is optional:

Information	Explanation
Phone #1	Your telephone number, up to 32 characters long
Phone #2	An alternative telephone number, such as a cellular phone, fax, or voice mail number, also up to 32 characters long
Office	A description of your office location, up to 32 characters
Department	A description of your department; 32 characters maximum
Notes	Any text you like, to a maximum of 128 characters

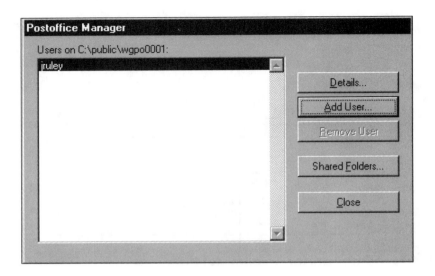

FIGURE 4.16 Postoffice Manager.

Connecting Your Computer to a Postoffice

Only an Administrator can add users to a postoffice. Once you've been added, you can connect to the postoffice this way:

1. Start the Windows Messaging application by double-clicking the Inbox icon on the desktop. The Windows Messaging Setup Wizard appears (Figure 4.17). Check the Microsoft Mail item in the list of information services, and click the Next button.

2. Enter the path to your postoffice. If necessary, click the Browse button, and look for it (it's normally named WGPO*nnnn*). Click the Next button.

3. Select your e-mail name from the list, and click the Next button. Enter your password and click the Next button.

4. Windows Messaging asks you for the location of your personal address book (.PAB) and personal folder (.PST) files. If you don't have them yet, it will create them for you. Click Next both times.

5. Windows Messaging confirms your setup. Click the Finish button. The Windows Messaging Inbox now appears (Figure 4.18), and you're ready to read and send mail.

Creating an Address List Once a Postoffice has been established, you'll want to get started creating messages. Windows Messaging provides an address book for you to store the most frequently used addresses. To maintain an address book, start the Windows Messaging Inbox and select Tools/Address Book. The address book (see Figure 4.19) appears.

Pick the address list you want from the Show Names From in drop-down box. To modify an existing name, right-click on it, and select Properties from the resulting context menu. To find

FIGURE 4.17 Windows Messaging Setup Wizard.

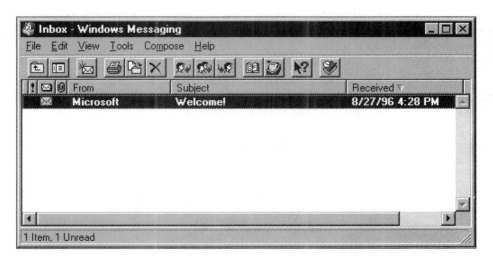

FIGURE 4.18 Inbox.

FIGURE 4.19 Address book.

a name, click on the magnifying glass button or select Tools/Find. To add a new address, select File/New Entry, and select the address type (normally Microsoft Mail Address) and the appropriate address book (normally your personal address book) from the New Entry dialog, and click OK. The New Microsoft Mail Address Properties dialog box appears. Enter the Alias (name), Mailbox (e-mail address), Postoffice, and Network. You can optionally check the Always send messages in Microsoft Exchange rich text format box. If you do, any messages to users of other mail systems will require a Microsoft Exchange gateway (see Chapter 8). Select OK to add the address or Cancel to return to the Address Book dialog box.

To remove a name from your personal address book, select the name, right-click on it, and select Delete from the resulting context menu. Names can be removed from the postoffice address list only by the Windows Messaging administrator.

Creating and Sending a Message

To create and send a message to one or more users in your Windows Messaging system:

1. Select Compose/New Message from the Windows Messaging Inbox. The New Message window shown in Figure 4.20 appears.

2. If you know the name(s) of the recipient(s), enter them in the To and Cc (carbon copy) boxes and go to step 4. If you do not know the names of the recipients, click on the To... or Cc... button as appropriate.

FIGURE 4.20 New message.

3. Windows Messaging displays the Address Book dialog box. It contains the names of the people in your Postoffice (the users to whom you can send a message) at the left of the window. Highlight the name(s) of the people to whom you want to send the message and click the To→ button (to add the name to the To: line) or the Cc→ button (to add the name to the list of carbon copy recipients). If you need to see the details for any user in the address list, select that user's name and click the Properties button. When all recipients have been entered, click on OK.

4. Type the subject of your message in the Subject line. This heading will appear when your message is displayed in the recipient's inbox.

5. Type the message in the area below the heading.

6. You can specify that Windows Messaging take action when you send your message. To set optional message handling options, select File/Properties. Choose Read Receipt or Delivery

Receipt and Save Copy in the Sent Items folder if you wish Windows Messaging to send you a message indicating the message was read/delivered or if you wish Windows Messaging to save the message (for possible resending later to the same or other users). Select the priority (high- and low-priority messages are displayed with a different icon in the recipient's Inbox). And choose the level of Sensitivity. When you are satisfied with the Properties, click OK.

7. To send the message, select File/Send.

Attaching a File to a Message

Besides sending plain text, you can attach one or more files to a mail message. Files can contain anything you like: sound, graphics, word processing or spreadsheet documents, Web pages, etc. Windows Messaging represents attached files by displaying an icon within the message area wherever you have positioned a file.

To attach a file to a message, compose the message text in the message area as described above. Then select Insert/File. Enter the name of the file you want to attach, or select it by browsing through the drive/directory listing. You can choose to insert the entire file as an attachment, insert text from the file as message text, or just insert a shortcut to the file's original location (which makes for smaller messages, but requires that your recipient have a live network connection to the file's location). When you are satisfied, click OK. If you choose to use an attachment or link, Windows Messaging displays an icon of the file, which you can reposition within the message area.

Replying to Messages

To read a message, select it from the list in the Windows Message Inbox and double-click on it. After reading the message, you can send a reply to the sender or, if the message was sent to multiple users, to all the recipients of the original message. To reply to *only the original sender* of a message, select Compose/Reply to Sender. Select Compose/Reply to All to send your message to *all recipients of the original message*. Windows Messaging automatically fills in the To name with the sender's name. The original message is also displayed in the message section; you can edit or delete it if you wish.

You can *add* names to the address list (in the To or Cc areas), entering them directly by clicking the To… and Cc… buttons as you would when creating a new message.

Enter your text in the message area, then select File/Send to send the message.

Windows Messaging Administration

Several tasks can be handled by the administrator of a Postoffice. These tasks include changing a password, reducing disk space, and moving a Postoffice to a new location.

Changing a User Password To change a Windows Messaging user's password, double-click the Microsoft Mail Postoffice icon in Control Panel. When the Microsoft Workgroup Postoffice Admin dialog box appears, select Administer an Existing Workgroup Postoffice, then click the Next button. Enter the Postoffice location (the default location will be filled in for you), and click the Next button. Then fill in the Mailbox and Password you entered when you created the postoffice, and click Next. The Postoffice Manager dialog will appear. Select the user name from the list, then click on Details. Enter the new password in the Password box and click on OK. Then click on Close.

Managing Postoffice Space As the number of users in your Postoffice grows, or as message volume increases, you will want to manage the disk space being used. You can also compress a Postoffice to recover some disk space.

To manage disk space, double-click the Microsoft Mail Postoffice icon in Control Panel. When the Microsoft Workgroup Postoffice Admin dialog appears, select Administer an Existing Workgroup Postoffice, then click the Next button. Enter the Postoffice location (the default location will be filled in for you), and click the Next button. Then fill in the Mailbox and Password you entered when you created the postoffice, and click Next. The Postoffice Manager dialog will appear. Click on the Shared Folders button.

To compress disk space, notify all Windows Messaging users with access to the folder, and ask them to close the folder on their workstations. *Do not begin compression until all users have closed their folders; otherwise, you could lose messages.* Click the Compress button to begin the disk compression. When Windows Messaging tells you that the compression is complete, click on Close.

Moving a Postoffice As a network changes or a Postoffice grows, you may find it necessary to move a Postoffice to a new location. To move a Postoffice to another drive or directory, notify all Postoffice users that they must sign out of the Windows Messaging system and advise them that you are moving the Postoffice. *Failure to have all users log out of the Windows Messaging system could result in data loss.*

Browse My Computer to find the WGPO*nnnn* directory of the drive where Windows Messaging is installed. WGPO*nnnn* is the standard (default) location of Windows Messaging systems. Select File/Cut. Browse the new location for the folder, and select Edit/Paste.

To share the Postoffice, select the WGPO directory, select File/Sharing…, and check the Shared As radio button. Verify that the name of the Postoffice is displayed in the Share Name box. Check the Re-share At Startup check box. Then click the OK button.

Advise the users of the new location (if you didn't do so before making the change), because they'll be asked for it the next time they log in.

Schedule Plus

Windows NT 3.*x* came with a 32-bit version of Microsoft's Schedule Plus 1.0 time management software. This is obsolete, and has been replaced by the newer Schedule Plus 2.0[1] application bundled in Microsoft Office 95.

---

1   The 2.0 version itself seems to be in the process of being replaced by Microsoft's new Outlook personal information management product, expected to debut with the Office 97 suite.

Chat

The Chat application lets you conduct an interactive conversation with another person on your network. Unlike Windows Messaging, in which users send text messages and await a reply, Chat provides two windows for immediate, real-time conversations. One window is used by you for entering text; the other window displays what the other user is typing.

To start the Chat application, select Start/Programs/Accessories/Chat. The main Chat window is shown in Figure 4.21.

Starting a Chat Session To start a chat session (conversation), click on the Dial button in the toolbar or select Conversation/Dial. Enter the computer name of the person you want to talk with in the Select Computer box. If the person answers, Chat displays a message in the status bar. You may begin typing in the top or left-most window. The response from the other user is displayed in the other window.

Note that the NetDDE service on which Chat depends is not started by default, because it may have an adverse performance impact on overall network throughput. If you can tolerate the overhead and want to be able to Chat at will, go to the Start/Settings/Control Panel, open the Services item, and configure the NetDDE service for Automatic startup.

Answering a Call If you are the party being called, you will hear a short sound, and a message will appear in the Chat status bar. If you are not running Chat, the program begins running minimized as a button on the taskbar, indicating that someone wants to start a conversation. To answer a call, click on the Chat taskbar button, if necessary, to open the application, then select Conversation/Answer.

FIGURE 4.21 Chat.

You and the person you are chatting with can enter text at the same time. As you type, your letters are visible to the other user, and vice versa. You can jump between windows—for example, you can copy text from the other user's window and paste it into your window. (To move between windows, select the other window with the mouse or press F6.)

The standard Windows NT text selection procedures (for example, highlight the text using the mouse or keyboard) are used in the Chat windows.

Ending a Chat Session To end a conversation, click on the Hang Up button on the toolbar or select Conversation/Hang Up. Either party can end a session at any time. If the other user hangs up before you do, Chat displays an informational message in the status bar.

To end the Chat application itself, select Conversation/Exit.

Print and Printer Management

Print Management has changed significantly in NT 4.0. The Print Manager application used in NT 3.x has been replaced by the Printers folder, shown in Figure 4.22, which contains icons for any printers you may have installed on your system and a template icon for new printer definitions called Add Printer. Once a printer has been installed, its icon will open to present a printer window with most of the same capabilities as the NT 3.x Print Manager.

Under the hood, NT 4.0 inherits the spooler-as-a-service printing model introduced in NT 3.5, but with a significant enhancement: rendering is now performed by the print server rather than by the client workstation. This change provides a significant enhancement in performance for the end user, because applications can return control as soon as a print job is spooled, without waiting for rendering to be completed. It also reduces network traffic.

The Printer Window, shown in Figure 4.23, displays a list of the documents being printed or in the print queue; it also lists the time the documents were generated and their size (the number of pages and the print file size in bytes).

Document Information

To see detailed information about a job waiting to be printed, select the document, then select Document/Properties.

FIGURE 4.22 Printers folder.

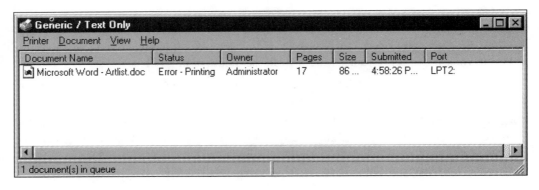

FIGURE 4.23 Printer window.

Managing the Print Queue

When you open a Printer Window associated with a printer, it shows you a list of the documents waiting to be printed, listed in the order in which they will be printed. To change the priority of a document, select it, and select Document/Properties; then adjust the Priority slider to give the document a higher or lower priority. Select OK to set the new priority.

To stop the printing of a *single* document, select the document, then choose Document/Pause. The Printer window displays "Paused" after the document description. To resume printing, select Document/Resume.

To stop printing a document *and* remove it from the print queue, select the document, then choose Document/Cancel. To remove *all* documents in the print queue, select Printer/Purge Printer.

You can temporarily stop printing *all jobs* by selecting the printer, then selecting Printer/Pause. The Printer window displays "Paused" after the printer description in the Printers list. To resume printing, select Printer/Resume.

Note: To see the most current print information, press F5 or select View/Refresh.

Creating a Printer Definition You can print a document on a printer only after you have created a printer definition and, if necessary, added the necessary print driver.

To create a new printer definition:

1. Select Add Printer from the Printers folder (Start/Settings/Printers). The Add Printer Wizard appears, as shown in Figure 4.24.

2. If you are installing a new printer locally, select the My Computer radio button. If you are connecting to a print server, select the Network Print Server button. Then click the Next button.

3. If you selected My Computer in step 2, you will see a list of local printer ports. Select the one to which your printer is connected. You will also have the opportunity at this point to add a port and associated print monitor software (which may be necessary for certain

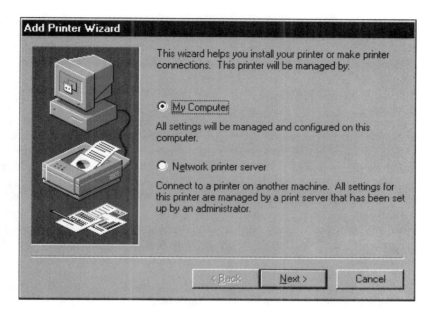

FIGURE 4.24 Add printer wizard.

specialized printers and fax cards—consult your print manufacturer's documentation for details) or configure a port (adjusting its timeout period, for instance). You can also Enable Printer Pooling, which has the effect of making several physical printers appear as a single print queue. After you are satisfied with your port settings, click the Next button and skip to step 5.

4. If you selected Network Print Server in step 2, you will see a Connect to Printer dialog. Browse the network, find the printer you want, and select it. Then click the OK button. If you are connecting to an NT print server and it has a compatible print driver installed, this will complete your installation. You'll get a "successfully installed" message and can just click the Finish button. Otherwise, you must install a print driver.

5. To install a print driver, pick the manufacturer and model of your printer from the list. If your printer isn't listed, try one of the Generic models, or get an NT 4.0 print driver diskette from your print manufacturer (NT 3.x print drivers are not compatible with NT 4.0). When you have the correct make and model specified, click the Next button.

6. Type in a name for your printer (NT will create a name using the make and model by default). Although you can type in a long, descriptive name that will work with NT and Windows 95 clients, DOS and Windows 3.x clients will be able to work with only printers that have DOS-style 8.3 (eight-character name plus three-character extension) names. You can also specify whether this printer is to be used as the default for all Windows applications

on your system by using the Yes and No radio buttons. When you are satisfied with the printer name and default settings, click the Next button.

7. The Add Printer Wizard asks if you want to share the printer, and if you do, asks you to designate the shared name for the printer. As with the local print name set in step 6, older DOS and Windows applications will work best with a short (8.3) name.

8. If you are sharing the printer, the Add Printer Wizard asks you to designate all the client operating systems that will be accessing the printer. By doing so, you enable your NT print server to download an appropriate print driver to each client, eliminating the need for local print drivers and significantly easing the most common administration problem encountered in network printing—improper drivers loaded at the client. Windows NT 3.1, 3.5/3.51, and 4.0 are supported through this method, as is Windows 95 (DOS, Windows 3.x, and OS/2 clients require local print drivers). Note that RISC-based NT systems use different print drivers from those in Intel-based systems, so in an environment with a mix of both Intel and RISC systems, you will need to load multiple drivers even if all clients are running NT 4.0. When you have all necessary client operating systems selected, click the Next button.

9. The Add Printer Wizard offers to print a test page. Printing it is not absolutely required, but is an exceedingly good idea. Then click the Finish button.

Removing a Printer and Disconnecting from a Network Printer To remove a printer from your system, including any associated print driver(s), open the Printers folder (Start/Settings/Printers), select the printer you want to remove, and select File/Delete. Select Yes to confirm your request. You can use the same steps to disconnect from a network printer.

Connecting to a Network Printer You can connect to a network print server using the Printer folder's Add Printer icon, as described above, but there's an even easier way to do it: browse the Network Neighborhood to find the computer and printer you wish to use, and double-click the printer's icon. A dialog box will appear asking if you want to perform the necessary setup steps to support the printer. Answer Yes, and it will all be handled for you!

To disconnect from a printer on your network, select Printer/Remove Printer Connection, or click on the Remove Printer Connection button on the toolbar. Select Yes to confirm your request.

Sharing a Printer To share a printer that is connected locally on a network, select the Printer window for the printer you want to share, then select Printer/Sharing... Designate it as shared, type in the name, and select appropriate drivers as in step 8 of Creating a Printer Definition, above. When you are satisfied with your settings, click OK to share the printer.

Setting the Default Printer To set a printer as the default printer, causing all document output to be directed to it, open its Printer window and select Printer/Set As Default Printer.

Security Options for Printers

A unique feature of Windows NT is the ability to track the users or groups accessing a printer. To audit a printer, open its icon in the Printers folder, select Printer/Properties, click the Security tab, and then click the Auditing button. Choose the user or group name you want to monitor. If the name is not listed, select Add, select the Names and Type of Access, then select Add.

Next, using the check boxes in the Events to Audit box, select the events you want to monitor, then select OK.

You can also change the permissions granted to a printer. Select Printers/Properties, then the Security tab, and click the Permissions button. To add a user or group name to the permissions, select Add. Select a name from the Name list and an access from the Type of Access pulldown list box, then click on OK.

To change the permission of a user or group, select the user or group name from the Name list in the Printer Permissions dialog box. Select the permission from the Type of Access pulldown list.

To delete a permission, select the user or group name from the Name list and select Remove. Click the OK button once to close the Permissions dialog box and again to close the Properties dialog box.

Fax Applications

One major problem area for those upgrading from Windows for Workgroups (WFWG) to NT is the lack of any native[2] fax support built in to the operating system. From version 3.11 on, Windows for Workgroups provided at-work fax support—which Windows 95 inherited—and of course, there are many fax applications for DOS and 16-bit Windows. With rare exceptions, these applications will not work under Windows NT. They depend on providing a "print-to-fax" driver, and NT's print driver architecture differs significantly from that in 16-bit Windows or DOS.

Fortunately, this problem area was seen as an opportunity by several independent software vendors, and over the last few years quite a few third-party fax solutions have appeared for Windows NT. They range from single-user systems all the way up to automated fax-back servers and enterprise fax routing solutions. A list[3] is provided in Table 4.5.

ClipBook

Windows NT's clipboard is an intermediate area used for cutting or copying data within or between applications. It's also part of a larger concept that extends the notion of copying between applications to copying between computers on a network. You can save the contents of your clipboard in a storage area called the Local ClipBook. Each item is stored on a separate ClipBook page, and pages can be arranged in several ways. In addition, you can share the contents of your Local ClipBook with those on your network, and access the contents of other shared ClipBooks.

---

2   Beginning with version 3.51, NT supports a limited form of built-in support for 16-bit applications, specifically Delrina's WinFax. Microsoft has announced that native support for MS At-Work fax (essentially a print driver coupled to the Windows Messaging Inbox) will be made available at some point after NT 4.0 ships, but as this book is written, we still haven't seen any sign of it.

3   The list is current as of this writing (August 1996); however, we cannot vouch for whether these applications properly support NT 4.0, which has a significantly different print spooler architecture from that of NT 3.51. We recommend that you check with the vendors.

Table 4.5 Fax Applications for NT

Product	Company	Address	Telephone	Notes
FacSys http://www .facsys.com	Optus	100 Davidson Ave. Somerset, NJ 08873	(908) 271-9568	32-bit fax server with 16- and 32-bit clients. Supports most e-mail systems. Class 1 and 2 fax modems. Single-user version under development.
Fax Sr. http://www .omtool.com	Omtool	8 Industrial Way, Salem, NH 03079	(800) 886-7845 (603) 898-8900	Multiuser fax print server. Multiplatform clients. Supports most e-mail systems (including MS-Exchange). Requires class 2 fax modem.
FaxFacts Server http://www .copia.com	Copia International	134 Avalon St. Wheaton, IL 60187	(800) 689-8898 (630) 682-8898	Extremely high-end fax-on-demand server. Many options.
Faxination Enterprise Server http://www .fenestrae.com	Fenestrae Inc.	7094 Peachtree Ind. Blvd., Suite 280 Norcross, GA 30071	(770) 446-2280	High-performance fax gateway for MS-Exchange.
FaxMaker http://www .gfifax.com	GFI Fax & Voice Ltd.	14 Pavillion Ct. 7 Nursery Rd London SW19 4JA, London, UK	(011) 44-181-9441108	Multi-line fax server with e-mail gateway, routing, voice-mail support. A dedicated fax gateway for MS-Exchange is also available.
FAXport WINport RASport http://www .lansource.com	LANSource Technologies	221 Dufferin St., Suite 310A, Toronto, Ontario M6A3J2 CANADA	(800) 677-2727 (416) 535-3555	Network fax and modem sharing servers, can use NT RAS connections. Supports many mail systems.
HyperKit http://www .vinfo.com /rlc	Response Logic Corp.	One Kendall Square S2200 Cambridge, MA 02139	(215) 558-2523	Development tools for voice, telephony, and fax services. Integrates with MS-Access database.

(Continued)

Table 4.5 (Continued)

Product	Company	Address	Telephone	Notes
LanFax **http://www .alcom.com**	Alcom Corp USA	1616 N. Shoreline Blvd. Mountain View, CA 94043-1316	(415) 694-7000	High-end 32-bit client/server fax, with inbound routing and server-based shared phone book. Supports DDE.
LG-Fax **http://www .net-shopper .uk/lg**	Lipp & Grau Software GbR	St.-Ulrich-Str. 22 D-80689 Munich GERMANY	(+49-89) 546-10684	Fax server with 16- and 32-bit clients. Address book, auto-redial.
Lightning Fax 4.0 **http://www .faxserver .com**	Interstar Technologies	5835 Verdun Ave., Suite 302 Verdun, Quebec H4H1M1 CANADA	(514) 766-1668	High-end fax server with WAN support, multiple fax card support, e-mail gateway, etc.
Telcom FAX 3.0 **http://www .ltc.com**	LTC	1541 E. Lake Rd. Skaneateles, NY 13152	(315) 673-1820	32-bit fax server with MAPI gateway. Supports class 1 and 2 fax modems. SDK.
Zetafax **http://www .zetafax.com**	Equisys Ltd.	45 Curlew St. London SE1 2ND UK	(+44-171) 403-2227	32-bit fax server with 16- and 32-bit clients. Requires class 2 modem.

Windows NT provides a ClipBook Viewer that lets you examine what is on the clipboard and what you have saved to the Local ClipBook.

To start the ClipBook Viewer application, Start/Programs/Accessories/ClipBook Viewer. You'll see the ClipBook application illustrated in Figure 4.25

The Clipboard Most Clipboard content is created when you select Edit/Copy from within an application. To save information from a character-based NT, DOS, or OS/2 application, open the application's control menu box (the icon in the upper left corner) or hold down the Alt key, and press the spacebar. Select Edit/Mark and mark the data you want to copy by using the arrow keys until the selection is highlighted. Select the control menu box again and select Edit/Copy.

To copy the contents of the Clipboard into a Windows-based application, move to the application and select Edit/Paste from the application's main menu. To paste the contents of the Clipboard into a character-based application, switch to the destination application and position the cursor or insertion point where you want the clipboard contents to be placed. Hold down the Alt key, and press the spacebar to display the Non-Windows-NT application's control menu. Select Edit/Paste.

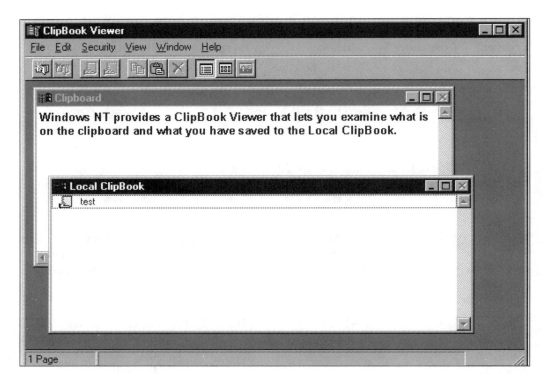

FIGURE 4.25 Clipbook.

You can also save screen images to the Clipboard. To save the contents of the currently displayed window to the Clipboard, hold down the Alt key, and press PrintScreen. To save the contents of the entire screen, just press PrintScreen.

To delete the current contents of the clipboard, activate the ClipBook Viewer, then select Edit/Delete (or press the Del key). Click on Yes to confirm your request.

To copy a page from a ClipBook to an application, first copy it to the clipboard. Select the page you want from the ClipBook, then select Edit/Copy or click on the Copy button in the toolbar.

By default, the ClipBook Viewer displays the data in its native format. You may wish to view the data in another format, such as to view the embedded codes in a word processing file. To view the contents of the clipboard in a different format, select the View menu and choose the desired format from those listed. To view the contents in its original format, select View/Default Format.

To save the contents of the clipboard to a file, select the ClipBook Viewer and choose File/Save As. Enter a file name with the .CLP file extension and click on OK. To open a Clipboard file, select File/Open, select the file, and click on OK. If the clipboard is *not* empty, the viewer asks if you want to clear the contents of the clipboard. Select No and save the clipboard, or select Yes to discard the contents and display the selected file.

You can also save the contents of the Clipboard to your local ClipBook. To do so, select the Local ClipBook window. Select Edit/Paste (or click on the Paste button in the toolbar) to place the contents in the local ClipBook. Type the name of the page in the Page Name text box. This name is used when you sort pages using the Table of Contents option. To share the page with other users, check the Share Item Now check box. Click on OK. If you opted to share the page, the Share ClipBook Page dialog box is displayed. Enter the options and select OK.

ClipBook Pages To share a page from your ClipBook with other computers, select the ClipBook page, then select File/Share… You can check the Start Application on Connect box if you want to have the application used to create a page start automatically when the page is connected. You can also set permissions on the page using the Permissions button. Once you're satisfied with the sharing properties, click the OK button.

To stop sharing the page, select it and choose File/Stop Sharing.

To use pages from another ClipBook that is shared on another computer, select File/Connect. Type in the name of the computer or select it from the Computers list, then click on OK.

To disconnect from the ClipBook, select File/Disconnect (or click on the Disconnect button on the toolbar).

In addition to sharing ClipBook pages, you can protect them. To set the access permissions for a ClipBook page, select the page, then choose Security/Permissions. Select the name of the user or group whose permissions you want to change, select the permission from the Type of Access pulldown list, and select OK.

To remove all ClipBook permissions for a group, select the user or group name and select Remove. To add permissions, select Add, select the user(s) and/or group(s), and select the permission you want to grant, then click on OK.

You can also take ownership of a ClipBook page. To take ownership, select the page you want, choose Security/Owner, and select Take Ownership.

Arranging ClipBook Pages You can arrange your ClipBook pages in three ways. To view ClipBook pages alphabetically by name, select View/Table of Contents. To view small images of each page, select View/Thumbnails. To view the entire contents of a ClipBook page, select View/Full Page.

Auditing ClipBook Pages Auditing allows you to keep track of who is using images in *your* ClipBook. To audit a ClipBook page, select the page, then choose Security/Auditing. Select the group or user name you want to track. Choose the event(s) you want to audit, then select OK.

To add a user or group to an existing audit list, click on the Add button, select the names of the group(s) or user(s) you want to add, and click OK. To remove a user or group, select the user or group name and click on Remove.

Network Operations from the Command Line: The NET Commands

Although it's usually easier to use the graphical utility programs like Windows Explorer and User Manager, sometimes a command-line interface is more convenient. The Windows NT NET commands fill this need. Essentially, every network operation that can be conducted from a graphical program can be done in this way. Aside from simple convenience, the Net interface has two major advantages: the syntax is consistent across all LAN Manager-derived networks, so users familiar with the LAN Manager, LAN Server, MS-Net, or Windows for Workgroups NET commands will immediately be comfortable in NT. Also, the NET commands can be employed in batch files.

Five of these commands are helpful for general use as command-line alternatives to the functions normally accomplished from Windows Explorer, the Printers folder, or the Control Panel. And one, Net Send, has no graphical equivalent. These end-user commands can be used as shown in the following sections.

Listing the Available Network Commands: *Net* If you type *net* at the command prompt, a list of the available commands will show on the display screen. This feature is handy when you can't remember the particular command you want, and you can use it in conjunction with net help to quickly find the command you want. A slightly better formatted list of commands will be printed if you type *net help* without any arguments.

Getting Help for Network Functions: *Net Help* and *Net Helpmsg* When you know you want to use a particular NET command, but can't remember the command syntax, typing *net help* <command> will provide a brief description of the command and its arguments. For instance, *net help view* prints the following message:

```
net help view
The syntax of this command is:

NET VIEW [\\computername | /DOMAIN[:domainname]]

NET VIEW displays a list of resources being shared on a server. When used
without options, it displays a list of servers in the current domain.

\\computername          Is a server whose shared resources you want
                        to view.


/DOMAIN:domainname      Specifies the domain for which you want to
                        view the available servers. If domainname is
                        omitted, displays all domains in the local area
                        network.
```

Just type *net help* without arguments for a formatted list of the net commands.

Note: Many of the screens displayed by net help *are quite long. If material goes by too fast for you to read, you may find the* \more *command helpful. For instance,* net help use \more *will display help on the* NET USE *command, but will do so one screen at a time.*

Viewing and Browsing the Network: *Net View* You can view lists of servers and browse shared network resources from the command line just as easily as you can from Windows Explorer. Type *net view* without any arguments for a list of servers. To view shared resources at a server, type *net view* <server name>. In a multi-domain/workgroup) network, type *net view* /DOMAIN for a list of domains and workgroups and net view /DOMAIN:<domain name> to see a list of servers in the specified domain or workgroup.

Net view is most often used in conjunction with the NET USE command to access shared resources on other computers. A typical use begins with *net view* (no arguments) to get a list of server names, then one views the resources on a server, and finally employs *net use* to access the shared resource in question. For instance:

```
net view

Servers on MAGNET1:

\\MIPS-LAB-SERVER
\\JOHNR-NT486-66

net view \\JOHNR-NT486-66

Shared resources at \\johnr-nt486-66:

Sharename   Type   Used as   Comment
---------------------------
disk-d      Disk   Z:
PUBLIC      Disk   Public Shared Space
```

One could then employ *net use* to access the Public share, for instance, by typing:

```
net use Q: \\johnr-nt486-66\public
```

Sharing Folders: *Net Share* Use the NET SHARE command to share folders from the command line. To share a folder, type *net share* <sharename>=<folder to share>. For instance, the command *net share disk-d=d:* will share the entire d: disk (and all subfolders) with the sharename disk-d. Other users (provided they have user accounts on your system) will be able to access this folder using the NET USE command or by appropriate actions in Windows Explorer. To designate how many users can access the share at any one time, set the */users:*<number> switch. This can be useful if, for instance, you are sharing data files that only one user can safely access at a time. Or you can use the */unlimited* switch if there is no upper limit you wish to enforce (this is the default). If you want an explanatory remark to be associated with a share, you can use the */remark*: "<your text here>" flag. Be sure to type the quote marks.

You cannot share printers the same way—you must use the Printers folder for this activity (Windows NT's printers are tied very closely to the Win32 subsystem, so a Windows driver must be selected before a printer can be shared).

You can delete both shared folders and shared printers from the command line by typing *net use* <sharename> */delete*. Doing so will eliminate the share and terminate any outstanding connections (functionally, this is the same as performing a "Stop Sharing" command in Windows Explorer or the Printer's window).

Typing *net share* without any arguments will display information on the shares currently active (including administrative shares, if you are logged in with administrative privilege). For example:

```
net share

Sharename   Resource      Remark
-----------------------------------------
ADMIN$      C:\winnt      Remote Admin
A$          A:\           Default share
C$          C:\           Default share
D$          D:\           Default share
E$          E:\           Default share
IPC$                      Remote IPC
NETLOGON    C:\winnt      Logon server share
Public      E:\Public     Advanced Server NTFS Volume Set
```

Connecting and Disconnecting Shared Folders and Printers: *Net Use* Just as Windows Explorer and the Printers folder allow you access to shared folders and printers graphically, the NET USE command gives you this capability from the command line. Without arguments, it will display a list of whatever resources are currently connected, as in the examples below.

Currently Used Shares Shares being used are displayed as follows:

```
net use
New connections will be remembered.

Status          Local name    Remote name
--------------------------------------------------
OK              Q:            \\johnr-nt486-66\Public
OK              Z:            \\johnr-nt486-66\disk-d
Disconnected                  \\johnr-nt486-66\IPC$
```

Terminating Shares The keyword */delete* will terminate use of a shared resource, so the command

```
net use /delete Q:
```

would terminate sharing on \\johnr-nt-486-66\Public and make the Q: device name available for other use. To reuse this device name for the folder \\mips-lab-server\Public folder, for instance, one could type:

```
net use Q: \\mips-lab-server\Public
```

Persistent Shares If a connection is meant to be retained in future sessions, you can add the */Persistent:* keyword, which is followed by Yes or No to indicate whether sharing is to be persistent or temporary. These keywords act as a toggle and will continue in force until they are changed. /Persistent: Yes makes connections persistent by default, while /Persistent: No makes them temporary. For example, this command:

```
net use Q: \\test_server\a_share /Persistent: YES
```

Creates Q: as a persistent connection to the home folder defined in User Manager. All further connections in the session will be assumed to be persistent until a net use command is issued with the */Persistent: No* keyword, such as:

```
net use R: \\test_server\temp /Persistent: NO
```

which will create R: as a temporary connection to \\test_server\temp. All further connections in the session will be temporary until a */Persistent: YES* is issued.

Passwords If the device one connects to is password protected (a passworded Windows for Workgroups share, for instance), the sharename should be followed by the password- or by an asterisk place holder, which will cause the system to prompt you for a password to be typed in. The latter is especially useful in batch .CMD files. For example, the command

```
net use Q: \\accounting\first_quarter *
```

will connect me to the accounting server's first_quarter share, if I type in the correct password when prompted to do so.

Connecting as Another User and Across Domains In some situations, it may be desirable to establish a connection under another username. For instance, JRULEY on one system might be JDR on another. In such a case, the */User:* keyword allows you to connect to a share using another user name. For instance, while logged in, JRULEY, can issue the command:

```
net use Q: \\accounting\financials /USER:jdr
```

to gain access under the JDR account on the \\accounting system. If the JDR account is a domain account for the CFO domain, then the command:

```
net use Q: \\accounting\financials /USER:cfo\jruley
```

would be used.

The Home Folder The */Home* keyword connects a user to his or her home folder as defined in the User Manager. Thus, the command:

```
net use Q: \\accounting /HOME
```

would connect Q: to a user's home folder on the accounting server.

Sending Messages: *Net Send* Windows Messaging and Chat are the usual methods for communicating between NT users, but there are times when it's preferable to reach many users with a single command. *Net Send* meets this need. It causes a pop-up window to appear immediately on the systems to which a message is addressed, carrying your message (which must be one line of simple text).

The simplest form of the command assumes that you want to send a message to only one user and that you know that user's name, in which case the command is, for instance:

```
net send jruley Hi There!
```

which will send "Hi There!" to the user named jruley on the network.

Sending a Message to All Members of a Workgroup If you want to send a message to everyone in your workgroup, just use an asterisk instead of the name. For instance:

```
net send * Who has my copy of Networking Windows NT?
```

would be an efficient way to see who in your workgroup has borrowed your copy of a very interesting book.

> *Note: This command uses network broadcasts that are not routed, and therefore will not work on routed networks and WANs.*

Sending a Message to All Users in a Domain It's often necessary to send messages to users of a particular Domain or Server. In a Windows NT Advanced Server Domain, you can send a message to all other domain users by using the /DOMAIN keyword. For instance:

```
net send /DOMAIN Warning: Server 2 almost out of disk space
```

would let everyone in your domain know that Server 2 has a problem. You can follow the /DOMAIN keyword with the name of a domain if you want to send a message to users in that domain. For instance:

```
net send /DOMAIN: accounting Backup System is Down for Maintenance
```

would alert all accounting domain users to the status of the Backup System.

Sending a Message to All Users Connected to a Server At times you may want to reach everyone else attached on your server, especially if you are the administrator and you know there is a problem. The /Users keyword meets this need, sending the message to all users of the system. Thus, the command:

```
net send /USERS Server going down in 5 minutes...
```

would perform the traditional service of scaring the wits out of everyone connected to your server.

Logon Scripts and Batch Files

Of course, the availability of the NET command-line interface makes possible quite sophisticated network-aware batch files and scripts in Windows NT. Indeed, there are additional, administrative commands beyond those documented here. Since the most frequent use of these commands is in logon scripts created and maintained by system administrators, they're documented in the *Batch Files and Logon Scripts* section of Chapter 3.

Conclusion

The basic networking features of Windows NT run the gamut from file and printer sharing through electronic mail and ad hoc client/server links (with Network DDE). You can perform most network tasks from the Windows Explorer, the Printers folder, and Control Panel, although the *net* command interface gives you a character-mode alternative.

With this chapter completed, you're ready to begin looking into the details of maintaining your Windows NT connections—which we will cover in Chapter 5.

For More Information

Custer, Helen (1993), *Inside Windows NT.* Redmond, WA: Microsoft Press, ISBN: 1-55615-481-X. Chapter 6 (on NT's networking features).

Feldman, Len (1993), *Windows NT: The Next Generation.* Carmel, CA: Sams Publishing, ISBN: 0-672-30298-5. See Chapter 6 for network coverage.

Microsoft Staff (1993–96), *Windows NT System Guide.* Redmond, WA: Microsoft Corp. The basic reference guide to Windows NT, which comes with all Windows NT systems.

Keeping Connected

Troubleshooting and Performance Tuning Windows NT

When you have finished reading this chapter, you will understand:

- The principles of preventive maintenance

- Performance monitoring and tuning procedures

- Basic mechanisms of Windows NT troubleshooting

- Windows NT Registry

- Tools provided with Windows NT 4.0 Workstation and Server

- Third-party tools and resources

- Getting technical support

You are *not* expected to feel comfortable facing the diagnosis of a fault in a Windows NT system on your own. No competent technician *ever* feels so confident. But you should feel comfortable taking a crack at it. You will understand the preventive maintenance techniques that will help you avoid trouble whenever you can, and you should know when to cry "uncle!" and call for professional help.

Read This First

The odds are quite good that if you've turned to this page, you're faced with a system that is not operating as it should and you are desperately seeking help. This is the worst possible time to read about troubleshooting procedures, but we're all too aware that it's often the only time we do. If you look carefully at the edge of the book, you will see that some pages have been tinted. These pages, later in this chapter, constitute a troubleshooting section listing the most common errors in Windows NT, their symptoms, and the steps you need to take to correct them. So, read the rest of this paragraph and then go ahead to the colored pages and the best of luck to you. But when you've finished that, when your bug is fixed, come back here and read the rest of this chapter because it will tell you how to avoid having to go through this again.

The preceeding sentence will strike some readers as an appallingly bad joke. It is not!

In many situations a complex piece of equipment or complex piece of software (such as Windows NT) is installed by someone whose most urgent consideration is bringing the thing up as fast as possible. Once installed it will run until it breaks, at which time that same individual will be desperately looking for help, and that's the reason for that first paragraph. But those who have taken the trouble to read a chapter like this ahead of time will know that there's a much better approach. This approach, taught by the United States Air Force among others, is called *preventive maintenance* or *PM*. The principle of PM is simple: Don't wait until the system breaks—fix it *before* it breaks. Replace parts that you know will wear out before they wear out.

How do you find out which parts of the system are wearing out and need replacement? By applying *actuarial statistics* and *the mathematics of fault prediction* (see Appendix 6 for details). Basically, you need to keep a maintenance log for the system, recording how performance varies over time, along with the date and time of any failures. By examining the log, you can generally predict the overall reliability of the system and perform maintenance tasks in advance of an actual failure.

There's a second benefit to PM. Because it forces you to undertake regular, scheduled maintenance, it also gives you the foundation for *performance tuning*—keeping throughput as high as possible by "tweaking" the system to eliminate bottlenecks. Windows NT gives us some particularly sophisticated tools with which to determine system throughput. For example, it's not necessary to go through any complicated calculation to determine the packets per second the server is handling. It is necessary only to go to the Performance Monitor and look at it. With this theory under our belts, we'll now take a look at the specifics in performance turning and troubleshooting in Windows NT systems.

Performance Tuning in Windows NT

As discussed in Appendix 6, the overall throughput of a system is an end-to-end process, a chain in which total system throughput is no greater than the throughput of the slowest individual component. So performance tuning generally amounts to the process of determining this component, referred to as a *bottleneck* that's "bogging" the system, and increasing its throughput either by changing system settings or by replacing the component with a faster one. In individual Windows NT systems the components that can be performance tuned (aside from components that will be tuned to suit individual preferences, such as the keyboard and the mouse) include the central processor, memory, disk, video, and network.

General Methods of Performance Tuning

The principal tools an administrator or technician will use to perform routine performance monitoring/tuning on Windows NT systems are the Performance Monitor (covered in Chapter 3), Configuration Registry Editor (covered later in this chapter), and Event Viewer (see Chapter 3). For version 4.0, Microsoft introduced a powerful new tool: Network Monitor (covered in this chapter). In the sections that follow we discuss which performance monitor counters to track, what threshold values to look for, and what steps you should take when a threshold value is reached. In some cases there will be little that you can do short of moving the user to a faster machine, for example: if you detect a CPU speed bottleneck. In other cases it may be possible to modify various Window NT configuration values to produce a performance improvement. You will generally do so using the Windows NT Configuration Registry Editor (a.k.a. REGEDT32.EXE), illustrated in Figure 5.1.

Be forewarned that the Configuration Registry has some features in common with a nuclear reactor. It is potentially an immensely powerful tool. It is also fairly dangerous. No, it won't irradiate you, but if it's not used with care, it can render a system unusable (effectively irradiating your career!). So always take great care when making a configuration change using the registry. In particular, make sure you have the *emergency repair diskette* for the system you are working on close at hand.[1] (This diskette is created during the installation process and may be recreated or updated using the *Rdisk* utility described later in this chapter.)

Performance Monitor

In what follows, we constantly refer to Performance Monitor (see Figure 5.2) *objects*. To review (Performance Monitor is covered in detail in Chapter 3), these are selections from the Objects pull-down list that appears in the Add to Chart (or Add to View) dialog box after you select Add to Chart (or Add to View) from the Edit menu. The pull-down lists all system objects that have registered themselves with the Performance Monitor service. Each object has an associated set of *counter* variables that can be charted or on which alerts can be set. In the sections on subsystem tuning that follow, we refer to these counters and to their parent objects.

---

1   Sometimes even the Emergency Disk won't help. We recommend using the Resource Kit's REGBACK and REGREST utilities (see Appendix 4) to keep separate copies of registry data in a nice safe place. You'll never know how much you need it until it's way too late.

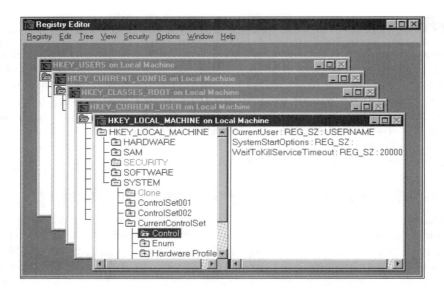

FIGURE 5.1 Registry editor. NT's configuration registry editor (REGEDT32.EXE) provides an interface to the registry—a redundant database of configuration information for the system, software, and users.

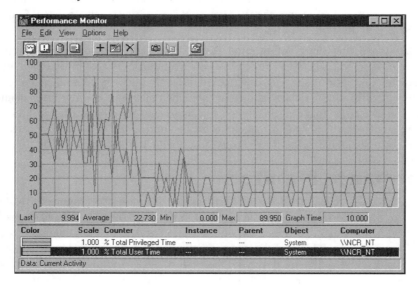

FIGURE 5.2 Performance monitor. NT Performance Monitor gives administrators and support personnel the ability to observe, monitor, and record data on a wide variety of system (and application software) components.

CPU Tuning

Since the central processing unit (CPU) is the "brains" of the system, it is not surprising that monitoring CPU performance is one of the most important functions an administrator can undertake. Windows NT provides a very high degree of capability to monitor the CPU, including measuring total CPU utilization, percent of time in privileged (operating system) mode, percent of time in user (application) mode, and frequency with which the system is *context switching* between tasks. All of these measurements can be extremely useful, and most can be monitored not only for the entire system but on a per-processor basis on symmetric multiprocessor (SMP) machines. The relevant counters to monitor for the *System Object* are:

- *% Total Privileged Time*—This is the percentage of the total system time (time for all processes in the system) that is being spent in "privileged" (that is, in operating system) mode. This measurement generally is a reflection of how much time the system is expending performing system-level tasks such as disk I/O and video display operation. If the system is bottlenecked at the CPU and this counter is high, there is a configuration problem in your system. To diagnose the problem further, see %Total DPC Time.

- *% Total User Time*—This is the percentage of system time that is being expended running user-level or application code. If the system is bottlenecked at the CPU and this counter is a high percentage, it may be possible to improve performance by changing the way applications are being used on the system. You can consider having in-house vertical applications rewritten in a more efficient way, for instance, or you may want to examine the way a user is operating on the system to see if some additional efficiency can be achieved.

- *% Total Processor Time*—This measurement indicates the percentage of system time the processor is spending doing useful work and is effectively the total of the percent privileged time and the percent user time. When this figure approaches 100%, it indicates that the processor has become a bottleneck in the system. Windows NT will then be forced to suspend certain tasks to give others time to run, and the system will slow down in much the way a time-sharing system slows down when too many users are logged into it. At this point, you have two alternatives: increase the number or speed of processors in a scalable processor system or move the user or server, as the case may be, to a faster CPU.

- *% Total DPC Time*—This percent measures the time the processor is spending in *Deferred Procedure Calls* (DPCs). DPCs are mechanisms for efficiently handling interrupts. Rather than executing interrupt code immediately, NT may elect to handle it in a DPC. DPCs run at a lower priority than hardware interrupts, so deferring execution can allow higher interrupt rates to be handled, but a *very* high interrupt rate can still bog the processor. Related counters worth checking include Processor Queue Length and Interrupts/sec.

- *Context Switches/Sec.*—This counter indicates how frequently Windows NT is performing a *context switch* between tasks. By default, Windows NT will task switch several times each second to give every task in a system a chance to run. If this counter become *very* high (around 1,000 context switches per second), it may indicate that Windows NT is blocking on one or more shared resources in the system—quite possibly a video resource. To diagnose this, observe the % Total Privilege Time and % Total User Time counters of the System object. If both of these are at or near 50% and the total processor time is at or near 100%, multiple threads within the system are contending for a single shared resource and are doing so with such frequency that the resource can't keep up (a form of *contention*, a topic described more fully in Appendix 5). This can happen, for example, if intensive use is being made of a video application and the video card is not fast enough to keep pace.

- *Processor Queue Length*—This measurement indicates the number of threads queued for execution on a processor (you must also monitor at least one Thread counter to generate Queue Length data; otherwise, it always indicates zero). Sustained values higher than two indicate congestion. You'll need to identify which process is causing the congestion, then reconfigure the process, switch to a faster system, or (if you have the capability) add a processor to your system.

- *System Calls/Sec.*—This counter indicates the frequency of calls to Windows NT system routines—not counting the graphical routines. If the preceding values are high—including Processor Queue Length and % Total Privileged Time at or near 50% and % Total Processor Time at or near 100%—but the System Calls/Sec. is low, in all probability, you have a video problem, particularly if you are running graphically intensive applications. See the section on video performance troubleshooting for more information.

- *Total Interrupts/Sec.*—This counter indicates the rate at which interrupts are being generated by hardware in the system for all processors. This indicator should tend to closely track with the System Calls/Sec. (with the exception of high mouse, keyboard, and serial port activity). If it does not, it may indicate that some hardware device is generating an excessive number of interrupts. Attempt to determine whether the device in question is the video card, the network interface card, the hard disk driver, or perhaps some other device, such as the mouse.

- *% Registry Quota in Use* — This indicator shows the percentage of registry quota currently in use by the system. This is a critical item to monitor on Primary and Backup Domain Controllers (PDC/BDC) because user accounts, system policies, and related information can cause a registry quota to become exhausted, especially on large networks. If this value begins to approach 100%, it's time to increase the total registry size (set in Control Panel/System's Virtual Memory tab). If this happens on an NT Workstation (or a Server not functioning as a PDC/BDC) you probably also want to examine the Registry to determine *why* it has grown so large.

Like the System object, the *Processor Object* provides indications of % Privileged Time, % Processor Time, % User Time, and Interrupts/Sec. However, it does so on a per-processor basis rather than on a system-wide basis. On a single-CPU system, the Processor counters should yield the same results as the System counters. On a symmetric multiprocessor (SMP) system, the Processor object will have multiple instances, and you can examine these instances (in particular, % Processor Time for all processors) to check the load balancing of applications across processors. All processors in the system should tend, on average, to report approximately equal utilization. If this isn't happening, you likely have a problem with one of your processor boards (or if you observe an imbalance only when running certain applications, such as older versions of Microsoft SQL Server, it may be a programming problem) and you need to investigate further.

Floating Point Performance

Unfortunately, Windows NT does not provide a direct counter for floating-point (FPU) operations, which would be useful in determining whether the system is being bogged by floating-point performance when running applications such as computer aided design (CAD). However, in general, if a system is performing an application known to be floating-point intensive and is indicating a CPU bogging condition (% Processor Time at or near 100%) with no other indication of a bogging condition (such as a high number of System Calls/Sec., high number of Interrupts/Sec., etc.), the odds are quite good that the system is floating-point bogged.

You need to investigate to see whether the system in question, in fact, includes floating-point processor hardware.[2] No 386-based or 486SX series Intel computers have built-in floating-point hardware, but all 486DX computers, all Pentium and Pentium Pro processors, and most RISC processors will have it built in. If a user is experiencing a CPU-bogged condition of this type and is operating on a 386 or a 486SX workstation, you may want to consider moving that user to a 486DX, Pentium, or RISC-based workstation to see if the problem clears up.

Windows NT *does* provide a performance counter for floating-point *emulation*; it's the System object's Floating Emulations/Sec. If the system shows signs of processor bogging (high %Total Processor Time) and Floating Emulations/Sec. is high, you are running a floating-point-intensive application on a processor that lacks hardware floating-point support.[3]

Memory Tuning

The *Memory Object* has the following counters to monitor:

- *% Committed Bytes in Use*—New for NT 4.0, this counter gives the ratio of Committed Bytes/Commit Limit, expressed as a percentage. If you observe virtual memory thrashing (see Pages Per Second, below), this is the counter to check: if it's running close to 100%, you need more memory! See the next item for an explanation of committed memory and the commit limit.

---

2   You can test for the presence of an FPU and profile its performance using WINDOWS Magazine's WINTUNE benchmark, available for download from http://www.winmag.com.

3   Or (on NT 3.51 and later systems) you may have a system that has a floating-point unit, but has been configured to *emulate* floating-point operation (e.g., an older model Intel Pentium chip, in which the FPU has been disabled because of the infamous divide flaw). You can check and change the emulation mode with the PENTNT command, covered in Appendix 5. Alternatively, you can edit the relevant registry entry: HKEY_LOCAL_MACHINE\ System\CurrentControlSet\Control\SessionManager\

ForceNpxEmulation. This is a REG_DWORD that accepts values of 0 (hardware floating-point), 1 (Pentium-only, *may* emulate FP divide instructions *if* a defective Pentium CPU is installed), and 2 (emulates all floating-point instructions).

- *Commit Available Bytes*, *Committed Bytes*, and *Commit Limit*—These three counters indicate the state of the virtual memory management subsystem. Commit Available bytes is an instantaneous indicator of the *available* virtual memory in the system (i.e., virtual memory not being *used* in the system). This value fluctuates with time and is interesting to monitor but does not provide a reliable indicator of total memory available. The Committed Bytes value, on the other hand, is an instantaneous indicator of the *total* amount of virtual memory committed—reserved memory space for which there must be backing store available. Commit Limit is the total amount of space that is available for committing and is generally equal to slightly less than the size of physical memory plus the size of the page file (just slightly less because of memory the system reserves to itself).

    Note: If the Committed Bytes counter approaches the Commit Limit, the system is running out of virtual memory, and it will become necessary to expand the page file. You can use this as an indicator to expand the page file manually, avoiding an automatic page file expansion and the associated deterioration of system performance.

- *Pages per Second*—This is an indicator of the total paging traffic in the system—the rate at which memory pages are being swapped between the paging file and physical memory. Systems with lots of physical memory will tend to show a zero value for Pages per Second. Systems operating with a minimal amount of physical memory (16MB in workstations, 24MB in servers) will generally show zero Pages per Second in an idle state but may show paging activity (100 Pages per Second or less) as applications are opened and closed in the system. A rise in Pages per Second to a sustained value above 100 indicates a *thrashing* condition, meaning that the system has reached a state in which the demands made on the virtual memory manager exceed its capacity—so more RAM is needed. Therefore, when the Committed Bytes indicator approaches within 10% of the Commit Limit, begin watching the Pages per Second to see if the system is thrashing.

- *Pool Nonpaged Bytes*—This counter measures the total number of bytes in the pool of nonpaged memory. Nonpaged memory is *reserved* and cannot be paged out into virtual memory (disk space) on demand. In effect, it's the total amount of memory the system is using that must at all times remain in the physical RAM. If this value rises to within 4MB of the total amount of memory in the system (for example, if it rises to over 12MB in a system that contains only 16MB of memory), performance is compromised.

    Whenever an application is launched from Windows NT, Windows NT temporarily requires a substantial amount of space for buffers, for loading subsystems (such as the 16-bit WOW system for 16-bit applications), and other activities. In an instantaneous state wherein less than 4MB of nonpaged pool is available, Windows NT will begin to "swap" severely in an effort to free up enough memory to get a new application started. In this situation, the best thing to do is provide the user with more memory in the system. You can also use this value in conjunction with the Working Set and Working Set Peak counters of the Process object(s) to determine the total amount of memory required by a particular user, which brings us to the *Process Object*.

- *Working Set*—This counter measures the total memory *used by an application*. It's particularly helpful in detecting memory hogs, as illustrated in Figure 5.3.

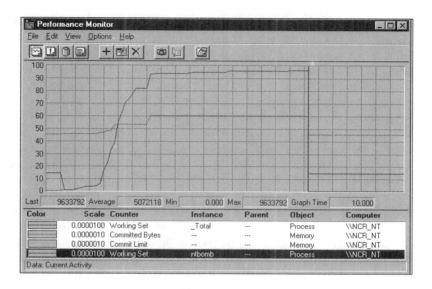

FIGURE 5.3 Performance Monitor, working set. Performance Monitor can be very useful in diagnosing memory hogs. Now that NTBOMB has been identified as the errant process, it can be shut down.

This seems as good a place as any to take a bit of time out and explore the entire subject of virtual memory in a bit more detail.

Memory hogs have been, unfortunately, all too common in Windows NT—until quite recently, Microsoft's own 32-bit VC++ compiler for Intel CPUs implemented a run-time memory allocater that did not return memory allocated by applications to the OS unless specifically instructed to do so. As a result, applications could exhaust system memory—*even virtual memory*—if they continually allocated and de-allocated large memory blocks.

If you encounter a memory hog (the symptoms are obvious: excessive memory paging when you are doing normally innocuous things such as moving the mouse, appallingly low Memory/Available Bytes, appallingly high Memory/Committed Bytes, and possibly also the dreaded "Low Virtual Memory" message discussed later in this chapter), you can determine which application is causing the problem with Process/Working Set, then simply shut that process down. *It is not necessary to restart Windows NT.*[4]

Virtual Memory and Swapping As described in Chapter 1, Windows NT is a virtual memory operating system, meaning that it can employ hard disk space as auxiliary memory to hold information that is not immediately required in RAM. The strategy that Windows NT uses to do this depends on the operation of several sections of memory known as memory pools in conjunc-

---

4   In the OS/2 1.*x* environment, rebooting servers nightly was a common practice because of a system-wide memory fragmentation problem. NT has no such problem, so although it may be necessary to shut down an ill-behaved application, it should never be necessary to reboot the computer.

tion with the cache manager. To begin with, there is a *non-paged pool* that stores memory that cannot be paged out to disk—that is, memory required to be immediately on hand in order for Windows NT system components and applications to perform their functions. This memory generally appears to run in a pool of 2 to 3MB in most configurations. There is also a *paged pool* of memory that is pageable and can be swapped to disk but is kept ready for immediate access. This generally will contain the memory pages that are being most frequently requested by system components or applications. Paged pool may vary in size from a few megabytes up to the total capacity of physical memory, depending upon the configuration and available free space.

Windows NT also caches disk activity within the virtual memory space and *can employ up to one-half of the physical memory's space to store disk cache information*. That is, on a 16MB system, up to 8MB will be employed for cache. When so many applications and system components are running and requesting memory that the system cannot fulfill those requests from within the range of pages available in the Physical Page Pool—the system will begin to *page* less frequently used pages out to hard disk, freeing them to fill those requests. This process will continue until the *commit limit* is reached. The commit limit specifies the total amount of memory that can be committed—that is, for which data space is required in either the physical memory or the virtual memory paging file—without expanding the paging file. When the commit limit is reached, Windows NT will attempt to expand the paging file.

Notice that we have two separate threshold situations involved here where the paging file becomes a consideration. In the first, Windows NT is paging information into the file without the commit limit being affected. In this situation disk I/O is *special cased* in a manner analogous to that used by Windows 3.1's permanent swap file. That is, if you have a 16MB system with 24MB set as the initial size for your paging file, the commit limit for the memory system will be about 37MB (24MB plus the physical memory, 16MB, less the space reserved for the Paged and Nonpaged Pools, which must be retained in physical memory). Until that commit limit is reached, Windows NT will perform *special case* I/O—essentially, raw reads and writes within the paged file space—a relatively efficient process. Paging will occur, but the impact on system performance will tend to be minimal.

When the commit limit is reached, however, Windows NT is forced to expand the paging file, and a completely different situation occurs, analogous in many respects to the temporary swap file in Windows 3.1. It is now necessary for Windows NT's system software to carry out *create* operations in an attempt to find more room on the disk. As a result, once the commit limit begins to increase, performance becomes abysmal. This a situation to be avoided at all costs, particularly in file servers, because it can rapidly reach a point where the system becomes totally bogged and almost useless. But we haven't quite hit the ultimate limit. That happens when Windows NT either reaches the maximum size of the paging file (set in the Control Panel/System/Virtual Memory) or worse, if Windows NT runs out of physical disk space because application and data files on the disk partition containing the paging file don't leave enough room for the page file to grow to its maximum size.

At this point it becomes impossible for Windows NT to fill the application and system requests for memory and you may expect a series of events, beginning with a "System low on virtual memory" alert that will escalate through various error messages until the system crashes. This need not happen. When multiple page files are available, Windows NT will distribute paged virtual memory more or less equally across all of them, allowing for more total paging *and* improving performance, provided that each swap file exists on a separate physical disk. Note, however, that creating multiple paging files on a *single* physical disk will slow the system down—page file I/O alternates between two separate locations on the same disk, keeping the disk head in constant motion.

The best performance can be achieved if the page file is on a partition or disk by itself—indeed, the ultimate performance can be achieved if a separate controller is available for the page file because this will allow page file operations to occur independently of other disk operations, which is something to consider when you are setting up large, multivolume file servers.

Why Not Just Add More RAM and Forget About Paging? You might think that the solution to all these paging problems is simply to add enough RAM to the machine to prevent it from ever carrying out paging operations, on servers particularly. We know from experience that this is probably not a wise strategy where Windows NT is concerned. Windows NT has been designed to be efficient—nay, stingy—in its use of memory resources. It likes to run with just a few megabytes of RAM available as a ready reserve pool for emergency use to maximize disk performance, which in Windows NT is outstanding.

Essentially, the Windows NT cache manager takes over as much as possible of the free physical RAM to use for disk caching. Even on systems with what one would expect to be rather large amounts of memory (e.g., 32MB) it turns out to be relatively easy to force Windows NT to engage in some swapping behavior, particularly during application start. When applications are loaded, Windows NT attempts to load the full binary image of the application in memory and in doing so begins to release pages from its pageable pool (with resulting flush operations on the disk cache). This is one reason that first-time users of Windows NT may *think* it's slower than Windows 3.1 (or OS/2 2.1). It really *is* slower, where application launch is concerned. Steady-state performance of applications after they're launched, however, is quite another matter.

It's not possible to configure Windows NT so that it won't engage in this behavior (although you *can* minimize it by adjusting the Control Panel/Network/Server configuration). As long as sufficient virtual memory is available to handle peak cache loads without exceeding the commit limit, this doesn't have any significant impact on performance. In fact it will not be noticed at all unless applications are continually started and stopped. Applications that just run in a steady state for the most part will be completely unaffected—indeed, they benefit from significantly higher effective disk performance because of the large disk cache size.

The one major performance situation to watch out for is that in which page file limits are not sufficient and Windows NT starts raising the commit limit. To avoid this hazard run Windows NT systems during a burn-in period for the first few days (or weeks) of operation, observe the commit limit, and note any increase in the page file size. If the page file size increases over and above the preset size during the burn-in, reset the Initial Page File Size in the Control Panel, increasing it by 20%. This strategy will take care of most peak loading situations, give you a little "head room," and minimize any performance impact due to further page file growth. You needn't do this if Windows NT did not expand the page file during the burn-in period, because it's probably already big enough.

In either case, observe the Commit Limit using Performance Monitor. Add 10% to that value and set it as a performance monitor alert on all servers and workstations. As an example, if the Commit Limit is 60MB, set an alert at 66MB. Make sure, of course, that the maximum page file size is *more* than 66MB and that there is sufficient free space on the partition containing the page file to store the additional space if it becomes necessary.

The steps outlined will, essentially, set a trip wire. When the system begins to expand its paging file, as soon as that 10% threshold is crossed, the alert will be transmitted and you'll likely have a chance to react to the problem. You'll want to react *quickly*, particularly if it happens on a server. Expansion of the commit limit doesn't indicate an imminent crash, but it indicates a fairly severe problem that will become *very* severe if you leave it alone.

Paging on Workstations Paging on workstations is a little different. The most common situation encountered is one in which a Windows NT workstation over time starts seeing a sufficient load so that the page file starts to increase, and an adequately configured system starts subjecting its user to severely frustrating behavior because whenever the user does *anything,* the page file grows (with associated thrashing).

Again, you can anticipate a problem situation by setting an alert based on a 10% growth in the Commit Limit. This isn't a crisis. For example, you have a basic Windows NT workstation outfitted with what would appear to be plenty of memory, say 24MB or double the 12MB Microsoft recommends. Initially, the system's user will to be delighted with its performance and may be running a suite of applications. Initially, the user will employ the system very much the way one would Windows 3.*x*. That is, the user will perform *task-switching* rather than *multitasking* on the system.

Over time the user finds that it's more convenient to start *all* of applications first thing in the morning, iconize the ones not immediately being used to buttons on the task bar, and just work away with the one on top, switching from application to application with the taskbar buttons as needed. This works fine, of course, in Windows NT. It is a preemptive multitasking system, and the intelligence built into NT's virtual memory subsystem is such that the applications that are iconized (and not in use) take up a minimal amount of memory.

At some point however, your user will find the threshold for the commit limit, regardless of how high you set this initial threshold. Even on a system with plenty of memory and a Pentium Pro CPU, which you would expect to be an excellent performer, you will find that System/% CPU Time is relatively low but that System/Pages per Second is intermittently hitting a relatively high value (in the hundreds of Pages per Second, at least) nearly every time a new application is started, often when an application is closed.

Problems occur because the *working set* for the user's applications exceed the memory available in the system with the page file at its default size. Windows NT then starts expanding the page file. It does this in a very stingy manner, expanding only a little bit at a time, which means it buys just enough room to have the crisis come again 10 seconds later (it would be awfully convenient if the system were designed so that administrators could selectively control the growth of the paging file or cause an alert to be displayed suggesting that the user resize the paging file or call the administrator).

Unlike the server situation, in which this condition presages a crisis, for end users it's probably not urgent. Moreover, it's likely that the Commit Limit problem will grow slowly over time. Because Windows NT workstations can be inspected remotely, you can sit on any workstation, and (with administrative privileges) open a Performance Monitor session on any other user's station. The most desirable approach is probably to log Commit Limit and Working Set sizes for users on an infrequent basis, such as once a week, observe users who are approaching their commit limit, and (when time is convenient) expand their page file for them. In this way they will never see the problem. You can also take advantage of this situation to observe the free space availability on the disk that holds the paging file and suggest that users move files as necessary to save enough room for the page file in case it needs to expand. In this way you achieve *invisibility*, that ultimate goal of administration discussed in Chapter 3.

Controlling Memory Use In most respects, Windows NT is a self-tuning operating system. At installation, certain configuration settings will be made to optimize performance for the amount of memory in the system. In most cases, these settings will provide the best performance, but there are exceptions.

By default, Windows NT Servers run a Large System Cache model, in which all available RAM not otherwise used by applications or the system is available for disk caching. Windows NT Workstations, by contrast, run a Small System Cache, in which the cache manager will page out least-recently-used memory in an attempt to keep 4MB of RAM free for application launch.

In some circumstances, you may want to change this behavior. For instance, if an NT Server is being used in nondedicated mode by someone running it as a desktop system, using the small cache model may speed local application performance (at the expense of Server performance). Likewise, NT Workstation users who spend most of their time running a preloaded set of applications, but rarely launching new ones, may benefit from a large cache model (especially on systems with limited RAM).

To control which model is set, use the NT configuration registry editor, and reset HKEY_LOCAL_MACHINE\System\CurrentControlSet\Control\Session Manager\Memory Management\LargeSystemCache (this is a REG_DWORD value). A value of 1 sets large cache mode, a value of 0 sets small cache mode.

Virtual Memory Settings Aside from large/small cache mode, you can tune NT's virtual memory subsystem using the Control Panel/System icon's Virtual Memory settings (see Figure 5.4). This lets you set the initial and maximum page file sizes, determine on which disk(s) page file(s) reside (as mentioned earlier, systems with multiple physical disks can benefit from having multiple page files), and control growth of the Windows NT configuration registry database.

Control Panel/Server To further refine NT memory use, you can select any one of the four optimization settings for Server operation (*Minimize Memory Used, Balance, Maximize Throughput For File Sharing,* and *Maximize Throughput For Network Applications*) from Control Panel/Network's Services tab. Select Server from the list of installed software and then click the Properties button, as illustrated in Figure 5.5. The first setting is obvious; it is designed for a maximum of 10 network connections and is suitable only for lightly used workstations. This setting should *never* be selected on a file server (unless it's doing local file services on a *very* small—10 clients or fewer—network). The Balance setting allocates memory for up to 64 sessions and is useful primarily for departmental servers. Maximize Throughput For File Sharing allocates as much memory as is required for file sharing (it has no inherent upper limit) and is the basic setting for Windows NT Servers. Maximize Throughput For Network Applications de-tunes the Windows NT Virtual Memory System to be less aggressive in reserving physical memory to provide a buffer

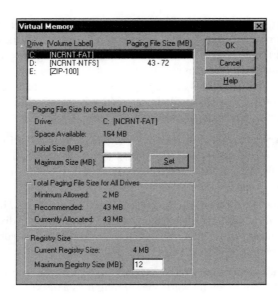

FIGURE 5.4 Virtual memory. NT's Paging File and Registry settings are adjusted in the Control Panel.

for application launch. This setting reduces swapping in systems and is a good choice for servers that run primarily network applications (such as SQL server). Indeed, this is probably the *optimal* setting for Server installations that have adequate memory (greater than 32MB).

Video Performance

The Windows NT Performance Monitor includes no specific video object. It is nonetheless possible to get an *indirect* indication of video activity in the Windows NT system. If the majority of video activity is in text-mode, the best way to do this is with the *Process Object*, which has the following counters of interest:

CSRSS is a Windows NT Executive subsystem that carries out graphical activities on behalf of text-mode applications (in versions of NT prior to 4.0, it did so for graphical applications as well). It contains one thread for each application. If CSRSS % Processor Time is continually absorbing a very high proportion of the overall system activity—that is, if one observes a high percent of processor time on the system and then traces this high percent processor time to CSRSS—in all probability, your system is being bogged by excessive text display. If you have multiple open text windows that display fast-changing data, consider minimizing them or at least reducing their size.

For graphical applications, the situation is more complex. With NT 4.0, Microsoft modified the video architecture to eliminate CSRSS as an intermediary process for graphics-based applications. All graphic operations are now carried out in the NT Executive. You can, however, get an indication of video load on your system by tracking the System Object/ % Total Privileged

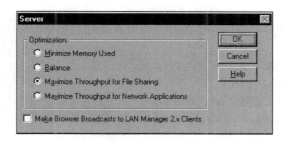

FIGURE 5.5 Server object in control panel/network. The Server Configuration dialog allows you to control the memory optimization settings of NT's built-in network services. You reach this dialog from the Control Panel/Network Settings, by selecting the Server object and clicking the Configure... button.

Time. If that's consistently very high while graphical applications are running, you are probably being bogged by a slow video card.

Disk Performance

Microsoft recommends monitoring two counter values when you attempt to determine disk performance. The first is *Average Disk Sec./Transfer* from the *Logical Disk Object* on any logical disk. The second is *Current Disk Queue Length*. Average Disk Sec./Transfer gives a direct measure of disk access speed, although determining a transfer *rate* will also require you to look at the *Average Disk Bytes/Transfer* to estimate the size of the block being transferred. Current Disk Queue Length gives a direct indication of the number of disk transfer requests that are being stored temporarily because the disk is unable to respond to the request. A sustained Current Disk Queue Length above one probably indicates that the disk is becoming a bottleneck in the system.

> *Note: It is not possible to measure any of these values without turning on disk counters (see the next paragraph).*

Because disk performance monitoring incurs a 10% to 15% overhead, it should not be permanently turned on unless it's absolutely necessary. Disk performance monitoring is something that you want to do only during maintenance intervals or when problems are suspected. It *may* be left on permanently on servers if, in fact, you can determine that a 10% disk performance hit will not materially affect overall responsiveness of the system. NT 4.0 implements an enhancement to disk counters that allows performance of individual drives in a RAID array to be measured and allows you to turn disk counters on for remote systems on the network. To see the options, type *diskperf -?* at the command prompt. It will show the following display:

```
DISKPERF======================

Starts and stops system disk performance counters.

Used without the command switches, DISKPERF reports whether disk
performance counters are enabled on the local or specified computer.
```

```
Enhanced Disk performance counters can be specified to report the
performance of the individual physical drives in a software striped
disk set. Normally software striped disk sets are reported as a single
logical and single physical drive. Note that when using the Enhanced
Disk performance counters, the Logical drive counters will not be
correct when measuring software striped disk sets.

DISKPERF  [-Y[E]  |  -N]  [\\computername]

  -Y[E]  Sets the system to start disk performance counters
         when the system is restarted.

     E   Enables the disk performance counters used for measuring
         performance of the physical drives in striped disk set
         when the system is restarted.
         Specify -Y without the E to restore the normal disk
         performance counters.

  -N     Sets the system disable disk performance counters
         when the system is restarted.

  \\computername        Is the name of the computer you want to
                        see or set disk performance counter use.
```

Thus, typing *diskperf -E \\MIPS40* will turn on enhanced disk counters the next time server MIPS40 is rebooted.[5]

Once performance counters have been enabled, you can begin to monitor counters from the *Logical Disk Object*:

- The *% Free Space* and *Free Megabytes* counters indicate respectively the percentage of disk space that is not filled and the number of megabytes of disk space that are not filled. If Free Megabytes falls near or below the space needed to hold the page file at its maximum size, the system might be unable to grow the paging file and will start giving you "Out Of Virtual Memory" indications. In general, it is probably wise to set alerts on % Free Space less than 5% on all drives on servers.

- *% Disk Time*—This counter indicates the activity of the disk drive, including both reads and writes as a percentage of total elapsed time. It is a good indicator for excessive disk activity. If this value achieves a sustained level greater than 50%, the disk is approaching a full duty cycle, and you may have a thrashing condition, indicating that some corrective action needs to be taken. You may wish to examine % Disk Time on all the volumes of a server to see how load is being balanced across the disk drives and consider moving files as necessary (particularly in database server applications) to try to equalize load on the drives on the system.

---

5   You can reboot systems remotely using the NT Resource Kit's SHUTCMD.EXE utility. See Appendix 4.

- The *Physical Disk* object provides a set of counters similar to those used for the Logical Disk objects. These will give you information about performance of a physical disk platter but will not give you information that can be broken down by partition and therefore is probably less useful in most circumstances. However, Microsoft does make one interesting recommendation,[6] which is to observe Average Disk Access Time for physical disks. If you have multiple platters available, particularly in a SCSI disk system in which the disks could be striped, striping will probably improve disk performance if average disk access time for the physical disk is less than average disk time divided by the number of disks available striped.

With respect to setting alerts on disk performance counters, again, bear in mind that turning on disk performance counters (using the *disperf -y* command syntax) will extract a 10% to 15% performance penalty on disks for which performance monitoring has been enabled. However, on servers for which you suspect that disk performance may represent a system bottleneck, it might well be advisable to turn on disk performance monitoring as a debugging aid and then set an alert on the Disk Queue value in the Logical Disk Object for any disks on which you suspect that performance may be a problem. Set the alert to trip if a sustained value greater than one is achieved. This will indicate that disk transfer requests are being received faster than the disk can accommodate them. Monitoring this value might indicate when a particular disk is accessed more frequently than the physical disk hardware can sustain, in which case you need to consider moving files around on the disk or replacing the existing disk setup with a stripe set.

You should also be concerned if you see a Disk Queue higher than one and cannot account for it. If the level of traffic is such that the disk ought to be able to handle it, consider monitoring Average Disk Bytes/Transfer and Average Disk Sec./Transfer. You can use this information by dividing Average Disk Bytes/Transfer by Average Disk Sec./Transfer. You will get a *transfer rate* in Bytes/Sec. Comparing this with the specifications for the disk drive may indicate if a disk drive is starting to lose performance due to wear, fragmentation, and so on. Periodic monitoring of this value and historical logging of this information on a month-to-month basis may help you determine when a disk needs to be reformatted to eliminate fragmentation or when the disk hardware is beginning to have problems.

Network Performance

Up to now we've been concerned with monitoring other parts of the system to detect and overcome system bottlenecks. But this is a book about networking, and as any network administrator knows, the odds are much higher that you will experience performance bottlenecks on your network than on almost any other component. The classic approach to this problem (other than guesswork, jiggling the network cables, and so forth, which are always good ideas if you're having a network problem on a workstation), is to break out the Protocol Analyzer, and this remains the preferred method of dealing with a wide variety of network problems (with NT 4.0, you might try Network Monitor first).

Where NetBIOS is used (NetBEUI, NBT, NBIPX), Windows NT actually provides built-in performance tuning that will give you almost (but not quite!) the same information you'd get from

---

6   In the Resource Kit. See Chapter 4, *"Optimizing Windows NT."*

a protocol analyzer. You can't get down into the wire and actually look at the bits in the packets, but you can look at data rates, and collisions. You can in fact perform a sophisticated level of system performance monitoring in the software itself. There are also performance counters that can be used in monitoring performance of some of the critical software components, including the LAN Manager workstation and the LAN Manager server. We examine all of those in what follows.

As you will recall from Chapter 1, the Redirector is a software component in the Windows NT Executive, which essentially acts as a traffic cop and determines when data transfers need to be handled by local resources (such as hard disks) and when they need to be handled over the network. It is, therefore, the component that sits nearest the center of the Windows NT network and is a good place to look for network bottlenecks.

Several parameters of the *Redirector Object* can be monitored here that may prove useful in problem detection and network turning:

- *Bytes Total/Sec.*—This value provides an overall indication of how busy the redirector is and provides the simplest direct measure of network performance (in combination with the same counter for the *Server* object, below).

- *Current Commands*—This counter is the number of redirector commands waiting in queue to be serviced. If it rises to a value significantly higher than the number of network cards in the system, you're dealing with a severely bottlenecked network server.

- *Network Errors/Sec.* —This counter indicates the number of serious network errors (generally collisions) being experienced in the system. You can look for further information in the System Error Log (using Event Viewer) because there will be an entry every time a network error is generated. In any case, if Network Errors/Sec. rises above zero on a well-behaved network (or above some small background value in a heavily loaded network), you have a problem somewhere in the subnet, and you'll need to trace it down.

- *Reads Denied/Sec.* and *Writes Denied / Sec.*—These counters indicate that a remote server's refusing to accommodate requests for *raw* reads or writes. Raw reads or writes are techniques that Windows NT uses to increase data rates in large data transfers. Instead of transferring packet frame information for each data packet, a *virtual circuit* connection is opened and a whole stream of raw data packets is transmitted, maximizing the throughput rate for the duration of the virtual circuit connection. If the server is running low on memory, it may refuse to participate in this kind of a connection because it cannot allocate the necessary local buffer space. Therefore, the Reads Denied/Sec. and Writes Denied/Sec. counters are direct indications of memory problems at the file server.

Obviously, the preferred solution to this problem is to increase the memory in the server (or at any rate, examine the file server and determine why it is running so low on memory that it's refusing to allocate space for raw reads and writes). If it is impossible to fix this problem promptly (i.e., you don't have extra RAM to put in the server or cannot immediately take it off-line), you can add *UseRawReads* and *UseRawWrites* values to the *Parameters* sub-key of the LANManWorkstation entry in the system registry and set them to False. This action will stop futile attempts to use raw I/O, thus increasing throughput. Again, however, the preferred method is to correct the problem at the server. One further registry setting that might help where networks are heavily used is to create a *UseNTCaching* value in the *Parameter* sub-key of the LANManWorkstation registry sub-key to True. This will cache I/O requests during file writes, reducing the number of requests transmitted across the network. In effect, repeated writes will be cached locally, and then a single request for transfer will transmit all the information across the network. When a network is heavily loaded, this setting may improve performance.

All Windows NT systems are to some extent servers, whether they are dedicated as file servers or functioning as desktop workstations. And operations in which services are provided and resources are shared are managed by the Server Object. This setup can be monitored from the *Server Object* in the Performance Monitor. Appropriate counters and indicated performance are as follows.

- *Bytes Total/Sec.*—This value provides an overall indication of how busy the server is and should probably be monitored on file servers because an increase over time indicates a need to expand server memory (or perhaps even to consider upgrading your server hardware).

- *Errors Access Permissions, Errors Granted Access, Errors Logon*—All of these indicate security problems. These may be as innocuous as someone forgetting a password but *could* indicate that someone's attempting to "hack" your system. In particular, a high value for Errors Logon may indicate that someone is trying to hack the system using a password-cracking program. You will want to examine the system security log (using Event Viewer), and you may want to enable auditing (from User Manager) to track what's happening. This is also a classic application for a protocol analyzer (sniff the LAN and see where those errors are coming from!), and in NT 4.0 you may want to fire up Network Monitor.

- *Errors System*—This counter will show the number of unexpected system errors that the server is experiencing and indicate that there is a problem with the server. Check to see whether the server is running out of memory and check the system error log to see if you have a hardware problem. If neither is indicated, call a Microsoft-certified professional technician or Microsoft technical support.

- *Pool Nonpaged Bytes*, *Pool Nonpaged Failures*, and *Pool Nonpaged Peak*—These counters give an indication of the physical memory situation with respect to the Server Object. Pool Nonpaged Bytes indicates the amount of non-pageable physical memory that the server is using; Pool Nonpaged Failures indicates the number of times it attempts to allocate memory that is not available. Any value above zero for the latter indicates that the physical memory in the system is too small. Pool Nonpaged Peak tracks the maximum value that Pool Nonpaged Bytes has reached since the server was started—a direct measure of how much memory the Server object needs. If you get an indication that the server is running out of memory, reset the Server Object in the Control Panel/Network settings and consider using the Minimize Memory Used optimization setting. However, doing so will reduce system performance and will likely prove inadequate where you are attempting to establish connections with more than five systems at once. Increasing the physical memory is always the preferred solution to this problem.

- *Pool Paged Bytes*, *Pool Paged Failures*, and *Pool Paged Peak*—These parameters give a similar indication for pageable memory used by the server. In this case, the solution to the problem may be to increase the page file size on the system (set in Control Panel/System's Performance tab—press the Change button in the Virtual Memory section).

- *Server Sessions*—This parameter counts the number of sessions currently open on the server—a direct measure of server activity (note that individual users can have more than one session open at a time).

- *Sessions Errored Out* and *Sessions Timed Out*—These parameters give an indication of the number of times that network errors are causing a session to be disconnected or, alternatively, the number of times that an administrative auto disconnect setting (from User Manager) is disconnecting users with idle connections. Sessions Timed Out may be useful on a system with a heavily loaded server that's experiencing memory problems.

- *Sessions Logged Off* and *Sessions Forced Off*—These parameters count the number of users who have logged off normally and those who were forced to log off (either by active intervention of an administrator or because of the time limits set in their profile). The latter counter may be useful on a system with a heavily loaded server that's experiencing memory problems.

There are also various *NetBEUI, NBT Connection, Appletalk, NwLink,* and *NetBIOS/IPX/SPX Objects*—which all provide similar counters, most notably *Bytes Total/Sec.* and *Packets/Sec.*, measuring respectively the total data transfer for all packets containing data and the total number of packets transmitted. You can work out the packet size by dividing an average of the Bytes Total/Sec. by Packets/Sec. If that number begins to change (particularly if it begins to drop), it probably indicates a *collision* condition in which you have a large number of packets that don't contain any data. Some of the protocol objects present additional counters that may be helpful in diagnosing specific problems. To see the counters and a brief explanation of what each does, start Performance Monitor, select Add to Chart, select the object, and press the Explain>> button. A Counter Definition will appear, as illustrated in Figure 5.6, and you can scroll through the list of counters to see what each indicates.

- Application-Specific Performance Counters—In addition to the standard NT counters, many applications—including those in Microsoft's BackOffice family—export their own counters that can be charted, logged, and tracked in exactly the same way as the built-in ones. Among the most valuable of these are the counters for IIS (covered in Chapter 7) and those from Microsoft SQL Server. If you have a server application, check the documentation for Performance Monitor support.

Performance Monitor-Logging

Besides using Performance Monitor to examine instantaneous counter values for troubleshooting, you can use it to create performance data logs over extended periods of time—which is particularly useful on servers. To do so:

1. Start Performance Monitor, and select View\Log.

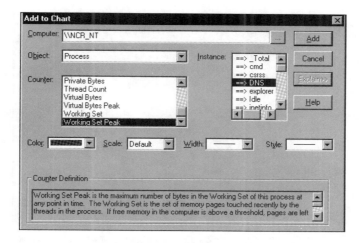

FIGURE 5.6 Counter definition. Performance Monitor counters have definition information associated with them, which can be displayed by clicking the Explain>> button on the Add to Chart dialog.

2. Select Edit/Add to Log, and add the Processor, Logical Disk, Memory, Redirector, and Server objects. (Note that using the Logical Disk object requires you to start disk performance counters as described earlier in this chapter.)

3. Select Options/Log. Specify a full pathname for your log file and how often you want to update the log (for example, once each 3600 seconds, which is once per hour).

4. Click the Start Log button. Performance Monitor will start collecting data, and as it goes, it will display the file size. You can minimize it to a button on the task bar and go on with other work. When you're finished collecting data (for example, after 24 hours), select Options/Log again, and press the Stop Log button.

To view the resulting data: select View/Chart, then Options/Data From..., and a file selector will appear. Type in the name of your log file. You may now add counters to the chart just as you would for a regular chart, but the data will come from the log file (you can also *export* data in comma-separated-variable format, which can be read in by most spreadsheets). For example, see Figure 5.7. This log was taken on a busy corporate e-mail server. It shows a typical diurnal cycle, with logons peaking in the morning and afternoon. Logging information like this can be a huge help in tracking how your system performs over time.

Some things to look for include Excessive Memory/Page Faults per Second (if the number is consistently 100 or higher, you need more RAM) and Processor/% Total CPU (if it is consistently less than 100%, you are not CPU bound and do *not* need to buy a faster system to improve server performance). Peak and average network throughput (Server and Redirector/Bytes Total per Second) will tell you if you're saturating your network and need to consider upgrading to 100-base-T or FDDI.

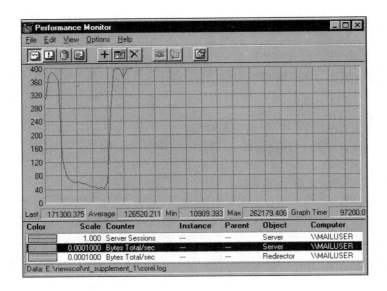

FIGURE 5.7 Long-term log. Performance Monitor can be used to log counter values over an extended period—in this case 24 hours of server operation.

A Final Word About Performance Tuning, Logging, and Maintenance History

The built-in tools (such as Performance Monitor and the configuration Registry Editor) in Windows NT are quite powerful and can make life much easier for a support professional who needs to maintain multiple servers and workstations. They can also, however, lead you into making a grave mistake. It's all too easy to install a Windows NT system, conduct some initial performance tuning, and then forget about it until something breaks, at which point one is left with no record of how well the system performed when it was installed.

Whenever a server is put in, you will most likely carry out an initial performance measurement (and tuning, if necessary). At that time, record the performance results you achieve in a *performance history*. This can be either a log document that is kept on the server (although if it is in electronic form, keep a copy somewhere else because even if the server goes down, you may need to access the maintenance information) or a separate physical record.

The point of the maintenance history is that the next time you need to conduct a performance tuning or routine check on the system, you have a *base of comparison*. That is, you know what the system performance was when you conducted the initial tuning and you know how it differs when you look at it later. This base can be enormously valuable in detecting problems. A routine performance tune-up once per month, for example, is probably a good idea. Values for basic performance criteria such as Nonpaged Pool and Paged Pool sizes from the Memory Object, Total Processor Time from the System Object, Logical Disk Available Space, Free Space, % Free Space, Average Disk Bytes/Transfer, Disk Queue and Average Disk Sec./Transfer, Netbeui Bytes

Total/Sec., and Packets/Sec., among others, will make it possible when you compare these values to identify when something that is going on with the system will need to be corrected eventually.

For example, if you find that the Nonpaged Pool is rising continuously, you know that eventually you must increase the physical memory in the system. If you find that the Paged Pool is rising consistently, you might need to expand the size of the paging file, consider adding more virtual memory to the system, consider distributing the paging file over multiple disks to improve performance, etc., etc., etc. Use your common sense. Keep a record of this information, and look at it periodically, think about it. That way you will not have to resort to using the troubleshooting information presented later in this chapter.

Windows NT Configuration Registry

Windows NT provides an advanced approach to configuration tracking and maintenance that can be an absolute godsend to system administrators. This approach is mediated through a special tool called the Configuration Registry Editor (REGEDT32.EXE), which is a full-featured database editor for the examination and manipulation of configuration registry information.

> *Warning: The Registry Editor is one of the most powerful administrative tools provided with Windows NT. It is also potentially one of the most dangerous. Editing registry entries and making changes to the registry blindly may render the system completely unstable. Use this tool with care.*

The Configuration Problem

How many times have you been faced with this problem? A Windows user comes to you and says, "My system won't work." You ask, "What did you change?" Your user says "Nothing!" You examine the system and find that it won't boot. You know that however sincere the user may be, *something* changed in the system because it booted before. After further discussion, you find that the user recently added some applications, removed others, and in all probability edited the CONFIG.SYS file, AUTOEXEC.BAT file, and/or any of the dozen or so *.INI files in the Windows\SYSTEM directory (or the PROTOCOL.INI file on a Windows for Workgroups or LAN Manager system). You are now faced with the nightmare of system administrators the world over—trying to correct configuration problems in the absence of any backup information at all. The odds are quite good that the solution to the problem will be to reinstall Windows, reinstall networking, and reinstall applications, because there really isn't anything else you can do.

Windows NT attempts to solve this problem with a *configuration registry*, a true database organized as a multiple tree structure and maintained individually on every Windows NT server or workstation. This database contains all (well, in theory *all*, but in practice *most*) of the information that is contained in the AUTOEXEC.BAT, CONFIG.SYS, *.INI files of a Windows system, or in the enormous CONFIG.SYS file of an OS/2 system, or in the PROTOCOL.INI file of a LAN Manager system. Furthermore, the data is inherently backed up. Multiple copies are maintained, and a special tool is provided for manipulating the data, which, among other things, organizes the data in a logical structure and makes it possible to access the data remotely—a dream come true for many system administrators. This tool is called the Configuration Registry Editor (REGEDT32.EXE).

The Bad News

The availability of a centralized configuration database and a proper tool for managing it is a dream come true for system administrators, up to a point. Unfortunately, the current implementation of the Registry Editor is less than perfect. It looks and behaves much like the Windows 3.*x* File Manager—neither the best nor the worst thing that one could think of to use as a model—but its most unfortunate feature is that (much like the various *.ini files it replaces), the Registry continues the system management tradition of providing configuration information in the form of thousands of incomprehensible key values that are not documented anywhere.[7] This situation is extremely frustrating and potentially dangerous. It means that when you first examine the Registry, you need to be very careful not to change anything. If you do, it's almost impossible to get the initial value back because there's no place to go look it up. It also means that finding the appropriate values to modify in a system is difficult.

Configuration Registry Structure

As mentioned above, the Configuration Registry is organized as a multiple tree database. This is stored in such a manner that it is fully backed up in a system, as we will see. Changes to the Registry are made through a Registry Editor, which enforces a high degree of *atomicity* in the database—you are guaranteed to see either an old or a new value for any registry key. You will never see a mixture of old and new values even if a system crash occurs. That's the good news.

Physical Data Structure

The registry is organized as a series of *hive* files, stored (with associated logs) in binary form on your computer's hard disk.[8] You can also back up the registry manually using REGBACK and REGREST from the NT resource kit, thereby providing yourself with a fallback in case the files become corrupt.

Fortunately, Windows NT goes to considerable lengths to make sure that the Registry doesn't become corrupted, and it provides a *last known good* configuration recovery menu during system start. So you will usually be able to recover at least to a previous known state in a system reboot (provided, of course, that nobody has been making dramatic Registry changes in an ill-thought-out manner).

Logical Data Structure

Because you will invariably access the Registry through the Registry Editor, the data structure of most importance is the logical data structure that you see when observing the Registry Editor. This is organized at the top level into five[9] registry *keys*, or five entry points into the four major

---

7   Except in the Windows NT Resource Kit. See Appendix 4 for details.

8   For details, see the *Windows NT Server Concepts and Planning Guide* (included in NT Server Books Online) or *Windows NT Workstation Resource Kit.*

9   It was four keys in NT 3.*x:* HKEY_CURRENT_CONFIG, which stores data for the current hardware profile, is new for NT 4.0.

tree structures that contain the system Registry information. HKEY_LOCAL_MACHINE is the tree structure describing the hardware and software configuration of the machine whose Registry Editor you are running or whose Registry you have loaded remotely. HKEY_CURRENT_USER is the Registry information applying to the currently logged-in user of the system. HKEY_CLASSES_ROOT is Windows NT's OLE database. HKEY_USERS maintains the list of users in the local machine's local login database and the security identification number (SID) for each user along with the program groups, control panel settings, environment variables, and so forth associated with each user's login. HKEY_CURRENT_CONFIG stores settable parameters (video display settings and network enabled/disabled) for the hardware profile currently in use.

Of the keys, by far the most useful for system maintenance is HKEY_LOCAL_MACHINE, which contains, again, the actual description of the system and the settings that would formerly have been found in CONFIG.SYS, AUTOEXEC.BAT, or *.INI file. This is the Registry key with which we are most concerned in this chapter.

The HKEY_LOCAL_MACHINE Key

Starting from the HKEY_LOCAL_MACHINE entry there are five sub-keys: HARDWARE, Security Account Manager (SAM), SECURITY, SOFTWARE, and SYSTEM. Of these, the SAM and SECURITY sections are of interest to us only insofar as we know that they exist. They cannot be accessed except through the appropriate APIs (in the case of SAM—the SECURITY entry cannot be accessed at all). These registry entries contain the security information used to validate logons into the system and to validate privileges and user access rights. They cannot be edited manually.

The HARDWARE key contains a description of the system, which is updated every time the system restarts. This is done through use of a *hardware recognizer,* one component of the Windows NT boot process. Examining the HARDWARE key, you'll find sub-keys for DESCRIPTION, DEVICEMAP, and RESOURCEMAP. A sub-key of the DESCRIPTION will be System, which will contain information about components such as the central processor (or processors) and the various adapters in the system. The DEVICEMAP sub-key will contain a list of the I/O devices in the system, as will the RESOURCEMAP sub-key. This information is used by the various Windows NT system software components, such as the network components and the Control Panel, which will examine the HARDWARE key in the Registry to identify any or all network cards in the system and test their settings. It can be used by an administrator to determine what hardware is in the system and the status of the hardware (this is better done using the Windows NT Diagnostics tool described later in this chapter), but obviously it can't be changed (other than if you change the hardware and restart the computer).

The SOFTWARE sub-key contains, first of all, the sub-key called Classes, which provides the software class associations used by Windows Explorer (the same data is pointed to by HKEY_CLASSES_ROOT); that is, it associates a three-letter file extension with a program. This is followed by a Description sub-key that appears to be used currently only as a temporary repository for Microsoft Remote Procedure Call (RPC) addresses and sub-keys for each vendor that supplies software to the system. In Windows NT systems today you are certain to find a sub-key called Microsoft—and there is some small probability that you will see sub-keys called

Lotus, Borland, or whatnot in the future (if you have the NetWare Requester for Windows NT installed, for instance, you'll see a Novell sub-key).

Within each vendor (such as Microsoft) sub-key you will see sub-keys for programs or components, and within those component sub-keys are sub-sub-keys for versions of the products. Within those sub-sub-keys you might find information about the product and product settings. From an administrator's point of view, the value of this information lies solely in that it does provide a central resource for determining the versions of software currently installed in the system. You can examine the SOFTWARE entries for each vendor, and if you click, for example, on the LAN Man Server entry under Microsoft, you'll see a sub-key called Current Version. Clicking on that will list description and installation date, major version, minor version, and other data. This information can be used by software such as Microsoft's SMS to automatically track and update software versions across the network.

If ODBC drivers are installed on your system, there will be an ODBC sub-key containing information about the drivers that are installed and the servers that are supported.

The SOFTWARE key will also contain a Secure sub-key (the purpose of which is not clear at the moment), a Program Groups sub-key listing any Windows (or NT) 3.*x* program manager groups that have been converted to links on the NT 4.0 desktop, and a Windows 3.1 Migration Status sub-key. This sub-key will indicate the status of any migration information for systems providing dual boot between Windows 3.1 and Windows NT that have been upgraded from a Windows 3.1 or Windows for Workgroups installation to a Windows NT installation (this key is really obsolete in NT 4.0 and may appear only if you've upgraded from NT 3.*x*).

After the SOFTWARE sub-key, there is only one more sub-key of the HKEY_LOCAL_MACHINE, the SYSTEM sub-key. This is the one that contains practically everything of interest to a support professional.

Opening the *SYSTEM* sub-key, we find a number of sub-sub-keys. The most important are the *ControlSets*: CurrentControlSet, ControlSet001, and ControlSet002. A ControlSet is a tree structure containing information on all the main services of a Windows NT system, including parameter settings. The system maintains a CurrentControlSet, which is the one currently being used in the system, and two fall-back copies representing previous configurations. During shutdown the CurrentControlSet will be copied into ControlSet001, so that it always contains the ControlSet in use when the system was last shut down. That, in turn, replaces ControlSet002 during system start if the system starts correctly. If the system fails to start correctly, an attempt will be made to start it using the earlier configuration. You could also have the option of doing this manually using the *last known good configuration* menu, which comes up during a Windows NT system start. This feature alone is immensely valuable to system professionals because it means the system automatically protects users from themselves. If you have a system that starts to misbehave, there is a very good chance that by reverting to one of the two last known good configurations, you will be able to recover.

In addition to the control sets, the SYSTEM key contains DISK, Select, and Setup sub-keys. The DISK sub-key contains a binary disk signature. The Select sub-key tells you which of the Control Sets is in use. Examining this list, you'll see entries for Current, Default, Failed, and LastKnownGood, which (by default on a system operating normally) will have a Current value of one, Default value of one, LastKnownGood value of two, and a Failed value of zero. If a configuration corruption is detected during startup, the Failed value will rise, and the system will attempt to use the last known good entry as the current entry instead of using the default entry.

The Setup sub-key of the SYSTEM key contains information about the Window NT system setup that was performed when the system was installed. This includes the network card, the type of setup performed, and the setup command line employed. There is an entry for system setup in progress. If you ever examine this entry and it is other than zero, something has gone dreadfully wrong, and it will indicate the path to the system setup files.

By far the most important information, again—from a support professional's point of view—is the information contained in CurrentControlSet, which we examine next.

The CurrentControlSet Key

CurrentControlSet contains four[10] sub-keys: Control, Enum, Hardware Profiles, and Services.

- The *Control* sub-key contains information such as the load order for the device drivers and services (in the GroupOrderList and ServiceGroupOrder sub-sub-keys) along with much of the Control Panel and Setup data. This will rarely be edited directly by an end user or administrator, but will simply reflect the settings set for the computer using other tools. So from an administrator's standpoint it is the Services sub-key, finally, that contains the parts that are a matter of concern.

- The *Enum* sub-key contains information used by NT's Hardware Enumerator at boot time to determine what hardware devices are attached to the system. The most useful portions of this key are found in the Enum/HTREE/ROOT/0 sub-key, which will contain two entries: a multi-string list called AttachedComponents and a dword value for FoundAtEnum (normally 1). This might be useful in troubleshooting a system that refuses to identify a peripheral. If it's not in the list, it wasn't enumerated, which means NT didn't recognize it. Enum/ROOT contains a series of entries listing all the devices NT looks for at boot time. Currently, all are listed as Legacy devices, presumably in preparation for the introduction of plug-and-play support in a future release.

- The *Hardware Profiles* sub-key contains numbered entries for every hardware profile on the system, each of which will have a Software and System sub-key of its own. These keys indicate only those items that have profile-specific settings—typically the display driver settings and settings for disabled services.

- The *Services* sub-key provides individual sub-keys associated with each subsystem or hardware device driver. Within each sub-key the linkage of the subsystem or driver to other devices appears in a sub-key, and there may be a parameters sub-key that will have any user-set parameters for the component. Some sub-keys will also have an auto-tuned parameters key associated with them, which will incorporate parameters dynamically tuned by the component itself.

---

10 As with HKEY_CURRENT_CONFIG, the Hardware Profiles sub-key is new for NT 4.0.

If you start the Registry Editor (by typing REGEDT32 from the command line) you will see the Registry Editor display containing within it the five windows containing the four Registry keys. Select the one called HKEY_LOCAL_MACHINE and double-click the HKEY_LOCAL_MACHINE key entry to list its sub-keys; double-click the SYSTEM sub-key; double-click the CurrentControlSet sub-key; double-click the Services sub-key. This will give you a list of all of the services and hardware components in the system. If you now double-click on the Browser sub-key, you'll see Parameters, Linkage, and Security. Double-clicking on Parameters will give you a list of parameters for the sub-key.

Note that this list is not necessarily complete—and this is one of the problems with the Registry as it currently exists. It's possible for a parameters entry in a sub-key entry for a component to be empty. This does not mean that there aren't any parameters. It means that the component is using the default parameters, whatever those might be.

On a particular Windows NT Server system, the Parameters for Browser are IsDomainMaster, which is a parameter of type REG_SZ (a string data type), is set to False; and the parameter MaintainServerList, which is again of type REG_SZ and is set to Yes (there is also a DirectHostBinding value listing the protocols to which the browser service is bound). Possible values for *IsDomainMaster* would be True and for *MaintainServerList* would be No. What these settings do, in fact, is determine the operation of the system browser, the component that determines the response to a *net view* command or to clicking to the Connect Net Drive icon in File Manager. IsDomainMaster determines whether the system in question stores the *browse list* or the list of systems that can be accessed on the local workgroup or domain.

In this case, even though the system in question is a backup domain controller for the Windows NT Server logon domain in question, it is *not* the domain browse master. In fact, one of the workstations on the system is functioning as browse master. However, because MaintainServerList is set to Yes, the system does maintain a list of the available systems and can act as fall-back to the browse master if it does not respond to a browse request from other workstations. (See the section on browsing in Chapter 9.)

To edit any of these entries, such as the IsBrowseMaster entry, it is necessary only to double-click on it. Because these entries are of the type REG_SZ, the String Editor will then appear, allowing you to type in a character string. Again, at this point we have one of the unfortunate problems with the Registry database. Obviously only certain strings will provide acceptable entries for string data types, yet there's nothing to indicate how a string should or should not be typed. In fact, the TRUE and FALSE values are uppercased, yes and no values are lowercased. You must find this kind of information by examination (for that matter, as this is written, we are unsure whether the choice of case is even significant—it may not be).

Another data type is REG_DWORD, the double-word data type, which contains a 32-bit binary value. Double-clicking on one of these, such as the LMAnnounce parameter in the LAN Man server sub-key, you will be presented with a Dword Editor, which will show the data in question in your choice of a binary, decimal, or hexadecimal representation. This can be of some use to you in setting a particular value because you can type it in using the most convenient form. Again, however, there is no explanation of what the acceptable values are. The *LMAnnounce* value, in point of fact, has legal values of zero or one, a one indicating that the system is to perform LAN Manager 2.*x*-compatible system announcements and a zero indicating that it is not. Fortunately, as with most entries in the system sub-key, it is not necessary to edit this value from the Registry Editor. You can edit the value, in fact, by using the Control Panel/Network Settings, Services tab: select Server from the list of installed network software, and click the Properties button. You will then see a screen offering a choice of four possible optimizations and a checkbox titled *Make Browser Broadcasts to LAN Manager 2.x Clients*. Checking this box and clicking OK will change the Registry value from zero to one, and if you return to the Registry Editor, you'll see, in fact, it updates itself and the LMAnnounce value will now be set to 0x1 as type REG_DWORD.

You will also notice a *Size* value in the LAN Man server sub-key. Size, which is a REG_DWORD, represents the server optimization value that has been selected from the Control Panel. Because the four possible values are one through four, it is obvious that a value of zero or five, for instance, would be illegal, yet there is nothing in the Registry Editor that would indicate this.

Why Go On and On About the Limitations of the Parameter Settings?

Why do we keep harping on the limitations of the parameter settings? Because it's *dangerous* to edit settings in the Registry Editor! *Never* do this if there is an alternative. *Do not* change the LMAnnounce setting with the Registry Editor—change it from the Control Panel. *Do not* change the server size from the Registry Editor—change it from the Control Panel. Whenever you examine a setting in the Registry Editor and consider changing it, try to find an alternative way to change it first. And these ways are usually available in one or the other of the Control Panel components on a Windows NT system.

There really *ought* to be a button associated with the Registry Editor that would examine the LMAnnounce parameter and tell you that it can be changed in Control Panel/Network Settings (much like the Explain>> button in Performance Monitor's Add to Chart dialog). And because that way of changing it is available, the ability to edit it directly ought to be disabled. There are, of course, circumstances in which you have no choice.

The registry also allows you to configure systems *remotely*. From the Registry Menu of the Registry Editor, you can perform a Select Computer, select another Windows NT server or workstation on the network, and edit that computer's Registry (though when you do so, only the HKEY_LOCAL_MACHINE and HKEY_USERS menus will be available). If you must set a parameter remotely, that may be the only way to do it. But this is something that must be done with extreme care—when you use the Registry Editor to make a parameter change, you run the risk of typing an illegal parameter or deleting a value and not being able to remember what it is. Possibly the worst thing that you could do would be to delete a value then wish to re-establish it—and re-establish the wrong type.

Suppose, for example, we delete the LMAnnounce parameter. Blindly looking at the registry editor and thinking about the LMAnnounce parameter—remembering that it only has two possible states, on or off—we might very well tend to restore it as LMAnnounce type REG_SZ with a value of True or False. That would not work properly. Worse, it might cause the browser to malfunction, rendering the system unstable. We repeat: *Do not make parameter changes using the Registry unless you have no alternative.*

Registry Value Types

The types of entries that can be accepted in a Registry value include:

- *REG_DWORD* is a double word value that can be represented as a decimal, hexadecimal, or binary number. By default, when displayed in the Registry, it will be displayed in hexadecimal format.

- *REG_SZ* is a Registry string value, and this will be a data string.

- *REG_EXPANDSZ* is a special string type used when you need to include environment variables within the string. For example, a legal REG_EXPANDSZ could contain the value %system root%/SYSTEM32/whatever. The %system root% environment variable will be expanded to the appropriate directory path at the time that the string is evaluated.

- *REG_MULTI_SZ* is a multiple string type. Double-clicking on a REG_MULTI_SZ value will bring up a multi-string editor with scroll bars, allowing you to enter multiple strings with one string on each line in the editor.

- *REG_BINARY* is used for binary data storage, and the Binary Editor is necessary to edit it. The Binary Editor can also be used to edit other types. It provides a bit-by-bit representation of the data similar to that used by the Dword Editor with the binary type selected. You can use the Binary String Dword and Multi-string options under the Edit Menu in the Registry to select whether the Binary String Dword or Multi-string Editor is used with a particular Registry entry, and all Registry entries are, in fact, 32-bit entries. Registry Names are not case sensitive, but they do preserve case, and they are unicode compatible.

Registry Capacity and Size

Currently,[11] the total size of the NT registry files is limited to approximately 2GB (the limit of NT's 32-bit address space) or the free disk space available on the system volume, whichever is less. However, NT continues to require a maximum registry size to be set (Control Panel/System, Performance tab—press the Change button in the Virtual Memory section) and indicates how large the registry has become in comparison to that maximum with the % Registry Quota performance monitor counter, described earlier.

One Last Time...

Finally, a reminder: the Registry is an extremely powerful tool. It's tremendously useful when properly controlled. But if you get in there and meddle around blindly, you will mess up your system beyond repair. Treat it with care.

---

11 NT 3.1 had a fixed maximum registry size of 8MB. NT 3.5 allowed the registry to be resized, but the ability to monitor the registry and set an alert if the maximum size was approached only appeared with NT 4.0.

Other Tools

Windows NT Diagnostics

One of the most overlooked tools for troubleshooting NT systems is a 32-bit version of the Microsoft System Diagnostics (MSD) program. NT's version of MSD is actually implemented as a Windows application with a graphical interface, and its executable file is therefore named WINMSD.EXE. To launch it, select the Windows NT Diagnostics item from the Start Menu's Programs/Administrative Tools folder (see Figure 5.8).

Using Windows NT Diagnostics Beginning with NT 4.0, WINMSD was redesigned and significantly enhanced. It now sports a Windows 95-style tabbed dialog user interface and provides more information about the system, and best of all, it can be used over a network to examine a remote system. This works because, unlike MSD on DOS systems, NT Diagnostics is actually reporting information from the NT registry.

The information available in WINMSD is extensive and includes:

- *Version*—The topmost tab on the WINMSD display shows system version information, including the NT version number, type (workstation or server) build and type (free or checked—the latter implies an instrumented kernel and is used mainly for development), CPU architecture, and multiprocessor support. It also displays the distribution CD's serial number and the name of the person to whom this copy of NT is registered.

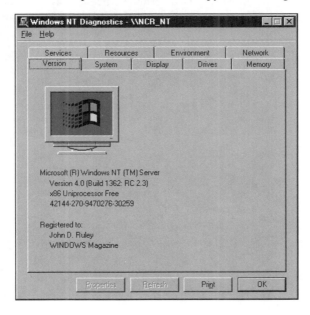

FIGURE 5.8 Windows NT diagnostics. NT includes a Windows-based system diagnostics application as a standard component. In NT 4.0 this tool can be used remotely as well as locally.

- *System*—This tab provides system-level information about the hardware on which WIN-MSD is being run, including vendor ID, Hardware Abstraction Layer (HAL) type, BIOS date, and a description of the CPU(s).

- *Display*—This tab lists the video BIOS date (if available), display processor and DAC (Digital-to-Analog converter) types, driver type and revision, currently set video resolution, amount of video RAM, vendor, and lists of all the associated files.

- *Drives*—This tab provides a tree display, sorted by drive type or drive letter, of each logical disk drive (be it a separate physical disk, logical disk partition, or network drive) known by the system. Double-clicking on any drive brings up a Drive Properties dialog (see Figure 5.9) showing general information including the drive letter, serial number, and disk space available and in use (displayed both in clusters and in bytes). A File System tab on the Properties dialog box gives general information about the file system (NTFS, FAT, CDFS, NetWare-Compatible, etc.) in use, including the maximum number of characters in a filename, and tells whether the namespace is case sensitive, supports Unicode, supports Compression, and so forth.

- *Memory*—This tab gives details on system memory utilization, including the total number of handles, processes and threads in use, amounts of physical RAM; kernel (non-pageable) RAM; committed RAM and page file space in use and available; and location and size of all page files. Most importantly, it records peak usage for both committed RAM and page-file space, providing a simple way to determine whether a system is running low on virtual RAM, which can then be changed with the virtual memory settings described earlier in this chapter.

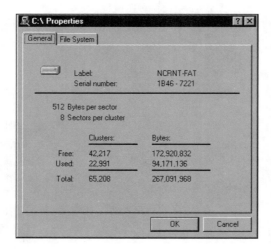

FIGURE 5.9 Drive properties. Selecting properties for a disk drive displays information about the drive, including its capacity and free space.

- *Services*—This tab displays essentially the same information as Control Panel/Services, with the additional refinement that it can display identical information for device drivers (when you press a Devices button on the bottom of the tab). Clicking the Properties button at the bottom of the NT Diagnostics dialog in this tab brings up a Service Properties dialog for the service or driver in question (see Figure 5.10), which displays the executable file associated with the service or driver, its start type, the user account with which it is associated (normally LocalSystem), any error associated with it, and its service flags (driver type, whether it runs in its own memory space, whether it can interact with the NT desktop). A dependencies tab allows you to see on what other services the service or driver in question depends (which can help in diagnosing why a particular service or driver fails to start.)

- *Resources*—This unique (and most useful!) NT Diagnostics' tab displays information about hardware resources, including interrupts (IRQ), I/O Ports, Direct Memory Access (DMA), Memory; and Device Drivers. For each type of resource, a list is displayed indicating the associated device driver, bus, and bus type. Clicking the Properties button when this tab is displayed will yield a Resource Properties dialog box (see Figure 5.11) giving details on the device driver that "owns" the resource and telling whether the resource is shared (for device drivers, the dialog lists resources owned by the driver). A check-box on this tab allows you to choose whether resources owned by the NT HAL are listed.

We cannot overemphasize the usefulness of the Resources tab. If you encounter a hardware problem such as a network card refusing to operate, after checking the physically obvious (i.e., making sure the network cable is actually present and connected), start Control Panel/Network's Adapters tab, and press the Properties button to view any card settings, such as the I/O port and IRQ. Then launch WINMSD, bring up its Resources tab, and see what driver owns those resources. If the two disagree, *believe WINMSD*. Both it and the

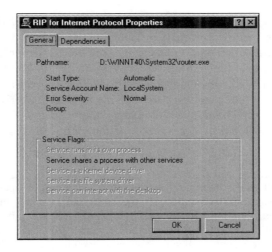

FIGURE 5.10 Service properties. Selecting properties for a service displays information about the service, including its startup type, security account, and service flags.

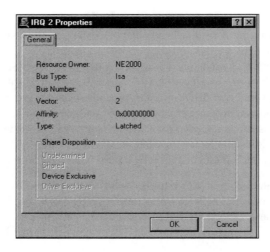

FIGURE 5.11 Resource properties. Selecting properties for a system resource (such as an IRQ) displays information about that resource, including the owning device driver, the interrupt vector, and whether the resource is shared.

Control Panel are getting their information from the NT Registry, but the Control Panel indicates the setting you *requested*, while WINMSD indicates the setting NT has actually *used*. Once you've identified such a problem, it's generally possible to correct it.[12]

- *Environment*—This tab displays all environment variables and values. By default it shows global (system-level) values, but a Local User button shows user-specific entries as well.

- *Network*—A close second in value to the Resources tab, the Network tab provides a wealth of network-specific information, including the network version, a list of logged-in users, transport-level protocols in use and associated Ethernet addresses, internal network Settings, and cumulative Statistics since system start. The Settings information is especially valuable—it corresponds to various registry entries for the Server and Workstation services, but centralizes them all in one place (and gives readable names for them!), which is of great value. Unfortunately, this value is somewhat lessened by the fact that WINMSD help provides no information on how to change any of the settings displayed.[13]

---

12 Doing so, however, can sometimes be frustrating. One author operates an obsolete NCR 486/33 as a combination PDC and router, the latter requiring two network adapters. When this system was configured to add a second SCSI card to support a backup device (IOMEGA ZIPdrive), the resulting conflicts among the network cards, SCSI cards, and motherboard devices eventually required replacing one network card with a different model. It *did* finally work, and it was WINMSD that solved the problem!

13 Once again, the only place to find that information seems to be the *NT Resource Kit*.

Using NT Diagnostics Remotely To view diagnostic information on a remote computer, use the File/Select Computer... menu. Most information displayed will be identical to that available if you run WINMSD locally. Exceptions may include certain details on the Display tab and Environment properties for the Locally logged-in user.

Task Manager

Like NT Diagnostics, Task Manager has been significantly enhanced for NT 4.0. You can now launch it by right-clicking in the taskbar at the bottom of the NT desktop (in an area not covered by an iconized application button) and selecting Task Manager from the resulting context menu. By default, it will appear with its Applications tab selected, as shown in Figure 5.12, which is useful mainly for shutting down hung applications. However, two other tabs are of special use in troubleshooting problems:

- *Processes*—This tab lists all processes running in the system. It's a much longer, and more detailed list than the top-level Applications tab (see Figure 5.13), providing process name (typically the name of the associated .EXE file, though some internal processes have descriptive names instead), ID number, and the amount of CPU time (as a percent of the total available) and memory in use by each process. This vastly simplifies troubleshooting memory hogs, because you need only bring up the Task Manager and look for them—processes using thousands of Kbytes are easy to spot! It also helps in diagnosing the occasional problem with one or more invisible and hung instance(s) of an application.[14] If a user

FIGURE 5.12 Task Manager—Applications. By default, NT Task Manager shows a list of applications running in the system. Note that the list contains only nine entries, despite the fact that some 30 processes are running.

14 Microsoft's Internet Explorer is a persistent example, in our experience.

complains to you that a program won't start, no matter how often he or she clicks on its Start menu entry or icon, examine Task Manager/Properties and look for the associated .EXE file. If you find it, use the End Process button to stop it (and any duplicates). In all probability this will solve the user's problem.

- *Performance*—This tab provides memory details (similar to those from the WINMSD memory tab) along with a graphic display of both CPU and memory utilization that's comparable to what you get with Performance Monitor's Processor and Memory objects. However, it's much faster to just launch Task Manager and look. Among other uses, this display makes it immediately obvious whether excessive disk activity (you don't need software to see that—look at the drive light) is being caused by virtual memory thrashing (Commit Change Total nearly equal to Limit and CPU utilization constantly high), in which case a change to virtual memory settings is called for. It can also help you diagnose a processor hog. If the user complains that his or her system seems excessively slow, first check WINMSD's Performance tab for consistently high CPU utilization when the system should be idle and eliminate thrashing as a possibility by checking that Commit Change Total is under the limit (as well as looking at the drive light and listening to the drives). Then switch to the Processes tab and see what process has the highest CPU value. It may even be a hung application with an invisible window. End that process, and performance is liable to improve (if it's a system process, you'll need to inspect the relevant settings to determine why it was using so much CPU).

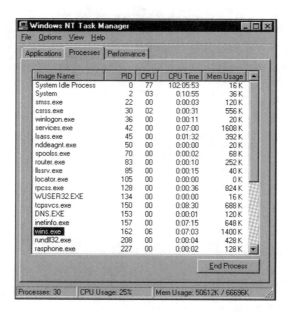

FIGURE 5.13 Task Manager—Processes. Selecting the Properties tab gives you a more detailed view of exactly what's going on in the system, including memory and CPU use broken down by a per-process basis.

Network Monitor: Wiretapping for NT LANs

A *protocol analyzer* has always been the network technician's tool of last resort. Basically one step above plugging an oscilloscope directly into the network cable, using a protocol analyzer shows you the actual packets on the wire. Implemented as a special-purpose computer (and a fairly simple one, at that), but packaged as a piece of test equipment, a protocol analyzer (colloquially, "sniffer") costs thousands of dollars.

Beginning with version 4.0, NT Server includes a new tool: Network Monitor, which amounts to nothing less than a protocol analyzer implemented in software!

Installing Network Monitor Network Monitor is implemented as a network service. As such, it's installed from Control Panel/Network's Services tab. Press the Add... button on that tab, and select Network Monitor Tools and Agent from the list. Then press OK. NT Server Setup will prompt you for a path to the files (in the /i386, /mips, /alpha or /ppc directory of the distribution CD or a network directory where you've already copied the same information), then copies the necessary files to your system directory. Then it instructs you to reboot your server. Do so.

After your server reboots, Network Monitor will be available in the Start menu's Administrative Tools folder. On startup, it displays an empty capture window (see Figure 5.14).

Capturing Data Before you can perform protocol analysis on your network, you need to capture some network data. To do so, Select Capture/Start. Network Monitor will allocate

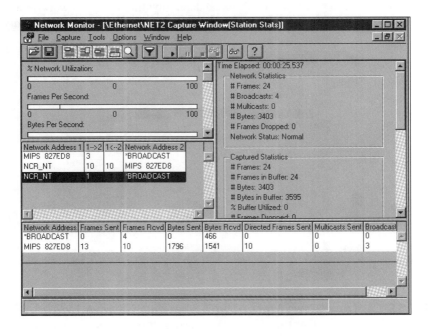

FIGURE 5.14 Network Monitor—Capture window. The Capture Window, initially displayed empty when Network Monitor starts, is the top-level display from which capture statistics are available.

buffers (you can control the size it allocates with Capture/Buffer Settings) and begin capturing data. If your network is busy, you'll see the network statistics numbers in the upper right corner of the display change rapidly.

If your network appears to be idle, go to another machine on the LAN that's connected to your server, log in, and browse the network. If that doesn't produce any activity, select Capture/Networks and pick a different network segment (Network Monitor monitors only one network at a time). If you're getting lots of activity but no actual frames captured, select Capture/Filter (see Figure 5.15), select the line below "[AND] (Address Pairs)," and Delete it.

When the Captured Statistics section on the right of the Capture Window shows a dozen or so frames captured, select Capture Stop and View. A Capture Summary will appear. Double-click the first line in the Summary. The Capture Summary window will shrink to make room for Detail and Hex windows (see Figure 5.16).

You can adjust the relative sizes of the Capture Summary, Details, and Hex windows—and you'll want to do so (in particular, make sure the Hex window has enough room to display about a dozen lines of text, because some frames require that much room). You'll find yourself looking at a lot of very cryptic data, but it's worth its weight in gold!

Analyzing Captured Data To completely understand what Network Monitor is showing you requires a full understanding of network protocols, something far beyond the scope of this book (or the experience of most technicians). But you don't need to understand protocols completely to gain *some* benefit (if you don't understand anything about network protocols or if what follows seems to be one incomprehensible acronym after another, read Appendix 2).

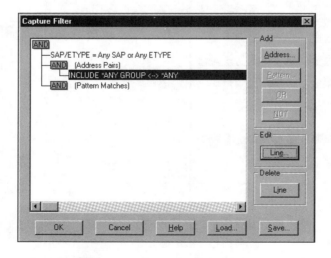

FIGURE 5.15 Capture filter. You can limit what data Network Monitor will capture through the use of a Capture Filter. This allows you to limit capture based on packet type, address, or even a particular text string or other byte pattern.

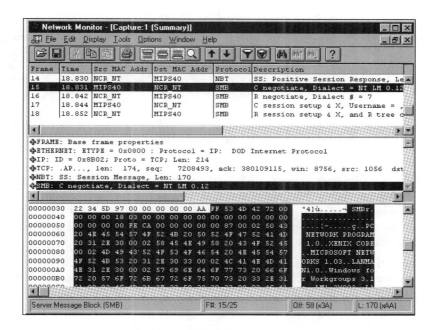

FIGURE 5.16 Capture detail. Once data is available, the detail view allows you to analyze it in depth, including what transport protocol was used, what kind of packet was captured, and the actual packet data is displayed in both Hex and ASCII (text) formats.

Browse your way down the capture display until you find an entry that lists SMB as the protocol (if you can't find one, run Capture/Start again, and execute a NET VIEW from the command line). You should see a display something like this (with minor variations):

```
7 34.743 NCR_NT          PANTHER40 SMB C negotiate, Dialect = NT LM 0.12
NCR_NT          PANTHER40 IP
--------------------------------------------------------------------------
+FRAME: Base frame properties
+ETHERNET: ETYPE = 0x0800 : Protocol = IP:  DOD Internet Protocol
+IP: ID = 0x75EC; Proto = TCP; Len: 214
+TCP: .AP..., len:  174, seq: 105127909-105128082, ack: 182164614, win: 8756,
src: 1285  dst:  139 (NBT Session)
+NBT: SS: Session Message, Len: 170
+SMB: C negotiate, Dialect = NT LM 0.12
--------------------------------------------------------------------------
00000:  02 60 8C 4C BC 99 00 00 1B 48 D2 AA 08 00 45 00   .`.L.....H....E.
00010:  00 D6 75 EC 40 00 80 06 68 28 0A 02 04 09 0A 02   ..u.@...h(......
00020:  04 01 05 05 00 8B 06 44 1F E5 0A DB 9C 86 50 18   .......D......P.
00030:  22 34 A5 A8 00 00 00 00 00 AA FF 53 4D 42 72 00   "4........SMBr.
```

```
00040:  00 00 00 18 03 00 00 00 00 00 00 00 00 00 00 00    ..............
00050:  00 00 00 00 FE CA 00 00 00 00 00 87 00 02 50 43    ............PC
00060:  20 4E 45 54 57 4F 52 4B 20 50 52 4F 47 52 41 4D    NETWORK PROGRAM
00070:  20 31 2E 30 00 02 58 45 4E 49 58 20 43 4F 52 45    1.0..XENIX CORE
00080:  00 02 4D 49 43 52 4F 53 4F 46 54 20 4E 45 54 57    ..MICROSOFT NETW
00090:  4F 52 4B 53 20 31 2E 30 33 00 02 4C 41 4E 4D 41    ORKS 1.03..LANMA
000A0:  4E 31 2E 30 00 02 57 69 6E 64 6F 77 73 20 66 6F    N1.0..Windows fo
000B0:  72 20 57 6F 72 6B 67 72 6F 75 70 73 20 33 2E 31    r Workgroups 3.1
000C0:  61 00 02 4C 4D 31 2E 32 58 30 30 32 00 02 4C 41    a..LM1.2X002..LA
000D0:  4E 4D 41 4E 32 2E 31 00 02 4E 54 20 4C 4D 20 30    NMAN2.1..NT LM 0
000E0:  2E 31 32 00                                        .12.
```

The top section (the one beginning 7 34.743 NCR_NT) is from the Capture Summary at the top of the display. It shows that this is frame #7, capture time 34.743, and it came from NCR_NT. Following on from there, we can see that the destination address was PANTHER40 (the machine on which this capture occurred), and the protocol was SMB (Server Message Block). A description of the packet is next.

The next section (the one beginning +FRAME) is the Detail window. It's actually a tree, so clicking any of the + characters will expand that line to show all the properties in question. Thus, clicking the first line yields:

```
-FRAME: Base frame properties
   FRAME: Time of capture = Aug 31, 1996 21:45:16.602
   FRAME: Time delta from previous physical frame: 4 milliseconds
   FRAME: Frame number: 7
   FRAME: Total frame length: 228 bytes
   FRAME: Capture frame length: 228 bytes
   FRAME: Frame data: Number of data bytes remaining = 228 (0x00E4)
```

From this window we can see when the frame (or network packet) was captured, along with other information. Clicking on down each + in turn will show us the packet's Ethernet properties, its IP properties (this packet was captured on an IP network), TCP and NBT properties, and finally its SMB properties.

Server Message Block (SMB) is the top-level protocol for NT's built-in networking: irrespective of the underlying name resolution protocol (in this case, NBT), control protocol (TCP), transport protocol (IP), and wire protocol (Ethernet), it's SMB that defines how NT does things like directory browsing. On another LAN the protocols could just as easily be NB-IPX, SPX, IPX and Token Ring, but the top-level protocol for NT is *always* SMB. Armed with that knowledge, let's look at the Hex dump at the bottom of the display:

```
00000:  02 60 8C 4C BC 99 00 00 1B 48 D2 AA 08 00 45 00    .`.L.....H....E.
00010:  00 D6 75 EC 40 00 80 06 68 28 0A 02 04 09 0A 02    ..u.@...h(......
00020:  04 01 05 05 00 8B 06 44 1F E5 0A DB 9C 86 50 18    .......D......P.
00030:  22 34 A5 A8 00 00 00 00 00 AA FF 53 4D 42 72 00    "4........SMBr.
00040:  00 00 00 18 03 00 00 00 00 00 00 00 00 00 00 00    ..............
00050:  00 00 00 00 FE CA 00 00 00 00 00 87 00 02 50 43    ............PC
00060:  20 4E 45 54 57 4F 52 4B 20 50 52 4F 47 52 41 4D    NETWORK PROGRAM
00070:  20 31 2E 30 00 02 58 45 4E 49 58 20 43 4F 52 45    1.0..XENIX CORE
00080:  00 02 4D 49 43 52 4F 53 4F 46 54 20 4E 45 54 57    ..MICROSOFT NETW
```

```
00090:    4F 52 4B 53 20 31 2E 30 33 00 02 4C 41 4E 4D 41    ORKS 1.03..LANMA
000A0:    4E 31 2E 30 00 02 57 69 6E 64 6F 77 73 20 66 6F    N1.0..Windows fo
000B0:    72 20 57 6F 72 6B 67 72 6F 75 70 73 20 33 2E 31    r Workgroups 3.1
000C0:    61 00 02 4C 4D 31 2E 32 58 30 30 32 00 02 4C 41    a..LM1.2X002..LA
000D0:    4E 4D 41 4E 32 2E 31 00 02 4E 54 20 4C 4D 20 30    NMAN2.1..NT LM 0
000E0:    2E 31 32 00                                        .12.
```

The last line in the Detail window (the one beginning +SMB) called this a Negotiate packet, and that's certainly what it looks like. Note the long list of compatible systems—a veritable history of Microsoft's network software: PC Net 1.0, Xenix, MS-Net 1.03, LAN Manager 1.0, WFWG 3.1, LAN Manager 1.2, LAN Manager 2.1, NT LM 0.12...

NT LM 0.12? Yes, the truth comes out! Elsewhere in this chapter, we've referred to the LanManServer and LanManWorkstation objects; that's NT's built-in networking. The 0.12 appears to be a new version numbering scheme.

Browsing down to later SMB packets (to make this easier, select Capture/Filter, double-click the Protocol==ANY line of the resulting Display Filter dialog shown in Figure 5.15, and disable everything except the SMB protocol, then click OK) will show things like the logon process (you'll see the workstation request \\panther40\ipc$) and eventually a list of servers on the network.

For certain commands, SMB will transmit native NT data, which is built on the international Unicode character set (see Chapter 1 and Appendix 1), so the names will appear as .P.A.N.T.H.E.R (the periods represent the zero-byte of the unicode character).

Following this same approach, you can examine various packets in the system, and by looking at them (in conjunction with a good understanding of the material in Appendix 2 and perhaps a good reference book on protocols) begin to make some sense of them. In trying to understand what the packets do, keep in mind that again, it's beyond the scope of this chapter (or even the whole book) to explain all the protocols you're likely to encounter, but some of the more interesting ones (all acronyms that follow are defined in Appendix 2 unless otherwise noted) will include the following:

- *RIP*, which carries router data on both IP and IPX networks

- *ARP*, which resolves DNS (whoever.whereever.com) names into IP (10.2.3.4) addresses

- *NBT* and *NBIPX*, which put NetBIOS (Microsoft's favorite protocol) onto the IP or IPX transport protocols

- *SAP*, which is used to announce service availability on IPX nets

- Microsoft Remote Procedure Call (*MSRPC*), which is used to carry out underlying operations (You'll frequently find that an SMB command packet is followed by several RPC packets.)

How can you troubleshoot with this? For starters, look for packet types that don't belong. For instance, if you're running an all-IP net, you shouldn't see any NBIPX, IPX, SPX, or SAP packets. The same applies for NBT, IP, TCP, UDP, and ARP packets on an all-IPX net. Look for an excessive amount of broadcast activity—typically UDP, NBF, or SAP packets. Those may indicate a browser problem.

Learning to use Network Monitor (or any protocol analyzer) takes time and patience. It often helps to exploit downtime when the net is idle or use a private subnet when you can control all traffic. You can turn on capture, perform some operation, stop capture, and view the results. Sometimes those can be very enlightening, as for example:

```
3588 1152.575 NCR_NT              PANTHER40 FTP Req. from Port 1341, 'PASS test'
NCR_NT           PANTHER40 IP
---------------------------------------------------------------------------------
+FRAME: Base frame properties
+ETHERNET: ETYPE = 0x0800 : Protocol = IP:  DOD Internet Protocol
+IP: ID = 0x7EFD; Proto = TCP; Len: 51
+TCP: .AP..., len:   11, seq: 111121206-111121216, ack: 188156601, win: 8675, src:
1341  dst:   21 (FTP)
+FTP: Req. from Port 1341, 'PASS test'
---------------------------------------------------------------------------------
00000:   02 60 8C 4C BC 99 00 00 1B 48 D2 AA 08 00 45 00    .`.L.....H....E.
00010:   00 33 7E FD 40 00 80 06 5F BA 0A 02 04 09 0A 02    .3~.@..._.......
00020:   04 01 05 3D 00 15 06 9F 93 36 0B 37 0A B9 50 18    ...=.....6.7..P.
00030:   21 E3 15 30 00 00 50 41 53 53 20 74 65 73 74 0D    !..0..PASS test.
00040:   0A                                                 .
```

This display is quite real—it was captured on a machine running the IIS FTP Service (see Chapter 7), which had been configured to allow both anonymous access and access by password. And here you see the password, *test*, in plain text, readable to anyone with a protocol analyzer.

Security Issues The subject of passwords brings us to the matter of security. As we said earlier, Network Monitor *is nothing less than a protocol analyzer implemented in software*. To put it another way, Network Monitor *is the NT network equivalent of a wiretap on a telephone line*. There is no greater risk to network security. Using Network Monitor, you or anyone else with access to the Administrative Tools group will have the ability to "sniff" any and all network packets sent to or from your server—not just simple protocols like ftp either (everyone knows that's insecure!). The following is an example of e-mail:

```
123 166.720 PANTHER40 NCR_NT          SMB R read & X, Read 0x74 PANTHER40
NCR_NT           IP
---------------------------------------------------------------------------------
+FRAME: Base frame properties
+ETHERNET: ETYPE = 0x0800 : Protocol = IP:  DOD Internet Protocol
+IP: ID = 0x2662; Proto = TCP; Len: 220
+TCP: .AP..., len:  180, seq: 189081087-189081266, ack: 112034892, win: 8760, src:
139 (NBT Session)  dst: 1355
+NBT: SS: Session Message, Len: 176
+SMB: R read & X, Read 0x74
---------------------------------------------------------------------------------
00000:   00 00 1B 48 D2 AA 02 60 8C 4C BC 99 08 00 45 00    ...H...`.L....E.
00010:   00 DC 26 62 40 00 80 06 B7 AC 0A 02 04 01 0A 02    ..&b@...........
00020:   04 09 00 8B 05 4B 0B 45 25 FF 06 AD 84 4C 50 18    .....K.E%....LP.
00030:   22 38 0A 06 00 00 00 00 00 B0 FF 53 4D 42 2E 00    "8.........SMB..
00040:   00 00 00 98 00 20 00 00 00 00 00 00 00 00 00 00    .....  .........
```

```
00050:   00 00 01 10 FE CA 03 08 40 2C 0C FF 00 00 00 FF    ........@,......
00060:   FF 00 00 00 00 74 00 3C 00 00 00 00 00 00 00 00    .....t.<........
00070:   00 00 00 75 00 00 00 00 6A 72 75 6C 65 79 00 00    ...u....jruley..
00080:   00 00 00 52 45 3A 20 45 2D 4D 61 69 6C 20 53 65    ...RE: E-Mail Se
00090:   63 75 72 69 74 79 00 00 00 00 00 00 00 00 00 00    curity..........
000A0:   00 00 00 00 00 00 00 00 00 00 00 00 33 00 35 00    ............3.5.
000B0:   17 00 1F 00 08 00 CC 07 00 30 30 30 30 30 30 30    .........0000000
000C0:   36 00 00 00 45 08 00 00 00 00 00 00 00 00 18 00    6...E..........
000D0:   00 00 00 00 00 00 00 00 00 00 00 00 00 00 00 00    ................
000E0:   00 00 35 F7 C8 00 00 00 00 00                      ..5.......
```

Note the address (jruley) and the title (RE: E-Mail Security). The message body itself isn't visible (it's in a packed binary format in one of the follow-up packets), but the point is surely made: *Network Monitor is a serious security risk.*

In fact, it's not as bad as all that. Microsoft took steps with NT Network Monitor to make sure it stays under control. To wit:

- *No promiscuous mode support*: Most sniffers employ a special network card operating mode in which the card becomes *promiscuous:* that is, captures any packet that goes over the wire, irrespective of whether it was intended for the card in question. Instead of doing this, Microsoft uses a new feature of the NDIS 4.0 driver specification to capture packets as they are sent from or received by your card. Thus, Network Monitor can capture *only* packets sent from or to one of your server's network cards.

- *Password protection*: In addition to placing Network Monitor *only* on NT Servers, and running it from the Administrative Tools group (which isn't available to end users), you can set capture and display passwords through Control Panel/Monitoring Agent. This will ensure that even among Administrative users, only those who know the passwords can use Network Monitor.

- *No remote operation*: NT 4.0 Workstations come with the same Network Monitor Agent as NT Server, but Network Monitor cannot connect to those agents. It can use them only for identification purposes (besides typing in capture and display passwords, Control Panel/Monitoring Agent lets you associate a text description with your network card(s), which can save puzzling out which Ethernet MAC address belongs to which workstation on the net). Network Monitor can be operated only locally. You must be physically present and logged in at the NT console to use it.

On the other hand, if you really *want* promiscuous mode support and remote operation, check out SMS Network Monitor, covered (briefly) in Chapter 8.

Disk Fragmentation

Since NT was first introduced, Microsoft's position on disk fragmentation has been as follows:

1. Use NTFS because it doesn't require defragmenting.

2. If you run a DOS-compatible FAT partition, boot DOS and use a DOS-based defragmenter (or an OS/2 defragmenter on HPFS partitions).

3. As a last resort, back everything up on tape, reformat your disk, and restore the tape.

Of course, NTFS does in fact require defragmentation. We've seen a 2:1 or better[15] performance improvement by defragmenting NTFS partitions, and other users (especially those running heavily used servers) report much the same results.

As it happens, this isn't the first time Dave Cutler and his ex-Digital crew have missed the boat on fragmentation. Cutler's VMS operating system had much the same problem on VAX computers, and Executive Software[16] eventually filled the gap with a line of *Diskeeper* products. In 1994 they brought the same technology to NT with *Diskeeper for Windows NT*. Separate versions are available for NT Workstation and Server, and a "Light"[17] version for NT 4.0 recently became available that's free for the download from Executive Software's Web site: http://www.execsoft.com.

Two caveats on Diskeeper: First, *read the release notes before installing it*. We periodically hear from users who've had files corrupted and blame Diskeeper. Invariably, they did not follow instructions. Diskeeper operates as a low-level adjunct to the NT file system drivers, and as such it cannot safely defragment files from applications (such as Oracle server) that bypass the file system and manipulate bits on the disk directly. This is documented in the release notes, and you can deal with it by adding the files in question to a list of files that Diskeeper will not touch. Second, be aware that in the past, each revision of NT (including not only major version number changes, but also service packs) has required a new version of Diskeeper. Again, Diskeeper acts as an adjunct to the NT file system—when Microsoft modifies kernel drivers that affect the file system, Diskeeper is affected in turn. With NT 4.0, Microsoft has provided "hook" APIs to the file system that *should* allow Diskeeper to work even if the file system changes. But to be on the safe side, check with Executive Software before applying an NT service pack or upgrade.

Undeleting Files

Currently, no file system undelete[18] programs for NT are available. However, three approaches *may* retrieve an accidentally deleted file. First, if you're using the DOS-compatible FAT file system, you can boot your computer to DOS (using either NT multiboot or a DOS boot diskette) and use DOS undelete software (likewise, for NT versions prior to 4.0, you can undelete files on HPFS partitions by using an OS/2 boot diskette and OS/2 disk utilities).

---

15 On the order of *5:1* for a heavily fragmented NTFS partition. See the "Windows NT" column in the August 1995 WINDOWS Magazine for details.

16 You can reach the company at (818) 829-6468.

17 Diskeeper Light differs from the full-up versions in that it implements a single-pass defragmentation scheme rather than automatic defragmentation in the background. The latter is a much better choice, especially on file servers.

18 There is, of course, the Recycle Bin on the NT Desktop, but it stores *only* files that are deleted using the Windows Explorer. Files deleted from the command line or under program control are, in a word, *gone!*

Alternatively, if you are not using NTFS disk compression, try the DiskProbe application from the Windows NT 4.0 Resource Kit.[19] Although this doesn't provide a simple undelete, it does provide a way to search the disk cluster by cluster for data on *any* partition type, including NTFS. If you find a cluster containing your data, you can copy it (and closely adjacent clusters) to a new file.

Finally, you can always restore a file from backup, provided you've been keeping regular backups.

Several vendors have expressed interest in providing a true undelete capability for NT, along with other disk maintenance tools. None is available at this writing. As and when such a utility ships, you can expect us to report it on our *electronic update*, at the location mentioned in the Introduction.

Resources

A variety of available command-line tools can be of help when you are trying to track down low-level protocol problems. Among these are the IP network utilities *ping, arp, nbtstat, netstat, nslookup, tracert, and route* (all covered in Chapter 6), and the IPX network utility *ipxroute* (Chapter 10).

The *Windows NT Resource Kit* (covered in Appendix 4) includes a very wide range of maintenance and support tools, including tools to back up and restore registry files, monitors for the browser and domain services, and even an upgrade for the single-CPU version of NT that adds multiprocessor support. (The hardware, needless to say, is not included!) These are covered in Appendix 4.

Microsoft *Systems Management Server* (SMS) provides a wide variety of troubleshooting and maintenance tools, including an enhanced version of Network Monitor that supports both promiscuous mode and remote operation (which makes it an even more effective network wiretap!), along with remote software installation/upgrade capability. With SMS version 1.2, Microsoft added remote control support for NT 3.51 and 4.0 as well. It's of interest primarily to larger sites and is covered in Chapter 8, where we also cover troubleshooting and maintenance of Microsoft's Remote Access Services (RAS) and other wide-area networking issues.

Finally, don't neglect the release notes that come with an NT distribution CD. Aside from whatever printed documentation you find, check the CD for .TXT and .WR* files. Currently, NT 4.0 setup copies README.WRI (general release notes) into \winnt\system32, while NETWORK.WRI (network card issues, and related material) and PRINTERS.WRI (printer issues) are copied into your \winnt directory.

NT Messages

Windows NT can produce a variety of messages during its normal operation along with a wide range of error messages. Prior to NT 4.0, you could expect all NT distribution CDs to include a Messages database in a run-time Microsoft Access format. Unfortunately, this does not seem to

---

19 Covered in Appendix 4.

be included with either NT 4.0 Workstation or Server. We *assume* it will be included with the NT 4.0 Resource Kit—and in any case, all editions of that kit have included an extensive manual on NT Messages. We cover the Resource Kit in Appendix 4.

Character Mode, Stop, and Hardware Malfunction Messages The ultimate worst-case situation you have to deal with in Windows NT is the "blue screen crash." This happens when the Windows NT kernel encounters a completely unrecoverable error either in the kernel software or in hardware. The system will stop and display a screen similar to that illustrated in Figure 5.17.

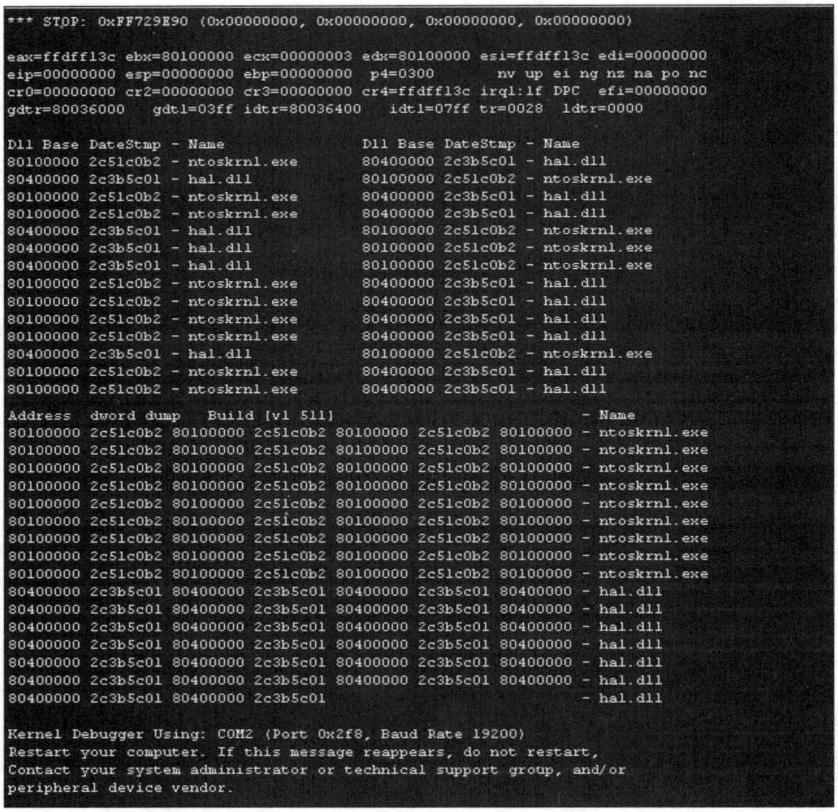

```
*** STOP: 0xFF729E90 (0x00000000, 0x00000000, 0x00000000, 0x00000000)

eax=ffdff13c ebx=80100000 ecx=00000003 edx=80100000 esi=ffdff13c edi=00000000
eip=00000000 esp=00000000 ebp=00000000 p4=0300     nv up ei ng nz na po nc
cr0=00000000 cr2=00000000 cr3=00000000 cr4=ffdff13c irql:1f DPC  efi=00000000
gdtr=80036000   gdt1=03ff idtr=80036400    idt1=07ff tr=0028   ldtr=0000


Dll Base DateStmp - Name                 Dll Base DateStmp - Name
80100000 2c51c0b2 - ntoskrnl.exe         80400000 2c3b5c01 - hal.dll
80400000 2c3b5c01 - hal.dll              80100000 2c51c0b2 - ntoskrnl.exe
80100000 2c51c0b2 - ntoskrnl.exe         80400000 2c3b5c01 - hal.dll
80100000 2c51c0b2 - ntoskrnl.exe         80400000 2c3b5c01 - hal.dll
80400000 2c3b5c01 - hal.dll              80100000 2c51c0b2 - ntoskrnl.exe
80400000 2c3b5c01 - hal.dll              80100000 2c51c0b2 - ntoskrnl.exe
80400000 2c3b5c01 - hal.dll              80100000 2c51c0b2 - ntoskrnl.exe
80100000 2c51c0b2 - ntoskrnl.exe         80400000 2c3b5c01 - hal.dll
80100000 2c51c0b2 - ntoskrnl.exe         80400000 2c3b5c01 - hal.dll
80100000 2c51c0b2 - ntoskrnl.exe         80400000 2c3b5c01 - hal.dll
80400000 2c3b5c01 - hal.dll              80100000 2c51c0b2 - ntoskrnl.exe
80100000 2c51c0b2 - ntoskrnl.exe         80400000 2c3b5c01 - hal.dll
80100000 2c51c0b2 - ntoskrnl.exe         80400000 2c3b5c01 - hal.dll

Address  dword dump   Build [v1 511]                    - Name
80100000 2c51c0b2 80100000 2c51c0b2 80100000 2c51c0b2 80100000 - ntoskrnl.exe
80100000 2c51c0b2 80100000 2c51c0b2 80100000 2c51c0b2 80100000 - ntoskrnl.exe
80100000 2c51c0b2 80100000 2c51c0b2 80100000 2c51c0b2 80100000 - ntoskrnl.exe
80100000 2c51c0b2 80100000 2c51c0b2 80100000 2c51c0b2 80100000 - ntoskrnl.exe
80100000 2c51c0b2 80100000 2c51c0b2 80100000 2c51c0b2 80100000 - ntoskrnl.exe
80100000 2c51c0b2 80100000 2c51c0b2 80100000 2c51c0b2 80100000 - ntoskrnl.exe
80100000 2c51c0b2 80100000 2c51c0b2 80100000 2c51c0b2 80100000 - ntoskrnl.exe
80100000 2c51c0b2 80100000 2c51c0b2 80100000 2c51c0b2 80100000 - ntoskrnl.exe
80100000 2c51c0b2 80100000 2c51c0b2 80100000 2c51c0b2 80100000 - ntoskrnl.exe
80400000 2c3b5c01 80400000 2c3b5c01 80400000 2c3b5c01 80400000 - hal.dll
80400000 2c3b5c01 80400000 2c3b5c01 80400000 2c3b5c01 80400000 - hal.dll
80400000 2c3b5c01 80400000 2c3b5c01 80400000 2c3b5c01 80400000 - hal.dll
80400000 2c3b5c01 80400000 2c3b5c01 80400000 2c3b5c01 80400000 - hal.dll
80400000 2c3b5c01 80400000 2c3b5c01 80400000 2c3b5c01 80400000 - hal.dll
80400000 2c3b5c01 80400000 2c3b5c01 80400000 2c3b5c01 80400000 - hal.dll
80400000 2c3b5c01 80400000 2c3b5c01                           - hal.dll

Kernel Debugger Using: COM2 (Port 0x2f8, Baud Rate 19200)
Restart your computer. If this message reappears, do not restart.
Contact your system administrator or technical support group, and/or
peripheral device vendor.
```

FIGURE 5.17 Blue screen crash. You should *never* see this display from NT under normal circumstances—if you do, then the system has become completely unstable, and will require a hardware reboot. The *** STOP 0x000000... message will identify the type of error involved, and it is followed by a register dump that can be helpful in identifying what's gone wrong with the system.

In a "blue screen crash," the first line displayed on the screen will generally be of the form

```
*** STOP 0x000000nn DESCRIPTION
```

The 0x000...number is a unique hexadecimal identifier that identifies the STOP message number and will indicate the cause of the crash. The text immediately following it is a text description of the crash. This will be followed by a system trace, including an identification of the address areas in which the crash occurred, register dump, and a system call tree indicating the various functions that are in the tree of system calls above the function in which the crash occurred. They are of value only to a system developer or hardware support engineer, but if the same crash occurs repeatedly, it may be worth writing it down, in particular the first two or three lines of information on the screen so that the information can be presented when you call Tech Support.

The follow-up to a blue screen crash generally involves making a change to the hardware settings in the system, removing hardware devices from the system, or taking other relatively drastic steps. The list of troubleshooting problems and work-arounds in this chapter gives some suggestions for certain well-known errors (such as the 0x0000000A IRQL problem) but the general nature of this kind of crash is that it's serious.

Hardware Malfunctions If a low-level hardware problem occurs on a system at such a level that Windows NT kernel cannot handle it at all (technically, a *non-maskable interrupt* or NMI), you're likely to see a message beginning "Hardware malfunction..." and ending "...call your hardware vendor for support." And the message says it all—call the vendor.

Status and Warning Messages Status and warning messages will appear as a Windows alert and indicate some specific matter of concern for the system. They may simply indicate some piece of system information that is of general interest such as "Password too complex." They may warn of a problem with some components of the system such as a "Printer Out Of Paper" message. They may report a more serious problem such as the "Access Denied" message that indicates that an application has tried to do something for which it doesn't have the necessary security permissions. Consult the Resource Kit's NT Messages manual for details on the specific message.

Network Messages Errors that occur within the network components of Windows NT and Windows NT Server will be identified as network errors and will have a four-digit number associated with them. In addition to the messages database you can get a brief description of each error by typing *net helpmsg* and the message number; for instance:

```
D:\>net helpmsg 2102

The workstation driver is not installed.

EXPLANATION

Windows NT is not installed, or your configuration file is incorrect.

ACTION

Install Windows NT, or see your network administrator about possible problems
with your configuration file.
```

But the explanation for this message in the NT Messages manual (or database) will be far more complete.

Online Troubleshooting Guides

Microsoft has a series of useful step-by-step guides to troubleshooting problems that are available from its Web site at http://www.microsoft.com/support (pick Windows NT Workstation or Server from the GO! List). Topics with online guides available include:[20] Applications, Directory Replication, Fault Tolerance, Licensing, Remote Access, Support Resources, User Profiles, File Systems, Joining a Domain, Printing, Setup, and Trust Relationships. In addition, there is some good troubleshooting information available in NT Server Books Online. Check under Troubleshooting in the Index for a list of topics.

Service Packs

Microsoft periodically makes fixes and upgrades available for NT as *service packs*. These are numbered, and you will find from time to time that a given piece of software may require that one be installed. You can find out about the latest service packs on Microsoft's Web site at http://www.microsoft.com/support (pick Windows NT Workstation or Server from the GO! List).

Two caveats about service packs: Once you have installed one, you must reapply it any time you install new components from your original NT setup CD (the service pack may include updates for the new component(s) you've installed). And there have been problems with some service packs—after all, they update system software, and it's all but impossible for Microsoft to check the update against all possible hardware/software combinations. It's wise to check the NT support newsgroups to see what problems have been reported before applying a service pack.

Getting NT Tech Support

Even the best technicians get in over their heads from time to time and must call in the support engineers. Unfortunately, calling for NT technical support can be expensive. Microsoft provided 30 days of free support for installation problems with NT 3.1, but dropped all free support in NT 3.5. With NT 3.51, support was reintroduced, but only the first call was free (and then only if you called on a setup issue). With NT 4.0, support has been increased to *two* free calls (again, setup-related issues only). After that, you're expected to pay.

Currently, Microsoft's least expensive telephone support for NT is $195 per incident (what Microsoft calls "priority support"). Microsoft justifies this pricing by calling NT a "Business Systems" product rather than a personal product, but it seems excessive for NT Workstation. Fortunately, Unisys offers a low-cost[21] support program for setup problems, and they cover all versions of NT on all platforms.

---

20 This list is current as of August 1996.

21 Just $30 per incident when we last checked. Call (800) 328-0440.

Larger organizations that want to purchase a support contract or one of Microsoft's higher-end "Premier" or "Select" support options may call Microsoft Product Support Services at (800) 426-9400. Microsoft can also refer you to a local "solution provider" if you prefer to deal with someone in your area.

Crash Recovery

Windows NT is a very reliable operating system, but it *can* crash because of errant drivers, hardware problems, or—rarely—undetected operating system (or application) bugs. Beginning with NT 3.5, you have some options for handling such crashes. The most important of these are the Recovery settings, controlled by the Control Panel/System object's Startup/Shutdown tab (see Figure 5.18).

In many cases, the most obvious of the recovery options is, of course, the one to automatically reboot after a crash. However, if the problem that caused the server to crash in the first place recurs, you can put your server into an infinite loop: reboot, crash, reboot, crash...

Obviously, you should enable the options to write a system event (and possibly to send an administrative alert) if you're enabling the automatic reboot feature. Enabling the memory

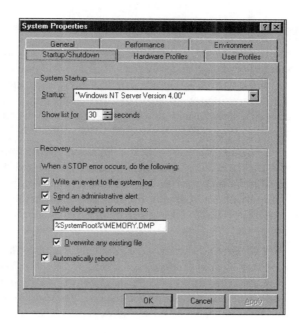

FIGURE 5.18 Recovery. NT 4.0 provides recovery options that may be used to control how an NT system behaves during and after a system crash. These options are set using the Startup/Shutdown tab in Control Panel/System.

dump feature can also help, though decoding it will most likely require cooperation from a Microsoft support engineer.

Incidentally, the crash recovery behavior of NT is controlled, like so much else, through the configuration registry. The HKEY_LOCAL_MACHINE\SYSTEM\CurrentControlSet\ Control\CrashControl key contains entries that match all the control panel settings. As we've said before, making these settings in Control Panel is preferable to making them directly in the registry, but if you're managing several servers on a LAN or WAN, you may find it simpler to set them using the registry editor.

DRWATSON and DRWATSON32

When applications crash in Windows NT, Dr. Watson will appear. This is a simplified run-time debugger application that (optionally) performs a crash dump and maintains a log of application errors. It is not of much immediate help, but if you find that an application is crashing repeatedly, having the logs available may help you (or more likely, the vendor) diagnose the problem. For more information, launch Dr. Watson manually by typing drwtsn32 at an NT command prompt, and press the Help button.

Making and Updating Boot and Emergency Repair Diskettes

You cannot create an old-fashioned, DOS-style boot into character mode for Windows NT, but you can nonetheless boot the operating system from a floppy[22] (although the NT systems files will still have to load from the hard disk), which can be a lifesaver if the boot sector on your hard disk accidentally gets overwritten. You can do this by running winnt32.exe (from the /i386, /mips, /ppc, or /alpha directory of the distribution CD-ROM) with the /ox command-line switch. You will need three formatted floppy diskettes to hold all the files.

Of course, a good support person covers all the bases, so having *both* the boot diskettes *and* an emergency disk is a good idea. The latter is normally created during the NT setup process, but if you need to make one later (or update the data on the original, which is a good idea, especially after you install any software packages or modify the user database on an NT Server), you can use the RDISK utility provided with NT versions from 3.5 on (see Figure 5.19).

> *Warning: If the Emergency Disk was created during the installation process and never updated, it contains the original registry settings for the computer, which most likely will include only default user accounts. Restoring the registry from such a diskette will destroy any user accounts created after the installation. Because NTFS tracks directory permissions based on security access rights, it can make acessing data impossible as well.*

---

22 On Intel systems only. On RISC systems, use the ARCS menu to execute NT setup directly from the CD, as described in Chapter 2.

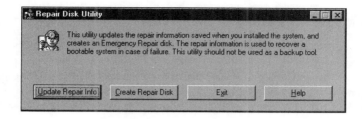

FIGURE 5.19 Repair disk utility. NT's RDISK utility allows you to create (or update) an NT emergency repair diskette. Used in conjunction with a book diskette, this allows recovery from a variety of serious system errors.

With the boot diskettes and Emergency Disk available, it is possible to recover from most "soft" errors (corrupt files) that prevent NT from starting up normally. Insert the NT Startup disk in your A: drive and reboot the system. When NT Setup starts, it will give you an option to carry out a new installation *or* repair an existing installation. Select the latter option. You will then be asked to insert the Emergency Diskette, which is used to recover Registry data. You will also have the opportunity to copy system files from the CD.

On Intel-based systems, you also need to make a *recovery diskette*. This is simply a formatted diskette onto which you have copied the key system files that may need to be restored in order for NT to boot (note that you will need to clear the system/hidden/readonly attributes to copy these files):

- *NTLDR*

- *NTDETECT.COM*

- *NTBOOTDD.SYS* (On systems with older SCSI drives—if the file doesn't exist, you don't need it.)

- *BOOT.INI*

- *BOOTSECT.DOS* (If you have a dual-boot Setup)

On RISC-based systems, the needed files are OSLOADER.EXE and HAL.DLL. Use the ARCS menu to create an additional boot option with the following values:

- OSLOADER= SCSI(0)DISK(0)FDISK(0)\OSLOADER.EXE

- SYSTEMPARTITION=SCSI(0)DISK(0)FDISK(0 or 1, depending on whether you want to boot from the first or second floppy drive)

- OSLOADPARTITION and OSLOADFILENAME to the same values they're set for in your regular boot menu

Troubleshooting Hit List

In any system as complex as Windows NT a broad range of errors and problems can occur. As we note in Appendix 6, the potential for errors increases enormously when the system is networked. So it's impossible for us to present a comprehensive list of the errors you are likely to encounter and directions for fixing them. However, certain errors are more likely to occur than others, so we present some of the most frequently encountered errors with suggestions about how to troubleshoot them and fix them.[23] We've arranged them by general category.

Failure to Boot

In general, when a Windows NT system that has otherwise operated correctly suddenly refuses to boot (or recover from a reboot), you have to expect that one of two things has happened. Either there has been a major hardware failure or something has changed in the configuration. Major hardware failures or boot problems that occur when a system is first created are generally of the type that we covered in the Troubleshooting section of Chapter 2, and we urge you to look there. The following are possible explanations for the problem:

- *Misconfigured System.* It's worth remembering that many problems that appear to be due to boot failure can actually reflect misconfiguration. For instance, if you change the video type in Windows NT Setup to one that's not compatible with your particular hardware, you may have a completely successful boot (NT is still running) but find yourself looking at a blank screen. So the best initial step to take with *any* boot problem is to try selecting the previous configuration from the Last Known Good configuration menu, or if that doesn't work, try using the Windows NT Emergency Diskette. Get the boot diskette originally supplied with Windows NT, insert it in drive A, reboot the computer, and when it asks whether you want to do an installation or attempt a repair, select repair and insert the emergency disk. The odds are good that this will allow the system to "heal itself." But if that doesn't work, some other boot problems that may occur include those listed below.

- *Unrecognized Partition Types and BOOT.INI.* When you install Windows NT on a system in which an unusual partitioning scheme is used or a partition type is presented that Windows NT does not recognize, it is possible for Windows NT to install but for the system partition to be incorrectly identified. The boot subsystem may assume that system files are on partition 0 when they are in fact on partition 1, for instance. Inspect the BOOT.INI file to make sure that it refers to the correct partition or logical disk drive and directory. You may also want to check and examine the arc system formatted syntax for the initial partition location. This will be in a format like:

---

23 Information in this section is from a variety of sources, including the Microsoft on-line Knowlege Base (go MSKB on Compuserve), the Microsoft TechNet CD-ROM, reports from Windows NT users, and our own experience with Windows NT over the past few years. We can't claim to have personally experienced every problem (or tested every fix) reported here, but we've had quite a few!

```
SCSI(0)DISK(0)RDISK(0)PARTITION(1)\WINDOWS="Windows NT".
MULTI(0)DISK(0)RDISK(0)PARTITION(1)\WINDOWS="Windows NT".
```

(The format here is BUS(*number*), where the bus can be SCSI or AT-bus, the latter represented by MULTI, the disk controller number, represented by DISK, the disk itself, represented by RDISK where R stands for Rigit, and the PARTITION.)

PARTITION(1) is most likely to be the cause of a problem here, although on some machines the controller, represented by DISK(0) could be the cause of the problem, as noted in the section on installation. Try changing the partition number to 2 in this case (PARTITION(0) refers to the entire unpartitioned physical disk) or to another partition number depending on the contents of your partition table (which you can examine using the *fdisk* program on DOS machines).

- *Boot NTLDR Not Found.* If for any reason the NTLDR file is deleted from the root of the C drive, Windows NT will be unable to boot. You can cure this situation by using the NT boot disks with the NT Setup *repair* option and copying NTLDR back on the hard disk from the recovery diskette.

- *NTDETECT.COM Deleted.* When Windows NT starts on x86 systems, it employs the NTDETECT.COM program to detect the hardware configuration on the system—which updates the hardware information in the Configuration Registry and begins to carry out the boot process. This insulates Windows NT from configuration errors that may occur when someone changes a hardware component. However, it also means that if NTDETECT.COM is deleted, the system will fail to boot, generally failing with a fatal general system error of 0x00000067-Configuration Initialization Failed. This can also indicate that an error has been introduced into the BOOT.INI file (an indicator for this is if an additional line appears in the BOOT.INI file besides those for NT and for any alternate operating systems that existed when NT was first installed). So check the BOOT.INI file as well. If the BOOT.INI file is found to be correct, you will need to restore the NTDETECT.COM file from the installation CD or recovery diskette.

- *Problems in the OS Loader.* If the BOOT.INI is sufficiently correct for the OS to start loading but then presents a bad path, it's possible that the OS Loader blue screen will start but will then fail with one of these errors:

  Could not read from the selected boot disk.

  The system did not load because it could not find the following file:...

  Either of these errors, again, indicates a problem with the BOOT.INI file, and as with NTLDR and NTDETECT.COM, the solution is to restore it from your recovery diskette.

- *Failure to Boot Back to a Previous Operating System.* On systems in which a dual boot is installed (NT+DOS, Windows 95, OS/2, etc.), NT uses a hidden file called BOOTSECT.DOS to store information about the physical layout of the hard disk so that the system can boot back into DOS (or other operating systems) from Windows NT. If this file is inadvertently deleted or cannot be found during an attempt to boot to an alternate operating system, the boot process will fail with the message: "Couldn't open boot sector file." Once again, to solve the problem, restore the file from the copy on your recovery diskettes.

- *OS/2 Boot Manager Problems.* The Boot Manager that IBM supplies with OS/2 versions 2.0 and 2.1, attempts to perform very much the same functions that the Windows NT Flexboot performs. Unfortunately, each tends to compete with the other to a certain extent, so it's possible that a system that has been set up with the OS/2 Boot Manager will fail to operate properly after the Windows NT Flexboot has been installed. You can get around this problem by booting OS/2 from the installation disk, pressing escape at the first opportunity to get to the OS/2 command line, bringing up the OS/2 fdisk, and reinstalling Boot Manager, adding entries for each of the bootable partitions in the system.

When Boot Manager is installed *after* the Windows NT Flexboot, it generally seems to operate correctly. OS/2 Boot Manager will give you the option either to boot DOS or OS/2—there won't be any mention of Windows NT, but if you boot to DOS, you will get the Windows NT Flexboot—giving you the option to use Windows NT or DOS. Another option is to avoid the use of the OS/2 Boot Manager entirely and instead use the OS/2 Dual Boot feature in conjunction with Windows NT, although this method does not give the same flexibility in terms of booting from multiple partitions on the disk.

A related common problem with the OS/2 Boot Manager is that the Boot Manager and Windows NT Flexboot may disagree on which drive letters represent which partitions in the system. The simplest solution is to install the OS/2 Boot Manager in the *last* partition on the drive and put Windows NT on the *primary* (first) partition at the start of the drive. Both systems will then agree on the drive letter assignments for all partitions (unless, of course, the "sticky drive letter" feature of Windows NT has been used to modify the drive letters used with Windows NT).

If you've tried all of the above and NT *still* won't start, it's time to call tech support, but to save yourself time (and possibly money), check the online troubleshooting guides mentioned earlier. Then check the "Before You Call..." topics in README.WRI. Then call technical support.

CPU Problems

Generally, a problem with the Central Processor Unit in a Window NT system will be detected during the installation process and the system will fail to install properly. Again, there are a few things to watch out for. The first—which again, is an installation problem—is to make sure you are installing on a CPU that supports NT. Windows NT requires a 25MHz 386 or higher processor. Note that for the 386 processor it does not support version B1 and earlier 386 chips. If you have such a chip you'll need a CPU upgrade. Also look for the following:

- *Machine Check Exception on Pentium Chips.* Windows NT machines equipped with early Intel Pentium (P5) CPUs may experience a *machine check exception fault* during operation, particularly if they have been in heavy use over an extended period of time. A machine check exception on the Pentium processor chip is an indication that the processor self-test hardware has detected an internal fault. It most commonly indicates an overheat condition. This is not unknown on early model Pentium CPUs, and it generally indicates a cooling problem in the system. The first solution, of course, is to turn the computer off and let it cool down. If the problem happens repeatedly, you may want to open up the case and make sure any on-chip cooling fan is operating and make sure that there isn't any obstruction in the airflow, and consider moving the system so that the airflow holes are not being obstructed by walls, desks, or other obstructions. Finally, contact your system manufacturer to see about some kind of an upgrade.

- *Poor CPU Performance.* This is a topic that really refers to the tuning section earlier in this chapter. If the computer is running but seems to be dead slow and the processor appears bogged with tasks that should not bog it, you may want to check to see first if the "turbo switch" (if any) is depressed. Second, you may need to reboot the computer and examine the CMOS register settings to see if the computer is set for one or more memory wait states. A computer operating in a one-wait state condition effectively is operating at a half the stated CPU clock rate, because after every clock cycle involving a memory access it will idle or "wait" one cycle to give memory a chance to stabilize. In the event that your system is using one or more wait states, try resetting to a zero-wait state condition. If the computer refuses to run, your memory is physically incapable of operating at the processor full speed, and the solution is to buy faster memory chips. Beyond that, refer to the section on *Performance Tuning* earlier in this chapter for suggestions on how overall system throughput may be increased.

COM Port Problems

Problems with serial (COM) ports will generally be due to one of the following mistakes:

- *Attempting to use one port for two applications.* Aside from the usual problems with improperly matched baud rate, parity, stop bits, and so forth, between an application and the device attached to a COM port, Windows NT presents one new class of problem. It absolutely, positively will *not* let you assign a COM port to another application or device when one is already using it. You can see this by looking at Control Panel/Ports. If you have a mouse installed on COM1 port for instance, the COM1 port will not appear in the Control Panel listing even though it does exist in the system. The reason is that Windows NT has assigned the COM port permanently to the mouse, and it will not allow that port to be used by any other application or service until and unless the mouse releases it.

You can determine which ports are assigned to devices in this way by inspecting the HKEY_LOCAL_MACHINE/HARDWARE/DESCRIPTION/System/Multifunction Adapter/0/Serial Controller entry (this may say EISA adapter instead of multifunction adapter on EISA machines, etc.), as illustrated in Figure 5.20.

The ports will be stored in a sub-key numbered from zero through one less than the number of COM ports. Zero through three respectively, for instance, represent COM1 through

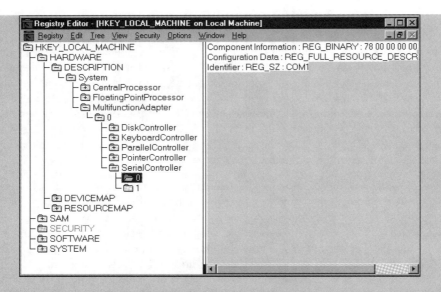

FIGURE 5.20 Registry editor. NT's system registry database is edited using the Registry Editor (REGEDT32.EXE). It allows registry "hive" files to be loaded, viewed, and modified. The particular registry "key" shown here displays information about COM port utilization on the system.

COM4. The device using the COM port will appear within the numbered sub-key for the COM port in question. If no hardware device is using the COM port, the next thing to look for is the possibility that you have some application or service using the port.

An example of this would be if COM1 is physically attached to a modem and you attempt to use COM1 from a communications program at the same time that Remote Access Services (RASs) are running bound to COM1 through the network's Control Panel. Windows NT won't let you assign the port to the communications program. The solution is to stop RAS (or the other service in question) using the Services applet in the Control Panel while you use the communications program, then close the communications program (or select another COM port temporarily) and start RAS again.

- *Incompatible Hardware.* Most other COM port problems will be improper matches between the COM port settings and the external device as mentioned above, or in rare cases, you may run into a COM port using a universal asynchronous receiver transmitter (UART) chip that is incompatible with Windows NT. The way to test for this is to attach a known good serial device (such as a dumb terminal or another computer running a terminal program) using a null modem cable to the port, run the Windows terminal, select identical baud rates, parity settings, and word lengths on both ends of the connection, and then try typing on the Windows NT system's keyboard. If only one or two characters appear on the other screen and the port appears to hang up and refuse to transmit, you need a new UART chip.

Machines known to have this problem include several models of DEC machines in the 300 and 400C series.

Some systems with 16550 UART chips may be incompatible with NT's support for a FIFO buffer. If you have a 16550 and are experiencing COM port problems (you may note an event log entry saying, "A FIFO was detected and enabled"), try disabling it with the Ports control panel applet (select the port in question, click Settings, then Advanced, and you'll find a FIFO checkbox).

• *COM3, COM4,—COMn Problem.* On machines that don't include a Micro-Channel Adapter (MCA) bus—virtually all machines except IBM PS/2 computers—COM3 and COM4 support is provided by sharing the same interrupt as COM1 and COM2 with two different port addresses. That is, COM3 has the same interrupt number as COM1 but is at a different physical port address. COM4 is at the same interrupt level as COM2, but at a different port. This works fine until you try to use both COM1 and COM3 (or COM2 and COM4) at the same time. Windows NT supports interrupt sharing by the two sets of ports but it cannot and will not permit devices to use the ports at the same time. As a result, you may find it impossible, for example, to attach modems to COM1 and COM3 and get two programs (for example, Remote Access Services and a terminal program or Microsoft Mail Remote) to work on both ports simultaneously. You can have one or the other, but not both.

• *Interrupt Conflicts.* Just as Windows NT is intolerant of multiple applications or devices trying to share the same COM port, it is *exceedingly* intolerant of devices attempting to share an interrupt. The usual indication of an interrupt problem is the refusal of Windows NT to boot (on rare occasions, it can crash *after* booting correctly during an attempt to perform a network login). The major symptom will be the Windows NT "blue screen" displaying error number 0x000000A: IRQ Expected To Be Less Than Or Equal. This indicates that two hardware devices in the system are set for the same interrupt level. It most probably will happen just after you've installed a network card or other physical device.

Remove the card most recently installed and reboot the computer. Examine the hardware manufacturer's settings for the device and attempt to find an interrupt level that is not used by other devices. A common cause of this problem is interrupt cards that are predefined at IRQ3, the interrupt used by COM2 and COM4. Therefore, if you have a second COM port in your machine IRQ3 is automatically disallowed. Common interrupts in most systems include:

• IRQ0 (timer)

• IRQ1 (keyboard)

• IRQ3 (COM2 and COM4)

• IRQ4 (COM1 and COM3)

• IRQ5 (LPT2)

• IRQ6 (floppy controllers)

- IRQ7 (line printer one)

- IRQ8 (system clock)

- IRQ13 (math coprocessor)

- IRQ14 (hard disk controller)

- IRQ15 (secondary disk controller)

You will need to select an interrupt number not used by any of these devices installed in your system.

> *Note: After making the change and restarting NT, start NT diagnostics, and check to see that the driver in question is actually using the IRQ you think it is!*

Malfunctioning Disk Drives

See the section on installation problems in Chapter 2 for information on the most common hard disk problems. Aside from the ones covered there, the problem that most frequently arises is failure to terminate a SCSI chain. Make sure that the last device in the chain is terminated and that there is terminating power. Failing this, if disk drives are misbehaving on Windows NT when they have been installed correctly and have been behaving themselves until now, check the BOOT.INI. Try reverting the configuration. Try using the emergency diskette. If none of that has any effect, you probably have a disk hardware problem and need to employ conventional hardware troubleshooting techniques (swap disk controllers, then disk drives) to isolate the bad component—then call your hardware vendor.

CD-ROM Problems

The most frequent CD-ROM difficulty with Windows NT is adding a CD-ROM into an installation that initially did not have a CD-ROM. Making Windows NT recognize the CD-ROM is fairly straightforward: from Control Panel/Devices, select the SCSI CD-ROM object and set the startup value to Automatic so that the service will start when the system boots. You may want to set the CD Audio entry to Automatic as well (for certain CD-ROMs, this may be required). Then shut down and restart NT. Other problems include the following:

- *CD-ROM Impacting Windows NT Performance.* Certain CD-ROM players, specifically those including the NEC Intersect series players, may have a dramatic impact on Windows NT performance when the CD-ROM is playing. This will occur because of the setting of a jumper switch on the CD-ROM reader that disables disconnects during read operations. Disk-read operations on CD-ROMs are very slow, and if a disconnect is not available, no other device has access to the SCSI interface card until the disk read is finished. Consult the hardware documentation for your CD-ROM reader and reset the jumper switch as necessary to enable disk connects during read operations.

- *Failure to Recognize Data on a CD.* Windows NT supports the ISO9660 CD-ROM format but does not support any format extensions. A series of extensions known as the *Rock Ridge*

CD-ROM format provides additional features that are used by CD-ROMs for some systems, in particular, UNIX systems that require long filenames and a complex directory structure and, unfortunately, the Macintosh Heirarchical File System (HFS) format. Windows NT's CD file system does not recognize these formats.

Printing Problems

Windows NT suffers from one unique set of printing problems in common with its COM port problems, which again arises because only one device can own an interrupt. A number of sound cards, including the SoundBlaster Pro card, by default use interrupt 7, the same interrupt that is typically used by the Line Printer 1 port. If Windows NT refuses to recognize a printer attached to LPT1, start a command line prompt, and type:

```
mode LPT1:
```

If you see the message "Device Not Found," IRQ7 is being subverted by another hardware device. You can check this using NT Diagnostics: select the Resources tab, press the IRQ button, and look for IRQ 7. It's normally invisible until you click the Include HAL Resources check-box, because the NT Hardware Abstraction Layer uses it. If you find it has been taken by another device, you must remove the offending device, change the settings on the device, or otherwise make an adaptation so that the interrupt conflict is eliminated. Other problems could be the following:

• *Cross-Platform Network Printing.* If RISC and Intel versions of Windows NT are mixed on a network, the usual Windows NT print driver approach in which the remote printer takes advantage of the print driver installed in the print server will fail because a MIPS RISC machine, for example, has no use for an Intel print driver. The indication will be an error message, when you attempt to connect to the printer, saying that the server does not have a suitable print driver installed. You then have the option to make a temporary print driver installation on the local machine or install print drivers for the other types on the print server.

For instance, if the print server is a RISC machine, you could install the Intel print driver. Alternatively if the print server is an Intel machine, you could install one or more RISC drivers, as described in Chapter 2.

Network Problems

Difficulties involving the network could involve the following:

• *Disconnection*—The most common symptom of a network card problem is that the user is unable to connect to the network. The most common cause is that the network cable is not plugged in to the card. So, the first thing to do if you suspect a network card error is to check the connection between the network cable and the computer and then the connection between the network cable and the wall. If it's a 10base2 (coax) Ethernet connection, make sure that the chain of connections isn't broken. The cable may be plugged in on the computer of the user who is reporting a problem, but it may be unplugged further down the line.

Of course, this will usually be easy to spot. If such a break in a 10base2 cable exists, *all* users on that side of the break will be disconnected, not just one. But that good first step is to be sure everything's connected. The next step is to run the Windows NT Event Manager and see if it's reporting any network errors.

- *Misconfigured network card*—If the network connection appears to be good and the other systems on the subnet are up, check to see whether you have a hardware or software error. The easiest way to do this is with PING (on TCP/IP networks) or the NET SEND[24] command (on NetBIOS networks). (Use of PING is covered the next boldface heading.)

In either case, you will want to determine whether the computer is in fact talking to the network at all. From this you can tell if you have a software problem with misconfigured networking software or a hardware problem in which the network is not working at all. In our experience the net send command is convenient for this because it operates at a very low level on the system. You can reliably expect a net send command to tell you if the network is properly installed. If the network is installed and network communications exist, but the computer is not being logged into the network properly, the net send will still reach the designated target system. For instance:

```
net send mips1 Can anyone hear me?
```

will print the message "Can anyone hear me?" in a pop-up window on the mips1 workstations or server. A second possibility is that net send will not give an indication on the target but will return with the message "The message was successfully sent to MIPS1." In this case, the low-level Windows NT software, driver, and transporter are all working properly—they are getting proper indications from the card—but for some reason the transmission is not getting out on the network. This indicates that the network cable is bad, and the signal is being blocked somewhere outside the computer.

- *TCP/IP Misconfiguration*—If DHCP is not in use, inability to "see" hosts on TCP/IP networks may indicate that the HOSTS or LMHOSTS database files (described in Chapter 6) contain bad information. Try accessing a local host (or router) using the TCP/IP "ping" utility, *using the four-number IP address of the host (or router) in question*. The syntax of the command is *ping* <ip-address>, as in the following example for a node with address 127.119.13.213:

```
ping 127.119.13.213
```

Do *not* use a ping to a DNS or HOSTS name (at least, not at first) because this may not be definitive. The command:

```
ping vax.cmp.com
```

---

24 In NT 3.1, it was possible to use net send /BROADCAST *text* without designating a target. This functionality has been removed from NT 3.5 and later versions. Assuming that you know the name of any one machine on the net, you can achieve the same effect with net send *MachineName text* or net send /domain:*domainname text*. For instance: *net send mips1 just testing* should print "just testing" on \\mips1, assuming nothing's broken.

will evaluate to the same command as ping 127.119.13.213 if and *only* if the vax.cmp.com DNS name properly evaluates to 127.119.12.213. By contrast, pinging "by the numbers" is an absolute—if it gives you no response, there is a very deep configuration problem.

If a "by the numbers" ping gives a response, try a ping to the name. If that doesn't work, check the Name Resolution settings in Control Panel/Networks TCP/IP Configuration to see whether DNS, WINS, or HOSTS naming is in use, and then check the status of the DNS server, WINS server (or HOSTS file) as appropriate.

If both pings work, but you still can't "see" the system in question using the built-in Windows NT networking, check the WINS and LMHOSTS file settings and the settings of any intervening routers. A useful diagnostic for systems that use Windows NT at each end may be to run the FTP Server Service on one end and attempt FTP client access from the other. If that works, the low-level linkage (and router, if any) are properly set up, and the problem *must* lie with Windows NT name resolution. See the troubleshooting section in Chapter 6 (particularly IPCONFIG and NBTSTAT).

• *Hardware (interrupt) Problems*—It is quite common to experience network problems on Windows NT machines if the network card is set to interrupt level 3. Normally, Interrupt 3 is used by the COM2 port and since Windows NT does not permit interrupt sharing if a network card is designated to use Interrupt 3, there are two possibilities: One is that you will see the infamous blue screen when NT boots up with "Error 0x0000000A—IRQ expected to be less than or equal." This is the most severe version (the other case is that NT starts, but the network refuses to run). In either case, take the network card out and reset it to a new IRQ setting. You'll also have to change the IRQ setting for the card in question in Control Panel/Networks.

It's possible that the computer will boot but the network card will refuse to function. In this case, again, you need to shut down the computer, take out the card, change the settings on the card, bring up the computer, change the settings on the Network Control Panel applet, and then shut down and restart Windows NT, and it should work. If it's not an interrupt problem and the network cables are believed to be good, you need to begin troubleshooting procedures to determine whether you, in fact, have any connectivity to the network card and try to determine where the break is occurring. You can use the PING application on TCP/IP networks or Net Send on NetBEUI and other SMB networks.

On rare occasions, there are network cards with programmable interrupt and I/O settings in which the low-level network software can see what appears to be a perfectly good network connection, yet will not work initially. It may be worth trying a warm boot by shutting down Windows NT and selecting the Restart When Shutdown Is Complete option, and then try Net Send again. If it operates correctly after the reboot, you have a network card that requires two passes to set the software configuration. You may want to consider reconfiguring the card with a hardware configuration (if that's possible), or you may need to tell the user that when he starts up in the morning, he needs to do a warm boot before he can expect to see his network.

If Net Send reports that the message is not being sent because of a network problem, this invariably indicates an error in the binding of the low-level network software to the network card. This *should* be accompanied by an entry in the System Event Log. (You did check the log, didn't you?) In any case, the problem is a low-level one. It indicates that, for whatever reason, the software is not recognizing the card. This may mean that you're using the wrong driver for the particular network card you have, or that the network card may be misconfigured. Take a close look at the network card to verify that the network settings match the settings in the Network Control Panel, and cross-check with NT diagnostics to verify that any resources such as IRQs and ports are in fact "owned" by the network adapter card driver (if not, you have a conflict!). Verify that you are using the correct driver, and try again.

Sound Card Problems

As with network cards, the most usual symptom for a soundboard problem is the user reporting that no sound comes out of the speakers, and as with network cards, the first thing to do is see that there is a speaker plugged in, that the speaker has power, that the speaker volume is turned up, and that in all other respects you have a situation in which sound should be coming from the computer. If it is not then you may want to look at the following:

- *Is the sound driver installed?* This may sound simple-minded, but Windows NT does not install sound drivers during installation by default, so you will very likely will have to install a sound driver for each system. You do this through the Control Panel Sound Driver's applet. Make sure that you are using the right driver for the right sound card. In particular, with Creative Labs SoundBlaster cards, you must be careful because there are several different versions of the SoundBlaster, and the drivers are not interchangeable. For example, the driver for a SoundBlaster Pro will not work with a SoundBlaster version 1.

- *Do you have an interrupt conflict?* Check the interrupt and port settings that are set in Control Panel/Multimedia's Devices tab (select your device and click the Properties button). Make sure those settings match any switches on the audio card. Use NT Diagnostics' Resources tab to verify that the interrupt and port settings are not in fact used by another device. Note that the original SoundBlaster uses IRQ7 by default. This is also the setting for LPT1, and as noted elsewhere, Windows NT does not tolerate interrupt overloading, so it is likely that if you've installed a SoundBlaster card and it refuses to work, you'll have to change the interrupt. If you can play .WAV files (an easy way to check this is with the Control Panel Sound applet setting system sounds on and using the test button) but you can't play .MID (MIDI) files, you may need to install the ad-lib midi driver. Because most sound boards have two independent audio chips on them, one for midi synthesis and one for wave audio, two drivers are typically required.

- If you are using a *Windows sound system* and have upgraded from Windows 3.1 or Windows for Workgroups, you may see the message "SOUND.CPL is not a valid Windows NT Image" and find that the Control Panel is not working properly. That's because the SOUND.CPL file installed by Windows is incompatible with Windows NT.

- As we noted in the section on CD-ROMs and SCSI, a number of sound card manufacturers incorporate a *proprietary CD-ROM interface* on the sound card. Windows NT supports most of the common ones, with either built-in drivers or ones from the installation's CD's DRIVERS library. See Chapter 2 for details.

Video Problems

The most common video problem arises when a user changes the video settings using Windows NT Setup to try to get a higher resolution and is suddenly presented with an image that is either grossly unstable or completely blank. The solution in either case is the same. Restart Windows NT going through the shutdown procedure if you can. (This is one case in which pressing the reset switch may be your *only* option.) When Windows NT starts, it will start with the character mode startup that ordinarily will survive a change in video resolution and will present you with a "Press Escape for Last Known Good Menu" option. Immediately hit the Escape key, and select Last Known Good Configuration. If the user has not repeatedly modified the installation (which is almost impossible with a video problem), this will get you back to the working video.

Another common problem with video drivers occurs when a user installs a new video board without resetting the driver, in which case, the only response is to use the VGA mode boot option and then install the proper driver.

Finally, remember that Microsoft changed the video driver model in NT 4.0. Past versions of NT supported "downlevel" video drivers with reduced functionality; but in 4.0 you cannot use an older driver, period.

Conclusion

We've reviewed the basic principles of *preventive maintenance* (PM—covered in detail in Appendix 6), examined the steps necessary for performance tuning in a Windows NT system, reviewed the tools used for tuning and troubleshooting—including those that are new or updated for NT 4.0—and presented a list of the most likely problems and their solutions. With this information at your disposal, you'll have a good idea of how to proceed when you're presented (inevitably) with your first Windows NT system crash. However, we reiterate that it's *far* better to apply PM principles and avoid the crash altogether!

For More Information

Microsoft Staff (1996), *Windows NT Server 4.0 Concepts and Planning.* Redmond, WA: Microsoft Corp. Covers many aspects of installation and operation.

Microsoft Staff (1996), *Windows NT Server 4.0 Network Supplement.* Redmond, WA: Microsoft Corp. Detailed information on network operation, including troubleshooting.

Microsoft Staff, *TechNet CD.* Redmond, WA: Microsoft Product Support Services (PSS). TechNet is a monthly publication on CD-ROM containing a digest of topics from the Microsoft Knowledge Base, the Net News publication, Resource Kits, and other information. TechNet is available from Microsoft sales. A one-year subscription (12 CDs) costs $295 and is worth every penny.

Microsoft Staff (1993–96), *Windows NT Resource Kit*. Redmond, WA: Microsoft Corp. The only source for detailed information on the Windows NT configuration registry and the best source of information on topics like performance monitor counters.

Microsoft Staff (1995), *Windows NT Training*, Redmond, WA: Microsoft Corp. This is a two-volume set with a video and diskettes, covering Windows NT support and troubleshooting issues. It's marketed as a self-paced training guide for professionals studying to take the Microsoft Certified Professional (MCP) examinations.

Connecting to the World with TCP/IP

After reading this chapter, you will understand the basic elements of NT's TCP/IP services. You will also know the following:

- How to install and configure NT's TCP/IP services
- How to build a Windows NT-based network using TCP/IP as the primary transport
- The basics of the TCP/IP applications provided with NT and how to use them to connect to UNIX and other TCP/IP-based hosts

Topics covered include:

- TCP/IP installation and configuration
- Name resolution: HOSTS, LMHOSTS, WINS, DNS
- Client utilities: telnet, ftp, rexec, finger, etc.
- Services: simple (Echo, Character Generator, Quote of the Day, etc.) and otherwise (TCP/IP Printing, etc.)
- Advanced topics: routing and SNMP

Underlying concepts such as network protocol stacks, protocol definitions, addressing, subnet masks, and routing are covered in Appendix 2. If you're unfamiliar with acronyms like IP, UDP, and TCP, read the appendix before proceeding.

Internet-specific features, including Internet Information Server (IIS) and Peer Web Server (PWS), are covered in Chapter 7.

How NT Uses TCP/IP

To review, the Transport Control Program / Internet Protocol (TCP/IP[1]) is probably the most widely used standard for networking in the world today. Originally developed under U.S. government sponsorship as a set of distributed protocols that could operate with disconnected hosts, it has evolved into the backbone for today's planet-girdling Internet.

The only problem, from a Windows NT point of view, is that Microsoft came late to the party.

As explained in Appendix 2, Microsoft's networking has historically been built on the NetBIOS API and various related protocols (NBF, NetBEUI). Without belaboring the relative advantages and disadvantages of that approach (for that, see Chapter 8), suffice it to say that the two approaches are basically incompatible, and NT's built-in networking is built around the Server Message Block (SMB) protocol, which in turn uses NetBIOS.

The basic compatibility problem between NetBIOS and TCP/IP arises as a result of a different approach to system identification on the network. NetBIOS uses *machine names* associated directly with hardware (typically Ethernet) addresses to identify nodes on the network, while TCP/IP uses the famous (if not infamous) four-digit dotted IP address.

So to use Windows NT's SMB-based networking features with TCP/IP, there must be some mechanism to translate between NetBIOS names and IP address numbers. That mechanism is called NetBIOS-over-TCP/IP (NBT).[2] When we speak of using TCP/IP protocol with Windows NT's built-in file/print sharing and related services, we are really speaking of NBT.

Three types of NetBIOS nodes can be used on a TCP/IP network by NBT. A b-node (broadcast node) sends *broadcasts* to query other nodes on the network for the owner of a NetBIOS name. A p-node (point-to-point node) uses directed calls to communicate with a *NetBIOS name server* for the IP address of a NetBIOS machine name. An m-node is a mixed node, one that uses broadcasted queries to find nodes and failing that, queries a p-node name server for the address. Once the node discovers the IP address associated with the name, it sends IP traffic directly to

---

1   See Appendix 2 for definitions of the protocols discussed in this chapter.

2   Defined by Internet Engineering Task Force (IETF) Requests for Comment (RFCs) 1001 and 1002. They're downloadable from http://www.internic.net.

it. The process of starting with a NetBIOS name and turning it into an IP address is called *address resolution,* and it can be accomplished in several ways:

- Domain Name Services (DNS), which associates numeric IP addresses with Internet-style names. Prior to NT 4.0, while NT systems could work with DNS names, a native DNS server was not included. NT Server 4.0 includes one, which for NBT purposes, is a p-node.

- Windows Internet Name Service (WINS), which dynamically associates numeric IP addresses with NetBIOS names (an NBT p-node). Prior to NT 4.0, WINS was limited to use in all-Microsoft (NT, Windows for Workgroups, Windows 95) environments. With NT Server 4.0, it is—*finally*—possible to combine DNS and WINS.

- The HOSTS and LMHOSTS, which statically associate numeric IP addresses with DNS-compatible names (the hosts file) or NetBIOS names (the LMHOSTS file). The HOSTS file plays no role in NBT; LMHOSTS essentially serves as a crutch. NBT checks to see if the name being addressed is in the file, and if so, uses it. If not, it will make a b-node broadcast hoping to find the name. This approach is now nearly obsolete, though there are still a few situations in which it must be used.

An additional complication is the assignment of the numeric IP addresses to nodes (workstations and servers). This process can be done either manually, resulting in a *static* assignment, or with the Dynamic Host Configuration Protocol (DHCP) in which blocks of addresses are *leased* to clients on a first-come, first-served basis. Typically, DHCP is combined with WINS, so an IP address is both dynamically assigned and automatically associated with a domain name. In NT 4.0, this can be combined with DNS, resulting in a dynamically assigned numeric IP address that is automatically associated with both NetBIOS and Internet names.

With that basic information out of the way, we can begin to look at the actual process of supporting TCP/IP on NT.

Installing and Configuring TCP/IP

Basic TCP/IP support is installed by default on NT Servers (and may be installed on NT Workstations) during the setup process. Or you can add it later using the Network item from the Windows NT Control Panel (Start/Settings). In what follows, we assume that you've already installed NT network support and a driver for your network card; if not, see Chapter 2.

Installing TCP/IP

1. To install TCP/IP, start Control Panel/Network. The Network dialog appears. To see if TCP/IP support is already installed, click the Protocols tab and inspect the list (see Figure 6.1). If you don't see TCP/IP Protocol listed, you can add it by clicking the Add... button. You will then need to make some decisions about exactly what sort of TCP/IP support you require.

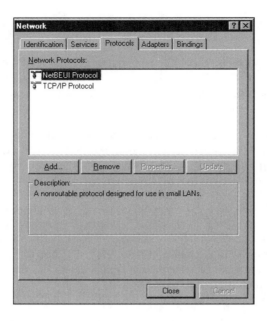

FIGURE 6.1 Protocols tab in Control Panel/Network. The easiest way to tell if TCP/IP support is installed on NT is to run Control Panel/Network and inspect the Protocols tab.

2 You will be asked if you want to use DHCP. If there is a DHCP server already configured on your LAN, press Yes.

3. Setup asks for the location of the Windows NT distribution files (the /i386, /ppc, /mips, or /alpha directory of your distribution CD or a shared network folder where the files have been copied). Verify that the path name given is correct and click Continue.

4. Setup copies the TCP/IP files to your computer and displays a message that it's installing TCP/IP and related services.

5. If you previously installed NT Remote Access Service (RAS), you will be asked if you wish to configure it to work with TCP/IP. Click OK if you want to use TCP/IP over dial-up lines (i.e., for Internet access). See Chapter 8 for details on RAS configuration.

6. The Network dialog's Protocols tab now lists TCP/IP. Click Close. A series of messages will be displayed, and the TCP/IP Properties dialog box will appear (see Figure 6.2) with the IP Address tab selected. You will be concerned mainly with three entries: IP Address, Subnet Mask, and Default Gateway. These three parameters identify the logical location of your workstation. (For more information on IP addresses, see Appendix 2.) When you first add TCP/IP to a network adapter, this dialog box is empty. If you've already set these parameters in a previous install, the dialog box will show them instead.

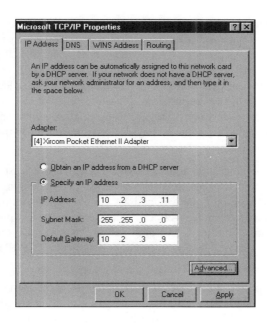

FIGURE 6.2 TCP/IP Properties: IP Address. The IP Address tab is used to set the IP address, Subnet Mask, and Default Gateway on a per-network adapter card basis.

The various elements of the dialog box, and their meanings and potential values, are explained below:

- Adapter—This drop-down box lists all the adapters in your system. If you have more than one network card, you can set the parameters for each of them here. Simply fill out the information for the first adapter, then select the next one from this drop-down list. NT will remember the settings for all the adapters. The number in parentheses before the adapter description is the load order of all the adapters in the system. An adapter with a (1) means that it is loaded first, (2) means second, and so forth.

- Obtain an IP address from a DHCP server—Select this check-box if you are on a network that supports Dynamic Host Configuration Protocol (DHCP). In such a situation, the remaining settings may normally be left blank; the DHCP server provides the necessary information at boot time.

- IP Address—Enter the four-number dotted IP address (explained in Appendix 2) for this specific adapter here. Each adapter gets its own unique address. Other machines use this address to find you when they have network traffic to send. Get your address from the network administrator. If you *are* the network administrator, get a valid block of addresses from your Internet Service Provider (see Chapter 7 for more information on this). When you receive your IP address from your network administrator, be sure to copy it carefully and confirm that it is correct. Do the same when you enter it into the dialog box—duplicate IP addresses on a network can cause all sorts of problems, including lockups.

- Subnet Mask—This number is used to mathematically "mask" IP addresses on your network. In other words, it eliminates those parts of an IP address that are alike for machines on your network (see Appendix 2 for a detailed explanation). *It is absolutely essential that this entry be correct.* If it is entered incorrectly, you will not be able to "see" the other machines on your network. Once you've entered the IP address, NT will automatically guess the appropriate subnet mask, based on the "class" of the address. You will need to modify this value only if you are using nonstandard subnet masks on your network. All systems using the same addressing schemes must use the same subnet mask in order to see each other.

- Default Gateway—This entry indicates where TCP/IP traffic should be sent when its address indicates that it needs to be forwarded to another logical or physical network. You must provide a default gateway address for every network adapter in your system. This address points to a router—either another computer or a piece of dedicated hardware—that is responsible for forwarding packets to hosts that are not on the currently selected adapter's subnet. Get this information from your TCP/IP network administrator.

7. For most installations, the above entries will be sufficient. However, some systems may require additional options. Such cases include assigning more than one IP address to a single network adapter, providing more than one gateway address, enabling PPTP filtering, and enabling IP security. If you don't require any of these options, click OK (and skip ahead to step 10).

8. The Advanced IP Addressing dialog appears (see Figure 6.3). Press the Add, Edit, or Remove buttons, as necessary, to modify the list of IP and Gateway addresses for your network adapter(s). The various elements of the dialog box, and their meanings and potential values, are explained below.

- IP Address—Each network adapter can have up to five IP addresses assigned to it. Multiple addresses are commonly used in networking environments with multiple domains and subnets sharing the same wire. Because IP is based on defined nodes and does not rely on broadcasting as NetBIOS, IPX, and AppleTalk do, it is possible to have many different IP networks on the same physical wire that are invisible to each other. Another common use for multiple IP subnets on one wire is the benefit of having multiple "virtual" FTP or Web servers on one machine (see Chapter 7 for ways this can be used with IIS/PWS).

- Subnet Mask—Each IP address may need a modified subnet mask. See Appendix 2 for an explanation.

- Gateways—You can add gateway addresses beyond the default address entered on the preceding dialog. You might need to do this if you're connected to multiple network segments.

- Enable PPTP Filtering—This setting will enable PPTP filtering (explained in Chapter 8) on the selected network adapter. *Select this setting only if you want to dedicate the selected network adapter to PPTP.* Once enabled for PPTP filtering, the adapter will ignore all other network traffic.

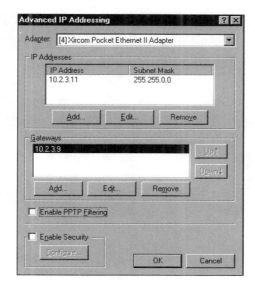

FIGURE 6.3 Advanced IP addressing. This dialog box allows multiple IP addresses to be assigned to individual network adapters and multiple gateways to be specified. It also controls whether IP security (simple filtering by port number and protocol type) is enabled and whether an adapter is dedicated to PPTP.

- Enable Security—Select this setting if you wish to explicitly control what combination of TCP Ports, UDP Ports, and IP protocols are allowed to be used with the selected network adapter. *For normal operation, this setting should not be selected.* If you choose to select it, press the Configure button to display the TCP/IP Security dialog box (see Figure 6.4). Unfortunately, you'll need a complete list of port and protocol numbers to use this dialog, and no such list is included in the NT documentation. See Chapter 7 for some suggestions on when and how to use these settings.

9. Click OK to exit the Advanced IP Addressing dialog box and return to the TCP/IP Properties dialog box.

10. If you will not be using DNS or WINS for name resolution or setting up IP routing, press OK to exit the TCP/IP Properties dialog box (skip ahead to step 14).

11. If your network supports DNS addressing (or if you will be using the selected network adapter with the Internet), select the DNS tab (see Figure 6.5). The various elements of this tab and their meanings and potential values are explained below:

   - Host Name—This is the name that others will use to connect to your workstation. By default, NT uses the system's workstation name (assigned during installation) as the TCP/IP hostname. If you want to change it, type in the new value here, but make sure you tell the other users so that they can update their HOSTS and DNS files.

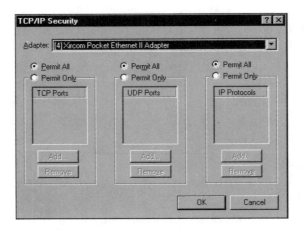

FIGURE 6.4 IP Security. This dialog box controls security settings on particular network adapter cards. You can permit all or permit only specific UPD and TCP ports and IP protocols. Note that you will need documentation on the UDP/TCP port and IP protocol numbers. Microsoft does not supply any such documentation with NT.

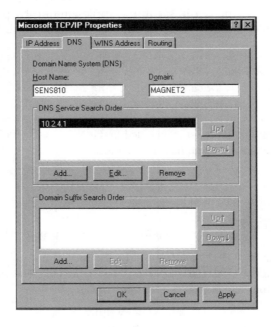

FIGURE 6.5 TCP/IP Properties, DNS tab. NT's DNS client configuration is controlled with this dialog.

- Domain—If you are in a TCP/IP domain, type in the domain name here (*this is not necessarily the same as your Windows NT Domain or Workgroup name*). Get this value from your network administrator. (See Appendix 2 for more information on TCP/IP domain names.)

  Combining the Domain Name and Host Name entries will give you a complete DNS name. For example, if your machine name is colossus and your domain name is forbin.com, your fully qualified domain name (FQDN)—equivalent through DNS to your numerical IP address—is colossus.forbin.com. Note that the ".com" part of this name indicates that this is a commercial enterprise. Other extensions are used to indicate other types of organizations; for example, .edu for educational institutions, .org for non-profit organizations, .net for networks, and .mil for military.

- Domain Name Service (DNS) Search Order—If you are using DNS, you must tell NT the IP addresses of the name servers you wish to use and their precedence. To add a DNS server to the list, type in the IP address in the edit box on the left and click the Add button. To change the search order for DNS queries, select the IP address from the listbox and click the up or down arrow buttons to move the server up or down the list as desired.

- Domain Suffix Search Order—If you are using DNS, you need to tell NT the TCP/IP domains in which you want to search. By default, NT will look in the domain you specify in the TCP Domain Name field discussed above. To add other domains, type them in the edit box on the left and click the Add button. To change the search order for DNS queries, select the domain name from the listbox on the right and click the up or down arrow buttons to move the domain name up or down the list as desired.

12. If you will use TCP/IP to connect with other Microsoft Networking (NT, Windows 95, Windows for Workgroups, LAN Manager) systems, select the WINS Address tab. The various elements of this tab and their meanings and potential values are explained below (see Figure 6.6).

    - Primary (and Secondary) WINS Server —As explained earlier, to use the TCP/IP transport protocol with NT's built-in networking, NetBIOS machine names must be mapped to the corresponding IP addresses for each machine. This mapping can be managed through the use of a text database called LMHOSTS, with DNS, or through a Windows Internet Naming Service (WINS) Server, which is the easiest method and the *only* method that supports dynamic IP address assignment through DHCP. You can specify a primary and secondary WINS Server address for each adapter to use. WINS is explained in detail later in this chapter.

    - Enable DNS for Windows Name Resolution—NT 4.0 allows you to convert NetBIOS names to IP addresses by using a text database called LMHOSTS, with DNS servers, with WINS servers, or a combination of the three. If you want to use DNS for NBT name-to-address mapping, enable this check-box.

    - Enable LMHOSTS Lookup—If you want to use the LMHOSTS file (explained in detail later in this chapter) for NBT name-to-address mapping, enable this check-box. The associated Import LMHOSTS button allows you to use a predefined LMHOSTS database.

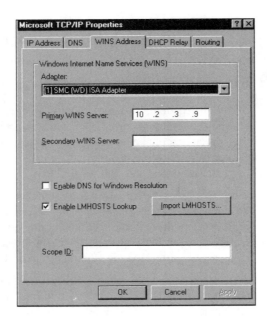

FIGURE 6.6 TCP/IP Properties, WIN Address tab. NT's WINS client configuration is controlled with this dialog box, which also determines whether an LMHOSTS file is parsed for name resolution (either in addition to or instead of WINS/DNS).

- Scope ID—This allows you to set a filter on the NBT traffic you want the machine to see. By default, this field is blank, and unless you are instructed by your network administrator to provide a value, leave it that way. Like subnet masks, the Scope ID must be consistent across all machines for the systems to see each other.

13. If your system will function as an IP router, select the Routing tab and check the Enable IP Forwarding box. Select this option only if your system has two or more network cards installed and operates as a gateway across subnets. See the section on Routing later in this chapter for details.

14. Click OK to close the TCP/IP Properties dialog box.

15. Click Close to close the Network object. The TCP/IP protocol is now installed. You will need to restart your system before TCP/IP services will be available.

HOSTS, NETWORKS, PROTOCOL, SERVICES, and LMHOSTS, Files

Although most configuration settings for the TCP/IP services are managed by the Network Control Panel object, there is a collection of files that can make life easier for your users.

These files are stored in the directory specified by the HKEY_LOCAL_MACHINE\ CURRENT_CONTROL_SET\Services\Tcpip\Parameters\DataBasePath entry of the Windows NT system registry (\winnt\system32\drivers\etc by default). The filenames and a description of their functions are listed in Table 6.1.

> **Warning:** *Unlike most other Windows NT configuration and settings files, the HOSTS, LMHOSTS, NETWORKS, PROTOCOL, and SERVICES files are not maintained in the Registry database, and fallback data for these files is not part of the "Last known good" data available on system restart. It is essential that administrators maintain backup copies of these files!*

HOSTS People have a difficult time remembering 32-bit binary numbers, which is why the IP address is most commonly represented by four 8-bit numbers instead. But even then, remembering a bunch of obscure number sequences can be a mental strain. TCP/IP allows users to use hostnames for systems instead, making life easier for its human users. For example, to connect to a host named VAX, you could type "telnet vax" instead of "telnet 192.155.13.116." if your host file is properly set up as shown below.

Windows NT TCP/IP uses a file called HOSTS to map IP addresses to well-known hostnames. The file is simple in structure, containing an IP address, the hostname, and (optionally) a comment preceded by a pound (#) sign. An entry in the HOSTS database file to substitute "vax" for IP address 192.155.13.116 would look like this:

```
192.155.13.116 vax      #Mapping for local VAX mini
```

Hosts you often connect with can be added to this database at any time. TCP/IP will consult the database when ever a hostname is passed to it (provided the proper Name Resolution Search Order setting has been selected, as described above).

Following are some helpful HOSTS file tips:

• Back up HOSTS before making changes. The copy can be placed in the same directory as the real HOSTS file and will protect you from inadvertent changes you might make during editing. HOSTS files can become large, with many entries, and they just won't work if the IP addresses are incorrect.

Table 6.1 TCP/IP Files for Windows NT

Filename	Description
HOSTS	Hostname to IP address database
NETWORKS	Network name to network number database
PROTOCOL	Protocol name to protocol number database
SERVICES	Application/service name to port number database

- Keep the HOSTS file up to date. Be sure to keep track of machines added to or taken from the network, and make sure your HOSTS file reflects these changes. To help automate this process, the administrator can use e-mail to send changes and updates that can be placed in the HOSTS file through copy and paste. If you can maintain exactly the same HOSTS file on all machines, the process of update is even simpler. The administrator can place the updated file directly into the machines directory with no user intervention using NT's native networking capabilities. Obviously, this is less critical if your network uses DNS, but be aware that the HOSTS file is the fallback for DNS name resolution if the DNS server is down, so even on DNS networks, periodically updating HOSTS is a good idea.

- Keep HOSTS entries in order. Because HOSTS files are read in the order they're written, place the entries covering your most frequently used hosts at the top of the file to speed searches.

- If you have a big HOSTS file, you might find it easier to maintain in a spreadsheet. To do this, update the spreadsheet, then save it as text—not the native format—of your spreadsheet. This way you can use the database and organizational functions of the spreadsheet on your library of IP names and addresses.

NETWORKS Just as you can create alias names for hosts, you can create alias names for networks. If you are in a complex environment, creating aliases helps you keep track of different networks. For example, you can type the command "NETSTAT -R", and see that network "Lab 10baseT" is up, rather than having to remember that 192.155.12 is the IP number for that network. To create an alias, the NETWORKS file would need the following entry:

```
Lab10baseT      192.155.12
```

PROTOCOL and SERVICES The remaining two TCP/IP files are not likely to require editing in normal use. PROTOCOL allows you to define the specifics of the IP, TCP, ICMP, and other protocol levels within the overall TCP/IP suite. If you replace (or augment) Windows NT's built-in TCP/IP protocol stack with a third-party stack, you may need to edit this file. SERVICES provides a similar capability for mapping application-level communication requests to a well-known TCP/IP port number. More information on these files can be found in Appendix 2, and in the Microsoft TCP/IP documentation included with Windows NT.

LMHOSTS The LMHOSTS format is identical to the HOSTS file described earlier, with a numerical IP address, a tab character, and a Windows NT name (and optionally, a comment); for example:

```
128.0.0.1      lm-machine
```

LMHOSTS is read by the NT system at startup and cached in memory, so any changes you make will not take effect until you either restart or execute NBSTAT -R from the command line.

Do not confuse the LMHOSTS database with the HOSTS database. Although they are similar in use and structure, they serve two entirely separate purposes. The HOSTS file is a database of TCP/IP host names and their corresponding IP addresses; while the LMHOSTS file is strictly for NetBIOS name to IP address mapping. Typically, the LMHOSTS file shows only a few systems. This does not mean that there are only a few nodes on the network, but that there are only a few remote nodes that must be addressed directly.

LMHOSTS simply acts to extend the realm of the broadcast area to include hosts that would otherwise be unreachable. By using this method, NT takes advantage of both the broadcasting and point-to-point architectures, without relying on a dedicated nameserver. Because broadcasting is necessary in the dynamic environments so typical of peer-to-peer LANs (because it's impossible to predict which systems will be available when), it is the preferred vehicle for name resolution. For example, if the primary domain controller were down, another would respond to any broadcast-based query, such as a login request, increasing network reliability tremendously without forcing users to place servers on every segment.

More specifically, name resolution takes the following steps to find a node's IP address:

1. NBT searches its internal cache for the NetBIOS name and IP address.

2. If the address is not found in the cache, NBT issues a b-node broadcast.

3. Failing a response from a local node, NBT searches the LMHOSTS file.

4. If no match is found, and if the client has been configured to use DNS servers in its name-to-address resolution scheme, NBT will then issue a DNS query for the NetBIOS name in question.

5. If a match is not found, NBT returns a name-not-found error to NetBIOS.

By understanding the sequence of events and also by knowing a few tricks that we're about to show you, you can customize your environment for both speedy responses and flexibility.

The Name Resolution Cache NBT first checks the local name cache for entries, so it is best to preload some names into the cache at boot time. Thus, your system won't have to wait for the local broadcasts to time out nor go through the trouble of having to check the LMHOSTS file. You can add a name to the cache by adding a "#PRE" command to an entry in the file:

```
192.155.11.10        marketing1    #PRE    #Marketing Domain Controller
```

Preloading the marketing1 server into NBT's cache speeds up the name resolution process considerably. Likewise, it's worth preloading the app1 and app2 servers if they're accessed frequently. In fact, you can preload every node on the network (up to a maximum of 100). There isn't much of a need to do this, however, because successful resolutions via broadcasts and lookups are also held in the cache for a while. If you need to preload more than 100 addresses (which you might in a large network), here's how to do so:

1. Start the Registry Editor by typing "REGEDT32.EXE" from the command line or the Start menu's Run item.

2. When the Registry Editor starts, select the HKEY_LOCAL_MACHINE key and find the SYSTEM tree.

3. Double-click the SYSTEM folder icon, and select the CurrentControlSet folder. Continue working down the tree until you get to the SYSTEM\CurrentControlSet\Services\Tcpip\ Parameters folder, and then select it.

4. Select Edit/Add Value. In the Value Name field, type the keyword MaxPreload and then select a Data Type of REG_DWORD. Click the OK button, and type the desired number of preloaded entries into the String Editor dialog box.

5. Shut down and restart the system after making these changes in order for routing to begin.

Items stored in the cache with the #PRE command never leave the cache unless forced. Using the NBTSTAT -R command will flush the cache and reload the first 100 #PRE entries from the LMHOSTS file.

Note that although the # symbol in the LMHOSTS file normally signifies a comment, Windows NT uses the #PRE string as a valid flag. This is for backward compatibility with LAN Manager servers that do not support selective preloading. They will ignore the #PRE command simply because they will not see it.

Specifying Domain Controllers Whenever a client attempts to log onto the network, broadcasting is used. Normally, a broadcast message follows the chain of events described above, but where domain controllers are involved, it is sometimes necessary to bypass normal channels. We certainly don't want domain controllers broadcasting password changes to every node on the network and all the nodes in the LMHOSTS file!

To signify that a system is a domain controller, put the #DOM flag in the LMHOSTS file:

```
192.155.11.10    marketing1  #PRE   #DOM:MARKETING
```

In this case, marketing1 is a domain controller in the MARKETING domain.

The #DOM keyword activates a pseudo-backchannel for communication between domain controllers. All domain controllers should have entries in their local LMHOSTS files for all of the other controllers within their domain. Also, if trust relationships have been established across separate domains, there should be entries for the primary controllers within the trusted domains (and perhaps for backup domain controllers as well).

In fact, you might want to set #DOM for all Windows NT Advanced Servers on your network. Otherwise, if the primary domain controller fails, a server that promotes itself to domain controller will not be able to use the backchannel for domain administration.

Sharing LMHOSTS Files Obviously, large networks with multiple trusted relationships and many hosts will have a hard time dealing with massive LMHOSTS databases. A couple of tricks can help in this situation. One is to use the #INCLUDE flag, which tells NBT to read not only the local LMHOSTS file, but other files as well. You could therefore point NBT to a shared LMHOSTS file on a departmental server or domain controller. For instance:

```
#INCLUDE \\marketing1\public\lmhosts
```

In this example, the local PC will incorporate any entries in the remote LMHOSTS file whenever a lookup is needed. Although you can point to as many remote databases as needed, keep the remote #INCLUDE list as small as possible. If you do this, make sure to give users at least read-only access to the shared file. Also, never reference drive letters for remote systems, but instead use the UNC names of the share point whenever possible (remember, remote drive letters can change!). For servers that need to share master copies, you can take advantage of NT's replication features to make sure that backups are always available (see Chapter 8 for details).

There are other tricks that you can do with the #INCLUDE command. For example, suppose marketing1 is down. You would not be able to read the remote LMHOSTS file. You would not want to put multiple #INCLUDE statements for each of the servers in the marketing domain, because that would increase your search time with no foreseeable benefit (the data in each file would be the same).

However, by enclosing a block of #INCLUDES with #BEGIN_ALTERNATE and #END_ALTERNATE commands, you can tell NBT to search the first available LMHOSTS file. Thus, if marketing1 were down, NBT would search marketing2's LMHOSTS file:

```
#BEGIN_ALTERNATE
#INCLUDE \\marketing1\public\lmhosts
#INCLUDE \\marketing2\public\lmhosts
#INCLUDE \\marketing3\public\lmhosts
#END_ALTERNATE
```

Windows Internet Naming Service

When you resolve IP addresses using an LMHOSTS file, broadcasts are issued first, and then the LMHOSTS file is consulted as a fallback. When you use Windows Internet Naming Service (WINS) however, the process is reversed. NBT queries are sent directly to a specified WINS server, and if that fails, then a broadcast is issued. This method improves response time and overall reliability of the network considerably. In essence, a WINS server is a p-node server, as defined in RFCs 1001 and 1002.

More specifically, name resolution takes the following steps to find a node's IP address when WINS servers are used on your network:

1. NBT searches its internal cache for the NetBIOS name and IP address.

2. If the address is not found in the cache, a p-node query is issued to the WINS server specified in the TCP/IP Configuration dialog box.

3. If the WINS server doesn't respond with an IP address for the host requested, a broadcast is issued on the local segments.

3. Failing a response from a local node, NBT searches the LMHOSTS file, if available.

4. If no match is found, and if the client has been configured to use DNS servers in its name-to-address resolution scheme, it will issue a DNS query for the NetBIOS name in question.

5. If a match is not found, a name-not-found error is returned to NetBIOS.

WINS servers have NetBIOS name-to-IP-address databases that are built automatically from a variety of sources:

- If you are using DHCP servers, they will inform all the WINS servers they know about of all the NetBIOS names and IP addresses in their databases. This makes the entire network less reliant on static information stored in LMHOSTS database files scattered around the enterprise.

- WINS clients that come up on the network register their NetBIOS names and IP addresses with the WINS servers specified. If a name is duplicated, it is rejected by the server, and the WINS client software informs the system manager of the error. This allows the WINS database to be centrally maintained and refreshed by clients scattered around the world.

- WINS servers also store local b-node query traffic so that they can answer on behalf of other devices. This means that nodes won't have to resort to broadcasts as often, because the WINS server will respond immediately with the cached information.

Because the WINS servers are populated by so many forms of network activity, they require almost no administration and are extremely reliable at the same time. This makes them the best choice for NBT mappings. A single WINS server that all clients point to can be used to enable browsing across an entire worldwide network, since the reliance on broadcasting has all but been eliminated.

Also, clients that do not have WINS software and (and therefore rely on broadcasting) can take advantage of the WINS servers, because the latter will respond to a broadcast on behalf of a remote system. This means that all NBT nodes now can know about any other node that the WINS server knows about, increasing your network's overall reliability.

Installing the WINS Server Service The WINS Server Service is installed from Control Panel/Network's Services tab. Click the Add button, select WINS Server from the list, and click OK. No additional configuration is required, because WINS is completely self-contained. Note that using WINS requires that you statically assign an IP address for it on your server—you cannot use DHCP to obtain the address.

Managing WINS WINS is managed with the WINS Manager application (see Figure 6.7) from the Start menu's Administrative Tools group. Fortunately, WINS management tends to be very simple—for all but the most unusual cases, WINS is maintenance free. Exceptions to this rule include scavenging the database, backing up and restoring the WINS database, establishing static mappings, and replicating the WINS database among multiple WINS servers. We will briefly examine each below.

Scavenging the WINS Database WINS data is stored in a Microsoft Jet (the underlying technology used in Microsoft Access and Exchange Server) Database engine. Over extended periods of time, the database can become cluttered with old data. WINS names that are not renewed will become extinct and then be automatically scavenged after a preset time (defined by the Extinction Timeout setting in Server/Configuration), but on rare occasions you may want to scavenge the database manually. To do so, select Mappings/Initiate Scavenging.

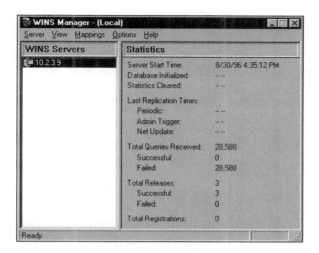

FIGURE 6.7 WINS Manager. The WINS Manager application (from the Start menu's Administrative Tools folder) is used to control WINS server settings.

Backing Up and Restoring the WINS Database As with any other server-side files, WINS database files require periodic backup (otherwise you run the risk of losing your mappings). To back up the database, select Mappings/Backup Database…, and enter a directory location to which WINS Manager will copy the database files (*Note: This must be a local path, not a network path.*) To restore the backed-up database, select Mappings/Restore Database.

Establishing Static Mappings In certain cases, it may be desirable to permanently assign an IP address to a particular system (especially if a system will be used on the Internet). In such a case, you create a static mapping, reserving a particular IP address for the use of a given system (identified by its NetBIOS name). To make such a mapping, select Mappings/Static Mappings… and click the Add Mappings button on the resulting Static Mappings dialog.

Replicating the WINS Database Large sites with multiple network segments will need to use WINS Replication to keep a consistent database of WINS names throughout the organization. To do so install one WINS Server on each network segment and configure each WINS server to act as a replication partner to another WINS server (partners can push or pull the database). Configuring WINS replication is beyond the scope of this book. For more information, see the WINS Manager online help and the NT Server *Network Supplement* (available in Books Online from the NT Server distribution CD).

Dynamic Host Configuration Protocol

Without a doubt, the biggest single problem with TCP/IP has traditionally been the need to assign a unique address number to *each and every node on the network*. Once that's done, the list of IP address assignments has to be maintained so that the uniqueness of each address is guaranteed. This can be (and *is*, for most people) an administrative nightmare. Almost every large network manager has had to track down duplicate IP workstation names at one time or another and can attest to the great indignity of it all.

"What would be really great," most administrators will tell you, "would be a database that not only tracks IP address assignments, but *makes* the assignments for you as needed." This is what the Dynamic Host Configuration Protocol (DHCP) does. Microsoft, Sun, and others wrote a series of RFCs (1533, 1534, 1541, and 1542) for DHCP that provides mechanisms for assigning IP addresses, host names, domain names, and other IP information to nodes dynamically.

Basically, at boot time, a client PC with DHCP software requests an address and other information from a DHCP server, stores the information for a certain amount of time, and periodically re-requests the information from the server. This provides administrators with a centralized address allocation tool, relieving them from having to manually make these assignments on a per-workstation basis.

Using DHCP servers provides several benefits to network administrators:

• Global network parameters such as domain name can be set for all nodes.

• Per-subnet parameters (such as default router) can be set for nodes on specific subnets.

• Pools of IP addresses can be set aside for use on a per-subnet or enterprise-wide basis.

• Lease terms can be established, forcing clients to renew their requests every so often.

There are also advantages at the client level:

• DHCP clients don't have to be configured for anything. When the node boots, it issues a DHCP broadcast request, which gets answered by all the DHCP servers on the network. DHCP-enabled routers automatically forward these requests, so you don't have to have DHCP servers on every subnet to take advantage of this.

• If you move a client PC to another subnet, it will automatically get the new subnet information, because the server can tell what subnet the client request came from.

Installing the DHCP Server Service The WINS Server Service is installed from Control Panel/Network's Services tab. Click the Add button, select DHCP Server from the list, and click OK. You will not need to do any additional configuration at this point, although you will need to use the DHCP Manager utility to add scopes, nodes, and other information.

DHCP Scopes DHCP groups nodes into logical entities called "scopes." Every subnet on an internetwork has its own scope, for example. You assign IP address ranges, subnet masks, and length of "leases" to each scope. You can also assign any of the DCHP options to each individual scope to be served, or you can assign them on a global basis. If a global setting and a scope-specific setting are both present, the DHCP server uses the scope-specific setting. If you assign these values to a specific node, those node-specific settings override the scope-level settings.

To create a scope, load the DHCP Manager utility from the Network Administration group. Select a server from the list presented, and then select Scope/Create. You will be presented with the following dialog box (Figure 6.8), which you must complete.

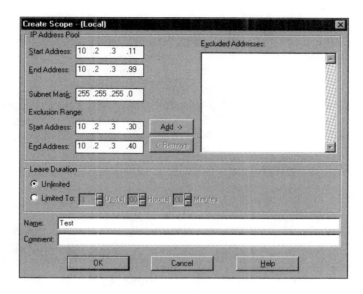

FIGURE 6.8 Create scope. Ranges of TCP/IP addresses, called *scopes,* are created and managed through NT's DHCP Manager application. Addresses in the range can be *leased* on login by a DHCP client.

The various elements of the dialog box and their meanings and potential values are explained below.

- Start Address—This is the first IP address to be used in this scope's pool of available addresses. If you were to place the entire class C subnet 192.155.11.0 into this scope, you would start with 192.155.11.1.

- End Address—This is the last available IP address to be used in this scope's pool of available addresses. If you were to place the entire class C subnet 192.155.11.0 into this scope, you would end with 192.155.11.254.

- Subnet Mask—This is the subnet mask of the IP address pool. Because each segment contains a unique subnet mask per address block, this is a required field. If you have broken a subnet into multiple subnets, you would need to create separate scopes for each of the resulting subnets.

- Exclusion Range—Just as you can specify a starting and stopping point for address ranges to include in the scope, you can exclude a block of addresses from the scope's include list. You can also exclude a specific address from the pool simply by defining the complete node address and clicking the "Add" button. If you need to exclude multiple ranges from the subnet, create multiple scopes with unique include lists instead.

- Name—You can give a name to your scope by editing this field.

- Comment—You can attach a description of this scope by editing this field.

Client Reservations Under certain conditions you may want to always assign the same IP information to the same node. For example, if you have SMTP mail gateways, FTP servers, DNS servers, or other frequently accessed systems that must always have a consistent host name and IP address, you would want to ensure that their information never changes.

One way to do this is to simply *not* configure these types of systems to use DHCP. However, there are many benefits to using DHCP beyond simple address assignment, as we'll see later in this chapter. In these instances, you would want to configure the node to use DHCP, but you would want to guarantee that it always received the same IP address. You can do so with *reservations*.

To add a client reservation, select Scope/Add Reservations. The dialog box in Figure 6.9 will appear. The various elements of the dialog box and their meanings and potential values are explained below.

- IP Address—The IP address to use with this client.

- Unique Identifier—This is the unique MAC (Media Access Control) address for the network adapter the client will use when requesting information from the DHCP server. The MAC address is the network-topology-specific address, such as the Ethernet address, or the Token Ring address of the network adapter.

- Client Name—This is the name you use to refer to the PC, and it should not be confused with the host name or the NetBIOS machine name.

- Comment—You can assign a comment to this machine by editing this field.

Other DHCP Options Many DHCP options can be defined beyond simple IP address assignment. You can make these assignments on a global basis, per scope, or per machine if you have defined any reserved clients. To set these options on a global basis, select a scope from the list of servers and then select DHCP Options/Global menu. The dialog box shown in Figure 6.10 will appear.

Several configurable options can be assigned to any DHCP client on boot. These options can be assigned globally, per scope, or per node when client reservations are used. Microsoft's

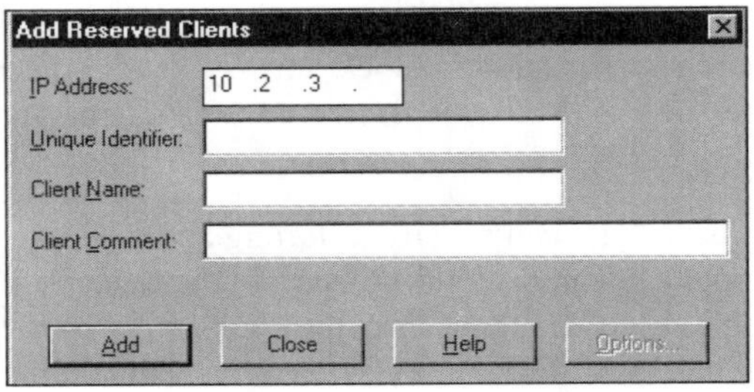

FIGURE 6.9 Add reserved clients. Settings for DHCP clients that require a particular "reserved" IP address are made in DHCP Manager's Add Reserved Clients dialog.

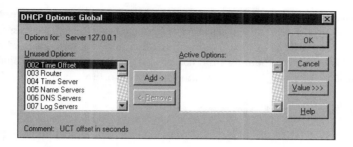

FIGURE 6.10 DHCP options: global. Network-wide DHCP settings are controlled from DHCP Manager's Global Options dialog.

DHCP client software does *not* support all of the DHCP options that are defined in the DHCP RFCs. All the ones that it does support, however, are listed below.

- Router—You can add a list of default routers that you want the clients to use. This option is best set on a per-scope basis, because you wouldn't want to assign a remote subnet a local default route.

- DNS Servers—You can specify a list of DNS servers and their preferences with this option.

- Domain name—You can specify the domain name you want a client to use. If you have multiple geographically or departmentally separated domains, you would probably want to assign this value on a per-scope basis.

- WINS/NBNS—You can specify a list of WINS servers and their preferences with this option.

- WINS/NBT node type—This option allows you to define the NBT node type (b-node, p-node, m-node, or h-node). For best operation, leave this setting alone.

- NetBIOS Scope ID—This option allows you to define the NBT Scope ID for the client.

Client Lease Times DHCP clients request information from DHCP servers when they are booted. If the client has local storage capabilities, this information is retained locally. If not, the information is requested every time the client boots.

This information is kept for a certain amount of time, referred to as a "lease." When the lease "expires," the information is considered invalid. Rather than wait for the lease to expire and then have to argue with the server and other clients over new lease information, the lease is renewed when 50% of the lease term has expired. Otherwise, the lease may expire, and the client may not be able to get another address for some reason, and the user would be "dead in the water" until another lease became available.

When clients renew their leases, they attempt to rebind the information. Just as the clients don't attempt to renew their leases after the lease expires, they don't attempt to rebind the information when it is too late. By default, clients attempt to rebind their information after 50% of the remaining lease term has expired. If the lease was renewed at exactly 50% of the lease term, this would first occur at 87.5% of the lease term (renewed at 50% of lease term - rebinded at 50% of remaining term = 87.5% of lease term). If another node contests the binding, the process is delayed until 50% of the remaining time has passed, and so on, until the binding succeeds. This allows multiple nodes to phase information back and forth without human intervention.

Domain Name Service

Domain Name Service (DNS) is one of the most convoluted subjects on the planet. It takes weeks to understand and a lifetime to master. However, once you set it up right, you rarely have to mess with it again. Also, the paybacks for running DNS servers are tremendous. You won't have to mess with HOSTS files scattered around your network anymore. If you're interested in DNS, there's a book called *DNS and BIND* (publisher information is listed at the end of this chapter) that is a must read.

Basically, DNS revolves around the concept of a client/server relationship similar to WINS. A DNS client wishing to communicate with a remote host issues a lookup request to a specified DNS server. If the DNS server knows the information (i.e., has it cached), it will return it. If it doesn't know the information (i.e., a client is asking for information about a host in a remote domain), it will query the remote domain's DNS server for the information on behalf of the client, and pass the resulting information back.

Each domain has a *primary* server that manages information for that domain. The primary DNS server reads information from a series of text files. These files generally contain subnet-specific information such as hostnames and corresponding IP addresses. The primary DNS server is the "authoritative" server for the domain.

There are also *secondary* servers that can read information from the primary servers, instead of from a collection of text files. Clients can point to these services for their inter-domain name resolution. If a client requests a remote host be looked up, the secondary server will issue the request to the remote domain's primary server on behalf of the client and return the information. It also caches the information for future use.

There can also be *caching-only* servers, which simply forward requests and cache the information for future use. They don't know anymore about the local domain than they do about the remote domains. However, because they are caching servers, they can retain the information for a long time, instead of having to constantly query other servers.

Every NT server should be configured as a caching-only server, and local clients should be pointed to it so that they will get fast responses to their queries, with no overhead required on the primary and secondary servers. Obviously, you'll need at least one primary DNS server for your domain. If you have geographically dispersed or heavily laden networks, you'll also do well to distribute secondary DNS servers throughout your network.

Unfortunately, DNS understands only static mappings (after all, it comes from the UNIX world, where you don't go around resetting IP addresses on your VAX every day). Wouldn't it be nice to have DNS naming combined with the flexible dynamic mapping provided by WINS and DHCP?

Microsoft Dynamic DNS

Prior to NT 4.0, Microsoft didn't ship a DNS Service with NT. One was available in the NT Resource Kit (and several more were available from third parties). One of the neat tricks supported by the DNS server in the Resource Kit was the ability to map WINS servers into the DNS database. For example, if you knew the NetBIOS name of a workstation you wished to PING or FTP to, but didn't know the IP host name, you could have the DNS server issue WINS queries on your behalf and return the corresponding IP address.

With NT 4.0, you no longer need the resource kit. DNS is a network service like DHCP and WINS, and it ships with NT Server.

Installing Microsoft DNS The DNS Service is installed from Control Panel/Network's Services tab. Click the Add button, select Microsoft DNS Server from the list, and click OK. You will not need to do any additional configuration at this point, although you will need to use the DNS Manager utility to add zones and configure the server.

Configuring Microsoft DNS As explained earlier, DNS is a complex and convoluted topic. We cannot hope to offer more than a trivial introduction here, but we can offer a *very* simplified procedure that may help you get started:

1. Start the NT 4.0 DNS Manager utility from the Start menu's Administrative Tools folder (see Figure 6.11).

2. Select DNS/New Server, and the Add DNS Server dialog box will appear. Type the name or IP address of the system on which you've installed the DNS Service. Then Click OK.

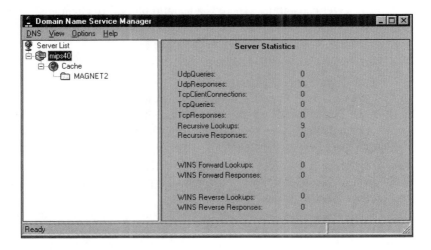

FIGURE 6.11 DNS Manager. New for NT Server 4.0, the DNS Manager tool from the Start menu's Administrative Tools folder controls the configuration and operation of NT Server's Domain Name Service (DNS).

3. With luck, you'll see a set of Server Statistics. If not, something went wrong with the service installation. Check the NT Server event log.

4. Right-click on the icon for the Server you just added and select New Zone... from the context menu. The Create new zone dialog box appears.

5. If your organization already maintains DNS servers, show the local DNS "guru" this display. He or she will know whether your server should control a primary or secondary zone and can help you configure it.

6. If you aren't already using DNS, select the Primary radio button, then click Next and follow the wizard's instructions to create a new zone. By default, the zone name will be the same as your NT domain name.

7. For more information, see Help/Table of Contents from the DNS Manager. It includes a long "how-to" list covering most anything you might want to know about Microsoft's implementation of DNS. You will undoubtedly want a reference book as well, and we cannot recommend *DNS and BIND* (see the citation at the end of this chapter) highly enough.

Utilities

If you are familiar with using TCP/IP utilities on a UNIX system, you will be right at home on an NT system. The utilities provided by Microsoft are of the standard variety with little difference from any others you may have used.

The utilities included with Windows NT allow you to take advantage of UNIX and other systems with TCP/IP server capabilities. There is a handful of TCP/IP client applications, such as Telnet, FTP, and Finger, and a set of Simple TCP/IP Services.

Telnet

Windows NT 4.0 provides a barely usable Telnet client application, about on par with TERMINAL.EXE. It's not meant to be a fully functional application, but instead a usable tool for people who require Telnet capabilities, but have not yet purchased a full-featured Telnet client. Typing "telnet" in a command window or from the Start menu's Run... item will start the Telnet application running. Figure 6.12 shows the Telnet client's main window.

To connect to a remote host, select Connect/Remote System... A Connect dialog box will appear, allowing you to select a Host, Port, and Terminal type for your connection. Enter the IP address or host name (if you are using DNS or have the host listed in your HOSTS file) of the system you want to connect to in Host Name. The Port will normally be Telnet, but you can select another port—for example, the quote-of-the-day (qotd) port—on systems that support it. Terminal type will default to VT100, but may be reset to another type if required.

Once the connection is made, Telnet operates very much like the Windows 3.x terminal application or HyperTerminal, for that matter. How you interact with a host depends on how the host is set up.

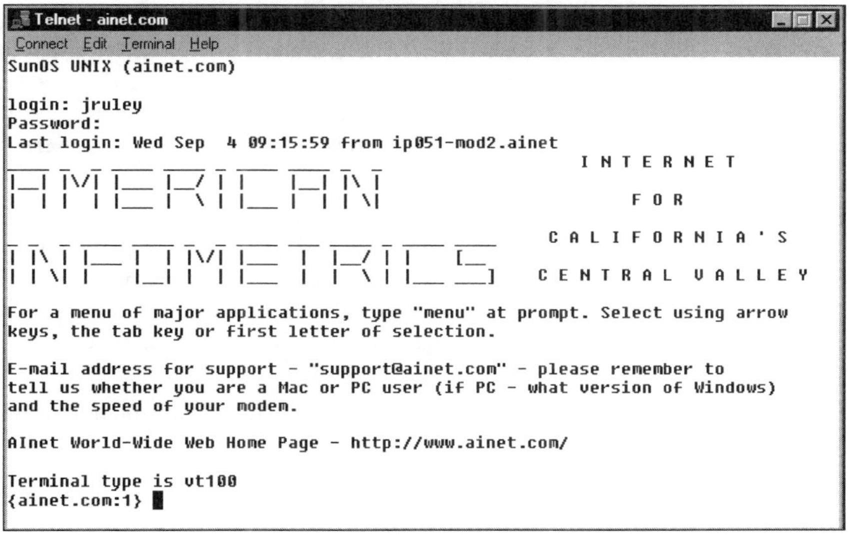

```
 Telnet - ainet.com                                          _ □ ×
 Connect  Edit  Terminal  Help
SunOS UNIX (ainet.com)

login: jruley
Password:
Last login: Wed Sep  4 09:15:59 from ip051-mod2.ainet
                                            I N T E R N E T
 |_| |\/| |_| |_/ |_| |\|
 | | | | |_ |\ | |_ | | |\|             F O R

 | |\| |_ |_| |\/| |_ |_/ |_            C A L I F O R N I A ' S
 | |\| |  |_| | | |_ |  |\| |_]         C E N T R A L   V A L L E Y

For a menu of major applications, type "menu" at prompt. Select using arrow
keys, the tab key or first letter of selection.

E-mail address for support - "support@ainet.com" - please remember to
tell us whether you are a Mac or PC user (if PC - what version of Windows)
and the speed of your modem.

AInet World-Wide Web Home Page - http://www.ainet.com/

Terminal type is vt100
{ainet.com:1} █
```

FIGURE 6.12 Telnet. Telnet (simple character-mode terminal) support is provided through NT's Telnet application.

For more information, see Telnet's on-line help.

RSH and REXEC

If you don't need a completely interactive session with a host, you can use the RSH and REXEC utilities to execute a single command on a remote system. These are non-interactive utilities, so you can't run a text editor or the like in this manner, but you can retrieve a directory listing, or type out a file, or execute any commands that don't require interaction.

RSH and REXEC are virtually identical. In fact, they provide the exact same service and even use the same command-line parameters. The difference between the two is based on authority. RSH uses the concept of trust between remote hosts, and REXEC does not. The latter requires a username and password to pass to the host for authentication before executing the command.

For example, assume that there are two hosts named GRUMPY and DOPEY. GRUMPY "trusts" the NT system, using either the .rhosts or /etc/hosts.equiv files. Users on the NT system could list the files in their home directories on GRUMPY by issuing the command *rsh grumpy ls*. Because the host GRUMPY trusts the NT system, it accepts the RSH request, logs in with a user's account, executes the command "ls," and returns the results. Then it logs the user out.

DOPEY, however, doesn't trust the NT machine. Users who want to run a program on DOPEY need to use the REXEC command. This requires the user to provide a username and password for the REMOTE command. Thus, to list the files in the user's home directory on

DOPEY, the user would type *rexec dopey -l username ls*. Then NT will ask for a password to go with the username entered in the command line. The username and password are sent over to DOPEY, which verifies the account, and if accurate, logs the user in and runs the command. Note that the REXEC utility will abort if no password is given, so if the remote user ID doesn't have a password, you can't use this program. RSH, however, allows you to use usernames with no password.

In order for a host to provide REMOTE command execution services, it must be running the appropriate remote server service programs. Currently, NT does not offer this functionality, so it can act only as a client. Furthermore, although the default action for the RSH command is to allow users to log in if no command has been passed on the command line, the RSH and REXEC utilities bundled with NT do not allow this. A command must be provided for the utilities to run.

For information on setting up trust between hosts, refer to the documentation provided with the system that will act as your server.

Finger

Another way to interact with a remote system is through the FINGER command. Finger is, essentially, a way to query a remote system for information in the form of text. The principal use of finger is to identify users on the remote system (hence its name), but it has gained popularity as a way of distributing any sort of information that a system administrator wants to provide. The traditional use of finger—identifying users—is simple. At the NT command prompt type:

```
finger username@host.domain.com
```

Depending on how the remote system supports finger, your results will vary. For example, the Massachusetts-based public access UNIX system "world" run by Software Tool & Die takes a finger request seriously:

```
finger bgaret@world.std.com
jgaret@world.std.com
[world.std.com]
world—The World—Public Access UNIX—Solbourne 5E/900 OS/MP 4.1A.3
5:14pm  up 24 days, 15:05,  69 users,  load average: 13.33, 15.51, 17.16
bgaret . Bill Garet              Login Fri 16-Jul-93 1:11AM from std-annex.sto
[3374,3374]  </users/bgaret>;  Group: bgaret
Groups: hamradio bgaret
bgaret has new mail as of Fri 16-Jul-93 4:58PM
last read Fri 16-Jul-93 8:24AM
```

Clearly, world.std.com provides plenty of information about the user. On the other hand, some system administrators consider finger a security hole, and disable it.

The other way that finger is used is to provide specific text files, but from your point of view it works the same. For example:

```
finger weather@iugate.ucs.indiana.edu
```

This will provide the text for the National Weather Service forecast for central and southern Indiana.

Transferring Data Between Hosts

The TCP/IP client utilities included with NT offer three programs to move files between hosts. RCP, the remote copy program, is the simplest, providing the same functionality as the DOS copy command between hosts. The other two, FTP and TFTP, are the client side of the FTP server discussed later in this chapter. These two programs allow the transfer of files through the standard TCP/IP File Transfer Protocol (FTP) by interacting with the remote machine's server and creating the necessary communications channels.

Remote Copy RCP stands for *remote copy* which is what this command is all about. You can exchange files with remote hosts or even copy files from one host to another without having to log onto them explicitly. RCP uses trust between systems, via either the .rhosts or /etc/equiv.hosts files on the remote systems. You can use explicit user names on the command line, but there must still be trust between the hosts and the NT system.

RCP also supports copying files on the local system, similar to the NT (or DOS) copy command line utility. To copy a file named SCHEDULE.TXT to the c:\accounting directory on the remote system, type the command "RCP SCHEDULE.TXT C:\ACCOUNTING\SCHEDULE.TXT".

To copy binary files, such as an executable program or a document with extended characters, use the "-b" option. To copy a file named PAYROLL.WKS from one directory to another, type the command "RCP -B PAYROLL.WKS C:\ACCOUNTING\PAYROLL.WKS." If the -b option is left out, RCP assumes that ASCII transfer is all that's needed.

To copy the same spreadsheet to the remote host GRUMPY, use the command "RCP-B PAYROLL.WKS GRUMPY:PAYROLL.WKS." To copy the file from GRUMPY to the local NT system, type the command "rcp -b grumpy:payroll.wks payroll.wks."

You can copy entire directory trees from one host to another using the RCP utility as well. If you need to move a bunch of files from a remote host to the local system, or vice versa, this is the quickest way to get the job done. To copy the entire accounting directory on GRUMPY to the NT system, type the command *RCP -B -R GRUMPY:/ACCOUNTING C:\ACCOUNTING*. This command will create a directory called c:\payroll on the local NT system and copy all the files in all of the subdirectories in GRUMPY's /accounting directory.

Like the RSH and REXEC services, the RCP utility is implemented as a client service only. You cannot RCP to and from the NT system from another system. Also, remember that the remote hosts with which you exchange files must trust the NT machine you are using. For information on setting up trust between hosts, refer to the documentation provided by the vendor of each system that you want to use.

FTP The FTP client software included with NT is of the simple command-line variety. It lets you establish a connection to the remote machine, log in as a user, and then interact with the host to locate and transfer files. FTP can be used for upload or download, and although it has many subcommands, you need to know only a few to use FTP effectively.

Establishing a Connection The first step in using the FTP client is to establish a connection. There are two ways to accomplish this. First, if you are not yet running the FTP program, is the command line:

```
ftp hostname
```

where *hostname* is the name or numerical IP address of the host to which you wish to connect. This will execute the FTP program and initiate the connection to the named host. If the FTP program is already running, the OPEN command will perform the same function at the FTP prompt:

```
ftp> open hostname
```

The prompt ftp> is displayed whenever the FTP program is running to indicate that it is active.

Logging In Once the connection to the remote host is established, you will be prompted to log in. Frequently, FTP sessions are of the "anonymous" variety. Anonymous FTP is a way to allow users without accounts on a particular machine to access a public directory (usually called "public" or "pub") to get or send files. Anonymous FTP is prevalent on the Internet. The first message you will see upon connecting is an informational message about the FTP server:

```
220 hostname Windows FTP Server <Version 1.0>.
```

This message provides the name of the machine (hostname), and the operating system/server software. Note the number in front of the message: 220. Each message sent by the FTP server is preceded by a message number. These numbers are used by the client software to determine the meaning of the message. The numbers are standard and can be used to determine what the server is saying with no ambiguity. The text messages are there for your benefit and may vary depending on the server.

Immediately after this informational message you will be prompted for a user name. This message comes from the client software, not the server. When you enter the name, the FTP program uses it as the argument for the "PASS" command. For example, if you answer the login prompt:

```
User hostname: anonymous
```

(where *hostname* is displayed by the client to remind you of where you are logging in, and "anonymous" is the user name that you entered), this is then translated by the FTP program and sent to the host as:

```
PASS anonymous
```

Before you saw the User prompt from the FTP program, the server sent a message asking for a login. It was intercepted before you saw it. If for some reason you want to see all the messages, you can use the VERBOSE command; just enter it at the ftp> prompt:

```
ftp> verbose
```

This will give you a full view of all the messages, which may be useful if you're debugging a system (or interesting if you're just curious). Here's what a successful login looks like:

```
C:\users\default>ftp 130.26.0.100
Connected to 130.26.0.100.
220 emsworth Windows NT FTP Server (Version 1.0).
User (130.26.0.100:): anonymous
331 Anonymous access allowed, send identity (e-mail name) as password.
Password:
230 Anonymous user logged in as ftpuser.
ftp>
```

In this example, the numerical address of the server named "emsworth" is used to connect directly from the command line. The user name anonymous is used; the password—which does not echo—is the real Internet e-mail address for the user logging in. This is traditional, because it allows administrators to contact the user if some sort of problem occurs. This is not enforced by the server, because it doesn't know who you are. The message that starts with 230 tells us that the login was successful and for information indicates that we were logged in as ftpuser. This is the account name that the system administrator assigned to anonymous FTP logins and determines various access permissions. Most commonly this will say guest, but it can be anything. The return of the ftp> prompt indicates that the FTP client program is ready for the next command.

Navigating on the Remote Host Once logged in you have access to the directory structure that the remote hosts administrator has made available to FTP users. If you know DOS or UNIX commands, FTP navigation will be old hat. The first thing you are likely to want to do is get a directory of the remote drive. You can do this in more than one way. The two simple ways are with the "DIR" and "LS" commands.

Which you will use depends on the file system in use there. FTP servers are running on just about every sort of machine that can be connected to the Internet. The most common type to see, though, is UNIX. Many FTP servers will even translate their non-UNIX file system into something that looks like one for FTP users. On a NetWare FTP server, the DIR command returns:

```
-   [RWCEAFMS] supervisor              20319       Aug 12 06:49    vol$log.err
-   [RWCEAFMS] supervisor              10423       Aug 12 06:50    tts$log.err
-   [RWCEAFMS] supervisor              20480       Aug 12 09:48    backout.tts
d   [RWCEAFMS] supervisor                512       Aug 13 09:49    login
d   [RWCEAFMS] supervisor                512       Aug 13 10:07    system
d   [RWCEAFMS] supervisor                512       Aug 13 09:49    public
d   [RWCEAFMS] supervisor                512       Aug 13 09:49    mail
```

This is a variation on a standard UNIX structure (the differences lie in the way the permissions are indicated). What's important to you, as an FTP user, is the lowercase d that precedes the letters in square brackets. This indicates that the entry is a directory instead of a file. The UNIX-style LS command is a quick directory that eliminates everything except the names:

```
vol$log.err
tts$log.err
backout.tts
treeinfo.ncd
login
system
public
mail
```

In this NetWare example, there is no indication that an entry is a directory. On many UNIX systems, a directory will be followed by a forward slash:

```
file
file
directory/
```

One thing to keep in mind as you connect to remote systems is that the file system in use there may be completely foreign to what you are used to. Some IBM mainframes, for example, use a flat system with no subdirectories and are very hard to navigate.

Once you determine what is available in the root directory of the remote host, you'll want to switch to the directory of interest. You will almost always have to do this, because it is rare that any files will be in the root directory on an FTP server. Once again your DOS experience will help out. The CD command is used to move to other directories. Remember, though, the DOS convention of "\" as a separator is exactly the opposite of the convention in UNIX world where "/" is used. Just type:

```
ftp> cd directory/directory
```

to switch the working directory. To find out where you are, use the PWD (print working directory) command:

```
ftp> pwd
257 "/sys" is the current directory.
Getting Files from the Remote Host
```

You have two choices in transferring files: one at a time or in a batch. The simple one-shot file transfer is done with the GET command. The syntax is very simple:

```
get remote-filename local-filename
```

It works just the way it looks, getting the remote file and storing it in the local file you've named. For instance, the command:

```
get myfile.dat c:\temp\myfile.dat
```

will cause the remote system to send MYFILE.DAT to your system's C:\TEMP directory. The batch method is very similar, using mget (multiple get). With mget, wildcards are allowed, which simplifies batch transfers. For example, to get all the files in the current directory that start with "my" use the command:

```
mget my*
```

Note that the wildcards are UNIX style, so this will get everything that starts with my, regardless of extension. The FTP program will prompt you for an OK on each file it finds that matches the wildcard criteria.

Sending Files to the Remote Host Sending files is done with get's COMPANION command, *put*. There is also an MPUT command, which (surprise!) does a batch-style (or multiple) put. These commands work the same way as get:

```
put local_filename remote_filename
```

that is:

```
mput c:\temp\myfile.dat myfile.dat
```

or

```
mput my*
```

just as in the previous example.

Manipulating Directories and Files FTP offers a set of commands to manipulate directories and files:

```
mkdir directory
```

Make Directory creates a directory on the remote host. This command will fail if you do not have sufficient permissions.

```
rmdir directory
```

Remove Directory removes a directory on the remote host. This command will fail if you do not have sufficient permissions.

```
delete filename
```

deletes a remote file. This command will fail if you do not have sufficient permissions.

```
mdelete filespec
```

Multiple Delete deletes a set of files specified by a wildcard. This command will fail if you do not have sufficient permissions.

```
rename filename
```

renames a remote file. This command will fail if you do not have sufficient permissions.

Configuration Commands There are a few FTP commands that help to make the FTP environment more suitable to your particular use.

```
ascii
```

puts FTP into ascii mode for transferring text files. This mode is needed because, for historical reasons, American Standard Code for Information Interchange (ASCII) text files are stored differently on UNIX systems than they are on other systems (including Windows NT). The UNIX convention is to follow each line of text with the ASCII linefeed (LF) character. Most other systems (including Windows NT) follow each line of text with a pair of characters: an ASCII carriage return (CR) and then an LF (a few systems use just the CR, as if matters weren't complicated enough already!). This mode does automatic CR/LF translation where appropriate, which is great for text files, but inappropriate for binary file transfer.

```
binary
```

This companion to ascii switches to binary mode, which transfers characters as a binary stream verbatim from the other system (without any CR/LF translation). *Failure to use this command is responsible for 90% of ftp errors*. FTP defaults to text (ascii) mode. If you are transferring any other kind of file, set *binary* before attempting to transfer data.

mode

displays the current mode—binary or ascii.

bell

toggles the bell indicating completed operations. This is useful if you are doing long transfers and want to know when they are complete.

hash

toggles the printing of a hash mark (#) for every 512 bytes of data transferred. This is useful if you have a slow connection or are transferring large files. It lets you know that things are progressing.

Ending an FTP Session To end a session simply type close at the ftp> prompt. This disconnects you from the remote machine. The OPEN command can then be used to begin a new connection. To close the connection and exit the FTP program, type bye.

Getting Help The help included with the FTP program is minimal, but still useful, at least as a reminder. Type help or? at the ftp> prompt for a list of available commands:

```
ftp> ?
Commands may be abbreviated.   Commands are:

!               delete          literal         prompt          send
?               debug           ls              put             status
append          dir             mdelete         pwd             trace
ascii           disconnect      mdir            quit            type
bell            get             mget            quote           user
binary          glob            mkdir           recv            verbose
bye             hash            mls             remotehelp
cd              help            mput            rename
close           lcd             open            rmdir
ftp>
```

For a little information on any particular command, type help *commandname* at the ftp> prompt.

```
ftp> help remotehelp
remotehelp      get help from remote server
```

The nature of FTP is that it translates local commands into a set of standard commands. Not all FTP server software supports the entire command set. If a command does not seem to be working, typing remotehelp at the ftp> prompt might shed some light with a list of supported commands.

TFTP The Trivial FTP program is a command line FTP client that allows simple transfers from the command line. It is useful for quick transfer operations and use in batch or command files.

TFTP does not allow user logins, which means that the remote file/directory must allow "world" access. The syntax for TFTP is:

```
tftp [-i] hostname <put|get> source file destination file
```

The -i option tells TFTP to use binary (image) mode instead of the default ASCII, which performs translations of control characters. Use binary mode to move compressed and executable files. Put or Get do just what their FTP counterparts do—transfer files to (put) or from (get) the remote host. The source and destination files are the names of the file on which the operation will occur (source) and where it will end up (destination). If no destination file is specified, the source filename will be used.

Other TCP/IP Tools

Windows NT includes a variety of UNIX-style command-line tools, including (among others) *arp. gdsset, ping, hostname, nbtstat, netstat, nslookup, tracert*, and *route*. All are defined in Windows NT Commands (from the Start menu's Help entry). Of these, ping, nbtstat, route, and nslookup are probably the most important. See the section on TCP/IP Tips and Tricks at the end of this chapter for advice on how to get the most from them.

Simple TCP/IP Services

Both NT Server and Workstation support simple services, including *daytime, echo, qotd,* and *chargen*. All are installed from Control Panel/Network's Services tab. Press the Add button and select Simple TCP/IP Services from the list. You will need to supply a path to the NT distribution files.

Once the Simple TCP/IP Services are installed, you may access them using telnet. For example, connecting to the qotd service yields the sort of display shown in Figure 6.13.

FIGURE 6.13 QUOTD service. NT comes with a variety of simple TCP/IP services, including Quote-of-the-Day, shown here.

TCP/IP Printing

Both NT Workstation and Server support a UNIX Line-Printer Daemon (LPD) service, which allows the server's printer(s) to be used by UNIX systems that support the companion Line Printer Redirector (LPR) application, which is also provided for NT when you install the service. TCP/IP printing is installed from Control Panel/Network's Services tab. Click the Add button, and select Microsoft TCP/IP Printing from the list. You will be asked to enter a path to the NT distribution files. NT will then copy the files onto your system. When it has finished, close the Network dialog and reboot your computer.

Once TCP/IP Printing is installed, any printer that is shared by the system becomes available to UNIX clients (and other NT systems on which the TCP/IP Printing Service has been loaded) via the LPR command:

```
C:\>lpr

Sends a print job to a network printer

Usage: lpr -S server -P printer [-C class] [-J job] [-o option] [-x] [-d]
filename

Options:
      -S server    Name or ipaddress of the host providing lpd service
      -P printer   Name of the print queue
      -C class     Job classification for use on the burst page
      -J job       Job name to print on the burst page
      -o option    Indicates type of the file (by default assumes a text file)
                   Use "-o l" for binary (e.g. postscript) files
      -x           Compatibility with SunOS 4.1.x and prior
      -d           Send data file first
```

Thus, the command:

```
C:\>lpr -S mips40 -P GenericT test.txt
```

sends the file *test.txt* to the printer named *GenericT* on print server *mips40*.

Multiple Adapters and IP Routing

NT Workstation (and NT Server, prior to version 4.0) can act as only a very basic router for users who have only a few segments and do not need dynamic routing capabilities. To use it this way, you must have multiple network adapters with TCP/IP enabled on all the ones you want to route IP traffic between. Then use the TCP/IP Configuration in the Control Panel/Network to turn on static routing between network adapters and then use the ROUTE.EXE utility to create static routing maps between the adapters. For information on configuring TCP/IP on multiple adapters, refer to the "Installing TCP/IP" section earlier in this chapter and the "IP Forwarding" section that follows.

NT Server 4.0 supports dynamic IP (and IPX) routing using the Router Information Protocol (RIP) and thereby can support more sophisticated networks. See the RIP for Internet Protocol entry later in this chapter for information on how to set up RIP on NT Server.

But first, let's review how IP routing works.

Routing on Small Networks After you have enabled routing and rebooted the system, your system will provide local routing services to the networks it knows about. You can then point other systems' default routes to the NT system. For NT Workstation (and pre-4.0 Servers), any network segments to which the NT system is not physically connected must be entered into the route table manually.

ROUTE.EXE is a command-line utility that lets you add or delete static routes between networks or hosts. You can define multiple routes to a destination, and if the first one fails, the second will kick in. You must define routes to all intermediate points along the way. For example, let's look at the simple network illustrated in Figure 6.14.

There are two network segments (192.155.11 and 192.155.12) and 3 nodes (x.2, x.3, and x.4). When NT was installed on nodes 192.155.11.2 and 192.155.12.4, the default router was given as node x.3, meaning that all nonlocal IP traffic will be passed to the server in the middle. However, by default, x.3 is unable to route the traffic. The network administrator must enable TCP/IP on each adapter in node x.3, and then enable IP forwarding as described later in this chapter. At that point, the node at x.3 will be able to forward traffic from 192.155.11.2 to 192.155.12.4 and vice versa.

Routing in Mildly Complex Networks Let's look at the more complicated setup shown in Figure 6.15. As in the example in Figure 6.14, node 192.155.11.2 points to 192.155.11.3 as the default route. However, node x.3 knows only about networks 192.155.11 and 192.155.12, because that's all it is directly connected to. Likewise, node x.4 knows only about networks 192.155.12 and 192.155.13. In order for packets from network 192.155.11 to reach network 192.155.13 (and vice versa), several things must happen.

First, nodes x.3 and x.4 must be configured to route, as in the example above with node x.3. Then, static routing entries must be defined for nodes x.3 and x.4, telling them about the remote networks. For node x.3, the command would look like this:
```
ROUTE ADD 192.155.13.0 192.155.12.4
```

This command adds a static route to node x.3's routing table. Then, any packet coming from subnet 192.155.11 destined for network 192.155.13 will get passed to node 12.4 for handling. In order for x.4 to return packets to network 192.155.11, it must be informed about the route as well (remember that NT doesn't support dynamic routing). Therefore, the following command must be given to node x.4:

```
ROUTE ADD 192.155.11.0 192.155.12.3
```

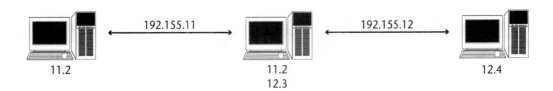

FIGURE 6.14 Routing-1. Simple network layout and routing.

FIGURE 6.15 Routing-2. Mildly complex network routing setup.

Now packets will make it from any node on any net to any other node on any other net. Believe it or not, this is a very simple example, and serves to illustrate the complexity inherent in multiple-segment IP networks. The more segments you add, the more systems you must manually configure. The static routing model breaks down after about five segments, at which point the administration and configuration becomes overwhelming. That's where RIP—supported by NT Server 4.0—becomes essential.

Routing in Very Complex Networks A very complex network, more typical of large corporate sites, is illustrated in Figure 6.16. Many departmental routers throughout a company are connected over a high-speed backbone with redundant links between the routers. All these routers have separate interfaces for multiple small networks. Workstations on each of the smaller subnets have a single adapter running TCP/IP, and they identify the nearest backbone router as their default router.

This method is the simplest to configure and maintain, because each of the routers is capable of updating the others via RIP or OSPF or some other router-to-router protocol. Since they

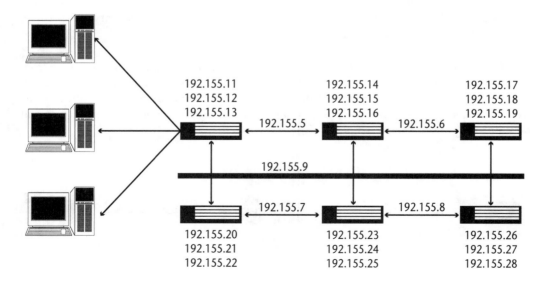

FIGURE 6.16 Routing-3. Large corporate or campus network.

are directly connected to each segment, the network numbers are seen automatically by the routers and forwarded out with no maintenance or configuration required. If a node on network 192.155.11 sends a request to a node on 192.155.28, the routers are capable of automatically forwarding and rejecting packets as needed. The clients simply point to the closest router as their default and let the network hardware do its work.

Purchasing and maintaining these dedicated routers is an expensive procedure, however, and many companies prefer to let other devices handle the routing work instead. Almost all the UNIX and NetWare implementations support RIP or other dynamic routing protocols, and by adding RIP support to NT 4.0, Microsoft has leveled the playing field for NT in this kind of environment (for more information on IP routing, refer to Appendix 2).

In some environments, users may see multiple routers on a single segment. This setup is similar to that shown in the example in Figure 6.16, wherein each router has multiple paths in case one fails. However, here we are speaking of multiple routers on the client's network, which might look something like Figure 6.17.

In this type of environment, users need to be able to define multiple default routes. In the event that one router fails, another router will be used automatically. NT allows this by adding multiple default routes in the TCP/IP Protocol section of Control Panel/Network as described earlier in this chapter. You must reboot the system after making these changes. You can also add default gateways after making the initial changes with the "ROUTE -S" command, although they are not permanently added to the registry.

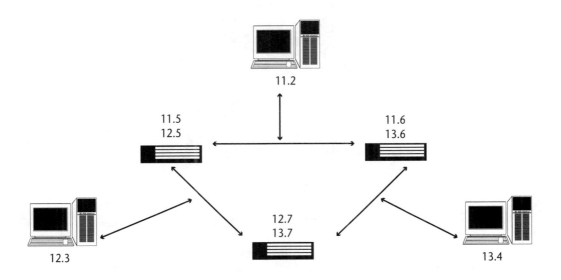

FIGURE 6.17 Routing-4. TCP/IP Routing in a redundant network.

It's important to note that you *can* have multiple default gateways for every network inter-face in your system. For example, if you have two dynamic routers each on two different seg-ments to which you are directly connected, you wind up with up to four default routers. If one of your adapters or subnets fails, you will still have two routers on the other segment that you can use. This is an expensive and unlikely wiring scheme, but it is completely possible.

Routing Support in Windows NT As was mentioned earlier in this chapter, both NT Workstation and NT Server support the use of multiple network adapters with TCP/IP for static routing (IP Forwarding). NT Server 4.0 also supports the Router Information Protocol (RIP) for automatic inter-router communication.

IP Forwarding Both NT Workstation and NT Server support simple forwarding of IP packets between network cards—all that's required for static IP routing. To enable IP forwarding, select Control Panel/Network's Protocol's tab, select TCP/IP Protocol from the list, and click the Properties button. The TCP/IP Properties dialog will appear. Select its Routing tab (see Figure 6.18).

Check the Enable IP Forwarding box on this page. IP traffic may then be routed between the network cards in your computer (each of which must have its own separate IP address) using the ROUTE command as described earlier in this chapter.

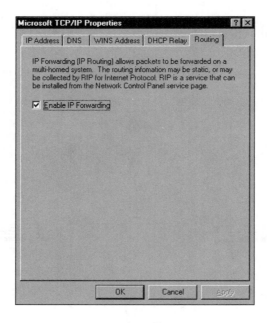

FIGURE 6.18 IP forwarding. Whether or not NT functions as a software router for IP traffic is controlled in this dialog box. Both NT 4.0 Server and Workstation support *static* routing; only NT 4.0 Server supports *dynamic* routing via Router Information Protocol (RIP).

RIP for Internet Protocol In addition to basic IP Forwarding (described above), NT Server 4.0 supports a *Router Information Protocol* (RIP) Service. This allows NT Servers to exchange router information with each other and other RIP routers.

The RIP Service is installed from Control Panel/Network's Services tab. Click the Add button, select RIP for Internet Protocol from the list, and click OK. No additional configuration is required, because RIP is completely self-contained. Note that using RIP requires that you statically assign an IP address for each network adapter on your server. You cannot use DHCP to obtain the addresses.

With RIP enabled, it is not necessary to use ROUTE to establish static routes for each and every system on your network. It is, however, necessary to assign default routes—the workstations have to know where the router is. In general, remember that RIP is used by routers (including NT Server 4.0, when so configured) to communicate among themselves. If your network has just two segments and a single NT Server to route between them, RIP won't help—there are no other routers!

SNMP SNMP stands for Simple Network Management Protocol, and that's exactly what it is. It provides basic administrative information about a device so that network administrators or SNMP management software can monitor the overall health of the network (as well as individual systems). To take advantage of NT's SNMP services, you must have an SNMP manager that can monitor and display SNMP alerts. Several such programs are available for a wide variety of platforms.

SNMP is installed from Control Panel/Network's Services tab. Click the Add button, select SNMP Service from the list, and click OK. After the system copies the necessary software to the hard drive, you are presented with the SNMP Service Properties dialog that is illustrated in Figure 6.19.

There are two methods that SNMP management software can use to collect information about devices. One way is to have devices send *alerts* to an SNMP manager or to any manager in the community. Another method is to have the SNMP manager poll devices every few seconds (or minutes or hours). There are benefits to both strategies, and it is likely that both are in use within your organization.

For example, when an SNMP device can send an alert to a management station, that device can do so as soon as something starts to fail. By the time a polling management station gets to a node that has started failing, it may be dead altogether, leaving no clue as to the cause of death. Conversely, devices that are in good health clutter the network with unnecessary alerts, and it's better to let a manager poll nodes when needed.

By default, NT's SNMP service does not send alerts. It does, however, support SNMP queries from any device in the "public" community (a community is a logical grouping of devices).

To enable the SNMP service to send alerts, select the Traps tab, type in the community name you wish to add, and click the Add button. Although "Public" is the default community for inquiries, it is not the default community for the sending of alerts. To make your system send SNMP alerts to devices within the "Public" community, add it here. If you have a departmental

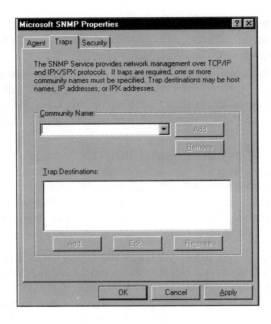

FIGURE 6.19 SNMP Properties, Traps tab. Simple Network Management Protocol (SNMP) can be configured to send management alerts to "communities" of SNMP users or to specific destination addresses.

SNMP community, add it here as well. A node can be in more than one community at a time; simply add additional community names as needed.

With the "Public" community added to the alert list, any management station within the community will receive the alerts and may also be able to make changes to your configuration. If you want to send alerts only to a specific management station, you can add it to the Trap Destinations list on the same tab by clicking the associated Add button. You will then need to designate the destination management station's IP or IPX address—and only that management station will receive the alerts (you can designate multiple destinations by clicking Add again).

Remember that by default NT will respond to any management station request that comes from the "Public" community. To disable this feature, or to add a new community name, select the Security tab (see Figure 6.20).

If you want to remove the "Public" community from the list, select it and click the Remove button. If you want to add another community to the list, click the Add button.

If you want to restrict the management stations that can query your machine for SNMP statistics, click the "Only Accept SNMP Packets from These Hosts" radio button and add the desired management stations to the list below it with the associated Add button. You will then need to type in the hostname or IP address of the management station you want to add.

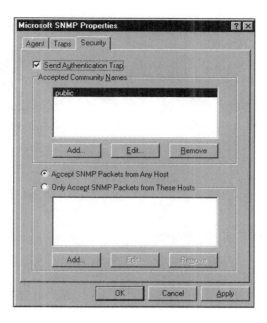

FIGURE 6.20 SNMP Properties, Security tab. Which SNMP communities do or do not have access to the system in question is controlled with this dialog.

The "Send Authentication Trap" check-box in the upper-left corner alerts managers that an unauthorized host is attempting to pull statistics from your machine. If a management station that does not belong to one of the accepted communities queries your machine and this option is checked, the SNMP Server will send an alert to the management stations listed in the Trap Destinations from the Traps tab.

You can customize additional information about your system for inclusion with SNMP alerts and responses from the Agent tab, and the dialog box shown in Figure 6.21 will appear. Type in either your name or the name of the system administrator in the "Contact" edit box. Type in a location, such as building, floor, or room number, in the "Location" edit box.

The Service group box consists of several check-boxes that allow you to detail various levels of specific information:

- *Physical*: Pertains to the low-level wire and physical network statistics. If your node acts as a part of the physical network (i.e., a repeater, bridge, or router), check this box.

- *Datalink / Subnetwork*: Applies only if you are acting as a part of a logical network, such as a bridge. The "Internet" check-box applies only if you are acting as an IP router. Errors generated within the higher-level network software are passed to the management stations if these check-boxes are enabled.

- *End-to-End*: Applies to devices that act as an end-node on the network. If you're running TCP/IP, you are acting as an end-node at least some of the time.

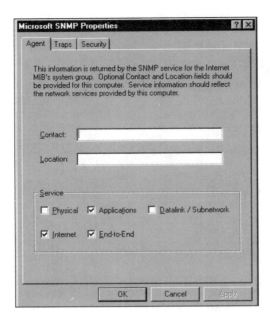

FIGURE 6.21 SNMP Properties, Agent tab. Optional information filled in on this dialog box indicates the system's location, a contact name (and perhaps phone number), and the role the system plays in the network.

- *Application*: These alerts have to do with TCP/IP-based application-generated errors, such as e-mail failures or FTP errors. All NT systems that use SNMP should have at least the "End-to-End" and "Application" check-boxes enabled.

- *Internet*: New for NT 4.0, this check-box should be enabled if you want SNMP to provide alerts for Internet-related services, including those from IIS/PWS (see Chapter 7).

TCP/IP Tips and Tricks

Personal experience is the best teacher, and we've had our share. Here are some notes on situations that have caused us no end of trouble. We hope they'll be helpful to you.

Changing IP addresses for an Entire Domain

This is the IP administrator's ultimate nightmare—changing the IP address for every single system in a domain, and in today's world of buyouts, downsizing, and ISP-of-the-month it *can* happen. Here's a procedure to make it easier (best done overnight at a site of any size):

1. Convert your network to DHCP and WINS, if you haven't already done so. Why? Because they minimize the number of places settings must be changed!

2. Log off all workstations.

3. Start DHCP manager.

4. Delete all reservations.

5. Delete all static mappings.

6. Note any scope properties you've set, and then delete all scopes.

7. Create new scopes (re-creating any properties mentioned above—for example, router settings) with updated addresses, mappings and reservations, as needed.

8. Start Control Panel/Networks.

9. Change IP addresses for all NICs in the server.

10. Manually edit the WINDOWS/SYSTEM32/DRIVERS/ETC/HOSTS and LMHOSTS files and correct them if necessary.

11. Reboot the server.

12. Start WINS Manager and view the database. It will probably show a mix of old and new IP addresses (if it doesn't, skip ahead to step 16).

13. Select Mappings/Initiate Scavenging.

14. Select Server/Configuration. Change the Renewal Interval to one hour, the Extinction Interval to 30 minutes, the Extinction Timeout to one hour, and the Verify Interval to 30 minutes. Then click OK.

15. Take a one-hour coffee break (this will allow WINS to update itself).

16. Manually edit the HOSTS and LMHOSTS files on all workstations. In most cases, nothing will be necessary (assuming they're set up to use DHCP and WINS, it all should be automatic), but in some cases there will be manual notations (for example, any workstation set up to permit SMS remote control to work across a router).

17. Reboot the workstations. Check connectivity.

18. Re-establish routing tables (ROUTE ADD whatever) as necessary.

19. Troubleshoot as needed (see below).

20. When everything works, reset the WINS manager configuration to reasonable values so that you don't kill your network with name server traffic.

IP Troubleshooting

On each server and station, run:

1. IPCONFIG to check the local IP addresses.

2. PING to check low-level connectivity. (Try it using the name first. If that fails, try the IP address. If it won't work with even the IP address, either the NIC drivers or routing is hosed. If ping works, but something high-level won't work, test with NBTSTAT.)

3. NET USE whatever to check high-level connectivity.

4. NBTSTAT -c to see what IP address the station *thinks* is associated with a name. If it has the addressing wrong, edit the LMHOSTS file (check HOSTS too) and/or WINS database, then use NBTSTAT -R to reset the addresses.

5. NSLOOKUP if you're using DNS. (See the nslookup section of the Windows NT command reference in Start menu's Help.)

Multi-Protocol Networks

A piece of advice from bitter experience: do your initial setup and troubleshooting with *just* IP, no other protocols. Trying to get everything running with a mix of IP and other protocols (in our experience, IPX) can be a disaster. Short of breaking out a protocol analyzer (on NT Server 4.0, you can always use Network Monitor), it's all but impossible to tell which protocols are routing properly and which are not. You may ultimately want to run multiple protocols, but get the system working with just IP first—then add any other protocols.

Conclusion

Windows NT's TCP/IP support provides a broad range of the most-needed TCP/IP features, including FTP and Telnet client support and the usual range of TCP utilities. In addition, Windows NT TCP/IP provides a routable protocol for use in large networks, and this feature is augmented by NT's built-in static router (and NT 4.0 Server's RIP) support, which allows a single computer with multiple network cards to functionally replace an expensive dedicated router in many (but not all) TCP/IP routing applications. Now that we've examined these pieces of the Windows NT network puzzle, we can put them to use on the Internet (Chapter 7) and in creating multi-domain enterprise networks (Chapter 8).

For More Information

Albitz, P. and C. Liu (1992), *DNS and BIND*. Sebastopol, CA: O'Reilly & Associates, ISBN: 1-56592-010-4. Great book for learning Domain Name Service (DNS).

Allard, J. (1993), *Advanced Internetworking with TCP/IP on Windows NT* (tcpipnt.doc). Redmond, WA: Microsoft Corp. (downloadable via anonymous ftp from rhino.microsoft.com). This 34-page paper on networking explains advanced TCP/IP topics for Windows NT, including static routing, in great detail.

Arick, M. (1993), *The TCP/IP Companion*. Wellesley, MA: QED Publishing Group, ISBN: 0-89435-466-3. Good end-user-oriented discussion of TCP/IP and utilities.

Black, U. (1992), *TCP/IP and Related Protocols*. New York: McGraw-Hill, ISBN: 0-07-005553-X. Mandatory desktop reference for the TCP/IP administrator.

Comer, D. (1991), *Internetworking with TCP/IP, Volume 1*. Englewood Cliffs, NJ: Prentice-Hall, ISBN: 0-13-472242-6. Mandatory desktop reference for the TCP/IP administrator.

Hunt, C. (1992), *TCP/IP Network Administration*. Sebastopol, CA: O'Reilly & Associates, Inc., ISBN: 0-937175-82-X. Mandatory desktop reference for the TCP/IP administrator.

Liu, C., et al. (1994), *Managing Internet Information Services*, Sebastopol, CA: O'Reilly & Associates, Inc., ISBN: 1-56592-062-7. An excellent book for people setting up Internet servers; covers FTP, Gopher, WWW, and WAIS server management techniques extensively.

Microsoft Staff (1993), *Microsoft Windows NT TCP/IP*. Redmond, WA: Microsoft Corp. (part of Windows NT documentation). Brief overview and reference on Windows NT TCP/IP functionality.

Internet Connections

7

Once you have finished this chapter, you will know:

- ⇗ How to connect your site to the Internet

- ⇗ What security precautions to take

- ⇗ How to configure the new Internet Information Server (IIS) and Peer Web Server (PWS) that come with NT 4.0 Server and Workstation, respectively

- ⇗ How to perform common IIS administrative tasks

- ⇗ Where to find further information on the Internet

Both the Server and Workstation editions of NT 4.0 come with everything you need to hook up to the Internet, though if you expect your site to function as an Internet *server* you will need NT Server.

Internet or Intranet?

If you set up an Internet server but permit access only by people inside your own company, you've created an *intranet*. There isn't much reason to distinguish between the two situations in most of this chapter, because most Internet technology applies just as well in the intranet situation.

Because an intranet isn't connected to the public Internet, some of the security concerns you might have are reduced. However, if your network is connected to the Internet through a firewall, it's critically important that the firewall not allow access to the intranet server. You can block outside access to the IP address of the intranet server or use a non-standard port for Web services and block that port. The section below on firewalls has more information on this subject.

Client-Side Tools

Both NT 4.0 Workstation and Server include Internet Explorer (IE) 2.0 on the CD. About a week after Microsoft shipped NT 4.0, it released the final version of Internet Explorer 3.0 on its Web site. It's a major improvement over IE 2.0 and includes support for ActiveX controls, so you'll want to download it.

The upside of IE 2.0, other than the obvious benefit of already having it, is that it's small, quick, and responsive. IE 2.0 pops up much more quickly than either IE 3.0 or Netscape Navigator 3.0. And if you're concerned about the security risks of Java, ActiveX, or JavaScript, IE 2.0 lets you rest easy because it doesn't support any of that. It's on par with Netscape 1.2 in terms of support for features like tables and probably can view 80% of what's on the Web with no compromises at all. If IE 2.0 was not installed during NT setup (it normally appears as an icon on the desktop), you can add it with Control Panel/Add Remove Software (where it's called "Internet Jumpstart Kit").

If you're coming from a UNIX environment and are familiar with command-line FTP and Telnet tools, you'll find those in NT 4.0 as well (see Chapter 6). Most people won't have much of a need for these, however, because FTP services are conveniently provided by Internet Explorer, and few will need to log in to a command-line session.

Making the Internet Connection

If your goal is to connect your own server to the worldwide Internet, you'll need a communications line, an Internet Service Provider (ISP), and some basic address and domain information. We'll cover the essential procedures in this section.

Internet Service Providers

If you'll pardon the analogy, the Internet is a lot like an illegal drug network. The people at the top run the Internet backbone, dealing with massive high-speed connections. They sell big chunks of bandwidth to ISPs, who divvy it up into even smaller parcels and sell that to companies needing "large" amounts of bandwidth such as a T1. The bigger ISPs also sell to smaller ISPs, who turn around and break the bandwidth up, selling dial-in services to people with low-speed modems.

The more bandwidth you plan to buy, the closer to the Internet backbone you're likely to be. That puts you at a double disadvantage if you go with a slow connection such as 28.8Kbps modems. Not only is the data rate low, but there are a lot more hops—from your ISP to his ISP to the big kahuna ISP—before packets make it to the Internet backbone where they can speed to their ultimate destination.

Communication Links

Your options for bandwidth are varied, as are the costs. The least expensive option is a plain phone line combined with a 28.8Kbps modem. Because your ISP is probably a local call away and most areas don't meter local calls, the telephone costs are essentially zero. Unfortunately, analog modems aren't a very feasible solution; you can't really serve more than two or three users simultaneously this way before response time becomes ridiculous.

One step up are ISDN digital lines, which offer up to 128Kbps performance and can support around eight simultaneous users with acceptable response times. Beyond that, you can go to a T1 line at 1.5Mbps that can offer decent service to as many as 100 users at once. Some ISPs offer fractional-T1 access to the Internet, but you'll still have to install a T1 to your site. You just won't be using its full bandwidth.

One new development worth asking your local phone company about is an Adaptive Digital Subscriber Line (ADSL). This technology is being touted as a faster, more flexible alternative to ISDN. In essence, ADSL is special short-haul modem technology that works over existing copper wire. One modem is placed at your site, and the other is located at your telephone central office. The modem in the central office is connected to standard Internet router equipment that is separate from the phone system. Because the distances between the modems are small—your central office is often just a mile or two away—ADSL can get speeds up to 5MB per second or so. The phone companies like it too, because, unlike ISDN, they don't need to buy an completely new multimillion-dollar phone switch to provide the service.

If you need more than a simple phone line, you have the added variable of dealing with the local phone company. ISDN has been available for a few years in large metropolitan areas, but it's still common in many areas to have a month's wait before you can have service installed. And when Windows Magazine (in New York) ordered a T1 line in mid-1996, there was a two-month wait before NYNEX (the local telephone company) could install it. Emerging technologies like ADSL are likely to have the same slow ramp-up and long waits for service connection as the phone companies stumble through the learning curve.

One way to circumvent the phone company is to locate your server at the ISP. Many ISPs will offer to keep your server at their site and connect it directly to their high-speed network—for a price. Besides the extra cost associated with this arrangement, there's the additional hassle of not being in physical control of the system. Some ISPs offer trained staff that may be able to help you resolve problems remotely, but make sure you're clear on what they will and won't do.

In every case except the simple dial-up modem (be it analog or ISDN), the connection you get will be connected to some special equipment called a CSU/DSU (channel service unit/data service unit). This equipment acts as a modem, converting the digital signal to an analog form that's sent over the phone line. The CSU/DSU output will typically be connected to an Ethernet router. The equipment you want to connect to the Internet is then plugged into the router's Ethernet segment.

Software and Administrative Setup

Once you've chosen an ISP and selected the bandwidth you need (and can afford), it's time to think about how you'll do the protocol and routing part of the work.

Most likely, you'll want to register a domain name so that your Web site and other services can be accessed as http://www.yourcompany.com. To do this, contact InterNIC (http://www.internic.com) and fill out a form. Domain name registration costs $50 a year, with the first two years being paid in advance. It's worth the cost, because otherwise you'll be using the ISP's domain, like http://www.isp.com/yourcompany. This makes it nearly impossible to change ISPs! Some ISPs will offer to register a domain name for you as part of a bundle deal. If you go this route, make sure that *you* own the domain name (your name is on the InterNIC form and not the ISP's). If the ISP owns the domain name, it could complicate moving to another ISP if you become dissatisfied.

The next requirement is to get a block of IP addresses. The more addresses you need, the greater the complications. The InterNIC also is involved in assigning and doling out blocks of IP addresses, but for small numbers of addresses you can usually go through your ISP. The catch here is, again, becoming locked into one ISP. The explosive growth of the Internet has meant that the backbone routers have millions of addresses to track. One way to reduce the load on those routers is for the backbone managers to assign blocks of IP addresses to specific ISPs and always route those addresses the same way. The problem comes for you, the customer, when you try to move to another ISP and have to change all the IP address assignments in all your systems.

Firewalls

Any private network that is connected to the Internet should go through some type of firewall. At minimum, a firewall provides the ability to filter out traffic that shouldn't pass between the Internet and your private network, such as messages between two computers within your private network. These are typical packet-router functions, and indeed most dedicated routers can provide basic firewall functions. However, there are benefits to more sophisticated arrangements.

Limited Access Quandary A firewall must balance ease of access with adequate security precautions. If you create restrictions on users that are unworkable given the needs of their jobs, they will find ways around the restrictions. Their workarounds may create security problems that are even worse. For example, most companies have dial-in or dial-out modem facilities, either on individual systems or in a shared modem pool. Users might use a modem pool to create their own dial-in access to the IP network, using their own PC as the router. These "backdoor" access paths to your network can let attackers make a complete end-run around your firewall security.

Another balancing act involves the position of your public Internet server. If you place the Internet server outside your firewall, it's open to just about any attack. Yet if you try to place the Internet server behind your firewall, the firewall restrictions must be loose enough for public Web, ftp, and other traffic to pass. One common solution involves a "perimeter network" or "sandwich" approach that uses two levels of firewall. The first level provides basic protection to your public Internet servers, and the second level screens traffic further before it enters your private network.

Packet Filtering Each packet on the network has information that a firewall can use to make decisions about security. First, there are two IP addresses in each message: source and the destination. For both incoming (Internet to internal network) and outbound (internal network to Internet) traffic a good firewall will let you filter by either or both. Skilled intruders can easily forge the source address, so filtering based on it won't always be foolproof.

Another important piece of information in a packet is the port number. When a packet arrives at a system, the port number helps to route the message to the right service on that system. For example, a port number of 80 is usually routed to the HTTP (Web) service. A firewall can block use of the standard HTTP service by blocking port 80. It would still be possible to use the HTTP service on a non-standard port, as long as both the source and destination system agreed on the port number.

One application of filtering is to discard "impossible" messages. For example, let's say a message arrives at your firewall from the Internet, and its *source* address is that of a legitimate system inside your firewall. How would a message from inside your firewall end up at the front door? This probably indicates that an attacker is trying to get the destination system to accept a message from a supposedly trusted system.

Using NT's packet filtering NT Server includes a limited ability to filter packets, on a per-adapter basis, using the port number, the protocol type, or a combination of the two. You configure this feature in Control Panel, Network, Protocols, TCP/IP Properties, IP Address, Advanced dialog. Check the Enable Security box, and click the Configure button.

One use for this feature would be as a poor man's firewall, where the NT system is acting as a router between two network cards. You might, for example, allow only mail and news traffic through from the Internet by permitting only the TCP and UDP protocols (6 and 17) and further restricting traffic to TCP on ports 25 and 119. The user interface for port filtering leaves a bit to be desired; you must know the decimal values for all the ports, protocols, and services. The most common port/protocol combinations you'll need to know are HTTP (80/TCP or UDP), FTP (20 and 21/TCP), mail (25/TCP), and news (119/TCP). Protocol numbers are 6 for TCP and 17 for UDP.[1]

NT's packet filtering feature *cannot* screen by source or destination address. For example, "only allow TCP packets with port 80 (HTTP) and a destination address of 10.124.201.8 (an HTTP proxy server)" isn't possible. And of course if someone manages to break into your system—for example, by exploiting some bug in your mailer software—that person may be able to circumvent the port restrictions you've put here. Given its security and filtering restrictions, NT's port filtering shouldn't be considered an adequate replacement for a dedicated router or complete firewall setup.

Proxy Servers Although packet filtering can provide basic protection, it still leaves a lot of your internal network visible to the outside world. For example, if each user in your private network wants to browse the Web, your firewall will have to let those packets through in both directions. You could try to restrict things a bit by permitting only packets that use the HTTP common port number of 80, but a fair number of useful Web servers use other port numbers. In essence, your firewall can't filter much unless your users are willing to sacrifice some communication ability.

One way around this problem is to add a *proxy server*. The proxy usually resides on a system that figuratively has one foot in the Internet and one foot in your private network. Instead of talking directly to a Web server on the Internet, for example, the users inside your network talk to the proxy server. The proxy server then forwards the request to the destination Internet server. The destination server sees only the proxy server; to the Internet your entire network appears to be one Web user (a really busy one).

With a proxy in place, the firewall can be much more restrictive. Only the proxy server is talking to the Internet, so a would-be attacker sees only one IP address from your network. All other addresses in your internal network can be completely screened by your firewall and are safe from direct attack. To keep the firewall tight, you need to have a proxy for each type of service that your internal network users want to access. At a minimum, that will include HTTP and FTP, but it may also include news (NNTP), mail (SMTP), or telnet services as well.

At the time this book was written, Microsoft was developing an NT-based proxy server, code-named *Catapult* for use on NT Server. Catapult can act as a proxy at the Windows Socket level, supporting any socket-based application (which includes most Internet applications). It can also function as a direct Web proxy. The Microsoft Web site should have the latest information on the progress of this product.

Many other vendors are already active in the proxy and firewall arena; one NT-based solution is made by Raptor Systems (http://www.raptor.com), another is part of Digital's Altavista product line (http://altavista.digital.com). Yahoo has a comprehensive list at http://www.yahoo.com/Business_and_Economy/Companies/Computers/Software/Systems_and_Utilities/Security/Firewalls.

---

1   These port numbers are documented in Internet Engineering Task Force (IETF) Requests For Comment (RFC) documents, available on the Web at http://www.internic.net (start with the Directory and Database Services link on that page). WAIS searching of the InterNIC site is also available.

Internet Information Server and Personal Web Server

NT Server includes Internet Information Server (IIS) 2.0, a full World Wide Web, FTP, and Gopher server for the Internet. NT Workstation offers a reduced-function version of IIS called Personal Web Server (PWS). Because the Peer Web Service (PWS) in NT Workstation is a subset of the full IIS in NT Server, the sections here cover both products.

Differences Between PWS and IIS

The basic differences between PWS and the full IIS are that PWS lacks the following features:

*   Access control via IP addresses

*   Virtual servers (multiple home directories for different domain names)

*   Logging to SQL/ODBC database

*   Bandwidth throttling

*   128-bit keys in Secure Sockets Layer (SSL), with both versions supporting 40-bit keys for SSL

In addition, PWS lacks a few of IIS's performance-enhancing optimizations such as caching of frequently used file handles. Microsoft also introduced some performance limits on PWS with the assumption that foreground application performance should remain a priority. That keeps the workstation responsive, but at the expense of Internet-service performance.

In practical terms, NT Workstation/PWS would serve perfectly well as a test bed for developing IIS applications or as an intranet Web server for a small group of users. Beyond that, either upgrade to NT Server/IIS or check out a third-party Web server. But before you do that, read the next section.

NT Workstation as an Internet Server?

Although NT Workstation is billed by Microsoft as a workstation operating system, it can easily handle the load that most Internet servers would see from World Wide Web (HTTP) or File Transfer Protocol (FTP) requests. The communication line between the Internet and the Web server is the limiting factor for all but the largest Web sites. This is especially true if your Web site uses anything less than a T1 line (1.544Mb per second) as its communication link. Although NT Workstation/PWS can't handle the load of NT Server/IIS, that's mostly because Microsoft specifically changed PWS to reduce its performance and limit its features.

Third-party vendors of Web servers such as Netscape Commerce Server and O'Reilly WebSite have been able to hold down the overall cost of their products by using NT Workstation as the basis for a Web server. Microsoft hasn't been pleased with this development. Its product strategy has been to bundle its own Internet server product, IIS, on only the higher-cost NT

Server product. Competitors have priced their Web servers so that the cost of NT Workstation plus the Web server is hundreds of dollars less than the cost of NT Server.

Microsoft's position is that the use of NT Workstation 4.0[2] as an Internet Web server violates the NT Workstation 4.0 license restriction that permits no more than 10 inbound connections. The result is that although there are few *technical* reasons you can't use NT Workstation 4.0 as the base for third-party Web server software, Microsoft says you will be in violation of your license if you have more than 10 connections. At the time this book was written, Microsoft hadn't clarified exactly what "10 connections" means in the context of Internet services.

For the additional cost of NT Server, you do get a good set of extra features, including FrontPage for managing your Web content; it's an excellent value overall. It's probably more rewarding to spend your time creating great Web content than interpreting the nuances of software license legalese, unless you're a lawyer.

Setting Up Internet Information Server

Preparation and Planning Before you actually begin the installation, review the settings here and in the Internet Service Manager (ISM) section that follows. Most of the choices you make at installation can be easily changed later in ISM, but subsequent work will be a lot easier if you do a bit of planning before running setup.

Choosing Services To Install IIS provides three services: World Wide Web (WWW or just Web), File Transfer Protocol (FTP), and Gopher. You can opt to install any or all of these services, and this section outlines the abilities of each.

By far, the World Wide Web is the most popular service on the Internet, mainly because companies like Netscape (and now Microsoft) have spent a lot of time improving the quality of Web browsers. Browsers now include support for FTP and Gopher protocols, so there isn't a need for a separate client-side utility if you decide you want to transfer a file or do a Gopher search. Given the popularity of the Web, nearly every IIS administrator will want to install the Web service.

The popularity of FTP predates that of the Web, but many of the basic duties of file downloading (from server to client) can be done by a Web browser as well. FTP's protocol is more robust and also kinder to network bandwidth than the HTTP protocol used for Web transfers. Bandwidth is an issue primarily if you will be posting large multi-megabyte files for downloading. In these cases, the FTP service is a good choice, as long as you can offer the files for *anonymous* download. When FTP logs users on for non-anonymous use, it requires that the password be sent over the Internet in unencrypted form, which makes it easy for an attacker to steal the password.

If you want to transfer files securely, the most convenient way is to use a Web browser and HTTP protocol in combination with Secure Sockets Layer (SSL) encryption. Receiving files (server to browser) is easy; just place a link to the file in a Web page, and the browser will download it. Sending files back to the server is a bit more difficult. Both IE 3.0 (but not 2.0) and

---

2   The language of the NTW 4.0 license agreement was changed for the express purpose of preventing such use, as explained in Chapter 1.

Netscape Navigator 2.0 or higher support a file upload feature in their forms support. However, IIS 2.0 doesn't provide the CGI/ISAPI program that is required on the server side to receive the file. (One server that does is O'Reilly's WebSite for NT.) Presumably Microsoft will provide an ISAPI[3] version of such an application at some point as an IIS upgrade.

You won't find much on Gopher in this chapter, because the Gopher service has essentially been killed off by the popularity of the Web. Gopher's claim to fame was its ability to act as a distributed index to information all over the Internet. However, with Web-based resources like Lycos, Yahoo, and AltaVista now available, Gopher isn't used much. If you're a fan of Internet history, you can get the latest FAQ file for Gopher by browsing the URL (Uniform Resource Locator) gopher://mudhoney.micro.umn.edu/00/Gopher.FAQ in your Web browser.[4]

File Locations and Permissions Here are some points to consider when you're deciding where to put files on your Internet server:

- *Web pages*: At this point, you need to be concerned only about choosing the root directory for your Web pages; the sub-structure can wait for later. If multiple people will be responsible for editing and updating Web pages, consider whether you'll want to have them edit the pages directly or do off-line editing on another system and submit the pages in an update procedure. If they edit the pages directly, you'll need to give them write access to the directories they maintain (and only those directories). Because NTFS disk partitions provide file/directory security and FAT partitions do not, all Web pages (and other Internet-accessible files) should be located on an NTFS partition. See the section on security later in this chapter for some of the reasons.

- *CGI and ISAPI programs*: Only a trusted administrator should be given write access to the CGI/ISAPI programs directory. This administrator should understand the function of any program placed into this directory. By default, the virtual directory name of this directory is /scripts, and the Web-based version of Internet Service Manager has this name wired into all its pages. Some software packages may assume that the scripts directory is named /cgi-bin, but you can easily appease them by adding that as another virtual directory alias for the /scripts directory. Again, CGI and ISAPI applications should be available *only* from NTFS partitions.

- *FTP directories*: The FTP directories should *not* overlap any directories used by the Web services if those directories are writable. If outsiders can upload new Web pages or CGI programs, they can create security holes. If you allow FTP uploads, make sure the disk that holds the upload directory has plenty of room. IIS does not provide an option to limit the size of uploaded files, so this disk may fill up. To prevent a server crash, keep the NT system files and virtual memory pagefile on a separate volume from that used for uploads (which should, of course, be formatted through NTFS[5]).

---

3 Internet Server API—see Appendix 1 for details.

4 As this was written (August 1996), the Gopher FAQ file hadn't been changed since May 1995. It really is a dying protocol!

5 On upload directories, consider setting *write-only* access. Set up a separate directory for downloads, and make arrangements to periodically inspect files and move them from the first directory to the second. This will provide some protection against *warez* attacks mentioned in the Internet Security section of this chapter.

- *Log files*: Log files can grow quickly on a very busy server. As with FTP directories, make sure you have enough space on drive to hold them and avoid putting them on the same volume with the NT system and virtual memory page files. (The default setup puts log files in the "C:\Winnt\System32\Log Files" directory, which breaks this rule.) Log files hold information that might be valuable to competitors or attackers, so don't put them in directories that are accessible by the FTP or Web services, and make sure they're protected with appropriate NTFS permissions.

Virtual Directories Both the Web and FTP settings in Internet Service Manager offer you a way to set up virtual directories that create a different-looking file structure for Internet users than actually exists on your hard disk. This is extremely useful, both for administrative maintenance and for security reasons. You'll find these settings inside the Directories tab of the Web and FTP services, in the *Directory/Alias/Address* list.

One very useful feature the Web server implements here is *virtual servers*. (PWS on NT Workstation does not offer this feature; it's available only with IIS on NT Server.) It lets you host multiple Web home pages with a single IIS server. For example, your company might have a site with the domain name www.acme.com. You decide to go into two new ventures: selling books and selling specialty foods. Instead of selling both from your existing domain name, you could create separate domains, one for www.books.com and one for www.foods.com. The DNS IP address resolution (see Chapter 6) would direct requests for any of these three domains to your single NT IIS server, but they would arrive at the server with different IP addresses. IIS chooses the home page based on the incoming IP address, which depends on the domain name you use.

If you don't specify an IP address when creating an entry, it's available to every IP address configured for the server. In our example with books and foods above, that means that you could share the /scripts directory and use the same shopping-cart program for both virtual servers. Of course, you could also create separate /scripts directories if you preferred.

URLs are showing up everywhere nowadays—business cards, TV commercials, cereal boxes—and it's good to keep them short so that people can remember and type them. Usually, that means you don't want to give people any more than a domain name and one extra thing tacked on the end of it, like "http://www.winmag.com/reclist." If you make users type "http://www.winmag.com/library/current/reviews/reclist," they'll inevitably type it wrong. From a site administration standpoint, though, the one-level hierarchy can be a nightmare for a Webmaster to manage.

That's where *virtual directories* come to the rescue. These let you create a directory that appears to be just one level below the domain name when used in a URL, but can actually be located anywhere—deep in a directory tree, on another hard disk, on a CD-ROM, even on another system on your network! Figure 7.1 shows the dialog you get when you create or edit an entry in the directory list.

You should think the implications over carefully before using a *networked* virtual directory because of its security implications. The other directory choices use the privilege of the default IIS account or prompt users to enter their own account information. With a networked virtual

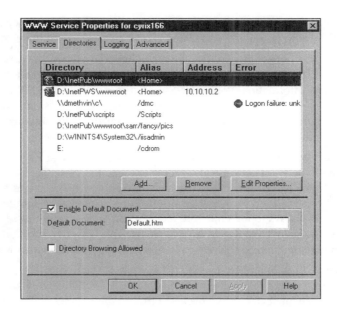

FIGURE 7.1 WWW Service Properties, Directories tab. This dialog from Internet Service Manager lets you view IIS directories.

directory, you enter the user name and password that should be used to log into the remote system; the privilege of the browsing user is irrelevant. Note, however, that the system containing the files must still be in the same NT domain as the system running IIS.

User Accounts IIS security is completely integrated into the security of Windows NT. The user names and passwords you use for IIS, including that of the default user, must be defined in NT's User Manager. If you are using IIS for an intranet server, this type of setup is excellent and offers good security with almost no effort on your part.

If, however, you are creating an Internet server that may have thousands of registered users, you'll probably want another layer of software to maintain and validate user logons. Otherwise, the information for thousands of users will be stored in the User Manager database, and whoever manages this database will have to be given administrative privileges for the entire system. Most UNIX-based servers handle Web-based accounts with a file that's separate from system accounts, and IIS will probably get this option in the future from either a third-party vendor or Microsoft itself.

In order to integrate with the standard Windows NT security scheme, the IIS service runs with the privileges of a special NT user account. In a typical Web and FTP server setup, most of the pages will be accessed without the user (of the Web browser) having to identify themselves or know a password; this is called *anonymous logon*. The installation program automatically sets up a special anonymous user account for IIS, which is named IUSR_*systemname* by default. Web pages should be readable by this account (and scripts should be executable) if you don't want the user to be asked for a password. For FTP access, users should log in with the name "anonymous." (Web browsers quietly do this for you when you specify ftp as the protocol.)

The username and password you specify for anonymous logon must be for an account (user) that already exists. IIS setup does this for you for the default account, but if you change the anonymous logon information, you'll need to do it manually, using NT User Manager. IIS doesn't define the account; it is used only to log on. Passwords, permissions, and restrictions for the account must be defined in NT's User Manager by someone with administrative privileges, just as for other accounts.

In a higher-security Web server, you can control access to individual Web pages or FTP directories based on the privileges of corresponding NT user accounts. (Note that users who want to log on through the Web or FTP services must be granted the *Log on Locally* right for the NT Server hosting IIS set in User Manager, Policies/User Rights; this is the default for the account IIS sets up.) If you want users always to log on before receiving any pages from this server, uncheck the *Allow Anonymous* option under password authentication. This is particularly useful in the intranet situation in which users will already have a valid user account for the domain where IIS resides.

IIS supports two kinds of authentication for passwords. The first is *Basic*, which sends both the username and password to the network in plain text. Basic authentication is a bad idea on the Internet, because people can attach a packet sniffer to the Internet and capture this information.[6] By capturing the logon packet, they can determine the Internet address of your system and

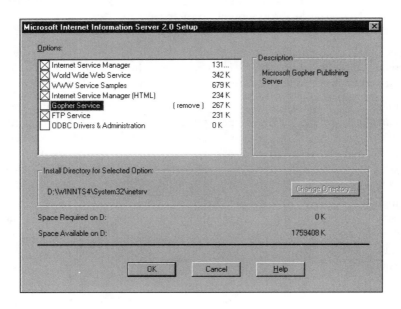

FIGURE 7.2 IIS 2.0 Setup. IIS 2.0 Setup allows you to determine which components are installed on your server.

---

6 See the "Network Monitor" section of Chapter 5 for a real-world example from a live NT Server running the IIS FTP service.

a valid account they can use to attack it. Fortunately, basic authentication can be made more bulletproof through use of the Secure Sockets Layer (SSL) protocol, described later in this chapter. SSL encrypts messages so that they can't be easily decoded, even if they're captured by a packet sniffer. If you decide to use Basic authentication, SSL is essential for any semblance of security.

Windows NT Challenge/Response, the second type of authentication, is more secure because it doesn't send the actual password over the network. However, at present only Microsoft's Internet Explorer supports Challenge/Response authentication. If you want Web users who have another browser—for example, Netscape Navigator—to be able to see your pages,[7] you must use Basic authentication. For intranet use, where you can control what browser is used, though, NT authentication may be the best approach.

Running the Installation The basic IIS setup is integrated into NT setup; you can just run setup, and somewhere around the middle of the process it will prompt you for the installation locations for the IIS files. If these are new directories it will also prompt you to create them. You can later change just about any of the setup decisions you make here, by either re-running setup or just changing some parameters in Internet Service Manager.

If you want to add or remove parts of IIS after the initial installation, select the "IIS Setup" item in the Start menu's Microsoft Internet Server folder. Unless you have a special need for it, remove the Gopher service to save space (see Figure 7.2).

The final step in your installation should be to go into Internet Service Manager and disable any services you don't plan on using immediately. Because most people plan to use the Web but not FTP or Gopher, disable the latter two if you installed them. Disabling them will prevent any security problems that might arise from having these services enabled but not configured properly.

FIGURE 7.3 Internet Service Manager. Internet Service Manager (ISM), from the Start menu's Microsoft Internet Server folder, is the primary tool used to manage IIS services.

---

7   At this writing (August 1996) Navigator was widely reported to have an 80% or greater share of the browser market, so supporting it is probably a good idea!

Internet Service Manager

Microsoft offers two versions of the Internet Service Manager (ISM). The first is a standard Windows application, located in the Start menu's Microsoft Internet Server folder (see Figure 7.3). It lets you administer any IIS or PWS server connected to your network, as long as you have an account with administrative privileges. The version of ISM that comes with NT Server can search for IIS servers on your network; the NT Workstation version of ISM requires that you enter the server name explicitly.

In addition, Microsoft offers a second version of ISM that you access through a Web browser. To start the HTML version of ISM, launch Internet Explorer and type *http://server-name/iisadmin*. (If you're logged onto the IIS server system, use *localhost* as the server name.) The HTML version of ISM is functionally identical to the Windows version, with a few user interface compromises to accommodate the limits of HTML. Figure 7.4 shows a typical screen from the HTML version of ISM. The remainder of this section shows screen shots from the Windows version of ISM, but the same features are available in the HTML version. The Windows version provides some useful security warnings that the HTML version does not, so you may want to use the Windows version until you're comfortable with IIS.

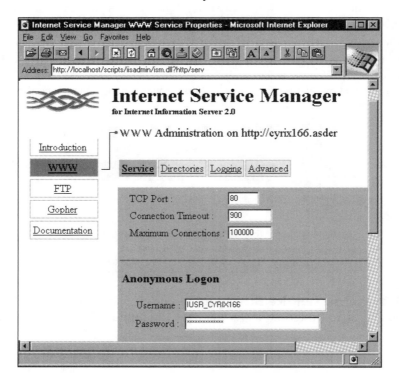

FIGURE 7.4 ISM Web page. Alternatively, you can manage IIS from a special Internet Service Manager Web page. Note that proper security settings are vital if you are using this method.

In this section, we cover the configuration of the Web and FTP services in detail. The Gopher service has essentially become obsolete, replaced by the powerful Web search engines and indexing sites. For in-house indexing of your Web content, see the section on Internet Search Server (Tripoli) later in this chapter.

Web Service Configuration

Service Tab Most Web servers use the standard *TCP port* value of 80, which is also the port value that is assumed by Web browsers unless you specify another port in the URL. (A URL that specifies port 2000, for example, would look like http://www.server.com:2000/test.) Changing the port value has implications for NT's packet filtering and for router and firewall traffic, so if you decide to use a port other than 80, coordinate the change with the administrator of your network equipment. See Figure 7.5 for the Service tab.

The *connection timeout* lets IIS clean up connections that aren't closed because of a protocol error. The default value of 900 seconds (15 minutes) is fine in most cases. Similarly, you aren't likely to need to change the *maximum connections* value from its default of 100,000.

The rest of the information in this property tab is related to user accounts; these issues were covered in the previous section.

Directories Tab You'll find many interesting features inside the directory options dialog box (see Figure 7.6). We focus first on the easy activities.

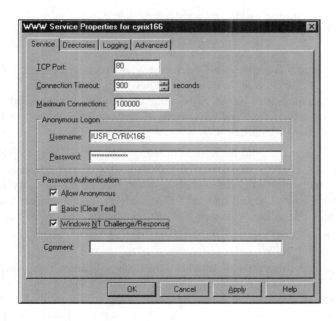

FIGURE 7.5 WWW Service Properties, Service tab. The ISM Service tab displays and controls settings for the IIS Webserver.

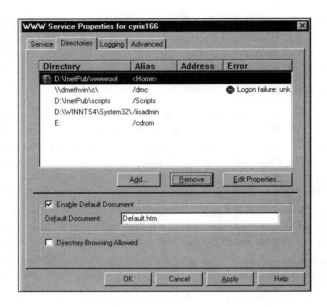

FIGURE 7.6 WWW Service Properties, Directories tab. This dialog box from Internet Service Manager displays and controls IIS directories. Default pages and virtual directories can be set here.

Usually you will want to check the *Enable default document* option, which provides a default document name if you specify only a directory. For example, it's more friendly (and easier to remember) if your Web site is "http://www.mycompany.com" than "http://www .mycompany.com/default.htm." If you're moving content over from another vendor's Web server, you may encounter default documents named "index.html." Otherwise, it's probably best to stick with the standard "default.htm."

Most of the time you should leave the *Directory Browsing Allowed* option unchecked to increase security. If you check this option and there isn't a default document in the URL the browser specifies, the server will return a listing of the files in the directory at that URL. This may include files that aren't linked into any HTML pages, such as backup files, or pages that aren't ready for public viewing. Although it might be convenient to have this feature in a few directories (especially download directories), IIS allows you to configure it only on a site-wide basis, so it's best to leave it off.

The advantages of using virtual directories were discussed earlier in this chapter; here we discuss the settings. The Directory Properties dialog box (Figure 7.7) lets you give the files in a virtual directory *Read* access, *Execute* access, or both. But it's a bit more complicated than that. Regardless of how you set these two check-boxes, the privileges granted to people requesting the file will additionally depend on the file's NTFS privileges for the user accounts under which they are logged in. For anonymous access, that will be the default IIS user account, IUSR_*systemname*.

Let's assume the default IIS user has the appropriate NTFS privileges for files in the directory you're setting up. And let's say a browser (user) using anonymous access requests a file in

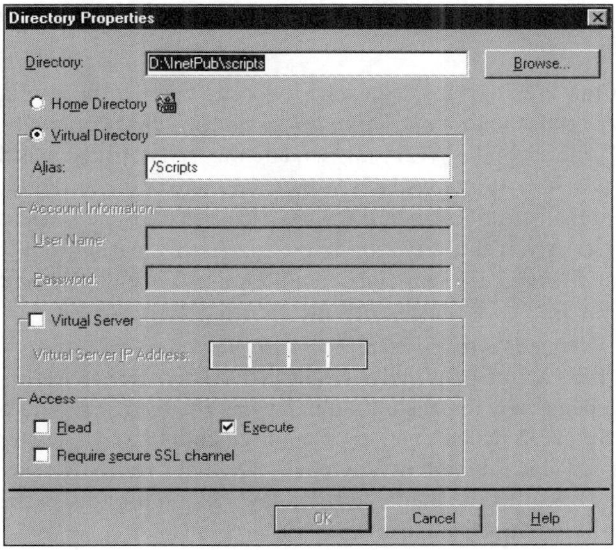

FIGURE 7.7 Directory Properties. ISM Directory Properties is where you control who can access an IIS Web directory and whether it will appear as a virtual directory or virtual *site* on a Web browser.

this directory. If the Execute access box is checked, IIS will first examine the requested file name to see if its extension matches one of the ones it knows how to execute as CGI or ISAPI-DLL applications. If the extension is on this list (say it's an .EXE file), IIS will try to run the associated command. If this file isn't executable (for example, it's an HTML file) and you have the Read access box checked, IIS will read the file and send it back to the browser. Even though the operating system obviously has to read the file to execute it, Execute Access doesn't require you to check the Read Access box!

Because either or both of these boxes can be checked, you can have a directory that is strictly executable, strictly read, or a mixture of both. (You could also check neither of the boxes, but we don't know of a good reason to do that.) The most secure approach is to avoid mixing content files such as HTML with program files such as EXEs and DLLs. This is especially true if many people will be creating content on the server. By having someone responsible for a set of directories exclusively dedicated to program files, it is much easier to track and control them.

Incidentally, the Read and Execute access properties apply not only to the top-level virtual directory, but to any of its physical sub-directories. Particularly in the case of executable files, you can use this feature to help you organize programs in a consistent way. Notice that the default installation of IIS takes advantage of this in the /scripts directory; the IIS administrative scripts are kept in a separate sub-directory.

The final check-box in the Access area is *Require secure SSL channel*. This option will be available only if you have installed one or more keys for use with Secure Sockets Layer. See the section on SSL and Key Manager later in this chapter for more information. If this box is checked, access to the directory will be allowed only if the browser can establish a Secure HTTP connection to the IIS server.

Logging Tab With the Web service, you have two choices for the format of log files (see Figure 7.8). Microsoft calls the first one *standard format,* which is compatible with the log files produced by IIS 1.0. The second is *NCSA format,* and this is the format used by most other Web servers that run on UNIX or Windows NT. At present, there is much more third-party support for NCSA log format than for IIS standard format. IIS uses a different file-naming convention for the two file types, so you'll always know the log file format by looking at the filename. When you switch log formats, IIS will close the old log and open a new one on the next hit to the server; one log file never contains both formats.

It's a good idea to have IIS *automatically open a new log* every day so that you can take the previous day's log file for off-line analysis and processing. Be aware of one complication, though. IIS doesn't open a new log file until the day has changed and there's a file request (hit) made to the server. So, if IIS doesn't get any hits for an entire day, there won't be a log file for that day. You might see that situation in a company intranet over the weekend, for example. If your server isn't very busy, just be prepared for a day with no log file, particularly if you write scripts to automatically process log files.[8]

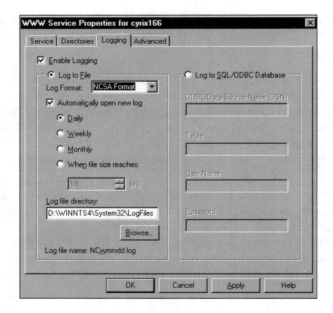

FIGURE 7.8 WWW Service Properties, Logging tab. Logging in IIS can use either Microsoft's proprietary format or industry-standard NCSA format.

---

8   Or, it might be easier to make someone come in and work over the weekend. (Just kidding.)

IIS offers the option of logging directly to an ODBC database (PWS does not have this option). Because of the overhead of making a database entry for each hit to the server in real time, Microsoft recommends that this option be used only for lightly loaded servers. As far as flexibility goes, it's usually best to create an ASCII log file. If you want to enter the data into a SQL database later, you can do it with a program that parses the log file and enters the records into the database in a batch. This could be done in the middle of the night when the load on your server would presumably be much lower.

Advanced Tab IIS lets you fine-tune access to the server through the options in the Advanced tab (PWS on NT Workstation does not offer these options). See Figure 7.9.

Typically, you would set the default here so that all computers will be *Granted Access*. In a high-security network, you could reverse the situation and deny access to everyone but the IP addresses (or address ranges) you list.

Using the IP address as a security filter is less than bulletproof. First, it is possible for someone to forge an IP address, so don't ever use this as your *only* security mechanism. Second, many sites are using dynamic IP address assignment (see the section on DHCP in Chapter 6, for example). If you try to filter out one particular person's IP address because of some suspicious or annoying behavior on your Web site, that person may have a different IP address by the next day.

There is a way to specify a *group* of IP addresses. In the exceptions list dialog, select "Group of computers" and enter the IP address and subnet mask for the range you'd like to

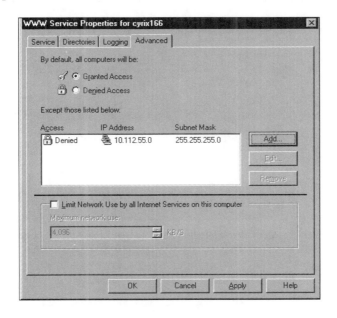

FIGURE 7.9 WWW Service Properties, Advanced tab. The ISM Advanced tab controls who is permitted access to the Web server and lets you limit overall IIS network bandwidth.

filter. For example, let's say your competitor was Acme Corporation and you wanted to deny its employees access to your Web site. If Acme had a Class C address of 192.14.30.0, you could enter that address into the exceptions dialog box with 255.255.255.0 as the subnet mask. Remember, though, that this would not prevent Acme employees from reaching your site through a different route, such as America Online.

The second option on the Advanced tab is the *Limit network use...* option. This option is echoed in the FTP and Gopher dialogs as well, but is really the same number no matter where you set it. It is used to control IIS resource use on a server that is shared with other services. See the section "Performance Tuning" later in this chapter for more information.

FTP Service Configuration

Service Tab The default *TCP Port* of 21 is typically the value you'll want to use. Changing the port value has implications for NT's packet filtering and for router and firewall traffic, so if you decide to use a port other than 21, coordinate the change with the administrator of your network equipment. See Figure 7.10.

Keep the *Connection Timeout* at 900 seconds. The *Maximum Connections* default of 1000 is fine unless you're concerned about excessive load on your server. For more discussion, see the "Performance Tuning" section below.

As with the Web, the most common way to use FTP is through anonymous connections. In this process, a user logs on to the FTP server with the user name *anonymous*. By checking

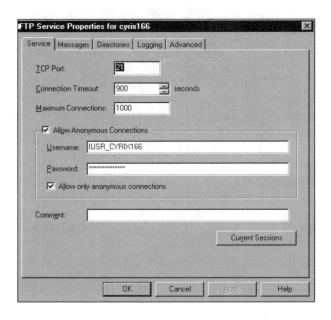

FIGURE 7.10 FTP Service Properties, Service tab. The ISM Service tab for the FTP server controls top-level settings.

Allow only anonymous connections, which is the default, you can prevent users from logging on using their NT user names and passwords. This is important because the FTP protocol sends plain-text passwords through the Internet. It would be possible for an attacker to steal this information by placing a packet sniffer on the wire. As mentioned in the Choosing Services section earlier in the chapter, a Web browser is a safer alternative to FTP for authenticated and secure logons.

You can view current FTP sessions by pressing the *Current Sessions* button. Most connections will be from anonymous logons, so the most useful information will be the IP From address and the connect time. This screen doesn't show what file is being transferred, but the log file will have an entry for each file transferred.

Messages Tab On most browsers, the *Welcome Message* is displayed before the directory listing at the root directory (see Figure 7.11). You can use this for quick reminder or update messages like "The latest version of DingBat is 4.02. Be sure to check the README file before trying an install." The *Exit Message* will typically be seen only by people who use a command-line FTP client, so don't put anything there that you actually want most people to see. If you have a busy site, it's good to give some hints in the *Maximum Connections Message* like "Try us between 5:00 p.m. and 8:00 p.m. EDT, when we're not as busy."

FIGURE 7.11 FTP Service Properties, Messages tab. The Messages tab lets you set a welcome message for FTP users, as well as an exit message, and a "so sorry" message for users who attempt to connect when the server is already fully subscribed.

Directories Tab As with the Web service, the directories tab lets you create virtual directories that provide access to other directory subtrees, devices, or network shares (see Figure 7.12). When you create a new directory in this dialog box, it appears to the remote FTP user to be located under the FTP root directory. For anonymous logons—the most common case—the permissions of the default user will determine what access is given to the directory. One exception is when the directory is a network share on another system. In that case you provide a user name and password to log into that system, and its permissions are used.

Remember never to share a writable FTP directory associated with the Web service. That would allow anonymous users to create Web pages on your Web site! This isn't a good idea at all, for reasons outlined later in the chapter.

Although IIS gives you a choice between the UNIX and DOS formats for listings, it's best to stick with UNIX because some FTP clients and Web browsers expect to receive this format and don't work well if you send them another format.

Logging Tab With the logging tab you can set whether activity of the FTP service should be logged and which directory should be used for the log file (see Figure 7.13). It's a good idea to keep a log, because it can tell you what files are most popular at your site. Logs can also be used to detect intrusions. A discussion of log files and how to analyze them follows later in this chapter.

Advanced Tab FTP's options in the Advanced tab are exactly the same as the ones offered in the Web service; you will find them described above.

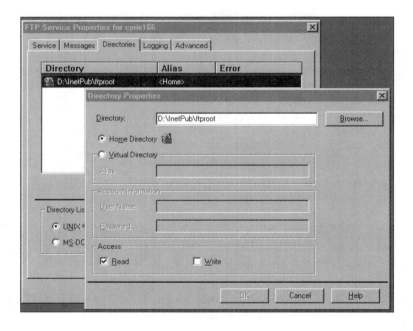

FIGURE 7.12 Directory Properties. Directory Properties for the FTP Service allows you to control access.

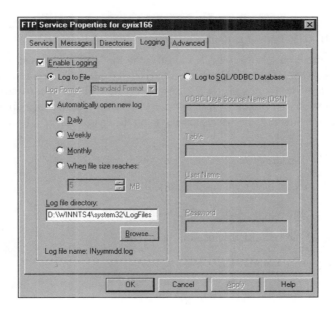

FIGURE 7.13 FTP Service Properties, Logging tab. IIS can log FTP activity in much the same way as Web activity.

IIS Administration

Once you have IIS up and running, you'll be dealing with day-to-day embellishments and maintenance duties. This section outlines procedures and tools for dealing with many of these common chores.

Log Files All the IIS services provide the option of logging their activity. Log files can provide valuable information about your Web site because they tell you what data is being accessed. Knowing what data is being used by your visitors, you can concentrate your design and development efforts to improve that data. Or you can encourage visits to the quiet parts of your Web site by placing links on the frequently visited pages. Log files can also tell you who is and isn't coming to get the information you offer.

Log files can also be used as part of a security auditing procedure, which is particularly important if you make use of CGI programs or other server-side applications. Any program executed by the server as part of a URL will be logged, and you can analyze the logs for suspicious-looking queries or program arguments.

IIS's handling of log files for the combination of Web and FTP services is a bit confusing but flexible once you understand it. The locations of log files can be configured separately for each service; they don't need to be the same directory. In the default setup, the Web and FTP services use Standard log format, and both Web and FTP events are logged in the same file, with a tag that tells what service made the entry. Standard log files are named in *YYMMDD*.log indicating the date that the log was started. The format of Standard log files is described in Microsoft's HTML-based documentation for IIS (/iisadmin/htmldocs/07_iis.htm).

If you switch the Web service to NCSA log format, the Web service will write its log entries to a file named NC*YYMMDD*.log. However, the FTP service will continue to write its entries into the Standard log file; there's no NCSA format for the FTP service. Microsoft doesn't document NCSA format, and a search of the Internet surprisingly didn't turn up a definitive document somewhere. Fortunately, the basics are easy to tell if you look at a few entries. The fields are:

- The requester's IP address

- A dash ("-") for a parameter we couldn't document

- The user name, but usually a dash ("-") for anonymous access

- Date and time of the request, enclosed in brackets

- The HTTP request in quotes

- A status code

- Size of the response packet, usually the size of the requested file plus overhead

  The status codes you're likely to encounter are:

  200 OK, successful transmission.

  302 Redirection to a new URL. The original page has moved.

  304 Use local copy. This tells the browser to use the copy it cached; the server does not send the file again.

  401 Unauthorized access. Invalid user name or password entered.

  403 Access denied. (For example, trying to read files in the /scripts directory if you have Read access turned off.)

  404 Not found. The requested URL doesn't exist.

  500 Server error.

If you enable log files, be sure to make enough disk space available for them. On a busy server connected to a T1 line, the log file for a single day's worth of activity can be over 50MB! If you're running a sleepy intranet, on the other hand, you probably won't have log files bigger than a few hundred kilobytes per day. As a conservative guess of the size of your log files, figure that each access to a Web page will generate about 1KB of log file entries. (There's a log entry for the HTML page itself, plus an entry for each graphic, sound file, or Java applet on the page.) If your company intranet serves 50 employees and each loads 20 Web pages over the course of a day, that would equate to a log file of about 1MB.

Once you've created a log file, you'll want to analyze it. Because the files are just plain ASCII, you can do some simple analysis by loading the log file into WordPad and searching for a particular file or IP address. That's a bit tedious, though, so you'll probably want to get a program to parse the file and generate reports. There are plenty of tools for analyzing log files; many are available free on the Internet. For an extensive list, see (http://www .yahoo.com/Computers_and_Internet/Internet/World_Wide_Web/Servers/Log_Analysis_Tools).

Typical reports or graphs that you can derive from log files include:

- Total hits (access to any file)

- Total visits (multiple accesses by the same IP address)

- Hit counts for individual files or directories

- Number of hits from each visitor (IP address)

- Traffic patterns by time of day

IIS/PWS also supports a set of NT Performance Monitor counters, which provide a tremendous amount of detail (the actual number of bytes sent and received, number of connections broken out as anonymous and non-anonymous, how much of the data was kept in cache, etc.). Tracking this information can help in performance tuning and maintaining your server. See the section on performance tuning later in this chapter.

Secure Sockets Layer IIS supports encrypted communication with Web browsers via the Secure Sockets Layer (SSL) protocol. To use SSL, you must obtain a security certificate specific to your server and your organization.

There are multiple steps to the process of getting a security certificate, and it takes at least a few weeks before you have a certificate that's ready to use. That's because the certificate authority (CA) needs to check out your organization to see if it's legitimate and to record information in case there's ever a dispute about the authenticity of your messages that have been encrypted by SSL. The certificates are usually good for one year; there's a fee for both the initial certificate and the renewal. The best-known CA is VeriSign (http://www.verisign.com), but many new companies are coming on-line as the awareness of security issues increases.

We obtained a demonstration certificate free from Nortel/Entrust simply by visiting its Web site (http:/www.nortel.com/entrust). The next day the certificate arrived via electronic mail, allowing us to test SSL without the expense of obtaining a truly verified certificate. New CAs are likely to offer similar deals that let you test out the technology. A good place to check is Yahoo, http://www.yahoo.com/Business_and_Economy/Companies/Computers/Software/Systems_and_ Utilities/Security. If you go to Internet Explorer 3.0 and select Tools/Options/Security, you can find a list of CAs there as well.

Here are the steps you take to create a certificate:

- Run Key Manager from the Microsoft Internet Server group (see Figure 7.14). Select the WWW service and choose Key/Create New Key from the menu. You'll be presented with a dialog box with information about your company and this server; note that the certificate is good for only this server and is linked to a specific IP address. Fill this in, and then create a (good!) password for your certificate. When you click OK, Key Manager creates a

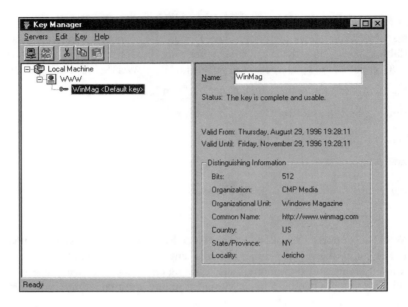

FIGURE 7.14 Key Manager Key Manager is used to configure IIS for use with Secure Sockets Layer (SSL) for encrypted transactions.

certificate request file (by default named c:\new key.req) that is your public key information. It's a text file; you can look at it, but it's just the ASCII representation of your original information, all hashed up.

- Send your key request file along with your application to a certificate authority (CA). The CA will require other information in addition to what you filled out in Key Manager. At minimum it will want to know the name and phone number of a contact at the company and of course how you intend to pay. Then wait a few weeks.

- After the CA has checked you out, it will send you the security certificate. This is simply another ASCII file with the hashed information. Open Key Manager again, select the key you created a few weeks before, and pick Key/Install Key Certificate from the menu. Key Manager will prompt you for the password you entered when you created the key, and the security certificate should now be installed.

Once you've installed a default security key, browsers can access your site via Secure HTTP protocol by typing https:// instead of http:// in front of the URL. Typically, you'd put these references into your page so that users wouldn't need to be bothered with remembering the difference. If you want to absolutely *require* that SSL be used with some or all of your pages, go the Directories tab of the Web service in Internet Service Manager. For each directory in which you want to require SSL, edit the properties of the directory and check the "Require secure SSL channel" box.

Perl and CGI Many day-to-day tasks involve repetitive work like changing information in some large set of files at your site or looking for certain patterns of usage in log files. It's certainly possible to write Visual Basic or C++ programs to do this kind of work, but it often takes nearly as long to write the program as it does to do the work by hand. What's needed is a programming language that can handle these tasks without a lot of lengthy setup and tedious programming work.

Perl is that programming language. Born in the UNIX community, Perl was designed for just the kinds of text-processing tasks you'll find yourself doing as a Web site administrator. Many good Web-related utilities are written in Perl, so you'll at least want to have a copy of the Perl program so that you can run them. After seeing what Perl can do, you'll probably want to try your hand at some programming as well.

You can get the latest set of executable files for NT Perl at http://www.perl.hip.com/. Two versions are available. One is a standard executable that can be used either for CGI applications or for standalone programs. The other version is an ISAPI DLL that you can use as a more efficient alternative to CGI programs.

ISAPI programs and CGI programs Many of the interesting activities you can do with a Web site depend on running a server-side program that can process requests from browsers. IIS supports two interfaces for running a program. The first, Common Gateway Interface (CGI), is a standard developed early in the evolution of the World Wide Web. CGI defines how information is passed from the browser to the server. A CGI program is an executable file or interpreted file such as Perl scripts. Information is usually passed to the program as part of the URL-like command-line arguments, but HTML forms can also use a method called POST that passes the information through the standard input file handle.

Microsoft has defined Internet Service API (ISAPI) applications as a higher-performance alternative to CGI. ISAPI applications are implemented as *dynamic link libraries* (DLLs) that run in the IIS address space, but otherwise the calling convention is the same as that for CGI programs. Here's the important difference: instead of starting and running a new copy of the program each time it's called from a URL, IIS loads the DLL *once*, keeps it in memory, and just passes the new arguments for each URL invocation. This makes ISAPI significantly faster than CGI.

Security is extremely important with ISAPI and CGI programs. In essence, you are letting Web users send you a command line to be run on your Web site.[9] If you don't check the input to these programs carefully, an attacker can easily break into your system. Be wary of getting an EXE (or DLL) file off the Internet and putting it into your programs directory. It's better to get the source code, understand what it does, and compile it yourself. Perl programs also offer a bit of reassurance, because you can see the source code. If you install commercial programs where you don't have the luxury of source code, check the vendor's Web site frequently for information about security-related bug fixes.

Only the virtual directories that you have marked with Execute access in the Web/Directories tab of Internet Service Manager can be used to hold CGI or ISAPI programs;

---

9   Indeed, Microsoft's ISAPI development kit includes an example program that *literally* allows a user to type in batch file-type command lines that are executed by the server!

by default the only program directory is /scripts. For security reasons it's better not to mix data files and programs so that you can keep a close eye on exactly what programs can be run on your server.

At installation, the only file extensions that are supported are DLL, EXE, and IDC files. (The IIS documentation says .BAT files are supported too, but they are disabled for security reasons.) You can add associations for other types of files by adding them to the IIS script map. For example, if you want to run Perl programs directly, you need to create an association for Perl script files. This must be done in the registry editor:

1. Start/Run REGEDT32.EXE.

2. Drill down to HKEY_LOCAL_MACHINE\SYSTEM\CurrentControlSet\Services\ W3SVC\Parameters\ScriptMap.

3. Add a new key of type STRING. The name of the key should be the name of the extension you want to map. For example, you would typically use ".pl" for Perl files.

4. Set the value of this key to the name of the command that should run when this type of file is encountered. For Perl used as CGI it would typically be "c:\perl5\perl.exe %s %s" or wherever you've installed the Perl executable. (The first %s is for the program name, and the second is for any arguments that might have been passed through the URL.)

> *Warning: Under no circumstances should you put an interpreter (such as PERL.EXE) in the scripts directory! This creates a serious security problem, because any user in the world can then run the interpreter and pass it an arbitrary program as command line arguments!*

Another IIS quirk may lead you to think you have to make the scripts directory readable when you really don't. (You really *shouldn't*—it's a security hole.) Let's say you mistype the command string that's associated with the extension when you enter it into the registry. When IIS tries to run the program, it will get an error. In this case, IIS then tries to read the file and return it to the browser as straight text. If you have (wisely) turned off Read access to this directory, IIS will complain that it can't read the file instead of telling you that the registry string is incorrect.

ISAPI Filters With a CGI program or ISAPI program, the browser makes an explicit call to the program via a URL. ISAPI filters are different because they do their work without any specific action on the part of the browser. As IIS processes requests from browsers, it passes the requests to any installed ISAPI filters so that they can process the file as well. Writing an ISAPI filter requires quite a bit of programming expertise; the basics of ISAPI are covered in Appendix 1.

Server-Side Includes The IIS Web service permits a form of *server-side include file* that lets you have the contents of one file inserted into another automatically. This is similar to the include-file feature of languages such as C. To use this feature, place the text

```
<!--#include file="FILENAME" -->
```

at the point in a HTML file where you want this second file's content to appear. The file name is treated in URL style and uses the virtual directories you have set up, so the filename should use forward-slashed names rather than DOS style. By default, files must have the extension of

.stm before IIS will process them for include directives. If you want all HTML files in your site to be processed for includes, you can edit the registry key HTML\SYSTEM\ CurrentControlSet\Services\W3SVC\ Parameters\ServerSideIncludesExtension and set the extension to ".htm" instead. Notice that the text of an include is actually an HTML comment. If the include doesn't happen for any reason, it won't be part of the visible text in the browser, but you will be able to see the include comment if you view the HTML source code.

Processing files for includes does cause a bit of a performance hit, but it's handy when you decide that the common site header in every one of your 200 HTML files needs to be changed. As an alternative, you might try the *include bot* feature of Microsoft FrontPage if you've elected to manage your Web content that way. You can also use Perl scripts to manage and globally change the content of files in lieu of using server-side includes, but you'll need to apply extreme discipline so that the common text has a consistent pattern you can find.

IIS does *not* support a feature called server-side execs that's common in many UNIX-based (and non-Microsoft NT-based) servers. With this feature, you can execute commands of the form

```
<!--#exec cgi="command_line" -->
```

and the command line will be executed. Whatever output results from the command line will be included on the page at the point where the exec command was located. If you're trying to port existing Web content that uses server-side execs, it's best to figure out exactly what the page designer was trying to accomplish. Often there will be other equally acceptable ways to do the job, although some of them may require significant redesign.

Although server-side execs are powerful and convenient functions, they present a massive security risk. For example, if a user's input is used as part of the output of an HTML page, that user could potentially type in exec commands as part of their input and get your server to execute them. This might be a particular danger in the case of a guest book or bulletin-board-like discussion forum implemented as Web pages.

Internet Search Server (Tripoli) At the time this book was being written, Microsoft was beta testing its Internet Search Server product for IIS, code-named Tripoli. Although it wasn't in finished form, the beta was available for downloading at Microsoft's Web Site, and it looked very promising. Tripoli lets you easily create a searchable index page for your Web content. The search uses an automatically updated index so that the actual searches are *fast*, even for large sites. When Tripoli is complete, Microsoft will make the final version available on its Web site.

Tripoli is managed by a set of Web pages, similar to the HTML version of Internet Service Manager. These let you control what parts of your Web site are indexed. You can schedule index generation at regular intervals, presumably during your Web site's slack periods. Tripoli also adds statistics that you can track in Performance Monitor, so you know the impact of search requests on overall performance.

Performance Tuning Microsoft has integrated the most important IIS statistics into NT's Performance Monitor, so it's easy to track the IIS effects on overall system performance and the relationship to other work the server may be doing. Figure 7.15 shows a sampling of the IIS-related information you can display in Performance Monitor (see Chapter 3 for a description of Performance Monitor and Chapter 5 for hints on its use).

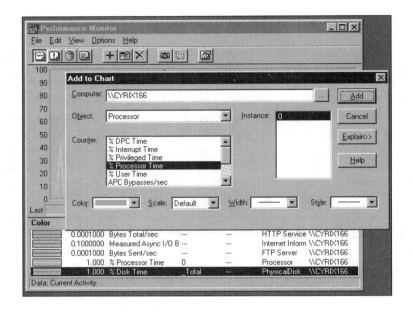

FIGURE 7.15 Performance Monitor. IIS exports a series of Performance Monitor counters that permit performance tuning and data logging.

In the case of an Internet-connected server, the speed of your connection to the Internet is likely be the most limiting factor. Even a T1 is only 1.5 megabits per second, or about 200KB per second at best. A BONDed ISDN line gives you a top-end throughput of only 16KB per second. So bandwidth is already limited enough in these cases. For an intranet, on which Ethernet speeds are typically available, IIS could potentially soak up a lot of server CPU time and network bandwidth. Limiting IIS network use will prevent an impending crisis, but it's an indication that either the server or network bandwidth is overloaded.

Internet Service Manager's Web, FTP, and Gopher dialogs all offer an option titled *Limit network use...* in their Advanced option tab. (This applies to IIS only; PWS doesn't have this option.) The limit that you set in any of those three places affects the total combined bandwidth used by all three services. This type of restriction is most useful if you're sharing the server with other services that you don't want to be overwhelmed by IIS if demand becomes high, such as a primary domain controller, file services, or SQL server.

Using Performance Monitor, you can monitor total bandwidth being used by IIS to find an appropriate cutoff level. Start Performance Monitor and select Edit/Add to Chart from the menu or click the plus sign on the toolbar. For the Object, select Internet Information Services Global; for the counter select Measured Async I/O Bandwidth usage. Measure the performance during a typical load period. To have any impact on the overall server performance, you'll need to choose a limit that is lower than the peak bandwidth usage during this period.

If you're providing large files for downloading, FTP sessions can cause quite a load on your network bandwidth and create slow response time for Web users on the same server. Again, you can use Performance Monitor to determine a reasonable restriction to FTP sessions that give Web users a fighting chance at bandwidth. Monitor the FTP Total Bytes/sec and FTP Current Connections counters, along with the IIS global counter for Measured Async I/O Bandwidth, HTTP Connections/sec, and HTTP Total Bytes/sec. If Web response seems unacceptably slow, go to ISM and set the FTP connections below the current value. If you're impatient and feel like being cruel, knock a few sessions off immediately; if not, you'll have to wait until they finish normally to see the effect of fewer sessions. If FTP sessions were hogging the line, you should see HTTP bytes/sec and connections/sec increase.

If you offer a lot of database or other CGI programs on your site, it's possible that network bandwidth won't turn out to be the limiting factor. This may become more common as more sites turn to online-database technology and active server-based content. In such cases, the server limits are likely to come from using up the CPU power or saturating the disk bandwidth. You can detect both of these problems by monitoring % Processor Time for the CPU and % Disk Time separately for each disk drive (see Chapter 5 for details). If any of these numbers push up toward 100% for more than a brief spike, you have a bottleneck.

Security

Although security issues have been discussed in conjunction with many of the Internet features of NT described already in this chapter, this section looks at the bigger issues you'll have to address when connecting a server to the Internet.

Here is the most important thing to remember: *You are connected to the world!* It's easy for your employees or customers to connect to your site through the Internet, but it's just as easy for a hacker halfway across the world to connect, too. Or perhaps the person who wants to break in is a business competitor who would find the information useful. Either way, you want to keep the "bad guys" out.

Why Worry?

Quite often, the first reaction to the issue of Internet server security is, "The worst thing that can happen is someone would crash our server; we don't keep important information on it." But think again, because the consequences of someone hacking into your server can range from inconvenience to catastrophe:

- *Misrepresentation*: An intruder may place files on your Web server that make false, slanderous, or misleading statements. For example, in an investment advisory service, the intruder could create a Web page with a phony "buy" recommendation for a stock. Or, the hacker could forge electronic mail messages that appeared to be from someone within the company. Suddenly, your mishap on the Internet has turned from a computer problem into an expensive legal one.

- *Loss of confidential or proprietary information*: Valuable information would obviously include customer credit card numbers if you do online commerce, but it could also include mailing addresses and purchase records. If you let customers upload data to your server, that data can be a target as well. If you keep early draft versions of sensitive Web pages on the server, an intruder could see those pages before a public announcement. Even your own Web server logs may be valuable to competitors, because they show what data is being accessed at your site.

- *Use of your system for "warez" distribution*: When hackers find an FTP server that accepts uploads, they will put pirated software on the server for downloading by others. If you don't maintain control over public directories, your site may become a haven for illegal software distribution, exposing you to another legal risk.

- *Denial of service*: Your server could crash or be so overwhelmed by the intruder's acts that it doesn't respond to legitimate requests. Given the legal and financial implications of the other options, this is probably about the *best* thing that can happen. And having your Web site taken out of commission is not so good.

You must build a good defense into your Internet server because it's nearly impossible to find and prosecute someone who breaks in electronically. It's too easy for people to cover their tracks on the Internet. Even if you do track down the culprit, the laws on computer crime aren't well tested. Worse, if the person isn't even in your own country, you'll end up dealing with a maze of international laws and treaties.

Intruder Attacks and Countermeasures

Just about every attack on a system can be traced to a handful of causes that, either alone or in combination, allow the attacker to penetrate a system. By exploiting known problems with software, and with the help of sloppy system administration, intruders are likely to be able to break into just about any system if they're persistent enough. If you're vigilant, you can make the job tough enough that most potential intruders will decide to find an easier target.

Known Software Problems All software has bugs. In the case of the Internet, those bugs can sometimes be exploited to break into your system or disable it in some way. The most famous software problem in the history of the Internet is the Morris Internet Worm incident in 1988; it was the first time that many in the general public had even heard of the Internet.

Most Internet security problems today are related to the UNIX operating system. There's nothing particularly wrong with UNIX that isn't also a problem with other operating systems. It's just that people have had 20 years, often with OS source code in hand, to probe the security of UNIX. In addition, most versions of UNIX include a wide variety of Internet services; each is another opportunity for bugs and security holes. Most of the problems are fixed in new shipping versions of the operating system. But even when bugs are fixed, many sites don't upgrade. Those sites can become targets for future attacks.

Even though UNIX has a strong lead on security problems, NT and IIS seem to be trying hard to make up for lost time. Since its original release in January 1996, for example, IIS 1.0 has had three patches released that fix various security-related problems. Two of these involved a problem with the execution of batch files that would easily let anyone in the world execute any DOS command on your server! (This same problem was also found—and fixed—in other NT Web servers, including Netscape's.) In IIS 2.0, the installation default that allowed you to run batch files as common gateway interface (CGI) programs has been removed, although the documentation erroneously indicates it's preinstalled.

As NT increases in popularity, there will be more people probing its problems and a larger base of knowledge on its weaknesses. The best defense is to keep up with the information released by Microsoft and the third-party vendors of your products. Whenever a new patch or update is available, find out if there are any security-related problems that it fixes.[10]

Programming Errors Operating systems and Web servers have their problems, but often the worst threats to security come from locally written CGI programs or ones written by inexperienced programmers and distributed over the Internet. Many of these programs don't validate the arguments that are passed to them in any way, and people who manipulate the input to these programs may be able to obtain files or information they shouldn't be able to access.

For example, let's say you install a CGI program called DISPLAY.EXE that generates an HTML page based on an input file that's specified as an argument to the program. A call to your CGI program might look like something like "http://www.acme.com/scripts/display .exe?test.dat." The program works fine and the formatting looks beautiful, so you make your new Web page available and go home.

Later that evening, someone comes to your Web site and sees you're using this new DISPLAY.EXE program. He also notices the argument looks a lot like a file name. And unfortunately for you, this program doesn't check for suspicious input. After a few false starts he types "http://www.acme.com/scripts/display.exe?../../../autoexec.bat" and out pops your AUTOEXEC.BAT file. (Formatted beautifully, of course.) Now he knows how far up the root of the current disk drive he is, so he tries "http://www.acme.com/scripts/display.exe?../../../ winnt/system32/logfiles/in961208.log," and the server starts delivering that day's log file. Now he knows who visited your site today. He can get a lot of other information the same way.

Does it seem incredible that someone could know enough to type just the right information? If you're like probably 90% of the people who install NT and IIS, you'll accept the defaults for the location of executables, HTML files, scripts, and log files, which makes breaking into the system and finding sensitive files even easier.

Each time this intruder runs the DISPLAY.EXE program, IIS puts an entry into the log file. If you are checking your log files regularly for suspicious use of CGI programs, you'll find this problem very quickly. For example, you should scan the log files for any use of the scripts directory that include the string ".." or other suspicious characters.

Sloppy Administration Between the struggle to get things up and running, the exhilaration of having them finally work, and the fear of doing something that will stop them from working, it's no wonder that many system administrators take the "if it ain't broke, don't fix it"

---

10 Check for NT Workstation and Server patches at http://www.microsoft.com. Check the NT Workstation, NT Server, and IIS pages as needed. Another good resource for security information is the World Wide Web Security FAQ at http://www-genome.wi.mit.edu/WWW/ faqs/www-security-faq.html.

philosophy when running Internet servers. As a result, many sites are less-than-stellar examples of security. Common errors include the following:

- *Passwords*: People use passwords that are easy to guess, such as "password" or their own name. They use the same password for all their accounts because it's too easy to forget different passwords for each one. NT's GUEST account should be disabled, because it allows anonymous access without a password. NT Server disables GUEST by default, but double-check to make sure it's disabled on your server.

- *Inappropriate permissions*: Many systems run with everyone given full access to files. As a result, someone who does break into a system, even on a low-privilege account, can do significant damage. (It's even worse if the disk uses the FAT file system, because security protections aren't even available.) Very few accounts should be given write access to files in the Web or FTP areas, and only an administrator should have the ability to install new CGI programs. It also goes without saying that NT-based Internet servers should use NTFS, which provides file/directory security, on their hard disks.

- *Lack of monitoring*: Both Windows NT and IIS have very good auditing and logging functions that you can use to detect intrusion. Unfortunately, people often don't use them. Many sites don't even do the simplest types of monitoring and maintenance, such as cleaning up leftover temporary files. You have to be aware of what's normal for your system so that you can detect the abnormal.

- *Unused but active services*: Every piece of software adds more complexity and more opportunities for break-ins. If you're using IIS only for its Web server, disable its Gopher and FTP services. The installation default, of course, is to run these services. If you don't turn them off, you've left the door open a bit.

Low-Level Attacks Data on the Internet can potentially pass through locations where someone has attached a packet sniffer to the line. That would let attackers see just what is going on between a remote client and your server. They could obtain any data that passed between the two, such as passwords or form data.

Even if your passwords are encrypted, other attacks are possible. One is "session playback." If a repeatable series of transactions occurs, for example, to log into your server, attackers can just record these actions during a legitimate session and then play them back whenever they want to attack. Another approach is to "hijack" a session as it occurs in real time. The attacker waits for the legitimate user to log in, then sends packets to the server with the valid information obtained by watching the logon process. This usually requires that the attacker intercept and block any subsequent requests by the legitimate user.

These kinds of attacks are relatively rare and also hard to set up. They require technically advanced hackers with physical access to the Internet at a point where they know your server's packets will pass. The best places to tap in are inside your own site; one company reported that it found a packet sniffer under the raised floor inside its computer room, connected to a dial-in modem line. Management suspected, but couldn't prove, that it was a night operator who worked only a few months and then quit. Unfortunately, the sniffer was only discovered *six months after he left the company*!

The new Point-to-Point Tunneling Protocol (PPTP), supported by NT 4.0, provides protection from these kinds of attacks by encrypting the entire message. PPTP is covered in Chapter 6. In a PPTP-encrypted message, all the attacker can see is the source and destination address. When combined with a firewall, as described in the next section, PPTP offers a very good level of protection from packet sniffing.

Creating Web Content

Editing Web Pages

Once you have your Web site up and running, the work really begins: creating the content and applications that will make people visit your site. This is true whether you're creating an Internet site or an intranet site. If you build a site with information that is useful and well organized, people will come to get it.

Microsoft includes its FrontPage Web page editing product with NT Server 4.0. FrontPage is much more than just an HTML editor, because it helps you manage the overall structure and content of the Web site. Tedious jobs like changing the look of your pages globally or catching all the references to a moved or renamed file are greatly simplified.

Still, sometimes you will want to drop into a low-level tool and edit with a tool that doesn't hide anything from you. That's especially true if you plan to make use of newer developments like Java or ActiveX. These technologies weren't quite cooked when FrontPage made its debut, so you won't get any tools or help working with these new types of active content. As crude as it sounds, we've found that Notepad is often the best tool for editing single files or making small editing changes. It's free, it's fast, and there's no learning curve.

Database Connections

IIS includes an Internet Database Connector (IDC) feature that lets you create dynamic HTML pages based on the contents of data tables. IDC is implemented as an Internet Server API (ISAPI) application that uses 32-bit ODBC to retrieve data from databases. Sample files and documentation are provide with IIS in the /samples/dbsamp/dbsamp.htm file under the location where you installed the wwwroot directory.

The basic approach of IDC is to have two files that control the HTML output. The first file has an extension of .IDC and describes the source of the data table and the fields you want to extract from it. A simple IDC file might look like this:

```
Datasource: Names
Username: admin
Template: names.htx
SQLStatment:
+Select FirstName, LastName
+From Names
```

An HTML template file, with an extension of .HTX, defines the format that is used to display the results of the data obtained when the query in the IDC file is executed. For the example above, the corresponding NAMES.HTX file might look like this:

```
<HTML>
<HEAD>
<TITLE>List of Names</TITLE>
</HEAD>
<BODY>
<%begindetail%>
<%if LastName EQ " "%>
<%else%>
<%FirstName%> <%LastName%><br>
<%endif%>
<%enddetail%>
</BODY>
</HTML>
```

The special tags enclosed in "<% ... %>" let you perform conditional actions and include the contents of fields you retrieved in the data query.

To perform the query, simply reference the IDC file in a link or as the action of a form:

```
<A HREF= "/scripts/names.idc">List the Names</A>
```

Using the examples from the IIS online documentation you can develop interactive databases that can gather information from users and store the information in a database.

Conclusion

IIS and the other Internet-specific features of Windows NT 4.0 Server (and to a lesser extent, Workstation) provide an unprecedented out-of-the-box capability to get your company on the Internet or create a private intranet. However, you must apply these features with care—or you may expose yourself to a severe security risk.

Further Reading

Chapman, Brent and Elizabeth D. Zwicky (1995), *Building Internet Firewalls*. Sebastopol, CA: O'Reilly & Associates, Inc., ISBN 1-56592-124-0.

Lehto, Kerry and W. Brett Polonsky (1996), *Introducing Microsoft FrontPage*. Redmond, WA: Microsoft Press. ISBN 1-57231-338-2.

Lemay, Laura (1994), *Teach Yourself Web Publishing with HTML in a Week*. Carmel, CA: Sams Publishing, ISBN 0-672-30667-0.

The Internet itself is one of the best sources of information about Internet issues. A good place to start is at Yahoo (http://www.yahoo.com) or one of the search engines such as AltaVista (http://www.altavista.digital.com). Here are a few of the best references we have found:

Internet Information Server

- news://comp.infosystems.www.servers.ms-windows

- news://microsoft.public.inetserver.iis

- http://rampages.onramp.net/~steveg/iis.html

Internet Security

- WWW Security FAQ, http://www-genome.wi.mit.edu/WWW/faqs/www-security-faq.htm

- Windows NT Security, http://www.somarsoft.com

- CERT advisories, http://www.cert.org

Firewalls and Proxies

- Network Computing, http://techweb.cmp.com/nwc/netdesign/series.htm

- http://www.williamette.edu/~dlabar/firewall.html

Enterprise Connections

After reading this chapter you will understand:

- Why enterprise networks are different from simpler LANs
- The need for administration across multiple domains
- Wide-area networking issues
- The need for routers and gateways
- The central importance of e-mail
- Multi-vendor issues
- Troubleshooting enterprise networks

You'll have a basic understanding of the principles involved in creating, operating, and maintaining networks characterized by size and complexity and the need for communications between multi-vendor platforms. You'll also know where to go for further information.

Enterprise Networks

Enterprise Networks—this term has come into general use only recently and has tended to displace more descriptive technical terms like *internetwork*. Fundamentally, the idea behind an enterprise network is that it makes all data from any network in an enterprise (that is, a corporation) available to users on all other networks provided, of course, that they have the necessary security privileges. The idea leverages the total information resources of an enterprise by making, for example, information from the shipping and receiving department available to management, an approach that is clearly essential if you are looking at, say, just-in-time manufacturing and wishing to maintain minimum inventory. These kinds of issues are becoming increasingly important as industries engage in downsizing or rightsizing operations.

From the system administrator's perspective, the central issues involved with enterprise networks are really three-fold. First is the issue of *communicating across great distances,* because the odds are high that an enterprise network will not exist within a single building. Second is the issue of *complexity,* because the enterprise network by its nature involves many servers and users. This issue is closely related to the third and most complex issue, *multi-vendor connectivity.*

Enterprise networks almost never comprise components from a single vendor, and it's unlikely that anyone will establish a totally Windows NT-based enterprise network (even Microsoft hasn't done this). So, there are issues of integrating the Windows NT networking components with existing networking components.

Because of the complex relationship among these issues, and the need to provide an administrative communications medium that includes them all, we consider that there is a fourth overriding concern on enterprise networks: *electronic mail.* In our experience, only electronic mail can possibly be used to provide reliable connectivity throughout the enterprise.

You can provide specific connections between different points in the enterprise for specific purposes—and we'll talk about how to do that—but the bottom line is that the only reliable way to connect *every* individual within the enterprise is to use some form of e-mail that works across all platforms. Because the workgroup-level Windows Messaging client and postoffice incorporated in NT is derived from Microsoft's *Exchange,* that's the main e-mail platform we'll talk about.

Windows NT in Enterprise Networks

Microsoft clearly had enterprise networking issues in mind when the Windows NT (especially Windows NT Server) networking architecture was conceived. Windows NT incorporates some unique features for use in enterprise networks that have never before been packaged into a single networking product. Among these are Windows NT Server's domain-wide administration features and a very important additional feature, *inter-domain trust*. This allows separate administrative domains of Windows NT systems to share user account information.

Windows NT also comes with Windows Messaging workgroup clients pre-installed (and NT Server adds support for a simple workgroup post office). These provide the essential electronic mail infrastructure just discussed. Unfortunately, even on Server systems, Windows NT does not provide the facilities necessary to connect multiple e-mail "post offices," so we will discuss what is necessary to expand on NT's built-in e-mail infrastructure. We'll also discuss the issues of providing connectivity between the MS Mail system and other e-mail systems the company may already have installed such as IBM PROFS or the UNIX-based simple mail transfer protocol (SMTP).

Windows NT also has a limited form of wide-area networking built in by its support for the remote access service (RAS) that is provided in a single-user version on basic Windows NT workstations and in a multi-user version on Windows NT Servers. This support is important because enterprise networks normally span many local area networks combined within a larger geographical area, making it impractical to string wires and physically connect all the elements of an enterprise. There must be some mechanism provided for connecting across the wider area. RAS allows you to do this via multiprotocol dial-up phone lines, Integrated Services Digital Network (ISDN), or x.25 packet switching links.

Windows NT also provides a high degree of multiprotocol support (as discussed in Chapters 6, 8, 9, and Appendices 2 and 4). In particular, the provision of support for the Transmission Control Protocol/Internet Protocol (TCP/IP) provides the necessary foundation for creating an enterprise network. As we will see, it is not practical to even consider constructing a Windows NT-based enterprise network without TCP/IP or the generally equivalent NetWare-compatible IPX/SPX protocol.

Finally, Windows NT and Windows NT Server support a very wide range of network clients, including DOS, 16-bit Windows, OS/2, Windows NT, UNIX, and Macintosh workstations. This support makes Windows NT, and particularly Windows NT Server (which has Macintosh support built in), an *ideal* platform for creating or expanding an enterprise network with a mix of client types.

The Search for Perfection

The preceding laundry list of features makes it sound as if Windows NT and Windows NT Server are a one-stop shopper's dream for enterprise network problems. Don't make the mistake of believing this! Windows NT has an excellent network architecture and is based on some very advanced technology. It's a good design, but the phrase "Jack of all trades, master of none" comes to mind.

Some major (though not fatal) issues with the Windows NT network architecture become apparent when you examine enterprise connections. In particular, Windows NT depends on either the TCP/IP protocol or Novell's IPX/SPX to provide a routable enterprise backbone, yet it modifies that protocol by transporting NetBIOS packets over it. As a result, the Windows NT subcomponents of an enterprise net always make up a separate network within an enterprise. You can, of course, incorporate Windows NT systems into an overall enterprise network management scheme based on IBM NetView or SNMP protocols, but the NT portion of the network will remain somewhat separated from other platforms.

We don't mean to say that it's impossible or outrageously difficult to incorporate Windows NT into an enterprise network. Sadly, doing so will present many of the same difficulties that incorporating any other proprietary networking into an enterprise network will. It's greatly to Microsoft's credit that it has provided *some* of the essential infrastructure as part of the Windows NT and Windows NT Server packages.

Enterprise Network Architectures

As we said earlier, the central facts of life for an enterprise networking environment are that such a network commands a large geographic area in which it is not practical to string physical wiring to connect all components of the enterprise, and in all probability, no standardization of the network hardware and software within the network's subnets. To put this in perspective, let's consider a hypothetical example.

A small growing company has, up to a point, grown its own local area network at the corporate headquarters (say in New York) and then opens a branch office (say in California). The existence of the branch office immediately creates some enterprise network issues. How are the branch office workers to be connected into the corporate headquarters? Some form of wide-area networking will be necessary. There's no realistic way to string private cable from New York to California, so dial-in support over modems will be needed. But will that be fast enough? If not, there are other possibilities extending all the way up to T1 dedicated telephone circuits (which amount to buying the dedicated wire from New York to California from the phone company at a rather hefty price). Finding the right combination of network hardware and software to achieve this connection efficiently and economically is one of the keys to enterprise networking.

The situation is further complicated if the company grows over a period of time or is taken over and integrated into another corporation. It's quite possible that our small company will have grown up using one networking system—for example, Novell NetWare—and the acquiring corporation has standardized on another networking system—perhaps DEC Pathworks. At this point, you are faced not only with the wide-area networking problems in connecting the new division into the corporate headquarters of the acquiring organization, but also with the problem of matching incompatible network protocols, transports, hardware, and who knows what else.

When Windows NT enters this networking picture, you're presented with some immediate opportunities because Windows NT Server includes some enterprise features, in particular, domain-wide management, inter-domain trust, and built-in wide-area network support.

Administrative Domains

One of the essential decisions that will face the network administrator attempting to carry out an enterprise network situation, whether the administrator is expanding an existing network to become an enterprise network incorporating new subnets that have been acquired through acquisition, or creating a branch office, or making some other change, will be deciding when to use the features that have been built into Windows NT, when to go outside and acquire other components, and most of all, what to use for the overall structure for the network. This is an administrative and management issue and a very important one, having to do with the relationships among the *administrative domains* that make up the network.

As we learned in Chapter 1, Windows NT can support two different administrative architectures. One is a *workgroup* architecture, essentially an ad hoc collection of more or less independent machines that happen to be linked on the same subnet. The second is an *administrative domain*. Administrative domains are characterized by the existence of a single Primary Domain Controller (PDC), which must be a Windows NT Server. All users log on to the PDC, and the PDC stores account information for all computers in the domain. This system greatly simplifies an administrator's responsibility because it's possible to *centrally* manage those user accounts for all users in the domain.

Of course, when one starts to consider an enterprise network, the domain structure begins to present some problems. It is possible, although unlikely, that an enterprise network can be managed as a single account domain. However, as you reach a very large number of users connecting over a very large network, you'll run into some severe problems. The first of these is the basic bandwidth limitation of the network hardware that's currently in general use. The most common network media today is IEEE 802.3 10Base2 (coax cabled) or 10BaseT (graded phone wire-cabled) Ethernet, which has a maximum capacity of 10 million bits per second. That sounds like a lot. But let's suppose an enterprise has built its entire network at its headquarters around a single Ethernet backbone (without routers[1]).

Our hypothetical enterprise has 1,000 employees. They all arrive between 8:30 and 9:00 a.m. on a Monday morning, turn on their workstations, and attempt to log in to the primary domain controller. Now, assuming (for argument's sake) that the login sequence requires an exchange of 10 data packets between the workstation and the server, each packet containing 1KB of information, the total information that needs to be transmitted through the company during this login "storm" will amount to just 10MB. Ethernet should be capable of handling this within just a few seconds, and we have half an hour, so it should be perfectly adequate. It isn't.

We've neglected the fact that for each one of those user logons the primary domain controller must perform disk accesses to locate the user's records in the database and update them. Because Windows NT employs a very efficient caching architecture based on its virtual memory system, it may be able to keep up with this example. At some point, if we expand the number of users to 5,000 or 10,000, we will saturate either the server or the network itself. Worse,

---

1   It may sound stupid, but even though this example is hypothetical, it's based on a real case!

as we've discussed earlier, the odds are quite high that not all parts of the company will be connecting over a 10Mbps Ethernet. Branch offices are likely to be transmitting their login information over wide-area network channels that will have variable speeds ranging from 9600 baud telephone lines up to T1 circuits that can approach Ethernet transmission rates.

If all the users in a large branch office are attempting to transmit their login information over a single 9600 baud phone line, you may find yourself with a very frustrated branch manager on the telephone. You might think that the solution is to avoid the use of domains altogether and use the workgroup model instead. That won't work in an enterprise network. The administration problems involved in supporting user accounts across a myriad of servers will quickly become totally unmanageable.

Fortunately, Microsoft has provided a rather elegant solution to this problem. In Windows NT Server domains, although only one server can be the primary domain controller for the user accounts, *any* server can support a login request and can *replicate* the primary domain controller's account database. For instance, our hypothetical branch office might have its own login controller (a Windows NT Server set up to replicate the database on the primary domain controller). This *login server* would then handle all the login traffic on Monday morning on its own over the local Ethernet. It would simply receive information from the primary domain controller on a regular basis (we'll discuss how to do this shortly).

The one problem with this approach is that creating or modifying user accounts requires interaction with the primary domain controller, so the administrator will wind up bearing the burden of communication over the wide-area connection. A workaround for this situation (which also provides for more centralization and control of the network) is for all administration to be handled in the corporate headquarters and for requests for changes in user accounts to be transmitted to the administrators by electronic mail.

There are variations on this approach, and Microsoft has taken these into account in Windows NT Server, which provides inter-domain trust. Inter-domain trust arises from the fact that it isn't always practical for an enterprise to have a single account domain.

Suppose that the branch office in our example grows to include several hundred people. At this point, even with the account database being replicated on the branch office server, there will be enough administrative traffic to become a real burden traveling across the wide-area networking link between the corporate headquarters and the branch office. If e-mail is used for communicating with the central MIS group that includes all the administrators, users will likely experience a certain amount of frustration and friction dealing with that distant and seemingly unresponsive MIS department.

At some point, with a large branch office you will wind up needing an administration group, essentially an MIS department in miniature, for the branch office. And the best solution, obviously, is to create a separate login domain and separate user accounts at the branch office. You then confront the same problem discussed when we defined the difference between workgroups and domains. A home office employee needing to access files on the branch office server will need *two* accounts: one at the branch office and one at the home office. For example, if the branch office handles West Coast regional sales, the West Coast branch office manager will probably need to have a user account at the home office to communicate with other branch managers and the sales department chief. Similarly, the sales manager at the home office will need to have access to directories on the branch office server.

The traditional way to handle this is that the MIS heads at the branch office and the home office will communicate and try to keep their user account databases in sync. Invariably, this method results in problems. It means an increased overhead both at the branch office and at the home office, and if an organization has many branch offices, the overhead at the home office can become overwhelming.

To get around this problem, Windows NT provides inter-domain trust. A *trust relationship* is created between the domain servers for two domains. These trust relationships are inherently *one-way*. Thus, the fact that the branch office trusts the home office does *not* imply that the home office trusts the branch office (although it is possible to arrange two-way trust). With two-way trust, our problem goes away; the West Coast regional sales manager has an account on the branch office domain server. The home office server trusts the branch office domain server.

Because the regional sales manager is a member of the sales manager's group, and sales managers have read/write access to the sales data directories, this individual *automatically* has access to the data directory on the home office server as well as on the branch server. With a trust relationship extended in the other direction, the head of the sales department at the home office will have the same kind of access on the branch server, not only in California but in any other branch the company has. The account management problem is essentially eliminated. The home office MIS group needs to maintain accounts only for people who have local access to the local server. Access to the remote servers is handled automatically. Only the trust relationships need to be maintained.

The only coordination required between the MIS director at the home office and the branch office MIS directors is first, that they maintain the trust relationships and second, that they agree on the group names. The need to manage separate user accounts for remote individuals is eliminated, which is a tremendous assist in a complex enterprise situation, particularly for organizations with many branch offices.

The only problem with inter-domain trust is that it works *only* with Windows NT Servers, not only at the home office but at all branch offices. You cannot extend inter-domain trust privileges to a NetWare server (without a radical change of control as provided by Domain Services Manager for NetWare—see Chapter 10) or a UNIX server or even to a LAN Manager server (in its current incarnation). Therefore, to provide inter-domain trust capabilities, it will be necessary to install a Windows NT Server for domain control at each branch that needs to be trusted or needs to trust the central office.

Windows NT Server Domain Administration Models

Given the existence of Windows NT Servers at the home office and all branch offices, trust relationships can be arranged a number of different ways to provide one degree or another of centralized administrative control over the network. Microsoft defines four basic models for trust relationships, as explained in the following sections.

Single Domain Model

The Single Domain Model is the most obvious of the models and essentially is the baseline case. There is just one user domain and one primary domain controller, which maintains *all* accounts for the entire enterprise. This model provides, obviously, the maximum degree of centralized administration and control and it can work for very large networks (up to around 10,000 user accounts) with judicious use of replication and fall-back servers to provide local logon capabilities for remote offices and divisions. The network traffic, however, will become considerable on this kind of networking scheme, particularly for organizations with branch offices that must replicate the primary database controller over a wide-area networking link and for organizations in which user accounts (particularly remote user accounts) change frequently.

Master Domain Model

In the Master Domain approach there may be more than one domain, but there is a single domain to provide central control, probably the MIS domain at the home office. All other domains trust the master domain. This model is ideal for organizations maintaining a centralized MIS department but supporting users at many branch office sites, and it can be used with very large networks (this is the approach that Microsoft itself uses). Users are members of local domains. They are *not* members of the central MIS domain. All user accounts are created in the central MIS domain, but because the remote domains trust the MIS domain, users automatically have access privileges on their local servers.

The administrator can define which servers and workstations the user is permitted to use at the time the user account is created. Requests for user account modification are communicated by electronic mail to the central account operators in Redmond, Washington (Microsoft's corporate headquarters). Local system administrators do not have account operator privileges and cannot create or modify user accounts, but they do have the necessary permissions to administer servers and to administer groups of users.

This approach provides central MIS control over the network, and a single central authority for creating and granting user access rights (with a high degree of security), while minimizing network traffic between central MIS and the remote sites and providing administrative flexibility at the remote sites. This scheme makes sense for large organizations.

Multiple Master Domain Model

The Multiple Master Domain approach, recommended for very large networks (more than 10,000 users), employs essentially the same logic as the master domain model, but allows more than one master domain. Each sub-domain trusts one or more of the master domains. The master domains may or may not trust each other (it would probably be most convenient if they do). In a very large organization this model would allow a distributed MIS environment in which there are central MIS groups for several divisions within the organization and would provide the benefits of the Master Domain Model without the need for centralizing all user accounts. Microsoft uses this approach. The central MIS department in Redmond is the global master domain, but there are geographically oriented user account domains for each area in which Microsoft has a major presence. Management overhead is reduced by having locally controlled second-tier domains throughout the organization. All of these trust the central user account domains. Thus, Microsoft gains the benefit of decentralized operations while retaining central control over user accounts, and because all user account domains trust each other, users throughout the organization have the benefits of enterprise-wide single login.

Complete Trust Model

The final model that Microsoft discusses is one that appears to make *no* sense for an enterprise network. In the Complete Trust Model all domains operate independently, but all domains trust all other domains within an enterprise. The idea is that there is no central MIS department. Instead, each domain is separately administered, but (by the maintenance of the necessary inter-domain trust links) users who have an account on any server will be able, with appropriate privileges, to use any other server in the enterprise.

The problem with this approach is that it depends *critically* on the diligence of the network administrators supervising each of the trusted domains in the organization. Laxness on the part of any one administrator (for example, in closing obsolete user accounts or enforcing password changes) can propagate throughout the network via the trust relationships, creating a large opportunity for security breach.

Because this type of networking is inherently insecure, we do not recommend it.

A Mixed Domain Model

In addition to the four models that Microsoft recommends, it's likely (especially as Windows NT capabilities are added onto existing networks or as subnetworks are acquired and incorporated into an enterprise running a Windows NT network) that a need to *mix* the various models will arise. In particular, a model we think makes some sense is a combination of the Single Domain and Master Domain Models. In this approach, one would have a more or less independent account domain with a local administrator, which also trusts a central Master Domain. Account control can be accomplished either locally *or* from the Master Domain. Local user accounts can be created locally; local or remote user accounts can be created by the Master Domain (i.e., the central MIS department).

This mixed approach may be advantageous in several situations. When Windows NT networks are initially added to an existing enterprise, it's unlikely that there will, in fact, *be* a Master Domain for the local domain to trust. Therefore, it will make sense to create an independent domain. Later, if the company accepts Windows NT as a standard, you're faced with the problem of grafting these independent subnetworks into the Master Domain Model. You can do this most conveniently by trusting the Master Domain servers then begin life with local user databases that can be supplanted (or augmented) by a remote account database at the Master Domain. There is no need for users who use only a particular domain server to have an account in the central MIS account database, and it may simplify things initially if they do not.

Similarly, when a remote site needs to be added to an existing Windows NT Master Domain or Multiple Master Domain network, it may not be possible (initially) for that branch network to be administered under the Master Domain Model—probably because the remote domain does not, in fact, *have* a Windows NT Server available initially as a domain controller. In this situation, it may be convenient to allow the domain to operate more or less independently and transport the foreign accounts from the existing network onto a Windows NT Server. Again, you're faced with essentially an independent network. By having this network trust the central Master Domain you gain the opportunity for remote administration and for access by users who have accounts in the remote network.

There is a problem with this approach, and that is synchronizing account database information between the local network administrators and the administrators in the Master Domain. It's possible in this kind of model to wind up having multiple user accounts: one presented from the MIS domain and one from the local domain. Cooperation between the administrators can prevent this from becoming a significant burden, and the overall security risks reflected by the Complete Trust Model do not occur because the trust relationships in this approach are essentially *one-way*. A variation on this approach would be to have the remote domains not only trust the Master Domain but be trusted by the Master Domain. It's not necessarily required for each of these domains in turn to trust each other. Such a two-way trust model will present something of a security risk, but not as great a one as the Complete Trust Model discussed earlier.

Selecting a Domain Model

From the preceding discussion, it should be clear that many factors—including company policy, location of branch offices, and the underlying network infrastructure—affect the choice of a domain model. Selecting the right model for your organization can be a complex task. Microsoft does provide some help with this, including a *Domain Planner* in the Windows NT Server Resource Kit. It's a "wizard" application that queries you for information about your network and the way you plan to use it, and then recommends a model and provides instructions for installing it. See Appendix 4 for more information on the Resource Kit.

Now that we've examined the basic administration models for Windows NT, let's take a look at the specific steps involved in creating the necessary inter-domain trust links.

Setting Up Inter-Domain Trust Linkage Relationships

Microsoft packages an excellent video on domain management with the Windows NT Server documentation kit (number 227-074-410, $69.95), which also includes eight volumes of printed NT documentation. Any NT Server site should have one of these kits (the full NT Server package with documentation includes the tape), and the tape will show you all the details on domain management in much greater detail than we can describe here.

The basic steps for establishing inter-domain trust links (assuming that you have administrative status on both the domain to be trusted and the trusting domain) are:

1. Start User Manager for Domains. Select Domain from User menu. The Select Domain dialog appears. Select the Domain to be Trusted from the list (or type it in if you can't see it).

2. Select Trust Relationships from the Policies menu. The Trust Relationship dialog appears (see Figure 8.1).

3. Click the Add... button on the lower (Permitted to Trust this Domain) list box and add the Trusting domain to the list. The Permit Domain to Trust dialog appears. At this point you will also have to type in (and confirm) an Initial Password for the trust relationship. This will be used only the first time the trusting domain is attached. At that point the system automatically changes the password on both systems, and the modified password (which you cannot change) will be used for further connections. Click Close to dismiss the dialog.

4. Select the User menu's Select Domain item, and select (or type) the *trusting* domain name.

5. Select Policies/Trust Relationships. The Trust Relationships dialog appears again. Click the Add button on the upper (Trusted Domains) listbox. The Add Trusted Domain dialog box appears. Type in the domain name to be trusted and the password from step 3.

6. Assuming steps 1 through 5 work properly, an information box will appear with the message "Trust relationship established with domain <domain name>." If not, examine the Event Log to see if an error occurred and carefully repeat steps 1 through 5.

Once these steps have been accomplished, administrators in the trusting domain can assign permissions to users and groups in the trusted domain at will. Administrators cannot, however, create or delete user accounts in a domain other than their own, nor can they assign rights to resources in the other domain (unless granted the right to do so by an administrator from the trusting domain). Some coordination between administrators is necessary to make the system work, but it's still a vast improvement over separately administering each server.

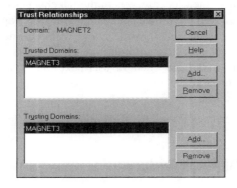

FIGURE 8.1 Trust Relationships dialog box. Inter-domain trust relationships in NT Server 4.0 are set from this dialog box from User Manager.

Performance Tip: Isolate Domain Controllers

You can improve login performance on enterprise networks by setting aside a separate server (it doesn't have to be a very big one) as the Primary Domain Controller.[2] Don't run any other services on that machine—don't even share directories on the network (other than for administrative access).

The PDC is a very busy server on a big network; it validates most logons and provides the master database that's replicated by other servers. If the PDC is busy validating logon requests, the performance of other services will suffer and vice versa. In fact, one of the few ways to seriously impair an NT Server network is to run SQL Server on a PDC, with the "Boost SQL Server Priority" box checked in SQL Server Setup/Set Server Options. That setting gives SQL Server exclusive priority over all other system tasks, including logon validation. It can render the PDC completely useless or (at worst) crash the PDC. That's why Microsoft recommends running SQL Server on a separate machine from the PDC. If you're running a very small network, you can go ahead and run both services on one machine; just don't check the boost box!

It may seem extreme to dedicate a server to handling user accounts, but if you're running a large network, the additional cost involved is negligible.

Replication

The mechanism Windows NT Servers provide for users to log on to machines other than the primary domain controller is called *account replication*. The way it works is actually relatively simple: every five minutes, the primary domain controller examines its account database to see if any changes have occurred. If they have, it transmits these changes to *every other Windows NT Server in the domain*. In this way all Servers in a domain maintain directory information that is within five minutes of being current across all servers. This also means that if for any reason there is a network failure that blocks out the primary domain controller, users can continue to log in using the information in their local servers (although changes to the user accounts, which have to be accomplished through the primary domain controller, won't work until the linkages are reestablished). Although Windows NT workstations within the network do not replicate the account database, they *do* cache the account information for the most recently logged-on user, so (even if no logon server is available when the user next logs in) the system will identify the user based on the information stored from the last logon and will permit the user to use the computer if the information matches.

With that information as background, let's examine the specifics of setting up the replication service in Windows NT.

Replicating Directories

In addition to replicating the user account structure, you can exploit the *replicator service* to copy other information between servers. This is necessary in a server domain that employs *logon scripts* because (obviously) you want to have users logon to any server in the network but

---

2   A tip from the MIS department at Sequent Computer Systems Inc.

still use the same script that you maintain on the primary domain controller. It can also be desirable if you need to maintain centrally controlled information that has to be broadcast to all servers in the network (policy statements, etc.)

Each Windows NT Server can maintain an *export* directory structure and an import directory structure. These directory structures normally include the logon scripts and data. You can add subdirectories into the directory structure if you want. However, *only one directory tree may be exported from each server*. Windows NT workstations cannot export but can *import* through the replication system. With replication in place, changes within the directory tree will be transmitted to other systems on the network either immediately when they occur or (at the administrator's discretion) after a two-minute stabilization period.

Proper operation of the replicator service is absolutely key to efficient use of logon scripts in NT Server networks. If replication is set up correctly, login scripts from the PDC can be automatically duplicated on servers throughout the enterprise, but if replication isn't properly set up, you have no way of knowing who does and does *not* have up-to-date scriptfiles. This problem becomes especially important if you deploy an enterprise-wide application such as Microsoft SMS (covered later in this chapter), which depends on login scripts.

Replication provides a transparent method for replicating the script information throughout a domain. It also can be employed to provide *automatic backup* of information. For example, one can replicate the critical data directory structures of a server, export that information, and import it on a backup server. You can use this in a variety of ways.

Do *not* view this replication approach as a panacea for providing automatic near-line backup of user directory information. One site that attempted to do this[3] by replicating all user directories on backup servers every six minutes found that it almost immediately saturated a 100-megabit-per-second FDDI backbone. It is simply not practical to use the replication mechanism for frequently changing data at existing data rates.[4] Use it on data that changes *infrequently* or data so important that you can't afford to risk its loss. For user information that changes on a minute-by-minute basis, consider some other mechanism for critical data backup; such as a near-line magneto-optical storage system.

If you've decided to exploit replication for cross-server account maintenance or for some other purpose, I'll explain how to get it running.

Step-by-step Instructions for Setting Up Replication

To set up replication export (assuming you have domain administrative privileges):

---

3   See *Enterprise Connectivity in a Multivendor Environment,* paper from 1992 TechEd conference, included on Microsoft's TechNet CD.

4   It might be possible if data can be transmitted over a *very local area network* (VLAN),which is essentially shared memory space in every computer on the VLAN (tied together with fiber-optic cable). The memory-mapped files described in Chapter 1 might well have something to offer in this regard.

1. Start Server Manager.

2. Select View/All (this will show both servers and workstations in the domain).

3. Select the server you wish to have export directories (typically the Primary Domain Controller). The Properties for <Machine Name> dialog box will appear, as shown in Figure 8.2 (functionally, this is the same as running the Control Panel Server object locally on <Machine Name>).

4. Click the Replication button. The Directory Replication dialog box appears (see Figure 8.3).

5. Click the Export Subdirectories radio button. The default path for export (typically \WINNT\SYSTEM32\REPL\EXPORT) appears in the From Path... field. You can edit the path if needed (note that you can export directories from only one directory).

6. If needed (to control replication of subdirectories and record-locking within the replication path), click the Manage... button. The Manage Exported Directories dialog box appears. This allows you to add or remove subdirectories from the export list, determine whether the entire subtree or only the top-level subdirectory is exported, determine whether replication can occur while the contents of the export directories are being changed, and "lock out" specific directories that you do *not* want to export (the first time through, you're well advised to click the Help button for a more detailed explanation). When you're satisfied with the export management settings, click the OK button.

7. By default, the system will export replicant directory data to *all* importing systems in the *local* domain. If that's what you want, click the OK button now and skip ahead to step 9.

8. If you want to limit which systems are permitted to import replicant data, or if you want to export data to systems outside the local domain, you will need to add these systems explicitly in the To List. You can do so using the Add button, which will display the Select Domain dialog. You may select just a domain name to export to all systems in the domain, or you can select specific systems.

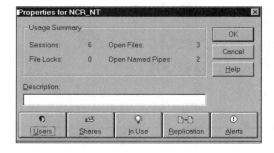

FIGURE 8.2 Properties dialog (from Server Manager). The Properties dialog from NT Server 4.0's Server Manager application duplicates the Server component in Control Panel, but from Server Manager, you can control servers over the network.

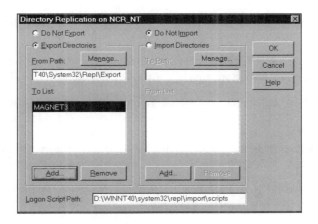

FIGURE 8.3 Directory replication dialog. Directory replication is set from this dialog box from NT Server 4.0's Server Manager application.

> *Note: In wide-area network systems selecting the domain may not be sufficient. You may need to select each system to be exported to explicitly.*

9. Click the OK button. The replicator service will be started, if it was not already running. If import has not been set up on any system(s), you will now need to set up replication import on the relevant system(s) (see the instructions that follow).

To set up replication *import* (assuming you have domain administrative privileges):

1. Start Server Manager from the Administrative Tools folder.

2. Select View/All (this will show both servers and workstations in the domain).

3. Select the server you wish to have import directories (typically all Backup Domain Controllers). The Properties for <Machine Name> dialog box will appear.

4. Click the Replication button. The Directory Replication dialog appears.

5. Click the Import Subdirectories radio button. The default path for import (typically \WINNT\SYSTEM32\REPL\IMPORT) appears in the To Path... field. You can edit the path if needed (note that you can import to only one directory, although that directory can be loaded with information from multiple *export* servers).

6. If needed (to control replication of subdirectories and record-locking within the replication path), click the Manage... button. The Manage Imported Directories dialog box appears. This allows you to add or remove subdirectories from the import list, determine whether the entire subtree or only the top-level subdirectory is imported, determine whether replication can occur while the contents of the import directories are being changed, and "lock out" specific directories that you do *not* want to import (the first time through, you're well

advised to click the Help button for a more detailed explanation). When you're satisfied with the import management settings, click the OK button.

7. By default, the system will import replicant directory data from *all* exporting systems in the *local* domain. If that's what you want, click the OK button now, and skip ahead to step 9.

8. If you want to limit the servers from which the system will import, or if you want to import data from servers outside the local domain, you will need to add these servers explicitly in the From List. You can do so using the Add button, which will display the Select Domain dialog. You may select just a domain name to import from all or you can select specific servers.

> *Note: In wide-area network systems selecting the domain may not be sufficient. You may need to select each server to be imported from explicitly.*

9. Click the OK button. The replicator service will be started, if it was not already running.

Enterprise Connectivity One: The Local Area Networks

An Enterprise Network is made up of one or more local area networks (typically many local area networks) connected through a backbone system or across wide-area network (WAN) links. The structure of the individual LANs that make up the enterprise network is similar to that of an isolated small business local area network, but there are some differences that come into play when multiple local area networks must be connected. In particular, protocol selection (a rather arbitrary choice in an isolated LAN), becomes a critical issue when applied to large-scale enterprise networks, and this is especially true for Windows NT and other Microsoft networking products because they depend so heavily upon NetBIOS broadcasts.

The Backbone Protocol

TCP/IP connectivity was discussed extensively in Chapter 6, and some readers may find it confusing that we chose to discuss TCP/IP networking *before* introducing the enterprise issues. The reason we did this is a very simple one: if you are doing enterprise networking with Windows NT, you *must* use either TCP/IP or IPX/SPX as the backbone protocol. You have no other choice.

TCP/IP and IPX/SPX are the only fully routable protocols that Windows NT can use for its native networking. You can connect two local area networks using TCP/IP routers, and traffic will be routed between the two TCP/IP networks, including the NBT (NetBIOS over TCP/IP) packets necessary for Windows NT native communications involving the Network Browser (File Manager or the administration tools or so forth). If the NWLink IPX/SPX Compatible Transport is installed, it's also possible to use IPX Routing (see Chapter 10) to place NT in the enterprise as a fully routed server. The other protocols supported by Windows NT, are not routable.[5] This is particularly true of NetBEUI whose virtual circuit architecture inherently limits it to operation over a single subnet. If the NetBIOS broadcasts on which NetBEUI depends were routed, a large-scale network could quickly be saturated by broadcasts not intended for any particular subnet, and because broadcasts are inherently not addressed to a particular location, it isn't possible to route them selectively. Therefore, the broadcasts are blocked at the router, and any subsystem requiring broadcasts (in particular the browser) cannot function across the router.

TCP/IP avoids this problem because the HOSTS and LMHOSTS databases (or a Domain Name Service or Windows Internet Name Service server[6]) provide addresses for any and all message traffic. This provision eliminates the need for broadcast announcements to locate a given machine and allows Windows NT to operate effectively through quite complicated routing situations.

Does This Mean No Other Protocol Can Be Used?

Just because TCP/IP or IPX/SPX is required as the backbone protocol does not mean that it must be the only protocol used in an enterprise network. There are significant advantages to using a multi-protocol solution. TCP/IP is quite complex (which is why we've devoted an entire chapter to it). And setting up and maintaining TCP/IP protocols is a significantly more complex task than setting up more standardized protocols like NetBEUI or IPX because of the complicated addressing scheme that has to be manually set up and maintained through the HOSTS and LMHOSTS database files. There's also a performance implication.

The NetBEUI protocol that Windows NT 3.1 used by default[7] is designed as a high-efficiency protocol for small networks. It provides a *virtual circuit* scheme for high-data-rate *raw* I/O transmissions between the server and the client. This works well on small subnets and delivers higher performance than TCP/IP (although it obviously militates, along with the broadcast issues discussed earlier, against use of NetBEUI over wide-area network links, where error handling can be a severe restriction). The NWLink IPX protocol has similar (though lesser) limitations and is even faster than NetBEUI. NetBIOS can be run over IPX, but only through eight routers; to prevent over propagation of NetBIOS packets, the packets are designed to die after eight router hops. In large organizations, this setup can present some difficulties, but for most organizations, NetBIOS over TCP/IP (IETF 1001/1002) or simple IPX/SPX protocols can suffice.

---

5   Actually, NWLink *is* routable to a limited degree. It generally will route one hop; that is, you can have machines on either side of a router that will "see" the other. If two routers are involved, however, it fails to route the essential NetBIOS broadcast messages. We hope this problem will be eliminated in future versions of Windows NT.

6   See Chapter 6 for more information.

7   Beginning with NT 3.5, IPX is the default protocol for NT Workstations, and IPX, TCP/IP, or both are typically used by NT Servers. NetBEUI, although retained for compatibility with earlier versions of NT and other Microsoft networking systems, is clearly on its way out.

What you *can* do is set up a mixed protocol network. Consider a network situation in which a central office local area network backbone needs to communicate with a remote office for account information. Either TCP/IP or IPX/SPX can deliver file, print, and NetBIOS connectivity for quite some distance through a router maze. Obviously, it's necessary for the central office backbone to run TCP/IP or routed IPX/SPX. Does this mean that one should run TCP/IP or IPX/SPX for *all* the clients on the remote network? The answer is probably no (particularly for TCP/IP), both for performance reasons and for simplicity of administration. Rather than doing so, run *two* network stacks in the remote server. The routed (TCP/IP or IPX/SPX) stack will be used for communications with the central office (including the necessary traffic for maintaining the account databases and communicating inter-domain trust links). The second protocol should be either NetBEUI or non-routed NWLink IPX, depending on the needs of the particular site. This will be used for connections between the remote server and clients on the remote LAN.

The implication of such a dual-protocol setup is two-fold. First, it means that the remote clients will be able to see *only* the remote server and will not be able to establish connections across the wide-area network to the central office. If such connections are necessary, a particular client will need to have the routed protocol installed as either a replacement for or augmentation of NetBEUI (or IPX) in that client. Alternatively, a Remote Access Services (RAS) connection could be established directly from the remote client into the central office–which may be preferable in certain situations.

Using dual network stacks in Windows NT computers presents no particular problems—it's simply a matter of loading and configuring the necessary protocols. Moreover, you can choose to manipulate the bindings using the Control Panel/Networks object and place the most heavily used bindings first in the list. This would mean, presumably, the NetBEUI (or IPX) bindings for the local traffic. Doing so will have the effect of performing what amounts to a primitive routing function. Any traffic that can be sent over the NetBEUI (or IPX) links will be sent that way. Traffic that cannot be sent over the local links will automatically go to the next step in the bindings to the routed portions of the stack for transmission that way. The result is effectively a routed network extending between the remote server and the central office that overlaps a local area network running between the remote server and its clients on the remote LAN.

The advantages of this approach are, first, better performance with a fast local protocol for all traffic on the LAN and routed protocols only for remote connection when needed; and second, a much reduced administrative burden, especially when the backbone protocol is TCP/IP. The network administrator at the remote site needs to maintain only routable connections (and for TCP/IP, the associated addresses) between the remote server and the central site. Most workstations on the LAN don't require this maintenance because they will use principally the much simpler local protocol stack. As a result, it is easier to plug and unplug computers as necessary. If a few users need connections extending into the central office, they can be provided with routable stacks, but the number of addresses needing maintenance will be minimized. And although it's true that today's DHCP and WINS-enabled TCP/IP implementation dramatically reduces the administrative burden traditionally imposed by TCP/IP, the higher performance of a local protocol more than makes up for the additional complexity of running two protocol stacks (especially if there's a problem with your DHCP or WINS server!).

Windows NT has an additional advantage in this kind of environment. The *static or RIP routing* capability it provides for IPX/SPX and TCP/IP is suitable for use at many branch offices. Rather than installing an expensive hardware router, one of the Windows NT servers can have two network cards installed and function as a router for connections to the central office (see Chapter 6 for details on IP routing, Chapter 10 for details on IPX routing).

Moreover, beginning with version 3.5, Windows NT supports TCP/IP and IPX WAN links. The Point-to-Point Protocol (PPP) and Serial Link Interface Protocol (SLIP) are supported, and no special hardware is required to connect the subnets (though you may want to use custom router hardware for optimal performance). See the "Remote Access Service" section later in this chapter for more information on NT's built-in WAN support.

If you're setting up a multi-protocol network, you'll need to tune the bindings appropriately. The following section explains how.

Step-by-Step Instructions for Tuning Multi-Protocol Binding

1. Start the Windows NT Control Panel, and double-click the Network icon. Then click the Bindings... tab (see Figure 8.4). The resulting display is a tree structure. To see the Bindings associated with any Service, click the [+] box to the left of the Service's icon.

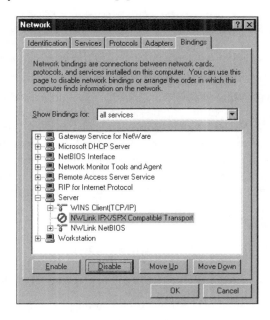

FIGURE 8.4 Control Panel/Network, bindings tab. In multi-protocol environments, you can control the order in which network bindings are executed using the bindings tab from Control Panel/Network.

2. Bindings at the top of the list are executed first, so in a mixed NetBEUI (or NWLink IPX) local protocol and TCP/IP environment, make sure that the local protocol bindings are at the top of the list. If the local protocol is not at the top, select the appropriate binding and click the Move Up button to "promote" it as necessary.

3. You can disable unused bindings (a step that may prove helpful in troubleshooting) rather than removing them. To do so, click on the binding step in question and click the Disable button.

4. Click the OK button. You will be returned to the Network Settings dialog. Click OK again to exit to the Control Panel. You will need to exit and restart Windows NT to apply the new bindings.

Services for Macintosh

Microsoft provides another unique capability in Windows NT Server by supporting Apple Macintosh computers as network clients out of the box. It uses *Services For Macintosh* (SFM), a combination of a Windows NT Server, file system driver, and network protocols that provides:

- Macintosh-compatible namespace on NTFS volumes

- Native (and fully routable!) support for AppleTalk network protocols

- Postscript emulation on non-Postscript printers (allowing Macs to leverage non-Postscript printers already on the network)

- Access to Apple Laserwriter (and compatible Postscript printers on the AppleTalk network) by Windows NT, Windows 3.x, DOS, and OS/2 clients

SFM is included with Windows NT Server—there is nothing additional to buy (with the possible exception of a compatible AppleTalk card for the server if you want to use LocalTalk[8] cabling to the Macintosh workstations). It requires no additional software on the Macintoshes (although it can provide better security if a Microsoft authentication package is used in place of the Macintosh's default authenticator—this is included with Windows NT Server). SFM does require approximately 2MB of additional disk space in the server, and directories to be made available to the Macs must exist on an NTFS drive (or CD-ROM).

Installing SFM

Install SFM from Control Panel's Network icon, as follows:

---

8   LocalTalk is the native form of networking built into all Macintosh systems since the 512KB "Fat Mac." It is less than one-fourth as fast as Ethernet, but for many users this lower performance is more than offset by its low cost. It's also possible to put Ethernet cards into most newer Macintoshes or to use a LocalTalk/Ethernet router to bridge Macintoshes into an existing Ethernet. Windows NT is compatible with all these solutions, although (as always) it's wise to check that any AppleTalk or Ethernet cards you're thinking about buying are listed in the current *Windows NT Hardware Compatibility List*.

1. Click the Add Software button, select Services for Macintosh from the list, and click Continue. You will be asked to specify the source directory for installation. The SFM files are then copied to your hard disk. Click the Close button.

2. NT Server will review the network bindings, and the AppleTalk Protocol Properties dialog box appears (see Figure 8.5). Designate the network card and AppleTalk Zone[9] to use for SFM. You can control AppleTalk routing from this dialog's Routing tab.[10] When you're satisfied with the network and Zone settings, click OK.

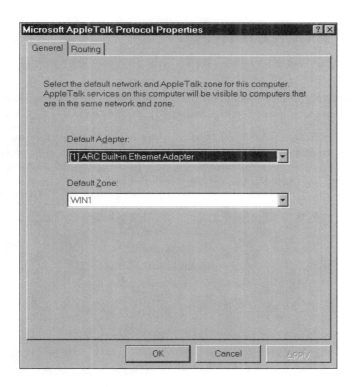

FIGURE 8.5 AppleTalk protocol properties. NT Server 4.0 provides AppleTalk protocol support as part of its Services for Macintosh (SFM) package. To use SFM, you must associate AppleTalk with a particular network adapter card and assign a default AppleTalk zone to the card.

---

9   AppleTalk *Zones* are used for routing, much as DNS zones are used with the TCP/IP protocol (see Chapter 6).

10 Details of AppleTalk routing are beyond the scope of this text. See *Windows NT Advanced Server—Services for Macintosh* (listed in "For More Information" at the end of this chapter) for a detailed discussion of this topic.

3. Close Control Panel/Network. You will be instructed to reboot the computer to start Services for Macintosh.[11]

After it's installed, SFM can be started/stopped/paused/continued from Control Panel/Services (or Server Manager/Services) like any other Windows NT service, and you will find an addition to the Start Menu's Administrative Tools folder, namely File Manager.[12] It has a special MacFile menu, as does Server Manager, and a MacFile icon has been placed in the Windows NT Control Panel. You will use these new features to control operation of the SFM service.

Creating SFM Volumes

Once SFM is installed, it's necessary to create an SFM-compatible "volume" that Macintosh clients can mount. This is done as follows:

1. Create the directory tree you want Macintosh systems to access using Windows Explorer, File Manager, or the equivalent command-line functions on an NTFS disk volume.

   Note: SFM volumes include all subdirectories of the root directory that's made accessible to Macs, and SFM volumes cannot overlap. You cannot share only part of a directory subtree, nor can you share a directory and also share its subdirectory with a separate volume name.

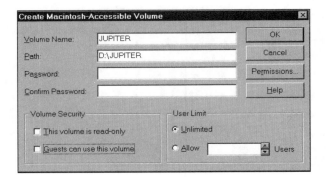

FIGURE 8.6 Create Macintosh-accessible volumes dialog. Create MacFile volumes within the name space of an NTFS partition using this dialog box from NT Server 4.0's File Manager.

---

11 However, it's our experience that you don't really need to reboot. Just use Control Panel/Services to start the File Server for Macintosh and Print Server for Macintosh services (you might also take this opportunity to create a user account for Macintosh printing, as described later). Unlike most of NT's network services, SFM doesn't appear to *need* a reboot!

12 When we first started updating this chapter for the third edition, we wondered how Microsoft integrated the MacFile menu into the Windows Explorer. The answer turned out to be that it isn't integrated at all!

2. Select the root of the directory tree you want to make accessible to Macs using File Manager, then choose MacFile/Create Volume. The Create Macintosh-Accessible Volume dialog box appears (see Figure 8.6). You may now declare the volume name, edit the path, and specify a password[13] that Mac users will have to issue for access to the volume. You may also designate a maximum number of users for the volume (the default is unlimited). Note that none of this affects the status of the NTFS directory that contains the volume—it's still a valid NTFS directory and can be accessed by PCs in the usual way.[14]

3. Click the Permissions button. This will bring up the Macintosh View of Directory Permissions dialog box (see Figure 8.7), which you will use to decide which users have permission to access the volume (this is in addition to the regular NTFS security settings, but be aware that Macs see access controls on a directory-by-directory rather than file-by-file basis). When you're satisfied with the permission settings, click OK to exit the MacFile Permissions dialog.

4. Click OK to exit the Create Macintosh-Accessible Volume dialog box. The volume is now available for access from Macintosh clients.

Once a MacFile volume is created, you can modify its settings by selecting it in File Manager and selecting MacFile/View-Modify Volumes. You can eliminate Macintosh access to the volume

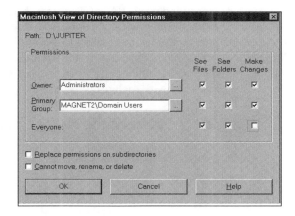

FIGURE 8.7 Macintosh view of directory permissions dialog box. Set MacFile directory permissions using this dialog box from NT Server's File Manager.

13 This *volume password* is a separate, additional, security measure for Macintosh users. It is *not* the same as the username and password, which still must be issued in order for Mac users to access the volume.

14 SFM extends the existing filename translation scheme that NTFS uses to present 8.3 names to DOS users to Macintoshes as well. Macintosh-created long names are treated as native NTFS filenames (with the exception of certain illegal characters, which are replaced). These are then translated into 8.3 DOS-compatible names for PC users. Windows NT users see the long filenames. NTFS filenames will appear exactly as created to Mac users, *provided* the names are 32 characters or shorter. If not, NTFS converts them to 8.3 names for the Mac users.

using MacFile/Remove Volumes (note that this removes the MacFile volume associated with the directory, *not* the directory itself—you do that with File Manager in the usual way).

You can use exactly the same procedure to make CD-ROM directories available to Mac clients—just skip the first step. (It's usually most convenient to share the entire CD, starting from the root directory, specifying read-only access. This allows you to change discs in the CD player without having to reset the MacFile volume sharing.)

SFM Printer Support

As mentioned above, SFM provide *Postscript emulation*, so that Macintosh users can take advantage of non-Postscript printers (such as the HP LaserJet), and also makes Macintosh printers accessible to PCs. SFM does this by exploiting the Windows NT Print Manager (and the associated print spooler) along with performing a little trick called "capturing" the Macintosh printers.

To understand how capturing works, you need to be aware that Macintosh printers are usually connected to the *AppleTalk Network* rather than to any particular Macintosh.[15] They're *Network Printers* in much the same sense as HP's LaserJet IIIs (which contains its own Ethernet card) is.

By capturing LaserWriter printers, Windows NT Server ensures that the administrator has control of all print jobs dispatched to that printer. It accepts jobs from only the Server (which in turn makes a *logical* printer available to both Macintosh and PC users). This setup has the additional benefit of avoiding the "Laserprep Wars" that can result from incompatible versions of the LaserWriter print drivers on Macintoshes attempting to access the same printer. Instead, Windows NT sends its own LaserPrep code with each print job.

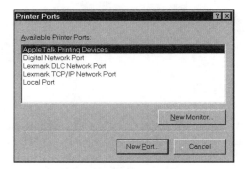

FIGURE 8.8 Printer ports dialog box. This dialog box, from the NT Server 4.0 Add Printer Wizard, allows AppleTalk network Printer support to be added as a class of NT printer port.

---

15 We are referring here to Apple's LaserWriter (and compatible) printers, not the various dot-matrix printers made by Apple.

Of course, using PC printers with Windows NT Server doesn't necessarily involve any form of capture because the printer is connected directly to the print server (or at least controlled by it). DLC printers *are* captured, in exactly the same way as Macintosh printers.

To set up an SFM printer on your Windows NT Server:

1. Select Add Printer from the Printers folder (Start/Settings/Printers). The Add Printer Wizard appears.

2. If you are installing a new printer locally *or connecting to an AppleTalk network printer,* select the My Computer radio button. If you are connecting to a non-AppleTalk print server, select the Network Print Server button and skip ahead to step 6. Then click the Next button.

3. If you are using a non-AppleTalk printer, skip ahead to step 5. For a LaserWriter (or other AppleTalk printer), press the Add Port button. This will present a Printer Ports dialog box (see Figure 8.8), from which you can select AppleTalk Printing Devices. Then click the New Port button.

4. Assuming you are connecting to an AppleTalk printer, you're now presented with an Available AppleTalk Printing Devices dialog box (see Figure 8.9). Select the Zone and printer from this list, and click OK.

5. If you selected My Computer in step 2, you will see a list of local printer ports. Select the one to which your printer is connected. You can also Enable Printer Pooling, which has the effect of making several physical printers appear as a single print queue. After you are satisfied with your port settings, click the Next button and skip to step 7.

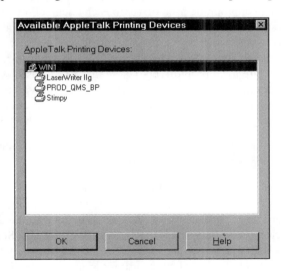

FIGURE 8.9 Available AppleTalk printing devices dialog box. This dialog lets an administrator designate an AppleTalk printer to capture.

6. If you selected Network Print Server in step 2, you will see a Connect to Printer dialog box. Browse the network, find the printer you want to connect to, and select it. Then click the OK button. If you are connecting to an NT print server, and it has a compatible print driver installed, this will complete your installation. You'll get a "successfully installed" message and can just click the Finish button. Otherwise, you must install a print driver.

7. To install a print driver, pick the manufacturer and model of your printer from the list. If your printer isn't listed, try one of the generic models or get an NT 4.0 print driver diskette from your print manufacturer (NT 3.x print drivers are not compatible with NT 4.0). When you have the correct make and model specified, click the Next button.

8. Type in a name for your printer (NT will create a name using the make and model by default). Although you can type in a long (up to 32 characters), descriptive name that will work with NT, Windows 95, and Macintosh clients, DOS and Windows 3.x clients will only be able to work with printers that have DOS-style 8.3 (eight-character name plus three-character extension) names. You can also specify whether this printer is to be used as the default for all Windows applications on your system by using the Yes and No radio buttons. When you are satisfied with the printer name and default settings, click the Next button.

9. The Add Printer Wizard asks if you want to share the printer and if so, asks you to designate the shared name for the printer. As with the local print name set in step 6, older DOS and Windows applications will work best with a short (8.3) name.

10. If you are sharing the printer, the Add Printer Wizard asks you to designate all the client operating systems that will be accessing the printer. By doing so, you enable your NT print server to download an appropriate print driver to each client, eliminating the need for local print drivers and significantly easing the most common administration problem encountered in network printing, which is improper drivers loaded at the client. Windows NT 3.1, 3.5/3.51, and 4.0 are supported using this method, as is Windows 95. (DOS, Windows 3.x, and OS/2 clients require local print drivers.) Note that RISC-based NT systems use different print drivers from Intel-based systems. In an environment with a mix of both Intel and RISC systems, you must load multiple drivers even if all clients are running NT 4.0. When you have all necessary client operating systems selected, click the Next button.

11. The Add Printer Wizard offers to print a test page. Doing so is not absolutely required, but is an exceedingly good idea. Then click the Finish button.

12. The printer should now be available to PC clients in the usual way. To make it available to Mac clients, one further step is needed: a user account for Mac printers must be created (do this with User Manager in the usual way). Once you've created the account, start Control Panel/Services, select Print Server for Macintosh, and click the Startup button. A Print Server for Macintosh dialog box will appear. Click the This Account radio button, and type in a user account name (and optional password) for Mac print jobs. Then click OK. You can now control whether Macintosh users have permission to use the printer with the Security tab of the Properties dialog for the printer in question.

Accessing SFM Volumes and Printers from Macintosh Clients

Before a Macintosh client can access an SFM volume, it must log in to the server in question using the Macintosh Chooser. Click the AppleShare icon, then the Zone where the server is located. This will present a list of file servers, from which the Mac user selects the name of the Server.

At this point a Connect to the File Server... dialog box appears. If Guest access has been enabled on the Server, the Guest button can be clicked. Otherwise, the Registered User button must be clicked, requiring the entry of a valid Windows NT username and password.[16]

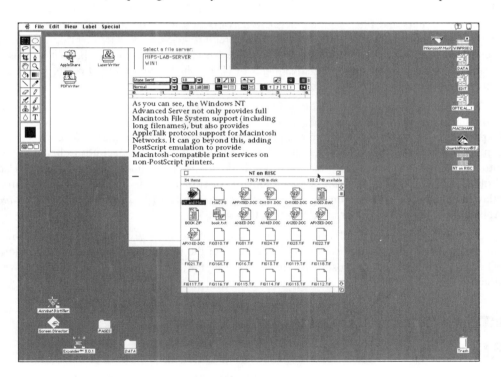

FIGURE 8.10 Macintosh access to NTServer 4.0. Macintosh users "see" NT Server files and directories as icons and folders on the Macintosh desktop.

---

16 Here we run into a security problem. Appleshare passwords are sent in cleartext over the network, which violates Windows NT's C2 security standards. All is not lost, however. Microsoft provides an alternate Microsoft UAM sign-on with password encryption. Its installation is detailed in the *Windows NT Server—Services for Macintosh* manual that's included with Windows NT Server full packaging.

Once this is done, a list of available volumes is presented, and the Mac user can mount one by selecting it and clicking the OK button, at which point an icon appears on the Mac desktop that represents the shared volume. The Mac user then accesses this icon in the usual way (see Figure 8.10) Macintosh workstations access Windows NT Server printers (including captured AppleTalk printers) through Chooser in exactly the way they use any other AppleTalk printer.

A Final Word About SFM

In summary, SFM is one of Windows NT Servers' best-implemented features. By simply installing SFM and configuring it properly, you can provide full file-and-printer sharing to Macintosh clients, while giving Windows NT, Windows, OS/2, and DOS clients access to the very same printers and files. To the enterprise network administrator, this represents a significant advantage over other network servers, which require add-on software or bridging to connect Macs and PCs to the same directories. The Windows NT Server approach to this is completely seamless, leverages the advantages of NTFS (including excellent performance and fault tolerance), and is extremely easy to set up.

Unfortunately, there are limitations. One of the most serious is that RAS *still* doesn't support AppleTalk. MS-Mail can support Macintosh clients, but the necessary client software must be purchased separately (you'll also need an MS-Mail Upgrade Kit because Mac clients aren't compatible with the Workgroup version of mail bundled with NT). Macintosh clients logged into a Windows NT Server also do not execute login scripts and cannot take advantage of User Profiles, nor can they participate in inter-domain trust relationships or "see" resources from other Windows NT systems (unless those systems also run SFM and have access to the *same* AppleTalk or AppleTalk/Ethernet network as the clients).

However, SFM is by far the *cleanest* approach we've seen for giving Macs and PCs simultaneous access to the same files. We consider it one of the best reasons for buying a Windows NT Server and hope that Microsoft will improve the support for Macintosh clients in future versions of Windows NT.[17]

Enterprise Connectivity Two: Electronic Mail

The most general method of connecting the LANs that make up an enterprise network is to connect them via one form or another of wide-area networking link or through an enterprise backbone. However, as we will see when we begin discussing WANs, the assumption that one can

---

17 We suppose it's too much to hope that Microsoft will exploit the SFM technology to give Windows NT *native* access to AppleTalk. That's a pity. It's completely routable yet avoids the incomprehensible addressing problems of TCP/IP. An optional native AppleTalk capability for both Windows NT *and* Advanced Server would go far toward making the dream of Mac-like plug-and-play connectivity a reality for PCs.

simply extend a network connection across low-data-rate media and get tolerable results is often false. Wide-area networking links are orders of magnitude slower than local Ethernet networks, slower still by comparison with, say, FDDI backbones. They're also expensive. In WANs you must pay for use of the wire rather than get (essentially) free use of the wire, once you've paid for installation, as is true of LANs.

Therefore, the least expensive and most flexible way to connect people in an enterprise system is often electronic mail (e-mail), which has the following advantages:

- Low-cost wide-area connections are possible by modem.

- Disparate systems can be connected with gateways.

- Connections are *asynchronous*. They don't require continuously operating links.

Windows NT includes built-in e-mail, which we discussed in Chapter 4. Unfortunately, the built-in e-mail that's included is not suited to enterprise use. It's a Windows for Workgroups-style *workgroup postoffice,* which cannot be connected to other postoffices, the key requirement for enterprise systems.

As we saw in Chapter 4, the postoffice is the basic building block of Microsoft Mail (which is included with Windows NT—though it's called *Windows Messaging*). It's the central storage point for messages, which are communicated between the postoffice and the clients. To create an enterprise mail system, you need a capability to *forward* messages between postoffices, along with some sort of *directory*, so that postoffices know what to do with messages intended for users outside the local postoffice. The workgroup postoffice built into Windows NT lacks this *store-and-forward* capability, but you can get it by upgrading to a full Microsoft Exchange Server postoffice.

Microsoft Exchange Server

In earlier editions of this book, we presented instructions at this point for upgrading from NT's workgroup postoffice to an MS-Mail 3.x postoffice—but there is now a significantly better alternative: Microsoft's Exchange Server (formerly called Enterprise Messaging Server, aka EMS).

With Exchange Server, Microsoft has moved from a simple shared-file mail architecture to a true client/server messaging system, which (to repeat what we said in the first edition) "will be NT-based, graphically administered, x.400/500 'standards'-based, and network-independent... Since EMS will be MS-Mail 3.2-compatible, gateways built to the current MS-Mail File API (FAPI) and clients written to the Messaging API (MAPI) will work with it too—and a new Gateway API (GAPI?) will make it easier to 'roll your own' solutions for special e-mail problems …"

All of our above expectations, we're delighted to report, are now true. Exchange Server really is a huge improvement over its predecessor, which leaves us with one problem: how do you get there from the Windows Messaging postoffice that comes with NT (or MS-Mail 3.x, if you've already upgraded to that)?

Upgrading to MS Exchange 4.0

Exchange Server Fortunately, Exchange Server 4.0 was designed from the outset to provide a clean migration from MS-Mail 3.*x* (and the 3.*x*-derived NT workgroup postoffice). Just install it according to the setup instructions.

> *Note: It is mandatory that you install Exchange Service Pack 2 or higher. Earlier versions do not understand the NT workgroup postoffice file structures.*

Exchange Server setup automatically migrates user accounts (which become NT user accounts on the Exchange Server, which should ideally be a BDC; accounts thus created will be automatically replicated throughout the domain), messages, and address books. It's a very straightforward process.

> *Note: This process is not reversible. If you migrate users to Exchange Server and then attempt to roll them back to MS-Mail 3.x or NT Workgroup messaging, access to messages will be lost. Migrating users to Exchange is a one-way process.*

The Exchange Client Although MS Exchange 4.0 must be upgraded to Service Pack 2 on the server, any available release of MS Exchange 4.0's client software will work. We do recommend upgrading to the most recent Service Pack because the original release has known bugs and executes much more slowly.

If you've been using the Windows Messaging Client for either peer-to-peer or MS Mail 3.*x*, the MS Exchange client software will examine your computer for pre-existing MS messaging client software and use the settings that it finds—thus preserving your personal address book and preferences. It will also migrate message files to the new PST format.

Installation

To install the MS Exchange client software:

1. Start the Exchange SETUP.EXE program (see Figure 8.11) from its distribution CD (or equivalent network resource).

2. When Setup finds the current settings for Windows Messaging client, choose the Next button.

3. Setup will also find any Global or Personal address book and convert it for use by Exchange.

4. Setup will then locate the message file that contains your prior mail and import it and any folders from the Windows Messaging Client into Exchange.

The MS Exchange client won't be able to display the updated personal folders and mail contents until MS Exchange Setup is completed. If the workstation onto which Exchange is being installed is a portable or notebook PC, it's a good idea to immediately make an off-line storage file. Start the Exchange Client, and:

1. Highlight the Personal Folder that was created, then select File/Properties.

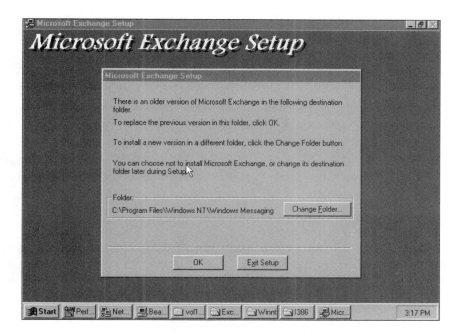

FIGURE 8.11 Exchange Server setup. It's possible to upgrade from NT Server's built-in "Windows Messaging" e-mail to Microsoft's Exchange Server during the Exchange setup process.

2. Click the Synchronization tab and press the Offline button.

3. A wizard starts that says that it can't find the Offline storage file, and asks you if you want to create one. You can choose the default file and path or substitute your choice of a file and path, as long as the file extension ends with .OST

Off-line use of the MS Exchange Client will then update the Exchange Server the next time you connect to it.

Compatibility Issue for MS-Mail 3.x Users

Although the migration process on both server and client is relatively straightforward, it isn't entirely trouble free. Problems with the Exchange Client include inability to connect using existing MS Mail Remote protocols by modem (remote mail in Exchange is accomplished through RAS/Dial-Up Networking), one-way conversion of mail files from the MS Mail 3.x format to Exchange format (making it impossible to revert if the Exchange client won't do what's expected), and incompatible attachment formats.

Microsoft has also distributed a white paper on migration from MS-Mail 3.x to Exchange, reporting the following:

- Mail 3.x clients are incompatible with Exchange servers.

- For compatibility, all message text from Exchange clients to foreign mail systems (including Mail 3.x) must be sent *twice*: once in Rich Text Format (RTF) and once as plain text for mail clients that do not understand RTF.[18]

- For *complete* compatibility in mixed Exchange and MS-Mail 3.x networks, binary attachments must be sent *twice*: as OLE 1.0 attachments for older clients and as OLE 2.0 attachments for the new ones.

Against all that, Exchange *does* offer powerful inducements. In particular, it offers the standards-based X.400/500 messaging mentioned earlier and a built-in UNIX-compatible SMTP gateway.

Other Mail Systems

Of course, if you're working for a corporation that's standardized on another mail system—UNIX Simple Mail Transfer Protocol (SMTP) or cc:Mail, for instance—the preceding discussion will have struck you as weird. Couldn't we just ignore MS-Mail, and substitute another mail system instead?

In principle, the answer is yes, provided, of course, that the necessary software runs under Windows NT. Because most such software is DOS- or Windows 3.x-based, it will probably work under Windows NT (and cc:Mail, at least, is planning to support Windows NT as a client platform directly, although the software was not available as this was written). Users of such e-mail systems may want to investigate running their existing client software on Windows NT.

RAS: Windows NT's Built-in WAN

LANs are fine for local connections, and e-mail can help with certain kinds of connections at any distance, but there comes a point when you need direct connection and you can't find (or buy) a long enough wire. That's when you must resort to *wide-area networking*, in which LAN-style connections are extended across phone company lines and other elements of the larger telecommunications system. Uniquely among today's operating systems, Windows NT comes with a limited-use WAN built in. It's called *remote access services* (RAS).

In NT 3.1, RAS was a *NetBIOS router* using a proprietary asynchronous extension of Microsoft's NetBEUI protocol. In NT 3.5 (and later versions) this was extended to a protocol-independent routing over Point-to-Point Protocol (PPP).[19] In effect, it takes the network

---

18 Ironically, *this* is a solvable problem. The issue with binary attachments is something of a necessary evil, but sending all the message text twice is ridiculous!

19 Microsoft's proprietary AsyBEUI protocol continues to be supported for backward compatibility, and Serial Link Internet Protocol (SLIP) is now supported as an alternative to PPP for TCP/IP networks. The change in RAS between NT versions 3.1 and 3.5 was nothing short of astonishing!

connections of the *RAS Server* (the machine on which RAS dial-in services are running) and extends them over a WAN connection to the *RAS Client* (a machine that's connecting to the RAS server using RAS client software).

Two different RAS servers are provided: a single-user version with NT Workstation, and a multi-user version with NT Server (the client software, which from NT 4.0 on is called *Dial Up Networking* for consistency with Windows 95, is the same in either case). Both NT Workstation and Server can function as RAS clients. A local user logged into the system console can connect over the WAN to another RAS server. The single-user RAS Server provided with Windows NT Workstation allows one user at a time to access the Windows NT system remotely over the WAN, while the Windows NT Server version supports multiple[20] users logged in at one time.

Both versions of RAS are installed from Control Panel/Network's Services tab, using a procedure that we'll examine shortly. First, there are some things you need to know about the different kinds of WANs that RAS can support.

Modems

The first, and least expensive, option is connecting by an asynchronous modulator/demodulator (modem). Widely available today are modems that will work at data rates up to 48Kbps, which is actually faster than most telephone systems can handle. The maximum data rate available on standard phone lines that are digitally switched (most offices) is currently 28.8Kbps (some older systems are limited to 9.6Kbps).

RAS works well with modems, although given the limitation of the low data rate, the resulting connection is useful mostly for transferring data files or administrative information on an intermittent basis. The major issues of concern in using modems with RAS are:

- Get fully compatible modems, preferably identical ones, at both ends of the link.

- Get modems that work *symmetrically*. Some older high-speed modems use a low-data-rate *back channel* for receiving that can be overwhelmed by RAS traffic (modern V.32 and V.32bis modems don't have this problem).

- Get modems that are compatible with Windows NT, for which the Windows NT Hardware Compatibility List[21] is indispensable.

Because modems can be used with normal telephone lines, you need only pay the usual telephone company connect charges for use of the line, which makes this approach by far the most economical if you don't require continuous high-speed connection. If you do, one of the other choices will probably suit you best.

---

20 NT Server 3.1 supported up to 64 users. NT Server 3.5 and 3.51 support up to 256, assuming you can come up with that many ports!

21 Available online at Microsoft's Web site (www.microsoft.com), as well as in the Microsoft Windows NT documentation.

RS-232 Null Modem–NT's "Zero-Slot" LAN

One interesting way to use RAS isn't really *wide*-area networking at all. If you replace the modem used for asynchronous communication with a widely available RS-232 *null-modem* cable, you get a wired connection good for speeds up to 115,000 baud (about 10% of Ethernet) that *doesn't require a network card*. This kind of approach can be useful in several situations. For one thing, given the fact that all Windows NT systems (not just Servers) can use RAS to support one user at a time, it makes a very convenient way to connect a portable computer running the DOS-based (LAN Manager) or Windows for Workgroups version of RAS.

Another possible application for RAS with null modem cable would be to provide a low-cost "zero-slot" LAN connections for up to 256 users on a Windows NT Server (with a Multiport RS-232 card installed, as explained below). Given the low cost of Ethernet cards and cable today, this probably won't be a common solution, but many sites have *miles* of serial cable left in the walls and ceilings from the 1970s and 1980s when connecting terminals to host mainframes was common. Multi-user RAS on Windows NT Server offers an effective way to reuse that cable where full Ethernet data rates aren't required.

Multiport RS-232 Cards

Windows NT Server can support multiple simultaneous remote WAN users on RAS, as mentioned earlier. Of course, it can't do this with just the communication ports built into most PCs. If more ports are needed, the solution is a multiport serial communications (RS-232) board.

Multiport boards include their own coprocessors and memory, eliminating the need for the main CPU to oversee all communications between the system and the outside world. You can use a multiport board to connect Windows NT RAS with modems or (using a *null-modem cable* as mentioned above) as a zero-slot LAN for local systems.

In any case, the vital issue in selecting a multiport board for Windows NT is to get one for which a Windows NT driver is available. Check the Windows NT hardware compatibility list before buying.

X.25 Links

If asynchronous modem data rates (14,400 baud) aren't sufficient, or if users spend so much time connected that long-distance telephone bills become a major expense, consider an *X.25 packet-switching network*. X.25 is a communications standard for digital switching of customer data over long distances. It provides data rates as high as 56Kbps or can multiplex many low-data-rate connections together into a single high-speed connection. There are two ways that Windows NT can use X.25: directly, through a *smart card*; or indirectly, through a Packet Assembler-Disassembler[22] (PAD).

---

22 Incorrectly called a *Peripheral Access Device* in Microsoft's documentation.

PADs are generally used for client connections and usually connect to a standard asynchronous modem, making it possible for remote clients to dial into a PAD, but have their data transmitted over the X.25 packet switch to the server, which can use either a PAD or a smart card. Because modem connections to PADs are limited to the usual data rates for asynchronous communication, you might think this is a waste of time, but it isn't.

To understand why, consider what's involved in connecting five remote users to a RAS server using conventional modems. Each user requires a modem and telephone line, and the server will need five modems (and a multiport serial card, described below). The total investment in equipment alone will run into the thousands of dollars, and if the phone lines get a lot of use (and remember that they're limited to just a few percent of Ethernet data rates, so things will happen slowly) the connection charges, especially if they're long-distance, will become quite a burden.

By using X.25, you can save money in this situation. The server gets a single X.25 smart card, and a leased line from the local telephone company connects it to an X.25 provider (such as Tyment, Sprintnet, or Telnet). Client systems connect to the server by modem, making a local telephone call to the X.25 provider's PAD in their area. The cost will be lower (*if* the system is heavily used), because the hourly charge by the X.25 provider is typically much less than that from the telephone company; and the line conditions are better (so the connection is more reliable).

For Windows NT clients, there's another advantage to X.25. By using a smart card at both ends of the connection, you can get much higher data rates (typically 56KBps) than from modems. For applications that require such data rates (and use of RAS for more than intermittent copying of small data files certainly qualifies!), these data rates can be not just convenient, but *essential*.

ISDN

The final option for using Windows NT RAS is *integrated services digital networking* (ISDN). In contrast to X.25 and standard telephone lines, ISDN was designed from the beginning for computer use and provides throughput as high as 128Kbps.[23] By comparison with X.25, ISDN is generally cheaper (at the maximum data rate) and gives higher throughput. It's almost certainly a better choice for remote clients who need high-speed connections. On the other hand, X.25 PADs offer great flexibility. A server with an X.25 smartcard installed can support a single high-speed client (itself connected with a smartcard) or a number of low-speed clients (using dial-in PADs). ISDN is also limited to the larger metropolitan areas, and is not generally available overseas.

Companies that make multiport boards, X.25 smartcards, and ISDN interfaces for use with Windows NT RAS include those listed in Table 8.1.

---

[23] ISDN typically provides two channels, providing a maximum of 64Kbps each. RAS supports using both channels at once, but be aware that most providers will bill for each channel separately.

Table 8.1 RAS Hardware

Vendor	Address	Telephone Number	NT Products
Comtrol Corp. www.comtrol.com	900 Long Lake Rd Saint Paul, MN 55112	(800) 926-6876 (612) 631-7654	Multiport Controllers
Consensys www.consensys.com	1301 Pat Booker Rd. Universal City, TX 78148	(905) 940-2900	Multiport Controllers
Digi International www.digiboard.com	11001 Bren Road E. Minnetonka, MN 55343	(800) 344-4273 (612) 912-3444	Multiport Controllers, ISDN cards
Eicon Technologies www.eicon.com	14755 Preston Rd. Suite 620 Dallas, TX 75240	(214) 239-3270	X.25 smartcards, ISDN cards, and multiport controllers
Equinox www.equinox.com	One Equinox Way Sunrise, FL 33351	(800) 275-3500 (954) 746-9000	Multiport Controllers
Link Technology Inc. www.linkisdn.inter.net	23 Crescent Dr. Holland, PA 18966	(215) 357-3354	ISDN Basic Rate and Multilink Adapters
Motorola Information Systems Group www.mot.com/mims/isg	20 Cabot Blvd. Mansfield, MA 02048-1193	(508) 261-4000	ISDN Modems
US Robotics www.usr.com	U.S. Robotics 8100 N. McCormick Blvd. Skokie, IL 60076	(800) 342-5877 (847) 982-5010	ISDN Modems
Xircom Inc. www.xircom.com	2300 Corporate Center Dr. Thousand Oaks, CA 91320-1420	(800) 438-4526 (805) 376-9300	Multiport Modem Boards

For more information on this topic, browse http://altavista.digital.com, select Advanced Search, and search for RAS near Hardware near "Windows NT" (if you're interested in a specific type of hardware, you might want to add that as well, ie: near ISDN or near x.25).

Installing Windows NT Remote Access Services

Now that we've looked into the various WAN options that RAS supports, let's see how it all works out in practice. To install the RAS server:

1. Start the Windows NT Control Panel and select the Network icon's Services tab.

2. Click the Add… button and select Remote Access Service from the list, then press OK. You will be asked to type a path for the NT distribution files. Once you've entered the path, Remote Access Service Setup copies the necessary files to your hard disk.

3. The Add RAS device appears (Figure 8.12). It may include a predetected device. If not, click the Install Modem[24] or Install X.25 PAD button. The former starts the Add Modem wizard, and the latter asks you to associate a COM port with an X.25 PAD driver. When your device is selected, press OK.

4. The Remote Access Setup dialog box appears. Click the Configure… button to bring up the Configure Port Usage dialog, which allows you to set whether RAS is used for dial-out only (the default for NT Workstation), dial-in only (the default for NT Server), or both. Click OK to return to the Remote Access Setup dialog box.

5. Click the Network… button to bring up the Network Configuration dialog box (Figure 8.13), which allows you to select the protocols that will be used for dial-out and dial-in. When you are satisfied with the setup, click the OK button. Note that protocol support for outgoing and incoming calls is completely separate. You can, for instance, arrange to dial out using only TCP/IP, but receive calls only on IPX. This dialog also allows you to control the authentication method used, with options varying from Allow Any Authentication, which is useful if you are

FIGURE 8.12 Add RAS devices. NT Remote Access Service requires selection of a communications device (modem, X.25 PAD, etc.) for operation. Use this dialog box.

---

24 Note that ISDN *modems* and null modem cable are considered modem types in NT 4.0, unlike in past versions in which all ISDN devices were treated as a special class of network adapter card. Multiport adaptors, X.25 SmartCards, and certain ISDN devices are still treated that way. All are installed from Control Panel/Network's Adapters tab.

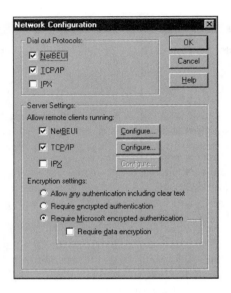

FIGURE 8.13 Network Configuration dialog (RAS). The network protocols that are transported over RAS and the way communication is authenticated are controlled from this dialog box.

setting up a RAS server that will be dialed into by a variety of clients. To Require Microsoft Encrypted Authentication, which provides the highest level of security, you may also select the Require Data Encryption check box, in which case data transported over RAS will be encrypted. Once you have selected the appropriate protocols and authentication, click OK.

6. For each selected Server Protocol, RAS will display a Server Configuration dialog box, the most complex of which is the one for TCP/IP (see Figure 8.14). At this point, you can determine whether dial-in clients have access to the entire network (default for NT Server) or just the local computer (default for NT Workstation). You will also need to make some protocol-specific settings. For TCP/IP, decide whether IP addresses are determined by DHCP (assuming, of course, DHCP is enabled on your LAN—see Chapter 6) or a static address pool is used. For IPX, determine how IPX network numbers and node numbers are assigned (online help is available to explain the various options). When you are satisfied with the protocol configuration, click the OK button to return to Remote Access Setup dialog. Click Continue to complete the setup.

7. Setup adds a Dial-Up Networking item to the Start menu's Programs/Accessories folder, and a Remote Access Administration creates a Remote Access Admin item in the Programs/Administrative Tools folder. You will use these items to run RAS after it's installed. Setup then informs you that RAS has been installed and suggests that you configure it using the Remote Access Administration program. Click OK to complete the setup, and then Close the Network Control Panel. A binding analysis will be performed, and

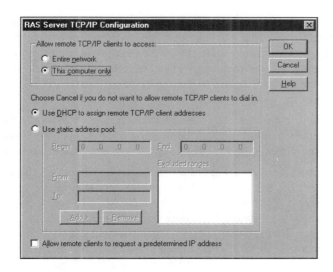

FIGURE 8.14 TCP/IP Configuration dialog (RAS). TCP/IP configuration for Remote Access is controlled from this dialog box. Similar dialogs allow configuring NetBEUI and NWLink IPX for remote operation.

depending on the options selected, one or more configuration dialogs may appear. When Network Setup is complete, you will be prompted to restart the computer. Do so.

Using RAS

Once RAS is installed, it's necessary to configure it using the Remote Access Admin program (see Figure 8.15) from the Start menu's Programs/Administrative Tools folder. You can start RAS using the Server/Start Remote Access menu (or start it from Control Panel/Services).

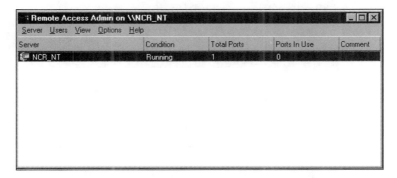

FIGURE 8.15 Remote Access Admin. Administrators control access to Remote Access Services (and settings such as dial-back) from NT Server's Remote Access Administration program.

Users/Permissions allows you to grant or revoke remote access permissions to any user of the server and to specify whether a *call-back* option is specified for any caller. Call-back is both a convenience and a security mechanism. It's convenient because the *set by caller* option lets remote users dial the RAS server then hang up and have the RAS server call them, which puts the burden of telephone connect charges on the server rather than the client. For people who will use RAS from home or the road, this can be a great convenience.

As a security feature, the *Preset To Call-back* option ensures that only authorized personnel connect, by hanging up on dial-in and then calling back to a preset number. This makes it practically impossible to hack RAS (unless the hacker has physical access to a RAS client).

With access permissions granted and dial-back set, you can access the system from other Windows NT, Windows, or DOS systems that support a remote-access client. To do so, install RAS on the client system and then select Dial-Up Networking (see Figure 8.16) from the Start menu's Programs/Accessories folder (this differs from NT 3.*x*, in which the program was called Remote Access and could be found in a special Remote Access Group in Program Manager). The first time this is done, you will be prompted to add an entry, which you can do using the New... toolbar button. This brings up a New Phonebook Entry Wizard that walks you step by step through adding an entry name, phone number, and description. You designate whether or not RAS is to log in using the user's current user name and password (if not, you will be prompted for the user name and password when RAS makes a connection).

If the default modem settings (entered when RAS is installed) are to be used, this is all that's required, and you can click the OK button to complete creation of the entry and then click the Dial button to initiate a connection. However, if a non-standard setting is to be used (modem connection on a system on which ISDN is the default RAS connection type, for instance) or a

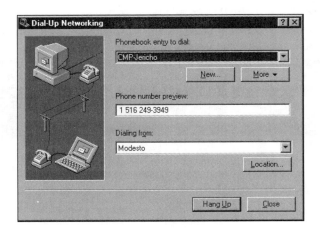

FIGURE 8.16 Dial-Up Networking. Remote users access NT Workstation (or Server) Remote Access Services through the Dial-Up Networking item in the Start menu's Accessories folder.

different port is to be used (outgoing dial through a single modem on COM1 while incoming calls are handled by a multiport board, for instance), you may need to edit the entry thus created. Do this from the Dial-Up Networking dialog's More button, and select Edit entry and modem properties from the resulting drop-down list.

You will see the Edit Phonebook Entry dialog (Figure 8.17), which allows you to designate the specific type of connection (PPP or SLIP, script, security settings, etc.) associated with this phone book entry. Again, when the entry is complete, the OK button returns you to the main Remote Access screen, from which you can initiate a RAS connections (using the Dial button), terminate it (with the Hang Up button), or designate the Location from which you're dialing (which controls whether dialing uses a prefix to reach an outside line).

When a connection is initiated (with the Dial button), the RAS client initializes the modem (or other connecting device), dials out (or performs the other steps necessary to make the connection), and waits for a response from the RAS server. The server and client then exchange user name and password information. (Note that when it is used with an NT RAS server, the password is not transmitted in cleartext. Instead, a hashed password is sent, which is based on an encryption scheme.) At this point, you're prompted for a user name and password. Assuming that the user name and security identifier match at both ends, the connection completes, and you have a complete network connection between the client and server (and a gateway to the rest of your network, if the server has been configured to permit access to the entire network).

Several things can go wrong with this process. In particular, if you haven't properly configured the RAS client or server for the modems it's using, or if the modems do not match (especially on high-speed connections), you're likely to get a message that RAS failed to authenticate. Our experience with this situation is that you should drop both the server and client back to a known connection state (we've found the Hayes-compatible 9600 baud setting

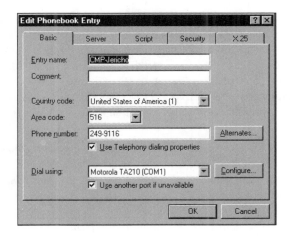

FIGURE 8.17 Edit Phonebook entry. Information about locations to be dialed is entered (or changed) with this dialog box.

to work for most modems), and try again. If it still doesn't work, check the configuration settings for RAS at both ends, check that the user who's attempting to dial in has in fact been granted remote access permissions at the RAS server, check for RAS-related error messages using the Windows NT Event Log (note that login errors will often show up in the *Security* log), and refer to the RAS documentation included with Windows NT for further suggestions.

RAS on the Internet

Because RAS supports PPP and SLIP protocols for TCP/IP networks—and TCP/IP is the core protocol for the Internet—it's possible to connect NT systems to the Internet using RAS. How this is done varies depending primarily on whether you're interested in using RAS on NT as a platform for Internet *client* software, such as ftp or Mosaic, or want to use RAS to create an Internet *gateway* (sometimes called a *node*) using NT Server.

To connect NT Workstation (or Server) to the Internet as a client, you must set up RAS with TCP/IP and arrange an account with a local Internet service provider (ISP). Providers are local Internet hosts that provide access (typically via dial-up modem lines) for a fee. Microsoft provides a list of providers in a *Remote Access and the Internet* helpfile that's installed with Windows NT Remote Access.[25] You'll need to arrange for an account that provides PPP or SLIP access and configure RAS to use that access. You'll probably also need to enable DNS support in your TCP/IP configuration, designating the provider's host system as your DNS server, and depending on how your provider works, you may need to designate a static IP address given to you by the provider.[26] You'll also need to set an appropriate security authentication mode (typically Accept Any Authentication) as specified by your provider.

If your provider supports PPP with Line Control Protocol (LCP) extensions, connection should be completely automatic, once everything is properly configured. If your provider requires SLIP or uses a non-LCP PPP implementation, you may have to type commands in a terminal window to complete the login sequence. Do this using the Edit Phonebook Entry dialog's Script and Security tabs. Select "Pop up a terminal window" in the former and "Accept any authentication including clear text" in the latter. (It may also be possible to automate this by entering the login commands in a \WINNT\SYSTEM32\RAS\SWITCH.INF file. Consult the *Remote Access and the Internet* helpfile Microsoft supplies with Windows NT RAS for more information.)

Using NT Server RAS to provide an Internet *gateway* is somewhat more complex. See "Making the Internet Connection" in Chapter 7 for bandwidth considerations. Also be sure to read the "Security" section of Chapter 7 and consult volume 2 of the *Windows NT Resource Kit* before attempting such an installation.

---

25 Another good source is Paul Gilster's book *The Internet Navigator,* listed in "For More Information" at the end of this chapter.

26 This is less common than it used to be. Most ISPs these days support dynamic setting of both IP and DNS Server addresses at connect time.

PPTP

Beginning with NT 4.0, RAS has been extended to support Point-to-Point Tunneling Protocol (PPTP). As described in Chapter 6 and Appendix 2, PPTP works by "wrapping" packets using a variant of PPP. Those packets are then transported over TCP/IP, unwrapped by the receiver, and transported on the LAN. Because PPP is transport-independent, any type of packet may be transported. The resulting connection between machines connected with PPTP is called a "virtual private network" because although it uses a public transport (TCP/IP), the PPTP packets are private (and may be encrypted).

Applications for PPTP Applications for PPTP are many and varied. A short list of the more obvious ones includes:

- Providing a mechanism for secure communication over the Internet (see for example, the section on Web-based Administration below).

- Using the Internet as a replacement for a PSTN[27] (Public Switched Telephone Network) as a RAS backbone, even for non-IP packets.

- Providing secure (encrypted) communications over in-house IP LANs. (Again, the Web-based Administration tool for NT Server is a good example.)

There are undoubtedly other applications. At this writing PPTP is so new that all the possible uses for it are not completely understood. In general, however, PPTP provides two vital capabilities: transporting non-IP packets over the Internet (and other IP networks), and providing security on public networks. For these reasons, it's an extremely powerful addition to the general capabilities of RAS.

Installing PPTP Install PPTP as a transport protocol: Open Control Panel/Network, select the Protocols tab, click the Add button, and select Point To Point Tunneling Protocol from the list. A PPTP Configuration dialog will appear (Figure 8.18), with which you specify the number of Virtual Private Networks (i.e., PPTP connections) supported by this system. By default this will be one. Servers that will use PPTP for more than simple administrative connections will require more. Then click OK.

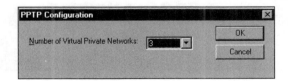

FIGURE 8.18 PPTP Configuration. The number of Virtual Private Network (VPN) connections to be supported by a RAS server running PPTP is entered via this dialog box.

---

27 For example, AT&T, MCI, Sprint—your local and long distance telephone carrier.

Once the PPTP Protocol is installed, RAS must be configured (indeed, if you install PPTP on a system that does not have RAS installed, it will be added automatically) for PPTP connections using Control Panel/Network's Services tab. Select Remote Access Services, and press the Properties button. The Remote Access Setup dialog shown earlier will appear. Press the Add button, and select VPN1, RASPPTPM from the list. Once it's added, it's configured like any other RAS port. You can set it to only receive calls, dial out, or both, and control which network protocols it supports. Also (very important!), you can determine whether it requires encryption.

This completes PPTP installation on the server. Just start the RAS Server using the Remote Access Admin tool.[28] On the client, add a phone book entry as described earlier, but pick Dial Using VPN1, RASPPTPM. When you dial that entry, type the IP address for the server running RAS with PPTP instead of a telephone number (see Figure 8.19).

On systems using RAS to connect to the Internet, you'll dial twice: the first time to your ISP (using a regular telephone number) and once that connection is established, to the PPTP server (using its IP address).

Advanced Uses of RAS

Besides providing interactive WAN connections for end users, RAS can be invaluable to administrators. As mentioned earlier in this chapter, using Windows NT Servers at remote locations invariably requires some sort of connection between servers to exchange user account information (and other replicated data). RAS is ideal for this, provided you can live with the available data rates.

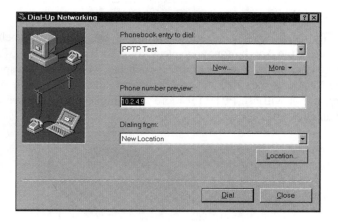

FIGURE 8.19 Dialing a PPTP Server. Client systems connect to PPTP servers in the usual way—except that an IP address instead of a telephone number is entered.

---

28 An alternative is to dedicate a network card to PPTP connections, as described in Chapter 6. This is a less general approach that will be of use only on systems with a dedicated connection to the Internet (or local IP net).

The key to using RAS *economically* for administrative connections is to have it connect only at preset times of the day—typically when the telephone (or other connection) charges are low, say between midnight and 4:00 a.m. You can do this by exploiting the fact that RAS is implemented as a Windows NT *service*, which can be started and stopped using either the Service Control Manager application in the Windows NT control panel or the *net start remoteaccess* command-line syntax from a command prompt or scriptfile. You can dial from the command-line using the *rasdial* command (type "rasdial /?" at an NT command prompt for more information). Because you can also start and stop the replicator service using *net start* and *net stop*, we have the makings for a completely effective periodic replication script:

```
net start remoteaccess
rasdial replicant_server
net start replicator
net accounts /sync[29]
```

The only problem is determining when it's safe to terminate the connection. Remember that the replicator operates every five minutes, so we suggest having a separate script that reverses these steps:

```
net stop replicator
rasdial replicant_server /DISCONNECT
net stop remoteaccess
```

If the first script is named REPLISTART.CMD and the second REPLISTOP.CMD, the commands:

```
at 12:00 am /EVERY Monday Wednesday Friday REPLISTART.CMD
at 12:15 am /EVERY Monday Wednesday Friday REPLISTOP.CMD
```

will get the job done.

Bridging

In the first edition of this book, we made much of NT 3.1 RAS's limitations—in particular, its support for only Microsoft's proprietary, non-routable NetBEUI protocol and its inability to *bridge* between LANs. The former limitation has been eliminated. The latter you can get around by two methods: either use *two* RAS servers, each of which dials the other (obviously, this requires two WAN channels, be they phone lines, X.25 links, or ISDN lines) or change the HKEY_LOCAL_MACHINE\System\CurrentControlSet\Services\RemoteAccess\Parameters\ NetBIOSGateway\RemoteListen parameter from 1 to 2 in the Configuration Registry. Making

---

29 Per Chapter 3, the /sync option on net accounts (equivalent to Server Manager's Synchronize Entire Domain command) *must* be executed locally on the Domain Controller. Therefore this script must be executed on the domain controller, or there should be another AT command that forces synchronization (e.g., at \\domain_controller 12:05 AM net accounts /sync).

the change causes RAS to function as a bidirectional gateway for NetBIOS-based[30] traffic and effectively bridges LANs over a single link, but it does so by forwarding *all* NetBIOS-based network traffic, which is virtually guaranteed to saturate the link on a busy network.

As a practical matter, if you're running anything but a very small WAN, you'll want to run a dedicated router; RAS works, but it loads the server that's running it proportionately to the network traffic. It's a good solution for small-scale applications, but if you need more bandwidth, the way to get it is with specialized hardware.

Dedicated Multiprotocol Routers

The principal alternative to RAS for Windows NT wide-area networking is use of a *multiprotocol router.* This is essentially a special-purpose computer whose sole mission is to take traffic in one protocol—for instance, NetBEUI, IPX or TCP/IP—and convert it to (or from) another protocol—such as X.25, PPP, or frame-relay. By using a pair of such routers, one can achieve higher-performance wide-area networking than that provided by Windows NT RAS.

An optimal multiprotocol router setup for Windows NT involves a routable backbone protocol (TCP/IP or IPX/SPX) and whatever secondary protocol is best suited to your particular needs. Determining the best protocol for your situation is beyond the scope of this book, but the general rule in WANs is that you pay for speed: low-data-rate dial-up lines (up to 28,800 baud) are relatively cheap; high-speed circuits tend to be extremely expensive.

Aside from determining which protocols are needed, selecting a router is largely a matter of features and price. You can pay from $2,000 to $25,000 for a router, depending on the features it provides. Aside from multiprotocol support, some routers provide simple network management protocol (SNMP)-compatible remote maintenance features, out-of-band (generally RS-232) console features, and varying degrees of upgradability. You would be wise to request literature from *all* the firms on the list in Table 8.2 before selecting a router for your network.

Because NT 3.5 and later supports PPP multiprotocol connectivity, getting a router that supports PPP dial-up connections will provide an additional level of flexibility—an NT-based client can use RAS to dial directly into the router! That capability can be a cost-effective approach in some situations: use dedicated routers for the home office and larger offices and NT RAS for smaller offices.

Shiva Netmodem

Another alternative that may work in smaller applications is the Shiva Netmodem. This is a high-speed modem with internal hardware that enables it to function as a network bridge. Models are available for both NetWare IPX/SPX and NetBIOS networking. The former is suitable for use with Windows NT's NWLink IPX protocol and the latter with NetBEUI. Unfortunately, although the Netmodem will *bridge*, it will not *route*, so all network traffic is transmitted from one net to the other, regardless of whether it's intended for non-local recipients. As a result, the Netmodem is

---

30 As is explained at some length in Chapter 6 and Appendix 2, NT's built-in file-and-print services are NetBIOS based, regardless of the transport protocol.

useful only for very small networks unless one can combine it with a separate router (in the IPX case—NetBIOS, of course, is not routable in this sense).

Management and Maintenance Issues

Managing and administering enterprise networks is not fundamentally different from managing LANs, although the complexity of the network tends to make the administrator's job a bit harder. Troubleshooting, on the other hand, takes on its own character where enterprise networks (especially WANs) are involved.

Microsoft provides a number of advanced administration tools with Windows NT Server that can make life for the administrator easier. These include *User Manager for Domains*, *Server Manager*, *System Policy Editor*, and *Remote Access Services Admin*. Client-based versions of these tools are available for NT Workstation, Windows for Workgroups, and Windows 95. (See the "Client-Based Administration Tools" section below.) The tools included with Server—building on those included with the base Windows NT product (Disk Administrator, Backup, Event Viewer, Performance Monitor, Network Monitor, and Registry Editor)—provide most of what you need to get an enterprise network up and running.

Server Manager

The most important of the NT Server administration tools is the Server Manager (see Figure 8.20). From this program, you can add computers to your Server domain, remove them from the domain, inspect the users, shares, replication, and alert status of any computer in the domain, synchronize user accounts across all servers in the domain, send messages (such as the ever-popular "Server going down in 3 minutes!"), or promote a server to be the Primary Domain Controller.

The way to perform all these tasks is fairly obvious. Select a computer from the list (which you may bring up to date at any time using the View/Refresh menu item), then either select a command to execute from the Computer menu or double-click the entry (equivalent to Computer/Properties) to bring up a Properties. It's equivalent to the Server dialog in the Control Panel and allows you to inspect (and control) logged-in user accounts, shared resources, connections, replication, and administrative alerts in exactly the same way. Perhaps the most critical use you'll make of this is controlling administrative alerts. Clicking the Alerts button brings up an Alerts dialog (see Figure 8.21) that lets you send administrative alert

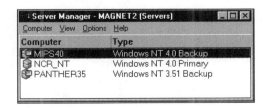

FIGURE 8.20 Server Manager. Administrators can view and control all NT Servers and Workstations in an NT Server domain from the Server Manager.

Table 8.2 Multiprotocol Router Vendors

Product	Vendor	Telephone	Comments
Various Models **http://www.acc.com**	Advanced Computer Communications 340 Storke Rd. Santa Barbara, CA 93117	(805) 685–4455	Central, branch, home-office, and remote routers
Various Models **http://www.cabletron.com**	Cabletron Corp. 35 Industrial Way P.O. Boc 5005 Rochester, NH 03866-5005	(603) 332-9400	Routers, hubs, switches, and other network components
Various Models **http://www.cisco.com**	Cisco Systems 170 West Tasman Dr. San Jose, CA 95134-1706	(800) 553-6387 (408) 526-4000	*De-facto standard central router for TCP/IP environments*
Various Models **http://www.digital.com**	Digital Equipment Corp. 111Powdermill Rd. Maynard, MA 01754-1418	(800) 344-4825, (508) 493-5111	Full line of hubs, routers (including OSI CLNP support for European applications), switches, concentrators, NICs, etc.
Various Models **http://www.hp.com**	Hewlett Packard Co. Roseville Networks Div. 8000 Foothills Blvd, Roseville, CA 95747	(800) 752-0900	Full line of NICs, switches, routers; also the OpenView LAN Management system
Various Models **http://www.ibm.com**	IBM Corp. One Old Orchard Rd. Armonk, NY 10504	(800) 342-6672	Full line of NICs, switches, routers—including Token Ring and SNA/DLC support; also NetView LAN Management
Various Models **http://www.network.com**	Network Systems Corp. (Division of Storage Tek) 7600 Boone Ave. N. Minneapolis, MN 55428	(612) 424-4888	Routers, bridges, hardware encryption systems, firewalls

Table 8.2 (Continued)

Products	Vendor	Telephone	Comments
NetWare Multiprotocol Router **http://www.novell.com**	Novell Corp. 1555 N. Technology Way Orem, UT 84097	(800) 453-1267, (801) 222-6000	Software-based (NetWare-hosted) IPX/SPX routers, mainly for use in NetWare LAN environments
Various Models **http://www.proteon.com**	Proteon Inc. Nine Technology Dr. Westborough, MA 01581	(800) 545-7464, (508) 898-2800	NICs, routers, switches, hubs.
Various Models **http://www.3com.com**	3Com Corp. 5400 Bayfront Plaza Santa Clara, CA 95052-8145	(408) 764-5000	Switches (including ATM), modems, high-performance NICs, routers (including PPTP support), hubs, etc
Various Models **http://www.xyplex.com**	Whittaker Xyplex Inc. 295 Foster St. Littleton, MA 01460	(800) 338-5316 (508) 264-9900	Hubs, repeaters, concentrators, switches (including ATM), gateways, ISDN products
Various Models **http://www.baynetworks.com**	Bay Networks, Inc. 4401 Great American Pkwy Santa Clara, CA 95054	(800) 231-4213 (408) 988-2400	Hubs, switches, and routers

Network Computing Magazine publishes an excellent annual review of routers from all major vendors. To subscribe, call (708) 647-6834, or browse their Web site at http://techweb.cmp.com/nc/current.

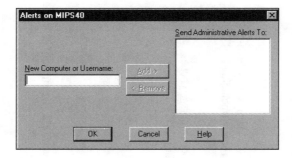

FIGURE 8.21 Alerts dialog (Server Manager). The Alerts dialog box, accessed from Server Manager's Computer/Properties menu, allows an administrator to determine where alert notifications are sent on the network.

information to specified computer or user names. This can be particularly convenient when the server's locked up and you want alerts to show up on your workstation.

You can control Services on the remote system(s) by selecting Computer/Services, which brings up a Services dialog that's identical to that from the Control Panel. This allows you to start/stop/pause/continue services on any Windows NT system in the domain and to determine the startup parameters (if any).

Server Manager also allows you to examine shared resource use on a per-user basis. Select Properties for the server you're interested in and click the Shares button. This feature was available to end users through File Manager in NT 3.*x*, but in NT 4.0 only administrators can see who is using a share.

User Manager for Domains

As we've now discussed at some length, the management of user accounts in Windows NT Server differs from that in NT Workstation, especially when inter-domain trust is involved. Not surprisingly, Microsoft provides a different version of User Manager for Server administrators. User Manager for Domains looks almost identical to Windows NT's User Manager, but provides several additional features.

The first feature is that you can select a domain to administer, from the User/Select Domain menu item. You will need administrative access in the domain you want to administer, of course. Once you select the domain, the list of user names in the main User Manager screen will update, showing the names of users and groups in the selected domain. Double-clicking on a user name brings up a User Properties dialog box (see Figure 8.22) that appears similar to the single-server version, except for the additional buttons on the bottom of the dialog box. These buttons allow you to specify the hours during which users may log in, the systems on which they're permitted to log in, the date that the account expires (this differs from the date the account's *password* expires), and whether the account is *global* or *local*.[31] In all

---

31   See Chapter 3 for an explanation of *local* and *global* user accounts.

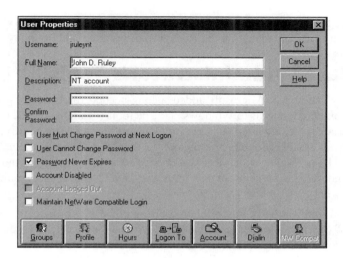

FIGURE 8.22 User Properties dialog. This dialog box, from NT Server's User Manager for Domains, allows administrators to control most aspects of a user's access to NT Servers and Workstations in the domain.

other respects, User Manager for Domains operates identically to the single-server version of User Manager (covered in Chapter 3).

User Profile Editor

Prior to version 4.0, NT Server supported a User Profile Editor that supported many, but not all, of the functions now provided by the System Policy Editor (see Chapter 4). This editor is now obsolete and is no longer provided.

Remote Administration

Although the tools just mentioned are shipped with Windows NT Server (and require one to be present on the network and configured as Primary Domain Controller), they do *not* have to be run from one. Indeed, you can run them from any Windows NT workstation on the network, even remotely, using RAS.

There are two ways to run these tools. The obvious way is to exploit the hidden ADMIN$ share that provides administrators access to the \WINNT\SYSTEM32 directory on all NT systems. Server Manager (SRVMGR.EXE), User Manager for Domains (USRMGR.EXE), and User Profile Editor (UPEDIT.EXE), among others, can be run remotely over the network (you could even set up a "Remote Admin" program group in User Profile Manager) from that location. We don't recommend this approach on slow WAN links (like RAS over modems).

There is one more setting that will help if you administer a Windows NT domain remotely. Server Manager and User Manager for Domains both support a "Low Speed Connection" option that saves time on slow data links by not displaying the full list of servers, users, and so forth. This option is also available on the RAS Admin program and on many other tools.

Client-Based Administrator's Tools

Beginning with version 3.5, Microsoft added a long-needed (and much appreciated) set of client-based administration tools to Windows NT. The tools (available in NT, Windows 3.*x,* and Windows 95 variants) include User Manager for Domains, Server Manager, Event Viewer, Print Manager for Windows NT Server, and an option to add a Security menu to the standard Windows 3.1/3.11 File Manager that lets you control access to directories and files on the NT server. The Windows 3.*x* versions of the tools are Win32 based and require Windows (or WfWG) 3.1/3.11 enhanced mode.

The practical implication of having such tools on client platforms is that remote administration of an NT Server no longer requires an NT Workstation, which is a distinct advantage, given the high cost of setting up a reasonably well-configured workstation for administrative use. There's also something to be said for running on the same client system as your end users. The client-based administrative tools do lack some of the full NT management features. There are (as yet) no Windows 3.*x* or Windows 95-based versions of NT's Performance Monitor, Disk Administrator, User Profile Editor, and Backup applications, and they currently provide no support for remote access to the NT command line.

Web-Based Administration

Beginning with NT Server 4.0, Microsoft has added yet another management option: administration of NT Server from an IIS Web page (see Figure 8.23). You can administer NT Server with a Resource Kit utility[32] that adds the necessary ISAPI scripts and HTML pages. You can then log in using any Web browser[33] and entering the address http://*YourServerNameHere/* NTadmin/NTadmin.HTM, you will see the administration tool for the server.

The tool is quite comprehensive, and allows you to perform a wide variety of tasks: creating and editing users and groups, adding workstations and servers to the domain, starting and stopping device drivers and services, viewing event logs, managing shared directories and printers, setting permissions on NTFS devices, examining the users who are logged in and seeing what server resources they are using, broadcasting a message, and even rebooting the server.

---

32 At the time this was written, the NT 4.0 Server Resource Kit was not yet available; however, Microsoft has posted a download for the Web-based admin tool on its NT Server Web page (http://www.microsoft.com/ntserver). Whether it will remain available for public download after the Resource Kit becomes available is not known.

33 The Web-based tool *does* require a browser that supports security, for obvious reasons. Options available include basic authentication, NT challenge/response, and SSL (see Chapter 7 for details). The browser that will work best with the tool, of course, is the latest version of Microsoft's Internet Explore; other browsers (e.g., Netscape Navigator) can be used if desired.

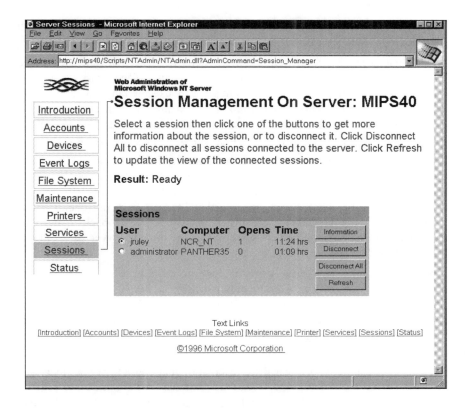

FIGURE 8.23. Web-based administration. NT Server 4.0 can also be administered through an IIS Web page as illustrated here. Note that IIS security settings are critical if this method is used. (See Chapter 7 for details.)

The great advantage to using this tool is, of course, that you can manage your server from any station on your LAN that has a Web browser installed, provided, of course, that TCP/IP is available and configured so that the systems can "see" each other. There is no need to install special software (like the client-based tools discussed earlier) on the station from which you want to manage NT Server. You can even use this tool on the Internet as long as a live Internet connection to the server is available.

The great danger of using the tool is that from a security point of view, HTML (the protocol used by Web browsers) is wide open. Unless Secure Sockets Layer (SSL) is used, your connection is not encrypted. For this reason, we do not recommend using the Web-based administration tool on the Internet unless SSL (or PPTP with encryption) is available.

Systems Management

Many observers expressed disappointment when NT 3.1 first appeared, noting that it lacked the kind of high-end systems management software required of a true enterprise operating system.

Systems Management Server (SMS), formerly known by the code name "Hermes," is Microsoft's answer. It's a powerful (and surprisingly, multiplatform!) enterprise management service.

SMS stores management information in a SQL Server database you can access using a specialized SMS administrator's program (essentially a highly customized query tool). Data is collected for the database automatically, through client software executed in conjunction with system login scripts. This data constitutes basic *configuration* data on all SMS-managed clients and servers, *inventory* data on software installed on the clients, and *audits* of specified software packages.

Each SMS site must contain a "site server," an NT Server running SMS software, as well as a SQL Server (which may or may not run on the same physical machine). Clients execute the SMS client software (a complex logon script) as part of their normal network server logon, and as necessary, they receive software updates and provide inventory/audit data in response to commands incorporated in the logon script. Inventory/audit data from the clients is stored in Management Information File (MIF) format files, which propagate back to the site server through the logon (and optionally, helper) servers. Finally, the site server stores the collected data in a SQL Server database.

Basic inventory data—such as the operating system version, processor type, and free disk space—on clients and servers is collected automatically at logon. Optionally, this can be expanded to include searching for specific files by name, size, and/or modification date, and files may be collected as well as detected. Once data is collected, queries may be executed against the resulting database, finding all copies of WINWORD.EXE with a date prior to 31/03/94, for instance, to generate a list of workstations that have not been upgraded to Word 6.0.

SMS also allows automatic (or nearly so) installation and upgrade of both locally installed applications and server-based network applications. You can create a *package*, which consists of all files required for the installation, including an installer (.BAT file, SETUP.EXE, or Microsoft Test script). SMS's client software includes a Test runtime and predefined packages for a host of Microsoft's own applications, and operating systems are supplied with the product. Shared network applications are supported through the creation of shortcuts to applications installed in and shared by a file server.

Once a package is created, SMS will automatically propagate the package to all designated clients, as simply as dragging an icon representing the package to a particular client, group of clients, or as the result of an explicit query against the site database.

SMS's inventory and remote installation features are complemented by an impressive set of troubleshooting tools that (for Windows 3.*x* clients) include examination of available DOS and Windows memory, a network PING test, remote file copy, remote execution of programs, remote control of the client console, and even remote reboot.

SMS also ships with an NT-based Network Monitor (formerly code-named "bloodhound") that has most features of a network "sniffer." It records network traffic, decodes it, and permits the troubleshooter to search captured packets in a wide variety of ways. It runs as an NT service and can be installed on any NT system on the network. SMS Network Monitor differs from the version included with NT Server 4.0 (see Chapter 5) in that it supports promiscuous mode (i.e., it will capture *any* packets it sees on the LAN, not just those sent to or from the SMS server) and can operate remotely in conjunction with network monitor agents on remote systems. In the language of Chapter 5, this makes SMS Network Monitor an even better network wiretap and a correspondingly greater security risk.

SMS limitations include its dependence on Microsoft SQL Server for Windows NT (Microsoft justifies this by pointing to SMS's membership in its Back Office suite), and the requirement that a Windows NT-based system be used to run the Administrators tools.

Although SMS doesn't provide true software metering (particularly for server-based network applications), its inventory and audit features do allow generation of a list of clients that have application components installed. In many cases this is just as valuable, and Microsoft is working with a third party[34] to provide add-on metering capability for those who demand it.

Experience with a small (three servers, fewer than a dozen clients) SMS test site showed that once the complicated installation process is completed (the release notes alone make up a 77KB Windows helpfile!), it's quite easy to use and extremely powerful. Indeed, some might say it's *too* powerful. SMS provides managers with a level of control over client PCs that may offend some end users. It needs to be deployed with some care.

SMS does *not* provide the kind of *network management* that's provided by products like IBM's NetView and SNMP-based systems. Microsoft's position is that plenty of other products are available for such uses; the issue of managing network *clients* hasn't been generally addressed. SMS 1.2, just being released as the third edition of this book went to press, adds the only currently available remote control for NT 3.51 and 4.0 systems, among many other features.

Troubleshooting Enterprise Networks

As we mentioned earlier, although administering an enterprise network is much like administering a very large LAN, troubleshooting problems in an enterprise environment is a different matter altogether, because enterprise networks are so much more complex than LANs. If a user can't see server in a LAN environment, there are only really four possible causes: the server's gone down, the wiring's bad, the network card's bad (more likely, the cable *to* the network card is unplugged—always check this first), or (*most* frequently) the software in the user's workstation is having a problem. There really isn't anything else to break!

Add a couple of routers and a WAN link to the connection, however, and you greatly multiply the possible causes of trouble. The WAN link might be down or just having line noise problems. One of the routers may have failed. A power glitch may restart a router with a bad routing table—and the list goes on and on.

As it happens, there's a fairly simple approach to troubleshooting these problems that we feel confident in recommending: it's used twice a year by the "network warriors" of INTEROP, who accomplish the amazing feat of creating a large (hundreds of routers, an FDDI backbone, and thousands of nodes) TCP/IP network–called ShowNet–*in just a few days*. That approach is to use the standard TCP/IP PING.EXE utility and little else.[35]

---

34 Express Systems Inc., whose telephone number is (206) 728-8300.

35 It's particularly instructive that the team does this even though *most* nodes on the INTEROP ShowNet support SMTP, NetView, or any of a dozen proprietary network management schemes.

The reason the INTEROP folks use this approach is that the huge network they put in really represents something of a worst-case multivendor net. Each node on the network terminates in a booth on the show floor, where vendors plug in whatever network hardware and software they're trying to sell. By using PING to get underneath whatever software the vendors are using, the ShowNet team isolates itself from the details of a particular vendor's software. Being isolated lets them concentrate on making sure that the cabling is good and the routers are properly configured. They start looking at the software, *only* after checking the hardware with PING.

We think this approach makes good sense for NT networks, especially because (as we discussed at some length at the start of this chapter) *all* routed NT networks *must* use either TCP/IP or IPX/SPX as the backbone protocol (and since IPX/SPX lacks any equivalent to PING, we're inclined to prefer TCP/IP!). We do think it makes sense to leverage NT's built-in tools as well (in particular, using Performance Monitor to check on network throughput, per Chapter 5), and it's *always* a good idea to look at the event log when a problem occurs. If the cause of the problem isn't immediately apparent, though, we suggest that a good place to start is to use PING from the workstation to the server. If PING gets through, you know the hardware's good, and you can start looking at the software. If not, you have a hardware (or router configuration) problem that must be solved first, before you look at any higher-level issues.

We also recommend that you look carefully at *out-of-band signaling* in enterprise networks, especially big ones. Out-of-band signaling means that you don't lock yourself into sending all administrative data and commands over the network itself because otherwise, if there's a hardware problem, it will stop the administrative data just as it stops the network traffic. There are basically three ways to get an out-of-band capability in a Windows NT-based enterprise network:

1. Use RAS on your servers. Set up a separate dial-in-only modem and line on each server (or one server in each closet) and grant access rights *only* to administrative users. This setup gives you a reliable "back door" to get into that server remotely and doesn't compete with user traffic on other RAS links you may have.

2. Configure a PC on the network to run a remote control program, such as PCanywhere for Windows. Again, with a dedicated modem line configured only for dial-in and with access restricted to administrators. This gives you access to the local network and can be especially useful in resetting a balky router (when you're on the wrong side of the router).

3. If you buy a multiprotocol router, get one with an RS-232 port and (again) put a dedicated modem on that port for administrative access. Doing so gives you direct control of the router from a remote location. (If you're using Windows NT's built-in static router feature, setting up RAS on the routing machine gives you the same capability.)

In any case, the point is to *give yourself a back door!* It doesn't matter whether your operation is standardized on NetView or SNMP or some other product; make sure there is a network-independent way to get in. You will save yourself from going on an emergency call.

> **Note:** *A back door is potentially a vulnerability point, and many MIS and IS management policies forbid them.*

Consider one more thing: on a really large enterprise system, there may be unattended servers (and routers) in locations that aren't easily accessible. Clearly, these are candidates for one of the back-door dial-in approaches we've just listed, but there's also a need for these systems to get the word out that they're in trouble.

If you're in charge of a truly mission-critical system that has to operate 24 hours a day, the ultimate way to handle this is, of course, the inevitable pager. Two applications that allow NT to interface with these useful (if annoying) systems are shown in Table 8.3, as are some other products of special interest to enterprise network managers.

Is NT *Really* Ready for the Enterprise?

You may find it interesting to compare the chapter you've just read with what we wrote in the first edition of *Networking Windows NT*. In the intervening couple of years, NT has gained client-side administration tools, an add-on management package (SMS), considerable third-party support (see Table 8.3), *greatly* improved built-in WAN connectivity, better e-mail options, and the ability to be administered from an Internet Web page. On the other hand, NT still lacks some enterprise essentials, such as per-user chargeback accounting. On the whole, we think that although NT has made great strides and is eminently suitable for use *in* the enterprise, it isn't yet the system we'd recommend as the *backbone* of the enterprise.

That situation is bound to change, however. Big-system features are coming for NT and from a variety of sources. For example, *clustering* (see Chapter 12) is coming to NT from several sources. As big-system technologies like clustering become available, we think the issue of whether NT is *really* an enterprise operating system will be answered!

Conclusion

We've examined the challenge represented by enterprise networks and seen how the features of Windows NT, especially Windows NT Server, can be used to ease the implementation of enterprise networks. We've explored what makes an enterprise network different from a LAN and determined that the governing factor is *complexity*.

Beyond sheer complexity, enterprise networks are characterized by geographic dispersion. They extend beyond one building or office complex (often beyond even one city, state, or country), requiring WAN connectivity. We've examined RAS, Windows NT's built-in WAN, which provides a reasonable alternative to dedicated multiprotocol routers in departmental applications.

We've also examined some special issues of interest to enterprise administrators, including Windows NT Server's built-in support for Macintosh computers, and issues involved in managing and maintaining enterprise networks, including remote administration and complex network maintenance.

By now, you should have a good feel for the features built in to Windows NT. The next three chapters extend these concepts beyond Windows NT's built-in networking as we examine what's involved in connecting Windows NT to other Microsoft SMB networks (Chapter 9), Novell NetWare (Chapter 10), and other networks, including UNIX, IBM's LAN Server and SNA systems, and Banyan VINES (Chapter 11).

Table 8.3 Windows NT Network Management Applications

Product	Company/Address	Phone	Comments
CA-Unicenter **http://www.cai.com**	Computer Associates One Computer Associates Plaza, Islandia, NY 11788-7000	(516) 342-5224	Advanced enterprise-wide client/server administration; Policy-based management
Various Products **http://www.seagatesoftware.com**	Seagate Software 37 Skyline Dr. Lake Mary, FL 32746	(800) 327-2232 (407) 262-8000	Batch operations, asset management, network alerts, remote install, software inventory, etc.
NAV Norton Your Eyes Only **http://www.symantec.com**	Symantec/Norton 1021 Torre Ave. Cupertino, CA 95014-2132	(408) 253-9600	Anti-Virus (*available online*), Encryption Software
NT ViruScan **http://www.mcafee.com**	McAfee & Associates, Inc 2710 Walsh Ave. Santa Clara, CA 95051	(408) 988-3832	Anti-Virus (*available online*)
Notify! **http://www.exmachina.com**	Ex Machina, Inc. 11 East 26th St.New York, NY 10010-1402	(212) 843-0000	Alphanumeric pager support for Windows NT; Supports TAPI, DDE, MAPI, Web, and various DMTF pagers
U-Page Pro **http://www.desktoppaging.com**	Desktop Paging Software, Inc. 547 Amherst St., Suite 402. Nashua, NH 03063	(603) 595-7500	Messages from PC to any wireless communications device; Mail-to-pager gateway also available
NT Anti-Virus (NTAV) **http://www.carmel.co.il**	Carmel Software Corp. POB 25055Haifa, 31250 Israel	(972) 4-841-6976	Client/Server anti-virus product
IncouLAN for Windows NT **http://www.cheyenne.com**	Cheyenne Software 3 Expressway Plaza, Roslyn Hts, NY 11577	(800) 243-9462 (516) 484-5110	NCSA-certified LAN-wide anti-virus product

Table 8.3 (Continued)

Product	Company/Address	Phone	Comments
Systems Management Server (SMS) **http://www.microsoft.com**	Microsoft Corp. One Microsoft Way Redmond, WA 98052	(800) 426-9400 (206) 882-8080	Described earlier in this chapter.
Polycenter AssetWorks **http://www.digital.com**	Digital Equipment Corp. 111 Powdermill Rd. Maynard, MA 01754-1418	(800) 344-4825, (508) 493-5111	Enhances SMS by providing multiplatform support to legacy systems
Quota Manager for Windows NT **http://www.ntp.com**	New Technology Partners, Inc. 40 South River Rd. Bedford, NH 03110	(603) 622-4400	Caps user files and directories at a fixed maximum size; Requires (and supports) NTFS
TME for Windows NT **http://www.tivoli.com**	Tivoli Systems, Inc. 9442 Capitol of Texas Highway North, Arboretum Place North Austin, TX 78759	(512) 794-9070	Automatic, unattended software installation / update / inventory

For more information on this topic, browse http://altavista.digital.com, *select Advanced Search, and search for "Network Management" near Software near "Windows NT" (if you're interested in a specific type of hardware, you might want to add that as well, i.e., near virus).*

For More Information

Gilster, Paul (1993). *The Internet Navigator*. New York: John Wiley. ISBN: 0-471-59782-1. An outstanding introduction to the Internet, including descriptions of most common services, and extensive lists of local providers. The book's one flaw is inadequate coverage of Mosaic/World Wide Web issues, but everything the author has to say about getting connected to the Internet still applies.

Microsoft Staff. *32-bit Applications Catalog*. Redmond, WA: Microsoft Corp. This is an electronic document (a large Windows helpfile) that lists dozens of Windows NT applications in categories ranging from desktop utilities to enterprise management. It's downloadable from Microsoft's Internet server (ftp.microsoft.com).

Microsoft Staff. *Windows NT Server—Concepts and Planning Guide*. Redmond, WA: Microsoft Corp. Detailed coverage of domain management, inter-domain trust, printer services, etc.

Microsoft Staff. *Windows NT Server—Remote Access Service*. Redmond, WA: Microsoft Corp. All the details of RAS, including specifics of use with modems, multiport cards, X.25 smartcards, and ISDN.

Microsoft Staff. *Windows NT Server—Services for Macintosh*. Redmond, WA: Microsoft Corp. The best (and only) reference on SFM.

Renaud, Paul (1993). *Introduction to Client / Server Systems*. New York: John Wiley. ISBN: 0-471-57774-X. Among other things (it's no accident we've cited him elsewhere in this book), Renaud has good coverage of end-to-end system management that's as applicable to Windows NT as it is to UNIX systems.

Microsoft
Connections

9

When you finish this chapter, you will understand how Windows NT's networking features arose from the old MS-Net/LAN Manager products. You will also know the following:

> How to connect NT clients with LAN Manager, LAN Server, and Windows for Workgroups or Windows 95 networks

> How to connect LAN Manager, Windows for Workgroups or Windows 95 clients to NT networks

> What is involved in operating a mixture of LAN Manager and Windows NT servers

> The difference between workgroups and domains

Microsoft Networks

Although Windows NT Workstation and Server are the most ambitious network products that Microsoft has ever built, they are not the company's only network products. In the recent past, Microsoft also offered its Windows for Workgroups product as a peer-to-peer network for sites with modest networking needs. Its successor, Windows 95, is already a great success as a small peer-network operating system. And despite Microsoft's coolness to OS/2, OS/2 LAN Manager was Microsoft's high-end networking solution until NT arrived.

All Microsoft network products use the Server Message Block (SMB) protocol (see Appendix 2), which gives them a baseline level of interoperability. In practical terms, that means any two Microsoft-based networks can usually share a network printer or directory. However, the differences between the products often mean that advanced features like security and system administration are not fully interoperable.

Microsoft's Early Networks

Microsoft is far from a newcomer to networking. It has been in the business since the early 1980s, when it offered its MS-Net product. Instead of selling MS-Net directly to end users, Microsoft licensed it to vendors, who then modified it—sometimes in incompatible ways—and resold it under many names. For example, IBM sold MS-Net as the IBM PC LAN Program; 3Com's version was called 3Plus.

LAN Manager

When Microsoft and IBM announced OS/2 in 1987, they also announced an OS/2-based network solution compatible with MS-Net. Microsoft called the product OS/2 LAN Manager. As with MS-Net, Microsoft licensed OS/2 LAN Manager to vendors like IBM (LAN Server), 3Com (3+Open), and Digital (Pathworks) that made their own enhancements and modifications.

In 1990, Microsoft made an important change in the way it sold networking products. It began to offer OS/2 LAN Manager as a retail product under the Microsoft name, but continued the licensing agreements with vendors like IBM, 3Com, and Digital. Since then, Microsoft has moved its networking emphasis from licensing to retail sales, capitalizing on the familiar Microsoft name.

Windows for Workgroups

Although you can still find Microsoft Windows for Workgroups (WfWG) being used as a low-end peer-to-peer network, it's being pushed out by Windows 95 and NT. WfWG is essentially Windows 3.1 with networking built in. In addition to having file-sharing features built into File Manager, Print Manager, and common dialogs, WfWG includes versions of Microsoft Mail and Schedule+ scheduling software in the box.

Windows 95

Microsoft's choice for a mass-market desktop operating system successor to Windows for Workgroups is Windows 95. It extends the networking capabilities of that earlier product, but most significantly replaces the Windows 3.1 look with a very different user interface that's now been adopted by Windows NT 4.0.

Using Windows NT with LAN Manager

As you would expect, because Microsoft wrote both LAN Manager and Windows NT, and the networking features in Windows NT are derived from those in LAN Manager, these products work together better than some of the third-party networking solutions that are discussed in Chapters 6, 9, and 10. Windows NT workstations can utilize the resources of LAN Manager Servers nearly seamlessly and LAN Manager workstations can make use of Windows NT Servers nearly seamlessly. There are a few rough edges—particularly when one tries to mix LAN Manager and NT Servers in the same domain—but there are workarounds. On the whole, it's a very usable system.

It's All the Same...

The networking features in Windows NT are advanced 32-bit versions of the networking features that Microsoft has built into the LAN Manager 2.x series. Windows NT and LAN Manager share many features in common, including: being based on SMB networking, using NetBEUI as the principal protocol (with TCP/IP as the enterprise protocol), and using NDIS device drivers. Many of the APIs and the data structures and even the syntax of the commands are the same. The systems are generally quite compatible, and the migration process from LAN Manager to Windows NT is not a difficult one.

Except When It's Not

The LAN Manager/NT situation is something of a good news/bad news story. The bad news is, first of all, that the structure and operation of the administrative domains differ and, as we will see, this difference can become a real problem when you start to mix LAN Manager (OS/2) and NT Servers. There's also a difference in the way that network browsing and announcement are handled. Microsoft has made it possible to reset Windows NT to use the LAN Manager-style browser service, but unfortunately, this is not a permanent solution either. There is also a difference in the way the passwords are handled in the two systems (a problem that LAN Manager and NT interoperation shares with Windows for Workgroups and NT interoperation). Finally, the directory replication mechanism differs, and in large networks this discrepancy can be a major issue. Take heart, however—Microsoft was not foolish enough to build a totally incompatible networking architecture into its new operating system.

In all probability, if you have an established LAN Manager system, your first experience with NT will be adding workstations.

Windows NT Workstations with LAN Manager Servers

Windows NT workstations work well with LAN Manager Servers. The one major issue of concern is the browsing service, which is activated when you go into the file manager and select Connect Net Drive or type *net view* from the command line.

Network Browsing in Windows NT This is as good a place as any to discuss the browse service. To understand the Windows NT situation, we should begin by understanding some basic facts about server message block (SMB) networking and the way LAN Manager works. Network browsing in the SMB system depends on a *broadcast* mechanism that uses APIs called mail slots. In the broadcast situation, whenever a LAN Manager Server or workstation is joined to the network, it begins by sending a class-2 mail slot message to all other machines on the local network segment, looking for a server. Servers will respond with a message directed back to the workstation announcing who they are. The workstation looks for the Primary Domain Controller (PDC), which is the center of administrative control in a LAN Manager network.

The major problem with this approach is that *broadcast announcements cannot be routed beyond the local subnet*. Otherwise, a complicated internetwork with many routers would spend most of its time doing nothing but broadcast announcements. Therefore, routers do not pass the broadcast announcements, creating a "double hop" problem. If you connect LANs, the LAN Manager-style browsing breaks down. Workstations in one subnet cannot see servers outside their subnet.

A variety of mechanisms have been attempted to get around this problem, and Microsoft is still working on resolving it. The ultimate solution appears to be use of TCP/IP as a standard internetworking protocol for multiple-hop networks (see Appendix 2 and Chapter 6). Aside from the double-hop problem, the use of broadcasts as a method of network browsing creates two difficulties. The first is, as stated earlier, that whenever a workstation logs into the network, it must broadcast its presence on the subnet. It will then sit for up to a minute waiting for a response from the domain controller. This can be extremely annoying. On a heavily loaded network it may be necessary for the workstation to make several broadcast announcements before the server will respond, causing a very frustrating situation for end users. Worse, on large LANs with many stations *race conditions* can exist where so many stations are attempting to logon at once that it's impossible for the server to keep up with them. This demand can actually have a significant impact on the overall network traffic.

Beginning with Windows for Workgroups and with the first beta versions of Windows NT, Microsoft began to eliminate the use of broadcast announcements during login. Instead, Windows NT and Windows for Workgroups employ the concept of a *browse master*. In the browse master scenario one station within the subnet (the primary domain controller and a Windows NT Server domain, or an elected Windows NT or Windows for Workgroups machine in a Windows for Workgroups/Windows NT Workgroup) maintains a list of all the other servers and workstations in the workgroup or domain. During login, instead of sending a broadcast message to all systems on the subnet, a workstation needs only to communicate its presence to the browse master, which in turn communicates the location of other systems, including the domain controller, to which the system sends a login message. No broadcasts are required.

Unfortunately, difficulties can still occur in this kind of networking. The whole process breaks down if the machine that has been selected as browse master is not turned on. In this condition, the machines that are turned on will attempt to contact the browse master, but "time out" after a preset interval and then conduct a *browse master election* (which involves the same broadcasts we were trying to get away from in the first place) in which they identify each other; the machine with the best performance characteristics will generally elect to be the new browse master.

To avoid having constant browse master elections, it is possible to force a machine to be a browse master. On Windows NT machines you can use the registry editor (REGEDT32.EXE) by opening HKEY_LOCAL_MACHINE\SYSTEM\CurrentControlSet\Services\Browser\Parameters, and creating an IsDomainMaster value, defining it as type REG_SZ, and specifying the text TRUE for the value of the string. This method will cause a machine to maintain the browse list irrespective of whether it is elected as a browse master. This is essential in a situation in which a remote workgroup does not have a domain controller associated with it.

Although Windows NT and Windows for Workgroups have migrated to a new manner of maintaining browse information, the existing installed base of LAN Manager 2.x systems have not. So whenever Windows NT is used in conjunction with LAN Manager computers, it is necessary to make a few adaptations. The most important of these is a parameter called Lmannounce (LAN Manager announce), which essentially forces a Windows NT (or Windows for Workgroups) machine to engage in the same behavior that a LAN Manager machine would. This doesn't mean that you will automatically wind up waiting one minute every time you login on a Windows NT workstation. The Windows NT machine continues to employ the browse master principle. It just adds the periodic broadcast messages the LAN Manager machines will need in order to see the Windows NT system.

To set LAN Manager-style broadcast announcements under Windows NT, run Network Settings in the Windows NT Control Panel, press the Services tab, select Server, press the Properties... button, and check the "Make Browser Broadcasts to LAN Manager 2.x clients" check-box at the bottom of the Server dialog.

LAN Manager Domains Are Windows NT Workgroups The various meanings of the word "domain" can cause some unfortunate confusion. The concept of an administrative *domain* is a simple one. This is a logical grouping of servers and workstations that are treated as a single administrative unit. In the LAN Manager environment all domain members share a centralized security account database that is controlled by the primary domain controller (PDC).

Unfortunately, in Windows NT we have a completely different type of domain controller and an incompatible domain system. As we'll see later, in a Windows NT Server domain, LAN Manager systems are essentially second-class citizens, and the PDC *must* be a Windows NT Server. Standard Windows NT workstations can participate in Windows NT Server domains only as domain members.

Does this mean that a standard Windows NT system cannot participate in a LAN Manager domain? No. Just as in Windows for Workgroups or Windows 95, the solution is to operate the Windows NT machine with a workgroup name but to set the workgroup name to the same name that is used for the LAN Manager domain. At this point, all the players are happy, and they can all talk. The Windows NT machine believes that it is part of a Windows NT workgroup. The LAN Manager machine sees the Windows NT machine as a workstation, not a server, in the domain. Everything works fine until the Windows NT machine tries to behave as a server by sharing files and printers.

Windows NT Systems as Servers in LAN Manager Domains Because Windows NT machines cannot participate as domain members, they cannot share security account information with the PDC and its cohorts. Therefore, a Windows NT machine takes the role of a stand-alone server or *peer* in a LAN Manager environment. That is, it must maintain its own user account database. This setup is very similar in principle to the existence of Windows for Workgroups machines within the domain. However, the Windows NT system operator incurs a greater responsibility and more difficulty because this person must have a true account database. There must be an account name and password for every individual who will attempt to use the shared directories and printers on the Windows NT machine. Therefore, stand-alone Windows NT machines present a significant administrative problem as part of LAN Manager domains. So, if you want to employ Windows NT Servers, upgrade at least one LAN Manager Server to a Windows NT Server (by implication, that means you will have two).

However, for light-duty purposes and for activities like printer sharing, you certainly can operate with the base Windows NT machine as a stand-alone server in a LAN Manager domain. As mentioned earlier, you must set the Lmannounce parameter to 1, using one of the two methods defined in the section above to avoid browsing problems. If you do not do this, LAN Manager workstations, be they OS/2 or DOS machines, within the domain will find it impossible to locate the Windows NT machine or its shared resources. Again, you must think of any such stand-alone NT system administratively. Windows NT machines sitting within LAN Manager domains are best thought of as *peers* (Version 2.0 of LAN Manager supported a special category of OS/2 machines as peers—stand-alone machines capable of resource sharing). This is very much the same approach that a Windows NT machine takes. It will work, albeit with some difficulty.

There are generally two approaches. One is to simulate share-level security. Windows NT does not support the Windows for Workgroups or Windows 95 style of resource sharing, in which any user with the necessary password can access a shared resource, but Windows NT does support a *guest account,* which is very similar to that used by LAN Manager systems. If you set the guest account to have a null password and give the guest account privileges for a shared printer, for example, all users will be able to access the shared printer, whether or not they have a user account on the print server (if the server does not recognize the user name at login, it will log in the user as a guest). This approach is fine for printers, but it's completely insecure, and therefore may not be a good idea for shared directories.

The alternative is to maintain a full user name and password list on the Windows NT machine, which represents a substantial job to expect an end user to perform. It is theoretically feasible to construct some kind of a batch file system that would automatically export account information from the LAN Manager Server to a Windows NT system (possibly using some of the same techniques that were discussed at the end of Chapter 4 where we introduced a batch file for automatically converting NetWare accounts to Windows NT accounts). However, Microsoft does not provide any such capability in the Windows NT box, and in any case, it represents a significant maintenance problem. Therefore, we do not recommend this approach.

It is possible to mix the two approaches: enable the guest account on Windows NT Servers for non-secure access and augment this method by maintaining user accounts *only* for users who require access to secure resources. Again, a major administrative burden will result because you must maintain these user accounts separately on each NT Server. If you must enforce user-level security from within Windows NT Servers that are part of a LAN Manager domain, it's time to upgrade the domain to a Windows NT Server domain.

Windows NT Server and LAN Manager

In the past, Microsoft has offered a special version of Windows NT Server (Windows NT Server Upgrade for LAN Manager) that not only includes additional migration tools for converting the user accounts, access controls, and even directories to work with NT, but also is priced considerably lower than the regular Windows NT Server package. Whether this will remain available for NT 4.0 is unclear at this writing.

Still, the idea of an upgrade to NT Server from LAN Manager shows us the method in Microsoft's madness. It's all very straightforward if instead of thinking *NT Server* you think *LAN Manager 3.0*.[1] As LAN Manager has migrated from version to version, it has acquired new features while retaining a certain degree of backward compatibility. Administrators have consistently needed to upgrade the primary domain controller to the latest version. The current situation is no exception, even though the name of the product has changed.

Windows NT Server functionally is the latest version of LAN Manager, and there is a definite need in a mixed environment to upgrade the primary domain controller to a Windows NT Server system. Fortunately, you don't need to upgrade *all* the servers in the system. It is perfectly possible to apply an NT Server as a domain controller and have it work with OS/2 LAN Manager 2.0 machines as backup controllers.

Note, however, that a significant issue arises if only one Windows NT Server functions as primary domain controller in a LAN Manager domain: What happens when the domain controller fails? Although the LAN Manager machines can participate as backup controllers and can *replicate* the user account database, they cannot export it to another Windows NT system. For this reason we strongly recommend that you upgrade *two* of your OS/2-based LAN Manager 2.x Servers to Windows NT Servers. The second machine should be regarded as the fall-back controller in case something goes wrong with the primary. The other LAN Manager Servers can continue to participate in the domain as well (although only a Windows NT Server can authenticate login requests from Windows NT Workstations participating in the domain).

PassThrough Permissions and Inter-Domain Trust The issue of inter-domain trust and multi-domain administration is discussed in more detail in Chapter 8. Suffice it to say that Windows NT Server brings a new and very powerful concept to enterprise system administration—a domain can be set to trust" the users of another domain, providing a mechanism for account management that spans many domains and (potentially) many subnets. That's the good news. The bad news is that LAN Manager does not support this capability, so when you mix LAN Manager and Windows NT Servers, you immediately create a problem. Fortunately, of course, existing LAN Manager systems do not employ inter-domain trust (because they don't

---

1   Actually, NT LAN Manager 0.12—see the section on Network Monitor in Chapter 5.

support it), so converting from a LAN Manager Server to a Windows NT Server as primary domain controller does not immediately create this problem.

However, when inter-domain trust services are instituted from the Windows NT Servers, or if an attempt is made to tie a LAN Manager domain to a Windows NT Server domain, you'll have problems. As a workaround, since the LAN Manager machines cannot support inter-domain trust, you can create *local* user accounts for the inter-domain trusted users. Essentially, this amounts to resorting to the LAN Manager-style of administration (which was to maintain duplicate accounts on each primary domain controller). This method is clumsy, but it's better than not working at all.

As described earlier, it is also necessary to employ Lmannounce=1 on the Windows NT machines that will be talking to the LAN Manager machines. Finally, with respect to *directory replication* (duplication of critical data on more than one server to maintain an ultimate degree of fault tolerance[2]), as described earlier, LAN Manager machines can *import* replicant data but they cannot *export* it to the Windows NT machine, so it's not really practical to use LAN Manager Servers as a backup to Windows NT Servers. As a result, again, we recommend that if the primary domain controller is converted to an NT Server, another machine also be converted to an NT Server (in effect, convert them in pairs). That way it is possible to step immediately from the NT Server primary to an NT Server fall-back and not miss a beat.

If all Windows NT Server primary domain controllers fail, you can have the replication data on a LAN Manager Server and then manually go through the necessary steps to restart the system using LAN Manager user accounts. The major issue here, of course, is that the LAN Manager user account database and the Windows NT account database are incompatible. As we will discuss a little further on, migration tools will automatically convert from the OS/2 LAN Manager account database to the Windows NT Server account database. The tools do not exist, however, to reverse that process. Just because the replication data exists on an OS/2 machine, it will not necessarily be easy (although in principle it is always possible) to re-establish the system with an OS/2 domain controller. In effect, converting from an OS/2 LAN Manager domain to a Windows NT Server domain is a one-way process.

These incompatibilities relate to another issue. Obviously, in implementing pilot programs many sites will wish to minimize the initial investment in the new technology. In these situations, it certainly makes sense to convert one LAN Manager machine to an NT Server, convert one more as a fall-back, and see how things work out. However, once it has been decided that Windows NT is an environment in which everyone is comfortable, the incompatibilities with the OS/2 machines will render it increasingly cumbersome to deal with them in the environment. It's also unlikely that Microsoft will see fit to significantly enhance the OS/2-based server products over time.[3] Administrators with large-scale systems are advised to contact Microsoft and ask about quantity pricing.

---

2   See Chapter 8 for replication details.

3   When *Networking NT* was written (1994), we were told that all OS/2-related development work had stopped at Microsoft.

LAN Manager Workstations and Windows NT Servers

The situation for workstations is ordinarily much cleaner than it is for servers. In general, LAN Manager workstations see Windows NT Servers, including both base product NT machines that are sharing resources and Windows NT Server machines, just as if they were LAN Manager Servers. There's little difference in the way they're handled. It is necessary to employ the Lmannounce parameter as discussed earlier so that the DOS, Windows, and OS/2 workstations will be able to see the NT systems.

Compatibility Issues Although operation of LAN Manager workstations and NT Servers is generally a clean process, there are a few things to watch for. The first of these is passwords. Windows NT systems employ a password validation mechanism that is case sensitive. That is, "PASSWORD" and "password" are not the same in a Windows NT environment, and if the uppercase version has been employed for a resource or a user account name, typing in the lowercase one will generate an error. To support backward compatibility with LAN Manager, Windows for Workgroups, or Windows 95 systems (which are not case sensitive), Windows NT detects, during login, that it is talking to a foreign, non-Windows NT system and uses a case-insensitive validation technique.

The case-sensitivity issue can lead to one unfortunate situation, if a user employs both Windows NT and LAN Manager systems to access a Windows NT Server. If the system has validated a user's login from a non-Windows NT machine, it will begin employing the case-insensitive logic and will continue to do so *even when the user transfers to a Windows NT machine*. But the Windows NT machine will transmit different characters, and the server may produce an error, even though the proper password has in fact been typed. The solution is simply to suggest to users that they always type the password the same way. If you always type the password in lowercase or you always type it in uppercase (or you always type it in one particular combination, as long as the combination stays the same), everything will work fine.

Also watch for login scripts from Windows and Windows for Workgroups machines. When a Windows or Windows for Workgroups user logs into a Windows NT (or, for that matter, LAN Manager) system in which the administrator has defined a logon script, the Windows 3.x machine initiates a virtual DOS session in which to execute the script. However, the virtual DOS system remains "live" for only approximately 30 seconds, which is not a configurable parameter. Therefore, if a script takes more than 30 seconds to execute, it will fail. The user will see an error message that the script has violated system integrity and will complain to the system administrator.

The solution for the 30-second limit is to keep your scripts short or disable script operation entirely when you have Windows users logging in. Remote users logging in over Microsoft's remote access services (RAS) or through a remote TCP/IP gateway traveling over async modem lines are especially affected because all operations will be slow over such a connection. You can disable the script support feature in the Windows control panel by running Control Panel. Choose the Network icon, choose the Networks button, select Microsoft LAN Manager in the

Other Networks In Use box, choose Settings..., and clear the "Logon to LAN Manager Domain" check-box. This is not an ideal solution, but it will get the job done.

Finally, watch for DOS and Windows workstations that hang during login because multiple processes are attempting to address the network adapter card while the card is handling an MS-DOS command. Microsoft supplies a TSR program called COMNDIS.COM that solves this problem. It's on the LAN Manager 2.2 installation disks in the LANMAN.DOS/NETPROG directory. If COMNDIS.COM is used, it should be the last thing loaded in AUTOEXEC.BAT, and it must start before any LAN Manager commands (except netbind).

COMNDIS.COM is not necessary with Windows for Workgroups, which uses a protected mode protocol stack and does not have the problem (unless it's used with real mode drivers, in which case COMENDIS might be desirable). In any case, try this solution only on those work-stations with a demonstrated propensity to hang when running with Windows NT (or LAN Manager) Servers.

How LAN Manager Clients Access Windows NT Servers In general, a LAN Manager client will see a Windows NT Server as if it were a LAN Manager Server. The same operations that are normally used on the client (File Manager from Windows, File Manager or the *net* command-line interface from OS/2, the NET.EXE program from DOS) will be used to access the Windows NT Server. All these procedures work very much the same for Windows NT as for LAN Manager, and in general, you can see the LAN Manager documentation for details.

We present here a very limited subset of the commands that are portable between (as far as we know) *all* versions of LAN Manager, Windows for Workgroups, Windows 95, and Windows NT. It's useful for a system administrator to be able to walk up to any station and carry out a minimal set of steps with a known response. However, there are better solutions for each individual environment, and we encourage you to consult the documentation for the system in question. Our portable command-line subset is as follows:

1. To use a shared resource from a LAN Manager, Windows NT, or Windows for Workgroups Server:

   net use device \\server name\share name

   Net use will permit you to redirect a network resource on a particular server and see it as a local device. Network resources include both shared directories and (LAN Manager only) printers. The syntax of this command is generally similar to the equivalent Windows NT command that is defined in Chapter 3. It works almost identically on all systems. As an example:

   net use m: \\mips-lab-server\WGPO

   will redirect the WGPO shared directory on \\mips-lab-server to local drive m:. Just typing net use by itself, with no arguments, will list any shared resources currently in use at the local workstation.

2. To browse shared resources (directories and printers) on LAN Manager, Windows NT and Windows for Workgroups, or Windows 95 Servers:

```
net view
-or-
net view \\server name
```

Without arguments, net view displays a list of servers on the local subnetwork. Net view\\server name displays a list of the shares on the server. Thus, the process of command-line browsing on any form of Microsoft network is generally to type net view to see the list of servers, net view and the name of a server to see the list of resources at the server, and net use local device name \\server_name\resource to access the resource. When resource sharing is finished, you can type net use device name /delete to terminate use of a shared resource.

3. To send messages on LAN Manager and Windows NT networks:

```
net send name message text
-or-
net send /DOMAIN:domain name message text
-or-
net send /BROADCAST message text
```

Net send provides basic messaging capabilities using class-2 mail slot broadcasts, as we described in the introduction to this section. In general, the form of the command is **net send** *name text*. For example:

```
net send Administrator How do I use this blankety-blank thing?
```

will send the text "How do I use this blankety-blank thing?" which will appear in a pop-up display on the workstation to which the Administrator is logged in.

4. To share resources on LAN Manager, Windows for Workgroups, and Windows NT systems:

```
net share sharename=local path
```

The syntax of the NET SHARE command is net share share name = directory specification. For instance:

```
net share disk-D=D:\
```

will share the D:\ device (and subtrees) with the share name disk-D. This is a completely portable syntax among all versions of LAN Manager. Various switches and flags will vary from version to version. On all versions of LAN Manger that support sharing, you can also type net share without any parameters to get a list of any shared devices and net share share name /DELETE to terminate sharing of a device.

Portable Administration With the four commands listed above an administrator can reliably get work done moving from system to system in a mixed LAN Manager network. LAN Manager DOS workstations, LAN Manager workstations running Windows, Windows for Workgroups systems (version 3.1 and 3.11), Windows 95 systems, Windows NT systems (Workstation and Server), and LAN Manager OS/2 systems (stand-alone servers, peers, and domain servers) all handle these four commands in generally the same way. The consistency is one of the nicest, if least understood, features of the entire LAN Manager system.

Integrating WfWG with Windows NT

From the network standpoint, the most important difference between WfWG and NT is that WfWG always uses share-level security to share resources between stations on a network. This approach is less secure and harder to manage centrally than the user-level security primarily used by NT. For compatibility reasons, NT also offers share-level security. If you already have a Windows for Workgroups LAN installed, you can add one or more NT systems and use share-level security equivalent to that used in Windows for Workgroups.

Workgroup or Domain? Taken on its own, Windows for Workgroups is a completely decentralized network that emphasizes sharing rather than security. You configure each WfWG system to be a member of a *workgroup*, which is primarily an organizational convenience. For example, when you browse the network within a File Open dialog in WfWG, you see the other users' names arranged in a two-level hierarchy based on the workgroup to which the users belong.

Workgroups do not figure into the WfWG security scheme. In fact, the only security options you have when sharing a directory on a WfWG PC are to make the directory read-only and to protect access (either read-only or read-write) with a password. All other WfWG, Windows NT, or LAN-Manager-compatible systems can connect to the shared directory, whether they're in your workgroup or not. The only way you can control who accesses the resource is by controlling the password for it.

The casually cooperative and decentralized nature of WfWG and its workgroup scheme lets users share files and devices with a minimum of hassle. However, if you're planning to use WfWG with Windows NT, you may want to make WfWG users part of a domain.

With Windows NT Server, a *domain* is a group of servers that use the same set of user accounts. Domains, unlike workgroups, are important contributors to security and system administration. The details of configuring WfWG users for workgroups or domains are presented later in this chapter. Chapter 8 contains a complete discussion of domains and their operation in Windows NT Server.

File Sharing

To set up file-sharing connections in Windows for Workgroups, use File Manager. The WfWG File Manager is visually very close to the one that was in NT 3.51 (see figure 9.1).

Sharing a Directory When you share a directory on a WfWG system, you can access the directory from any WfWG, Windows NT, or other LAN-Manager-compatible system on the network. In addition to the obvious use in sharing a hard disk directory, you can share floppy drives, Bernoulli removable disks, or CD-ROM drives this way.

From File Manager, select Disk/Share As from the menu or click on the toolbar icon of a hand holding a folder. You'll get the dialog box shown in Figure 9.2.

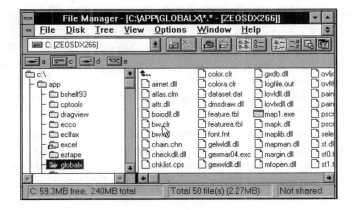

FIGURE 9.1 File Manager. The Windows for Workgroups File Manager is very simi-lar to the NT 3.x File Manager.

Enter the name of the directory you want to share. The share name must be unique for this system, but does not need to be unique network-wide. That is, other computers could share a resource with the name EXCEL, because each share name will always be associated with (and qualified by) a particular computer name.

If you want to share the directory only temporarily, for example, so that someone can copy a few files, clear the Re-share at Startup check-box. If this box is checked, WfWG will auto-matically re-share the directory each time you restart your system.

WfWG offers only two levels of access: read-only and full. You can require that someone who wants to use the directory provide a password for either or both types of access. Remember

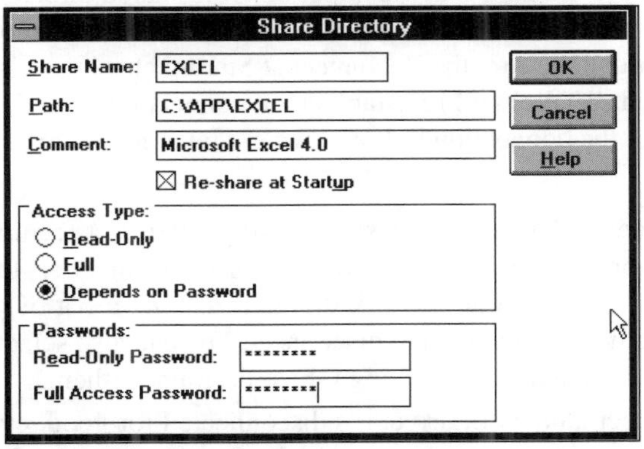

FIGURE 9.2 Share directory dialog. You control Directory Sharing in Windows for Workgroups through this dialog, which appears when you select the "Share As..." menu item (or speed button) in File Manager.

that full access allows anyone to delete or rename files and subdirectories below the shared directory. Also, although NT lets you share a directory multiple times by different names (and potentially different passwords), WfWG lets you share a particular directory only once.

Once you've shared a directory, File Manager's directory tree will give you a visual clue that the directory is shared by using the folder-in-hand icon rather than the standard folder icon. Also, if you click on a directory that is shared, the right side of File Manager's status bar will show you the share name mapping.

Stop Sharing a Directory Before you stop sharing a directory, be sure that all users currently using the directory are notified and asked to stop using it. Otherwise, if you stop sharing a directory that is in use, those users connected to it could lose data. You can find out who is using files in one of your shared directories by selecting the directory, choosing File/Properties from the menu, then clicking the Open By button.

You can either select Disk/Stop Sharing from the menu or click the toolbar icon of a hand holding a grayed-out folder. Select the directory you want to stop sharing from the list in the dialog box. If other people are currently using the directory, you'll get a warning that they might lose data if you continue, and you will be asked for confirmation.

Using a Remote Directory Windows for Workgroups is flexible about letting you make connections to other PCs. You can either set up these connections from File Manager ahead of time or wait until you need a file and make the connection at that point.

To connect to a remote directory from within File Manager, select Connect Network Drive from the Disk menu or click the toolbar button showing the network drive icon. You can also get to this dialog box through the File Open and File Save dialogs used by most applications. If the application uses the standard dialog, there will be a button labeled "Network..." you can click to bring up the Connect Network Drive dialog (see Figure 9.3).

Regardless of how you get to the Connect Network Drive dialog, it works the same way. If you click on one of the system names in the upper box, the shared directories on that system are displayed in the lower box. You can double-click one of the directories to establish the connection. Before you do, though, be sure the Reconnect at Startup check-box is set the way you want it. If this box is checked, WfWG will re-establish the connection each time you restart the system. If it's not checked, the connection will end when you exit Windows and never come back to bother you.

Stop Using a Remote Directory To stop using a remote directory, select Disk/Disconnect Network Drive from File Manager's menu or click the toolbar button that shows an X-mark over a grayed-out network drive. You'll get a list of your network connections; just double-click the one you want to disconnect. You can also select multiple connections by control-clicking on them and then clicking OK to disconnect them.

When you disconnect a network drive, it's disconnected for good, even if you checked the Reconnect at Startup check-box when you were in the Connect Network Drive dialog originally. That option applies only when you exit Windows with drives connected, then restart Windows. It's logical when you think about it.

What's not so logical is that File Manager has a little bug. If you have File Manager running and then create your first connection outside File Manager—for example, through a batch

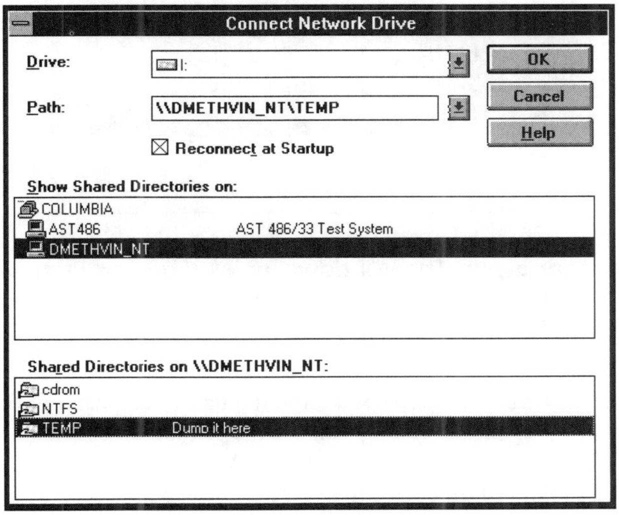

FIGURE 9.3 Connect net drive dialog. You use a shared directory on a Windows for Workgroups system with this dialog, which appears when you select the "Connect Net Drive..." menu item (or speed button) in File Manager.

file or File Open dialog inside an application—you won't get a drive icon for that connection inside File Manager. Also, the menu option and button to disconnect drives stay grayed out, which of course makes it hard to disconnect anything. If you exit File Manager and restart it, though, you'll see all your connections and be able to pull the plug on any of them.

Printer Management

A Windows for Workgroups system can share any printers that are locally attached to it. However, each PC that wants to share a printer must install the Windows printer driver for that printer locally. It's usually easiest to install drivers for all your printers on every PC when you install WfWG so that you won't be hunting for installation disks when you'd rather be printing.

Print Manager is a vital part of the WfWG printer sharing scheme, not just for establishing connections but also for maintaining them. You must start Print Manager and keep it running to share printers. This is different from the situation with File Manager, which establishes file shares but does not need to be running for those shares to work. If you're connected to a printer that many other people use, it would be a good idea to put a Print Manager entry in your Program Manager StartUp folder.

Figure 9.4 illustrates a typical Print Manager window.

Sharing a Printer To share a printer, select File/Share Printer from Print Manager's menu or click the toolbar icon that shows a hand holding a printer. You will then see the dialog box shown in Figure 9.5.

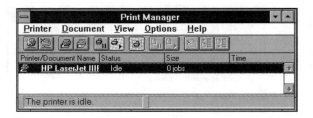

FIGURE 9.4 Print Manager. The Windows for Workgroups Print Manager controls network printers the same way as the NT 3.x Print Manager. The two systems differ, however, in their use of printer drivers.

Select the printer you want to share and assign it a name. You can optionally assign a password that other users must enter before they can use the printer. Select Re-share at Startup if you want the printer to be shared each time you start Print Manager. If you clear this check-box, the printer will be shared only until the next time you exit Print Manager.

Stop Sharing a Printer You can use either the menu selection Printer/Stop Sharing Printer or the toolbar button showing a hand with a grayed-out printer. Either way, you'll then get a dialog box showing all the printers you are currently sharing. Select the printer you want to stop sharing, then click OK.

Using a Remote Printer Note once again that to use a remote printer you will need to have a driver for that printer on your local system. (This isn't true for Windows NT, which can automatically obtain the driver from the system that shares the printer.)

To make the connection, select Printer/Connect Network Printer from the menu or click on the toolbar icon showing a printer with a network wire connected to it. There might be a slight delay while Print Manager polls the network for available printers, then you will get the dialog box illustrated in Figure 9.6.

Many applications will also let you select a network printer from a Print dialog or Print Setup menu selection. This is the most convenient option if you use a certain network printer only occasionally. You will need to check the specific application to see if it supports network printers directly.

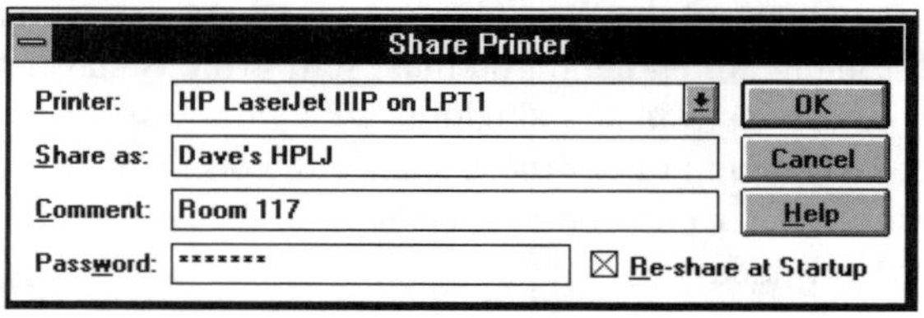

FIGURE 9.5 Share printer dialog. You control Printer Sharing in Windows for Workgroups from this dialog, which appears when you select the "Share As..." menu item (or speed button) in Print Manager.

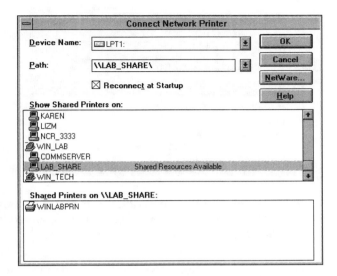

FIGURE 9.6 Connect network printer. You control use of network printers by a Windows for Workgroups system from this dialog, which appears when you select the "Connect to Printer..." menu item (or speed button) Print Manager.

Stop Using a Remote Printer To terminate a remote printer connection, select Printer/Disconnect Network Printer from the menu or use the toolbar button that depicts a network-connected printer with an X-mark next to it. You will get a dialog box with your current network printer connections. Select the printer you want to stop using, then click OK.

Windows for Workgroups Utilities

In addition to the bread-and-butter utilities like File Manager and Print Manager are other applications that make it easier to exchange data and messages with other users and to diagnose problems.

Mail and Schedule+ The versions of Microsoft Mail and Schedule+ that are provided with WfWG work fine with the Windows NT versions. It's usually best to set up the mail post office on a Windows NT system, then share the post office directory so that the WfWG systems can use it.

Chat The WfWG Chat utility is a split-screen message utility for point-to-point conversations over the network. It interoperates with and looks identical to the Windows NT version. At present, WfWG does not come with a broadcast messaging utility that would let you receive a note such as "Main server going down in 5 minutes" from a Windows NT system.

NetWatcher NetWatcher (illustrated in Figure 9.7) lets you see what connections other PCs have to your PC and when those connections were last active. You can also forcibly break connections.

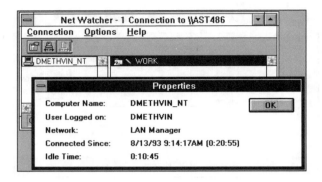

FIGURE 9.7 NetWatcher application. The Windows for Workgroups NetWatcher provides a degree of control over remote network connections, which is similar to (but more limited than) the Server applet in the NT Control Panel.

WinMeter WinMeter (illustrated in Figure 9.8) shows the CPU time use on a computer. One color is used for local applications, and another for the server component. This is a quick way to see if a PC is being bogged down by access from remote users. You can control the amount of CPU time remote users can get through the Network section of Control Panel.

Integrating Windows 95 with Windows NT

In its networking aspects, Windows 95 is an evolutionary step from Windows 3.1 and Windows for Workgroups. The core of the Windows 95 operating system still has some 16-bit code so that it can be maximally compatible with Windows 3.1 and DOS, but many of the core functions are now implemented as 32-bit protected mode software. As a result, Windows 95 offers greater reliability, better performance, and easier setup than Windows 3.1. However, its robustness and security are still below the level of those for Windows NT, a point that even Microsoft emphasizes as one of the advantages of NT.

Choosing a Protocol Out of the box, Win95 supports most of the networking environments and configurations you're likely to want. In addition to support for Microsoft's own NetBEUI and SMB protocols, Win95 supports IPX/SPX and Novell's NCP protocols, so you can easily connect to NetWare Servers. Multiple protocol stacks can be used with a single networking card,

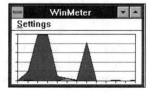

FIGURE 9.8 WinMeter application. The Windows for Workgroups WinMeter application provides a visual indication of system activity, which is similar to (but more limited than) that provided by the NT Performance Monitor.

so you can use NetBEUI/SMB for peer sharing with NT and IPX/NCP for NetWare. Win95 takes care of all the details after you've set up the protocols.

If you prefer, you can use TCP/IP as your transport protocol with Win95. Drivers are included in the box, as are interfaces for sockets (WinSock) and remote procedure calls (DCE RPC). If you have WINS and DHCP Servers on your network, Win95 workstations can be configured to query these servers to obtain their network addresses and names.

For absolute compatibility, Windows 95 does offer you the ability to use 16-bit real-mode client drivers such as Novell's NETX. You might be tempted to use this solution if you have an unusual TSR or DOS program that depends intimately on Novell's driver, but don't do it. First, the 16-bit software will have lower performance and be less reliable than the built-in support. Second, you can have only one protocol stack per network card if you use real-mode drivers. Finally, Win95's remote management capabilities aren't available if you use a real-mode driver. All of these are serious drawbacks, so it's better to remove or replace the offending code that requires old drivers.

You would expect Win95 workstations to work very well with Windows NT, but they also work well with Novell NetWare. With either type of server, you can configure a Windows 95 workstation so that it will pass the user name and password on to the server for verification. The support for Novell's NCP API is good enough that you can run Novell's own DOS-based tools from Win95 to configure a NetWare Server connection. Fortunately, you won't often need to do that because most common operations like attaching to a NetWare printer are supported through Win95's graphical interface. NetWare Servers aren't second-class citizens anymore.

Managing Windows 95 Users As with WfWG, Win95 can use pass-through security to validate logons using the server's password capabilities. The tradeoffs associated with this approach are described in the section labeled "User Account Management" later in this chapter. Because many Win95 network admin features depend on user-level security, it's highly recommended for all but the smallest networks.

Once you have set up user-level security, you can use the *user profiles* feature to greatly simplify management of Win95 workstations. On a user-by-user basis, you can control whether the user can use, change, or even *see* many features of Win95's interface. For example, you can prevent the user from changing the screen saver options so that a password-protected screen saver can't be easily defeated. You can disable peer services so that users can't share their personal printers or hard disks. And if you have users who share a pool of PCs, such as in a classroom environment, settings will follow users as they log in from PC to PC.

File Sharing

The Explorer interface in Windows 95 (and now NT 4.0) is very different from the old File Manager used by Windows for Workgroups or Windows NT 3.5. For a new user it's often easier to use, especially because it provides many ways to access the same features. If you think semi-logically and don't mind experimenting by right-clicking and double-clicking, you can probably find a way to do everything you formerly did in File Manager.

Sharing a Directory When you share a directory on a Win95 system, you can access the directory from any system on the network that has a protocol stack compatible with yours. You can share directories, floppy drives, Bernoulli removable disks, or CD-ROM drives.

To share a directory or device, right-click on it in Explorer and select Sharing. You'll get a dialog box that lets you select the share name and type of access. Remember that Win95 clients that share resources do not employ user-level security; you must use share-level security.

Using Remote Files The simplest way to use shared files in Windows 95 is to simply use the full UNC name when you are inside an application. So, instead of mapping the U drive to \\ATT3360\DATA and then specifying a file name of U:\MYFILE.DAT, just type the name \\ATT3360\DATA\MYFILE.DAT. If you don't know the entire path, but know the share name, most file dialog boxes will let you type \\ATT3360\DATA*.*, then click OK, and you can browse from there.

However, you probably have older 16-bit Windows or DOS applications that won't take kindly to newfangled UNC names. In this case, you can set up a drive mapping. In Explorer, select the directory you want to map and click the Map Network Drive button. Alternatively, you can right-click the My Computer icon and map drives from there. You can unmap the drives from the same two locations. Drive mappings are shown under the My Computer window, which is usually the most convenient place to examine and remove them.

If you have a remote file or folder that you use frequently, you can put a shortcut to it on the desktop. To do this, double-click the Network Neighborhood and browse the network for the item you want to access. Using the mouse, click and drag the item out onto the desktop. On the menu that appears, click Create Shortcut Here. You can now double-click this icon to access the file or folder.

Printer Management

Windows 95 makes many improvements over Windows for Workgroups in the management of shared printers. First, you do not need to have Print Manager active to share or use remote printers. Second, the drivers for network printers can be dynamically downloaded to the workstation when you connect to the printer. This capability eliminates the need for the system administrator to install printer drivers on every workstation.

In Win95, Connections to networked printers are implemented essentially as temporary shares that are active for only as long as it takes to send the file to the network printer. This is particularly important for NetWare Servers, for which every attached user counts against the license limits for that server.

Sharing a Printer To share a printer on a Win95 workstation, click the Start button and select Settings>Printers. (You can also get to this window through Control Panel or My Computer.) Right-click on the name of the printer you want to share and select Properties. Go to the Sharing tab and set the information for the way you want to share the printer.

If you have a NetWare network, you have another alternative for sharing a printer attached to a Win95 workstation. With Peer Services for NetWare Clients installed, you can set up the workstation to de-spool print jobs from a queue on a NetWare Server. That way, you can subject the print jobs to the standard NetWare user restrictions but still have the printer attached to the workstation.

Using a Remote Printer To use a remote printer, open the Network Neighborhood and find the name of the printer you want to use. Right-click on it and select "Capture Printer Port" from the menu. Then select the printer port (such as LPT1) you want to assign to this printer. Alternatively, you can create a shortcut for this printer on your desktop. To print a file you can either open the application, load the file, then select File/Print from the application's menu, or just drop the file onto the printer shortcut.

If you use a Win95 workstation that is connected to a network only sporadically, such as a notebook PC, the deferred printing capability may prove useful. If you print to a printer that isn't currently available, the print job will be spooled on the local PC. When the PC is reconnected to the network, the print job will restart and be sent to the printer.

User Account Management

Although neither Windows for Workgroups nor Windows 95 provides user-name-based security when used by itself in a peer-to-peer arrangement, either can be integrated nicely into the Windows NT security scheme. You have essentially three options when you are integrating WfWG/Win95 users and NT Workstation or NT Server systems. Your decision in implementing user accounts should balance the need for security against convenience and hassle-free access to resources. Also remember that a very secure system will require someone to administer the user accounts and set permissions appropriately.

Option 1: No Accounts, Share-Level Security If you have an established WfWG system or if security is not a critical issue, you can add the Windows NT and NTAS Servers to your network and use share-level security to make their resources available to the network. These new servers will simply show up in the browse lists as do all the WfWG/Win95 computers. To users, it just looks as if you've added another machine to the network, but there's no change at all in their work habits.

This first option works because of the behavior of the Windows NT "Guest" account. If the user name and password for a WfWG/Win95 user don't match exactly with the user name and password of the NT system, you are granted Guest access anyway.

On an NT Server, the Guest account is disabled by default to increase the security of the network. If you want to use this option on NT Server, you'll need to enable the Guest account. To do this, run User Manager and double-click on the account named Guest. By default, the Account Disabled check-box will be checked. Un-check it to make shared resources available to those who don't have accounts on this system (or domain, depending on how you've set up security). Now, any shared resource for which the group "Everyone" has been given access in File Manager will be accessible to all users on the network.

Option 2: Windows NT User Accounts If you require more security than option 1 allows, you can get it by creating an account on each of your Windows NT systems for every WfWG user. The password should be the same password users use to log into their WfWG system. Whenever a WfWG user connects to a resource on a Windows NT system, it will use that user's name and password rather than the Guest account to validate security.

You can, of course, have a hybrid of options 1 and 2 in which most of the users use the Guest account permissions and you create only a few accounts for users who need more (or less) access. For example, to restrict access to certain shares, give the Everyone group the No Access permission, and override this by giving Full Access (or other) Permissions to specified groups of users. Be warned, however, that this approach can become unwieldy if you have many users and/or NT systems. At some point, you may want to move to option 3, not for security, but for simplicity of account management.

Option 3: Domain Login Option 3 is the most secure way to run a WfWG system with NT Server. You actually set up the WfWG/Win95 system so that it logs onto your network domain when WfWG starts. To implement this approach, first create the domain and user accounts under NT Server. The user accounts should match the names of the users of the WfWG/Win95 systems you want to add.

The next step is to set up the clients. On a WfWG system go into Control Panel and open the Network dialog. Click on the Networks button at the bottom of the dialog; a list of installed networks should appear. Select LAN Manager from the Other Networks in Use list and click on the Settings button. The Dialog illustrated in Figure 9.9 will be displayed. Check the check-box labeled Log On to LAN Manager Domain, and enter the domain name. Wind your way out by clicking OK on all the dialog boxes.

On a Win95 client, right-click the Network Neighborhood icon and select Properties. Under the Access Control tab, select User-Level Access Control. In the box under this setting, type in either the server name in UNC style (\\servername) or the domain name if you are using domain-level security.

Although option 3 is the most organized and secure approach, it does have its share of caveats. Users need to come to this dialog to change their passwords so that the domain controller is informed of the change. (You can also use the NET PASSWORD command from a DOS prompt; see the section in this chapter on the NET command.) Don't depend on domain login to keep local information on a WfWG system safe. A knowledgeable person can disable domain login and boot the system by removing the LMLogon entry in the [network] section of SYS-TEM.INI. At the very least, someone could boot the system into DOS and copy sensitive files.

Command-Line Network Interface

Windows 95 and Windows for Workgroups include a DOS command-line interface (NET.EXE) that gives you access to many of the resource sharing features. They are particularly useful inside automated batch files.

A summary of the most useful NET commands is given in the following sections. You can get a complete list of commands and their options by typing **NET /?** or learn details on a specific command by typing **NET <command> /?**.

NET CONFIG The NET CONFIG command gives you a summary of this PC's network information, which is very useful while you're trying to debug things. A typical display looks like this:

```
C:\WFWG> NET CONFIG
Computer name                    \\AST486
User name                        DMETHVIN

Software version                 3.1
Redirector version               2.50

Workstation root directory       C:\WFWG
Workgroup                        COLUMBIA
The command completed successfully.

C:\WFWG>
```

NET LOGON NET LOGON logs this system into the workgroup. If you don't supply a user name or password on the command line, you will be prompted for them. Any NET USE commands that you specified as PERSISTENT (and the ones specified as "Reconnect at Startup" inside File Manager) are reconnected at this time.

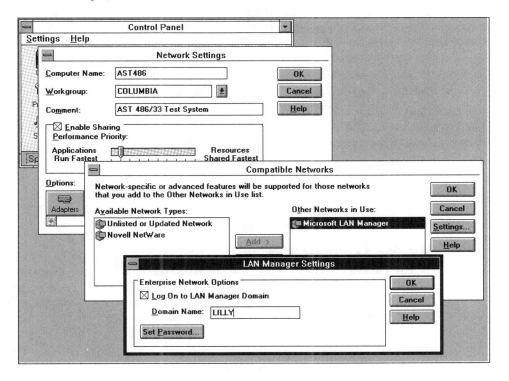

FIGURE 9.9 Lan Manager setting dialog. This dialog, accessed from the Windows for Workgroups Control Panel/Network Settings, allows the specification of a LAN Manager (or NT Server) logon domain and associated password.

NET LOGOFF The NET LOGOFF command logs you off the workgroup and breaks any network connections.

NET PASSWORD NET PASSWORD Changes your logon password. If you don't enter the old or new passwords on the command line, you'll be prompted for them. You can specify computer, domain, and user names if you also want to change your password at an NT Workstation or an NT Server domain. Otherwise, the password will be changed only in your local password file (<systemname>.PWL in the \WINDOWS directory).

NET PRINT The NET PRINT command lets you display the print queues on printers you are sharing and also lets you delete a print job that you have submitted to a printer but that hasn't yet printed.

NET TIME NET TIME lets you synchronize your computer's clock with the clock on a Windows NT system or Microsoft LAN Manager time server. This command is especially handy as part of each system's AUTOEXEC.BAT file to make sure all the clocks on the network are in sync.

NET USE The NET USE command establishes or breaks connections to network files and printers, and it has numerous options that are explicitly documented in the online help. If you enter NET USE with no arguments, it will display your current connections.

You can make a connection persistent by specifying the option /PERSISTENT:YES. This means that WfWG will re-establish the connection each time the network is started. Normally, NET USE will save the password along with the persistent connection. If you prefer to re-enter the password each time the computer starts, specify /SAVEPW:NO.

Other options of NET USE let you manage your persistent connections. You can display your persistent connections that will automatically be created the next time you start this system, clear the list of persistent connections, or make all your current connections persistent. This last option is useful so that when you get your connections set up the way you want them, you can take a "snapshot" for later sessions.

Migration from LAN Manager to Windows NT Server

If you're running LAN Manager Servers today, how do you go about moving to Windows NT? Note that we are discussing migration from LAN Manager to Windows NT *Server*, not "Migration... to Windows NT *Workstation* because you can't migrate to the workstation. To retain LAN Manager's centralized account management it is essential to move to an NT Server environment.

As stated above, Windows NT Servers cannot participate as members of OS/2 LAN Manager domains. They can participate only as members of a Windows NT Server domain, so you need to upgrade at least one system to a Windows NT Server. As we recommended earlier, if you upgrade one, you had better upgrade two. The first matter then is to set up a machine as a Windows NT Server. You probably won't want to do this with the machine being used as the primary domain controller in the OS/2 network, for obvious reasons. You can convert the accounts from the OS/2 LAN Manager system to NT Server accounts using the PORTUAS.EXE utility included with Windows NT Server software. This command has the syntax:

portuas-l `file name`

where filename specifies the LAN Manager 2.x NET.ACT file. Of course the filename is always NET.ACT, but you must use the full network path name. For example:

`portuas-l\\primary_server\admin\net.act`

You can use two flag variables: -u followed by a user name will specify a single user or group to port if you don't want to port the entire user account base. This makes sense, particularly in setting up a pilot project in which only a certain group of people will initially be exposed to the Windows NT Server environment. The second is -v, which displays all messages and which we recommend. This will give you a notification of any problems.

You must have administrative privileges to run portuas for which you can find further information in the on-line help system for NT Server and in the NT Server documentation.

Once the user accounts are converted, it is necessary to restore the OS/2 access control list to Windows NT access rights. At this point, of course, we have a major issue with respect to the file system, because access rights at the directory and subdirectory levels require NTFS on Windows NT. Therefore, when you migrate from an OS/2 LAN Manager system to a Windows NT Server, it is necessary for the NT Server to have an NTFS volume for the administrative information. This conversion requires using the ACLCONV.EXE utility. This command has the syntax:

aclconv `/data: datafile /log:logfile`

where datafile specifies the full path name for the OS/2 LAN Manager BACCACC.ACL datafile (created through the use of the OS/2 LAN Manager BACKACC command) and logfile specifies a file wherein aclconv will log information about failed conversions. For example, the command:

`aclconv/data:\\primary_server\admin\baccacc.acl /log:error.log`

will convert the BACCACC.ACL file in the ADMIN directory on the OS/2 LAN Manager primary server to directory permissions on the current NTFS volume and will store information about failed conversions in the ERROR.LOG file. You would then inspect the ERROR.LOG file and carry out any missing conversions manually. Note that the drive letter for the NTFS volume in which the ACLs are being restored must be the same as the drive letter on the original machine. You cannot restore the permissions from a C: drive on a LAN Manager OS/2 Server onto a D: NTFS volume on a Windows NT Server.

In summary, the steps necessary to convert from a LAN Manager OS/2 Server primary domain controller to a Windows NT Server as primary domain controller are:

1. Take the primary domain controller off-line. You will probably want to do this after hours when fewer users will need to be forced off the system.

2. Back up access permissions using the LAN Manager for OS/2 BACKACC command.

3. Share the administrative disk drives on the OS/2 system and make them accessible to the Windows NT system.

4. From the Windows NT system issue the PORTUAS command to port the user accounts from the LAN Manager for OS/2 system.

5. Use the OS/2 LAN Manager BACKACC command to back up the permissions on the directories on the server.

6. Transfer them to the Windows NT system using the ACLCONV command.

Conclusion

What used to be called LAN Manager networking (and Microsoft would now like to call Windows networking) is in a state of flux as represented by the changed names, browsing specification, APIs, and so on. Any time there's change there's a certain amount of confusion—and no doubt we've added to that confusion here.

It's worth noting that the migration problems introduced by Windows NT are certainly no worse than those faced by people upgrading from NetWare 3.x to NetWare 4.x. And it also seems clear that LAN Manager/Windows networking has a bright future. The Windows NT Server has been embraced as a database application server by every major vendor of client/server database software. Hardware manufacturers are lining up to supply platforms for servers and for high-end workstations.

The move to TCP/IP as the standard networking protocol, which began with LAN Manager 2.1, is accelerating under Windows NT, driven in part by NT's rapid acceptance as an alternative to UNIX on the Internet. On the whole, the advantages of incorporating Windows NT into LAN Manager and Windows for Workgroups networks far outweigh any disadvantage. This is a system to which you can migrate with confidence.

For More Information

Microsoft Staff (1993), *Windows for Workgroups Resource Kit*. Redmond, WA: Microsoft Corp. The encyclopedic guide to every setting in every initialization file in Windows for Workgroups. Also discusses the overall WfWG architecture and the differences between real- and enhanced-mode operation of WfWG.

Microsoft Staff (1995), *Windows 95 Resource Kit*. Redmond, WA: Microsoft Corp. As above, for Windows 95.

Microsoft Staff (1993–1996), *Windows NT 4.0 Server Concepts and Planning Guide*. Redmond, WA: Microsoft Corp. A solid and well-written introduction to Server issues including administration, replication, fault tolerance, and user environment management. A bit weak on the details of migration from LAN Manager, this book nonetheless contains essential information. If you begin an NT Server installation without reading this book, you are making a serious mistake.

Microsoft Staff (1993–1996), *Windows NT Server System Guide*. Redmond, WA: Microsoft Corp. All the details are written here.

Novell Connections: Windows NT and NetWare

After reading this chapter, you will understand the fundamental similarities and differences between Windows NT's built-in networking and the networking services provided by both Microsoft and Novell for NT-to-NetWare connectivity. These include:

➲ Microsoft's NWLink IPX/SPX Protocol, included with both NT Server and Workstation, which lets Windows NT provide access to NetWare clients and a way for NT to act as a gateway to NetWare resources.

➲ Microsoft's Gateway Services for NetWare (GSNW), included with NT Server, which uses the NWLink IPX/SPX Protocol stack to provide access to shared directories and printers on NetWare servers with standard (for Windows NT) NDIS drivers. Besides shared file and printer access (like Novell's NetWare Client for Windows NT), GSNW provides command-line access to NetWare resources through the Windows NT net command interface and supports most DOS-based NetWare utilities. It also provides the foundation for Microsoft's NetWare Migration Tool (also included in NT Server), which provides server-side utilities that simplify integrating NT Server into NetWare environments.

➲ Microsoft's Client Services for NetWare (CSNW), which is included with NT Workstation, and Novell's NetWare Client for Windows NT, which lets NT clients access shared directories and printers on NetWare servers. It also supports both non-standard (for Windows NT) Open Datalink Interface ODI) drivers and Windows NT standard Network Device Interface Specification (NDIS) drivers.

➪ Microsoft's Services for NetWare add-on to NT Server, which includes File and Print Services for NetWare (FPNW), a product that allows Windows NT Server to emulate a Novell file server, and DSMN (Domain Services Manager for NetWare).

➪ Wide-Area Network (WAN) connectivity to NetWare LANs via Remote Access Service (RAS). NetWare users have several options that allow either tunneled connectivity through the Internet or intranets or the use of dial-up modems, frame relay, X.25, or ISDN connections.

➪ Methods you can use to successfully deploy Windows NT Server into an heterogeneous but largely NetWare enterprise network.

The NetWare Story

Defending one's preferred network platform has taken on quasi-religious significance in many corporate Information Technology (IT) shops. But it's a fact of life—probably obvious to everyone reading this book—that the story of PC-based local area networking is largely the story of one company: Novell. Its great contribution was to eliminate the link between proprietary network hardware and software that characterized virtually all networking systems in the 1970s.

Until Novell's initial offerings in the early 1980s, connectivity between personal computers was monolithic, and the phrase "open systems" was an oxymoron. Usually a single vendor's wiring, network interface components, and operating procedures were used to connect personal computers. With NetWare, Novell crystallized the notion of a Network Operating System (NOS) that could work with hardware from many vendors.

Although initially popular with mainly network interface card vendors, who had Original Equipment Manufacturer (OEM) relationships with Novell, NetWare itself soon became independent of the OEMs. A strong secondary products market began and continues to flourish in NetWare-certified networking products that range from PCs through software and peripherals such as tape drives.

Until version 3.0, NetWare came in both dedicated and nondedicated versions. Nondedicated denoted the ability for the server console (the central file and print storage site) to also support a foreground DOS session. Although a version of nondedicated NetWare exists to this day (it runs on IBM's Warp Connect), other versions of NetWare proved to be unstable in nondedicated use.

This concept of dedicated versus nondedicated resource sharing is important because of its historical contrast with Microsoft's (and IBM)'s preference for nondedicated file and printer sharing. From an early point, Microsoft's networking philosophy treated file and printer sharing as just another process that runs with other user applications on a PC. The peer-to-peer structure that evolved as a result contrasts with Novell's server-centric approach.

NetWare NOS Advantages

NetWare is an incredibly efficient low-level architecture with a number of unusual features. It uses an unprotected memory model,[1] executes all processes in a single shared memory space, uses a variety of memory cache allocations, and employs special techniques, such as *elevator seeks*, that make it extremely efficient as a file-and-print server. In effect, NetWare exploits its own limitations. It may not provide virtual memory or preemptive multitasking, but it also doesn't have the overhead associated with such features. As a result, NetWare gives good performance in low-memory configurations where a Windows NT Server won't run at all.

Performance comparisons of Windows NT with NetWare on a given single-processor Intel-based server have traditionally favored the NetWare machine. If it has enough memory to run NT Server, it has *more* than enough memory to run NetWare. And NetWare will usually get better results from whatever disk drives and controllers are built into the machine than NT will.[2] NT can offset this shortcoming with such features as symmetric multiprocessing,[3] or by

---

1   Unlike the processes of NT, and those of most other modern operating systems, all NetWare processes operate in kernel mode (ring 0), sharing a common linear memory address space. This setup provides better performance by eliminating time-consuming *ring transitions* when user-mode applications call kernel-mode services, but it can decrease system reliability, especially when running third-party applications (in NetWare 4.*x*, Novell also supports running NLMs in user mode, but this is rarely done because it reduces performance—you just can't have it both ways!).

2   NT Server 4.0 has reduced the difference significantly. Microsoft has begun moving to a model similar to NetWare's for low-level services like file/print sharing. Such services are implemented as threads in the NT Executive, eliminating the overhead from ring transitions in previous versions. However, NT Server still needs more memory than NetWare for reasonable performance.

3   The long-awaited NetWare Symmetric Multiple Processing (NetWare-SMP) was finally delivered in late 1995. However, many comparative limitations are imposed: NetWare SMP is available only via OEM, such as Compaq and NCR, and it must be customized for a specific configuration. NT Server, by contrast, has built-in support for up to four CPUs in systems from a variety of vendors off the shelf, and it can often recognize and use additional processors during and after installation (versions of NT for more than four CPUs do have to be customized by the OEM, just as NetWare-SMP does).

abandoning the Intel processor to another line of CPUs, but few sites are willing to pay such a price to equalize NetWare's performance advantage in the kind of departmental setting in which it and NT Server compete.

Finally, prior to the advent of Windows NT 3.51 Service Pack 2, NetWare's built-in routing gave it an important competitive advantage over Windows NT. A multiprotocol router in NT Server now allows it to perform the same type of routing that NetWare provides—but with certain limitations that we'll discuss later.

NetWare as an Application Server

The notion of running a "back-end" application, such as a database, on the server, with user interactions handled by a client program running on one or more desktop systems is called *client/server computing*. A server used in such an environment is called an *application server*. Over the last few years, NT has become popular as an application server platform—in some cases, at the expense of NetWare.

Long before the release of NT 3.1 in 1993, Novell offered client/server programmers a way to build powerful server-side applications: NetWare Loadable Modules (NLMs), which allow developers to add processes either as utilities or as server-side applications to the NetWare server environment. Unfortunately, although developing NLMs isn't especially difficult, it represents a unique programming paradigm. The NetWare software architecture bears little resemblance to DOS, OS/2, Windows, UNIX, or NT. That uniqueness implies a rather steep learning curve and requires more of a commitment than many vendors have been willing to make.

NLMs aren't preemptible as NT services are. NetWare isn't event driven. Instead, applications running in the NetWare server poke their heads up every so often and look for other processes that require attention.[4] For that reason and because of the unprotected memory model mentioned earlier, it eventually became necessary for Novell to *certify* server applications to ensure that an ill-behaved application couldn't take over the machine and not relinquish it for other applications (and services) to use or overwrite memory in use by other processes.

Applications developed on traditional servers, such as Oracle's relational database (developed on UNIX) and IBM's Lotus Notes (developed on OS/2), have generally been less than successful in the NLM market. By contrast, each of these products has had much greater success on Windows NT. Only low-level service (fax servers, remote access, and other communications-oriented server applications) NLMs have fared well under NetWare.

NetWare Today

Novell's fifth-generation NOS, NetWare 4.*x*, introduced the concept of the NetWare Directory Service (NDS). NDS was designed to meet several needs: replace the complex multiple file

---

4   This model is known as *cooperative multitasking*, as contrasted with NT's *preemptive multitasking*.

user and managed object schema of the NetWare 3.*x* *bindery,*[5] provide a standards-based (quasi-ANSI X.500) directory system for single-point administration of many servers in many locations, and allow very large numbers of users and resources to be managed centrally. These capabilities, coupled with improved security, allowed NetWare 4.*x* to slowly take hold, and after several frustrating iterations it has now become largely stable.

Today, Novell's NetWare NOS accounts for some 70% of the local area networking market, although co-opted[6] market research firms all agree that the market share of NT-based servers is increasing dramatically. But homogeneous NOS installations have always been rare, and one of Novell's attractive qualities has been heterogeneous connectivity.

Unfortunately, in NT's first year on the market, Novell proved slow to support its use in NetWare environments. Microsoft eventually stopped waiting for Novell to provide NT connectivity and developed its own. Although Novell now provides client-oriented upgrades for NetWare on NT, its support for Windows NT has been late, leading to a great deal of administrator frustration.

Windows NT's built-in Server Message Block (SMB) networking is inherently incompatible with Novell's NetWare Core Protocol (NCP).[7] That incompatibility initially handicapped connectivity to NetWare, but Microsoft eventually took the initiative to add NetWare connectivity after Novell delayed delivering the necessary network redirector software.

Microsoft then developed the components needed to place an NT Server or Workstation into virtually any NetWare LAN and achieve user connections to or from NT. Novell has responded by making available NT Client Requester kits to connect NT Workstation (but not server as of this writing) to NT. No server-side components have been forthcoming from Novell, however, and management of NT systems using Novell's current NDS and "Green River" (also known as NetWare 4.11) administration tools are in beta test.

> **Warning:** *If you're reading this chapter, you probably have a NetWare server and need concrete advice on how to connect a Windows NT system to it. We will do our best to help you do that. In the process, we will recommend some things that do not have the blessing of either Novell or Microsoft. This entire subject area is an extremely complicated and fluid one for reasons that will become apparent. The relationship between Microsoft and Novell is complex and, as of this writing, less than amicable and is likely to remain so.[8]*
>
> *In view of the companies' relationship, please bear in mind that this is the one chapter of this book most likely to be overtaken by events. You are strongly advised to*

---

5   Novell's name for a central user and resource-sharing database. Prior to NetWare 4.0, each NetWare server maintained its own bindery, which made multi-server management somewhat difficult. NetWare 4.0 NDS provides enterprise-wide single-user accounts, much like NT Server Domain accounts.

6   Because they receive lots of money from both Novell and Microsoft!

7   See Appendix 2.

8   Note that this statement hasn't changed since our first edition was published back in 1994!

check what we have to say for yourself. At each stage, wherever possible, we have given you reference information to direct you to the very latest and most up-to-date information. Please treat this chapter as a starting point. It's vitally important, if you are to succeed in establishing and maintaining a good NT-to-NetWare relationship, that you develop and maintain your own active up-to-date sources of information.

Why Connecting Windows NT to NetWare Is Difficult

The facts of life are sometimes unpleasant. One unpleasant fact of life for Microsoft is that while Windows was becoming the dominant desktop environment, NetWare was becoming the dominant NOS. This situation is unfortunate from the point of view of the Windows NT user because Microsoft proceeded to make a number of rather engaging attempts in the networking field over the last few years. A whole series of products (described in Chapter 8) was introduced over the last few years with little success, ending with the technically impressive—but commercially unsuccessful—LAN Manager 2.x series.

The reason for Microsoft's lack of success is simple: NetWare provides a shared resource networking environment that in many respects is very similar to the kind of desktop operating system Microsoft has provided with DOS, while Microsoft made the mistake of trying to deliver something that might be better technically but didn't work as well for the end user.

A serious problem resulted for NT users: Microsoft and Novell invented their own communication protocols, and competitive pressures (coupled with arrogance) prevented timely, interoperable software from coming to market. The two protocols in question[9] can occupy and transverse the same network connecting wires, but they cannot be moved around the network in the same way or make sense of one another.

Whatever the origin of the problems, the components necessary to bridge NT Server or Workstation into NetWare LANs has become dramatically simplified, and we'll explain how a grouping of Microsoft and Novell products fills in the connectivity blanks.

Microsoft's NWLink Protocol Stack

Beyond redirecting simple shared files and printers, there's the larger matter of providing seamless NetWare client/server connectivity to NT 4. Microsoft's NWLink protocol stack takes care of this—while providing the low-level infrastructure needed by all of Microsoft's other NetWare connectivity applications. NWLink is installed by default during a typical installation of NT 4.0 Server or Workstation. The NWLink protocol is less trouble to set up than TCP/IP and offers better routing capability than Microsoft's older NetBEUI protocol. Microsoft documentation recommends installation of NWLink in any network running NetWare. We emphatically agree!

NWLink is a NetWare-compatible protocol stack that provides full 32-bit IPX/SPX connectivity from an NT Server or Workstation. In effect, it lets existing NetWare DOS, Windows,

---

9   SMB and NCP—see Appendix 2 for details.

and OS/2 clients access Windows NT Server in much the same way that they access NetWare servers. The NWLink protocol stack is the foundation for several different applications that are bundled inside NT Server 4.0 to provide connectivity, NetWare emulation, or various migration capabilities to NT. NT Workstation uses the NWLink protocol as the foundation for its NetWare client services.

NWLink does not provide any file or printer sharing of its own. Various services that we'll describe fit NT into a NetWare LAN or WAN and its resources. NWLink isn't monolithic: the full NetBIOS protocols that emulate NetBIOS over the IPX protocol are supported, the various levels of the Windows Network and Sockets APIs are supported, and Named Pipes are supported. Because all of these are implemented on top of an IPX/SPX stack (mostly using NetBIOS calls), a simple NetBIOS redirector in the client machines, such as Novell's IPX/NETX combination, provides a surprisingly high level of connectivity. More advanced client software, such as Novell's NetWare 32-bit Requester software, can also be used in a LAN/WAN in which Windows NT is desired to be placed.

The NWLink software also forms the basis for another application, called IPXROUTE.EXE. IPXRoute has the ability to read the source and destination of IPX/SPX packets coming into the NT Server and move the packets to another destination, usually another network cable segment or WAN device.

NWLink is more than sufficient for use as an application server, the role traditionally filled in NetWare environments by an NLM executing in the NetWare server. For example, consider a company that runs its financials or customer service database using a high-end product, such as Oracle's Workgroup Server for NT or Microsoft SQL Server. In that sort of environment, access to shared directories is meaningless. What you want is a way to link the client software in the workstations to the host database, exactly the capability that NWLink provides. Users log only to the application processes, and not to the server itself.

For all practical purposes, you can think of this approach primarily as a means for Microsoft to provide NetWare users with access to network applications running on Windows NT servers. File access and printing can be used as well, although Internet services will still require TCP/IP client services. Fortunately, those TCP/IP client services (largely WinSock and TCP/IP applications) are available in most desktop operating systems, especially MS Windows products. And Windows NT Workstation users get the benefit of being an equal member with Windows 3.x and 95 users on a LAN.

When NT Server is an application server in a NetWare LAN or WAN, however, NWLink supports the ability to be seen as another NetWare resource to NetWare users where desired, to the point of being able to emulate a NetWare file server with an optional product called FPNW (which we describe later).

NT versions from 3.5 on have a rewritten NWLink stack that gives much better performance. In NT 3.1, both NWLink and the TCP/IP implementation were based on an NT port of a UNIX-style streams interface, which was easy for Microsoft to get running but didn't give great performance. The new protocols are pure NT-native implementations. NWLink from NT 3.5 onward also supports multiple networks and SPX-IPX. In NT 4.0, the protocols have been rewritten again—this time to support automatic configuration of IPX routing and frame choice.

But the fact remains that what most users want is a way to access their NetWare server(s) and NT application server resources, and although NWLink provides the all-important low-level plumbing for such a client requester, it doesn't understand NetWare Core Protocol (NCP) packets. Translating the NCP packets into a method that Microsoft Network users will understand requires a network redirector—which we cover later in this chapter.

Configuring NWLink

If you selected NWLink at installation time as a protocol to include in NT Server or Workstation, a wizard will later guide you to a screen with a number of choices that represent selections needed to make NWLink work (see Figure 10.1). The defaults in NWLink are usually sufficient for most NT installations in which NetWare is present.

Two parameters are chosen by default: the Internal IPX Number for the network and automatic detection of frame types. The Internal IPX Number is a unique number that identifies the network and needs to be changed only where more than one NT Server will be used in a

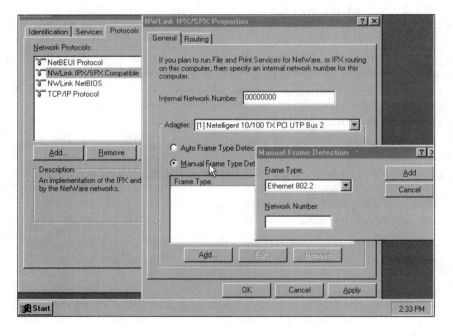

FIGURE 10.1 NWLink properties. You may configure Microsoft's NWLink IPX/SPX protocol directly from Control Panel/Network Settings by picking the protocol from the list and clicking the Properties button. This dialog box is then displayed, allowing you to select the network card bound to the protocol, the network number, and the frame type. It's also possible (though not recommended) to set these parameters using the Registry Editor (REGEDT32.EXE).

NetWare LAN using NWLink protocol or where administrative policy allocates that number. The numbers are often allocated where network management software or network testers need to identify servers by their Internal IPX Numbers. An Internal IPX Number is required for routing purposes (it can still be the 00000000 default number), but it must be *unique*. Each NetWare service requires a unique IPX number to identify it to the IPX protocol. The Internal IPX Number identifies the server to workstations, print servers, and other NetWare IPX fileservers on the network.

The frame default is 802.2. This frame type works for most networks, and NT has the ability to watch the frame types via the network cards or WAN devices attached in order to detect other frame types and add them to its list. If automatic frame type is used, it increases the delay in being able to attach NT system when it is first powered up because it will be spending a few moments detecting the network on which it resides. If frame types are chosen manually, it will respond without having to go through a discovery cycle.

You can assign frame types and IPX network numbers to use or choose an automatic configuration. Choosing the frame types matters only if you want the multiprotocol router (that's explained later) to route specific frames. Novell's LAN Workgroup software uses a special frame type called Ethernet_II; if you're using Windows TCP/IP applications that use WinSock or WinSock32 (virtually all non-Novell TCP/IP applications), the frame type used (and the one that will be automatically selected for you) is Ethernet 802.2, the same frame that NetBEUI uses.

The method for connecting to an NWLink-serviced application varies from application to application. In general, an application that exploits NWLink will need to set itself up using a name recognized by the NetWare bindery. Microsoft SQL Server for Windows NT ships with a DLL that does this by sending out a Service Advertising Protocol (SAP) packet via IPX that gets picked up by any NetWare server on the LAN. The server loads the SAP information into the bindery. Client applications can then use standard NetWare APIs for a list of servers to see the NT Server.[10]

Post-Installation NWLink Options

The network number will be 0 by default and should be left at 0 except under the circumstances described earlier. IPX network numbers are comparable to TCP/IP subnet addresses, but are set dynamically at runtime. Setting the network number to zero initially causes NWLink to send a RIP (Routing Information Protocol) broadcast message, which will be responded to by the local subnet server (which will send the network number). If no server responds, the default setting of 0 will be retained, indicating that IPX packets are intended for the local subnet, which is compatible with the client software in most IPX implementations.

Each network adapter in the system must have a *unique* IPX network number, so if there's more than a single network card in your NT server or workstation, you'll need to increment or

---

10 Programmers interested in implementing this kind of system should see the article on Windows Sockets in the July 1993 issue of *Microsoft Systems Journal*. You might also check Stardust Technologies, an interoperability testing lab for Winsock (http://www.stardust.com/).

match the IPX network numbers for each network card. Each adapter set to 0 will spawn a reply from the network that *usually* causes the correct network to be assigned. If an NT system (3.*x* or 4.*x*) no longer detects a given frame type and uses another one, you may get a router error message on all Novell Servers and IPX network monitors on the LAN.

If this happens, static IPX network addresses should be set. To correct the router error message problem, it's necessary to find the device that's complaining about the problem and reset it. In the case of a NetWare server, use the "RESET ROUTER" command. With print servers or other devices that cannot be command reset, the devices must be rebooted (HP LaserJets and LexMark print servers are notorious for complaining in this way).

For most users of NT server or workstation, the defaults are correct. We recommend changing the default settings only after it's been verified that connectivity to NetWare isn't working. Usually when this happens, a new frame type (802.3 or Ethernet_II) must be added.

NWLink Performance Tuning and Advanced Settings

Besides the three basic settings discussed earlier, a number of parameters can be set for NWLink in the Windows NT Registry. A detailed description of these parameters (and their uses) is beyond the scope of this book, but you'll find them detailed in Microsoft's online Knowledge Base.[11] Settings are available for controlling the use of NetBIOS-over-IPX traffic (used if NWLink is employed for interconnecting Windows NT systems, as well as for application services to NetWare clients), controlling a variety of low-level IPX and SPX behaviors, and controlling RIP (or static) routing of NWLink traffic. NWLink also makes a variety of performance counters available for use with the Windows NT Performance Monitor application—including packet-level performance of IPX, SPX, and NetBIOS packets transmitted over NWLink (see Figure 10.2). These can be used for performance tuning and maintenance in much the same manner as the other network parameters detailed in Chapter 5.

The IPX Router

Routing is the act of examining packets, determining their destination, and sending them either directly to the destination address (if its on the local subnet) or on to another subnet as necessary. Routing allows filtration of packets across several network devices, usually two or more network cards. In addition to network cards, WAN devices such as high-speed serial ports that are connected to WAN circuits need routing capabilities.

Routing is also performed by hardware routers whose functions are dedicated to routing. We suggest that larger networks investigate hardware routers (see Chapter 8) where a large number of networks must be routed. In smaller networks, however, it's possible to use internal routing to balance the load of users on each network cable segment attached to an NT Server.

---

11   Available on the Microsoft Web site at http://www.microsoft.com/kb/, and on Microsoft's TechNet CD (see "For More Information," at the end of this chapter).

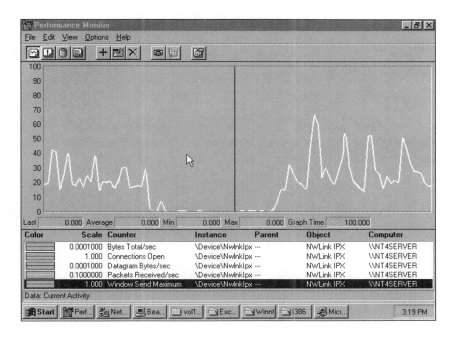

FIGURE 10.2 Performance Monitor NWLink Object. Microsoft's NWLink IPX/SPX protocol provides a number of useful Performance Monitor counters that can be exploited by Network Administrators in NetWare environments.

Microsoft now includes an IPX router with NT Server. The type of router that Microsoft uses is called a RIP Router, because it uses the Router Information Protocol (RIP) to determine where packets have come from and if they should be sent out via another network device attached to the NT Server. RIP routing is performed regardless of the frame type or type of network card involved (types include Ethernet, Fast Ethernet, and Token Ring). Adding RIP for IPX also enables SAP (Service Advertising Protocol), which causes NT Server to announce its presence on the network(s) to which it's connected. SAPs from the locally connected network can be suppressed, but that's necessary usually only for WAN links where rebroadcasting SAPs is expensive (from consuming slow link bandwidth).

Installing IPX Routing

RIP for IPX support is available only on NT 4.0 Server. The RIP Service is installed from Control Panel/Network's Services tab. Click the Add button, select RIP for Internet Protocol from the list, and click OK. Once RIP for IPX is installed, to enable LAN-to-LAN routing:

1. Choose the Network icon in the Control Panel.

2. In the Protocols tab, select NWLink IPX, then click the Properties button.

3. Click the Routing Tab, check Enable RIP Routing, and click OK.

You can also enable NetBIOS routing over IPX, although the packets used for NetBIOS over IPX have a time-to-live of eight routers. This means that the normally unroutable NetBIOS, running on top of IPX, can be routed only to destinations eight routers away (which is fine for most LANs).

IPXROUTE

Troubleshooting of IPX routing is aided with a utility called ipxroute.exe. The command *IPXROUTE TABLE,* for example, shows the internal IPX routing table that the IPX router process believes it's seeing:

```
C:\>ipxroute table

NWLink IPX Routing and Source Routing Control Program v2.00

Net Number          Ticks      Hops    Interface Net Number    Interface ID
------------------------------------------------------------------------------
002e3bba              47         4          c2c08204              1

C:\>
```

The command *IPXROUTE SERVERS* displays the known servers that the router has seen if the server uses the SAP protocol described earlier:

```
C:\>ipxroute servers

NWLink IPX Routing and Source Routing Control Program v2.00

IPX Address              Server Type      Server Name
--------------------------------------------------------------
c2c08204.be82d8000000       1600          NCR_NT
c2c08204.be82d8000000       1614          NCR_NT!!!!!!!!!A5569B20ABE511
                                          CE9CA400

004C762832

C:\>
```

Just type *ipxroute /?* for a list of the parameters IPXROUTE responds to:

```
C:\>ipxroute /?

NWLink IPX Routing and Source Routing Control Program v2.00

Display and modify information about the routing tables
used by IPX.

IPX Routing Options
-------------------

IPXROUTE servers [/type=xxxx]
IPXROUTE stats   [/show] [/clear]
```

```
IPXROUTE table

  servers        Displays the SAP table for the specified
                 server type. Server type is an integer value.
                 For example use IPXROUTE servers /type=4 to display
                 all file servers. If no type is specified,
                 servers of all types are shown. The displayed
                 list is sorted by server name.

  stats          Displays or clears IPX router interface statistics.
                 If no option is specified, statistics are shown.
                 To clear the statistics specify /clear.

  table          Displays the IPX routing table. The displayed
                 list is sorted by network number.

Source Routing Options
----------------------

IPXROUTE board=n clear def gbr mbr remove=xxxxxxxxxxxx
IPXROUTE config

  board=n        Specify the board number to check.
  clear          Clear the source routing table.
  def            Send packets that are destined for an
                 unknown address to the ALL ROUTES broadcast
                 (Default is SINGLE ROUTE broadcast).
  gbr            Send packets that are destined for the
                 broadcast address (FFFF FFFF FFFF) to the
                 ALL ROUTES broadcast
                 (Default is SINGLE ROUTE broadcast).
  mbr            Send packets that are destined for a
                 multicast address (C000 xxxx xxxx) to the
                 ALL ROUTES broadcast
                 (Default is SINGLE ROUTE broadcast).
  remove=xxxx    Remove the given mac address from the
                 source routing table.

  config         Displays information on all the bindings
                 that IPX is configured for.

All parameters should be separated by spaces.

C:\>
```

More information on IPXROUTE can be found in the NT Command Reference (from the Start menu's Help entry).

What the IPX Router Can't Do

The IPX router doesn't support LAN-to-WAN-to-LAN routing. This means that the router doesn't support scenarios wherein a network card is the first router point, then a WAN device is routed from the first router point to a second network card. NT Server when configured with RAS may encounter this scenario because packets coming in from a network card may go through a RAS interface (which cannot route remotely) to a second network interface card. In a way, this is helpful because the RAS connection isn't polluted with RIP and SAP traffic. It also means that you must use another (preferably hardware) router to perform many types of WAN routing. The benefit of using a hardware router is that you'll be using the CPU inside the hardware router to perform routing instead of wasting CPU cycles inside the NT Server.

Another downside to NT's IPX router is that it cannot be load balanced. In a NetWare LAN, IPX wants to connect at the lowest available IPX network number. This means that one network card usually gets the majority of traffic because of its lower IPX network address. If two network cards are connected to an Ethernet switch, as an example, users will always gravitate to the lower IPX address card.

Novell uses a special technique called IPX network number spoofing that's included in its BALANCE.NLM module to balance the load across two or more network cards configured to talk to an Ethernet or Token Ring switch, evening out the workload. In these cases, routing is often turned off, and the network cards may have the same IPX network address. Microsoft's IPX router has no equivalent.

The Next Step:
Adding a Network Redirector

Although NWLink provides a NetWare-compatible transport protocol, it still doesn't enable NT users to see shared resources on a NetWare server. That's because NT's default redirector (the Workstation service) talks in SMB packets rather than NCPs. To see and use NetWare resources, an additional redirector is necessary. Microsoft supplies two: Gateway Services for NetWare (GSNW) on NT Server, and Client Services for NetWare (CSNW) on NT Workstation.

Unlike earlier versions, NT 4.0 redirectors are capable of seeing NDS resources (see Figure 10.3) as well as an older NetWare resource list called the bindery. Prior versions of GSNW and CSNW knew how to address NCP only via bindery emulation mode.

GSNW

Gateway Services for NetWare (GSNW) is an NT Server redirector that can translate between Microsoft's SMB protocol and Novell's NCP. GSNW depends on NWLink to understand the plumbing of communications, then translates and makes apparent NetWare resources. In doing so, it opens up the NetWare world to users of Microsoft Networking who don't have NetWare client services. GSNW amounts to a superset of CSNW (Microsoft's NCP redirector for NT Workstation), which we describe later in this chapter. CSNW lacks GSNW's SMB translation capability.

GSNW is required when other NetWare-related services, such as Domain Services manager for NetWare (DSMN), are used. The NetWare resources that are thus made visible to Microsoft

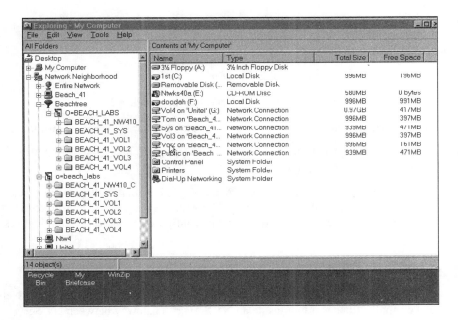

FIGURE 10.3 NetWare 4.0 NDS Trees. Microsoft's upgraded CSNW and GSNW redirectors for NT 4.0 have the ability to offer NetWare Directory Services information to the Explorer and other applications.

(SMB) users are secured largely through NT Server's security mechanisms. A single gateway user account bridges (and acts as a proxy agent) for NT to either a NetWare server or Novell's NDS. The resources available through this account represent the highest level of accessibility that will be available through this method.

Technically, GSNW is an SMB (Server Message Block) to NCP (NetWare Core Protocol) bridge. Gateway Services for NetWare enable NT Server to find NetWare services and IPX/SPX devices on a LAN. GSNW can see IPX SAPs (Service Advertisement Protocol messages), which are used by NetWare/IPX file servers, print servers, and other devices to announce their presence and network location to other devices on a network.

GSNW Installation Instructions

During a default initial installation, GSNW *isn't* installed onto NT Server. The NWLink IPX/SPX Compatible Transport must be installed and configured prior to a GSNW installation. There are two ways to install GSNW: through the Properties Sheet of Network Neighborhood and via the Control Panel's Network icon. If the NT Server in which GSNW is to be installed has any legacy or third-party NetWare client services, they must be removed first.

To install GSNW, log on to the NT 4 Server as a member of the Administrators Group, and follow these steps:

1. Start/Settings, Control Panel.

2. Double-click the Network icon in the Control Panel.

3. Click the Services Tab, then the Add… button.

4. Select Gateway (and Client) Services for NetWare, then click Add.

5. A dialog box will appear that asks you to type the path to your NT 4 Server installation files.

6. Once copying is completed, the server will request to be re-booted, and GSNW won't be ready until the system has restarted.

After you have re-booted the server, GSNW process is installed, but NetWare services and resource access won't be available until individual resource gateways are configured for them. Each NetWare bindery server must be individually configured with each individual resource that's desired.

Creating a Gateway

Gateways through GSNW are shares in which GSNW acts as an agent for Microsoft Network (SMB) users or applications residing inside an NT Server. A gateway between NT Server and a NetWare server can be accomplished after a group is created on the target NetWare Server called Ntgateway. This group can be created via Novell's NWAdmin or NetAdmin programs for NetWare 4.x, or via Syscon for NetWare 2.x and 3.x. The group needs to be created for each bindery server (or just once for NDS servers).

> *Note: Unless your server is running the Novell32 Requester for NT, it's not possible to make these changes from the server console with NWAdmin or NetAdmin, because they won't run under GSNW. Syscon, however, can be used to add the Ntgateway group as necessary.*

The user account used in conjunction with GSNW shares must be a member of the NetWare server's Ntgateway group with sufficient NetWare rights (set via NetWare's SYSCON, NETAD-MIN, or NWADMIN commands) for the NetWare resources that will be used through the gateway. Whenever NT Server restarts, the aforementioned user account will log on to the NetWare server (or NDS) using that account. If the password expires or the account is deleted, the gateway's link to NetWare will be broken. The user account that GSNW uses can be changed at your convenience.

> *Note: This user account will be used by all NT/WFWG/Win95 users when they are using GSNW to access the NetWare server! This account must be a member of the NTGATEWAY group on the NetWare server. The currently logged-in NT user account must also have permission to access the NetWare server and must have permission to create a share on the NT server.*

Each NetWare resource that you want to use via GSNW must have a gateway and a share name that Microsoft Network (SMB) users will identify with the resource. Security for each share made this way can be established by share name to the level you desire. Printing is the only exception to the resource shares provided by GSNW.

Once installed, GSNW can be configured as follows:

1. Start the Control Panel/GSNW applet. The Gateway Service for NetWare dialog box appears (Figure 10.4).

2. Set a Preferred Server and Print Options exactly as described for CSNW, above.

3. To control Gateway operations, click the Gateway... button. The Configure Gateway dialog box appears (see Figure 10.5).

4. To re-share a NetWare volume, click the Enable Gateway check-box. Then enter a valid NetWare account name and password into the appropriate fields (confirming the password in the field supplied for that purpose), and click the Add... button. The New Share dialog appears (see Figure 10.6).

5. You may now create a Windows NT sharename for a NetWare volume. Enter a sharename in the appropriate field and a properly formatted UNC name in the Network Path field (it helps to have a command prompt window open—type *net view /network:nw* to see a list of available NetWare servers, *net view \\server /network:nw* for a list of shares on a particular server). You can optionally add a comment, which will appear in lists of shares (this might

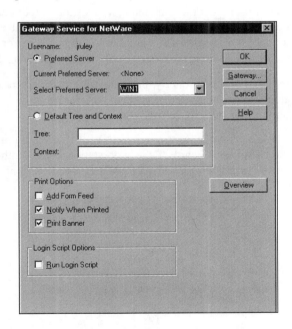

FIGURE 10.4 Gateway Service for NetWare (GSNW) Control Panel.
Microsoft's GSNW is managed from this dialog box. In addition to the preferred server and printer options supported by CSNW (and controlled using the very similar CSNW control panel), gateway functionality is supported.

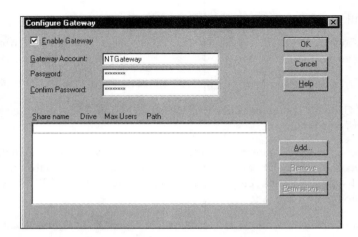

FIGURE 10.5 Configure Gateway dialog. GSNW gateway functionality is controlled through this dialog.

be a good way to alert users that the sharename in question is redirected), and designate a drive letter for local use. You can also designate a maximum number of users for the re-shared drive (you may want to restrict this number to minimize performance impact on the server in question or to meet the legal requirements of your NetWare license agreement).

6. Click OK. If everything worked properly, the share will be accepted. If you've designated an invalid pathname, user, or password, you'll get an error message. Go back to step 4 or 5 (as appropriate) and try again.

You can share NetWare print queues through GSNW if desired, but a preferred method is to use the standard Add Printers Wizard at the workstation level. If the workstation has a NetWare (NCP) redirector, such as Microsoft's CSNW or Novell's Client for NT, installed, we

FIGURE 10.6 GSNW New Share dialog. Once gateway functionality is enabled, it becomes possible to re-share NetWare directories using this dialog box.

suggest that users connect directly to the NetWare print queue. Where users have only the built-in Microsoft Network client software, a share must be provided through GSNW to the NetWare printer resource. NWLink provides users the ability to find NetWare printer resources (on bindery or NDS NetWare file or print servers).

GSNW Benefits

Before GSNW became available, all client systems in mixed (NT and NetWare) environments had to run two network protocol stacks: one for NetWare (NCP) and another for NT (SMB). This was true even if both networks ran the same underlying protocol. You could use NWLink as NT's only protocol driver, which meant that all the traffic for both NT and NetWare went over the wire as IPX packets, but every client still needed two requesters: one for NetWare and another for NT.

With GSNW, you can eliminate the need for dual stacks. All the clients run NT requesters, and all access to the NetWare server is through the gateway (an NT server that talks to the NetWare server using NCP). It's a good idea, but it has one serious limitation: because every request made of the NetWare server has to be translated, there's a substantial performance hit. Thus, GSNW isn't something you'd want to use as the only way for a large number of users to connect to NetWare, but it does make sense in a number of special situations.

The driver inefficiency but popularity of GSNW caused Microsoft to increase the efficiency of the GSNW code, and performance problems have become negligible. Now, GSNW has become one of the important glue components between NetWare and NT Server.

NetWare Migration Tool

Having the ability to use NetWare volumes as a client and to re-share them as a server provides NT with useful capabilities in a NetWare environment, but from the administrator's perspective, it does nothing to offset the single greatest difficulty of running a mixed network: maintaining two (possibly more, depending on the network setup) sets of user accounts and user resources such as printers.

To deal with this situation (and to make it as easy as possible for NetWare administrators to migrate their LANs to NT), Microsoft introduced the NetWare Migration Tool with NT Server 3.5. This tool has recently been upgraded in conjunction with FPNW (described next) and will no doubt continue to be enhanced as long as NetWare and NT compete with each other. The Migration Tool doesn't have to be used to replace a NetWare server, although it can gather information for use with FPNW.

The most popular use for NetWare administrators of the tool will be to rapidly populate NT Server with user accounts that will equal the accounts (except for passwords) from the migration NetWare server candidate. In larger networks, such migration is a non-trivial exercise; Migration Tool automates this process.

Windows NT Migration Tool for NetWare can automatically migrate NetWare users and groups, directory structures (including permissions), login scripts, and print queues. NDS information that has no equivalent to the NT Domain structure cannot be migrated, of course—there's no place to use this information and currently, NT cannot be controlled under NDS.

Resolving the Models

There are three possible models that must be united into a single model for migration. The Novell bindery-based, mixed, and homogeneous NDS environments must be resolved into the Microsoft Domain model during the planning stages of the migration if the Migration Tool will be used to completely replace NetWare functionality on a network.

NetWare migration information is always sent to an NT Primary Domain Controller (PDC), because the PDC is the primary source of information in any NT domain. In a multi-server bindery-only network (NetWare 2.*x*-3.*x*), the servers are migrated either into a single domain, or several trusted domains, or into a large single domain with a number of BDCs. The two approaches are actually quite similar.

The NetWare bindery model requires discrete information storage about users and objects on the bindery server. An obscure product from Novell called NetWare Naming Services acts as a proxy agent to replicate information in a group (recommended to be eight or fewer servers) of NetWare bindery servers. NetWare Directory Services has a root server that contains information for subsidiary servers. The subsidiary servers contain partitions of the directory service's content that are equal to or less than the entire NDS structure. These replicas of the NDS tree of resources are similar to BDCs, but needn't contain the "carbon copy" of information that BDCs contain of the PDC in Microsoft's model.

NDS also contains a wider variety of descriptive objects and resources that are represented by the NDS objects than the information replicated through the Microsoft Domain model. Further, because only partitions representing fractions of user and resource information need to be replicated through the NDS model, wide-area network traffic is reduced compared with that in single Microsoft domains.

Where a mixed NetWare bindery and NDS environment is to be migrated, each bindery server must be migrated to fit the Domain Model, but only one NDS server need be migrated if it's the primary NDS server (top of the tree) for user resources. Only the media on other servers needs to be migrated because the primary NDS server will contain all user resource information.

A homogeneous NetWare NDS environment is usually the easiest to migrate because the primary NDS server usually contains all of the network user, group, print server, and other information; subsequent servers under the NDS tree need only have their media (volumes) migrated. Where NDS environments are highly partitioned, such as the partitioning found in WANs, it is possible to have conditions under which a member server of an NDS tree has information that cannot be found in the Primary; therefore, it's up to the administrator of the tree to resolve migrating the branches.

What Migration Doesn't Transfer

Several kinds of NetWare user properties have no equivalent in NT and cannot be transferred if File and Print Services for NetWare (FPNW) isn't used. These user attributes are lost during a migration:

- Limiting Concurrent Connections

- Grace Logins

- Restrict User Disk Volume (space)

- Station Restrictions (user must log on at a specific station)

Some NetWare user attributes that can be described as either global or individual properties cannot be transferred as individual properties because they are global properties under NT Server:

- Require Password

- Maximum Password Length

- Days Between Forced Password Changes

- Require Unique Passwords

- Intruder Detection/Lockout

The following are NetWare user attributes that have direct NT Services equivalents and are retained:

- Account Expiration Date

- Account is Disabled

- Allow User to Change Password

- Account Use Time Restrictions

When a migration is performed to an NT Server running FPNW, station restrictions are still lost, but three other attributes can be transferred:

- Limiting Concurrent Connections

- Grace Logins

- Login Scripts (retained for each individual user account)

The migration process does not convert the NetWare Supervisor or Workgroup Manager account status to the NT Server equivalent (Domain Administrator); users of Supervisor or equivalent accounts must be re-established as members of the Administrator Group under NT Server. Workgroup Manager and User Account managers must be added to the Account Operator Group, the NT equivalent.

Comparing File Rights and Attributes

When files are transferred during a migration, several types of NetWare-specific file rights and attributes are lost, while others are either retained (in a DOS-equivalent status) or converted to an NT status. As an example, there is no NetWare Create or File Scan Status. Directories or files that have these attributes can have Read-only status (for Create inhibition) or Hidden (for File Scan inhibition).

Performing a Migration

The Migration tool is run in conjunction with GSNW and requires that you be logged in as both administrator on the NT server to which you're migrating and supervisor on the NetWare server from which you're migrating. To start the Migration Tool, choose Start/Programs, Administrative Tools, Migration Tool for NetWare.

The details of using the Migration Tool are far too involved to cover here. Fortunately, the Migration tool's online Help is excellent, written in a tutorial format that makes operation easy to understand. However, we do want to mention one feature that serves as a tremendous confidence builder: Trial Migration With Logging. This lets you carry out a complete dry run to see what happens, without actually creating user accounts, copying files, or translating login scripts. If you begin with the Overview section of the Migration Tool's Help file and practice using it with Trial Migration, you'll quickly gain the confidence to try it for real. The logs are very useful, and as many trial iterations can be performed as you like until you're confident that the migration steps are complete.

There are several drawbacks to using the Migration tool to fully migrate a NetWare server. First, it requires two complete servers, at least temporarily. You must have enough disk space on the NT server to store the complete directory structure (and files) from the NetWare server, which can be a real problem on a large LAN. (In such a case, it may pay to consider a stepwise migration, initially duplicating only the users and groups, then the login scripts, then parts of the directory structure, then more, in each case, giving users access to the remaining, unmigrated directories [and printers] through the NetWare gateway.)

File and Print Services
for NetWare: FPNW

File and Print Services for NetWare is an optional suite of programs that allows an NT Server to emulate a NetWare 3.x server for file and printer sharing. When coupled with the NetWare Migration Tool, an NT 3.x or 4.x server becomes a file-and-print NetWare server for most purposes and an easy way to adapt an NT Server for use on a NetWare LAN. FPNW is sold with DSMN (see below) as *NT Server Services for NetWare* at an extremely low price (US $149 in North America), but it may increase overall system-wide cost for two reasons. First, FPNW users on NT Server are affected by NT Server license fees, which have a cost associated for each concurrent user of the NT Server (currently about $30 per head, less expensive on larger LANs—see the sections on NT Server licensing in Chapters 1 and 2 for details).

A second cost implication of FPNW revolves around the use of network shared software. If an additional FPNW NT Server is deployed, many network software package vendors consider it a basis for separate server licensing costs.

Despite the per-head costs, there are several reasons for using FPNW, the most prominent of which is to take advantage of in-house training and understanding of NetWare as a production working environment. FPNW is capable of supporting NetWare login scripts (though certain syntax and keywords used in login scripts won't work with it), NetWare utilities such as Map, Attach, Slist, Userlist, Nlist, Pconsole, and others. A NetWare or FPNW Public directory must be in a client user's PATH for most commands to work.

FPNW is capable of correctly emulating a NetWare 3.x server for file-and-printer sharing but doesn't support the use of NLMs. For most uses, an FPNW-controlled NT Server looks to the world like a NetWare file server, but certain agents that aren't used in FPNW are expected by other genuine NetWare servers. These agents generally control communications, and the most famous example about the missing agents is the absence of a NetWare SNMP agent. This absence thwarts certain network management packages, Novell's Managewise among them.

Certain network-based tape backup packages may also expect an FPNW NT Server to react like a NetWare server, but NetWare's bindery and other NetWare-specific files will be missing, producing either lots of error messages or outright failure.

Users of Novell's NetWare for Macintosh cannot access NT Server resources easily; there is no equivalent FPNW resource, and Mac users are largely forced to use NT Server with Services for Macintosh (SFM), which is covered in Chapter 8.

Overall, FPNW does a very good job of server emulation, however. When it is coupled with the Migration Tool, Microsoft has made it very convenient for you to deploy NT Server, especially when it's at the sacrifice of a NetWare license.

Domain Services Manager for NetWare: DSMN

An optional add-on to Windows NT Server, Domain Services Manager for NetWare allows a NetWare server to be entirely under the control of an NT Server Primary Domain Controller. In one step, DSMN removes the bindery from a NetWare 2.x or 3.x file server and adds the NetWare server to an NT Domain. Once moved by DSMN, the NetWare server has only a skeletal bindery but has the advantage of being able to still run NLMs, which is convenient for many organizations with legacy components.

The primary advantage of DSMN for most organizations is that there's a single logon to all resources, and these resources are under the control of the Domain structure. Although it's considered an alternative to Novell's NDS single-logon methodology, DSMN has been found in our experience to be cumbersome when used for administrative control of NetWare resources.

Once the bindery is removed from the NetWare server, only NT Administrative programs can be used for user administration. There is no way to undo the move at this writing. If NetWare servers that have been attached via DSMN were part of another directory service initiative, such as Banyan System's StreetTalk for NetWare, they can no longer be used because the directory services for the NetWare servers have been moved to the Microsoft Domain.

On the whole, we can recommend DSMN only for those sites that have made an irrevocable decision to switch from NetWare to NT. It may then be of some help in easing the migration process by letting you retain NetWare servers as platforms for legacy NLM-based applications while converting to NT's domain-based management scheme.

CSNW

CSNW (which used to be called NetWare Client Services or NWCS when first introduced as an add-on to NT 3.1) is Microsoft's NCP redirector for Windows NT 4.0 Workstations. It lacks GSNW's ability to function as an NCP-to-SMB bridge but allows NT users to see and utilize shared resources on NetWare servers. The primary advantage of using CSNW (by comparison with Novell's NT client) is that Microsoft Networks users may use UNC naming conventions to access both NetWare and NT Server resources. For example, they can use the command:

```
net use x: \\server\sharename
```

A second advantage is that NT users need use only a single protocol stack, saving available memory and resources.

Install CSNW for NT Workstation by right-clicking Network Neighborhood or clicking the Network Icon in the Control Panel. Choose Add Service, and choose Client Services for Novell NetWare.

Using CSNW

In most respects, using CSNW is no different from using Novell's NetWare Client for Windows NT or using Windows NT's built-in networking, for that matter. You can access NetWare volumes (shared directories) or printers from Network Neighborhood (see Figure 10.7) or the command line, and you can access NetWare printers from Print Manager or the command line.

From the command line, you can view NetWare servers using the Windows NT NET VIEW command with the /NETWORK:NW switch. For instance, the command:

```
net view /network:nw
```

gives the following response on our network:

```
Resources on NetWare(R) Network
--------------------------------
\\OPTICAL1
\\WIN1
The command completed successfully.
```

Net view also lets you inspect shared resources available on a server. For example, the command:

```
net view \\win1 /network:nw
```

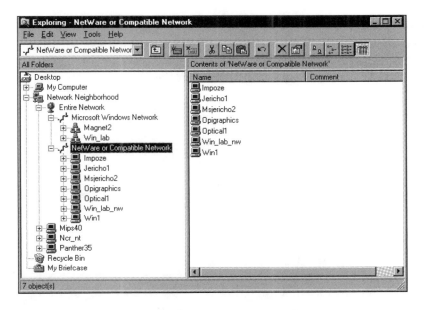

FIGURE 10.7 Explorer viewing NetWare LAN. With a NetWare redirector loaded, Windows Explorer sees NetWare shared directories exactly as NT Server Shares.

gives this response:

```
Shared resources at \\win1


-----------------------------
Disk            \\win1\BOOKSHELF
Disk            \\win1\CDROM
Disk            \\win1\DATA
Disk            \\win1\SYS
The command completed successfully.
```

To access shared directories, you use the NET USE command, in much the same way as it's used with the built-in Windows NT networking (documented in Chapters 3 and 4). For example, \\win1\bookshelf can be associated with the drive letter w: with the command:

```
net use w: \\win1\bookshelf
```

If your NetWare and Windows NT accounts have different user names, use the /user switch to set your NetWare user name:

```
net use s: \\win1\sys /user:jruley
```

See the "Network Operations from the Command Line: The NET Command Interface" section of Chapter 4 and "Administrative NET Commands" in Chapter 3 for more information on command-line network access in Windows NT.

Access to NetWare Utilities

CSNW allows you to access DOS-based NetWare utilities from the NT command line. Utilities like SYSCON, SLIST, WHOAMI, and SEND can all be run from a Windows NT command prompt with CSNW running. Here's an example of an CSNW session:

```
C:\users\default>net use z: \\win1\sys
The command completed successfully.


C:\users\default>z:

Z:\public>slist
Known NetWare File Servers          Network    Node Address Status
---------------------------         -------    ----------------
OPTICAL1                            [   122] [        1]
WIN1                               [   112] [        1]   Default

Total of 2 file servers found

Z:\public>whoami
You are attached to server WIN1, connection 20, but not logged in.
Server WIN1 is running NetWare v3.11 (100 user).
```

Note, however, that newer Windows-based tools like NWCAdmin can be run only from Novell's NetWare Client for NT.

Novell's Client for NT

The history of NetWare Client for NT releases is that they lag the shipping dates of the NT products by six months or more. However, Novell released a series of beta client software for NT within a week of Microsoft's production release. Although the software is called NetWare Client for Windows NT Workstation 4.0 (NCNT), the software is backward compatible with Windows NT 3.51 (server or workstation).[12]

There are several implications to using Novell's client software under Windows NT. Many NetWare administrators are more comfortable with client-side releases of redirector software from Novell than from Microsoft. NetWare users believe the Novell releases are more complete in their ability to recognize and utilize NetWare services than is Microsoft's implementation of NetWare redirectors.

There is some truth to the claim that Novell's releases are more complete. Although CSNW can now read and understand NetWare NDS tree objects, CSNW is still unable to log in as a full

---

12 Information about NCNT for NT 4.0 is based on experience with a July 1996 beta release, and updated information should be checked at the electronic update Web page mentioned in the introduction. Among other things, it is unclear at this writing what level of ODI driver support will be provided. The documentation for the beta indicates that Novell has not been testing this version of NCNT with ODI drivers!

NDS client. Therefore, CSNW users cannot use the NetAdmin or NWAdmin NDS administration software.

Another advance in the NCNT is its ability to allow users to have access to two or more NDS trees *concurrently*. Although CSNW allows this capability, prior releases of all NDS client software from Novell have prohibited client-side access to more than one NDS tree at a time.

The beta NCNT release also includes the ability to administrate another product that was in beta release at the time of this writing, Novell's NetWare 4.11 release, code-named "Green River." This 32-bit administration package is similar to a recent 32-bit interim release of the NWAdmin software for Windows 95 and is a vast improvement over the NWAdmin release that is included with NetWare 4.00–4.10 (see Figure 10.8).

The ODI Problem

Early versions of Novell's Client for Windows NT broke with Microsoft's NDIS standard for network drivers and introduced Novell NetWare 4.0-compatible Open Datalink Interface (ODI) drivers. One could make many arguments about the relative merits of NDIS and ODI, but the main point to be aware of is that NDIS is Microsoft's standard system, and ODI is Novell's.

There's one major advantage to using ODI drivers, over and above any possible performance enhancement: the 32-bit revision (F) drivers in question are *the very same drivers used*

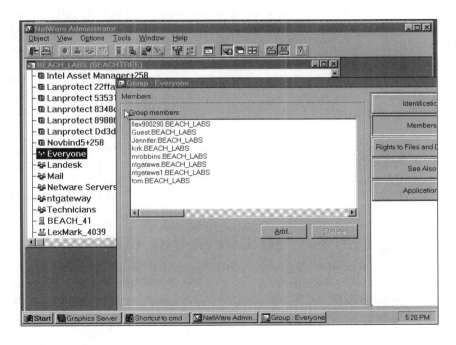

FIGURE 10.8 NWADMIN. A newly updated NetWare Administration program is included with Novell's NetWare Client for NT.

by NetWare 4.0 servers. This arrangement can be extremely convenient for administrators in a NetWare 4.0 environment because if you have NetWare 4.0 server drivers for your standard network cards, you can use these same drivers with Windows NT systems.

However, there are two problems with using Novell's ODI drivers in a Windows NT environment. First, although over 100 different revision (F) 32-bit Open Datalink Interface (ODI) network drivers are available at this writing, not all drivers are available for all Windows NT platforms (in particular, we have yet to see any drivers for the PowerPC architecture), so you'll need to make sure that both your network card and CPU architecture are supported. The second problem is that, although the driver .LAN files work perfectly with Windows NT, they require a customized OEMSETUP.INF file[13] for Windows NT setup to install them. As of this writing, OEMSETUP.INF files are available for about 100 network cards. Novell has said that it's working on a tool to create these files automatically, but it hasn't announced whether or not this will be made available to the public. Effectively, this means that Novell's ODI drivers are useful in an NT environment *only* if the vendor also supplies the Windows NT.INF file for the driver in question.

One or Two Network Cards?

Another problem with the need to use ODI drivers is that the ODI/NDIS incompatibility causes problems if you want to run *both* the NetWare redirector *and* built-in Windows NT networking, which was designed to work with NDIS. This problem arises because both ODI and NDIS want to "own" the network card—something that doesn't work out very well if you have only one network card in your system.

One solution is to use two network cards in the same machine: one bound to ODI for NetWare, and the other bound to NDIS for NT. This approach works and provides better performance and higher reliability than a single-card approach. But it's expensive, and it creates a configuration problem (you can't run both cards at the same interrupt level and I/O address, for instance).

A single network card solution has been made available by Novell. This uses a custom "shim" driver called ODINSUP, which acts as a translator layer between the ODI network card drivers and the Microsoft NDIS system. Therefore, it's possible to run one network card, ODINSUP, and the proper ODI driver, and have it run with both the NetWare NT Client and Windows NT's built-in networking.

Installing the Novell Client for NT

Two forms of installation are available for NCNT: administrative and diskette. The administrative installation is invoked via a network server (NT or NetWare servers). The administrative files occupy about 13MB of disk space, and the diskette installation requires 14 diskettes.

The NetWare Client for NT must replace CSNW if it has already been installed. Perform installation by invoking SETUPNW.EXE from either diskette or the administrative installation subdirectory/folder. During installation, users are prompted for their preferred tree and their

---

13   Documented in the Windows NT Device Driver Development Kit.

context. If these blanks are left empty, they can be filled in later via the Control Panel/Network's Services tab. Select Novell NetWare Client for Windows NT and click Properties (see Figure 10.9).

The installation process also respects System Policies if they have been set so that variables such as Preferred Server, Context, and other NDS-specific options can be automatically chosen during installation. Prior CSNW network drive mappings and other network-specific settings are also undisturbed during the installation processes. Novell warns installers that network card driver upgrades may be necessary to make specific network cards function correctly, but this problem is not new for either Microsoft or Novell.

A second, one-time installation process installs the Windows NT client files to an NDS server, as well as the NetWare Application Launcher (similar to the Microsoft Office Shortcut Bar), Land the NetWare Administrator. The final component is a new NDS Partition Manager that runs under Windows NT.

Using Novell's Client for NT with NWLink

Novell's Client for NT can be used concurrently with NWLink in both Windows NT 4.0 Workstation and Server, though in the latter case, it does replace CSNW. GSNW links are undisturbed and are still required for Microsoft Network clients of NT Server to see NetWare

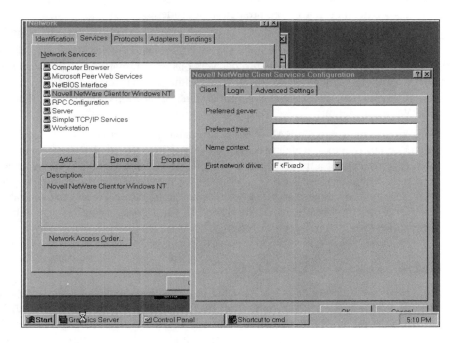

FIGURE 10.9 NetWare Client Services configuration. Configure Novell's NetWare client for NT using this dialog box, which you can access from Control Panel/Network's Services tab.

resources. Because GSNW uses NWLink, the resources aren't as visible for Microsoft Networks clients as they are for NCNT clients.

The choice between CSNW and NCNT is likely to be an identity choice rather than a functional choice. The CSNW software is more mature than prior offerings and now sees NetWare Directory Services resources. Overall, CSNW behaves as a fully participating client on a NetWare-based network.

The advancements in NetWare control software and the ability to use more than one NDS tree concurrently make the NCNT software attractive for largely NetWare installations. Although we can't recommend placing beta product into production, the NCNT client software didn't misbehave during the tests we made of it. The only strong criticism of the NCNT client software is that it will not become production software until this book is well into print.

NetWare and RAS

Microsoft originally developed a gateway feature for NWCS (which subsequently evolved into GSNW) as a response to user complaints at the impossibility of accessing NetWare servers over RAS in NT 3.1. That happened because NT 3.1 RAS functioned purely as an SMB gateway. It used Microsoft's proprietary AsyBEUI protocol, which could not redirect NCPs. Curiously enough, even while Microsoft was perfecting GSNW, it was eliminating the original need for it from the clients by extending RAS to be protocol independent.

Beginning with NT 3.5, RAS uses the industry-standard Point-to-Point Protocol (PPP) and transparently handles all types of connections: SMBs, NCPs, and UNIX-style IP. (It also retains AsyBEUI for backward compatibility with older versions and supports SLIP as an alternative protocol for TCP/IP connections.) As a result, dialing into an NT server (or PPP-compatible router) using RAS on an NT client gives you all the same connections you'd have on the LAN, including NetWare connections.

NetWare support built into the RAS client is consistent with Microsoft's view of RAS as a client-to-server connection tool, which makes a lot of sense in a central office environment with mobile users. But what about a true wide-area network (WAN) situation, in which you need to connect offices? Combining RAS with GSNW could be the answer: run one high-speed data link between the central office and an NT server at the remote office. Access the central office NetWare server(s) over that link using RAS. Then use the NetWare gateway to re-share the NetWare directories to users on the remote office LAN.

Connectivity Strategies

As a client in NetWare environments, NT Workstation sees the resources of a NetWare LAN in the same way as Windows 95/3.x, Macintosh, or OS/2-Warp Connect users do. No special considerations that differentiate NT Workstation from other clients have appeared. NT Server use in a NetWare environment, however, can be different. Although NT Server can be deployed with defaults into many NetWare LANs, it takes either a dual-protocol stack (NetWare and NDIS) or use of FPNW to make NetWare clients customers of NT Server.

NT Server can be dropped into many NetWare LANs with just the defaults to NWLink chosen. NT discovers how to adjust to NetWare's IPX layout in a LAN quite well. Optional File and Print Services might not be necessary for NetWare-only clients to use NT server products, such as Oracle for Windows NT or SQL Server. The test for whether licenses will be necessary usually revolves around whether users will be accessing NT file and print services. If users do access NT Server file and/or print services, they need the associated NT Server client license.

NT Workstation is limited to 10 concurrent users and doesn't include Gateway Services for NetWare, just the Client Services for NetWare. It also cannot be used as a platform for FPNW/DSMN. Because of these limitations, NT Workstation can't be used as an effective replacement for small (e.g., under 10-user) NetWare servers.

Products such as Microsoft Exchange Server require GSNW for connectivity to NetWare users. Exchange uses RPCs (Remote Procedure Calls) over IPX that require GSNW, and it's likely that you'll run into more applications that require such connectivity to service NetWare users over time.

NetWare and NT Tomorrow

Fault tolerance has become an important facet of NetWare environments, but early versions had many limitations. Novell's System Fault Tolerant (SFT) III is a concept in which two servers can be mirrored together. If one server fails, the other server continues running, and the failure is transparent to users and processes. NetWare Version 3.11 SFT-III had many limitations that made it incompatible with many programs and protocols. Novell solved those problems in NetWare 4.x, but by that time, NT was already on the scene, and NT-based clusters[14] promised to neutralize this as a marketing advantage.

NetWare also remains limited to Intel x86-family processors, although proof-of-concept ports to other target processor families have been demonstrated.

Novell has announced its intention to eventually bring NT Server under NDS control, and Microsoft has discussed making NDS controllable under its competing Directory Services/LDAP initiative.[15] At this writing, neither company is expected to bring production components together in 1996, but either (or both) may do so soon after. Because the products are only vaguely defined, any opinion we might offer on their relative merits at this point would be sheer speculation.

Conclusion

In this chapter, we've reviewed the history of Novell NetWare and discovered the products and applications that both Microsoft and Novell have produced to enhance NetWare connectivity with NT and applications that Microsoft has developed to migrate in or away from NetWare. We've examined several approaches from Novell (the NetWare Client for Windows NT), and Microsoft

---

14 See Chapter 8.

15 See Chapter 12.

(the NWLink protocol, Migration Tool for NetWare, and the alphabet soup of GSNW, CSNW, FPNW, and DSMN). All the approaches have unique advantages and disadvantages. Never before has NT NetWare connectivity been either as easy or as robust as in Windows NT 4.0.

This entire field is in a state of flux, and new developments happen daily. Indeed, as we go to press, there are rumors that Novell will finally deliver NetWare Directory Services (NDS) on Windows NT and even port NetWare file and print services to NT—in effect making NT a NetWare-controlled server. Still, the highest level of interoperability that's afforded by common directory services that are plainly and usefully compatible may be elusive for years. Readers are urged to check our Electronic Update (available from the Web page specified in the Introduction), watch the trade magazines, and check Novell's support forum, *NetWire*, on CompuServe for further developments.

For More Information

Novell's Web site: http://www.novell.com; anonymous ftp at ftp.support.novell.com

Clarke, Dan (1993), *The Complete NetWare Construction Kit*. New York: John Wiley & Sons, Inc. ISBN: 1-471-58259-X. Clarke's information on NT is one sided, but this book provides an invaluable practical overview of NetWare.

Custer, Helen (1993), *Inside Windows NT*. Redmond, WA: Microsoft Press, ISBN: 1-55615-481-X. Custer's description of the TDI-layer redirector is essential in understanding how the various kinds of NetWare connectivity fit into NT.

Microsoft Staff *TechNet CDs*. Redmond, WA: Microsoft Product Support Services (PSS). TechNet is a monthly publication on CD-ROM containing a digest of topics from the Microsoft Knowledge Base, the Net News publication, Resource Kits, and other information. This is the best place to find out about such new features as FPNW and to benefit from the experience PSS has in supporting those features.

Novell Staff, *Novell Standard Encyclopedia Professional Edition* (NSEPRO) CD-ROM, Novell, Inc. (yearly subscription). This is a dual-CD-ROM technical information database for troubleshooting, online manuals, and nearly a gigabyte of resource files, patches, fixes, and example files available in several languages.

Brainshare Presentation Books (1995), Provo, UT: Novell Inc. Novell's annual Brainshare conference is comparable to Microsoft's Tech*Ed. Brainshare presentations cover many aspects of the NetWare world, including NDS and the NetWare Client for Windows NT.

Other Connections

When you finish reading this chapter, you will have a better idea of where to go for further information on connecting Windows NT 4.0 to other networks and vendor-specific platforms, including:

- IBM LAN Server/ Warp Server
- IBM SNA networks
- DEC VMS and Pathworks
- Banyan VINES
- Advanced UNIX (X/Windows and NFS) networks
- Artisoft LANtastic networks

As we've noted in past editions, vendors are constantly struggling to deliver updated connectivity products for Windows NT as Microsoft adds (and changes) features with each new version. Although we were unable to fully test any of the products listed here, we present what information we were able to acquire about each. We *strongly* recommend that you contact the vendor directly for more information before purchasing any connectivity products.

IBM LAN Server/Warp Connect

When IBM and Microsoft were on civil terms, IBM licensed Microsoft's LAN Manager product, modified it, and sold the resulting product as IBM LAN Server. Since then, the relationship between the two firms has become less collegial, but LAN Server networks still share a common core base with the SMB-based networking that's built into Windows NT and other Microsoft networking products. In fact, it's quite possible to use LAN Server clients on Windows NT LANs (see Figure 11.1) and Windows NT clients on LAN Server networks.

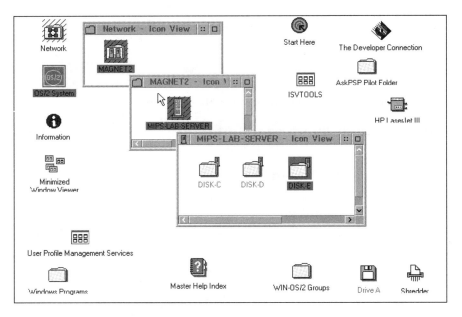

FIGURE 11.1 LAN Server (OS/2). IBM LAN Server 3.0 for OS/2 provides a networking environment that's functionally equivalent to and compatible with NT's built-in networking for file and printer sharing. Advanced management features of the two networks, however, are incompatible.

Aside from the fact that it uses IBM's OS/2 Warp instead of Windows NT as the base operating system, LAN Server (and its close cousin Warp Server—LAN Server bundled with OS/2 Warp) is actually quite similar to NT (and other Microsoft networks) in operation.

The most critical element in getting LAN Server and Windows NT networks to interoperate is protocol selection. As it happens, IBM's OS/2 NetBIOS protocol (the LAN Server default protocol) is functionally equivalent to NetBEUI (the Windows NT default protocol), and because both systems use SMBs, they interoperate quite well at the resource-sharing level.

Beyond that level, however—especially for the administration and management programs—LAN Server and Windows NT are quite different. Windows NT workstations can operate in LAN Server environments as peers, but cannot participate in LAN Server domain management. Similarly, LAN Server systems can operate as members of Windows NT workgroups, but not as members of Windows NT domains. The situation is similar to that described for Microsoft Windows for Workgroups in Chapter 9: LAN Server systems can function nicely as clients in the NT network, but cannot be effectively managed as servers and vice versa.

LAN Server and Warp Server are available from IBM Corporation. Call IBM at (800) 342-6672 or browse http://www.ibm.com for more information.

IBM Systems Network Architecture Environments

Although IBM mainframes and minicomputers have taken a beating lately as companies move applications to PC networks, there are still plenty of mainframes out there, and they have lots of important data on them. High-end IBM systems use Systems Network Architecture (SNA) to communicate with terminals and other computers, so there's a need for solutions to connect these SNA-based networks to NT.

Microsoft offers SNA Server for Windows NT as its solution for connecting NT (and other PC operating systems) to SNA. SNA Server installs on an NT Server and provides a protocol *gateway* between the LAN and the SNA network (see Figure 11.2). It supports 3270/5250 terminal emulation, LU6.2 Advanced Peer-to-Peer connectivity, and LU0 protocols. It also supports IBM's NetView network management system. A 3270/5250 terminal emulator is bundled with the product (it offers only basic functionality).

Third-party vendors provide much more extensive terminal emulator support. Other vendors offer competing products as well. Contact and product names are listed in Table 11.1.

Table 11.1 SNA Support Products

Product Name	Company	Phone	Type
5250 Elite for SNA Server **http://www.andrew.com**	Andrew Corp. 10500 W. 153rd St. Orland Park, IL 60462	(800) 328-2696 (708) 349-3300	IBM-5250 (AS/400) Terminal emulation

(Continued)

Table 11.1 (Continued)

Product Name	Company	Phone	Type
Extra! for Windows NT **http://www.attachmate** **.com**	Attachmate Corp. 3617 131st Ave. SE Bellevue, WA 98006	(800) 426-6283, (206) 644-4010	3270 terminal emu- lation, mainframe application integration (HLLAPI), intranet support
IRMA Workstation	Digital Communications Associates 1000 Alderman Dr. Alharetta, GA 30202	(800) 348-3211, (404) 740-8428	Terminal emulation
Access 3270 **http://www.eicon** **.com**	Eicon Technology Corp. 9800 Cavendish Blvd. Montreal, Quebec H4M-2V9 CANADA	(514) 745-5500	3270 terminal emulation, developers kits
TeamWARE HighWay **http://www.icl.com**	ICL Inc. 11490 Commerce Park Dr. Reston, VA 22091	(703) 648-3300	SNA/OSI Server, router, related services
Graphics 3270 **http://www.intergraph** **.com**	Intergraph Corp. Huntsville, AL 35894-0001	(800) 345-4856, (205) 730-5441	3270 terminal emulation
TCP3270 **http://www.3270** **.mcgill.ca**	McGill Systems Inc. 550 Sherbrooke St. W. Suite 1650 Montreal, Quebec H3A-1B9 CANADA	(514) 398-4477	3270 terminal emulation through telnet
SNA Server **http:/www** **.microsoft.com**	Microsoft Corp. One Microsoft Way Redmond, WA 98052	(800) 426-9400, (206) 882-8080	As described in text
NS/Elite NS/Print Server NS/Portfolio Manager **http://www.netsoft.com**	NetSoft 31 Technology Drive Irvine, CA 92718	(800) 352-3270 (714) 753-0800	Terminal emulation, mainframe-to-LAN printing, remote admin.
RJE 3770 BSC 3780	Passport Communications P.O. Box 162370 Austin, TX 78716-2370	(512) 328-9830	RJE (mainframe batch), 3780 emulation

Table 11.1 (Continued)

Product Name	Company	Phone	Type
3780Link **http://www.serengeti** **.com**	Serengeti Systems 2306 Lake Austin Blvd. Austin, TX 78703	(800) 634-3122, (512) 345-2211	RJE 3780/2780 emulation
RUMBA Office **http://www.walldata** **.com**	Wall Data Inc. 11332 N.E. 122nd Way Kirkland, WA 98034-6931	(800) 915-9255 (415) 812-1600	Terminal emulation, mainframe application integration
Passport **http://www.zephyrcorp** **.com**	Zephyr Development Corp. Summit Tower 11 Greenway Plaza, Suite 520 Houston, TX 77046-1102	(800) 966-3270 (713) 623-0089	3270 emulators

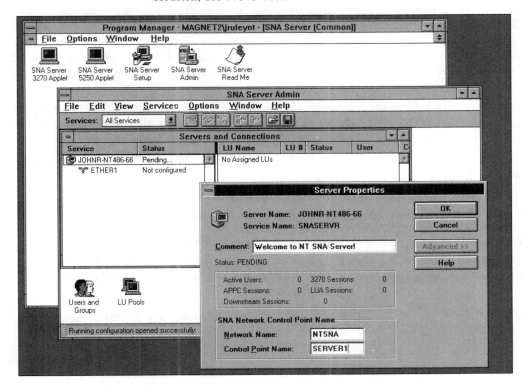

FIGURE 11.2 SNA Server. Microsoft SNA Server for Windows NT functions as a gateway between SNA networks and LANs. It's implemented as an NT service and takes full advantage of the NT APIs to provide graphical administration, integrated security, and other advanced features. A large number of 3270 terminal emulator vendors support this product.

To find additional products in this category, browse http://altavista.digital.com, select the Advanced Search option, and search for *"Windows NT" near (SNA or 3270)*.

Digital Equipment Corporation Pathworks

Like IBM's LAN Server, Digital's Pathworks is based on Microsoft's LAN Manager technology, which simplifies the problems of interoperability with Windows NT. Pathworks clients on any platform can access Windows NT or Windows NT Advanced Server systems, as well as Pathworks servers based on the VMS, Ultrix, SCO UNIX, or OS/2 operating systems.

Pathworks for Windows NT is offered for Intel, MIPS, and Digital's own Alpha AxP processors, and it interoperates with existing Pathworks clients (Windows 3.1/95, DOS, OS/2, and Macintosh).

One of the most significant interoperability items in Pathworks is the support for Digital's DECnet protocol at the network transport layer. This support can coexist with TCP/IP and NetBEUI protocols on the same server or workstation. DECnet events can be viewed through the standard Windows NT Event Viewer and Performance Monitor tools. Device drivers are provided for Digital's networking cards, including its FDDI (Fiber Distributed Data Interface) EISA card.

In addition to support for NT's user- and administrator-level tools, there is a Pathworks for Windows NT Developer Kit that provides API support for Pathworks Sockets and other Digital-specific networking protocols. The Windows NT APIs for WinSock, NetBIOS, and remote procedure calls are also supported when DECnet is used as the network transport protocol.

The vendors shown in Table 11.2 supply products intended for use in a Digital-oriented network environment.

Table 11.2 Suppliers of Digital-Oriented Network Products

Product Name	Company	Phone	Type
KEA! 340/420 http://www.attachmate.com	Attachmate Corp. 3617 131st Ave. SE Bellevue, WA 98006	(800) 426-6283, (206) 644-4010	VT340/420 terminal emulation
PATHWORKS, http://www.digital.com	Digital Equipment Corp. 111 Powdermill Rd. Maynard, MA 01754-1418	(800) 344-4825, (508) 493-5111	NT support for Digital's flavor of networking (as described in text)
SuperLAT http://www.meridiantc.com/	Meridian Technology Corp. 11 McBride Corp. Ctr. Dr. Chesterfield, MO 63005-1407	(800) 463-6682, (314) 532-7708	LAT protocol support

(Continued)

Table 11.2 (Continued)

Product Name	Company	Phone	Type
SmarTerm SuperLAT **http://www.persoft.com**	Persoft, Inc. 465 Science Dr. P.O. Box 44953 Madison, WI 57344-4953	(800) 368-5283, (608) 273-6000	VT340 terminal emulation, LAT protocol support
VX/DCL VX/RMS VX/SMG etc. **http://www.sector7.com**	Sector 7 USA Inc. 609 Castle Ridge Rd. Suite 300 Austin, TX 78746	(512) 306-8311	Complete line of VAX/VMS- compatible utility and porting applica- tions for NT, UNIX systems
Reflection **http://www.wrq.com**	Walker, Richards &Quinn 1500 Dexter Ave. North Seattle, WA 98109	(800) 872-2829 (206) 217-7500	Digital VT240/340 terminal emulation

To find additional products in this category, browse http://altavista.digital.com, select the Advanced Search option, and search for *"Windows NT" and ((VT240 OR VT340 OR VAX OR LAT OR VMS) near Emulat*).*

Banyan VINES

The VINES (VIrtual NEtworking Software) network operating system from Banyan Systems has long been a viable alternative to Novell and Microsoft networks, especially for large installations. Its biggest strength is the StreetTalk network name service, which lets users use resources on the network without needing to know where the services are located.

VINES server software is based on a version of AT&T UNIX, modified and supplemented by Banyan to provide a wide selection of network services. VINES can run on symmetric multiprocessor (SMP) systems with up to eight processors. Banyan sells VINES either preinstalled as part of a hardware-software bundle or as a software-only product.

Because VINES uses the standard Microsoft NDIS network driver model, it can coexist with NT's standard networking and use the same network card. VINES NT support includes the VINES IP transport protocol that is most commonly used by Banyan's networks. Most NT network operations are supported through VINES IP, including client/server applications such as Microsoft's SQL Server.

The Banyan VINES Toolkit provides 32-bit versions of the VINES APIs. Existing Win-16 or DOS applications that use VINES APIs are also supported. The WinSock API is supported if you use Microsoft's TCP/IP transport on NT systems and then install FTP Software's PC/TCP on DOS or Windows systems that are running VINES. Although similar, the Microsoft TCP/IP and Banyan VINES IP protocols are not interoperable.

At the user and application level, Banyan takes advantage of Windows NT's Network Provider APIs to integrate VINES networking smoothly into the environment. For example, VINES StreetTalk names show up in the browse list when you connect a network drive, along with the system and share names from NT's built-in networking.

In 1996, Banyan delivered a native implementation of StreetTalk for NT, allowing NT Servers to participate co-equally with VINES Servers and providing all the benefits of the StreetTalk directory.

For more information, call Banyan at (800) 222-6926 or (508) 898-1000—or browse its Web site at www.banyan.com. The Vines client for NT is downloadable by Banyan VIP plan members (it costs $99 including the toolkit), and extensive information on StreetTalk for NT is available.

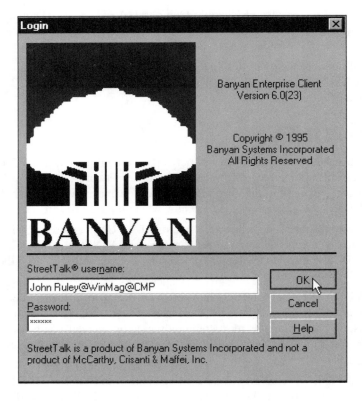

FIGURE 11.3 VINES Client for Windows NT. Banyan's VINES client for NT 4.0 is implemented as an NT service. It supports the VINES StreetTalk directory service, which is now in beta-test for NT Server.

UNIX Connections
(NFS, TCP/IP, X Windows)

Although Windows NT supports the TCP/IP protocol and offers a simple set of TCP tools (see Chapter 6 for more information), its UNIX connections could be better. Third-party companies long established in this field offer an expanded set of utilities that include NFS client software and X Window Server software, as shown in Table 11.3. (Note that Internet products, such as Webservers, are covered in Chapter 7.)

Table 11.3 UNIX Connectivity Products

Product Name	Company	Phone	Type
EXcursion **http://www.digital .com**	Digital Equipment Corp. 111 Powdermill Rd. Maynard, MA 01754-1418	(800) 344-4825, (508) 493-5111	X Server
Distinct TCP/IP Tools/NFS X/32 **http:www.distinct .com**	Distinct Corp. P.O. Box 3410 Saratoga, CA 95070	(408) 741-0781	TCP/IP and NFS software
X Server SuperTCP Suite **http://www .frontiertech.com**	Frontier Technologies Corp. 10201 N. Port Washington Rd. Mequon, WI 53092	(800) 929-3054 (414) 241-4555	TCP/IP, NFS, X Server software
InterDrive **http://www.ftp.com**	FTP Software, Inc. 100 Brickstone Square, 5th Floor Andover, MA 01810	(800) 282-4387 (508) 685-3300	NFS Client and Server
eXceed/NT **http://www .hummingbird.com**	Hummingbird Communications, Ltd. 1 Sparks Ave. North York, Ontario M2H-2W1 CANADA	(416) 496-2200	X servers, NFS, and TCP/IP utilities (recently acquired Beame & Whiteside)
DiskShare-NFS, PC-NFS Client **http://www .intergraph.com**	Intergraph Corp. Huntsville, AL 35894	(800) 345-4856, (205) 730-5441	NFS server NFS client (licensed from SunSoft)

(Continued)

Table 11.3 (Continued)

Product Name	Company	Phone	Type
XoftWare/32 Chameleon32/NFS **http://www .netmanage.com**	NetManage Inc. 10725 North DeAnza Blvd. Cupertino, CA 95014	(408) 973-7171	X Server, NFS, and TCP/IP utilities (recently acquired AGE logic)
Slnet **http://www .seattlelab.com**	Seattle Labs 9606 N.E. 18th St. Bothell, WA 98011	(206) 402-6003	Multi-user telnet with common NT command shell

To find additional products in this category, browse http://altavista.digital.com, select the Advanced Search option, and search for *(NFS or "X Windows") near "for Windows NT"*.

LANtastic

Artisoft's LANtastic software and network protocols are not compatible with Windows NT's built-in networking, and until recently, the company did not support NT. However, the LANtastic Ethernet boards are supported by NT because they are compatible with Novell's NE2000 board. If you were willing to abandon LANtastic, you could get an NT network running by installing Windows NT on your high-end systems, and Windows for Workgroups (or Windows 95) on the less capable ones.

While preparing this edition, however, we were delighted to discover that Artisoft has just announced plans to support NT throughout its LANtastic and CoSession Remote product lines (Artisoft's Visual Voice telephony toolkit already supports NT). Release dates and details were not available when we went to press. For more information, call Artisoft at (800) 846-9726 or browse http://www.artisoft.com.

Client/Server, Distributed Computing, and the Future of Windows NT

In this chapter, you will learn:

- ➪ What characterizes client/server computing
- ➪ How Windows NT compares with other client/server platforms
- ➪ Why Windows NT is well suited for use in a client/server environment
- ➪ Why and how Microsoft plans to migrate Windows NT to a distributed client/server model (via the Cairo project), including the DFS technology preview for NT Server 4.0

Along the way, we'll provide examples of client/server applications for Windows NT from several different client/server categories.

Paradigm Shifts and the Rise of Client/Server Computing

It's often said that we're now in the "fourth generation"[1] of computing. Although deciding just what constitutes a "generation" in data-processing terms is difficult, it's certainly true that we're now into the fourth major paradigm for using computer resources. These paradigms have (so far) been as follows:

- *Batch Processing*: The model for most computer use until the mid-1970s was that of queues of users waiting in line to submit "jobs," which were programs and data for the computer to run (typically, a punched card deck) for execution on the computer. This model was a reflection of the sheer cost of computing. Typical systems like IBM's 360/370 or Control Data's Cyber-700 cost upwards of $1 million, required dedicated support staffs numbering in the dozens, and represented a major cost center at any organization. The only way most corporations could afford such systems was to have many people use the computer during the course of a single day.

- *Host-centric Remote Processing:* Batch processing's major problem was that it required all users (or their assistants) to physically take their jobs to the computer. In the mid-1960s, IBM developed a way around making this trip called Remote Job Entry (RJE), which basically allowed an organization to have several card readers for batch processing in several locations. At least RJE made for shorter lines! However, as the cost of electronics dropped, a more sophisticated idea developed, called *time-sharing.* In this approach, many users could share a computer that would execute each user's job in a round-robin manner. Unlike the batch (or RJE) approach, however, instead of running each job to completion, a certain amount of time would be spent on one person's job, then it would be *suspended* while the computer worked on someone else's.

Because the computers were far faster than the terminal users (who initially communicated through teletypewriters at a speedy 11 characters per second), many people could use a single computer *at the same time*. This model persisted for years (it still exists today in many UNIX environments, and there are some who want to bring a variant of the concept back on the Internet, where they call the terminal a *network computer*), but the constantly falling cost of electronics caused the teletypewriter to speed up and evolve into a video display terminal (VDT) that could operate at much higher speeds. As more electronics became available inside the VDT, another paradigm shift occurred.

---

1   Thus we use 4GL for *fourth-generation language* when referring to client/server development tools.

- *Shared Resource Servers:* Eventually, several companies—notably, IBM and Hewlett-Packard—added fairly sophisticated logic to their VDTs, making them into *smart terminals*, but it took someone outside the world of mainframe computing to envision the ultimate end result of this combination: adding microprocessor-controlled logic *and* substantial local storage to the VDT made it into a completely separate unit—the *personal computer* or PC. Initially, PCs were used mainly on a stand-alone basis (or as a VDT replacement, running *terminal emulation* software), but the need to share expensive resources like hard disk drives and printers led to the idea of *resource sharing*. In this model, expensive resources are centralized on a *server*, and those resources are accessed by desktop computers (PCs) connected back to the servers over some sort of network hardware. This is the model that today is typified by Novell NetWare.

- *Client/Server Computing:* Inevitably, the rise of shared-resource servers provoked a reaction from the makers of classical host (i.e., mainframe) systems. The first to react was IBM, which arrived at an idea called "Connectivity" (note that capital "C"). Connectivity, in IBM-speak, meant that the PC was to be treated as the terminal that would normally be connected to the host (using the aforementioned terminal emulation software). But IBM went a step further. Because it was using quite sophisticated page-oriented VDTs in its host-centric systems by this time, it wasn't all that much of a stretch to view the attached PC as an *intelligent client*, which would interact with a host-based *server* to accomplish the computing task at hand. The resulting *client/server* paradigm has gradually displaced the others as the mechanism of choice for high-value (especially *mission-critical*) computing tasks.

Why Is Client/Server Computing Important?

You may well ask why the client/server model has become so pervasive in high-end systems. The reason, in brief, is that it exploits the power available at *both* the client(s) *and* the server, and it does so *while keeping network traffic to a minimum.*

An example may make this capability clear. Let's consider a typical line-of-business application, say, travel agents querying an airline database for flight availability. If this application is host based, every keystroke issued at every agent's terminal must be transferred over the network and handled by the host.[2] The host then must react, even if the keystroke(s) it receives are incorrect (or simply irrelevant). Even if every user of such a system *always* enters data without introducing errors (a virtual impossibility), as the usage of the system rises, the amount of network traffic rises until, at some point, the network (which is usually the slowest component in the system) saturates. At this time the *queuing effect* comes into play (see Appendix 6), with

---

2   Eventually, some designers decided to offload the host by putting sufficient electronics to handle one full screen (or *page*) of information at a time without host interaction, giving us *page-oriented terminals* (sometimes called *smart terminals*), of which IBM's 3270 is the prime example.

results familiar to everyone who has ever worked on such a system; i.e., response slows down (with the side effect that impatient users make more errors, which have to be processed and slow the system down still further).

Now consider the very same application implemented using client/server principles. Instead of a VDT, the agent has a personal computer, which runs an appropriately designed client/server *front-end* application. The user never accesses the host computer directly. Instead, the query on the host database is developed in an interaction between the agent and the front-end application, and only when this interaction is complete does the front-end interact with the host. Network traffic is minimized because *only* the bare minimum information needed to fulfill the query gets passed over the network (indeed, more sophisticated front-end applications have their own local data store and fulfill some of the requests from that rather than passing all queries through to the host).

If you're still not convinced that client/server computing is important, here's one more thought: *whenever you browse the World Wide Web, you're using a client/server application*!

Types of Client/Server Computing

For historical reasons, the client/server model has been applied in three widely disparate environments. Windows NT can play in all of them (of course), but its unique features are most fully exploited by only one, as we will see.

IBM SNA

Not surprisingly, as the company with the most to lose from the rise of microcomputers, IBM was the one that invented a way to link them to larger systems. IBM's approach, part of its *Systems Network Architecture* (SNA) specification, basically replaced the page-oriented IBM-3270 or -5150 terminals used with mainframe-based applications with a PC. Initially, the PC just replaced the terminal (running appropriate emulation software), with little advantage gained; but the availability of computing power on the desktop gradually came to be used as a way to offload processing that didn't *have* to be done in the mainframe. This process of migrating computation to the desktop was eventually formalized in the *Advanced Program-to-Program Communications* (APPC) specification of SAA in 1984 and is still in use today.

The APPC networking approach basically amounts to using the old IBM-3270 page-oriented terminal protocol as a mechanism to transfer data between client and server. A front-end application, which may look totally unlike a 3270 terminal screen (in fact, it will often provide a Windows interface nowadays) will nonetheless send 3270 keystrokes to the host computer, which responds by sending information to the front-end application as if it were a 3270: one screen at a time. Windows NT brings to this environment all the features that make it a good platform for mission-critical applications, but there's little to differentiate it from other advanced operating systems for this sort of use. In any case, the days of SNA/APPC networking are probably numbered.

Windows NT doesn't support SNA networks directly, but it's significant that one of the first applications Microsoft announced for Windows NT was SNA Server and that it arrived with substantial third-party support from terminal emulation vendors. SNA Server for Windows NT is covered (briefly) in Chapter 11 of this book, as are some connectivity products designed to help integrate NT in an SNA environment. To find other products in this category, browse http://altavista.digital.com, select Advanced Search, and search for *SNA near software near "Windows NT."*

X/Windows

Yet another approach to distributing computer power is provided by the X/Windows system that's become popular in UNIX networks. X/Windows was originally developed by the Massachusetts Institute of Technology and is now controlled by the X/Consortium sponsored by MIT. The X.11 standard defines X/Windows interfaces, which provide a client/server *graphics interface* for host-based applications (known as X/Clients). An X/Client is written with the use of the X.11 APIs and protocols and communicates through those protocols to X/Server software in the workstation computers. The workstations respond, in turn, by taking the action requested by the X/Server, drawing on the screen, in most cases. This is a powerful concept: it's as if you could execute a Windows application on someone else's computer, yet have the application draw on your screen and respond to your keyboard and mouse. (More to the point, because one X/Client can access many X/Servers, X/Windows provides unique *multi-user* capabilities for graphics software.)

Much like IBM's SNA/APPC approach, although X/Windows has its place, that place is primarily on the desktop. It's designed to maximize the effectiveness of host-based programs by making the workstations do all the work of drawing their own screen displays. Again, Windows NT is well suited to this kind of application in the general way that it's well suited to any high-end desktop use, but there's nothing special about it as a platform for X/Servers. Although no X/Server is shipped in the Windows NT box, several are available from third parties, and we cover a representative selection in Chapter 11.

Aside from X/Server software (and sometimes hardware: Digital's Multia is a good example) that turns Windows NT into a relatively expensive X/Terminal, there are several products that offer a capability to access NT applications from an X-based (or low-end PC) client, as shown in Table 12.1.

This class of *multi-user Windows servers* offers some unique capabilities. All three applications in this class permit end users to run software without installing a local copy. NTrigue, which requires only an X/Terminal (or X/Server software) has become Microsoft's preferred solution to providing compatibility with UNIX systems. Among other things, Exchange Server is supported this way. Citrix WinFrame's ICA protocol does a sufficiently good job of data compression to allow applications to be remotely executed over the Internet (the company has an online demonstration of this available on its Web site). Microsoft has licensed ICA for use with Internet Explorer 3.0 and in future Microsoft operating systems.

The model that WinFrame, WinDD, and NTrigue play in is called *thin client*: Only the multi-user client software (in WinFrame's case, Microsoft's Internet Explorer 3.0 Web browser; for NTrigue, any X/Terminal) must run on the client; all applications execute on the server. In many ways, this model is a throwback to the centralized mainframe computing model, but it

Table 12.1 Multi-User Environments for Windows NT

Product	Company	Phone	Comments
WinFrame **http://www.citrix.com**	Citrix Systems 210 University Dr., Suite 700 Coral Springs, FL 33071	(800) 437-7503 (305) 755-0559	Provides access to Windows NT from low-end (286 or better) PCs. Online demo available. Citrix's ICA Protocol has been licensed by Microsoft, and Internet Explorer 3.0 includes WinFrame client support.
Ntrigue **http://www.insignia.com**	Insignia Systems 2200 Lawson Lane Santa Clara, CA 95054	(408) 327-6000	Access to Windows NT from any X/Terminal (no client software needed).
WinDD **http://www.tek.com**	Tektronix Inc. Video and Networking Division P.O. Box 1000 Wilsonville, OR 97070-1000	(800) 835-6100 (503) 627-7999	Access to Windows NT from selected X/Terminals (requires client software).

may well have a role to play on the Internet. Technologies like WinFrame allow vendors to offer online previews of their products and provide a way to run basically *any* Windows application with nothing but an ICA-enabled Web browser. This might well turn out to be a good fit with Microsoft's forthcoming *Windows CE* (formerly code-named *Pegasus*) platform for hand-held computers and dedicated "Network Computers."

Client/Server Databases

The preceding two sections could make one wonder what, if anything, justifies Microsoft's advertising of Windows NT as *the* operating system for client/server computing. Is it all just hype?

No!

You'll remember that IBM actually started the client/server movement by employing PCs to replace page-oriented terminals in applications like order entry. At about the same time, a number of companies began looking at applying minicomputer technology on the other end of that connection, the host computer.

Minicomputers of the late 1970s and early 1980s approached mainframe hosts in both processing power and storage capacity. In effect, you could replace a mainframe host with a minicomputer directly (as many people did, especially using Digital's VAX series of minis), making it possible for big corporations to *downsize* by putting applications that heretofore ran on mainframes onto minis—and *most* of these applications involved databases.

Think about virtually *any* major line-of-business application—insurance claim processing, payroll, accounts receivable, airline reservations—and you'll realize that a major part of the job is maintaining (and manipulating) a database. For reasons that we will get to shortly, most of these databases are described as (more or less) *relational*, and virtually all use some form of *structured query language* (SQL) as the mechanism to get data in and out (don't worry too much about the precise meaning of those buzzwords just yet; we'll get to them soon). So virtually all downsizing involves moving SQL databases from mainframes to minis—or at least it *used* to.

Some years ago, Novell got the idea of putting a database on its NetWare servers. That database was Btrieve, and it was neither relational nor SQL, but it grew into a SQL NetWare Loadable Module (NLM). At around the same time, several companies—a major one being Sybase systems—started moving minicomputer SQL onto PCs (386s and 486s turned out to be plenty powerful to run the same UNIX operating system that runs on most minis), and this trend turned the downsizing movement into a virtual avalanche.

The same money that will buy one mainframe or 10 minis will buy *a whole lot of PCs*.

While all these changes were going on in "back room" data center operations (and making life sheer hell for MIS departments, minicomputer makers, and eventually even for IBM), another revolution was taking place on computer desktops. Apple's Macintosh, Microsoft's Windows, and (to a lesser extent) IBM's OS/2 got users to expect a graphical interface to their applications and forced them to buy really powerful systems to run the graphics.

Isn't a powerful desktop system *exactly* what you need for client/server? Why fiddle around with 3270 emulators or X/Windows? Why not write a Windows- (or Mac- or OS/2-)

based front-end application that sends SQL commands and has enough intelligence built in to format the database queries itself? This sounded like such a good idea that a handful of companies have overturned most of the information systems business doing exactly that. Now let's see where Windows NT fits into all this.

Client/Server Databases and SQL

First, we'd like to define Structured Query Language (SQL) and explain why it's important. SQL was invented (like so much else in the computer industry) by IBM, as a lingua franca for *relational databases*. Relational databases basically seek to protect us from ourselves.[3] Non-relational databases are usually organized as some form of sequential list, an approach that works well until the list becomes very large or very complicated (sometimes, parts of the list are *pointers* to other lists, which complicates things in a hurry). Relational databases are organized in such a way that you can always be *certain* that a properly formatted query will have an answer. It may be a ridiculously huge answer, but there will be one.

SQL is the mechanism that ensures that the queries are properly formatted. It's a special language for data access that makes it *impossible*[4] to issue an illegal query. Moreover, by convention, modern SQL implementations include transaction-locking mechanisms that ensure database integrity even if a query fails. The query isn't *committed* until all aspects of the transaction are complete.

The point you need to understand is that *most* serious, large-scale databases for business use are relational, and *all* use some form of SQL. A wide range of such databases is available for Windows NT. The range is so wide, in fact, that we can't hope to print a complete list, so Table 12.2 lists only the largest players in the client/server SQL database field.

To find other products in this category, browse altavista.digital.com, select Advanced Search, and search for *database near "windows nt."* You can also find client/server database performance benchmark results on the Web. Browse http://www.tpc.org.

Client/Server Development Tools

The client/server database products listed in the table are, for the most part, simply *database engines*. They provide the underlying foundation on which an application may be built, but do not constitute, by themselves, a useful business application. To create such an application, it's necessary to couple the database engine to a *client application*, which is typically developed to meet the special needs of a particular business.

The range of tools available for such development is immense, grows rapidly, and is now undergoing radical changes as client/server development evolves to embrace the Internet. In past editions, we attempted to provide a list, but doing so has now become practically impossible.

---

3   See *SQL Self-Teaching Guide* by Stephenson and Hartwig (listed in "For More Information" at the end of this chapter) for further explanation.

4   Almost impossible—human error knows few absolute limits!

Table 12.2 Windows NT Database Software

Product	Company/Address	Phone	Comments
SQLBase **http://www.centurasoft.com**	Centura Software Corp. 1060 Marsh Road Menlo Park, CA 94025	(800) 444-8782 (415) 321-9500	PC-based client/server database (formerly Gupta Corp.)
CA-OpenIngres **http://www.cai.com**	Computer Associates One Computer Associates Plaza, Islandia, NY 11788-7000	(516) 342-5224	Mission-critical RDBMS with intelligent query optimizer, rule system, resource controls
DB2 **http://www.ibm.com**	IBM Corp. One Old Orchard Rd. Armonk, NY 10504	(800) 342-6672	Scalable client/server database (available on mainframe and PC platforms)
Informix **http://www.informix.com**	Informix Software Inc. Bohannon Drive Menlo Park, CA 94025	(800) 331-1763 (415) 926-6300	Fully relational database server; does not require a database administrator
Microsoft SQL Server **http://www.microsoft.com**	Microsoft Corp. One Microsoft Way Redmond, WA 98052	(800) 426-9400 (206) 882-8080	High-performance multithreaded NT-native RDBMS with replication, e-mail integration, and advanced administration
Various Products **http://www.oracle.com**	Oracle Corp. 500 Oracle Pkwy. Redwood Shores, CA 94065	(800) 672-2531 (415) 506-7000	Extensive RDBMS line that spans the range from personal to enterprise
Sybase SQL Server **http://www.sybase.com**	Sybase 6475 Christie Ave. Emeryville, CA 94608	(800) 879-2273 (510) 922-3500	High-performance RDBMS, suited to mission-critical OLTP

All the client/server database vendors in Table 12.2 provide development environments for their own platforms, and many can work with other databases. Contact the vendors for more information. Or browse http://www.altavista.com, select the Advanced Search option, and search for *client near server near tool* near "windows nt."*

Other Client/Server Applications

Aside from general-purpose databases, many line-of-business and special-purpose applications exploit the client/server model to fill a business need. Coverage of such products is far beyond this book's scope. Again, browsing the Web can be useful. Given a product category like *manufacturing*, it's always possible to search (using Altavista's ubiquitous Advanced option) for *manufacturing near software near "Windows NT."* Searching through Microsoft's InfoSource database (currently available only on CD, but soon to be available from Microsoft's Web site at http://www.microsoft.com) may also prove helpful.

The Future of Windows NT

Although the Windows NT core was developed by Dave Cutler and a mixed team of ex-Digital employees, ex-OS/2 developers, and Microsoft marketers, a longer-range plan to exploit NT as a base for advanced capabilities has been under way, led by Microsoft Business and Personal Systems' Executive Vice President Jim Allchin (formerly of Banyan systems). The code name for this advanced development work is *Cairo*. In past editions, we've speculated on how Cairo might develop, but this time we're on much more solid ground. Many features originally intended for Cairo have already appeared in NT 4.0. Many other features are being demonstrated in technology previews or developers' kits. It looks as if Cairo really may ship by the end of 1997!

Before we discuss the specifics of Cairo, let's review just how far the PC has come.

NT: Windows Beyond the Desktop

Today's desktop PC remains as it began: a single-user computer for personal productivity, even though a 200MHz Pentium Pro system has several orders of magnitude higher performance than a first-generation PC! Consider the comparisons in Table 12.3.

Table 12.3 The Changing Desktop PC

Feature	IBM PC-XT (1983)	High-End PC (1996)	Ratio
RAM	640KB	32MB	Over 40:1
Hard disk	10MB	2GB	200:1
CPU speed	4MHz (8086)	200MHz (Pentium Pro)	50:1
Video RAM	32KB (640x200, 1 bpp)	700KB (1024x768, 8bpp)	Over 20:1

Such machines are capable of undertaking tasks well beyond those of earlier PCs, yet most common PC tasks today are essentially the same as they were in 1983: word processing, database management, spreadsheets, communications (granted, in 1996 "communications" has a somewhat different meaning than it did just two years ago when only specialists had heard of the Web).

Are there fundamentally new and different applications to which the power of today's PC may be applied, or are we just modernizing the look and feel of yesterday's software?

Workstations When Microsoft changed the name of NT's entry-level version to include the term "Workstation," many observers assumed this was a bit of marketing fluff designed to obscure the evident overlap between the low end of the NT marketplace and the high end of the Windows 3.*x* (and later, Windows 95) market. This was partly true, but it also represented a real effort by Microsoft to make NT viable as a platform for the applications traditionally run on UNIX workstations in (among other things) engineering environments.

Engineering workstations are used mainly on a desktop by one person, for applications beyond personal productivity. In UNIX environments, it's not uncommon to see *two* machines on each engineer's desk: a workstation on which design applications are run and a separate PC on which to write reports. Intergraph Corp. (which produced the first commercially available RISC workstations in 1984, based on a proprietary UNIX derivative and custom RISC hardware), among others, has exploited this opportunity by introducing true NT-based workstations for its high-end CAD applications. NT offers several advantages in such environments: support for "legacy" DOS, Windows, and (with the addition of suitable X/Server software) X-based applications; reasonably high performance (Intergraph does not currently use RISC processors in its NT-based systems, preferring an SMP approach using standard Intel hardware); a familiar "Windows" look and feel; and of course, NT's inherent security and reliability.

Intergraph's workstations are sold as high-end computer-aided design (CAD) platforms for use in architecture, highway design, naval architecture, mapping/GIS, civil structural and design engineering, plant design, map design, cartography, photogrammetry and map publishing, electronic design automation (EDA), integrated data publishing (catalogs, documentation, etc.), and utilities management, among other fields. Intergraph's customers include the governments of Hong Kong (Hong Kong airport design), Kuwait (Intergraph supplied the Defense Mapping Agency with detailed maps for Operation Desert Storm), 40 of the 50 state highway departments, the US Navy, Bechtel, several retail chains, numerous architects, many telephone and electric companies, and many others.

In 1992, Intergraph CEO Jim Meadlock decided to back NT as a platform, initially planning to support it on a RISC CPU, but eventually switching to Intel's Pentium, which Intergraph uses in single-, dual-, and quad-processor configurations. Its new hardware and applications began shipping in 1993, and by the end of 1994, the entire product line (some 400 applications, more than are available for NT from any other vendor, including Microsoft) were running on NT.

Intergraph's success in moving its UNIX customer base to NT Workstation (the company reports many customers' only complaint about NT is that Intergraph isn't moving to it fast enough!) speaks volumes about its viability as a technical workstation platform.

NT has also gained a foothold in the video post-production "ghetto" outside Los Angeles and specialized software, formerly found on platforms ranging from Commodore's late, lamented Amiga to Silicon Graphics range of proprietary UNIX workstations, is now appearing on NT. One example is Elastic Reality,[5] the makers of image-editing software used in movies including "Jurassic Park," "Forrest Gump," "Babylon 5," and "SeaQuest DSV," among others. This is full-blown professional-grade image editing, not a "toy" morph application, and it's available on all NT platforms. If you need to create a Hollywood monster, NT is now a perfectly viable alternative to UNIX.

Servers Local-area-network (LAN) file and print servers have traditionally been viewed as merely PCs with oversized hard disks. The move to "enterprise networking" is causing this view to change, much to NT's benefit. Traditional server operating systems, such as Novell's NetWare 3.*x,* treat each server as a separate administrative unit, which becomes a nightmare when a corporate network grows to include, perhaps, *dozens* of LANs and *hundreds* of servers. Advanced operating systems like NT Server (and Novell's NetWare 4.*x*) provide domain-wide management, in which groups of servers are administered as a single unit, and any given user requires just one account for the entire domain.

We spent an entire chapter (8) and much of another (6) detailing how NT works in an enterprise environment. Suffice it to say that although NT isn't perfect, it clearly is competitive with other imperfect solutions, such as UNIX.

Mainframes In certain applications (especially database services) NT-based systems are beginning to compete with, and in some cases replace, mainframe computers. Sequent Computer Systems'[6] WinServer line—computers with up to six processors running in parallel— can compete with (and in some cases *beat*) mainframe computers in database performance. They're ideally suited for use in applications like decision support (DSS) and online transaction processing (OLTP). As a result, some surprising customers are moving to the NT camp. Among them are Australian Commonwealth Bank, National Westminster Bank, CompuServe Inc., Citicorp, and the Irish Post Office.

This movement will not stop with six-processor systems. Sequent's next generation of NT-based servers will use larger per-CPU cache memory and faster processors, including Intel's Pentium Pro, in exotic Distributed Symmetric Multi-Processing (DSMP) designs, to deliver performance measured in tens of thousands of transactions per second. Sequent believes such systems will be necessary to handle global electronic commerce (OLTP over the Internet) in the next century.

Candidly, NT isn't completely ready for use in such applications today. The problems mentioned in Chapter 8—including the lack of chargeback accounting features, disk (and other subsystem) quotas, and cluster support—makes NT less than a perfect mainframe platform. Still, NT has been on the market for just three years at this writing. One wonders how these limitations will fare as NT matures.

---

5   Located at 925 Stewart St. Madison, WI 53713; (608) 273-6585.

6   Located at 15450 S.W. Koll Pkwy. Beaverton, OR 97006-6063; (503) 626-5700.

RISC Desktops and Personal Mainframes Moving further from today's off-the-shelf technology, we begin to encounter more exotic possibilities. One that's often predicted is the RISC-PC, using the CPU architecture of a UNIX engineering workstation on the desktop. It's an attractive idea—so attractive that three generations of vendors have attempted it to date: Mips Technologies (and partners) Advanced RISC Consortium (ARC), Digital's Alpha, and now IBM, Motorola, and Apple's Power-PC.

It's interesting that established NT vendors like Intergraph and Sequent are using Intel CPUs in applications in which many observers expected to see RISC processors. Nevertheless, it's *possible* that one of the RISC players will eventually fabricate an extremely high-performance processor at a cost low enough to provide a competitive advantage. Such a development could only redound to NT's benefit because it's the only CPU-neutral system in the Windows family. Microsoft's recent development of a technology (WX86—see Appendix 5) that would let such a system execute unmodified Windows 95 (i.e., 32-bit Intel) binary applications makes such a concept even more attractive.

A more exotic (and silly-sounding) concept is an NT-based *personal mainframe*. As the cost of technology falls, mainframe power, and mainframe applications like DSS and OLTP, may become available to individuals (or at least small companies). Such a development may be essential if widespread electronic commerce is ever to become a reality. Ordering products, be they pizza slices or auto parts, over the Internet *is* after all, an electronic transaction. As we write,[7] Microsoft is rumored to have a *small business server* project in the works. This could combine NT Server with some of Microsoft's Internet-related offerings (principally the *Merchant* electronic commerce product and the *Catapult* proxy server) to provide a near-turnkey business-on-the-Web solution.

And that same solution could be attractive to anyone running a home-based business or trying to manage a home network. The ideal way to protect your children from pornography on the Internet (or your employees from spending all their time on net-based games) is to set up your own proxy server!

Cairo Finally, there's the future according to Jim Allchin: Windows NT *everywhere*, in a distributed client/server environment. The code-name for this effort is *Cairo*, and as this chapter is written, the project is in something of a state of flux.

Up to the spring of 1995, Cairo was assumed to be a major Windows NT upgrade with three major features: an OLE-based user interface, an object-oriented file system, and distributed processing support. In March 1995 Microsoft announced that a version of Windows NT (which eventually became 4.0) would enter beta with the new user interface within 90 days of Windows 95's release—and it became clear that Cairo actually referred only to the file system and distributed processing features. Then the Internet "arrived." The next section provides some background into the development of Cairo through the leadership of Microsoft's Bill Gates.

---

7   September 1996.

Information at Your Fingertips

Some three years ago at Comdex, Gates presented a concept he called "Information at Your Fingertips" (inevitably given the unfortunate acronym IAYF). This was a general concept based on the following ideas:

- Ubiquity of computers

- "More personal" PCs

- Data made independent of location

- Greater use of non-traditional data types like voice and live (or animated) video

He didn't just give a slide show and make a speech; he illustrated the concept with an impressively produced multimedia video presentation to drive home his points. This demonstration showed computers in a much wider range of situations than just traditional desktop use, and truly mobile (including pen-based) computing was a big part of the presentation, as were "multimedia" elements like videoconferencing and video memos sent by electronic mail. But at the heart of the presentation lay a very powerful concept: end users should not need to know (or care) where and how data is stored.

In an example from another medium, the first episode of *Star Trek, The Next Generation*[8] had one character bring up a map of the ship's internal layout by saying, "Tell me the location of Commander Data," *not* something like "Display MAPFILE\PERSONNEL\LOCATION\DATA," as we'd do today. The computer, *not the human operator,* did the locating.

Gates handled his COMDEX presentation a little differently. Instead of employing a File Manager-style interface to find files, he (and the actors in his IAYF show) used a query-based interface that worked a lot more like our *Star Trek* example. Rather than remembering (and regurgitating) the directory path to a file, they used a combination of dates, subjects, media type, and creator name fields to create a query, and the result of that query was the information in question—truly information at your fingertips!

But that was all staged. Does IAYF have any bearing on reality? And if so, where does Windows NT fit in?

Distributed Computing

Earlier in this chapter we examined the classical host-based and shared-resource models of computing and saw how client/server computing naturally grew out of a combination of those two approaches (and the need to minimize network traffic). Let's consider a *fifth* model of computing that, to a certain degree, competes with client/server computing. This is the *distributed computing* model.

---

8 A production of Paramount Pictures.

In distributed computing, computing resources are distributed throughout the machines on the network, and computation is done at whatever location happens to be convenient. In particular, most computational models for distributed processing attempt to *equalize* resource utilization across the network. For instance, if computation work needs to be done, the system finds an idle processor and does the work there.

The beauty of distributed computing is that it can fully leverage *all* network resources in a way that is impossible for any of the other models to achieve. Even the client/server model, with all the advantages we discussed earlier, can leverage the resources of only a *particular* client and a *particular* server to accomplish a *particular* task. It doesn't matter that there may be over 100 CPUs on your network sitting idle; if the server's bogged, no work will get done.

You can achieve a limited degree of distributed processing with multiple servers (for example, having database functions provided by a database server, file functions provided by a file server, etc.). The limitation of this scheme is that you're still locked into the client/server model for any *particular* process. If the database server becomes overloaded with requests, the system will slow down, even though the other servers are idle.

There's no way in a multiple client/server model to distribute the database server functions among other servers on the system—a single bogged server can slow down the entire network. In a Windows NT environment with properly designed server software that exploits symmetric multiprocessing, we can try to throw a bigger server at the problem, but at some point, even the largest SMP will run out of steam.

What's needed is a way to distribute the functions of the database server among multiple servers on the network. *That's* the goal of distributed processing.

From a programmer's perspective, the key element in any distributed computing scheme is a Remote Procedure Call (RPC). Windows NT provides a powerful RPC implementation[9] that's partly compatible with the Open Systems Federation's Distributed Computing Environment (DCE) RPC. Using RPCs, a programmer can write a program that will call functions transparently, without knowing whether the functions are executed on the local computer or on another computer on the network.

The present Windows NT implementation lacks any way of assigning the RPCs such that neither the programmer nor the computer user (nor ideally the system administrator) will need to know the specifics of which machine receives the assignment. Perhaps another example will help to clear up this issue. It's common in the publishing business to run out of disk space on the production file server (or servers) as an issue is produced. This used to happen at *Windows Magazine* constantly. As the production staff finished a particular issue, they created a large number of PostScript images, which take up a great deal of disk space. They would consistently overshoot the production server's disk capacity by about 100MB, yet have over a dozen workstations on that same network with a total excess disk capacity far greater than 100MB. Why couldn't they use the excess disk capacity on the other machines on the network?

---

9   Documented in Appendix 1.

With Windows NT this is now possible in an ad hoc way. Each system can have a public shared directory, and by manually distributing files onto those public shared directories, users could take advantage of the excess disk capacity. Yet this would create an administrative nightmare. If you're looking for a particular file, do you look for it on \\johnspc, \\davespc, or \\main_server? What's needed, again, is a mechanism for adding a level of indirection. That is, one needs the ability to refer to a disk storage location, say \\DistributedDiskspace, without being concerned about its physical location.

Distributed File Systems Years ago the UNIX community tackled the problem of referring to a disk storage location. The solution is a *distributed file system*, a file system that spans more than one computer. Several such systems exist: DCE/DFS and the Andrews File System are the most popular. Because DCE/DFS is built on DCE/RPC, and NT's RPC is almost (but not quite) DCE/RPC compatible, many people have suspected that Microsoft would come up with an almost-but-not-quite DCE/DFS.

Shortly before this edition of went to press, Microsoft provided a technology preview for its very own DFS.[10] It's illustrated (from the end user's perspective) in Figure 12.1.

What's shown here is a single directory tree distributed over three servers. The server running DFS (on which the /dfs share is located) is a MIPS R4000-based RISC system running NT

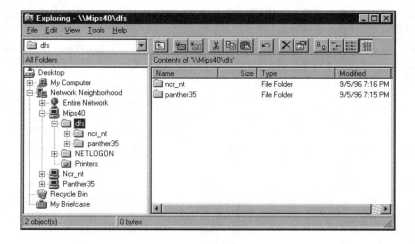

FIGURE 12.1 Distributed File System (DFS). To the end user, DFS shares appear as ordinary directory structures, displayed as a set of folders in the Windows Explorer. In this case, however, the NCR_NT and PANTHER35 directories are in fact located on different physical servers from MIPS40, which hosts the DFS share. Other than the folder names (which we selected deliberately to illustrate how DFS works), there is no indication of a file's physical location.

---

10 It's currently downloadable from the http://www.microsoft.com/ntserver page on Microsoft's Web site. Check the *electronic update Web page* referred to in the introduction for the latest location.

Server 4.0, and two others (both Intel-based): NCR_NT, also running NT Server 4.0, and PAN-THER35, running NT Server 3.51. That last server is significant, because NT 3.51 has no support (built in or added on) for DFS. For that matter, NCR_NT wasn't running any DFS software when this screenshot was captured, and DFS could have handled a NetWare server just as easily.

How does DFS work? Rather than functioning as a true network file system, Microsoft's DFS implementation acts as a network *directory*. It provides a vital additional level of indirection for network directories. When a client accesses a DFS directory or file, the DFS server resolves the reference to the physical location of the file. For the setup illustrated in Figure 12.1, for example:

DFS Directory Entry: **Resolves To...**   **Physical Location:**

\\MIPS40\DFS\PANTHER35\2ED   ⟶   \\PANTHER35\C$\2ED

Note that what you name a DFS directory is entirely arbitrary. Here, the server name was used to illustrate the process. We could just as easily use a more descriptive name:

DFS Directory Entry: **Resolves To...**   **Physical Location:**

\\MIPS40\DFS\"Networking Windows NT"\2ED   ⟶   \\PANTHER35\C$\2ED

Now we begin to see the power of the approach. Suppose we move the files from this server to another one—only the physical location changes. As long as we update the DFS Directory Entry to reflect the new location, *end users need never know that a change has taken place*. We can make this move using a new DFS Administration tool as shown in Figure 12.2.

This tool provides a very straightforward means of associating DFS directories with physical locations.

So far, so good (and a very powerful capability indeed!). What remains to be added is object support in the local NT file system.

OLE and DCOM Distributed computing involves more than just redirecting directories. The same concept can obviously be applied to printers, but what about programs?

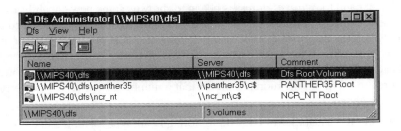

FIGURE 12.2 DFS Administrator. DFS is administered through a new administration tool, as shown here. Unlike end users, Administrators see both the logical and physical directory structures and can change the association between them at will.

Existing, monolithic applications can, of course, access objects in the DFS name space. Such applications just see directories and filenames. The fact that the names are being resolved by DFS is transparent to the application. But there's much more that can be done by a program specifically written to understand objects.

Microsoft realized this some time ago and began creating the foundation for an entirely new type of user interface. This foundation is the Distributed Component Object Model (formerly called Network Object Linking and Embedding), which is Microsoft's third-generation object model. OLE 1.0, introduced in Windows 3.1, provided simple data object capabilities. One could, for instance, embed a Paintbrush picture in the middle of a word processing document. Double-clicking on the picture then brought up the Paintbrush application with the picture loaded, so that it could be edited by the recipient.

OLE 2.0 extended the OLE 1.0 concept by providing an object-oriented name space (and thereby providing the all-important additional level of abstraction needed for distributed computing to become really effective). In both OLE 1.0 and 2.0 objects could be either *embedded in* or *linked to* a parent document. An object embedded in a parent document had its data embedded within the parent file (among other things, this had the side effect that one could now receive relatively short word processor documents that took up megabytes of disk space because of an embedded Paintbrush picture).

A slightly more sophisticated alternative to embedding the data was to link it. In a linked object, the only thing embedded in the parent document was a *reference* to the file linked to the document. Unfortunately OLE 1.0 understood only how to refer to direct physical addresses. These could, in fact, be network addresses. Even with Windows 3.1 it was possible (through the Object Packager, for instance) to provide a link to a network object, but you had to specify the precise physical address of the network object. The all-important additional level of abstraction was still lacking.

OLE 2.0 *did* provide abstraction, in the form of a *moniker*. An OLE 2 moniker is just a name that refers to an object without being specific as to its location. The name could be resolved either to a physical address or to a relative address. Monikers that expanded to absolute addresses worked exactly the same way that the absolute addresses did in OLE 1.0. Monikers that expand to *relative* addresses began to show us some new capabilities. For example, if you used relative addressing on an embedded Paintbrush object that referred to the same directory in which the parent word processing document was kept, moving the contents of the directory would *not* break the link (because the new directory still contained the Paintbrush picture). That may not sound like much of an improvement, but the fact that you now had a level of indirection through the moniker meant that a number of extremely powerful capabilities could be provided.

In addition to the capability of embedding foreign data types within a document, OLE 2.0 provided several completely new features. Through *OLE Automation* it became possible for applications to expose their computational functions as OLE 2.0 objects. These objects could then be addressed by other OLE 2.0-compatible programs and documents in much the same manner as a Custom Control is accessed from Visual Basic. For example, Windows 95 and NT

4.0 provide system-level spell checking using an OLE Automation object that is accessed as needed by applications (such as the e-mail client).

OLE Automation isn't for end users. Properly using OLE 2.0 within an embedded application requires the use of some kind of application scripting capability, which is why Microsoft has invested such heavy resources in its applications division developing Visual Basic for Applications (VBA) as a consistent scripting language for use between Microsoft applications. (With luck, it will finally be deployed with all of them in MS-Office 97!) Doubtless, other companies will eventually follow suit in one way or another.

Let's consider a more powerful possibility. After all, OLE Automation deals with objects, and it's irrelevant that the object contains code now rather than data. That's the whole point of an object.

This feature of object-oriented models is called *polymorphism*. It means that you don't distinguish between code and data; both are just objects. So it's possible to refer to the OLE Automation objects using monikers in exactly the same way that the data objects can. Based on what we've discussed so far, this merely means that you can access the objects through link structures and that the links won't break when you move them from directory to directory. That's because at this point we're looking at OLE 2, which lacks one important element. We're looking at it without an all-important *Object Server*, which is exactly what Allchin's Cairo project has been working on.

Detour to the Internet So far, we've talked about OLE, and in the second edition of this book, we went on at this point to explain how OLE 2.0 would be extended to work on the network, with Cairo providing the necessary name space. That is in fact exactly what's going to happen; but with a wholesale change to the names, reflecting a major change in Microsoft's strategy.

On December 7, 1995, Microsoft held a press conference in Seattle to announce its Internet strategy, which was followed by a flurry of announcements (including those covering the products and features covered in Chapter 7). Among other things, Microsoft started changing names at this point, and what had been referred to as Network OLE became Distributed Common Object Model (DCOM).

Why the name change? Microsoft made the change for at least two reasons. The first was to help distinguish the back-end distributed-processing (OLE automation on the LAN) from simple embedding of data objects in a document. From the end user's perspective, DCOM does nothing to extend the OLE 2.0 capabilities already present in applications. Second, it hoped to distinguish between what was widely seen as a proprietary Microsoft approach and a (hopefully) more standards-based one: COM, in contrast to OLE, has broad industry support.

For present purposes, don't let the name change bother you. DCOM really is just Network OLE, renamed for the Internet.

Cairo: DFS, DCOM, and NTOFS An early beta version of Cairo was shown at Microsoft's 1993 Win32 Professional Developers Conference. At that time, Cairo looked much like NT 4.0—it had a Windows 95-style user interface—but it also offered DFS and a new object-oriented file system (OFS) that allowed for rich query capabilities.

When Microsoft decided to deliver the new user interface on NT 4.0, that fell out of the Cairo specification, but DFS and OFS were still lacking. In fact, we now know that client-side DFS support *was* added to NT 4.0, and a DFS add-on to NT Server is now available as a downloadable technology preview as described above. The rich query functionality is also available, in the Internet Search Service add-on to NT Server (see Chapter 7). OFS seems to be all that's lacking at this point.

In fact, we are told that OFS has been abandoned as a separate file system. Instead, object capabilities are being added to NTFS, creating a hybrid New Technology Object File System (NTOFS). This system will allow, finally, the rich query capabilities of Internet Search Server to migrate directly into the operating system. When you explore a directory in Cairo, you'll actually be executing a query against NTOFS.

Microsoft has also said that it plans to replace NT's existing security object monitor subsystem with a system based on MIT's *Kerberos* distributed security system. Kerberos introduces the concept of a *security server* on a network that validates security requests against networked objects in much the same way that the Windows NT Security Object Monitor validates attempts to access internal objects in the system. The significance is that the physical location of an object becomes unimportant in determining its security context. Just because a particular object exists in the local file system on your computer, you do not necessarily have the right or the capability to access it.

Distributed security makes sense in the context of a truly distributed architecture like the one we've been describing. A compound document might wind up containing many linked objects from many directories, but the compound document *as a unit* will have an owner and will inherit the highest security certification level of any component (there may be embedded objects within it that are public, but they will be confidential if the overall container document is confidential).

Moreover, a confidential document *owned* by one person may not be read by another person unless either the security administrator for the system or the owner has granted the right to read the document, even though that person might have confidential level access. This confidentiality would be appropriate (indeed essential) in upgrading Windows NT Cairo security to Department of Defense B-level standards, which would permit it to handle information at the Secret classification level. It would also be useful in secure operations such as banks or in the handling of financial information.

Of course, everything that we've said about the brave, new Windows Cairo world has concentrated on the new features. In the second edition, we pointed out that for Cairo to have any chance of actually being shipped, Microsoft would have to find a way to present these new capabilities while maintaining backward compatibility with the existing Windows NT system. And indeed, as Figures 12.1 and 12.2 show, exactly that is happening: DFS can handle NT 3.51 Servers and redirect them, even though NT 3.51 has no built-in DFS support.

On the other hand, something has happened that we did not—indeed, could not—anticipate: many of the advanced capabilities expected for Cairo are being delivered first on the Internet. Internet Search Server is one example, and another is the Web-based NT Server administration tool discussed in Chapter 8. It was predictable that such a tool would appear for Cairo. After all, with DCOM there is no reason administration couldn't be conducted remotely (indeed, NT

Server has always had remote administration features). Microsoft's interest in (one might almost say obsession with) the Internet has driven some of these features into the market in advance of the complete system as a whole.

Another point that we can begin to sense, based on Microsoft's early technology demonstrations (and Internet-based deliveries) is that many Cairo features will require NT Server. Indeed, rather than the broad distributed processing approach that we originally expected Cairo to represent,[11] it seems that Microsoft has moved to a mixed model, what we might call a *distributed client/server* approach. To get the benefit of DFS, Kerberos, and the like you will need at least one NT Server available somewhere on the local LAN (or perhaps at your Internet Service Provider). This requirement represents in part a recognition by Microsoft that it simply isn't practical to run a completely anarchic distributed environment—central point management is impossible if there is no central point (in this case, local server) to manage. It also may represent an attempt to protect NT Server as a source of income.

Other Cairo Features: Clusters, Plug-and-Play, 64-bit Support Besides NTOFS, DFS, and DCOM; features that Microsoft intends to field "in the Cairo time frame" include Clusters, Plug-and-Play, and 64-bit large memory model support. Clusters have been used in the mainframe world for years as a cost-effective way to combine fault tolerance and scalability. In a cluster, several servers are tied together, sharing certain resources (in particular, hard disks) and are treated as a unit. For example, two servers can share two disk drives using standard SCSI. Each server has a controller on *both* disks. Users see the two disks as part of a single virtual device, so a NET USE shows just one entry called (for instance) Cluster1. You access the disks as though both are connected to a single server called Cluster1; that is, \\Cluster1\disk1 and \\Cluster1\disk2.

With both servers operating, disk performance is enhanced because each drive is *actually* handled by a separate server (the cluster software masks this activity from users). However, if one server goes down (Digital demonstrated this at the 1994 Comdex trade show by physically disconnecting power on one server *during a disk access*), there's a short delay, and the other server takes over.

The beauty of this technology, as compared with alternatives like proprietary ultra-reliable systems (NetFrame, for instance) is that it's *cheap*. Standard servers and disks are combined to create a redundant cluster. Microsoft licensed Digital's cluster technology as part of a broad cross-licensing deal in 1995 and expects to field a first-generation software-only 2-node failover cluster for NT Server (code-named *Wolfpack*) by the end of 1996. A more sophisticated, scalable cluster should be available next year. In the meantime, Digital has continued to work on the technology and has announced that a combined hardware/software cluster upgrade kit for selected NT-based Digital servers will be available by the end of 1996.

Aside from clusters, one of the most anticipated additions to NT in the Cairo time frame will be plug-and-play support. This technology, first deployed by Microsoft in Windows 95,

---

11 And that Microsoft still seems bent on marketing. Microsoft's just-announced 1996 Professional Developers Conference is subtitled *The Renaissance of Distributed Computing.*

combines intelligent hardware devices with dynamically loadable device drivers. To give an extreme example, on a plug-and-play-equipped portable, it is possible to add a hardware device and install the requisite driver *without rebooting the computer*. This capability will hugely improve NT's support for portables, and we're fascinated by the prospect of applying plug-and-play technology to servers.

Finally, there's the issue of 64-bit memory support. When the first edition of this book was written in 1993, the idea of a single PC with more than 4GB of physical RAM seemed ludicrous. We should have known better. For a real-world example, you need look no further than http://altavista.digital.com. If you select the first (Altavista) entry at that site, you will be shown a description of how Digital manages to index the entire Web each and every night, using a 30GB database index. To allow reasonable performance when one is searching that index, some 6GB of it is cached—in physical RAM—at any one time.

If you'll review NT's 32-bit memory management (Chapter 1) you'll find that NT can address no more than 4GB of physical RAM—and half of that is reserved for the operating system itself. The most memory that any application can ever use is therefore 2GB, which is one-third of what Altavista currently requires (and we have no doubt that requirement will grow over time) . . .

The ultimate solution to this problem is, of course, to make NT a true 64-bit operating system, but that will require significant work and undoubtedly won't happen until mainstream processors (probably Intel's P7) support a true 64-bit mode of operation. In the meantime, the NT developers are working on a simple extension (analogous to HUGE model in 16-bit programming) that will let applications address memory beyond NT's 2GB limit. That extension will be delivered with Cairo, most probably in the Server version (though sooner or later someone will undoubtedly think of an application for it on Workstation as well!).

Conclusion: The Operating System Designed to Connect

We began this book by defining Windows NT as the operating system designed to connect. We then examined a wide variety of the features and functions of Windows NT that indeed meet this specification. We've provided as much information as we think possible as of this writing on administration and maintenance features and as much information as was made available to us on connectivity to third-party products like NetWare, TCP/IP, and Banyan VINES. Now we've closed out with some information on where the Windows NT product is headed in the foreseeable future.

We hope you've found this book readable, interesting, and most of all, useful. If you would like to write us about the book—perhaps with suggestions for future editions or comments on the current one—please do so in care of:

John Wiley and Sons

605 Third Ave.

New York, NY 10158

Or you may write to our individual electronic mail addresses:

John Ruley   jruley@cmp.com

Dave Methvin   dmethvin@cmp.com

Tom Henderson   thenders@cmp.com

Martin Heller   mheller@bix.com

Be sure to check out our *electronic update* Web page (discussed in the Introduction), and remember never to be afraid to try out new features, because *the best way to learn is by doing*!

For More Information

Renaud, Paul (1993), *Introduction to Client/Server Systems*. New York: John Wiley & Sons, Inc. ISBN: 0-471-57774-X. Excellent overview of client/server theory. It's a bit thick for the average reader, but worth working through if you really want to understand the topic.

Steele, Tammy (1993), "The Win32 Story: Targeting Windows 3.1, Windows NT, Chicago, and Cairo with the Win32 API," *Microsoft Developers Network News,* Volume 2 Number 5, Redmond, WA: Microsoft Developer's Network. Good (if limited) overview of the relationship between Chicago, Cairo, and OLE 2.0 for developers.

Stephenson, Peter and G. Hartwig (1992), *SQL Self-Teaching Guide*. New York: John Wiley & Sons, Inc. ISBN: 0-471-54544-9. Solid introduction to SQL, focusing on user (and programmer) issues rather than on theory. Invaluable in understanding the SQL Server manuals.

Programming NT Networks

1

In the rest of this book, we've concentrated on matters of concern to end users and system administrators, but there are network issues for programmers as well. Although it's not possible to cover network programming in depth (that's a topic for another book entirely!), we endeavor here to give a solid general overview. First, we'll talk about the issues and APIs that apply to all server processes, and then we'll discuss network, interprocess, and Internet programming.

One thing to note: NT's APIs have changed, with new functionality appearing in each release of the operating system. This overview will be as complete as possible, but given the rate at which new APIs appear, we recommend that you keep yourself informed by checking Microsoft's Web site, and/or by reading *Microsoft Developers Network News, Microsoft Systems Journal,* or another periodical source.

Networks and Services

Many network-specific programs act as servers for multiple clients. On UNIX systems, they might be *daemons*; and in Windows NT, they are typically *services*. Windows NT has considerable support for services. It allows them to start when the system boots, to continue when users log in and out, to have different privileges from those of the current user, to use a standard interface, and to use a standard way to report errors. It also gives them a standard way to post run-time statistics.

The service control manager is the piece of the NT system that allows services to start at boot time and continue operating across logins. It also provides the services for a standard user interface. The event logging subsystem gives services a standard way to report not only errors, but also warnings and benign system events. NT's event browser provides the interface for a user or administrator who needs to examine and act on system events.

Services can post run-time statistics by exposing blocks to the performance monitor. Performance counters are queried through the registry and are available both locally and across the NT network.

When writing servers, consider supporting internationalization by using the UNICODE character set. Unfortunately, not all clients support UNICODE, so it may be necessary to support multibyte character sets on some clients, using the character set translation APIs.

Server performance can be critical. Beginning with version 3.5, NT supports an optimized mechanism for asynchronous file I/O known as I/O completion ports, which is accessed through the *CreateIoCompletionPort* and *GetQueuedCompletionStatus* functions combined with ordinary Win32 file I/O. NT versions from 3.5 on also support the *SetThreadAffinityMask* function, which allows a given thread to run only on certain CPUs in a multi-processor system, and the *SetPriorityClass* function, which allows you to tell the system something about your process's time-critical status.

Both SetThreadAffinityMask and SetPriorityClass need to be treated with great care: they are dangerous power tools with sharp edges and no safety shields, intended for use only by trained professionals. If you find yourself resorting to setting a high or real-time priority class to get the performance you need, for instance, consider the possibility that your service architecture may need to be redesigned to accomplish your goals in a way that allows the rest of the system to run, too.

Service Control Manager

A service is an executable object that is installed in a registry database maintained by the service control manager. The services database determines whether each installed service is started on demand or automatically when the system starts up. It can also contain logon and security information for a service so that a service can run even though no user is logged on.

Win32 services conform to the interface rules of the service control manager. Driver services conform to the device driver protocols for Windows NT. The service control manager functions are listed in Table A1-1. A discussion on device drivers is beyond the scope of this work.

Table A1.1 Win32 Service Control Manager Functions

Function	Action
ChangeServiceConfig	Change service configuration parameters
CloseServiceHandle	Close Service Control Manager object
ControlService	Send a control to a service
CreateService	Create a service object
DeleteService	Remove service from SC Manager database
EnumDependentServices	Enumerate services dependent on device
EnumServicesStatus	Enumerate services in SC manager database
Handler	Control handler function of a service
LockServiceDatabase	Lock specified SC Manager database
NotifyBootConfigStatus	Notify/respond to acceptability of boot configuration
OpenService	Open an existing service
OpenSCManager	Connect to service control manager
QueryServiceConfig	Get service configuration parameters
QueryServiceLockStatus	Get service database lock status
QueryServiceObjectSecurity	Get service object security descriptor
QueryServiceStatus	Get service status
RegisterServiceCtrlHandler	Register service control request handler
ServiceMain	Main function of a service
SetServiceStatus	Update service status to SC Manager
SetServiceObjectSecurity	Modify service object security descriptor
StartService	Start running a service
StartServiceCtrlDispatcher	Connect thread as dispatch thread
UnlockServiceDatabase	Unlock specified database

The service control manager is actually an RPC server, so you can control services on remote machines. You can write three kinds of programs that would use service control functions: a Win32 service process, which provides executable code for services and provides status information to the service control manager; a service configuration program, which manipulates the service control database; and a service control program, which starts a service and controls a running service.

The SDK SERVICE sample demonstrates a simple service process, a client for it, and a program to install and remove service processes. SIMPLE.C is a service process that echoes and mangles input it receives on a named pipe. CLIENT.C sends a string on the named pipe and displays the resulting echo. And INSTSRV.C demonstrates using CreateService and DeleteService.

A Win32 service process must include a main function that immediately calls the StartServiceCtrlDispatcher function to connect the main thread of the process to the Service Control Manager. It also needs an entry point function, ServiceMain in Table A1.1, for each service that can run in the process, and a control handler function, Handler in Table A1.1, for each service that can run in the process. The actual names for the service entry points are determined by the dispatch table passed to StartServiceCtrlDispatcher:

```
VOID main() {
    SERVICE_TABLE_ENTRY dispatchTable[] = {
        { TEXT("SimpleService"), //first service in list
        (LPSERVICE_MAIN_FUNCTION)service_main },
        { NULL, NULL }        //NULLs terminate list of services
    };

    if (!StartServiceCtrlDispatcher(dispatchTable)) {
        StopSimpleService("StartServiceCtrlDispatcher failed.");
    }
}
```

The actual name for the handler is determined by the main service entry point and registered with the service control manager through use of the RegisterServiceCtrlHandler function:

```
VOID service_main(DWORD dwArgc, LPTSTR *lpszArgv) {
    DWORD                  dwWait;
    PSECURITY_DESCRIPTOR   pSD;
    SECURITY_ATTRIBUTES    sa;

    // register our service control handler:
    //
    sshStatusHandle = RegisterServiceCtrlHandler(
                            TEXT("SimpleService"),
                            service_ctrl);
    if (!sshStatusHandle)
        goto cleanup;
```

A simple service process might include all the code it needed to do its job in its own executable. A more complicated service process might well spawn additional daemon processes. For instance, you could write a service process that accepted an SQL query on a named pipes, submitted the query to a separate database process through named shared memory, signaled the database that a query was pending using an event, and returned the query result to the originator via the named pipes.

It might also be possible to write a generic service process that did nothing but start and stop other processes. For instance, you might have a character-mode OS/2 server process that you want to run on your Windows NT system. You could make it look and act like a real NT server process, even though it runs in the OS/2 subsystem, by writing a small NT service process to start and control it. The OS/2 process would handle its own interprocess communications.

It's really fairly easy to turn a service application of any kind into a true Win32 service process. Consider doing this for any server application that should run independent of the current user—which applies to most network services. When it comes time to test your service, use the SC application supplied with the Windows NT SDK to communicate with the service control manager.

Also consider making your service configuration program a Control Panel applet. A Control Panel applet resides in a DLL, typically is given the CPL extension, and includes a standard callback entry-point function named CPlApplet, which must be exported. The application needs to include the CPL.H header file for the definition of the messages that Control Panel sends to the applet.

You can find all the information you need to write your own Control Panel applets in the Win32 SDK help by searching for "Control Panel Applications Overview." From there, you can browse through the successive help topics or investigate the cross-references. There is a fairly complete example included in one of the help topics as well, although it won't make much sense until you've read the preceding topics. In any case, doing a control panel applet isn't difficult once you have the information.

Event Logging

One issue many server applications face is how to display error conditions. Often, the server process has no user interface and can't even be sure it is running on a machine with an active screen. A standard message box might pop up on a screen that is powered down or hidden in a closet.

Event logging provides a standard, centralized way for applications (and Windows NT) to record important software and hardware events including not only error conditions, but events that ought to leave an audit trail. The Windows NT Event Viewer offers a standard user interface for viewing the logs, and the event logging functions provide ways to examine and back up the logs as well as to report events. The Win32 event logging functions are listed in Table A1.2.

Table A1.2 Win32 Event Logging Functions

Function	Action
BackupEventLog	Saves an event log in a backup file
ClearEventLog	Clears the event log
CloseEventLog	Closes an event-log handle
DeregisterEventSource	Closes a registered event handle

(Continued)

Table A1.2 (Continued)

Function	Action
GetNumberOfEventLogRecords	Gets number of records in event log
GetOldestEventLogRecord	Retrieves number of oldest record
OpenBackupEventLog	Opens a handle to a backup event log
OpenEventLog	Opens an event-log handle
ReadEventLog	Reads entries from an event log
RegisterEventSource	Returns a registered event-log handle
ReportEvent	Writes an event-log entry

Events are classified as information, warnings, and errors. All event classifications have well-defined common data and can optionally include event-specific data. For example, information can assert that a service has started or is stopping, that a process connected or disconnected, or that some specific action was performed.

For example, we might have a process that is controlling a soda machine. Information might record that the machine was filled or that a column of cans was changed to a different kind of soda. Information might also record each transaction on the machine such as what kind of soda was dispensed, what coins were tendered, and what coins were given in change. A viewing process for the soda machine's event log would be able to deduce the machine's exact status, plot historical usage, and predict future usage for ordering purposes.

Warnings are used for recoverable problems. For our soda machine, we might want to log a warning when any column drops below three cans or when the machine gets low on change. Errors are used for nonrecoverable conditions that might cause an application to fail. For the soda machine, that might be running out of soda in any column, running out of change, or being unable to keep the soda cold.

Of course, you can use event logs for more serious purposes as well. Windows NT itself uses the event log for conditions like driver failures to load, disk drive time-outs, and network errors. It also uses the event log to keep an audit trail (if the administrator enables it) of users logging in and out, security policy changes, system restarts, and so on.

Performance Monitoring

Network administrators often need to monitor network and disk server performance in order to maintain and tune their facilities. Windows NT has a useful Performance Monitor program in the Administrative Tools group. True to the open spirit of Win32, the key functions used by the Performance Monitor are exposed in the API and available for anyone to use. They are listed in Table A1.3.

Table A1.3 Win32 Performance Monitoring Functions

Function	Action
RegConnectRegistry	Connects to registry on a remote system
RegQueryValueEx	Retrieves the type and data for a specified value name associated with an open registry key
QueryPerformanceCounter	Obtains performance counter value
QueryPerformanceFrequency	Returns performance counter frequency

Why would anyone want to reinvent the Performance Monitor? You might, for instance, want to write a more statistics-gathering program or an alarm panel. The statistics-gathering program might collect selected performance numbers from a list of machines on the network at predetermined intervals and save them in a database. A companion program would process the saved data on demand, computing means and standard deviations, displaying time series graphs, histograms and scatter plots, and otherwise making sense of the network's behavior over time. The alarm panel would scan the network at intervals and send a message to the designated administrator when hard disks were full or performance figures fell outside their normal range.

NT's high-resolution performance counter functions allow you to access the system's high-speed timer. QueryPerformanceFrequency tells you the number of counts per second for the timer, and QueryPerformanceCounter tells you the current reading of the timer. These functions are similar to the C library function *clock* and the associated constant CLOCKS_PER_SEC, but might give you better time resolution.

NT's *system* performance numbers are accessed through the registry, although they are not actually stored in the registry. You can get system performance information by calling RegQueryValueEx with the key HKEY_PERFORMANCE_DATA. If you wish, use RegOpenKey to open the HKEY_PERFORMANCE_DATA handle, but remember to use RegCloseKey to close the handle when you're done with it.

Using RegQueryValueEx with HKEY_PERFORMANCE_DATA causes the system to collect the data from the appropriate system object managers. To collect data from a remote system, use RegConnectRegistry with the name of the remote system and the HKEY_PERFORMANCE_DATA key to retrieve a key usable with RegQueryValueEx to actually retrieve performance data from the remote system.

RegQueryValueEx returns a PERF_DATA_BLOCK structure followed by one PERF_OBJECT_TYPE structure and accompanying data for each type of object being monitored. The system being observed defines objects that can be monitored, which are typically processors, disks, and memory.

The performance data block describes the performance data returned by RegQueryValueEx:

```
typedef struct _PERF_DATA_BLOCK { /* pdb */
    WCHAR           Signature[4];
    DWORD           LittleEndian;
    DWORD           Version;
    DWORD           Revision;
    DWORD           TotalByteLength;
    DWORD           HeaderLength;
    DWORD           NumObjectTypes;
    DWORD           DefaultObject;
    SYSTEMTIME      SystemTime;         //time of measurement in UTC format
    LARGE_INTEGER   PerfTime;           //actual data value counts
    LARGE_INTEGER   PerfFreq;           //timer counts per second
    LARGE_INTEGER   PerfTime100nSec;    //data value in 100 ns units
    DWORD           SystemNameLength;
    DWORD           SystemNameOffset;
} PERF_DATA_BLOCK;
```

The PERF_OBJECT_TYPE structure describes the object-specific performance information:

```
typedef struct _PERF_OBJECT_TYPE {   /* pot */
    DWORD   TotalByteLength;
    DWORD   DefinitionLength;
    DWORD   HeaderLength;
    DWORD   ObjectNameTitleIndex;
    LPWSTR  ObjectNameTitle;
    DWORD   ObjectHelpTitleIndex;
    LPWSTR  ObjectHelpTitle;
    DWORD   DetailLevel;
    DWORD   NumCounters;
    DWORD   DefaultCounter;
    DWORD   NumInstances;
    DWORD   CodePage;
    LARGE_INTEGER PerfTime;
    LARGE_INTEGER PerfFreq;
} PERF_OBJECT_TYPE;
```

The PERF_OBJECT_TYPE structure for an object is followed by a list of PERF_COUNTER_DEFINITION structures:

```
typedef struct _PERF_COUNTER_DEFINITION { /* pcd */
    DWORD   ByteLength;
    DWORD   CounterNameTitleIndex;
    LPWSTR  CounterNameTitle;
    DWORD   CounterHelpTitleIndex;
    LPWSTR  CounterHelpTitle;
    DWORD   DefaultScale;
    DWORD   DetailLevel;
    DWORD   CounterType;
    DWORD   CounterSize;
    DWORD   CounterOffset;
} PERF_COUNTER_DEFINITION;
```

The PERF_INSTANCE_DEFINITION is used to define each instance of a block of object-specific performance data. Not all counters have instances. For instance, memory objects don't have instances, because the system has only one memory. Disk objects do have instances, because the system can have more than one disk.

```
typedef struct _PERF_INSTANCE_DEFINITION { /* pid */
    DWORD ByteLength;
    DWORD ParentObjectTitleIndex;
    DWORD ParentObjectInstance;
    DWORD UniqueID;
    DWORD NameOffset;
    DWORD NameLength;
} PERF_INSTANCE_DEFINITION;
```

Finally, the object-specific data is held in a PERF_COUNTER_BLOCK structure:

```
typedef struct _PERF_COUNTER_BLOCK { /* pcd */
    DWORD ByteLength;
} PERF_COUNTER_BLOCK;
```

The names of the objects and counters, as well as the text that explains their meaning, are kept in the registry. To access them, open the registry node:

```
\SOFTWARE\Microsoft\Windows NT\CurrentVersion\Perflib\<langid>
```

The language node (langid) is the ASCII representation of the three-digit hexadecimal language identifier. For example, the U.S. English node is "009." This node, once opened, can be queried for values of either "Counters" or "Help." The names of object types are included in the Counters data. The Help data supplies the Explain text. The Counters and Help data are stored in MULTI_SZ strings, listed in index-name pairs; for example:

```
2       System
4       Memory
6       % Processor Time
10      Read Operations/sec
12      Write Operations/sec
```

Navigating the performance registry tree is somewhat complicated. You can find some working code samples, however, in the Win32 help file: search for "Performance Monitoring Overview," then select the item "Using Performance Monitoring." The two sections of the help file that follow give examples that display counters and their titles.

Security

Windows NT has a centralized security facility in which all named objects, and some unnamed objects, have security descriptors (SDs), and all users and processes have access tokens and security identifiers (SIDs). Security descriptors include information about the owner of the object and an access-control list (ACL), which contains access-control entries (ACEs) that identify the users and groups allowed or denied access to the object.

When you program Windows NT, you access objects by getting handles to them, then using the handles. The security process applies when you try to get the handle: the system compares your access token with the object's access-control entries, and grants you a handle only if at least one ACE exists that allows your token access and additionally no ACE exists that denies your token access.

There can be two kinds of access control lists in a security descriptor. A system ACL is controlled by the system administrator. A discretionary ACL is controlled by the owner of the object.

With sufficient privilege, you can manipulate access programmatically, often by adding a discretionary ACL to an object's security descriptor. The functions to manipulate SDs, ACLs, ACEs, tokens, SIDs, and related objects like audit alarms are listed in Table A1.4.

Table A1.4 Win32 Security Functions

Function	Action
AccessCheck	Validates a client's access rights
AccessCheckAndAuditAlarm	Validates access, generates audit and alarm
AddAccessAllowedAce	Adds ACCESS_ALLOWED_ACE to ACL
AddAccessDeniedAce	Adds ACCESS_DENIED_ACE to ACL
AddAce	Adds an ACE to an existing ACL
AddAuditAccessAce	Adds SYSTEM_AUDIT_ACE to ACL
AdjustTokenGroups	Enables/disables groups in a token
AdjustTokenPrivileges	Enables/disables token privileges
AllocateAndInitializeSid	Allocates and initializes SID with subauthorities
AllocateLocallyUniqueId	Allocates an LUID
AreAllAccessesGranted	Checks for all desired access
AreAnyAccessesGranted	Checks for any desired access
CopySid	Copies an SID to a buffer
CreatePrivateObjectSecurity	Allocates and initializes a protected SD
CreateProcessAsUser	Creates a new process and its primary thread as a specific user
DdeImpersonateClient	DDE server impersonates client
DeleteAce	Deletes an ACE from an existing ACL

Table A1.4 (Continued)

Function	Action
DestroyPrivateObjectSecurity	Deletes a protected server object's SD
DuplicateToken	Duplicates an access token
EqualPrefixSid	Tests two SID prefixes for equality
EqualSid	Tests two SID security IDs for equality
FindFirstFreeAce	Retrieves a pointer to first free ACL byte
FreeSid	Frees an allocated SID
GetAce	Retrieves a pointer to an ACE in an ACL
GetAclInformation	Retrieves access-control list information
GetFileSecurity	Gets file or directory security information
GetKernelObjectSecurity	Retrieves kernel object SD
GetLengthSid	Returns length of an SID
GetPrivateObjectSecurity	Retrieves protected server object SD
GetProcessWindowStation	Returns process window-station handle
GetSecurityDescriptorControl	Retrieves SD revision and control info
GetSecurityDescriptorDacl	Retrieves SD discretionary ACL
GetSecurityDescriptorGroup	Retrieves SD primary group information
GetSecurityDescriptorLength	Returns SD length
GetSecurityDescriptorOwner	Retrieves SD owner
GetSecurityDescriptorSacl	Retrieves SD system ACL
GetSidIdentifierAuthority	Returns ID authority field address
GetSidLengthRequired	Returns required length of SID
GetSidSubAuthority	Returns subauthority array address
GetSidSubAuthorityCount	Returns subauthority field address
GetThreadDesktop	Returns thread desktop handle
GetTokenInformation	Retrieves specified token information
GetUserObjectSecurity	Retrieves server object SD information
ImpersonateLoggedOnUser	Lets the calling thread impersonate a user

(Continued)

Table A1.4 (Continued)

Function	Action
ImpersonateNamedPipeClient	Pipe server acts as client
ImpersonateSelf	Gets impersonation token for calling process
InitializeAcl	Creates a new access-control list
InitializeSecurityDescriptor	Initializes a security descriptor
InitializeSid	Initializes an SID
IsValidAcl	Validates an access-control list
IsValidSecurityDescriptor	Validates security descriptor
IsValidSid	Validates an SID
LogonUser	Attempts to perform a user logon operation
LookupAccountName	Translates account name to SID
LookupAccountSid	Translates SID to account name
LookupPrivilegeDisplayName	Retrieves a displayable privilege name
LookupPrivilegeName	Retrieves a programmatic privilege name
LookupPrivilegeValue	Retrieves LUID for privilege name
MakeAbsoluteSD	Creates absolute SD from self-relative
MakeSelfRelativeSD	Creates self-relative SD from absolute
MapGenericMask	Maps generic access to specific/standard
ObjectCloseAuditAlarm	Generates audit/alarm when object is deleted
ObjectOpenAuditAlarm	Generates audit/alarm when object is accessed
ObjectPrivilegeAuditAlarm	Generates audit/alarm on privileged operation
OpenProcessToken	Open process token object
OpenThreadToken	Open thread token object
PrivilegeCheck	Tests client security context for privileges
PrivilegedServiceAuditAlarm	Audit/alarm on privileged system service
RevertToSelf	Stops impersonation
SetAclInformation	Sets information in an ACL
SetFileSecurity	Sets file or directory security

Table A1.4 (Continued)

Function	Action
SetKernelObjectSecurity	Sets kernel object security
SetPrivateObjectSecurity	Modifies existing SD
SetSecurityDescriptorDacl	Sets DACL information
SetSecurityDescriptorGroup	Sets SD primary group information
SetSecurityDescriptorOwner	Sets SD owner
SetSecurityDescriptorSacl	Sets SACL information
SetTokenInformation	Sets various token information
SetUserObjectSecurity	Sets security-descriptor values

You can readily find security example programs in the Win32 SDK help files and in the CHECK_SD, EXITWIN, REGISTRY, SIDCLN, and TAKEOWN samples. If you want to deny all access to an object, you can add an *empty* discretionary ACL to its security descriptor. If you want to allow all access to an object, you can give it a NULL discretionary ACL. Note the difference between empty and NULL here: empty means there is an ACL, but it has no entries; NULL means there is no ACL.

Using Threads and Processes

Network programs, and particularly server programs, often need to be designed using multiple threads of execution and/or multiple processes to work efficiently and scale well. It is important to understand the difference between threads and processes. An application can contain more than one process; a process can contain more than one thread.

A thread is the basic entity to which the NT operating system allocates CPU time. A thread can execute any part of the application's code, including a part currently being executed by another thread. All threads of a process share the virtual address space, global variables, and operating system resources of the process.

A process, in turn, is an executing application that consists of a private virtual address space, code, data, and other operating system resources, such as files, pipes, and synchronization objects that are visible to the process. To complete the circular definition, a process also contains one or more threads that run in the context of the process.

Designing multitasking applications is more of an art than a science, and not an easy art at that, but you can approach it using a few rules of thumb. First, anything that you think of as a background task is a good candidate to be in a *thread of its own*. Printing a document, for instance, can be done by a background thread, as can recalculating a spreadsheet or reformatting a document.

Anything that can usefully be spread over multiple CPUs—and that's often the case for network server tasks—should use *multiple threads*. For instance, some image-processing tasks use a lot of CPU time and operate on only a few pixels at a time. It would be relatively simple to spawn multiple threads and use all the CPUs in a multiprocessing system for such a task.

Anything that needs to be independent and responsive might usefully be given its own thread. For instance, you might want to assign a thread to each character in an animation, a thread to each independent window in an application, or a thread to each client of a service, as long as you don't wind up with too many running threads. We'll explain what constitutes too many threads in just a moment.

Finally, you might want to consider using threads in situations in which an application spends a lot of time waiting for something to happen. Without threads, the application must chew up CPU time checking some state; with threads, you can simply have a thread waiting for one or more events to happen or for one or more resources to become available and rely on the system to block the thread from running at all until it can usefully do so.

When Not to Use threads

When *wouldn't* you want to use threads? In some cases using threads just makes things slower, and in other cases threads can't help because a resource is serialized. And in yet other cases multiple threads make accessing global data unsafe, requiring synchronization delays that wipe out the original advantage of using a threaded model.

For instance, all input is serialized in Win32 systems by USER32, so there's no point in having multiple threads handling input: one input thread will suffice. A printer is inherently a serial-access device, so one thread for printing is enough. But printing should be a background task, and handling input should be a high-priority foreground task, so printing and user input shouldn't really be handled by the same thread.

How can threads make things slower? If you understand the overhead involved in using threads, you can balance it off against the gains you make with threads. Each time you spawn a thread you create a new stack, a new register set, and another contender for the current time slice. In addition, you create complications every place the threads can interact. At some point, the cost of adding another thread on a given configuration will exceed the benefit of having that thread. It's a difficult point to predict at design time, but it's not to hard to determine experimentally.

Spawning a Thread

Before you can experiment, however, you have to know how to spawn a thread. Using the Win32 API set, you'd call CreateThread. If you're using Visual C++ without MFC, Microsoft recommends that you call the run-time library functions _beginthread or _beginthreadex instead of CreateThread to avoid incurring memory leaks in C run-time functions. If you're using MFC, Microsoft recommends that you use AfxBeginThread or construct a CWinThread object and call its CreateThread member.

In the Win32 API, you'd call SetThreadPriority to designate the priority of a foreground or background thread. Using MFC, you can set the thread priority as part of the AfxBeginThread call; you can also distinguish between worker threads and user interface threads by the form of AfxBeginThread call you choose. A worker thread is the sort of thread you'd use for background printing; a user interface thread handles user input and responds to user events.

You create a worker thread by passing AfxBeginThread the address of your thread procedure. You create an MFC user interface thread by first deriving a class from CWinThread, declaring it with DECLARE_DYNCREATE and implementing it with the IMPLEMENT_DYNCREATE macro. You then pass your derived class to AfxBeginThread, which creates and initializes an object of your class, then starts the thread by calling CWinThread::CreateThread. AfxBeginThread takes great care to properly release objects if any step of the process fails.

How Many Threads?

Now that we know how to create a thread, we can think about our thread model. The simplest is of course the default: one thread for the whole application. That's what we want to get beyond.

A second obvious model uses a thread per distinct function. In a program that does a dozen or so distinct functions, this model can work well as long as the synchronization issues can be addressed. A thread per function can help utilize multiple CPUs in SMP systems, but this thread-per-function model doesn't allow for highly CPU-bound tasks.

When you have a CPU-bound task that can be decomposed, you might want to invoke a third model: a thread per CPU. Find out how many CPUs are in the system using GetSystemInfo, then spawn that many low-priority threads for the CPU-bound task. You don't need to worry about counting your other threads—the CPU-bound threads will soak up all the background processing time, and the other threads will get in when they need to.

For a server, you can consider spawning a thread per client. This is a natural thing to do when handling named pipes, sockets, and so on. A thread per client will scale until you have too many threads—that is, when the time the system spends switching from thread context to thread context becomes a significant part of the total CPU time. In general, you don't want to have more than 20 or 30 runnable threads in your process contending for the CPU. In other words, you aren't going to create a usable server for 1,000 clients using 1,000 threads.

Worker threads can be made to handle more than one client, at some cost in code complexity. For instance, each thread in an ftp server might be able to handle 10 to 20 sockets if it performed asynchronous or overlapped I/O on the sockets and disk files; a total of 30 threads handling 20 sockets each would serve 600 simultaneous ftp client sessions. Worker threads can also use *I/O completion ports*, a special form of overlapped I/O introduced in Windows NT 3.5, to achieve even higher file transfer performance, both on disk file handles and on sockets.

Synchronizing Your Threads

We will not discuss Dining Philosophers or Petri nets here, but if you want to know more about concurrent programming, we can recommend some reference books.[1] Synchronizing multiple concurrent threads and/or processes is a nontrivial task, requiring a good deal of knowledge and experience as well as care and patience.

The three worst problems people face in this area are data corruption, race conditions, and deadlock conditions. You typically get data corruption when two threads or processes are trying to change the same data at the same time. You get race conditions when one thread relies on another thread to complete some action, without having any synchronization between the two threads.

The process works if the second thread wins the race by completing its action before the first thread needs it; otherwise, you're out of luck. You get a deadlock condition when both threads need to obtain two resources to continue, and each thread obtains one resource and waits forever for the other.

You typically fix data corruption problems across threads by guarding the data with *critical section* objects. If you have data corruption problems across processes, you can fix the problem by guarding the global data or global resource with *mutex* objects. You can also use *interlocked increment* calls to change data atomically: instead of using the C increment construct *count++* in a thread, you'd use the system call InterlockedIncrement (LPLONG lplVal) to increase the value of a variable by one without any possibility of another thread interrupting the operation. Similarly, you'd use InterlockedDecrement and InterlockedExchange calls instead of the equivalent C language constructs.

You can often solve race conditions by synchronizing things among threads and processes using *events* or *semaphores*. If one thread or process needs another to get to a certain point, it can wait for an event to fire, which is set by the other thread or process. The waiting thread would use WaitForSingleObject on the event handle; the other thread would signal the event with SetEvent.

---

1   Some good references on concurrency are Ben-Ari, M., *Principles of Concurrent Programming*. Englewood Cliffs, N.J.: Prentice-Hall, Inc., 1982; and Bic, L. and A. Shaw. *The Logical Design of Operating Systems*. Englewood Cliffs, N.J.: Prentice-Hall, Inc., 1988. For Petri nets, look at Murata, Tadao. "Petri Nets: Properties, Analysis and Applications." Proceedings of the IEEE 77 (April 1989): 541-580; Peterson, James L. *Petri Nets and the Modeling of Systems*. Englewood Cliffs, N.J: Prentice-Hall, 1981; and Reisig, W. *A Primer in Petri Net Design*. Berlin: Springer-Verlag, 1992.

You can find additional material on concurrent programming and Petri nets applied to Windows NT in a series of articles by Ruediger Asche on Microsoft's Development Library CD-ROM. *Multithreading for Rookies* introduces the whole topic. *Using Multithreading and C++ to Generate Live Objects* and *Synchronization on the Fly* deal with concurrent programming. *Compound Win32 Synchronization Objects* expands on the theme and explains how to build useful synchronization structures like reader/writer locks from Win32 primitives. *Detecting Deadlocks in Multithreaded Win32 Applications*, *The Implementation of DLDETECT.EXE*, and *Putting DLDETECT to Work* cover Petri nets. Another article, *Multiple Threads in the User Interface,* by Nancy Cluts, deals with the issues involved in using threads that run window procedures and process message queues.

Events tell you something happened; semaphores are used to allow N things to happen, and no more. For instance, a database might limit itself to 20 users. It could set a semaphore to an initial value of 20 and make each user claim the semaphore before giving access.

You usually fix deadlocks by standardizing the order in which objects are claimed, by using critical sections, by using mutex objects, by using the WaitForMultipleObjects system call, or by some combination of the above. For instance, you might need write locks on two database tables in order to perform a proper debit and credit to an accounting system. You could assign a mutex to each table for a write lock. If two threads claimed the mutex objects in different orders, you could easily get a deadlock condition. But if the threads always claimed the two mutex objects simultaneously with a WaitForMultipleObjects call, no deadlock would be possible.

Sorting Out NT Interprocess Communications

Windows NT, and specifically its 32-Windows subsystem, Win32, contains a plethora of inter-process and networking mechanisms of varying degrees of complexity. The fledgling Win32 network programmer often makes one feel like a kid in a candy store. Let's start by briefly tasting each networking, interprocess communication, and related mechanism: NetBIOS, WNet, mailslots, MAPI, pipes, RAS, sockets, RPCs, DDE, NetDDE, OLE, memory-mapped files, security, service control, event logging, and performance monitoring.

The NetBIOS function supports raw IBM NetBIOS, a very low-level protocol controlled by network control blocks (NCBs). According to Microsoft, NetBIOS is in Win32 primarily for compatibility with existing systems written to NetBIOS that need to be ported to Windows and Windows NT. On the other hand, NetBIOS will work whether your Windows NT system is communicating via NetBEUI, TCP/IP, or IPX/SPX. Various NetBIOS commands allow the use of communication sessions with individual partners, as well as datagram broadcasts to specific recipients or entire networks. The Win32 NetBIOS function works in Win32s as well as Windows NT; other implementations of NetBIOS are available for DOS, OS/2, and 16-bit Windows.

The WNet functions allow you to enumerate, connect, and disconnect from network resources (shares). One of the WNet functions also gives you access to the current network user name. The WNet functions work in Win32s as well as Windows NT.

A mailslot is a one-way interprocess communication (IPC) mechanism, amounting to a temporary pseudofile, which works over a network. Mailslot communications are not guaranteed to be reliable, because they use the datagram, but they are convenient for broadcasting messages throughout a domain. Mailslots do *not* work in Win32s.

MAPI is the Messaging Application Program Interface. It gives an application a simple way to send messages and files to network users via the Microsoft Mail application included with every copy of Windows NT and Windows for Workgroups. Don't confuse MAPI with mailslots: MAPI is really the programmatic interface to Microsoft Mail; mailslots are a system-level inter-process communication mechanism. MAPI is supported in 16-bit Windows and in Windows NT, but not in Win32s.

A pipe is a communication conduit with two ends: a process with a handle to one end can communicate with a process having a handle to the other end. Win32 supports both named pipes and anonymous pipes; only named pipes can work over a network. Named pipes were the preferred IPC mechanism in OS/2, so applications ported from OS/2 to Windows NT often use named pipes. Pipes are inherently reliable—they use a protocol that lets you know that each message has been received—and are therefore preferable to mailslots when reliability is important. Named pipes can be a two-way mechanism, but mailslots are strictly one-way mechanisms. However, pipes cannot broadcast messages to multiple clients: for broadcasting, mailslots are preferable to pipes. Named pipes are not supported in 16-bit Windows or in Win32s.

Remote Access Services (RAS) allow one Windows NT machine to connect to another over a serial line, modem, X.25 connection, or ISDN connection. Although the Windows NT RAS applets probably will allow most people to use RAS well enough, it is possible to use the RAS API functions to control the process from within another program, which might make sense for applications involving remote reporting and wide-area networking. RAS services are not supported in Win32s.

Sockets are standard networking mechanisms that originated in Berkeley UNIX. More recently, the Windows Socket (WinSock) specification codified extensions to Berkeley Sockets for the Windows environment. Windows NT implements a 32-bit version of Windows Sockets. Sockets allow for a wide variety of network addressing schemes and protocols, although they were historically associated with TCP/IP. Sockets are supported in Win32s as well as in Windows NT and most UNIX implementations. Implementations of 16-bit Windows Sockets are available from several vendors.

The Windows NT Remote Procedure Call (RPC), a partial implementation of the OSF DCE (Open Software Foundation Distributed Computing Environment) specification, is conceptually a simple mechanism for distributed computing, but is by its nature complex to program and debug. The NT implementation of RPC includes a Microsoft implementation of the Interface Description Language (IDL) compiler, used for specifying the interface to remote procedures and generating the required local stub functions; RPC run-time libraries, which let the local stubs call the remote procedures; and the actual network transport used by the client and server run-time libraries.

RPC can use a variety of transports, network address formats, and protocols. Windows NT RPC 1.0 supports TCP/IP, named pipe, NetBIOS, and Local Procedure Call transports. Network addresses can be in IP, DECNet, or OSI formats as needed. The RPC protocol can be NCA connections or NCA datagrams. The exact combination of protocol, address format, and transport used by a given connection is specified by an ASCII *protocol sequence*, which is combined with the actual endpoints to form a *binding*. RPC *naming services* allow a client to find a server on the network.

NT RPCs are supposed to work with DOS and Windows clients and UNIX servers as well as other NT RPC clients and servers. The DOS/Windows client software ships with the NT SDK, although it needs to be installed separately from the native Windows NT tools. It is not clear whether NT RPC servers will work with all UNIX clients, because the UNIX clients might rely on DCE services not present in the NT RPC implementation. RPC is not supported in Win32s.

Dynamic Data Exchange (DDE) is an old local Windows interprocess communication protocol that is supported in Windows NT in both 16-bit and 32-bit form. NetDDE is an enhancement to DDE that allows it to work over networks. DDE works in Win32s and 16-bit Windows as well as in Windows NT.

Object Linking and Embedding (OLE) is a different enhancement to DDE to support compound documents and application programmability. OLE is expected to be the basis for directory services in Cairo, just as OLE is already the basis for shell interaction in Windows 95. OLE automation can be considered a universal mechanism for remote control of applications, and the underpinning for common objects.

The basic mechanism underpinning OLE is COM, the Common Object Model. COM itself is actually quite simple: a COM server program is required to export an IUnknown interface that contains three methods, AddRef, Release, and QueryInterface. AddRef and Release are used for reference counting so that the system can release a COM object when all its clients have finished with it. QueryInterface is used to gain access to the COM object's other useful interfaces.

Using these three simple methods, clients and servers using COM can work together efficiently without crashing because of version incompatibilities. COM is a key part of Microsoft's system strategy, and most of Microsoft's newer applications and services use and/or support COM. In particular, ActiveX™ is little more than a new name for existing OLE and COM technology.

OLE automation adds another layer to COM in order to support programming environments like Visual Basic. In addition to QueryInterface, OLE automation servers support IDispatch and IClassFactory interfaces.

Networked OLE, or distributed COM (DCOM), was introduced in Windows NT 4.0. This mechanism allows COM to work over RPC; from the programmer's viewpoint, enabling DCOM is simply a matter of specifying a remote server instead of a local server.

OLE is such a large subject that we can't even outline it in an appendix like this one. Your best bet for including OLE in an application is to use your compiler's Wizard or Expert tools to generate the correct OLE options for your application framework, and add your code to that.

Memory-mapped files are Windows NT's answer to shared memory, which is not supported because each process in Windows NT has its own address space. Although not useful as a network connection, memory-mapped files are useful as a high-bandwidth interprocess communications method on a single machine, which might well provide a network service. For instance, memory-mapped files could be used to implement the high-bandwidth part of a database server involving several processes; one of these processes could then accept queries and send results over the network using named pipes or another network transport. Memory-mapped files are supported in Win32s as well as in Windows NT.

Windows NT has built-in security designed to be certifiable at the US C2 level. Although security functions are not specifically interprocess or networking functions, it is often in networking applications that the programmer must pay attention to security issues. Similarly, the Windows NT Service Control Manager, Event Logging, and Performance Monitoring services are not specifically for networks, but are often used in programming for networks.

Windows NT also includes the full LAN Manager API, although this is not considered part of the Win32 API. Existing LAN Manager code can be ported to Windows NT with little more than some code tweaks and a recompile. More information on the LAN Manager

API under Windows NT can be found in DOC\SDK\MISC\LMAPI.HLP on the Windows NT SDK CD-ROM.

In the balance of this appendix, we briefly examine the functions provided by each of the service groups mentioned above. When appropriate, we will go over simple examples of their use.

A few other function groups deserve mention, but are not generally important enough to merit their own sections. First, telephony: Microsoft provides a 32-bit development kit for TAPI, the telephony API, and TSPI, the telephony service provider interface. The TAPI kit is currently part of the Win32 SDK. You can also find out more about TAPI and TSPI by looking at the specifications, available on MSDN.

SNMP, the Simple Network Management Protocol, is supported in Windows NT as a layer on top of Windows Sockets. SNMP is good for making your application manageable in a heterogeneous environment, especially one in which UNIX management station software is already present. On the Windows NT SDK CD-ROM, you can find slides explaining SNMP extensions in the file PDC\SLIDES\ROSAT251.PPT, and code samples in the directory PDC\SNMP.

Aside from the new Internet-related features, Windows NT 4.0 introduces a number of features not directly related to network programming, including cryptography APIs and Win95-style shell APIs. For information on those see the Win32 SDK or MSDN CDs, or refer to the Microsoft Win32 development Web site at http://www.microsoft.com/win32dev.

NetBIOS

There is one and only one function to support NetBIOS in Win32, and that is NetBIOS. It takes one parameter: a pointer to a network-control block (NCB) structure, which holds all the semantic content for the service. The NCB contains a command, a return code, information about the network environment, and a pointer to a buffer that is used for messages or for further data about the network:[2]

```
typedef struct _NCB { /* ncb */
    UCHAR   ncb_command;        /* command code            */
    UCHAR   ncb_retcode;        /* return code             */
    UCHAR   ncb_lsn;            /* local session number    */
    UCHAR   ncb_num;            /* number of network name   */
    PUCHAR  ncb_buffer;         /* address of message buffer */
    WORD    ncb_length;         /* size of message buffer   */
    UCHAR   ncb_callname[NCBNAMSZ];
                                /* blank-padded name of remote */
    UCHAR   ncb_name[NCBNAMSZ];
                                /* blank-padded name of local  */
    UCHAR   ncb_rto;            /* receive timeout/retry count */
    UCHAR   ncb_sto;            /* send timeout/system timeout */
    void (*ncb_post) (struct _NCB *);
                                /* POST routine address     */
    UCHAR   ncb_lana_num;       /* lana (adapter) number    */
```

---

2   This and succeeding reference materials in this appendix are based on information supplied by Microsoft in its Win32 documentation from the *Windows NT System Development Kit*.

```
    UCHAR   ncb_cmd_cplt;    /* 0xff => command pending    */
    UCHAR   ncb_reserve[10]; /* reserved, used by BIOS     */
    HANDLE  ncb_event;       /* signaled when ASYNCH completes */
} NCB, *PNCB;
```

The Win32 implementation of the NetBIOS function includes some enhancements that are not part of the IBM NetBIOS 3.0 specification and a few differences in implementation from IBM NetBIOS 3.0. The enhancements allow POST routines to be called from C and allow for completion notification using a Win32 event object. The differences are minor.

The NCB_command member of the NCB structure specifies the command code and a flag in the most significant bit (the ASYNCH constant) that indicates whether the NCB is processed asynchronously. The command codes have the actions given in Table A1.5. Note that the symbolic NCB command names used here, which match those in the NB30.H file supplied with the Win32 SDK, might be somewhat different from the symbolic names defined for DOS NetBIOS programming environments.

Table A1.5 NetBIOS Commands

NCB Command Code	Action
NCBACTION	Enable extensions to the transport interface. NCBACTION commands are mapped to TdiAction. When this value is specified, the ncb_buffer member points to a buffer to be filled with an ACTION_HEADER structure, which is optionally followed by data. NCBACTION commands cannot be canceled through NCBCANCEL.
NCBADDGRNAME	Add a group name to the local name table.
NCBADDNAME	Add a unique name to the local name table.
NCBASTAT	Retrieve the status of the adapter. When this value is specified, the ncb_buffer member points to a buffer to be filled with an ADAPTER_STATUS structure, followed by an array of NAME_BUFFER structures.
NCBCALL	Open a session with another name.
NCBCANCEL	Cancel a previous command.
NCBCHAINSEND	Send the contents of two data buffers to the specified session partner. For Windows NT, this is equivalent to the NCBCHAINSENDNA command.
NCBCHAINSENDNA	Send the contents of two data buffers to the specified session partner and do not wait for acknowledgment. For Windows NT, this is equivalent to the NCBCHAINSEND command.

(Continued)

Table A1.5 (Continued)

NCB Command Code	Action
NCBDELNAME	Delete a name from the local name table.
NCBDGRECV	Receive a datagram from any name.
NCBDGRECVBC	Receive broadcast datagram from any host.
NCBDGSEND	Send datagram to a specified name.
NCBDGSENDBC	Send a broadcast datagram to every host on the local area network (LAN).
NCBENUM	Enumerate LAN adapter (LANA) numbers. When this value is specified, the ncb_buffer member points to a buffer to be filled with a LANA_ENUM structure.
NCBFINDNAME	Determine the location of a name on the network. When this value is specified, the ncb_buffer member points to a buffer to be filled with a FIND_NAME_HEADER structure followed by one or more FIND_NAME_BUFFER structures.
NCBHANGUP	Close a specified session.
NCBLANSTALERT	Notify the user of LAN failures that last for more than one minute.
NCBLISTEN	Enable a session to be opened with another name.
NCBRECV	Receive data from the specified session partner.
NCBRECVANY	Receive data from any session corresponding to a specified name.
NCBRESET	Reset a LAN adapter. An adapter must be reset before any other NCB command that specifies the same number in the ncb_lana_num member will be accepted. The IBM NetBIOS 3.0 specification documents several NCB_RESET NCBs. Win32 implements the "NCB.RESET Using the Dynamic Link Routine Interface." Particular values can be passed in specific bytes of the NCB. More specifically: If ncb_lsn is not 0x00, all resources associated with ncb_lana_num are to be freed. If ncb_lsn is 0x00, all resources associated with ncb_lana_num are to be freed, and new resources are to be allocated. The byte ncb_callname[0] specifies the maximum number of sessions, and the byte ncb_callname[2] specifies the maximum number of names. A non-zero value for the byte ncb_callname[3] requests that the application use NAME_NUMBER_1.
NCBSEND	Send data to the specified session partner. For Windows NT, this is equivalent to the NCBSENDNA command.

Table A1.5 (Continued)

NCB Command Code	Action
NCBSENDNA	Send data to specified session partner and do not wait for an acknowledgment. For Windows NT, this is equivalent to the NCBSEND command.
NCBSSTAT	Retrieve the status of the session. When this value is specified, the ncb_buffer member points to a buffer to be filled with a SESSION_HEADER structure, followed by one or more SESSION_BUFFER structures.
NCBTRACE	Activate or deactivate NCB tracing. Support for this command in the system is optional and system specific.
NCBUNLINK	Unlink the adapter.

The ncb_retcode member of NCB specifies the return code. This value is set to NRC_PENDING while an asynchronous operation is in progress. Once the operation is completed, the return code is set to one of the values listed in Table A1.6.

Table A1.6 NCB Return Codes

Return code	Meaning
NRC_GOODRET	The operation succeeded.
NRC_BUFLEN	An illegal buffer length was supplied.
NRC_ILLCMD	An illegal command was supplied.
NRC_CMDTMO	The command was timed out.
NRC_INCOMP	The message was incomplete. The application is to issue another command.
NRC_BADDR	The buffer address was illegal.
NRC_SNUMOUT	The session number was out of range.
NRC_NORES	No resource was available.
NRC_SCLOSED	The session was closed.
NRC_CMDCAN	The command was canceled.
NRC_DUPNAME	A duplicate name existed in the local name table.

(Continued)

Table A1.6 (Continued)

Return code	Meaning
NRC_NAMTFUL	The name table was full.
NRC_ACTSES	The command finished; the name has active sessions and is no longer registered.
NRC_LOCTFUL	The local session table was full.
NRC_REMTFUL	The remote session table was full. The request to open a session was rejected.
NRC_ILLNN	An illegal name number was specified.
NRC_NOCALL	The system did not find the name that was called.
NRC_NOWILD	Wildcards are not permitted in the ncb_name member.
NRC_INUSE	The name was already in use on the remote adapter.
NRC_NAMERR	The name was deleted.
NRC_SABORT	The session ended abnormally.
NRC_NAMCONF	A name conflict was detected.
NRC_IFBUSY	The interface was busy.
NRC_TOOMANY	Too many commands were outstanding; the application can retry the command later.
NRC_BRIDGE	The ncb_lana_num member did not specify a valid network number.
NRC_CANOCCR	The command finished while a cancel operation was occurring.
NRC_CANCEL	The NCBCANCEL command was not valid; the command was not canceled.
NRC_DUPENV	The name was defined by another local process.
NRC_ENVNOTDEF	The environment was not defined. A reset command must be issued.
NRC_OSRESNOTAV	Operating system resources were exhausted. The application can retry the command later.
NRC_MAXAPPS	The maximum number of applications was exceeded.
NRC_NOSAPS	No SAPs available for NetBIOS.
NRC_NORESOURCES	The requested resources were not available.

Table A1.6 (Continued)

Return code	Meaning
NRC_INVADDRESS	The NCB address was not valid. This return code is not part of the IBM NetBIOS 3.0 specification. This return code is not returned in the NCB; instead, it is returned by the NetBIOS function.
NRC_INVDDID	The NCB DDID was invalid.
NRC_LOCKFAIL	The attempt to lock the user area failed.
NRC_OPENERR	An error occurred during an open operation being performed by the device driver. This return code is not part of the IBM NetBIOS 3.0 specification.
NRC_SYSTEM	A system error occurred.
NRC_PENDING	An asynchronous operation is not yet finished.

The ncb_lsn member of NCB specifies the local session number, ncb_buffer points to the message buffer, and ncb_length specifies the size, in bytes, of the message buffer. ncb_callname specifies the string that contains the remote name, and ncb_name specifies the string that contains the local name. Trailing space characters should be supplied in both names to pad the length of the strings out to the length specified by the NCBNAMSZ command.

ncb_rto sets the receive time-out period, in 500-millisecond units, for the session and is used only for NCBRECV commands. Likewise, ncb_sto sets the send time-out period, in 500-millisecond units, for the session and is used only for NCBSEND and NCBCHAINSEND commands. A value of 0 implies no time-out.

ncb_post specifies the address of the routine to call when an asynchronous NCB finishes. The completion routine is passed a pointer to the completed network-control block.

ncb_lana_num specifies the LAN adapter number. This zero-based number corresponds to a particular transport provider using a particular LAN adapter board. ncb_cmd_cplt specifies the command-complete flag, which has the same as the ncb_retcode member. ncb_reserve is reserved and must be set to zero.

ncb_event specifies a handle to a Windows NT event to be set to the signaled state when an asynchronous network-control block finishes. The event is signaled if the NetBIOS function returns a nonzero value. The ncb_event member of NCB must be zero if the ncb_command member does not have the ASYNCH value set or if ncb_post is non-zero. Otherwise, NRC_ILLCMD is returned. In other words, you can't ask for more than one notification that a NCB request has completed: it must be synchronous, signal an event, or call a completion routine.

The event specified by ncb_event is set to the non-signaled state by the system when an asynchronous NetBIOS command is accepted and is set to the signaled state when the asynchronous NetBIOS command finishes. Using ncb_event to submit asynchronous requests requires fewer system resources than using ncb_post. Also, when ncb_event is non-zero, the pending request is canceled if the thread terminates before the request is processed. This is not true for requests sent with ncb_post.

Only manual reset events should be used with NetBIOS. A given event should not be associated with more than one active asynchronous NetBIOS command.

How can we use NetBIOS? The *very* simple example below doesn't actually *do* anything, but does illustrate working successfully with NetBIOS from Win32. We'll start by initializing the session and adding a name, which you normally do from the server:

```
#define WIN32
#include <windows.h>
#include <nb30.h>
#include <stdlib.h>
#include <stdio.h>
#include <memory.h>

#define NSESSIONS  1
#define NNAMES     1
//...

char chNameBuffer [ NCBNAMSZ ];
unsigned char ucRc;
int i;
NCB ncb;
//...

//  Code to initialize chNameBuffer should come here (not shown)

//....

/* reset NetBIOS session */

memset(&ncb,0,sizeof(ncb));
ncb.ncb_command = NCBRESET;
ncb.ncb_callname[0] = NSESSIONS;
ncb.ncb_callname[1] = NNAMES;
ucRc = NetBIOS (&ncb);

/* Add a Name */

memset(&ncb,0,sizeof(ncb));
ncb.ncb_command = NCBADDNAME;
memcpy (ncb.ncb_name, chNameBuffer, NCBNAMSZ);
ucRc = NetBIOS (&ncb);
if (ucRc )
        return (1);
```

The server would normally start a session and post a receive at this point, assuming it uses connections and not datagrams. Basically the server now has to wait for the client. The client first has to find the server by name:

```
struct {
    FIND_NAME_HEADER fnh;
    FIND_NAME_BUFFER fnb;
    } fn;

/* Find the Name   */

memset(&ncb,0,sizeof(ncb));
memset(&fn.fnh,0,sizeof(fn.fnh));
memset(&fn.fnb,0,sizeof(fn.fnb));
fn.fnh.node_count = 1;
fn.fnb.length = sizeof(fn.fnb);
ncb.ncb_command = NCBFINDNAME;
memcpy (ncb.ncb_callname, chNameBuffer, NCBNAMSZ);
ncb.ncb_buffer = (PUCHAR)&fn.fnh;
ncb.ncb_length =  sizeof(fn);
ucRc = NetBIOS (&ncb);
```

Now we can send a datagram or establish a session and send messages. When the server is all done, it needs to delete the name:

```
/* Delete the Name */

memset(&ncb,0,sizeof(ncb));
ncb.ncb_command = NCBDELNAME;
memcpy (ncb.ncb_name, chNameBuffer,   NCBNAMSZ);
ucRc = NetBIOS (&ncb);
```

If you're already familiar with NetBIOS programming from DOS, Windows, or OS/2, you probably now understand the Win32 NetBIOS function well enough to use it. If you aren't familiar with NetBIOS programming and need to use it from Windows NT, you'll want to consult a good NetBIOS programming book, but expect to have to mentally translate systems.

The Win32 NetBIOS function, unlike DOS, doesn't require you to issue interrupts. Unlike Windows, it doesn't require you to call it from assembly language, from a DLL, or with locked NCBs. Unlike OS/2, it doesn't require you to call additional functions. Like all of those, however, it requires NetBIOS names to be padded with blanks, so you'll want to use a function like CopyToBuffer to work with them:

```
void CopyToBuffer ( char *pchDest , char *pchSrc)
{
    register count;

    /* Check for null pointer */
    if ((!pchDest) || ( ! pchSrc))
        return ;

    /* set the name field with nulls */
    memset ( pchDest, 0x20, NCBNAMSZ);
```

```
/* copy from source to destination */
count = NCBNAMSZ;
while ((*pchSrc) && ( count))
{
    *pchDest++ = *pchSrc++;
    count--;
}
return;
}
```

You can build entire client/server systems using only NetBIOS, although no one would call that a convenient way to develop new programs. Fortunately, Win32 supports a number of other network mechanisms.

WNet

The WNet group of functions allows you to explicitly manipulate network disk and printer connections and other network resources from your applications. They allow you to add some of the functionality of the Windows Explorer, net use, and net view to your own programs. The WNet functions are listed in Table A1.7. To use any of these functions, you need to link to MPR.LIB, the multiple provider router library.

Table A1.7 WNet Functions

Function Name	Action
WNetAddConnection	Redirects a local device to a network resource
WNetAddConnection2	Redirects a local device to a network resource
WNetCancelConnection	Breaks an existing network connection
WNetCancelConnection2	Breaks an existing network connection
WNetCloseEnum	Ends a network resource list
WNetConnectionDialog	Starts a network connection dialog box
WNetDisconnectDialog	Starts a network disconnection dialog box
WNetEnumResource	Continues listing network resources
WNetGetConnection	Gets name of network resource
WNetGetLastError	Returns last error for network functions
WNetGetUser	Gets the current network user name
WNetOpenEnum	Starts listing network resources

Note that WNetAddConnection and WNetCancelConnection are already obsolete: they are present in Win32 for compatibility with Windows for Workgroups programs and have been replaced with WNetAddConnection2 and WNetCancelConnection2, respectively, which are considerably more flexible. WNetAddConnection2 and the resource enumeration functions WNetOpenEnum, WNetEnumResource, and WNetCloseEnum use the NETRESOURCE structure to describe network resources:

```
typedef struct _NETRESOURCE {   /* nr */
    DWORD   dwScope;         //connected, global, or persistent
    DWORD   dwType;          //any, disk, or print
    DWORD   dwDisplayType;  //domain, generic, server, or share
    DWORD   dwUsage;         //connectable or container
    LPTSTR  lpLocalName;    //i.e. H: or LPT3:
    LPTSTR  lpRemoteName;   //remote network name
    LPTSTR  lpComment;      //provider-supplied comment
    LPTSTR  lpProvider;     //provider name
} NETRESOURCE;
```

If you want to give control of network connections to the user, use the WNetConnectionDialog function to put up a dialog box, enumerate the network resources and display them, and allow the user to connect to resources:

```
DWORD dwResult;
dwResult = WNetConnectionDialog(hWnd, RESOURCETYPE_DISK);
if(dwResult != NO_ERROR) {
    MyErrorHandler(hWnd, dwResult, (LPSTR)"WNetConnectionDialog");
    return FALSE;
    }
```

In general, the alternatives to RESOURCETYPE_DISK are RESOURCETYPE_PRINT and RESOURCETYPE_ANY. WNetConnectionDialog, however, works only with RESOURCETYPE_*DISK*. It brings up the standard "Map Network Drive" dialog (Figure A1.1). One wonders whether some future version of the function will implement printer browsing as well.

One more function in this group bears comment. WNetGetUser does more than meets the eye. It not only can find the current default user name, but it can also find the user name used to establish any given network connection:

```
DWORD WNetGetUser(lpszLocalName, lpszUserName, lpcchBuffer)
LPTSTR lpszLocalName;   /* address of local name to get user name for */
LPTSTR lpszUserName;    /* address of buffer for user name */
LPDWORD lpcchBuffer;    /* address of buffer-size variable */
```

If you use NULL for the local name, you get the current user name for the process. If you specify a share name, you will get the user name used to connect to the share. If there are multiple connections with multiple names, you'll get one of the user names, but there's no telling which one.

Closely related to the WNet and security APIs are some group and user control APIs with Net prefixes. These are not LanMan APIs, even though they appear to be from their naming. The

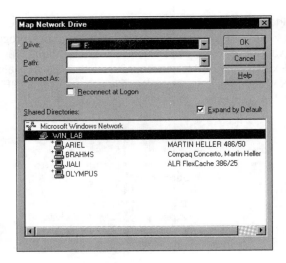

FIGURE A1.1 WNetConnectionDialog. The WNetConnectionDialog Win32 API function generates the familiar Connect Network Drive dialog used to associate drive letters with network resources in NT.

global group APIs—NetGroupAdd, NetGroupSetUsers, NetGroupAddUser, NetGroupSetInfo, and so on—control global groups of users in a way that can be used across domains. The local group APIs—NetLocalGroupAdd, NetLocalGroupSetMembers, NetLocalGroupAddMember, and so on—control sets of users with common permissions in the security database. User APIs—NetUserEnum, NetUserGetGroups, NetUserGetLocalGroups, NetUserAdd, NetUserDel, NetUserGetInfo, and NetUserSetInfo—control individual user accounts in the security database.

Mailslots

As we mentioned earlier, mailslots are convenient for broadcasting messages and other one-way communications tasks. Only three API functions are needed to support mailslots, as shown in Table A1.8; the rest of the mailslot functionality is performed with standard file functions, because mailslots act as pseudofiles.

Table A1.8 Mailslot API Server Functions

Function	Action
CreateMailslot	Creates a mailslot
GetMailslotInfo	Retrieves mailslot information
SetMailslotInfo	Sets mailslot read time-out

Note that, unlike real files, mailslots are temporary. When every handle of a mailslot is closed or the process owning the last handle exits, the mailslot and all the data it contains are deleted. The data in a mailslot message can be in any form, within the length limit set when the mailslot was created.

A server process creates a mailslot with the CreateMailslot function, which returns a handle to the mailslot:

```
HANDLE CreateMailslot(lpszName, cbMaxMsg, dwReadTimeout, lpsa)

LPCTSTR lpszName;              /* address of string for mailslot name */
DWORD cbMaxMsg;                /* maximum message size                */
DWORD dwReadTimeout;           /* milliseconds before read timeout    */
LPSECURITY_ATTRIBUTES lpsa;    /* address of security structure       */
```

The lpszName parameter to CreateMailslot is required to be of the form \\.\mailslot\[path]name and must be unique. The name may include multiple levels of pseudo-directories separated by backslashes. For example, both \\.\mailslot\example_mailslot_name and \\.\mailslot\abc\def\ghi are valid names. The cbMaxMsg parameter specifies the maximum message size that can be written to the mailslot, in bytes; zero means that the size is unlimited.

dwReadTimeout specifies the amount of time, in milliseconds, a read operation can wait for a message to be written to the mailslot before a time-out occurs. A value of zero means that reads return immediately if no message is present. A value of MAILSLOT_WAIT_FOREVER, defined as -1, means that reads to the mailslot never time out.

lpsa is a security descriptor for the mailbox (we discuss security descriptors a little later). Most of the time you can safely use NULL for the security descriptor, which causes the object to get default security attributes. You'll need a real security descriptor if you want to pass the mailbox handle to child processes or you actually want to restrict access to the mailbox to authorized processes.

To open a mailslot from a client process, use the mailslot name, with FILE_SHARE_READ and OPEN_EXISTING specified as flags. If the mailslot is local to the client, its name is the same one used when it was created; for example, \\.\mailslot\name. If the mailslot is remote, you can specify \\computername\mailslot\name, \\domainname\mailslot\name, or *\mailslot\name. The last two forms are used for domain-wide broadcasts: the * form broadcasts in the local system's primary domain, and the \\domainname form broadcasts in the specified domain. If you use either domain-wide broadcast form, you cannot write more than 400 bytes at a time to the mailslot.

Note that opening a mailslot from the client side can return a valid handle even if the mailslot doesn't exist. And remember that mailslot communications use datagrams, which are not inherently reliable. Don't use a mailslot for a message that absolutely, positively must get through.

Once you've opened the mailslot, you can write messages to it using WriteFile and the handle returned from CreateFile. The server reads messages with ReadFile. The only other functions that can be used with mailslots are GetMailSlotInfo, SetMailSlotInfo, GetFileTime,

SetFileTime, and DuplicateHandle. Mailslot clients should restrict themselves to CreateFile, DuplicateHandle, WriteFile, and CloseHandle.

MAPI

Although mailslots are good for sending transient one-way interprocess messages and message broadcasts, they are inappropriate for persistent messages, reliable messages, and applications that require two-way communication. For persistent, reliable one-way messages, it might be better to use MAPI, the Messaging Application Program Interface. (For transient, reliable two-way interprocess communications, named pipes might be a better choice.)

MAPI is a set of high-level functions that applications use to create, manipulate, transfer, and store messages. MAPI provides a common interface, which application developers use to create mail-enabled and mail-aware applications independent of the underlying messaging system. In addition to a message store interface used to create and manage collections of messages, MAPI also includes an address book interface for access to mail recipients and distribution lists.

MAPI comes in two flavors: Simple MAPI and Extended MAPI. Simple MAPI is built into Windows NT and Windows for Workgroups, as Microsoft Mail comes with both systems. You can add Simple MAPI capabilities to a Windows 3.1 system by adding Microsoft Mail to the system. Extended MAPI, also called MAPI 1.0, requires a *Windows Messaging Subsystem*, such as Exchange.

Extended MAPI augments Simple MAPI with additional functions for advanced addressing and folder and message management. Applications can use Extended MAPI to create and deal with large and/or complex messages, to access portions of a directory service, and to organize and search a large store of messages.

CMC, the Common Mail Calls interface, offers an alternative to Simple MAPI. CMC was designed to be vendor independent and to work specifically with Lotus VIM as well as Microsoft MAPI mail systems, so that using CMC should be preferable to using Simple MAPI in new applications. In practice, however, Lotus provides MAPI-to-VIM mapping layers for VIM mail systems, so that applications written to Simple MAPI often work properly with cc:Mail and Notes as well as with MsMail and Exchange post offices.

The Simple MAPI functions are listed in Table A1.9. To use these functions, you will need to include MAPI.H and dynamically link to MAPI32.DLL (from a 32-bit application) or MAPI.DLL (from a 16-bit application).

Table A1.9. Simple MAPI Functions

Function	Description
MAPIAddress	Addresses a Mail message.
MAPIDeleteMail	Deletes a Mail message.
MAPIDetails	Displays a recipient details dialog box.

Table A1.9. (Continued)

Function	Description
MAPIFindNext	Returns the ID of the next (or first) Mail message of a specified type.
MAPIFreeBuffer	Frees memory allocated by the messaging system.
MAPILogoff	Ends a session with the messaging system.
MAPILogon	Begins a session with the messaging system.
MAPIReadMail	Reads a Mail message.
MAPIResolveName	Displays a dialog box to resolve an ambiguous recipient name.
MAPISaveMail	Saves a Mail message.
MAPISendDocuments	Sends a standard Mail message using a dialog box.
MAPISendMail	Sends a Mail message, allowing greater flexibility in message generation.

The following code will allow you to dynamically link to the MAPI service DLL and get the address of the single function needed to mail-enable an application, MAPISendDocuments:

```
#ifdef WIN32
#define MAPIDLL "MAPI32.DLL"
#else
#define MAPIDLL "MAPI.DLL"
#define SZ_MAPISENDDOC "MAPISendDocuments"
extern ULONG (FAR PASCAL *lpfnMAPISendDocuments)(ULONG, LPSTR,
        LPSTR, LPSTR, ULONG);
extern HANDLE hLibrary;

int FAR PASCAL InitMAPI() {
  if ((hLibrary = LoadLibrary(MAPIDLL)) < 32)
    return(ERR_LOAD_LIB);
  if ((lpfnMAPISendDocuments= GetProcAddress(hLibrary,
      SZ_MAPISENDDOC)) == NULL)
    return(ERR_LOAD_FUNC);
  return(0);
}
```

Once you've successfully linked to MAPI32.DLL or MAPI.DLL and retrieved a pointer to MAPISendDocuments, add a Send menu item to the File menu of your application. Enable the menu item when there is a current document in the application, and disable it when there is no current document.

When the menu item is picked, you'll need to process it. If yours is an MDI application, you might want to offer a choice between "Send current document" and "Send all documents."

Whether you are sending a single document or multiple documents, the logic for each document is the same: save the current file as a temporary, call MAPISendDocuments for the temporary file, and finally delete the temporary file. The following code snippet calls MAPISendDocuments:

```
ulResult = (*lpfnMAPISendDocuments)(hWnd, ";",
 lpszFullPathToTemporaryFile, lpszTemporaryFileName, OL);
```

Amazingly, that's all there is to mail-enabling an application. The user, if not already logged into Mail, will see a login dialog and then a mail dialog with the file already listed, like the one shown in Figure A1.2. Where did all that user interface come from? From MS-Mail. You're actually using MAPI to tap into MS-Mail, which is acting as the mail service provider.

That's quite a bit of application to get from one function call. If you want to send documents or mail messages without involving the user or you simply want more control over the message, you can use an alternate function, MAPISendMail:

```
ULONG MAPISendMail(lhSession, ulUIParam, lpMessage, flFlags,
        ulReserved)
LHANDLE  lhSession;        //session handle, 0 or from MAPILogon
ULONG  ulUIParam;          //parent window handle, or 0
lpMapiMessage  lpMessage;  //pointer to MapiMessage structure
ULONG  flFlags;            //specify whether to display login and send
```

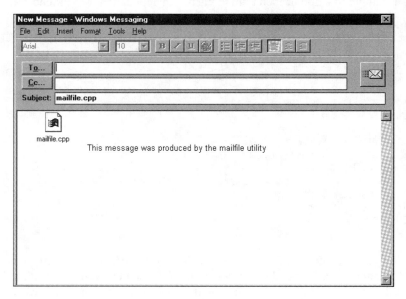

FIGURE A1.2 MAPISendDocuments. The MAPISendDocuments Win32 API function generates the Send Mail dialog shown here. This allows applications to be mail-enabled with a minimum of programming.

```
                            //message dialogs, and whether to use a default
                            //MAPI session if it exists
ULONG   ulReserved;         //must be 0
```

You can use MAPISendMail to accomplish much the same end as MAPISendDocuments, if you wish:

```
long err;
MapiFileDesc file = {0, 0, "c:\tmp\tmp.wk3", "budget17.wk3", NULL};
MapiMessage note = {0,NULL,NULL,NULL,NULL,NULL,0,NULL,0,NULL,1,&file};
err = MAPISendMail (0L,0L,&note,MAPI_DIALOG,0L);
if (err != SUCCESS_SUCCESS )
      printf("Unable to send the message.\n");
```

Or, you can use MAPISendMail to send a completely automated message:

```
MapiRecipDesc recip[2];
MapiFileDesc file = {0, 0, "c:\budget17.wk3", "budget17.wk3",
      NULL};
MapiMessage note = {0,NULL,
  "Attached is the budget proposal.\r\nSee you Monday.\r\n",
  NULL,NULL,NULL,0,NULL,2,NULL,1,&file};

recip[0].ulReserved = 0;
recip[0].nRecipClass = MAPI_TO;
recip[0].lpszName = "Sally Jones";
recip[0].lpszAddress = NULL;
recip[0].ulEIDSize = 0;
recip[0].lpEntryID = NULL;

recip[1].ulReserved = 0;
recip[1].nRecipClass = MAPI_CC;
recip[1].lpszName = "Marketing";
recip[1].lpszAddress = NULL;
recip[1].ulEIDSize = 0;
recip[1].lpEntryID = NULL;

note.lpRecips = &recip;

err = MAPISendMail (0L,0L,&note,0L,0L);
if (err != SUCCESS_SUCCESS )
  printf("Unable to send the message.\n");
```

None of the other Simple MAPI functions is any trickier than this. You would use MAPILogon and MAPILogoff to control sessions; MAPIFindNext, MAPIReadMail, MAPISaveMail, and MAPIDeleteMail to read and dispose of incoming mail; and MAPIAddress, MAPIDetails, and MAPIResolveName to assist the user in addressing outgoing mail. MAPIFreeBuffer is needed to release memory allocated by MAPIAddress, MAPIReadMail, and MAPIResolveName.

Pipes

A pipe is a communication conduit with two ends: a process with a handle to one end can communicate with a process having a handle to the other end. Pipes can be one way, with one end read-only and the other end write-only, or two-way with both ends of the pipe able to read or write. Pipes are similar to mailslots in that they are written to and read from like files. Win32 supports both anonymous (unnamed) pipes and named pipes. The pipe functions are listed in Table A1.10.

Anonymous Pipes Anonymous pipes are unnamed, one-way pipes intended to transfer data between a parent process and a child process, or between two child processes of the same parent process. Anonymous pipes are always local: they cannot be used over a network. The CreatePipe function creates an anonymous pipe and returns two handles: one to the read end and one to the write end of the pipe. The read handle has only read access to the pipe, and the write handle has only write access to the pipe. To communicate through the pipe, a handle to one of the ends must be passed to another process. Usually, this is done through inheritance, in which a child process inherits a handle from its parent process.

To read from the pipe, a process uses the read handle in a call to the ReadFile function. To write to the pipe, a process uses the write handle in a call to the WriteFile function. Neither ReadFile nor WriteFile returns until the specified number of bytes has been read or written or until an error occurs. Asynchronous I/O is not supported for pipes. An anonymous pipe exists until all handles to both read and write ends of the pipe are closed by the CloseHandle function.

Table A1.10. Pipe Functions

Function	Action
CallNamedPipe	Multiple pipe operations
ConnectNamedPipe	Waits for a client to connect
CreateNamedPipe	Creates an instance of a named pipe
CreatePipe	Creates an anonymous pipe
DisconnectNamedPipe	Disconnects server end of a named pipe
GetNamedPipeHandleState	Returns named-pipe handle information
GetNamedPipeInfo	Returns named-pipe handle information
PeekNamedPipe	Previews pipe-queue data
SetNamedPipeHandleState	Sets pipe read and blocking mode and controls local buffering
TransactNamedPipe	Reads and writes a named pipe
WaitNamedPipe	Waits for a named pipe

Named Pipes Named pipes are considerably more flexible than anonymous pipes. Named pipes can be one way or two way, they can work over a network, and a server process can use a named pipe to communicate with one or more client processes.

The server process uses CreateNamedPipe to create one or more instances of a named pipe. All instances of a named pipe share the same pipe name, but each instance has its own buffers and handles and provides a separate conduit for client/server communication. When a client process specifies a pipe name in the CreateFile or CallNamedPipe functions, it connects to an instance of the pipe. As a result, multiple client processes can use the same named pipe simultaneously. It is entirely possible for a single process to act as both a named pipe client and server.

The CreateNamedPipe function offers a number of options:

```
HANDLE CreateNamedPipe(lpName, dwOpenMode, dwPipeMode,
    nMaxInstances, nOutBufferSize, nInBufferSize, nDefaultTimeout,
    lpSecurityAttributes)
LPCTSTR lpName;                                 /* address of pipe name      */
DWORD dwOpenMode;                               /* pipe open mode            */
DWORD dwPipeMode;                               /* pipe-specific modes       */
DWORD nMaxInstances;                            /* maximum number of instances */
DWORD nOutBufferSize;                           /* out buffer size in bytes  */
DWORD nInBufferSize;                            /* in buffer size in bytes   */
DWORD nDefaultTimeout;                          /* timeout time in milliseconds */
LPSECURITY_ATTRIBUTES lpSecurityAttributes;     /* security attributes       */
```

The pipe name at creation has the form: \\.\pipe\pipename. The pipename part of the name can include any character other than a backslash, including numbers and special characters. The entire pipe name string can be up to 256 characters long. Pipe names are not case sensitive. When a client connects to a named pipe over a network, it uses the name form \\servername\pipe\pipename. If the pipe is local, the \\.\pipe\pipename can be used by the client.

The pipe's open mode can be PIPE_ACCESS_DUPLEX, PIPE_ACCESS_INBOUND, or PIPE_ACCESS_OUTBOUND, corresponding to bidirectional data flow, flow from client to server, and flow from server to client, respectively. A pipe can optionally use write-through and/or overlapped mode, which can vary for different instances of the same pipe.

FILE_FLAG_WRITE_THROUGH, which enables write-through mode, affects write operations only on byte-type pipes, which we'll explain shortly. Write-through mode keeps the system from buffering data written into the pipe: in write-through mode, any function that writes to the pipe returns only when the data is actually transmitted across the network to the remote computer. Write-through mode improves reliability at the expense of efficiency.

FILE_FLAG_OVERLAPPED, which enables overlapped mode, allows functions that perform read, write, and connect operations to return immediately. Overlapped mode allows one thread to service multiple instances of a pipe or perform simultaneous read and write operations on the same pipe handle. The alternative to overlapped mode, assuming that you want your named pipe server to handle multiple clients, is to spawn a thread per client.

In addition to directionality, write-through, and overlap, a named pipe's open mode can include any combination of security access flags, which can be different for different instances of the same pipe. The three possible security access flags are: WRITE_DAC, which gives the caller write access to the named pipe's discretionary ACL; WRITE_OWNER, which gives the caller write access to the named pipe's owner; and ACCESS_SYSTEM_SECURITY, which gives the caller write access to the named pipe's system ACL. An ACL is an access control list, the basic security control structure in Windows NT. A discretionary ACL is controlled by the owner of the object; a system ACL is controlled by the system administrator.

All of the above options apply to the named pipe's *open* mode, specified in the second parameter to CreateNamedPipe. A named pipe's *pipe* mode, specified in the third parameter to CreateNamedPipe, determines the pipe's type, read mode, and wait mode.

We mentioned earlier that a pipe must be in byte mode for write-through mode to be effective. PIPE_TYPE_BYTE means that data is written to the pipe as a stream of bytes. The alternative, PIPE_TYPE_MESSAGE, means that data is written to the pipe as a stream of messages. A pipe's write mode has to be the same for all instances.

In addition to a type or write mode, a named pipe has a read mode and a wait mode, which can differ among instances. PIPE_READMODE_BYTE is valid no matter what write mode was specified for the pipe. PIPE_READMODE_MESSAGE works only for a message-type pipe: the pipe data has to be written as messages to be read as messages, but messages can always be broken down into bytes.

PIPE_WAIT enables blocking mode, which means that transactions do not complete until there is data to read, all data is written, or a client is connected. Blocking pipes can in fact wait indefinitely. For non-blocking pipes, enabled by PIPE_NOWAIT, ReadFile, WriteFile, and ConnectNamedPipe, always return immediately. Non-blocking mode is basically there for compatibility with LAN Manager: if you want to enable asynchronous pipe I/O, use FILE_FLAG_OVERLAPPED in the open mode.

The fourth parameter to CreateNamedPipe specifies the maximum number of instances that can be created for the pipe, in the range of 1 through PIPE_UNLIMITED_INSTANCES. The fifth and sixth parameter size the pipe's output and input buffers, in bytes; the system will actually round the suggested sizes to allocation boundaries and limit them to some range.

The sixth parameter assigns the pipe a default time-out value, in milliseconds. The final parameter points to a SECURITY_ATTRIBUTES structure; it can be NULL if you want the pipe to have a default security descriptor.

The server calls CreateNamedPipe, the first time specifying the pipe's maximum number of simultaneous instances. To create additional instances, the server calls CreateNamedPipe again.

Once a pipe instance is created, a client process can connect to it by calling either CreateFile or CallNamedPipe. If a pipe instance is available, either returns a handle to the client end of the pipe instance. If no instances of the pipe are available, a client process can use WaitNamedPipe to wait for one to become available, then try CreateFile again.

CallNamedPipe is a client function that combines connecting to a pipe instance (and waiting for one to be available, if necessary), writing a message, reading a message, and closing the pipe handle. CallNamedPipe can be used only with a message-type pipe.

The server process uses ConnectNamedPipe to determine when a client process is connected to a pipe handle. If the pipe handle is in blocking mode, ConnectNamedPipe does not return until a client is connected.

Both clients and servers can use ReadFile and WriteFile with pipes. Alternatively, ReadFileEx and WriteFileEx functions can be used if the pipe handle was opened for overlapped operations.

PeekNamedPipe performs a non-destructive read on a pipe, and also reports information about the pipe instance. TransactNamedPipe, which works only with message-type pipes in message-read mode, writes a request message and reads a reply message in a single operation.

DisconnectNamedPipe is a server function to close the connection to the client process; it makes the client's handle invalid (if it has not already been closed) and discards any unread data in the pipe. The server can avoid closing the connection before the client has read all the data by calling FlushFileBuffers prior to calling DisconnectNamedPipe. Once the client is disconnected, the server can either call CloseHandle to destroy the pipe instance or call ConnectNamedPipe to let a new client connect to this instance.

GetNamedPipeInfo returns the type of the pipe, the size of the input and output buffers, and the maximum number of pipe instances that can be created. GetNamedPipeHandleState reports on the read and wait modes of a pipe handle, the current number of pipe instances, and so on. SetNamedPipeHandleState function sets the read mode and wait modes of a pipe handle, maximum number of bytes to collect (for a client), and/or the maximum time to wait before transmitting a message.

In summary, named pipes are reliable network pseudo-files of the form \\servername\pipe\pipename. They can be unidirectional or bidirectional, buffered or unbuffered, overlapped or synchronous, and contain byte or message streams. For compatibility with LAN Manager, pipes can be non-blocking, but normally you should use blocking pipes and enable overlapping if you want asynchronous I/O. Servers can create multiple instances of a pipe and vary some of the pipe's parameters on an instance-by-instance basis; they can spawn a thread per synchronous pipe instance, or use a single thread to service multiple asynchronous pipe instances. Clients connect to a single instance of a pipe at a time.

Named pipes are reliable and have good performance for communications across a network. Because a single named pipe server can optionally connect to multiple clients, named pipes can be the basis of any client/server application requiring 1-to-1 or 1-to-N connections in which it is reasonable for each client to establish its own connection. Named pipes would be a reasonable choice of transport for a database server, a transaction-processing system, a multi-user chat application, or a multi-player game. Named pipes would not be a reasonable way to implement a message broadcast facility; that would be better implemented with mailslots, which don't require each receiver to explicitly connect to the sender.

Microsoft supplies code for a multithreaded server service (and associated client) in the MSTOOLS\SAMPLES\SERVICE directory of the SDK.

You might also want to examine the SDK example programs NPSERVER and NPCLIENT, which together implement a primitive multi-user chat system. In the Windows NT SDK, you'll find them under the \MSTOOLS\SAMPLES\NAMEPIPE directory; in Visual C++ for NT, you'll find them under \MSVCNT\SAMPLES.

Remote Access

The Remote Access Services (RAS) functions offer the opportunity to develop applications that log into physically distant networks over modems and phone lines or over better connections like X.25, ISDN, and T1 links. The RAS functions are listed in Table A1.11. RAS is an attractive alternative to developing your own remote access protocols or setting up bulletin board systems for remote reporting.

The RAS API exposes the high-level functions used by the Windows NT RAS applets: functions to dial to and hang up from remote networks, functions to list the active connections and the entries in a RAS phone book, and a function to report the status of a connection. This set of functions is simple, so we won't show you a code sample; you won't have any trouble figuring out how to use the functions yourself. Once you have a connection established, you can use the WNet services to connect to remote hard disks, and then use ordinary file services to transfer information to the remote server.

Sockets

Aside from being the standard network programming mechanism in Berkeley UNIX, sockets are quite flexible and fairly simple to use. The Windows and Windows NT implementation of sockets includes some extensions to make sockets more efficient, but you really have to use only the initialization and termination routines (WSAStartup and WSACleanup) from the Windows extensions.

The basic Berkeley-style socket routines included in Windows Sockets are listed in Table A1.12. The so-called "database" or "getXbyY" functions are listed in Table A1.13, and the Windows extensions are listed in Table A1.14.

Table A1.11. Remote Access Functions

Function	Action
RasDial	Establishes a RAS connection
RasDialFunc	Callback function called by RasDial on state changes
RasEnumConnections	Lists active RAS connections
RasEnumEntries	Lists entries in a RAS phone book
RasGetConnectStatus	Reports current status of a RAS connection
RasGetErrorString	Converts RAS error code to error string
RasHangUp	Terminates a RAS connection

Table A1.12 Berkeley-Style Socket Routines

Function	Action
accept( )	An incoming connection is acknowledged and associated with an immediately created socket. The original socket is returned to the listening state.
bind( )	Assign a local name to an unnamed socket.
closesocket( )	Remove a socket descriptor from the per-process object reference table. Blocks only if SO_LINGER is set.
connect( )	Initiate a connection on the specified socket.
getpeername( )	Retrieve the name of the peer connected to the specified socket descriptor.
getsockname( )	Retrieve the current name for the specified socket.
getsockopt( )	Retrieve options associated with the specified socket descriptor.
htonl( )	Convert a 32-bit quantity from host byte order to network byte order.
htons( )	Convert a 16-bit quantity from host byte order to network byte order.
inet_addr( )	Convert a character string representing a number in the Internet standard "." notation to an Internet address value.
inet_ntoa( )	Convert an Internet address value to an ASCII string in "." notation (i.e., "a.b.c.d").
ioctlsocket( )	Provide control for descriptors.
listen( )	Listen for incoming connections on a specified socket.
ntohl( )	Convert a 32-bit quantity from network byte order to host byte order.
ntohs( )	Convert a 16-bit quantity from network byte order to host byte order.
recv( )*	Receive data from a connected socket.
recvfrom( )*	Receive data from either a connected or unconnected socket.
select( )*	Perform synchronous I/O multiplexing.
send( )*	Send data to a connected socket.
sendto( )*	Send data to either a connected or unconnected socket.
setsockopt( )	Store options associated with the specified socket descriptor.
shutdown( )	Shut down part of a full-duplex connection.
socket( )	Create an endpoint for communication and return a socket descriptor.

* The routine can block if it is acting on a blocking socket.

Table A1.13 Socket "Database" Functions

Function	Action
gethostbyaddr( )*	Retrieve the name(s) and address corresponding to a network address.
gethostname( )	Retrieve the name of the local host.
gethostbyname( )*	Retrieve the name(s) and address corresponding to a host name.
getprotobyname( )*	Retrieve the protocol name and number corresponding to a protocol name.
getprotobynumber( )*	Retrieve the protocol name and number corresponding to a protocol number.
getservbyname( )*	Retrieve the service name and port corresponding to a service name.
getservbyport( )*	Retrieve the service name and port corresponding to a port.

* The routine can block under some circumstances.

Table A1.14 Windows Asynchronous Socket Functions

Function	Action
WSAAsyncGetHostByAddr( ) *WSAAsyncGetHostByName( )* *WSAAsyncGetProtoByName( )* *WSAAsyncGetProtoByNumber( )* *WSAAsyncGetServByName( )* *WSAAsyncGetServByPort( )*	A set of functions that provide asynchronous versions of the standard Berkeley getXbyY() functions. For example, the WSAAsyncGetHostByName() function provides an asynchronous message based implementation of the standard Berkeley gethostbyname() function.
WSAAsyncSelect( )	Perform asynchronous version of select().
WSACancelAsyncRequest( )	Cancel an outstanding instance of a WSAAsyncGetXByY() function.
WSACancelBlockingCall( )	Cancel an outstanding "blocking" API call.
WSACleanup( )	Sign off from the underlying Windows Sockets DLL.
WSAGetLastError( )	Obtain details of last Windows Sockets API error.
WSAIsBlocking( )	Determine if the underlying Windows Sockets DLL is already blocking an existing call for this thread.

Table A1.14 (Continued)

Function	Action
WSASetBlockingHook( )	"Hook" the blocking method used by the underlying Windows Sockets implementation.
WSASetLastError( )	Set the error to be returned by a subsequent.
WSAStartup( )	Initialize the underlying Windows Sockets DLL.
WSAUnhookBlockingHook( )	Restore the original blocking function.

You initialize Windows Sockets by calling WSAStartup. You'll find the appropriate logic in the WM_CREATE section of MainWndProc in the WSOCK.C sample application Microsoft supplies with the Windows NT System Development Kit (SDK). A client can connect to a server by calling socket with the required socket type and the desired protocol, as shown in the WM_COMMAND / IDM_CONNECT case of MainWndProc; by identifying the server, which is done in FillAddr in the example; and by calling connect, shown in the IDM_CONNECT case.

Note that connecting a socket is expensive. If performance matters, do it once per connection and maintain the open connection as long as necessary.

A server waits for a connection with socket, bind, and listen, as shown in the IDM_LISTEN case. When a client connects, the server calls accept. The WSAAsyncSelect function causes window messages to be sent when socket events, like incoming data, need to be handled. Alternatively—most appropriately in a threaded application—the server can use select to determine when a socket needs to be read, or simply use recv or recvfrom to read the next data packet. This is demonstrated in AcceptThreadProc. To send data, use send or sendto, as shown in case IDM_SENDTCP.

In fact, you can and should write threaded socket applications without using select, which is inherently inefficient. By using a plain recv in a thread per client model, or by using recv with I/O completion ports in a thread per N client model, you can achieve much better performance than you can with select or WSAAsyncSelect.

The functions recv and send work only with connected stream sockets, the rough equivalent of NetBIOS sessions or named pipes. The functions recvfrom and sendto can also work with datagrams, the unreliable protocol that also allows broadcasting. You can use datagram sockets in the same sort of applications you would use NetBIOS datagrams or mailslots.

If you are using connected sockets in Windows NT 3.51 or later, you can optimize file transfers by using the new TransmitFile function, which reads the file data directly from the system's cache manager and avoids the buffer-copying overhead incurred by calling ReadFile and Send.

Sockets provide no inherent security mechanism, but Windows NT sockets support SSPI, the Security Support Provider Interface, which returns security "blobs" for the client and server to exchange. An SSPI server is provided in Windows NT 3.5 and above, and SSPI clients are included in Windows NT and Windows 95, and available for Windows 3.1.

Many socket programs falter on the issue of protocol dependence. The "RNR" APIs in NT (beginning with version 3.5) and Windows 95 allow for service registration and name resolution and are particularly useful when you are establishing sockets. EnumProtocols obtains information about network protocols active on a local server; GetAddressByName returns the local address information needed to bind the protocol to a socket and is more powerful than the socket function gethostbyname.

One final note: sockets can be used locally as well as across a network. In fact, they run very fast on a local machine and offer a good alternative to pipes as an interprocess communication mechanism.

For further information on socket programming read through WSOCK.C, browse the WinSock help, and have a look at PDC\SLIDES\TREAD251.PPT for tips on making your socket-based application perform as well as it can.

Remote Procedure Calls

Remote Procedure Calls (RPCs) are simultaneously the simplest and most complicated network programming mechanism supported by Windows NT. They are the simplest in concept: a program on one machine asks another program, possibly running on another machine, to perform some function on its behalf, in a way that looks a lot like an ordinary function call. But these calls are the most complicated in practice; defining the interface to a remote procedure requires a whole separate specification language (IDL), and implementing the call requires several layers of services.

The *RPC Programmer's Guide and Reference* is completely separate from the five-volume *Win32 Programmer's Reference*. The RPC manual and the MIDL compiler come with the Windows NT SDK; they do not come with Visual C++ for Windows NT. Table A1.15 lists the RPC API functions, but the API functions don't give you the whole picture.

In addition to the RPC API functions, you need to understand the Interface Definition Language (IDL), bindings, attributes, and transports. You can get all this from the Microsoft RPC documentation, but you'll find it hard going unless you're already familiar with another implementation of RPCs, such as the Open System Foundation's Distributed Computing Environment (OSF DCE) standard for UNIX. Following is a walk-through of "Hello, World," done with RPCs at the most basic level (as basic as Chapter 2 of the RPC manual, but more concise), so that you'll be ready to attack the Microsoft RPC materials on your own.

The example uses a HelloProc function to write the string, then it makes HelloProc a remote procedure.

The first step in setting up a remote procedure is to define the interface in IDL. An IDL file also needs a unique identification string, which you generate by running UUIDGEN, a tool that comes with the NT SDK. A minimal IDL file for HELLO might look like this:

```
[ uuid (6B29FC40-CA47-1067-B31D-00DD010662DA), version(1.0) ]
interface hello
{
void HelloProc([in, string] unsigned char * pszString);
}
```

Table A1.15 RPC API Functions (1.0)

RpcAbnormalTermination	RpcMgmtEnableIdleCleanup	RpcNsGroupDelete	RpcRevertToSelf
RpcBindingCopy	RpcMgmtInqStats	RpcNsGroupMbrAdd	RpcServerInqBindings
RpcBindingFree	RpcMgmtIsServerListening	RpcNsGroupMbrInqBegin	RpcServerInqIf
RpcBindingFromStringBinding	RpcMgmtSetComTimeout	RpcNsGroupMbrInqDone	RpcServerListen
RpcBindingInqAuthClient	RpcMgmtSetServerStackSize	RpcNsGroupMbrInqNext	RpcServerRegisterAuthInfo
RpcBindingInqAuthInfo	RpcMgmtStatsVectorFree	RpcNsGroupMbrRemove	RpcServerRegisterIf
RpcBindingInqObject	RpcMgmtStopServerListening	RpcNsMgmtBindingUnexport	RpcServerUnregisterIf
RpcBindingReset	RpcMgmtWaitServerListen	RpcNsMgmtEntryCreate	RpcServerUseAllProtseqs
RpcBindingSetAuthInfo	RpcNetworkInqProtseqs	RpcNsMgmtEntryDelete	RpcServerUseAllProtseqsIf
RpcBindingSetObject	RpcNetworkIsProtseqValid	RpcNsMgmtEntryInqIfIds	RpcServerUseProtseq
RpcBindingToStringBinding	RpcNsBindingExport	RpcNsMgmtHandleSetExpAge	RpcServerUseProtseqEp
RpcBindingVectorFree	RpcNsBindingImportBegin	RpcNsMgmtInqExpAge	RpcServerUseProtseqIf
RpcEndExcept	RpcNsBindingImportDone	RpcNsMgmtSetExpAge	RpcStringBindingCompose
RpcEndFinally	RpcNsBindingImportNext	RpcNsProfileDelete	RpcStringBindingParse
RpcEpRegister	RpcNsBindingInqEntryName	RpcNsProfileEltAdd	RpcStringFree
RpcEpRegisterNoReplace	RpcNsBindingLookupBegin	RpcNsProfileEltInqBegin	RpcTryExcept
RpcEpResolveBinding	RpcNsBindingLookupDone	RpcNsProfileEltInqDone	RpcTryFinally
RpcEpUnregister	RpcNsBindingLookupNext	RpcNsProfileEltInqNext	RpcWinSetYieldInfo
RpcExcept	RpcNsBindingSelect	RpcNsProfileEltRemove	UuidCreate
RpcExceptionCode	RpcNsBindingUnexport	RpcObjectInqType	UuidFromString
RpcFinally	RpcNsEntryExpandName	RpcObjectSetInqFn	UuidToString
RpcIfIdVectorFree	RpcNsEntryObjectInqBegin	RpcObjectSetType	YieldFunctionName
RpcIfInqId	RpcNsEntryObjectInqDone	RpcProtseqVectorFree	
RpcImpersonateClient	RpcNsEntryObjectInqNext	RpcRaiseException	

The top line of the file, the IDL header, contains the unique ID and the version number in square brackets. The last three lines of the file, the curly brackets and the declaration, constitute the IDL body. The non-C data in square brackets in the declaration gives additional information about the interface. In this case, pszString is an input string variable.

In addition to an IDL file, you need an ACF (Application Configuration File). A minimal ACF file for HELLO might look like the following:

```
[implicit_handle(handle_t hello_IfHandle)]
interface hello
{
}
```

The IDL file contains the interface definition, but the ACF contains RPC data and attributes that don't relate to the transmitted data. In this case, a binding handle is defined, which the RPC client uses to connect to the server. The interface name has to match the interface name given in the ACF file; the interface body is empty.

Compiling the IDL and ACF files with MIDL generates client and server C stub files and an include file. The stub files generated are fairly complicated; they're C programs to handle the client/server interaction over the network with RPC function calls. For instance, the client and server stubs for *HelloProc* look like this:

Hello_C.C (HelloProc client stub generated by MIDL)

```
#include <string.h>
#include "hello.h"
handle_t hello_IfHandle;
extern RPC_DISPATCH_TABLE hello_DispatchTable;
static RPC_CLIENT_INTERFACE ___RpcClientInterface =   {
   sizeof(RPC_CLIENT_INTERFACE),
   {{0x906B0CE0,0xC70B,0x1067,{0xB3,0x17,0x00,0xDD,0x01,0x06,0x62,
   0xDA}},   {1,0}},
   {{0x8A885D04L,0x1CEB,0x11C9,{0x9F,0xE8,0x08,0x00,0x2B,0x10,0x48,
   0x60}},   {2,0}}, 0,0,0,0 };
RPC_IF_HANDLE hello_ClientIfHandle =
       (RPC_IF_HANDLE) &___RpcClientInterface;
void HelloProc(unsigned char *pszString)
   {
   unsigned char * _packet;
   unsigned int    _length;
   RPC_STATUS _status;
   RPC_MESSAGE _message;
   PRPC_MESSAGE _prpcmsg = & _message;

   ((void)( _packet ));
   ((void)( _length ));
   _message.Handle = hello_IfHandle;
   _message.RpcInterfaceInformation =
               (void __RPC_FAR *) &___RpcClientInterface;
   _prpcmsg->BufferLength = 0;
```

```
   if (pszString == (void *)0)
       RpcRaiseException(RPC_X_NULL_REF_POINTER);
   tree_size_ndr(&(pszString), _prpcmsg, "s1", 1);
   _message.ProcNum = 0;
   _status = I_RpcGetBuffer(&_message);
   if (_status) RpcRaiseException(_status);
   _packet = _message.Buffer;
   _length = _message.BufferLength;
   _message.BufferLength = 0;
   tree_into_ndr(&(pszString), _prpcmsg, "s1", 1);
   _message.Buffer = _packet;
   _message.BufferLength = _length;
   _status = I_RpcSendReceive(&_message);
   if (_status) RpcRaiseException(_status);
   _status = I_RpcFreeBuffer(&_message);
   if (_status) RpcRaiseException(_status);
   }
```

Hello_S.C (HelloProc server stub generated by MIDL)

```
#include <string.h>
#include "hello.h"
extern RPC_DISPATCH_TABLE hello_DispatchTable;
static RPC_SERVER_INTERFACE ___RpcServerInterface = {
  sizeof(RPC_SERVER_INTERFACE),
  {{0x906B0CE0,0xC70B,0x1067,{0xB3,0x17,0x00,0xDD,0x01,0x06,
  0x62,0xDA}}, {1,0}},
  {{0x8A885D04L,0x1CEB,0x11C9,{0x9F,0xE8,0x08,0x00,0x2B,0x10,
  0x48,0x60}}, {2,0}}, &hello_DispatchTable,0,0,0 };
RPC_IF_HANDLE hello_ServerIfHandle =
  (RPC_IF_HANDLE) &___RpcServerInterface;
void __RPC_STUB hello_HelloProc(PRPC_MESSAGE _prpcmsg)
  {
  unsigned char *pszString = (void *)0;
  unsigned long _alloc_total;
  unsigned long _valid_lower;
  unsigned long _valid_total;
  unsigned char * _packet;
  unsigned char * _tempbuf;
  unsigned char * _savebuf;
  RPC_STATUS _status;
  _packet = _prpcmsg->Buffer;
  ((void)( _alloc_total ));
  ((void)( _valid_total ));
  ((void)( _valid_lower ));
  ((void)( _packet ));
  ((void)( _tempbuf ));
  ((void)( _savebuf ));
  RpcTryExcept
    {
    _tempbuf = _prpcmsg->Buffer;
    // recv total number of elements
```

```
      long_from_ndr(_prpcmsg, &_alloc_total);
    if (pszString == (void *)0)
      {
      pszString = MIDL_user_allocate ((size_t)
    (_alloc_total * sizeof(char)));
      }
    data_from_ndr(_prpcmsg, (void __RPC_FAR *) (pszString),
    "s1", 1);
    }
  RpcExcept(1)
    {
        RpcRaiseException(RpcExceptionCode());
    }
  RpcEndExcept
  if (((unsigned int)(((unsigned char *)_prpcmsg->Buffer)
  - _packet)) > _prpcmsg->BufferLength)
RpcRaiseException(RPC_X_BAD_STUB_DATA);
  RpcTryFinally
    {
    if (_prpcmsg->ManagerEpv)
      {
    ((hello_SERVER_EPV *)(_prpcmsg->ManagerEpv))
      ->HelloProc(pszString);
      }
    else
      {
    HelloProc(pszString);
      }
    _prpcmsg->BufferLength = 0;
    _prpcmsg->Buffer = _packet;
    _status = I_RpcGetBuffer(_prpcmsg);
    if (_status) RpcRaiseException(_status);
    }
  RpcFinally
    {
    MIDL_user_free ((void __RPC_FAR *)pszString);
    }
  RpcEndFinally
  }
```

You are not, however, saved from writing all the RPC code. In this application, the client is responsible for connecting to the server. You notice that the default protocol sequence used is for a named pipe, \pipe\hello:

from HELLOC.C (hand-written client code)

```
RPC_STATUS status;
unsigned char * pszUuid            = NULL;
unsigned char * pszProtocolSequence = "ncacn_np";
unsigned char * pszNetworkAddress  = NULL;
unsigned char * pszEndpoint        = "\\pipe\\hello";
unsigned char * pszOptions         = NULL;
```

```
unsigned char * pszStringBinding    = NULL;
unsigned char * pszString           = "hello, world";
unsigned long ulCode;
int i;
//...
  status = RpcStringBindingCompose(pszUuid,
      pszProtocolSequence,
      pszNetworkAddress,
      pszEndpoint,
      pszOptions,
      &pszStringBinding);
  printf("RpcStringBindingCompose returned 0x%x\n", status);
  printf("pszStringBinding = %s\n", pszStringBinding);
  if (status) {
      exit(status);
    }
  status = RpcBindingFromStringBinding(pszStringBinding,
&hello_IfHandle);
  printf("RpcBindingFromStringBinding returned 0x%x\n", status);
  if (status) {
      exit(status);
    }
  printf("Calling the remote procedure 'HelloProc'\n");
  printf("Print the string '%s' on the server\n", pszString);

  RpcTryExcept {
      HelloProc(pszString);   // make call with user message
    }
  RpcExcept(1) {
      ulCode = RpcExceptionCode();
      printf("Runtime reported exception 0x%lx = %ld\n", ulCode,
      ulCode);
    }
  RpcEndExcept

  status = RpcStringFree(&pszStringBinding);
  printf("RpcStringFree returned 0x%x\n", status);
  if (status) {
      exit(status);
    }

  status = RpcBindingFree(&hello_IfHandle);
  printf("RpcBindingFree returned 0x%x\n", status);
  if (status) {
      exit(status);
    }
```

Boiled down to its essentials, the above code amounts to composing the binding string, establishing the binding, calling the remote procedure through its stub, freeing the binding string, and freeing the binding.

In addition to establishing its own binding prior to calling the remote procedure, the client has to provide callback routines so that the RPC libraries can allocate and free memory. In this case, they are trivial:

```
void __RPC_FAR * __RPC_API midl_user_allocate(size_t len)
{
  return(malloc(len));
}

void __RPC_API midl_user_free(void __RPC_FAR * ptr)
{
  free(ptr);
}
```

On the server side, you need to write code to set the protocol sequence, register the interface, and listen for a client. The protocol used must match on client and server:

```
RPC_STATUS status;
unsigned char * pszProtocolSequence = "ncacn_np";
unsigned char * pszSecurity         = NULL;
unsigned char * pszEndpoint         = "\\pipe\\hello";
unsigned int    cMinCalls           = 1;
unsigned int    cMaxCalls           = 20;
unsigned int    fDontWait           = FALSE;
int i;
//...

 status = RpcServerUseProtseqEp(pszProtocolSequence,
      cMaxCalls,
       pszEndpoint,
       pszSecurity);  // Security descriptor
 printf("RpcServerUseProtseqEp returned 0x%x\n", status);
 if (status) {
    exit(status);
   }

 status = RpcServerRegisterIf(hello_ServerIfHandle, //interface
     NULL,   // MgrTypeUuid
     NULL);  // MgrEpv
 printf("RpcServerRegisterIf returned 0x%x\n", status);
 if (status) {
    exit(status);
   }

 printf("Calling RpcServerListen\n");
 status = RpcServerListen(cMinCalls,
      cMaxCalls,
      fDontWait);
 printf("RpcServerListen returned: 0x%x\n", status);
 if (status) {
    exit(status);
   }
```

```
if (fDontWait) {
    printf("Calling RpcMgmtWaitServerListen\n");
    status = RpcMgmtWaitServerListen(); // wait operation
    printf("RpcMgmtWaitServerListen returned: 0x%x\n", status);
    if (status) {
        exit(status);
    }
}
```

You'll need to provide midl_user_allocate and midl_user_free callbacks on the server side; they're the same as on the client side. And finally, you'll need a way to tell the server to shut down, which we've omitted here for brevity. (You'll find it in the Microsoft MSTOOLS\SAMPLES\RPC\HELLO sample.)

If we build the client and server and run the server we'll see:

```
RpcServerUseProtseqEp returned 0x0
RpcServerRegisterIf returned 0x0
Calling RpcServerListen
```

Then the server will stop. If we run the client on another machine or in another CMD session on the same machine, the server will continue and display:

```
hello, world

Calling RpcMgmtStopServerListening
RpcMgmtStopServerListening returned: 0x0
Calling RpcServerUnregisterIf
RpcServerUnregisterIf returned 0x0
RpcServerListen returned: 0x0
```

What the client will display in its CMD session is:

```
RpcStringBindingCompose returned 0x0
pszStringBinding = ncacn_np:[\\pipe\\hello]
RpcBindingFromStringBinding returned 0x0
Calling the remote procedure 'HelloProc'
Print the string 'hello, world' on the server
Calling the remote procedure 'Shutdown'
RpcStringFree returned 0x0
RpcBindingFree returned 0x0
```

Obviously, that was an awful lot of work to make "Hello, World" display. On the other hand, a great deal of the work was done with a few lines of IDL and ACF code, and the resulting client/server application works not only on a single Windows NT machine, but between two NT machines linked by a network, and between a DOS or Windows client and a Windows NT server. In addition, it works on a variety of network transports: in addition to named pipes, the NT implementation of RPC supports NetBIOS and TCP/IP transports. The Windows implementation supports all three of these plus DECnet, and the DOS implementation supports all the aforementioned plus SPX. There is no Win32s implementation of RPCs, however, at least in version 1.1 of Win32s.

We don't have space to cover many of the refinements you'll need to know about to write good distributed systems with RPCs, but there are a few tips you might want to consider to get decent run-time performance.

- Don't block threads in your RPC server.

- Keep the number of round trips to a minimum: combine functions to the highest level that makes sense.

- Shut down your idle connections.

- Don't adjust your thread priorities.

- Disable thread library calls in your DLLs.

- Avoid allocations in your server.

Despite substantial propaganda to the effect that RPCs are the best network mechanism since sliced bread, the high development cost and mediocre run-time performance of RPCs prompts us to recommend caution in selecting this mechanism. If you are already using RPCs, or if RPCs are clearly the most appropriate fit to your architecture, by all means use them. But if you are looking for high-bandwidth communications, other mechanisms may turn out to be better choices.

DDE and NetDDE

DDE is the principal mechanism for interprocess communication in 16-bit Windows. The Microsoft Windows Dynamic Data Exchange (DDE) protocol defines a method for communicating among applications that takes place as applications send messages to each other to initiate conversations, to request and share data, and to terminate conversations.

In the *hot link* form of DDE transfer, the *server* application sends data to the *client* application whenever the data changes; this guarantees that the derived form of the data (perhaps a table in a word processing document) will always reflect the current state of the original data (perhaps a spreadsheet). A variation of this, the *warm link*, notifies the client when the data has changed, but sends the data only if the client wants it, so the client can control the rate at which it receives data. A simpler mechanism, the *request*, is equivalent to a single copy operation from the server and a single paste operation to the client, without the need for the intermediate step of putting the data on the clipboard.

DDE also supports a back-channel transfer, the *poke*. And *execute*, perhaps the most intriguing DDE mechanism of all, allows one application to control another.

DDE supports a *client-server* architecture in which both client and server programs carry on multiple *conversations* with other applications. Each conversation has a *topic* and may include multiple *advisories*, each of which refers to an *item*. The application is responsible for keeping track of ongoing conversations and advisories; conversations are uniquely identified by the window handles of the client and server.

Windows NT and Windows for Workgroups continue to support DDE as an interprocess communication protocol and additionally support NetDDE, a special form of DDE that allows it to work across the network. Because of NT's security requirements and change from 16-bit handles to 32-bit handles, a few new DDE functions have been added in Win32. They are listed in Table A1.16.

The functions PackDDElParam and UnpackDDElParam allow the 32-bit program to pack and unpack parameters in the DDE message's lParam; use them instead of MAKELONG, LOWORD, and HIWORD. ReuseDDElParam and FreeDDElParam allow you to manage the dynamic memory used for packing parameters. The two impersonation functions allow a DDE server to take on the security attributes of its client: this is useful when a server has more privilege than the client and needs to maintain security.

Although you can still program DDE by sending messages, the preferred method for programming DDE is to use the Dynamic Data Exchange Management Library (DDEML). (Both methods are explained in Chapter 5 of *Advanced Windows Programming*. See "For More Information" at the end of this appendix.) For your convenience, the DDEML functions are listed in Table A1.17.

Table A1.16 New DDE Functions in Win32

Function	Action
DdeImpersonateClient	Impersonates a DDE client window
DdeSetQualityOfService	Specifies DDE quality of service
FreeDDElParam	Frees a DDE message lParam
ImpersonateDdeClientWindow	Impersonates a DDE client window
PackDDElParam	Packs data into a DDE message lParam
ReuseDDElParam	Reuses a DDE message lParam
UnpackDDElParam	Unpacks data from a DDE message lParam

Table A1.17 DDEML Functions

Function	Action
DdeAbandonTransaction	Abandons an asynchronous transaction
DdeAccessData	Accesses a DDE data object
DdeAddData	Adds data to a DDE data object
DdeCallback	Processes DDEML transactions
DdeClientTransaction	Begins a DDE data transaction

(Continued)

Table A1.17 (Continued)

Function	Action
DdeCmpStringHandles	Compares two DDE string handles
DdeConnect	Establishes a conversation with a server
DdeConnectList	Establishes multiple DDE conversations
DdeCreateDataHandle	Creates a DDE data handle
DdeCreateStringHandle	Creates a DDE string handle
DdeDisconnect	Terminates a DDE conversation
DdeDisconnectList	Destroys a DDE conversation list
DdeEnableCallback	Enables or disables one or more DDE conversations
DdeFreeDataHandle	Frees a DDE data object
DdeFreeStringHandle	Frees a DDE string handle
DdeGetData	Copies data from a DDE data object to a buffer
DdeGetLastError	Returns an error code set by a DDEML function
DdeInitialize	Registers an application with the DDEML
DdeKeepStringHandle	Increments the usage count for a string handle
DdeNameService	Registers or unregisters a service name
DdePostAdvise	Prompts a server to send advise data to a client
DdeQueryConvInfo	Retrieves information about a DDE conversation
DdeQueryNextServer	Obtains the next handle in a conversation list
DdeQueryString	Copies string-handle text to a buffer
DdeReconnect	Re-establishes a DDE conversation
DdeSetUserHandle	Associates a user-defined handle with a transaction
DdeUnaccessData	Frees a DDE data object
DdeUninitialize	Frees an application's DDEML resources

NetDDE is a minor variation on DDE that can be used by all DDE-aware applications. Normally, you establish a DDE conversation with an application on a topic and specify items within the topic. With NetDDE, the true application and topic are maintained in a DDE share, which is kept in a database. You establish a DDE conversation indirectly, by connecting to the special application NDDE$ on the remote machine, using the share name as the topic. This is the way the ClipBook applet works: it establishes a DDE share for each ClipBook page on each machine.

NetDDE acts as a redirector for DDE and communicates over the network using NetBIOS. In Windows NT, NetBIOS can work on any transport protocol. When NetDDE establishes the conversation, it retrieves the DDE share and connects to the real application and topic locally. Then the applications can exchange data on the actual items, and neither application needs to explicitly be aware of NetDDE.

On the other hand, a network application that is aware of NetDDE can browse for shares, establish its own shares, and delete its own shares. The Network DDE Functions are listed in Table A1.18.

With the exception of the functions that deal with trusted shares and security, the Win32 NetDDE functions are also supported in Windows for Workgroups. They are not, however, included in Win32s. Accessing them in Windows for Workgroups programs requires you to have a copy of NDDEAPI.H and NDDEAPI.LIB or dynamically link to the functions in NDDEAPI.DLL.

Table A1.18 Win32 Network DDE Functions

Function	Action
NDdeGetErrorString	Converts net DDE error code to error string
NDdeGetShareSecurity	Obtains net DDE share's security descriptor
NDdeGetTrustedShare	Retrieves net DDE trusted share options
NDdeIsValidAppTopicList	Validates net DDE app and topic string syntax
NDdeIsValidShareName	Validates net DDE share name syntax
NDdeSetShareSecurity	Sets a net DDE share's security information
NDdeSetTrustedShare	Applies trust options to a net DDE share
NDdeShareAdd	Adds a net DDE share
NDdeShareDel	Deletes a net DDE share
NDdeShareEnum	Lists net DDE shares
NDdeShareGetInfo	Obtains information about a net DDE sharer
NDdeShareSetInfo	Modifies an existing net DDE share's info
NDdeTrustedShareEnum	Lists trusted shares in calling process' context

Table A1.19 Win32 File Mapping Functions

Function	Action
CreateFileMapping	Returns handle to a new file-mapping object
FlushViewOfFile	Flushes a byte range within a mapped view
MapViewOfFile	Maps a view into an address space
MapViewOfFileEx	Maps a view into an address space
OpenFileMapping	Opens a named-file mapping object
UnmapViewOfFile	Unmaps a file view

Should you build networked applications with NetDDE? If you want them to work on Windows for Workgroups and Windows NT machines, or they already support DDE, certainly. If you need to access other environments, no. And if you have a high-volume communications application and care about transfer rate, consider another mechanism.

If you're interested only in networked communications, you can skip the rest of this appendix. On the other hand, there's more to network programming than the core communications functions, so you might want to read on.

File Mapping (Memory-Mapped Files)

File mapping does not work over a network quite the way you might hope, but it is often used for interprocess communications, partly because it allows high-rate local communications and partly because it is very similar to a UNIX mechanism often used to implement databases. Sixteen-bit Windows allows you to pass pieces of global shared memory among processes: file mapping is as close as Windows NT comes. The Win32 file mapping functions are listed in Table A1.19.

File mapping actually has two uses. The first is to let you treat a file like memory: mapping is the copying of a file's contents to a process's virtual address space. The copy of the file's contents is called the file view, and the internal structure the operating system uses to maintain the copy is called the file-mapping object.

The second use is data sharing. Another process can create an identical file view in its own virtual address space by using the first process's file-mapping object to create the view. Any process that has the name or a handle of a file-mapping object can create a file view. Note that you can map named files or simply ask for shared memory backed by the system paging file. The signal that you want shared memory backed by the page file is a file handle of *(HANDLE)FFFFFFFF*.

The following example demonstrates data sharing using file mapping. As you can see, the process creating the shared memory uses CreateFileMapping and MapViewOfFile, while the process sharing the memory uses OpenFileMapping and MapViewOfFile:

```
//-----------------------------
// In creating process
//-----------------------------
hFileMapping = CreateFileMapping(
        hFile,                  //file handle to map
        NULL,                   //security
        PAGE_READWRITE,         //protection
        dwSizeHigh,             //high 32 bits of size
        dwSizeLow,              //low 32 bits of size
        "NameOfFileMappingObject");
assert(hFileMapping);
base = MapViewOfFile(
        hFileMapping,
        FILE_MAP_WRITE,         //access mode
        dwOffsetHigh,           //high 32 bits of file offset
        dwOffsetLow,            //low 32 bits of file offset
        dwSizeToMap);           //size to map, 0 means whole file
// base points to mapped view of file
assert(base);
//...

//-----------------------------
// In sharing process
//-----------------------------
hFileMapping = OpenFileMapping(
        FILE_MAP_READ,          //access mode
        FALSE,                  //inherit handle?
        "NameOfFileMappingObject");
assert(hFileMapping);
base = MapViewOfFile(
        hFileMapping,
        FILE_MAP_READ,          //access mode
        dwOffsetHigh,           //high 32 bits of file offset
        dwOffsetLow,            //low 32 bits of file offset
        dwSizeToMap);           //size to map, 0 means whole file
//
// base points to mapped view of file.
// Note that the value of base
// is not necessarily the same in both
// processes sharing the file
// mapping object.
//
assert(base);
```

When the processes are done with the mapped file, they should call UnmapViewOfFile to remove the map from their address space and flush any dirty pages to the disk image of the file. Processes that need to commit portions of the shared file map to disk without unmapping the file can use FlushViewOfFile as needed.

NT and the Internet

As you already know from reading this book, several of the enhancements in Windows NT 4.0 have to do with the Internet: the addition of Internet Information Server (IIS) and Internet Explorer (IE) are only the most obvious. As you look deeper into the system, things get more and more interesting for programmers. For instance, IE 3.0 has a mere 15KB executable file, IEXPLORE.EXE, usually installed in "C:\Program Files\Plus!\Microsoft Internet."

That 15KB EXE is nothing more than a frame window and message pump for a COM (ActiveX) document object, IExplorer Browser, which has the OLE class identifier CLSID_IExplorer and is implemented in shdocvw.dll. IExplorer Browser, in turn, uses another ActiveX control, MSHTML.DLL, to implement HTML viewing and calls the OLE Hyperlinks object, CLSID_OAHyperLink, to implement generalized hyperlinking.

On the server side, IIS supports standard CGI programming and also exposes its own DLL-based interface, ISAPI. ISAPI extensions serve the same purpose as CGI programs but run in threaded DLLs; ISAPI filters intercept key IIS events and allow for extensive customization of the Web server.

ActiveX™

Most of the Internet extensions to Windows NT and Windows 95 have been gathered under the umbrella of ActiveX, which is basically a new name for OLE and COM. ActiveX controls are the technology previously known as OLE Controls and known before that as OCXs; ActiveX controls are also COM objects. ActiveX documents are the same as OLE document objects, and ActiveX document containers are the same as OLE document containers.

As we've just seen, IE is built with ActiveX documents and controls; there is little more than an illusion of an IE application. The ActiveX component-based approach opens up many opportunities for programmers, because every level of the system is exposed and available for use.

ActiveX controls can also be used to enhance Web pages. They are touted as being easier for users than Netscape Plug-Ins because the browser downloads and installs them automatically; they are also touted as being more efficient than Java applets. ActiveX control security and packaging issues are still being resolved as of this writing; so are Java applet security issues and Java just-in-time compiler performance issues.

Advanced developers might want to consider creating their own ActiveX controls. It's relatively easy to do so using Visual C++'s OLE Control Wizard or using Visual Basic 5.0, but the resulting controls might be fatter than you'd like for downloading from the Internet. It's much harder to develop lean and mean ActiveX controls, because you'll have to really understand OLE and COM, but if that criterion is met, it's a reasonable thing to do using Microsoft's ActiveX Control Framework or ActiveX Template Library.

ActiveX also includes scripting support, and IE fully supports scripting. OLE Automation is still supported, and both VBScript and JavaScript have been implemented in IE 3.0. VBScript is a free subset of Visual Basic for Applications with "unsafe" constructs removed; JavaScript is a Java-like scripting language.

Internet Client Programming

With so many options available for Internet client programming, the problem becomes one of selecting the appropriate level for the task at hand. Many people's first reaction to the beta versions of the ActiveX SDK has been to write it off as a confusing mess, but that impression needn't last forever.

You can use Internet Explorer's OLE automation interfaces to control it from a program written in a language with OLE automation support such as Visual Basic or C++. This is quite simple to implement, but your program's window will be separate from the browser window. Having a separate window for your control program may be appropriate if it needs its own user interface, but it may be undesirable in some cases.

Because IExplorer Browser is itself an ActiveX document object, you can add it to any document object container program. Writing such a container program is trivial in many languages, including Visual Basic, and the container can hold many document objects and controls, not just IExplorer Browser, so the user interface possibilities are wide open.

In fact IExplorer Browser is also a container, designed to hold MSHTML, which does the actual HTML display. If you don't need the extra capabilities of the IExplorer Browser object, you can simply contain MSHTML in your own program.

MSHTML doesn't solve every possible Internet client problem, however. The Internet Control Pack (ICP), available at http://www.microsoft.com/icp/, offers a collection of ActiveX controls to implement Internet protocols. At the lowest level, it offers controls for WinSock TCP connections and UDP streams. For retrieving remote files, the ICP includes an FTP (File Transport Protocol) client control. It contains a POP (Post Office Protocol) control to handle incoming mail and an SMTP (Simple Mail Transport Protocol) to send outgoing mail. For reading Usenet news, the ICP includes a NNTP (Network News Transport Protocol) client control.

The ICP offers separate HTML and HTTP controls. The HTTP control requests and retrieves information from Web servers, and the ICP HTML control displays the information. By contrast, MSHTML combines both functions. Currently, MSHTML can display more complex HTML (Version 3.0 with Microsoft IE extensions) than can the ICP HTML control (Version 2.0).

Uniform Resource Locators (URLs) express names and addresses of objects on the Internet. Monikers define names and addresses of objects in OLE/COM. URL Monikers tie the two together so that a program can retrieve the contents of a URL by binding it to a moniker.

The setup may sound a little odd, but it turns out to be fairly convenient. For one thing, URL monikers are implemented asynchronously, so your code can continue in parallel with a download from the Internet. For another, the amount of code you have to write to implement the functionality is minimal. It's manageable enough that we can show you the guts of a complete example, the PROGRESS sample from the ActiveX SDK. You should, of course, consult the full sample for all the details, but the essential bit is the implementation of DoDownload::DoDownload in progress.cpp:

```
HRESULT CDownload::DoDownload(HWND hwndStatus, HWND hwndProgress, HWND
hwndText)
{
    IStream* pstm;
    HRESULT hr;

    hr = CreateURLMoniker(NULL, m_url, &m_pmk);
    if (FAILED(hr))
        goto LErrExit;

    m_pbsc = new CBindStatusCallback(hwndStatus,
            hwndProgress, hwndText);
    if (m_pbsc == NULL)
        {
        hr = E_OUTOFMEMORY;
        goto LErrExit;
        }

    hr = CreateBindCtx(0, &m_pbc);
    if (FAILED(hr))
        goto LErrExit;

    hr = RegisterBindStatusCallback(m_pbc,
            m_pbsc,
            BSCO_ALLONIBSC,
            NULL);
    if (FAILED(hr))
        goto LErrExit;

    hr = m_pmk->BindToStorage(m_pbc, 0, IID_IStream,
(void**)&pstm);
    if (FAILED(hr))
        goto LErrExit;

    return hr;

LErrExit:
    if (m_pbc != NULL)
        {
        m_pbc->Release();
        m_pbc = NULL;
        }
    if (m_pbsc != NULL)
        {
        m_pbsc->Release();
        m_pbsc = NULL;
        }
    if (m_pmk != NULL)
        {
```

```
      m_pmk->Release();
      m_pmk = NULL;
      }
  return hr;
}  // CDownload::DoDownload
```

What's going on here? First we create a URL moniker from the URL string member of the DoDownload class, filling the m_pmk member with a pointer to an IMoniker. Then we create an object of class CBindStatusCallback, which is defined elsewhere as a public class derived from the standard OLE class IBindStatusCallback, using the window handles passed to the method for initialization of the CBindStatusCallback instance. Then we create a binding context, and register the bind status callback in the binding context. (By the way, you may want to copy the implementation of CBindStatusCallback from this sample for your own use.)

Finally we call the moniker's BindToStorage method and return. This is where the real work begins and lights start to flash. The CBindStatusCallback instance will get calls to its OnStartBinding, OnProgress, OnDataAvailable, and OnStopBinding methods. The OnDataAvailable method gets to actually read from the data stream, using the bound IStream's Read method; the OnProgress method has a chance to update the user interface to reassure the user that the transfer hasn't died.

Now, URL monikers are *not* completely simple and certainly not easy to understand when you first look at them in detail. Programming with URL monikers and OLE callbacks isn't the most straightforward method, but you may get used to it. If not, you can either work with the higher-level ActiveX controls described above or the lower-level Win32 Internet (WinInet) Functions.

In fact, the URL moniker COM methods themselves call WinInet, at least on Windows NT and Windows 95. On Macintosh and UNIX systems, URL monikers may be implemented some other way but should *work* the same way. That is, the COM interfaces aren't supposed to change from system to system, even if the implementations are different.

The WinInet functions are designed to make getting a file from the Internet as easy as getting a file on a LAN, and largely they succeed. InternetOpen initializes the application's use of the Internet DLL and returns an HINTERNET session handle; to end your use of the DLL, call InternetCloseHandle on the session handle. You can't call the ordinary Win32 CloseHandle function for this purpose, because the handles returned by WinInet functions are incompatible with normal Windows file handles.

To open a URL that starts with http:, ftp:, or gopher:, you can call InternetOpenUrl with an open session handle, the URL string, and any header strings you need to supply, and you'll get back an Internet file handle. You can then call InternetReadFile with the file handle as many times as you need to retrieve the full file, and finally call InternetCloseHandle to close the connection.

That's about as simple as it will get. The bad news is that InternetOpenUrl doesn't always give you as much control as you need; the good news is that you can drop down to slightly more complicated levels that will give you more control.

For one thing, you can define a function to receive status reports, using InternetSetStatusCallback. When you're dealing with the Internet, any stage of any operation can fail, so it's important to let the user know what's going on. A status callback function gets codes like INTERNET_STATUS_RESOLVING_NAME; it can display appropriate messages in a status bar window, advance the state of a progress meter, turn on lights on a simulated control panel, or whatever you like.

You can also delve deeper into the guts of the http, ftp, and gopher protocols. You can, for instance, obtain the contents of a Web page starting with InternetOpen to initialize the DLLs, then InternetConnect to open a session on the desired Web server. If that succeeds, you can perform a HttpOpenRequest to construct a request for the file path part of the URL with the verb "GET" to read a page, or another verb to perform a different operation, such as posting a query. As part of the request you can specify a list of file types you are willing to accept, and flags to control caching, handle reuse, and the format of some returned information. You can optionally add free-format request headers (for POST and SEND operations) before actually transmitting the request packet with HttpSendRequest.

It's useful to find out how much information you're about to get back at this point: you can accomplish this by calling HttpQueryInfo with flag HTTP_QUERY_CONTENT_LENGTH. Then you can allocate an adequate buffer and call InternetReadFile to actually obtain the data, and call InternetCloseHandle on your http file handle.

In a real Web browser, you will then need to format the HTML page for display and send back additional requests for embedded images and other references. If the user clicks a reference, you'd use that as the URL for a new connection request.

You might close the original connection before opening a new connection, or if you wanted to optimize access speed, you could manage a cache of recent connections. When you were done, however, you'd need to close the handle of all the connections and then finally close the session handle.

WinInet supports ftp and gopher protocols at roughly the same level of detail as http. One additional twist is the use of GopherFindFirstFile or FtpFindFirstFile to begin a directory listing and InternetFindNextFile to continue either kind of directory listing. GopherOpenFile or FtpOpenFile opens a file handle, and InternetReadFile or InternetWriteFile can be used to read or write the actual data. FtpGetFile and FtpPutFile do this at a slightly higher level; FtpDeleteFile and FtpRenameFile give you file-level control on the remote directory; FtpGetCurrentDirectory and FtpSetCurrentDirectory let you navigate the server; FtpCreateDirectory and FtpRemoveDirectory let you manipulate the server's directory structure; and FtpCommand lets you issue an arbitrary server command.

Internet Server Programming

The Internet Information Server (IIS), discussed in Chapter 7, can be extended programmatically in several ways: CGI programs, ISAPI extensions, and ISAPI filters. CGI, the Common Gateway Interface, is supported by almost all Web servers; ISAPI, the Internet Server API, is supported as of this writing only by IIS and Purveyor, although other vendors have announced plans to add ISAPI support to their Web servers.

CGI is a standard, portable interface for transferring information between Web pages and the underlying system. CGI programs can be implemented in any language capable of processing command line and environment strings and writing formatted text to standard output. That includes not only compiled languages like C and C++, but also interpreted languages like Perl and even command shell batch files. Because CGI programs written in shell languages and Perl are so common, they are often referred to as scripts. By default, you'll find scripts for IIS installed under the Scripts virtual directory; on most other Web servers, scripts are installed under the cgi-bin virtual directory.

Covering CGI programming in its entirety would be a Herculean task, because of all the different language and support library options. One good place to start is the Web itself: search Yahoo or any other Web indexing engine for "CGI" and you'll find references to numerous online manuals and support libraries, or start with the tutorial found at http://hoohoo.ncsa.uiuc.edu/cgi/.

Another good place to start is your local technical bookstore, where you'll probably find a good selection. For example, the book *Introduction to CGI/Perl* by Brenner and Aoki will help ease you into CGI programming using Perl and Brenner's cgi-lib.pl support library, one of the most common choices of language and support library today.

Writing CGI scripts in C or C++ is refreshingly easy after writing GUI programs; they are basically console applications. CGI programs can be called with three possible actions: a GET method from a form, a PUT method from a form, and an ISINDEX query. With the GET method, the program takes its input from the environment variable QUERY_STRING. With the PUT method, the input comes from the stdin stream. Use the environment variable CONTENT_LENGTH to determine how much data to read. With an ISINDEX query, the input comes from the command line.

Output from the CGI program goes to the stdout stream. It starts with a header, which is typically "Content-type: text/html" followed by a blank line. It then continues with standard HTML tags and body.

Each client request launches a separate instance of a CGI program. As we discussed in the section "Using Threads and Processes," the process-per-client model doesn't scale well to many simultaneous clients. ISAPI extensions offer the chance to use the slightly better thread-per-client model. ISAPI extensions reside in a DLL with two required exports: GetExtensionVersion and HttpExtensionProc. The former call lets the server know the extension DLL's version numbers and description string on initialization, and the latter call is basically the equivalent of the extension's main routine. Information is passed to HttpExtensionProc through its single parameter and extension control block pointer. The extension control block structure basically carries the major information that would be passed in environment variables to a CGI program.

The ISAPI program can request additional information by name through the GetServerVariable call, read information from the body of the Web client's HTTP request with a ReadClient call, send information to the HTTP client with a WriteClient call, and return locations, redirection, and status information to the server with a ServerSupportFunction call.

ISAPI filters have two required entry points, GetFilterVersion and HttpFilterProc, and are called automatically for any of eight events: when the server is reading raw data, when the server has preprocessed the headers of the request, when the server is authenticating the client, when the server is mapping the URL to a physical location, when the server is sending raw data back to the client, when access is denied, when the server is writing to the log file, and when the session with the client is ending. Callbacks can be limited to sessions on secure or nonsecure ports. Because the entry points are different for ISAPI extensions and ISAPI filters, the two may be combined into a single DLL.

Writing ISAPI extensions is fairly easy; writing ISAPI filters is a bit harder. ISAPI extensions are called once per client request with all the data they need available to them at once. ISAPI filters are called many times per client request, need to carry state information from event to event, and can't count on events always coming in the expected sequence or carrying all the information needed. On the other hand, ISAPI filters can be very flexible and efficient once developed, acting like very tightly integrated extensions to IIS.

Distributed COM

As we discussed earlier, COM, the Common Object Model, is a way for software components to interact with each other. A COM client can use whatever interfaces are actually present in a COM server at run time without crashing when faced with older or newer versions of the server, using IUnknown::QueryInterface as a late binding mechanism.

COM servers can be *in-process*, which means that they are DLLs that run in the address space of the calling program, or *out-of-process*, which means that they are EXEs that run in their own address space. COM uses a system of marshaling stubs and proxies to pass information between address spaces for out-of-process servers. Distributed COM (DCOM) extends the marshaling mechanism to work across the network as well as across address spaces, using RPCs. Therefore, it requires very little extra work from the programmer.

You can actually make DCOM work with legacy code simply by enabling DCOM support in the registry. You can add a \CLSID\{...}\RemoteServerName key for the server in question, and/or you can add a \CLSID\{...}\ActivateAtStorage key, and the system will activate the specified remote server instead of a local server. The remote server can be specified as a DNS name or a NetBIOS name; DNS names are preferred for location independence and obviously required for use over the Internet. The ActivateAtStorage key says that the system should run the server wherever the data is.

Windows NT 4.0 includes the DCOMCNFG tool for setting these registry keys. Use the Location tab under the properties for a given COM server to specify whether the server may be run on the computer where the data is located, on the local computer, and/or on a specific remote computer. See Chapter 3 for more information on using DCOMCNFG.

Explicitly invoking DCOM from your client software is not much of an incremental effort over invoking COM. The new structure COSERVERINFO can be passed to CoGetClassObject,

CoCreateInstanceEx, CoGetInstanceFromFile, and CoGetInstanceFromIStorage. If a NULL COSERVERINFO pointer is passed to these functions, they consult the registry; if a valid COSERVERINFO pointer is passed, it is used. The class context parameter to these same functions must include the CLSCTX_REMOTE_SERVER flag to enable remote activation.

The typical edit that will make a COM client aware of DCOM is to change existing CoCreateInstance calls to CoCreateInstanceEx calls and fill in the COSERVERINFO structures. That's not a big barrier. On the other hand, it opens up dramatically the possibilities for building distributed systems, both on LANs and on the Internet.

Conclusion

This appendix looked briefly at Windows NT security, services, event logging, and performance monitoring. We examined a road map to the different NT interprocess communication mechanisms, then went over the details of programming the individual mechanisms. Finally, we examined the Internet programming options introduced in Windows NT 4.0.

In a few cases, we've given enough information for you to actually write programs. In the rest of the cases, we only got you started. You'll find more information in the Win32 SDK help files and the MSDN and ActiveX CDs on Microsoft's Web site at http://www.microsoft .com/win32dev and http://www.microsoft.com/intdev, and in the references listed below.

For More Information

Arick, M. (1993), *The TCP/IP Companion*. Wellesley, MA: QED Publishing Group, ISBN: 0-89435-466-3.

Brenner, Steven, and Edwin Aoiki (1996), *Introduction to CGI/Perl*. New York: M&T Books, ISBN 1-55851-478-3.

Brockschmidt, Kraig (1994), *Inside OLE 2*. Redmond, WA: Microsoft Press, ISBN: 1-55615-618-9.

Chan, Chuck, Margaret Johnson, Keith Moore, and David Treadwell (1994), "Write an NT WinSock Service," *Byte*, December.

Heller, Martin (1995), "Tips and Tricks on Developing Killer Server Applications for Windows NT," *Microsoft Systems Journal*, August.

Heller, Martin (1993), *Advanced Win32 Programming*. New York: John Wiley & Sons, Inc., ISBN: 0-471-59245-5.

Heller, Martin (1992), *Advanced Windows Programming*. New York: John Wiley & Sons, Inc., ISBN: 0-471-54711-5.

Microsoft Windows NT Software Development Kit (1993), *Remote Procedure Call Programmer's Guide and Reference*. Redmond, WA: Microsoft Corp.

Microsoft Windows NT Software Development Kit (1993), *Programmer's Reference*, Volumes 1–5, Redmond, WA: Microsoft Corporation.

Nance, Barry (1990), *Network Programming in C*. Carmel, CA: Que Corporation., ISBN: 0-88022-569-6.

Sinha, Alok, and Raymond Patch (1992), "An Introduction to Network Programming Using the NetBIOS Interface," *Microsoft Systems Journal*, March–April.

Sinha, Alok, and Raymond Patch (1992), "Developing Network-Aware Programs Using Windows 3.1 and NetBIOS," *Microsoft Systems Journal*, July–August.

The OSI Seven-Layer Model, Windows NT's Network Architecture, and Networking Protocols

Operating systems don't normally know much about networks. They understand I/O, but may not care exactly how the data got in or where it's going. Windows NT is different in this regard, because it *does* know about and understand issues pertinent to networking.

When a product such as Windows NT comes to the marketplace, potential buyers want to be assured that it will be compatible with the hardware and software they already have. One way to ensure compatibility is to develop the product in accordance with industry standards. This appendix explains, in basic terms, industry standards such as the OSI Reference Model and some common protocols, and it shows you how Windows NT fits into the basic scheme followed by other computer industry vendors.

The Need for Standards

The purpose of networking software is to move information between devices. This process usually consists of transmitting requests from one device to another, carrying out the request, and then returning the results to the original device. Sometimes these devices are on the same local area network; sometimes they are located on different segments of a wide-area network (one that connects separate network sites, such as buildings or even cities). These devices are usually computers, but they can also be printers or any other type of networked machine.

To handle these requests, the network software has to determine how to reach the destination device. Then it has to put the request into a form that can travel across the network and be understood by the destination device. Once the request has arrived safely, it must be checked for errors, put into a form the device can use, and be properly executed. Then the return information (if there is any) must be put back into proper transmission form and returned to the original sending device.

The networking industry is constantly searching for viable standards that the various members of the industry can use as they design new hardware, new operating systems, new protocols, or other new concepts. Once certain standards have been accepted within the industry, it becomes easier for manufacturers to create products that work well together. In this way, information can eventually be transmitted anywhere in the world, no matter whose equipment is being used to send, carry, or receive it. This ideal scenario has yet to be achieved, but vendors such as Microsoft are working with other vendors, including competitors, to make this kind of transparent communication possible.

The OSI Reference Model

The OSI Reference Model is a communications structure defined by the International Organization for Standardization, or ISO (the real name is French). The ISO is a voluntary, international standards organization whose communications protocols are widely accepted. (A protocol is a set of rules that make it possible for all computers that know these rules to communicate with each other.) Founded in 1946, ISO comprises standards bodies from more than 75 countries. Similar organizations include ANSI (American National Standards Institute), which represents the United States in the ISO; ITU, the International Telecommunications Union (formerly known as CCITT), an international committee that sets communications standards; and IEEE (Institute of Electrical and Electronics Engineers), who have set many standards used in LANs.

In 1978, the ISO published the Open Systems Interconnectiseven-layer model," has become the basis for designing and evaluating methods of communication between devices. The O dissimilar devices.NetBIOS Frames (NBF)The lowet level of the NetBEUI protocol stack is the NBF protocol. NBF provides both the transport- and network-layer functions, and provides the raw connectivity services between devices. When network I/O occurs, the upper layers (either NetBIOS appSI Reference Model has been helpful to the networking industry as manufacturers of networking products strive for compatibility between their products and those of other vendors. It gives independent vendors a common set of criteria to discuss implementation techniques.

As a set of protocols, however, the official implementation of each layer as a standard has been under development for many years, with very few actual implementations commercially available. Top-down standards, burdened by bureaucracy, achieve popularity much more slowly than grass-roots de facto standards, usually created by vendors in leadership positions in their industry niches.

The seven layers of the OSI Reference Model are numbered consecutively from the actual physical hardware connections (layer 1) up to the layer that services the applications, or programs, that run on the network (layer 7). Each layer communicates only with adjacent layers. The model is shown in Table A2.1.

The Seven Layers

The OSI model describes seven levels of communication that occur between network devices, as follows:

- Level 1 (the physical layer) is concerned with the actual transmission of data over the local area network. This layer comprises the physical media used in interconnecting different network components. Examples of such media are fiber optics, twisted-pair cable, and coax cable. The RS-232 interface is a Level 1 standard for microcomputers.

- Level 2 (the data link layer) is concerned with the transmission techniques used to place the data on these different media. This layer is responsible for gaining access to the network and transmitting data packets from one device to another. Examples of transmission techniques include tokens and error-detection codes. This layer retransmits data packets that fail to reach their destination.

- Level 3 (the network layer) is responsible for finding the workstation to which the data is addressed. If there are several possible routes the data could take across the LAN, the network layer must choose the best one. Level 3 is the highest layer that understands the physical configuration of the network.

Table A2.1 Layers of the OSI Reference Model

Layer	Client		Server
7	Application	<--- virtual communication --->	Application
6	Presentation	<--- virtual communication --->	Presentation
5	Session	<--- virtual communication --->	Session
4	Transport	<--- virtual communication --->	Transport
3	Network	<--- virtual communication --->	Network
2	Data Link	<--- virtual communication --->	Data Link
1	Physical	<--- virtual communication --->	Physical

- Level 4 (the transport layer) provides reliable transportation of data. This layer is responsible for converting messages into the required formats for transmission over the network. If the transmission isn't successful, the transport layer may request a retransmission.

- Level 5 (the session layer) establishes a connection so that one application (or user) can communicate with another application on another device. This layer also queues incoming messages and terminates connections. It recovers from an abnormal termination.

- Level 6 (the presentation layer) must make certain that the commands and the data of an application can be understood by other computers on the network. In other words, it converts one format to another. It also provides data encryption and compression mechanisms.

- Level 7 (the application layer) refers to direct interaction with application processes. This layer consists of the messages that applications use to request data and services from one another. This layer provides distributed processing services, including file transfer, database management, and network control.

OSI and Windows NT

Because of the multivendor environment in which many users must work, the standards laid down in the OSI Model have influenced Windows NT development. Windows NT offers what Microsoft calls "built-in networking." This means that Windows NT users can communicate with other personal computers without a separate network operating system. (The term operating system, or OS, refers to the software that controls a personal computer. The term network operating system, or NOS, refers to the software that manages a network or server.) You can share data with other users, send and receive messages, and use a remote printer without any of these machines having to become a server. In other words, Windows NT can function as a peer-to-peer network. In addition to communicating with other computer users in your own workgroup, you can communicate with servers on other types of networks, such as Novell's NetWare or Banyan's VINES.

When your Windows NT workstation communicates with another workstation, both machines use a seven-layer system based on the OSI Model. When you send a transmission over the network, it passes down each layer on your machine, travels across the network, then passes up each layer on the receiving machine until it reaches the layer that can properly handle your request.

There are three distinct layers of activity within Windows NT's network subsystem. At the bottom, a set of device drivers (OSI layers 2 and 3) provides hooks into network adapters (OSI layers 1 and 2). Above that, protocols (OSI layers 4 and 5) bind to the device drivers to provide well-defined means to communicate with other systems. Finally, network redirectors provide user- and application-level (OSI layer 6 and 7) interfaces to other systems using those protocols.

Any of these layers can act in a many-to-many relationship with the neighboring layer. Multiple adapters can service a single protocol, or multiple protocols can run over a single adapter. Likewise, multiple redirectors can run over a single protocol, or a single redirector can run over multiple protocols. However, redirectors and adapters can't speak to each other directly. They must use a common protocol in between them and communicate directly with it. In effect, the protocol layer becomes a traffic cop, saying who can send data where and over what media.

Above each of the layers are "interfaces," which provide virtual portholes for layers to communicate through. The NDIS Interface, for example, maps network adapters to protocols, while the TDI Interface maps redirectors to protocols. If multiple redirectors are in use, a Provider Interface maps incoming network requests to the appropriate redirector.

Windows NT Network Architecture

Just as a computer needs a video adapter to display output, it also needs a network adapter to communicate over a network. The network media may be coaxial cable, modems, and phone lines, or even radio waves broadcast over the air. Regardless of the media, the operating system and the computer must have a way to communicate with the hardware that provides the network signaling.

This communication is handled through device drivers loaded at boot time. These drivers tell Windows NT what type of communications media is in use, the speed of the link, and other important information. Parameters stored in Windows NT's Registry tell Windows NT how to communicate directly with the adapter, so that it knows when the network needs servicing. A NIC (Network Interface Card) may use hardware interrupts (the same as a keyboard) to grab the CPU's attention. It may also use shared memory (like most SCSI cards) for the exchange of data between the system memory and the NICs memory. It may also use port addresses (like serial ports) for data I/O. Information stored in the Registry tells Windows NT how the adapter is configured and how to communicate with it.

To the user, this information is represented and configured in the "Network" object within Control Panel. Network adapters are installed, adjusted, and removed here. (For more information, refer to Chapter 2). Multiple adapters can be installed. As long as the adapters don't conflict with each other or any other peripherals within the computer, they can all be used. However, they are completely useless without protocols to take advantage of them.

Network Device Interface Specification (NDIS)

The NDIS Interface provides a way for protocols to bind to the underlying network adapters. Without this layer, each protocol would have to implicitly know about each adapter and the network media it used. By providing an interface between the NICs and protocols, the latter has only to send data to the interface for processing. It in turn has already registered information about the specific adapters and can make changes to the data as needed.

Another benefit of using the NDIS Interface is that multiple adapters can be bound to a single protocol, or conversely, multiple protocols can use a single adapter. In the earlier days of networking, using multiple protocols meant you *had* to use multiple adapters, because each one would be locked to another. The NDIS Interface provides a virtual network layer that protocols can address. The virtual layer then passes the data to the appropriate adapter.

Transport Protocols

Webster defines a protocol as "the code of ceremonial forms and courtesies... accepted as proper and correct in official dealings." That about defines network protocols as well. A protocol is simply a well-defined method for computer systems to use when communicating with other devices. Two computers must use the same protocol in order to communicate.

Different protocols are suited to different kinds of network environments. For example, Microsoft's NBF transport protocol uses "names" for computers as the primary method of distinction between systems. Although this makes the network easy to use and diagnose, other problems are introduced that limit the protocols' effectiveness on large networks. In contrast, TCP/IP uses a 32-bit binary addressing scheme, which makes it quite effective, but a nightmare for users to interact with (at least, without the help of a directory service that can provide friendly names).

A protocol is generally implemented as a background process, such as a TSR under DOS, or as a daemon under UNIX. With Windows NT, protocols run as threads within a privileged subsystem, as a part of the NT Executive (see Chapter 1).

The Transport Driver Interface

Some network software—like Windows NT's native networking—lets users run multiple protocols. This makes it more effective in complex environments. Just as the NDIS Interface provides a single point of communication between NICs and protocols, the Transport Driver Interface (TDI) provides a link between redirectors and protocols. Without this interface, the redirector software would need to explicitly understand each of the protocols and its capabilities. Whenever a new protocol was introduced, the redirector would have to be rewritten.

For example, Windows NT's native network software can run over NBF, TCP/IP, or IPX transport protocols (plus third-party transports like Digital's XNS). It doesn't have to know anything specifically about all of these protocols, however. It simply needs to communicate with the TDI, which handles the necessary conversion and spoofing needed to make the network software work over the appropriate protocol.

The biggest problem with this design is that there must be a virtual protocol for the redirector to address. In Windows NT's case, that protocol happens to be based on NetBIOS, which isn't very robust. In order for TCP/IP or IPX to act like NetBIOS, lots of trickery has to occur, and you wind up with hybrid protocols like NetBIOS-over-TCP (NBT). You lose a lot of the features that came with the underlying protocols by using a lowest-common-denominator approach such as this.

Redirectors

Although the protocol does the majority of the grunt work in finding and communicating with other systems, the network redirector handles the presentation of resources on the network and also acts as the component that communicates directly with the Windows NT kernel.

Under Windows NT, network redirectors run as file system drivers, the same as FAT, NTFS, and CD-ROM file system drivers. This capability allows network resources to appear exactly the same as any device that is physically attached to the system. When an application makes a call for a file or device, the application doesn't need to know anything about the device, because the underlying file system management subsystem handles all the communications.

For example, Windows NT Explorer doesn't understand network concepts explicitly, but instead relies on the redirector to handle requests for it. Since all file system requests are passed to the Windows NT Executive, when you open a folder, the Executive looks to see if the resource is local or remote. If remote, it passes the request to the redirector, which passes it to the remote system. That system processes the request and returns some sort of data. The redirector then passes the data back to the Executive for presentation to the application that requested it. A redirector can communicate with remote systems using any protocol that both systems understand and have configured.

Provider Interface

Just as you can bind multiple protocols to multiple adapters, you can also bind multiple redirectors to multiple protocols. For Windows NT to present and understand these different networks cleanly, a method for making them all look the same had to be devised. The result is the Provider Interface.

The Provider Interface is really made up of several smaller modules, each of which provide specialized services. The Multiple Provider Router (MPR) tracks what network a request is for and coordinates communication between the application and network.

Another module is the WNet API, which provides a consistent "look and feel" to different vendors' networks (see Appendix 1 for details). NetWare resources typically look like *server/resource:,* while NFS resources are represented by */server/resource*, and Microsoft LAN Manager, Windows NT, and Windows 95 resources look like *server**resource*. Part of the WNet subsystem maps all network resources into the Microsoft favored and built \\server\resource format, which is called the Universal Naming Convention (UNC).

The WNet subsystem, in conjunction with the MPR and several other modules, combine to form the Provider Interface. This allows you to use Microsoft's LAN Manager software as well as Novell's NetWare, Banyan's Vines, or any other redirector, with almost any Windows NT application, without the developers having to code in support for all these networks directly. If you're using only one redirector, you won't need the Provider Interface layer, although portions of it may be in use anyway.

Popular Network Protocols

Different network protocols exist for a reason. Each provides a different level of functionality in different areas. One protocol may work well for a certain kind of network, but be completely unsuitable for a different network that seems to be similar on the surface. There are a few key areas of concern that span all protocols, however. Memory consumption, bandwidth utilization, level of functionality (simple data transport verses applications), and scalability are all very important.

For example, your network may need only to read and write files from a relatively small file server, meaning you want fast transport performance and little else. To get that performance, you may pick a protocol that uses little memory and carries no application overhead. Another network may need to allow users to log in to interactive hosts and transfer large amounts of data. For these users, a protocol rich in functionality and features is more important than size or performance.

On a Windows NT network, the most likely transport protocols to be encountered are Microsoft's NBF, Novell's IPX, and the Internet-standard TCP/IP. NBF is the smallest, fastest, and easiest to use of the three, but it's also the least feature rich and the most limiting in large environments. Novell's IPX, although also small and fast, has the capability to run in complex networks that cannot be supported by NBF. Finally, TCP/IP is the most complex and scalable of the lot, but isn't very small, tends to be slower than the others, and can be difficult to set up (see Chapter 6 for details).

NetBIOS and NetBEUI

Historically, the NetBIOS user interface (and its transport protocol, NBF) have been Microsoft's preferred protocols. The resulting stack is very much a moving target, because it has been redefined, rebuilt, and repackaged many times in many products, including MS-NET, LAN Manager, Windows for Workgroups, and now Windows NT.

NetBIOS actually stands for Network BIOS, and as a user interface it literally extends the notion of a PC BIOS to the network. When IBM (which developed NetBIOS) started work, its goal was to develop a simple network protocol for small networks of PCs. The protocol would provide APIs for the development of network-specific applications that could communicate on a machine-to-machine or application-to-application basis. Also, the network naming system would allow for human-assigned names of devices, like "MyServer," which is easier to remember and work with than a complex numbering scheme. Unfortunately, like the PC itself, this simple yet limited design would prove to haunt users even today.

NBF was (and continues to be) a broadcast-intensive protocol. Since the assumptions were that there were only a few nodes on the network and that devices would be appearing and disappearing at random (as PCs are apt to do), it was best to be able to locate a device with a broadcast rather than with any sort of centralized registry. Unfortunately, broadcast packets don't work very well in today's router-based networks, because the routers don't pass packets that aren't specifically destined for another network segment. And since the NetBIOS naming structure is non-hierarchical, devices can't specify remote network segments. Thus, the only way to make NetBIOS work in large networks is to bridge the various segments into a single virtual network. Unfortunately, this reliance on broadcasting limits its use to relatively small networks, because large bridged networks don't work very well either.

When Microsoft chose NetBIOS as the basis for its first-generation LAN software (called MS-Net), it added another component specific to its software, called Server Message

Blocks (SMBs). Although SMBs are covered in more detail later in this appendix, suffice it to say for now that SMBs provide network-specific functionality to the mix, beyond what NBF provides by itself (indeed SMBs can be transported by IP or IPX just as easily as by NBF—as we will see.)

Today's NetBEUI stack doesn't look much like its progenitors. What started out as a single, monolithic protocol is now segmented into three unique components: the NetBIOS API, SMBs, and the NBF transport protocol. Figure A2.1 shows the various modules and the way they interrelate.

Many people confuse NBF with NetBIOS. It's important to remember that the term NetBIOS generally refers to an API for network applications, and does not specify how data is moved between systems, but only how data is packaged and acquired by applications. NetBIOS packets can actually use any transport—and Microsoft has them do exactly that with its NetBIOS-over-TCP (NBT) protocol. NBF refers specifically to the transport protocol originally designed for use with NetBIOS.

NetBIOS the API NetBIOS-based applications, such as the Chat applet bundled with Windows NT, work with the NetBIOS APIs. These high-level applications are not generally concerned with users, but interact with workstation names instead. When a NetBIOS-based application needs to communicate with a counterpart application, it locates the partner device and initiates the dialog. When the applications are finished, they disconnect, sometimes gracefully, sometimes not.

NetBIOS applications range from simple Chat-like applets to mainframe gateways and multi-user databases. Any application that needs to communicate with another can use the NetBIOS APIs to do so. Lotus's Notes server for Windows is a NetBIOS application, for example. Also, Microsoft Mail for Windows NT can support NetBIOS. As a result, one NT mail client can notify another client that new mail has been sent, using a NetBIOS message. The normal method requires that the recipient workstation check the inbox on a fileserver's shared drive for any unread messages.

Server Message Blocks When two Windows NT (or LAN Manager or Windows for Workgroups) nodes communicate, they use X/Open standard Server Message Block (SMB) protocol. SMB provides a well-defined method for servers and nodes (called "consumers" in the SMB definition) to communicate with each other, similar to the way that NetBIOS-based applications do.

FIGURE A2.1 NetBEUI stack. Microsoft's NetBEUI protocol stack has three layers: the NetBIOS API, Server Message Blocks (SMBs), and the NetBIOS Frame (NBF) transport.

The SMB specification contains a dictionary, more or less, of commands specific to network I/O. For example, if a user wants to open a file that resides on a server, the SMB command "SMBopen" is passed between the two systems. This occurs at the redirector level, of course, because all the user did was double-click on the file.

SMB commands exist for a wide range of functions and provide a quick and cost-effective way to do the most common network functions. Commands exist for things like login security, printing, and working directly with files and directories. In other words, the SMB protocol is the heart of the network, providing a common language for all the clients and servers to use.

The commands that make up the SMB specification can be thought of as lowest-common-denominator commands. Because the SMB spec assumes that there will be different types of machines on the network, the use of "extension protocols" is allowed to streamline operations significantly. For example, two DOS PCs would both use the DOS extension when speaking with each other, while two NT systems would use the NT extension, and so on. This allows nodes to communicate in the most efficient manner possible, while also guaranteeing compatibility between dissimilar devices.

NetBIOS Frames The lowest level of the NetBEUI protocol stack is the NBF protocol. NBF provides both the transport- and network-layer functions and provides the raw connectivity services between devices. When network I/O occurs, the upper layers (either NetBIOS applications or SMB transactions) pass data directly to NBF for processing. NBF then encapsulates the data into frames, locates the device(s) it needs to communicate with, and hands the data to the NIC for delivery.

NBF also handles the error correction services if needed, although through different mechanisms. Some services are established as connection oriented, meaning a detailed and highly monitored conversation is held through a virtual circuit between two systems. Other services are established as connectionless, using datagrams. In this situation, packets are sent and then forgotten about. This is generally used in situations in which repetitive broadcasts get sent frequently, such as status updates and the like.

NBF is the weakest link in the NetBEUI stack. Like NetBIOS itself, NBF is non-routable, meaning that it can communicate only with devices that it sees on the immediate subnet or one that is bridged into a virtual subnet. However, because no overhead is required for maintaining routing tables or the like, NBF is extremely small and fast—ideal for small networks of fewer than 100 devices. Also, because NBF was designed by IBM with Token Ring in mind, the default frame size of the packets is 4096 bytes, which allows for great throughput on networks that can handle it.

IPX and Complementary Protocols

Novell's protocol set is considerably different from NetBEUI, mostly in that it is somewhat larger and much more usable in complex environments. Indeed, its design called for multiple network segments from the start, and the use of numbers instead of names, for both networks and resources. Devices still have names, but these are seen at the higher-level redirector, not by the lower-level protocols themselves.

The heart of the NetWare protocol suite is based largely on Xerox's XNS (Xerox Network System). In fact, the two are almost identical, with the exception of some slight differences in some of the sub-protocols. For example, Novell's IPX (or Internetwork Packet Exchange) is based on Xerox's IDP (or Internetwork Datagram Packet). Novell did not copy the entire stack, however, because XNS includes sub-protocols for things like mail handling and the like. Many of the secondary protocols were not needed in the PC environment, and others were not even published until after Novell did its initial developments. Many other networking products are based on XNS, including VINES, Ungermann-Bass, and older 3Com software. Indeed, Microsoft's own internal network used XNS for years—and in some places still does.

The NetWare protocol suite looks something like Figure A2.2.

IPX IPX, the protocol most generally associated with NetWare, resides at the bottom-most layer of the stack and provides the "network" functions for the rest of the suite. In this instance, the term "network" refers to the network layer of the OSI model.

IPX tracks the various network segments that are available and directs the delivery of data accordingly. If a recipient node is local, the data is handed directly to it, and if remote, the data is handed to a router for delivery. IPX provides other network-layer functions, such as encapsulation of higher-level protocols, and is the single data-moving protocol for the NetWare environment. IPX does not guarantee delivery or provide error-correction services, however. These functions are left to the transport protocols, SPX and PEP.

Another aspect of IPX is that it determines packet sizes based on the "strength" of the media to which it is attached. Although the minimum (and theoretical maximum) size of an IPX packet is 512 bytes, if two nodes are directly attached to an Ethernet segment, they will use 1024 byte packets. If they are both on Token Ring, they will use 4096 byte packets. IPX routers, however, always convert the packets back to 512 bytes. Novell routing also allows for making packets more efficient, by limiting the "white space" in packets by using a technique called sparse packeting, where the total length of the packet can be cut to the size of the packet envelope plus the data within it. This is done largely for router efficiency.

SPX, PEP, and NCPs SPX (or Sequenced Packet Exchange) is an API similar to NetBIOS. Applications can use SPX to pass data directly between systems or applications. This process is

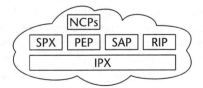

FIGURE A2.2 IPX/SPX stack. Novell's IPX/SPX stack has Netware Core Protocol (NCP) APIs at the top layer, Sequenced Packed Exchange (SPX), Packet Exchange Protocol (PEP), Service Advertisement Protocol (SAP), and Routing Information Protocol (RIP) in the second layer, and the Internetwork Packet Exchange (IPX) transport in the bottom layer.

assisted by SPX's virtual circuit capabilities, which provide guaranteed delivery of data over IPX. SPX does not acknowledge all packets, but instead uses a "window" method and acknowledges all the packets it has received within the window and conducts error-recovery based on keeping track of the *sequence* of the packets that have been received.

Another higher-level transport protocol is PEP (Packet Exchange Protocol), used exclusively for the delivery of NCP (NetWare Core Protocol) commands. NCPs are similar to SMBs in that they provide a dictionary of I/O-related network commands. NCPs are the heart of the NetWare server system and are guarded by Novell as if they were the crown jewels. PEP is considered a part of the NCP subsystem and is just as undocumented.

PEP provides error-correction services with the use of "timers." When a packet is sent from PEP, an internal timer is started within NCP, and no other NCP packets are generated until a response is received. If the timer expires, PEP rebuilds the packet, and NCP restarts the timer. This handshaking and waiting consumes lots of NCP utilization bandwidth, but guarantees that the packets get delivered. On small LANs, this goes unnoticed, but in large or exceedingly complex networks, performance can suffer tremendously.

SAP The advertisement of network devices and resources is managed by the Service Advertisement Protocol (SAP), naturally enough. SAP provides information about servers, routers, intelligent printers, and the like. Although SAP is really an application-level protocol, it uses IPX directly. Other sub-protocols, such as NCP and SPX, rely on SAP for information as well.

Because NetWare is a number-based network, there must be a way to translate human-defined device names into the device's "real" numerical address. SAP provides this registry service. When a program or service becomes available, SAP picks up on it and creates an entry in its tables. Although this dynamic name-keeping registry makes life easy for users, the constant updating of information can consume network bandwidth very quickly, because every device has its own SAP tables. For users in a WAN environment, filtering SAP entries at your routers is a good way to get your bandwidth back. SAPs can also be spoofed at routers: the service is advertised, but wide-area network wires aren't consumed with transmitting their packets—just their ghosts.

RIP Remember that IPX is a network-layer protocol. It doesn't know anything about other networks, other than the fact that they exist. When IPX has a packet for a remote subnet, it passes it to the closest router and forgets about it. RIP (or Routing Information Protocol) provides the routing services for IPX packets. When a node first comes onto the network, it issues a RIP request to find out what network number it is on.

If it is on multiple networks and configured as a router, it will send out a RIP update to all the nodes on the network, advertising the routes it can offer. Routers send out RIP updates every 60 seconds, telling other devices what networks it knows about. If a router doesn't send out an update within an allotted time, the router is assumed to be down, and the entry is removed.

IPX networks are non-hierarchical, meaning all routers must know how to get to every other network segment. As networks grow, this setup becomes an unmanageable and extremely overhead-expensive way to track remote networks. Novell has developed a link-state routing protocol called NLSP (for NetWare Link State Protocol), which works much better in extremely complex networks. Rather than routers continuously broadcasting information about every other network and router they know of, they send out only information that has changed, which greatly reduces the amount of bandwidth required.

The TCP/IP Protocol Suite

First and foremost, TCP/IP is not a single protocol, but a term used to define a variety of protocols that act in union to provide a variety of connectivity functions. These protocols are all very specific in function, ranging from the mundane task of providing transport services to more esoteric ones that provide extended management functions.

Most network operating systems use a very small set of proprietary protocols. For example, Microsoft's Windows NT uses NetBEUI and SMBs for almost all of its network services, and Novell uses IPX, SPX, and NCP for its connections. These very small and very functional protocols allow the network operating system to streamline their operation, resulting in very fast file and print sharing.

However, these protocols by themselves don't allow for much of anything else. By themselves, neither a Windows NT nor a NetWare file server will allow a remote user to log in to the server and run an interactive application within the server's memory (though third-party products are available to do this—see Chapters 11 and 12). You must run the application on a client PC, perhaps running the program from the server's shared filesystem, but that's as far as it goes. Thus the server is very contained and is highly optimized for the specific function of file and print sharing.

TCP/IP on the other hand offers an incredible breadth of services. Users can share files and printers, just as they can with NT or NetWare. They can also use terminal emulation services to execute applications on remote machines, allowing them to harness large system horsepower for specific applications. TCP/IP is a highly scalable set of protocols, and users can choose to implement any subset they wish, as either client or server services.

Another important aspect of TCP/IP is the issue of "openness." Although Microsoft uses the publicly available SMB specification for communicating, it incorporates proprietary network services into other aspects of the product. You can't put just any SMB-based client into a Windows NT-based domain and expect it to work. Novell is even worse, because it guards its proprietary NCPs as if they were the crown jewels (though as we point out in Chapter 10, it has proved possible to reverse-engineer them).

Both Microsoft and Novell license their server products to run on a variety of platforms, including minicomputers and mainframes, but you as a user must run that network service on each host and client in your organization—an exceedingly expensive and ungainly prospect at best. By comparison, TCP/IP is a fully public specification. Addenda to the specifications can be offered by anybody (even you), and the process is completely public. Thus, many companies already offer integrated TCP/IP protocols and services on their platforms. This makes it easy for an end user to connect resources without relying on any one vendor.

TCP/IP's third great advantage is that it is a very robust set of protocols, including transports that are highly efficient in wide-area networks. NBF (and, to a lesser degree, IPX) was designed for LAN use. NBF is non-routable, meaning that users on one network wire can't see servers on another unless the two segments are "bridged" into a single logical network wire. This doesn't work well in WAN environments. NetWare's IPX is a completely "routable" protocol. However, Novell's higher-level NCP relies on explicit acknowledgments for all network packets sent, which is ungainly over slow WAN links. Neither protocol set is appropriate for use on the Internet.

TCP/IP was originally written for connecting hosts over WANs and therefore is both routable and efficient. These benefits apply to LANs just as well, making TCP/IP a good choice for both small and large environments and explaining why TCP/IP protocols form the core of the Internet.

These three elements (scalability, openness, and robustness) make TCP/IP an attractive choice for users in mixed environments. They can run the same protocols and services on almost all of their host and client systems. For this reason, many customers have made TCP/IP a check-off item for network purchases: No TCP/IP support—no purchase. No wonder Microsoft put TCP/IP into the basic Windows NT package! Of course, all is not rosy with TCP/IP, and we'll explore these limitations alongside its advantages.

A Very Brief History of TCP/IP Back in the "big iron" age of commercial computing (the late 1960s), most companies bought a single large computer for their data processing needs. As needs expanded, they rarely bought a different system from a different vendor. Instead, they added on to their existing platforms or replaced them with newer, larger models. Cross-platform connectivity was essentially unheard of, nor was it expected by customers. They were generally too busy just trying to keep these newfangled computers running.

These systems used proprietary networking architectures and protocols. For the most part, networking in those days consisted of plugging "dumb" line printers or terminals into a "smart" multiplexer or communications controller. And just as the networking protocols were proprietary, so were the network nodes. To this day you still can't plug an IBM terminal into a DEC computer and expect it to work. The architectures and protocols are completely incompatible.

In an effort to help major research sites share resources, the Advanced Research Projects Agency (ARPA) of the Department of Defense (DOD) began coordinating the development of a vendor-independent network to tie the sites together. The logic behind this effort was obvious: the cost and time to develop an application on one system was too much for each site to re-engineer the application on other incompatible systems. Because each facility used a different computer with proprietary networking technology, the need for a vendor-independent network was the first priority. In 1968, work began on a private packet-switched network, using Honeywell-based communications hardware.

In the early 1970s, authority of the project was transferred to the Defense Advanced Research Projects Agency (DARPA). DARPA began developing and implementing protocols that would allow for the connection and use of the various systems. Although the original protocols were written for use with the ARPA network, they were designed to be usable on other systems as well, and significantly, DARPA was concerned to make sure that the protocols were *very* robust (reportedly, in part at least so that surviving network nodes could continue to operate after a limited nuclear attack!). In 1981, DARPA placed the resulting TCP/IP protocol suite into the public domain. Shortly thereafter, it was adopted by the University of California at Berkeley, which began bundling it with its freely distributed version of UNIX. In 1983, DOD mandated that all new systems connecting to their networks use TCP/IP, thus guaranteeing its long-term success.

During the same time period, other government agencies like the National Science Foundation (NSF) were building their own networks, as were private regional network service providers. These other networks also used TCP/IP as the native connection mechanism, because it was both a completely "open" protocol and readily available on a number of different platforms.

When these various regional and government networks began connecting to each other, the term "Internet" came into play. To "internet" (with a lowercase "i") means to interconnect networks. You can create an internet of Macintosh networks using AppleTalk and some routers, for example. The term "Internet" (with a capital "I") refers to the global network of TCP/IP-based systems, originally consisting of the ARPA and regional networks. Any organization (or *anyone* for that matter) can join the Internet, and extensive information on that topic is provided both at the end of this appendix and in Chapter 7.

TCP/IP's Architecture This anarchic peer-to-peer structure is purposefully designed directly into TCP/IP's architecture. Consider the distributed nature of TCP/IP, in contrast to the classic top-down security model of other host-based architectures of the time. Most systems had a hierarchical structure that permeated throughout the entire computing architecture. Everything was managed by the central host, including the network services themselves. Two nodes couldn't communicate without sending data through the host (an approach that DARPA could hardly accept for a network designed to survive a war!).

With TCP/IP, *there is no central authority!* Nodes communicate directly among themselves, and each maintains complete knowledge about the available network services. If any host fails, none of the others knows or cares (unless it needs data from the down machine). This setup is fairly similar to Windows NT's basic server design, in which servers are relatively independent of each other (Windows NT Server unifies servers into a single logical domain, however, which eases management, but also breaks the independence of each system).

Addressing To identify themselves in this peer-to-peer environment, nodes are given explicit addresses that identify not only the computer, but the network segment that it is on as well. For example, the address 192.123.004.010 specifies node number 10 on network 192.123.004. Another node on the same network segment might be numbered 20, and so on. Networks and the nodes on them are separate entities, with separate numbers.

Host 10 from the example above might also be connected to network 192.123.005 on a different network adapter. This host could then act as a router between networks 192.123.004 and 192.123.005. Routers perform the task of moving traffic between networks. A node that needs to send data to another node on another network will send the data to the router, and the router will send the data to the destination node. If the destination isn't on an immediately connected network, the router will send the data to another router for delivery. This network-based routing scheme allows devices to keep their local overhead low. Otherwise, they'd have to remember how to get to each node, which would require a tremendous amount of processing and memory. Network-based routing requires much less in terms of end-node resources.

Each node's address is actually a 32-bit binary number (like 11000000 01111011 00000100 00001010). For convenience, this is broken into four 8-bit fields, called octets. TCP/IP represents these binary octets with their decimal equivalents (192.123.004.010 in this case). This makes life much easier for humans (computers may have no trouble dealing with 32-bit binary strings, but people sure do!).

The four octets signify different things in different networks. Some sites have only a single large network, but millions of nodes. They would use the first octet of the address to identify the network and the remaining three octets to identify the individual workstations. This arrangement is known as a "Class A" address. The most common users of Class A addresses are network service providers, who maintain extremely large and flat networks with thousands of endpoints.

Another site may have thousands of nodes, split across many networks. They would use a "Class B" addresses, in which the first two octets (or 16 bits) are used to identify the network, and the remaining two octets identify the individual nodes. Universities and large organizations are the most common users of Class B addresses.

Finally, the most common address is the "Class C" address, in which the first three octets (or 24 bits) are used to identify the segment, and the last octet is used to identify the workstations. These are good for users with only a few dozen nodes on many separate networks. This address type is most often found in LAN environments, which average around 40 nodes per network segment.

When a Class A network connects to a Class B network, there must be some way for the router to recognize the difference between the two. Otherwise, it would think that traffic originating from the Class C network and destined for a Class A node would be identifiable by the last octet. In truth, the Class A node is identified by the last three octets, a significant difference. Without this knowledge, the router would attempt to locate the three-octet network that the one-octet host is on. In actuality, it should be trying to send the data to the one-octet network that the three-octet host is on.

TCP/IP uses the first three bits of the first octet to identify the class of network, allowing devices to automatically recognize the appropriate address types. Class A addresses are identified by the first bit being set to "0," leaving only seven other bits for identifying the network portion of the address (remember that Class A addresses use the first octet to identify the network and the remaining three octets to identify the nodes). Because only seven bits are available, there can be only 128 possible networks. Network numbers 000 and 127 are reserved for use by software, so there are really only 126 possible networks (001 through 126). However, 24 bits are available for identifying nodes, for a maximum of 16,777,124 possible node addresses for each of these networks.

Class B addresses are identified by having the first two bits set to "0." Because they use the first two octets to identify the network, this leaves 14 bits to identify each network segment. Thus, there are a possible 16,384 Class B addresses, ranging from 128.001 to 191.254 (numbers 000 and 255 are reserved).

Class C addresses are identified by having the first three bits in the first octet set to "0." These addresses use the first three octets to identify the network, so there are 21 bits available. The possible network numbers range from 192.001.001 through 254.254.254, a whopping 2,097,152 possible segments. However, with only one octet left to identify the nodes, there can be only 254 possible devices on each segment.

Out of Addresses? All told, there are over 4.7 billion possible host addresses. That sounds like plenty, but unfortunately, the four-octet structure causes some major restrictions. Every time a Class A address is assigned to an organization, almost 17 million host addresses go with it. If all 126 of the Class A addresses are assigned, over 3 billion of the 4.7 billion possible addresses are gone. If all of the 16,000 Class B addresses are assigned, another billion host addresses are gone as well. Whether or not all the workstation addresses are actually put to use is irrelevant; they have been assigned to a specific network, and cannot be used again.

Class C addresses represent the biggest problem, however, for two reasons. First, there are fewer of them (only about 500 million possible node addresses are available). Second, they are the most popular because they reflect the size of the majority of the LANs. However, every time a Class C address is assigned to a network segment, 254 possible node addresses go with it. Remember that a new network number is required for every separate network. People who have three segments and only 60 nodes are therefore wasting over 700 possible workstation addresses (3 segments x 254 node addresses = 762 addresses - 60 active nodes = 702 inactive addresses). Clearly, at this rate, the available workstation numbers will run out soon (in fact, at the current rate of depletion the available addresses are just about gone!).

To some readers, the logic for having different "classes" of addresses may seem vague at best. With the current design, there are only 2,113,662 possible networks. If all networks used the first 24 bits (without using "class bits") to identify the segment, there would be a possible 16,777,124 networks, with 254 nodes on each of them.

Remember, however, that TCP/IP networks are inherently router based. It requires much less overhead on the part of nodes and routers to remember a few networks than many. Having to process 16 million networks would quickly overwhelm the router databases, and network traffic would slow down tremendously. Having network classes allows routers to deal with large networks easily, and performance is maintained.

Remember also that the original architecture of the Internet consisted mostly of large networks connecting to each other. It was easy to give one address to milnet (a network of unclassified military hosts) and another to NSFnet (the National Science Foundation's network). By doing this, routers have to remember only another router's address in order to pass data to literally millions of hosts.

For us, however, the potential side effects of address depletion are frightening. No new organizations could connect to the Internet, and the existing networks couldn't expand. A new version of IP has been developed to overcome most of these limitations. However, it will be several years before IPng (next generation, or IP v6) will be implemented on enough commercially available equipment for you to take advantage of it on an enterprise-wide basis.

Subnet Masks There are ways to get more mileage from a single network number, however. Remember that the 32-bit binary address is divided into four logical 8-bit octets. There's nothing to prevent you from changing this structure. Although you can't change the binary values of the address itself, you can change the way that your software interprets it. The interpretation of the address is called the "Subnet Mask."

For clarification, let's look at the host address 192.123.004.010. This is a Class C address with the first 24 bits identifying the network number (3 bits for the Class C identifier, and 21 bits for addressing). The remaining eight bits identify the host. You could just as easily set the subnet mask so that the first 30 bits identify the network and the remaining two bits identify the host.

Because the first 24 bits in a Class C address identify an organization, the remaining eight bits can be used any way that organization sees fit. If it wishes to use the bits for identifying hosts, it certainly can. However, another option would be to assign some of the remaining eight bits to *sub*-networks. In essence, the network portion of the address gains another field, while the range of host numbers possible shrinks.

For example, suppose our imaginary company, Windows Inc., has both Ethernet and token ring networks. However, it has only a single Class C network address of 192.123.004. Rather than use the last octet to identify 254 hosts on a single network, it decides to add a subnet mask to its address by "borrowing" the first bit of the last octet. This creates two subnets, with 128 possible hosts in each of them.

Now when Windows Inc. looks at the network numbers, it sees the following:

```
Segment         Network Address    Node Addresses*
Ethernet        192.123.004        001 - 127
Token Ring      192.123.004        128 - 254
```

* Numbers 000 and 255 are reserved.

Remember, however, that devices on the network don't see this logical breakdown automatically. Based on the Class C identifier in the head of the address, they still think that the last eight bits of the address represent a host. All the devices on a network segment must be told about the mask.

The subnet mask uses a very simple algorithm. If a bit mask is set to 1, it is part of the network number. If the bit mask is set to 0, it is part of the host number. Therefore, the subnet mask for our example above looks like 11111111 11111111 11111111 10000000. Shown in Table A2.2 are the default subnet masks for the different network classes.

Table A2.2 Default Subnet Masks

Class	Subnet Mask
A	11111111 00000000 00000000 00000000
B	11111111 11111111 00000000 00000000
C	11111111 11111111 11111111 00000000

The subnet mask for a node is appended to its binary address when processed by routers. Just as the router would look to see if network 192.123.004 were locally attached before forwarding the packet, it would now look to see if the subnet mask of the destination network matched as well. If the subnet mask doesn't match the local network, the data is forwarded to another router that does match.

For subnet masking to work, all the devices on a subnet must support it. Some older TCP/IP client programs don't support subnet masking, so make sure that they do before you try this. By the way, some software packages convert the binary subnet mask values into their decimal equivalents for ease of use. For example, Windows NT doesn't show the default Class C subnet mask, but rather shows it as 255.255.255.0 instead, the decimal equivalent of the binary octets. Again, this is to make life easier for us humans.

Sub Protocols Like the IPX and NetBEUI stacks, TCP/IP is a collection of protocols that span the OSI reference model from top to bottom. There are application-specific protocols such as Telnet and FTP, a collection of maintenance protocols, at least two major transport protocols, and one network-layer protocol. Figure A2.3 shows the major sub-protocols in the TCP/IP suite.

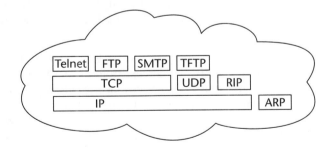

FIGURE A2.3 TCP/IP stack. The TCP/IP protocol suite includes Telnet, File Transfer Protocol (FTP), and Simple Mail Transfer Protocol (SMTP) at the user-interface layer; Transmission Control Protocol (TCP), User Datagram Protocol (UDP), and Routing Information Protocol (RIP) in the middle; and two transport protocols, Internet Protocol (IP) and Address Resolution Protocol (ARP).

IP and ARP IP, or the Internet Protocol, is the basic building block for all TCP/IP traffic and works at the network layer of the OSI reference model. It is where the internet address assignment, and the layer of software responsible for determining how packets are passed to other networks are realized. Other than that, IP is a fairly boring protocol. All it does is get internet packets from one node to another, across the best route possible.

IP converts internet addresses into "real" network addresses, such as Ethernet addresses, through the use of ARP (Address Resolution Protocol) and RARP (Reverse Address Resolution Protocol). An ARP packet will be sent with the destination IP address in the header, and if the receiving node is online, it will send back a response packet containing its real network address. RARP is used when a node needs to find out the IP address corresponding to a node's real address. Either way, when an ARP or RARP reply comes back, the node stores the address in a cache buffer for reuse.

TCP and UDP The protocols that provide the transport-layer services are TCP (Transmission Control Protocol) and UDP (User Datagram Protocol). Because IP provides no error-recovery or control services, applications that need it go through TCP, and those that don't go through UDP. Almost all applications use TCP or UDP for the delivery of data, both of which pass packets to IP for delivery. Very few applications speak directly with IP.

TCP provides error correction through the use of a connection-oriented transaction. A "start" packet is built and sent to the destination node (via IP), and when an "okay I'm ready" packet comes back, a monitored conversation between the hosts and/or applications begins. If a packet is lost or corrupted, TCP resends the data. The size, time-out interval, and other critical factors are determined by TCP, judging the strength of the media that the node is connected to.

UDP on the other hand, simply sends the data and forgets about it. If no error-correction or monitoring services are needed, an application is best off using UDP because it's much faster and requires less overhead than TCP. Like TCP, UDP makes decisions about packet sizes based on the strength of the underlying media and passes the fully contained parcel to IP for delivery. This is what makes IP so boring; it just delivers the data because all the big decisions have already been made for it.

RIP RIP may look familiar because it is the exact same Routing Information Protocol that NetWare uses with IPX, and like IPX RIP, it's derived from the XNS source code. It was not originally a part of the TCP/IP suite, but Berkeley included it with its distribution, and it has since become one of the most popular routing protocols around. It also carries many of the same limitations that Novell's version has, and there are many, many alternatives available. If you use a non-RIP routing protocol on a router, however, you need to make sure that you use it on *all* of them, because that's how they communicate with each other.

Early versions of Windows NT included only static IP routing, in which an explicit table of router addresses was maintained. RIP support for both IPX and IP was introduced with the *Multi-Protocol Router* (MPR) component of Service Pack 3 for NT 3.51, and in NT 4.0, it's built in to NT Server (see Chapter 6 for details).

Name Resolution: HOSTS, WINS, and DNS Once your system knows how to connect to the outside world, you are ready to start communicating with other systems. Although you can use

IP addresses for communicating with other TCP/IP resources, this is undesirable for several reasons. First and foremost, IP addresses change quite often. Second, working with machine "names" is much easier than trying to remember 32-bit sequences of numbers.

Until quite recently, the most common mechanism for assigning names to IP resources was the use of a text file called "HOSTS" (on NT systems, this file is located in the \winnt35\system32\etc directory). Another mechanism that is much more flexible and easier to manage in large environments is the Domain Name System (DNS). DNS servers manage hierarchical databases of IP addresses, host names, and networks. IP nodes use a DNS resolver to query the DNS server for IP addresses whenever a host name is used. If a resource moves to another network, or if the IP address changes for any other reason, the network administrator has only to update the DNS server's database, and all subsequent client queries are correctly resolved. If you've been on the Internet, you already know about DNS: names like whatever.com are DNS addresses.

The major problem with DNS is that it's static. Although HOST files don't have to be maintained separately on each node, there's still a list at the DNS server, which centralizes the problem of maintaining addresses but doesn't eliminate it completely. Various schemes have been attempted to get around this problem. Microsoft's first attempt, introduced in NT 3.5, was Windows Internet Name Service (WINS), which provides dynamic association of IP addresses with NetBIOS names. A companion Dynamic Host Configuration Protocol (DHCP) service allows the IP addresses themselves to by dynamically "leased" on a first-come, first-served basis.

The problem with WINS is that nobody but Microsoft uses it, so if you run an all-Microsoft (NT, Windows 95, Windows for Workgroups) network, it will work fine, but you will have great difficulty if you need to talk to anything else. To address this problem, Microsoft introduced a WINS-DNS converter in the NT 3.51 resource kit. A perfected version of that converter, now called Dynamic DNS, is built into Windows NT Server 4.0.

You can find more information on NT's implementation of TCP/IP and related services (including WINS, DHCP, and Dynamic DNS) in Chapter 6.

WAN Links: PPP and SLIP Two additional protocols of special concern to users of Windows NT's Dial-Up Networking/Remote Access Services (RAS) are Point-to-Point Protocol (PPP) and Serial Link Internet Protocol (SLIP), both of which can be used to establish a wide-area network (WAN) connection over dial-up lines, ISDN, x.25 networks, or similar services.

Both PPP and SLIP are characterized by relative insensitivity to line noise and to delays in receiving packets. They're designed to "punch through" in situations where LAN protocols would probably fail.

Of the two, PPP is far more flexible. It operates by "wrapping" TCP, IPX, or NBF transport packets inside PPP's own packet format and transports the resulting wrapped packet over the WAN link. At the other end, the packet is unwrapped, and the original transport packets are transmitted on the LAN. Once a connection is established, operation is completely transparent to applications—they see perfectly normal TCP, IPX, or NBF packets (although the packets may arrive a bit more slowly than on the LAN).

SLIP is less flexible. It's basically an extension of IP to operate over slow links, so it supports only IP networks. It also tends to be less immune to line noise. NT RAS basically supports SLIP for compatibility with UNIX-based WAN servers (it also provides an even less flexible proprietary Asynchronous NetBEUI transport for compatibility with older versions of RAS). If you're setting up a new WAN with NT, use PPP!

Getting Connected to the Internet Connecting to the Internet requires you to follow some very specific procedures. First, you must decide whether you will connect your network directly to a service provider's network or connect on a per-user basis using SLIP or PPP dial-up systems. You can also connect directly to the Internet backbone if you're sponsored by a government agency.

If you use a service provider for a full-time link, you will likely be given everything you need for the connection. This will include a block of registered IP addresses, a domain name, and a router. You will pay for the one-time setup fees and a monthly service charge. You may also pay the telephone line charges, unless they are part of the monthly service fees. Each service provider does business a little differently, so shop around for the deal that works best for you and your budget.

Once you are set up with this connection, however, managing your Internet resources is entirely up to you. You must take care of your DNS servers, allocate IP addresses to your clients, and make sure that mail is being routed correctly. Hiring somebody to manage all of this can cost you much more than the line charges.

If you choose to buy individual dial-up accounts, you will be faced with less management work, but more choices. Most dial-up service providers give you an interactive account on a UNIX system on which you read mail, access newsgroups, and run your Gopher and WWW browser clients. Some providers give you a SLIP or PPP connection, however, which allows you to run Windows-based applications on your local PC, acting as an extension of their network. Either way, you will be under the service provider's domain, and your resources will be managed for you.

You can find specific information on connecting NT systems to the Internet in Chapter 7.

PPTP One of NT 4.0's most exciting new features is support for Point-to-Point Tunneling Protocol (PPTP), which takes the PPP concept one step further: it actually puts a PPP "wrapper" around PPP packets. Operationally, the difference between PPP and PPTP is just this: to establish a PPP link, you dial a telephone number; to establish a PPTP link, you "dial" an IP address.

Just as with PPP, PPTP packets are "wrapped," transported to the other end of the link (in this case, the system identified with the IP address mentioned in the last paragraph), and "unwrapped" there. The result is a "virtual private network" between the two systems passing the PPTP packets. To keep the link truly private, PPTP supports a range of security options up to and including encryption of all packet data.

The implications of this capability are tremendous. PPTP has the potential to revolutionize the way businesses use remote networking. See Chapters 6, 7, and 8 for more on this exciting technology.

For More Information

Malamud, C. (1990), *Analyzing Novell Networks*. New York: Van Nostrand Reinhold, ISBN: 0-442-00364-1. Great low-level peeks at what goes on in NetWare LANs.

Miller, M. (1991), *Internetworking*. Redwood City, CA: M&T Books, ISBN: 1-55851-143-1. Solid reference material on XNS, IPX, and TCP/IP protocols.

Arick, M. (1993), *The TCP/IP Companion*. Wellesley, MA: QED Publishing Group, ISBN: 0-89435-466-3. Good end-user-oriented discussion of TCP/IP and utilities.

Black, U. (1992), *TCP/IP and Related Protocols*. New York: McGraw-Hill, ISBN: 0-07-005553-X. Mandatory desktop reference for the TCP/IP administrator.

Albitz, P. and C. Liu (1992), *DNS and BIND*. Sebastopol, CA: O'Reilly & Associates, Inc., ISBN: 1-56592-010-4. Great book for learning about the Domain Name System (DNS).

Estrada, S. (1993), *Connecting to the Internet*. Sebastopol, CA: O'Reilly & Associates, Inc., ISBN: 1-56592-061-9. Essential guide for getting yourself or your organization connected to the Internet.

Appendix

Legacy
Applications

With some exceptions, Windows NT will run applications compiled to run in DOS, Windows 3.1, and character-based OS/2 1.3. In addition, it supports the POSIX API (a generic subset of the UNIX API) so that application source code written to POSIX can be recompiled and run under Windows NT. This appendix details the operation and limits of compatibility for legacy applications.

Chapter 11 of the *Microsoft Windows NT System Guide* details the settings and operation of many aspects of legacy applications. Information is also available in the *Windows NT Resource Kit Volume 1*, Chapters 13 and 15. This appendix supplements the information in those sources.

Non-x86 Limitations

If you plan to make heavy use of legacy applications, be aware of important limitations with Windows NT on non-x86 (e.g., MIPS R4000/4400, Intergraph Clipper, DEC Alpha or other RISC-based) systems. (In this appendix, x86 refers to the Intel 386, 486, Pentium, and Intel-compatible chips produced by Cyrix, AMD, NexGen, and others.) Non-x86 systems use emulation software to interpretively execute the x86 instruction set. Two problems exist with this approach: performance and emulation level. Because the emulator must execute multiple non-x86 instructions to interpret one x86 instruction, it is slower by a factor of about 10 than a native application. So although the MIPS R4400 is about the equal of the Pentium for native Windows NT applications, it's only about as fast as a 386/25 when running a Windows 3.1 application.

What may be a more important limitation for many people is that the emulation software on the non-x86 versions of NT does not emulate 386 instructions. That means it runs Windows 3.1 in standard mode, not 386 enhanced mode. Similarly, the emulator cannot run 386 DOS extended applications. Native OS/2 1.3 applications are not supported at all on non-x86 platforms, even though they generally do not use 386 instructions. If you have an EXE file compiled as an OS/2 family mode (bound) application (which combines both DOS and OS/2 executables in a single file), it will run on a non-x86 platform, but execute the DOS code in the EXE file, not the OS/2 code.

Finally, although DOS applications run on non-x86 systems, they can do so only in a window. The full-screen operation provided by x86 systems assumes VGA hardware compatibility that isn't present on non-x86 systems. (Conceivably, some x86 systems might not offer VGA compatibility either, but that's not true at present.)

DOS Support

NT uses the virtual-86 feature of the 386 and 486 chip to provide a separate virtual machine for each DOS application you run. Most DOS applications will run under NT with no problem, but device drivers and low-level utilities may not. This was a conscious design decision by the NT designers to trade compatibility for security and system stability. If NT let DOS software access hardware directly, it could put hardware into an unstable state or corrupt the hard disk, so some poorly behaved DOS apps will not run under NT.

However, if the definition of a "poorly behaved DOS app" means that it accesses the hardware directly, nearly all DOS apps are poorly behaved. Most of them write directly to VGA video buffers, reprogram the timer chip, or access the serial port hardware. Therefore, NT makes this most basic PC hardware available through Virtual Device Drivers (VDDs). A VDD virtualizes hardware so that each DOS application believes it is using the actual hardware when it really is not. Therefore, NT can arbitrate access to the real hardware device when multiple DOS applications (or DOS and NT) try to access it.

There are two major trouble areas in DOS support under NT:

- *Specialized hardware that requires custom device drivers or TSRs.* This hardware includes high-resolution DOS video drivers, the fax section of the Intel SatisFAXtion 400, video capture boards, and many scanners. You cannot install DOS-based drivers for network cards, tape drives, or CD-ROMs in NT, because these typically interface to custom hardware. These devices should be installed under NT and accessed in DOS through the NT support. The SYSTEM32 directory includes special versions of the network redirector and MS CD-ROM extensions that are used with DOS and loaded in the AUTOEXEC.NT file (see below). Vendors need to write VDDs for any hardware they want to be supported under NT, using the Windows NT Device Driver Kit.

- *Utilities that require low-level access to disk drives.* These utilities include disk-compression software like Stacker and DoubleSpace and the disk doctor tools in Norton Utilities or PC Tools. These utilities present security and integrity risks, and assume things about the structure and layout of the disk that aren't necessarily true under NT. If you require these types of utilities, you will need to find NT equivalents. To perform an operation like disk defragmenting on a FAT disk volume, reboot into DOS and run the application from there.

The DOS compatibility built into NT is basically at the level of DOS 5.0, although the Get DOS Version API call actually returns 5.32 as the version number. Most applications aren't sensitive to DOS versions, so this shouldn't be a problem. However, if you have your system set up to dual-boot between a DOS 6.0 and NT, you will find that many DOS 6.0 utilities fail with an "Incompatible DOS version" error if you try to run them in NT. Most of those utilities (like MORE or FIND) have equivalents in NT. You can overcome these version incompatibilities by using the SETVER.EXE utility that comes with DOS (version 5 and later). Load SETVER in the CONFIG.NT file as described below.

When you log on, NT reads the AUTOEXEC.BAT file from the boot drive and sets any environment variables it finds for later use by DOS or NT applications. It also adds directories from any PATH statement onto the end of the path that NT uses. NT sets the path so that its SYSTEM32 directory is searched before any other directory, so 32-bit equivalents to DOS commands will be found first.

Each time you start a command prompt window or launch a DOS application from Windows NT Explorer, NT reads the CONFIG.NT and AUTOEXEC.NT files in the SYSTEM32 directory to configure the environment for the new application. These files are similar to their DOS analogs and let you configure each DOS session for maximum memory or to load a particular set of TSRs or device drivers. Chapter 11 of the NT System Guide details the commands available in these two files. Each DOS session has its own environment, complete with high memory area. As with DOS, you can specify commands to load TSRs or device drivers into high memory. Because hardware devices aren't mapped into the high memory of these virtual DOS environments, you may be able to put much more into high memory than in true DOS.

Like Windows 3.1 and Windows 95, NT supports Program Information Files (PIFs) for DOS applications. In fact, you can use the same PIFs you have been using under Windows 3.1, although NT ignores most of the DOS and Windows parameters. It does use the start-up directory, EMS/XMS memory usage, priority, shortcut keys, and display usage (details are in Chapter 11 of the NT System Guide). You can also specify different AUTOEXEC and CONFIG files, rather than the ones in SYSTEM32, that can be used to initialize DOS before running this particular application. For example, if you have a particularly memory-hungry DOS application, you could create a custom CONFIG.NT file to remove CD-ROM and/or network support to save memory.

The new NT shell goes to great lengths to make the process of setting 16-bit DOS executables easy, but there is one confusing thing. If you right-click a DOS EXE file and select Properties, you'll get the full set of *default* properties for DOS files. If you then change the properties, NT will make a corresponding PIF file for you, because that's where the settings are actually stored. PIF files should be kept together in the same directory with the associated EXE file. To change the properties of a PIF file, right-click on the PIF and select Properties. You'll see a property dialog box similar to the one in Figure A3.1.

If you are using an NTFS volume, NT creates DOS-compatible names for any files that violate the DOS 8.3 naming convention. When DOS applications are using files on NTFS, they see only the DOS-compatible names. The following rules are used:

- Lowercase letters are converted to uppercase.

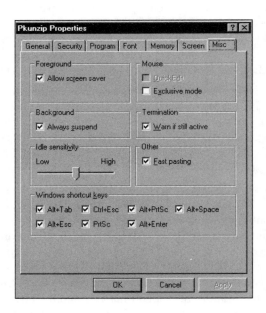

FIGURE A3.1 PKUNZIP properties. Right-clicking on the Program Information File (PIF) icon associated with a DOS application in Explorer and selecting Properties from the resulting context menu allows you to edit properties for the .PIF in question, which controls how the associated application will be executed.

- Characters that aren't legal in DOS files are converted to underscores (_). (NTFS uses the 16-bit Unicode character set, whereas DOS uses 7-bit ASCII.)

- Spaces are removed.

- If the name has more than one period, all but the last (rightmost) are removed.

- The name is truncated to its first (leftmost) six characters before the period.

- The extension (after the period) is truncated to three characters.

- A tilde and sequence number (e.g., ~1) are added to the name to create a unique file name. If a single digit doesn't produce a unique name, the name is truncated to five characters and a two-digit sequence number is used.

Table A3.1 shows some examples, assuming that the files here are created in order (which affects the sequence numbering).

If you are not sure what DOS filename will be produced from the long name, you can select the file in Explorer, right-click, and select Properties (see Figure A3.2). The General tab includes the MS-DOS name of the file. Or, type DIR /X from the command prompt to see both the long and short names.

In truth, though, much confusion will be saved in mixed (DOS and NT) environments if you stick to using DOS-style 8.3 names. Doing so eliminates the need to remember that "Monthly Report.DOC" on the NT system is the same as "MONTHL~2.DOC" in DOS!

Windows 3.x Support

NT's support for Windows 3.x is similar to Windows enhanced mode on x86 systems, but adds several significant improvements. (See the section at the beginning of this appendix for a discussion of non-x86 system limitations.) As with Windows 3.x enhanced mode, virtual memory is supported.

Table A3.1 Sample DOS-Compatible File Names

NTFS Name	DOS Name
This.Is.A.Very.Long.Name	THISIS~1.NAM
This Is A Very Long.Too	THISIS~1.TOO
This is a very_big.name	THISIS~2.NAM
Monthly Budget.DOC	MONTHL~1.DOC
Monthly Report.DOC	MONTHL~2.DOC

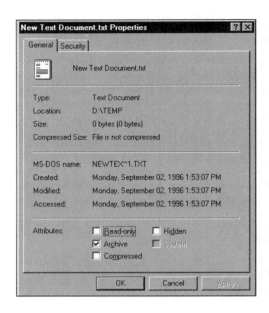

FIGURE A3.2 File properties. NT supports legacy applications by automatically generating DOS-style "8.3" file name equivalents to long file names in the New Technology File System. You can see both versions of the file's name by viewing the file's properties in Windows Explorer.

One major advantage to running 3.1 applications under NT is that they are not limited to a tiny pool of 128KB system resources as they are in Windows 3.*x*. This means that a Windows NT system can have more Windows 3.*x* apps running simultaneously than can Windows 3.*x*. It also means that a resource-hungry program like Microsoft Excel 5.0 can have *many* more worksheets open at once. For example, under Windows 3.*x* you can open only about 30 empty Excel worksheets before running out of system resources; under NT we've opened more than 470 (yes, that's four hundred seventy) before running out of paging file space. By increasing the paging file space (or adding more physical memory) we could go even higher.

As with DOS support, Windows 3.*x* applications cannot access hardware directly. The primary problem area you're likely to encounter here is with applications that add their own drivers to the [386enh] section of SYSTEM.INI. As with DOS emulation, if these drivers control custom hardware, you will need to contact the vendor to see if there is an NT driver. However, some vendors include drivers that simply work around problems with the standard Windows drivers, the most common one being COMM.DRV. You may find that you can run such applications successfully under NT without the driver (NT's built-in comm support is superior to that in Windows 3.*x*).

When you install Windows NT, it looks to see if you already have Windows 3.*x* (or Windows for Workgroups) installed on your system, for example, in C:\WINDOWS. If so, it suggests you install NT in the same directory. There's little danger that installing NT will cause your Windows 3.x setup to misbehave; nearly all the NT files actually go into a new \WINDOWS\SYSTEM32 directory, and NT uses its own registry database (rather than WIN.INI or SYSTEM.INI) to save system settings.

The advantage of installing Windows NT and Windows 3.x in the same directory is that NT will set up your Windows 3.x applications for you. The first time you log onto NT after doing a same-directory install, NT will create program groups that are equivalent to your custom groups in Windows 3.x. Each time NT is booted, the system updates its Windows 3.x configuration based on the WIN.INI, SYSTEM.INI, and REG.DAT (Object Linking and Embedding) information. When NT is running Windows 3.x apps, they will be able to use the information in your existing Windows setup, including private INI files in the \WINDOWS directory and application-specific settings in WIN.INI. Whether you install an application in Windows 3.x or NT, you will be able to run it in either environment.

If you choose to install NT in a location other than your Windows 3.x directory (for example \WINNT), running 3.1 applications under NT can be a bit more complicated but still quite possible. One simple approach is to re-install the application under NT but specify the same destination for the application files. This will usually re-create any changes required to INI files in the \WINNT directory without actually having a second copy of the application on disk. Remember that if you don't install NT and 3.1 in the same directory, the INI files can get out of sync. That is, if you boot into 3.1, change some settings in an application, and later run that application in NT, you may find those settings are not changed.

In Windows NT 3.51, you could use the settings for icons in Program Manager to set the startup environment of a program, such as the default directory. With NT 4.0, you do this by creating a shortcut. All the items on the Start button are shortcuts, so you can change these in the same way as Program Manager icons. Or you can create a custom shortcut and put it on the desktop or in any directory. To set the program's properties, right-click the desktop and select Properties. You'll see a set of property sheets that let you change startup and execution environmental settings.

From version 3.5 on, NT has had the ability to run each 16-bit Windows application in a separate memory space. Although each DOS application always runs in its own memory space, by default 16-bit Windows applications run in a single memory space for compatibility reasons. However, there are two definite advantages to separate memory spaces for 16-bit applications. First, a 16-bit application that crashes or locks up its own message queue will not affect other 16-bit applications. Second, each separate memory space also has a separate thread of execution, so they can be preemptively multitasked. The two biggest drawbacks of separate memory spaces are that they confuse some applications (utilities, mostly) that expect a single address space and they consume more system memory.

With the introduction of the new shell, procedures for running a Win16 program changed a bit in NT 4.0. You can choose from three options to launch a Win16 program in a separate memory space:

• From a command window, run the program using a command line of the form CMD /C START /SEPARATE *programname*.

- Run the program using the Start button's Run dialog, and check the "Run in separate memory space" option. Note that this option can be changed only if Windows NT determines the executable file you specify is a Win16 application; otherwise, it will be disabled (see Figure A3.3).

- Create a shortcut to the file using Explorer. In the shortcut's Properties dialog box on the Shortcut tab, check the "Run in separate memory space" option (see Figure A3.4).

Windows 95 Support

With version 4.0, Windows NT has essentially the same user interface as Windows 95. However, there are still many differences hiding just below the surface, and they can complicate your life if you run in a mixed Windows 95/NT environment or, even worse, want to boot one system between the two.

It is quite simple to install both operating systems on one PC and dual-boot between them. However, if you are doing so, we recommend that you stick to the FAT file system because Win95's lack of support for NTFS could create a migration hassle if you try to use it. Don't use FAT for NT if you plan to run NT as an Internet server, though; it's not secure.

Part of the new requirements for Windows 95 and NT applications is that they include an uninstall procedure that cleans up the files and registry entries. There's a catch if you run multiple operating systems, though. Even when you install them on the same system, each version of Windows (NT Workstation, NT Server, 95) keeps a separate registry file. That means if you install an application with one version of Windows, it will not work when you boot into one of the other versions. You must go through the install process with each operating system so that the registry settings are correct for that environment. You can usually specify the same location for the application's program and data files. However, be aware that with most applications

FIGURE A3.3. Start Menu/Run... Dialog. Like all versions of NT since 3.5, NT 4.0 supports running 16-bit Windows applications in separate sessions. This support allows such applications to be pre-emptively multitasked and prevents them from blocking one another. Designate an application to be run in a separate session using the Separate Session check-box shown here or the /separate switch with the *start* command-line function.

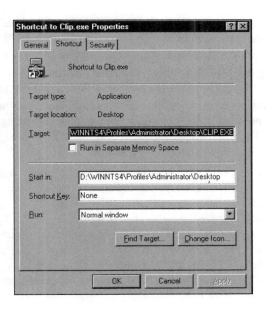

FIGURE A3.4 Shortcut properties. You can start a 16-bit program in a separate memory space by designating that option in properties for an associated shortcut icon in NT Explorer.

you'll be able to uninstall only once; you'll have to choose which operating system gets that honor. You can probably clean out the registry settings manually in the other ones, but the job is tedious.

Microsoft's Windows 95 logo program says that any Win95-logo application must also run on NT. However, there is an escape clause: Microsoft seems willing to make exceptions for utilities that it judges to be too Win95-specific to work under NT without significant changes. Thus, an undelete utility or disk formatter might be able to gain a Win95 logo but be completely unable to run on NT.

To some extent, Microsoft's inconsistent implementation of the Win32 API on the two platforms may encourage vendors to exercise that escape clause. For example, although Win32 and its NT implementation have API calls to format a floppy disk or to get hard disk geometry (sectors, tracks, cylinders, and the like), the Win32 implementation on Win95 uses a different and incompatible method based on the legacy DOS/BIOS APIs.

OS/2 1.3 Support

On x86-compatible systems, NT runs 16-bit OS/2 character-based applications out of the box. It won't run OS/2 applications that depend on Presentation Manager (even some character-based apps do), and it won't run 32-bit OS/2 applications. NT doesn't run OS/2 applications at all on non-x86 systems (see the first section in this appendix). However, Microsoft has an add-on package available that provides presentation manager support (see the next section).

When you start NT the first time, it looks at the CONFIG.SYS file on the boot disk. If it detects OS/2 commands, NT will add entries for PROTSHELL, COMSPEC, and OS2LIBPATH to the registry based on the entries in this file. These go into the NT environment along with the NT and DOS environment settings; you can examine them all using the System applet in Control Panel. Nearly all other commands in the CONFIG.SYS file are ignored by NT. (Chapter 11 of the *NT System Guide* details how they are handled.)

Most likely, you will need to deal with CONFIG.SYS changes when an OS/2 application installs itself and changes this file. To handle this situation, Microsoft created an unusual approach: an OS/2 application (it *must* be an OS/2 application) can edit the file named C:\CONFIG.SYS. In response, NT retrieves the OS/2 configuration data from the registry and puts it into a temporary text file. When the file is closed, NT parses the file and updates the registry. If you don't have an OS/2 text editor, you can't get NT to perform this magic. However, you can examine the OS/2 CONFIG.SYS by using REGEDT32 to edit the key HKEY_LOCAL_MACHINE\ SOFTWARE\Microsoft\OS/2 Subsystem for NT\1.0\config.sys (see Figure A3.5). Be aware, however, that Microsoft does not recommend changing the file in this way.

Like NT, OS/2 generally insulates applications from the hardware through device drivers. However, OS/2 has a "trap-door" that allows applications to perform I/O directly to devices,

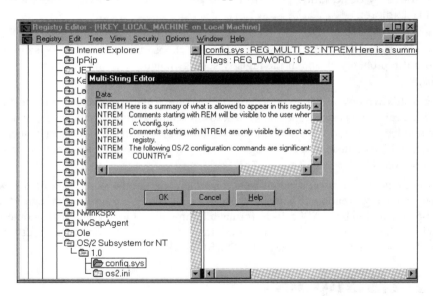

FIGURE A3.5 Registry Editor. The NT Registry includes a complete OS/2 CONFIG.SYS file, which can be edited with either an OS/2 text editor (the preferred method) or the appropriate sub-key in the Registry Editor.

called IO Privilege Level (IOPL). OS/2 applications that require IOPL will not run under NT. Although OS/2 device drivers are not supported under NT, you can map an NT device so that it appears as an OS/2 device using the DEVICENAME command in CONFIG.SYS. This approach should allow most 16-bit OS/2 application software to run correctly.

OS/2 Presentation Manager Support

Users needing a greater degree of OS/2 application support should investigate Microsoft's Presentation Manager subsystem add-on kit.[1] The kit replaces and enhances NT's OS/2 subsystem, allowing OS/2 1.2/1.3 Presentation Manager (PM) applications to execute under Windows NT. PM applications do *not* share the Windows NT desktop with other (Win32, DOS, OS/2 character mode, POSIX, Win16) applications. Instead, there is a single OS/2 full-screen desktop managed by the Presentation Manager Shell (PMSHELL.EXE) application. All PM applications share that desktop (see Figure A3.6).

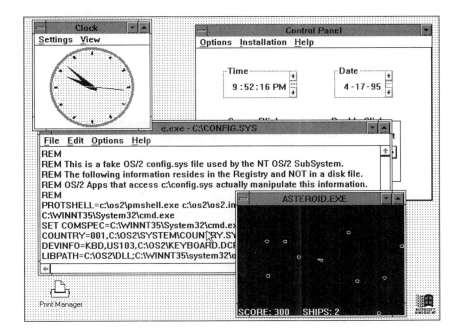

FIGURE A3.6 Presentation Manager subsystem. Microsoft's Presentation Manager add-on for NT 3.51 supports running graphical OS/2 1.2 and 1.3 applications in a separate screen group from NT applications. An upgrade of the subsystem for NT 4.0 is under development.

1   At this writing (August 1996) Microsoft has announced that the PM subsystem will be ported to NT 4.0, but has not said when it will be available. The information presented here is based on experience with versions of the PM subsystem for NT 3.5 and 3.51.

In addition to requiring a separate desktop, the PM subsystem enforces some other limitation on PM applications, including:

- All PM applications share a single event queue. Thus, if an application "hangs" it will probably hang the entire subsystem.

- Applications are not permitted to perform direct hardware access. Such access will hang the application (see Figure A3.7) and in all probability require that the PM subsystem be restarted.

- Only VGA-compatible video drivers and display resolutions are supported by default (the PM subsystem documentation includes a special procedure—launching PMSHELL.EXE with a /w command-line switch—to reconfigure the subsystem for other display resolutions).

- Printing requires an OS/2 print driver (half a dozen are supplied with the subsystem), and only the PMPRINT queue manager is supported. Printing to shared network printers is possible if the relevant print queue is redirected to a network printer from the NT command line.; that is:

```
net use LPT1: \\win1\edit_pcl
```

redirects the queue associated with LPT1: to \\win1\edit_pcl. PM-based printer-sharing applications are not supported.

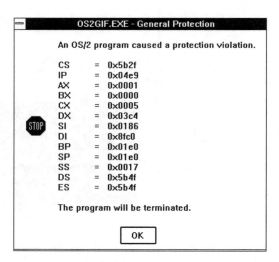

FIGURE A3.7 Protection Fault in Presentation Manager application.
Attempting to execute a PM application that directly accesses hardware may result in this dialog box. Unfortunately, this usually hangs not just the application, but the entire subsystem, requiring you to shut it down and restart it.

- Interprocess communication between PM applications is supported using all the methods supported by OS/2, including shared memory. Communication between PM applications and Windows (16- and 32-bit) applications, however, is limited to the clipboard (text and bitmap formats only), named pipes, mailslots, and NetBIOS. DDE between PM applications and other applications is not currently supported.

- PM applications do not recognize many of the standard NT control panel settings, including those for screen appearance, mouse settings, and communication ports. These must be set from the PM Control Panel included with the subsystem. Time and date settings are global and may be made from either the PM or NT control panel. Other NT control panel settings are unlikely to be recognized by the PM subsystem (see Figure A3.7).

Note that these restrictions are *in addition* to those imposed by the normal, character-mode OS/2 support provided in Windows NT. (OS/2 applications are supported only on Intel processors. Ring-2 IOPL code is executed at ring-3, and interrupt suspend/resume applies only to the OS/2 subsystem, *not* to the entire system.) The subsystem is also provided without the OS/2 file manager, desktop manager, and command prompt. Instead, PM applications have been launched from a PM group in Windows NT Program Manager (presumably in NT 4.0 and later systems, this will become a Start menu folder). The PM subsystem maps OS/2 groups to Presentation Manager groups, but does not support drag-and-drop between PM applications and the NT desktop.

On the whole, the level of integration provided by the PM subsystem is quite a bit less sophisticated than that provided for other types (Win16, OS/2 character mode, or POSIX) of legacy application in NT. However, the subsystem *does* work, and that may be all that matters if you depend on a particular PM-based application. A few final notes about the PM subsystem:

- You may need to reinstall it after updating NT with a service pack.

- You will probably need a new version if you upgrade from one version of NT to another (release of PM subsystem updates has lagged new NT versions by a few months).

- Non-U.S. users should check with Microsoft before purchasing the subsystem for use with a national-language version of NT (at this writing[2] only English and French system messages are supported, though it's possible to support several foreign keyboard layouts using a procedure in the PM subsystem documentation).

Finally, a note about installation: the PM subsystem is installed through use of a batch file (INSTALL.CMD) that creates an OS/2 directory in the root of drive C: and copies files into it. This method can have highly undesirable side effects if executed on a system that's been set up to dual-boot between OS/2 and NT—it may render the OS/2 installation unusable. Back up any such OS/2 files first before installing the PM subsystem. Another point of note: PM applications (including the subsystem itself) are best closed from within the subsystem. Although it's possible to shut down applications from the NT desktop, the procedure is time consuming and (at this

---

2   Originally written for the second edition, April 1995.

writing) somewhat unreliable. The best way to close down the subsystem is to invoke the PM task manager (by clicking the right mouse button from within the PM desktop) and select the Shutdown PM button.

POSIX Support

Windows NT has already begun to make inroads into areas where the UNIX operating system is currently used. To increase the attractiveness of Windows NT to the UNIX community, Microsoft has added a large degree of UNIX compatibility to the operating system. Another impetus for Microsoft is that the U.S. government favors the use of UNIX-compatible systems in many projects. Windows NT could not compete for many government projects without UNIX compatibility.

For an example of the encroachment of NT into UNIX territory, you don't need to look any further than the NT Resource Kit. On the CD that comes with the kit, there's a set of the basic UNIX utilities such as grep (see Appendix 4 for further details). Third-party providers such as MKS Systems and Hamilton Labs offer even larger sets of UNIX-compatible utilities.

There are actually many different versions of UNIX in addition to operating systems that are UNIX-like but not licensed to use the UNIX name. In the mid-1980s the Institute for Electrical and Electronics Engineers (IEEE) sponsored a committee to define the UNIX environment in a vendor-neutral way that would promote standardization. By 1990, that work progressed into International Standards Organization (ISO) standard IS-9945, but commonly called POSIX. A family of POSIX standards defines the system API, graphical interface, command shell language, tools (like grep and awk), security, and networking. However, most of these are still being defined. One of the few parts of POSIX that is fully standardized is POSIX.1, the C-language API to system services. This is the part of POSIX that Windows NT currently addresses.

The POSIX support in Windows NT is different from other legacy application support because it is not at the binary (EXE-file) level, but at the source-code level. Source code must be recompiled on Windows NT using the POSIX compatibility libraries. For an end user with shrink-wrapped applications this is not feasible, but it's standard procedure for the UNIX developers that Microsoft is targeting with POSIX compatibility.

UNIX developers are also familiar with another tradeoff created by POSIX: portability versus functionality. The POSIX.1 API standard is bare bones, mostly providing access to the file system and the ability to start and communicate with other processes. There is simple tty-style I/O, but nothing like the event-driven graphical interface that is the basis of both Windows 3.*x* and Windows NT. (UNIX systems often provide a graphical user interface called X Windows, but this is outside the scope of POSIX.1 and covered instead by the unfinished POSIX.2 standard.)

Generally, the POSIX libraries are just thin wrapper functions that translate POSIX API calls into their Windows NT equivalents. The operating systems use models that are similar enough that there are not major problems in most translating operations. Because POSIX applications are compiled with a Windows NT 32-bit compiler, their performance can be quite good compared with that of 16-bit DOS or Windows 3.*x* applications.

POSIX applications generally expect a file system that behaves like a UNIX file system. NTFS has some features designed specifically for maximum compatibility with POSIX. For example, NTFS is normally case preserving when one is creating files, but not case sensitive when one is opening files. Thus, you can save a file to an NTFS partition as "DaveM.DOC" but open it later using the string "davem.doc." However, when using the POSIX subsystem you must specify the capitalization exactly, because a POSIX application expects the file system to be both case sensitive and case preserving. Using POSIX you can, in fact, create a file named "DAVEM" and a different one called "DaveM" in the same directory.

You can start POSIX applications as any other application, either by typing the application name from a command line or through Windows Explorer.

Conclusion

As the third edition of this book went to press, Softway Systems[3] had announced an initiative to deliver an add-on (called OpenNT) that will deliver full POSIX.2 support for Windows NT. OpenNT is intended to replace or enhance NT's built-in subsystem—and Softway intends to provide a variety of enhancements to it, including full X/Windows libraries.

For More Information

Microsoft Staff (1996), *Windows NT Server 4.0 Concepts and Planning.* Redmond, WA: Microsoft Corp. Chapter 14 (Concepts and Planning) gives details on NT's built-in Win16, OS/2 character-mode, and POSIX support.

Microsoft Staff (1994), *Microsoft Windows NT Add-on Subsystem Release for Presentation Manager (PM).* Redmond, WA: Microsoft Corp. The combined documentation (overview and release notes) for the PM subsystem amounts to just 26 pages. It's available *only* when you purchase the subsystem.

---

[3] Browse Softway's Web site at http://www.softway.com or call (415) 896-0708 for more information.

The Windows NT Resource Kit

4

Throughout the chapters in this book, we've referred to utility software, documentation, and tools that Microsoft packages in the Windows NT Resource Kit. The kit was first made available a few months after the release of NT 3.1 and has since been updated for NT 3.5 (in its second edition) and NT 3.51 (third edition). As we write,[1] the NT 4.0 editions—there are two this time, as we shall see—are due out in just a few months. We expect that future editions will appear more or less annually.

The kit is so extensive that we cannot hope to cover it in detail here. Instead, we present a brief overview of its contents, with some notes on items we find particularly interesting.

---

[1] September 1996.

In brief, the NT resource kit is a positive gold mine of tricks, tips, and utility software. The most recent (NT 3.51) edition included a five-volume set of books (*Windows NT Resource Guide*, *Windows NT Networking Guide*, *Optimizing Windows NT*, *Windows NT Messages*, and *Version 3.51 Update*), one CD, and several diskettes, at an "estimated retail price" (Microsoft no longer quotes list prices) under $150. For NT 4.0, there will apparently be two separate versions of the resource kit: one for NT Workstation (probably at the above price or a bit less) and a more extensive version for NT Server (probably at a somewhat higher cost).

In our opinion, the programs and other information on the CD alone are easily worth the $150 price of past kits. They include Helpfiles that completely document all variables set using the configuration registry editor (REGENTRY.HLP), give technical specifications (including settings and a visual diagram) of all NT-compatible network cards (NTCARD*xx*.HLP), list all Windows NT-compatible hardware (HCL*mmmyy*.HLP), and document the tools on the CD (RKTOOLS.HLP). Tools available in past versions of the kit have included a graphical interface for the AT command-line function that lists all scheduled batch jobs (WINAT.EXE), a graphical monitor for domain servers (DOMMON.EXE), and a graphical monitor of domain browser activity (BROWMON.EXE) along with the Server Manager for Domains, User Manager for Domains, and User Profile Editor tools from Windows NT Advanced Server. All these were in addition to administrative tools for use with Services for Macintosh in Advanced Server environments.

The resource kit also includes a reasonably complete suite of POSIX 1.0-compatible command-line utilities including ar, cat, cc, chmod, chown, cp, devsrv, find, grep, ld, ln, ls, make, mkdir, mv, rm, rmdir, sh, touch, vi, and wc, although we cannot recommend them because of the POSIX subsystem's many limitations. (We suggest that users with a need for UNIX-style utilities investigate the *Hamilton C-Shell* and *MKS Utilities* packages discussed in Chapter 3, Table 3.3 and that users serious about the POSIX subsystem investigate Softway Systems' OpenNT tools, discussed in Appendix 3.)

End-user-oriented utilities have included an editor for creating your animated cursors (ANIEDIT.EXE), a multiple "virtual" desktop tool (TOPDESK.EXE), a graphical UNIX Uuencode/decode tool (NTUUCODE.EXE), and a Windows-based interface to the CompuServe Information Service (WINCIM.EXE), among others.

Network and administrative tools include a mechanism for getting user input in batch files (CHOICE.EXE), a tool for dumping the event logs as a text file (DUMPEL.EXE), a tool for disabling floppy disks in high-security environments (FLOPLOCK.EXE), a Simple Network Management Protocol (SNMP) Management Information Block (MIB) compiler, crude tools for operating a network-based modem pool (WINVTP.EXE), a command-line interface to services (NETSVC.EXE), a per-user file permissions command-line utility (PERMS.EXE), and a secure (relatively speaking) remote command-line for Windows NT in the second edition, available as both a command-line program (REMOTE.EXE) and an NT "service" background application (RCMD.EXE).

In the first edition of *Networking Windows NT*, we speculated that it should be possible to write a "universal" service application that would allow any compatible program to be treated as a network service (started and stopped remotely, etc.). Evidently Microsoft was listening or had the same idea; in the resource kit's second edition, SRVANY.EXE appeared. It does exactly what we'd suggested, and provides a simple but powerful way for administrators to convert batch jobs, DOS (or OS/2) executables, and even Windows (16- or 32-bit) applications into manageable network services.

Other tools in earlier kits included Microsoft's Computer Profile Setup (CPS), which was theoretically useful when a standard Windows NT configuration was installed throughout an organization—though we've never used it or encountered anyone who did. The new kit for NT Workstation will apparently replace CPS with a new *Windows NT Deployment Guide* and tools (in particular, SYSDIFF.EXE, as described in Chapter 2). The guide and tools are also provided on the NT Server distribution CD.

Beginning with the resource kit's second edition, Microsoft added a complete set of Internet services (many developed at EMWAC, the European Microsoft Windows Academic Centre, operated by Edinburgh University) including World Wide Web (WWW), WAIS, gopher, and DNS Services. These services are redundant with those provided by the Internet Information Server/Peer Web Server components in NT 4.0 Server/Workstation, and we expect them to disappear from the NT 4.0 edition.

Other tools in the kit include a command-line utility to create new user accounts, Dynamic Host Configuration Protocol (DHCP) management tools, tools to compact and manage the "Jet" database used by (among other things) the message database, and a screen saver for use in secure environments that logs the current user off automatically after a fixed period of inactivity.

The resource kit also includes the invaluable NT Messages database (which could also be found in the SUPTOOLS\WINNTMSG directory of the NT 3.*x* distribution CD, but has been dropped from the NT 4.0 CD). By installing the database on a server and then sharing the database directories, you can enable remote users to access the database, and this is by far the most convenient way to get access to the Windows NT system messages. (See Figure A4.1.)

With NT 3.51, Microsoft expanded the tools available in the kit, adding a POP3 Mail Server (suitable for use on the Internet), Telnet Server, PCMCIA Support, the NT 3.51 Shell Technology Preview (which provided an NT 4.0 look and feel), and NT 3.51 Service Pack #1 on the CD. Utilities, which were provided *only* on CD in the 3.51 resource kit (the four diskettes in previous versions were eliminated), included many new items. Most significant were both Perl 5 and REXX scripting languages (filling a major hole in past kits). Other utilities included the following:

- A GUI-based automatic login setting tool (which eliminated a tedious registry hack)

- Security Configuration Manager (to verify C2 compliance)

- A command-line tool for posting text to the clipboard

- An event log report generator

- A batchfile tool to write entries in the NT event logs

FIGURE A4.1 NT Resource Kit. Microsoft had not yet updated the Resource Kit for NT 4.0 by the time we went to press, but practically all the NT 3.51 Resource Kit utilities work under 4.0, and new kits for NT 4.0 Server and Workstation should be available by the time you read this.

- A new datalog service

- A Page Fault monitor

- A Profile control panel object that allows one (administrative) user to manage multi-system logons throughout an NT network

- A tool to enumerate remote users from the command line

- Console-mode remote file copy

- A UNIX RSH Server (which lets any RSH client execute commands on an NT server—a potential security risk)

- SETUPMGR.EXE, which creates answer (batch) files for unattended setup on NT workstations

- SHUTCMD.EXE, and SHUTGUI.EXE, which allow remote shutdown of NT systems

- SNMP monitor and browser, SOON.EXE (a *time-relative* version of the AT command)

- Many new troubleshooting tools including a TDI tracer, command-line (and batch) tools for managing WINS databases, and so forth

Some of the NT 3.51 resource kit tools are obsolete in NT 4.0. For example, *inet.exe* works exactly like net.exe, but with DNS names (i.e., inet view \\ftp.microsoft.com will show the volumes on microsoft.com and inet use x: \\ftp.microsoft.com\data gives you direct access to the ftp server as though it were a normal network drive). That capability is built into NT 4.0's redirector. Likewise, the PCMCIA control panel is now provided with NT 4.0, so including it in the 4.0 version of the resource kit would be redundant. And because NT 4.0 has no Program Manager, it has no use for PUTINGRP.EXE, which was used to create program group icons.

Aside from documenting custom installation options, including SYSDIFF.EXE, we know that the NT 4.0 Server Resource Kit will include a Web-based Administration Tool for NT Server, as described in Chapter 8. Undoubtedly there will be other new tools as well.

The Resource Kit Books

The five books included in the resource kit are essential for NT administrators and highly recommended for advanced end users. The *Resource Guide* contains up-to-date information on NT setup, printing, configuration (registry) management, and migrating Windows, OS/2, and POSIX applications to NT. *Windows NT Messages* documents all error and warning messages generated by Windows NT and its subsystems. *Optimizing Windows NT* provides vital information on Performance Monitor objects, disk cache tuning, and high-performance graphics programming, and it documents the NT registry. (It's also the best written of the books. Where else can you find an author suggesting,"There are many ways to make a computer go faster—such as dropping it from a fourth-floor window."?)

Windows NT Networking Guide, which first appeared in the resource kit's second edition, collects supporting information formerly found in various supplemental NT documents, adding some details not available elsewhere. Among other things, it covers the following:

- NT's PPP-based RAS architecture with extensive information on writing and debugging RAS scripts

- How to write logon scripts, including use of environment variables and considerations for the various client operating systems Windows NT supports

- Implementation details of NT's NetBIOS Frame (NBF) core network protocol and other supported protocols, including TCP/IP, Data Link Control (DLC), NetWare-compatible IPX/SPX, IBM host-compatible System Network Architecture (SNA); and the net-library and DB-Library protocols used by NT databases

Support professionals will find information on NT's NetLogon service—including user authentication and domain discovery for both local and networked systems—and a much-needed chapter on NT's network browser invaluable for solving problems when NT, WFWG, and DOS/LAN Manager users cannot "see" each other on an otherwise functional LAN.

The *Networking Guide*'s Chapters 10 through 22 provide some 270 pages of detail on NT's TCP/IP implementation, beginning with an overview and ending with NT on the Internet. This information is essential for anyone attempting to implement an NT-based Internet server. It completely documents NT's TCP/IP implementation, the way it relates to standard IP models, the way it's used with NBF, and the Internet-related services discussed earlier.

Coverage includes exotic topics: WINS hub replication frequency in multinational WANs, DNS-to-WINS name translation, setup and maintenance of NT's LMHOSTS name resolution file, hidden registry settings for the FTP service, TCP/IP-related performance monitor counters, use of NT as an IP router, and the setup for an Internet "firewall" to minimize security risks.

Version 3.51 Update coverage includes information on then-new *concurrent connection* licensing, ways to certify an NT system as C2 Secure (complemented by a C2 security planning and evaluation tool), a new SNMP MIB builder tool, substantial troubleshooting information (including sections on making tape backups run faster, notes on particular tape drives, viruses, and ESDI hard disks with more than 1024 cylinders). We anticipate that a forthcoming *Version 4.0 Update* will include comparable information on NT 4.0.

The resource kit does have some weaknesses, including limited information on Internet security and third-party routers, poor e-mail coverage (Chapters 8 and 9 of Volume 1 cover the workgroup post office included with NT, but don't discuss upgrades), and limited troubleshooting information.

Conclusion

It's impossible to overestimate the value of the NT Resource Kit. It is a tremendously valuable set of tools and documentation and is by far the least expensive investment that an NT site can make in support (it costs about as much as one support call to Microsoft). Even without seeing the 4.0 edition as this is written, we are confident enough to give it, once again, our highest recommendation.

System Design and NT Performance

The portable architecture of Windows NT discussed in Chapter 1 makes it possible to use a variety of different types of computer with this advanced operating system. Selecting the right type of computer for a particular Windows NT application is a matter of cost versus performance and could dramatically affect the cost-effectiveness of a Windows NT installation. Alternatives supported by the current release of Windows NT—over and above standard single-processor PC-compatible systems—include Symmetric Multiprocessor (SMP) and Reduced Instruction Set Computer (RISC) systems.

Why Not a Conventional PC System?

Before we examine the more exotic alternatives, it's worth considering just what might drive you to a decision to purchase a more exotic design. After all, the conventional PC architecture systems are well understood, technically mature, and—let's not ignore the most important feature—*cheap*.

The basic reason to consider an unconventional architecture is absolute performance. In a conventional PC-compatible system performance is limited because only a single central processing unit (CPU) can be used in each machine, and the performance of that CPU is limited to the highest performance of the highest-performing available Intel microprocessor (currently the 200MHz Pentium Pro). In order to understand why you might wish to consider moving to an unconventional architecture, we need to consider the performance limitations of the Intel chips.

Integer Performance

The most commonly used measure of a CPU's performance is the figure of Millions of Instructions Per Second (MIPS). This is a direct measure of the computational performance of any microprocessor chip. It refers to the number of individual instructions or steps that can be executed in a single second. Such steps might include fetching a data word from memory, performing an addition or subtraction, or comparing one data word to another. Computer programs are nothing more than a collection of such steps, so any given program will execute twice as fast on a machine that performs at twice as many MIPS. Intel microprocessors capable of running Windows NT span a considerable range of MIPS in their current configurations. The minimum system for running Windows NT currently is a 25MHz Intel 486 processor capable of somewhere in the vicinity of 15 MIPS. The highest-performance processor currently available is a 200MHz Pentium Pro, which employs instruction reordering and parallel execution to achieve over 400 MIPS.

A particular characteristic of the Intel architectural design that effects its integer performance is that Intel processors have, up to now, been designed according to a Complex Instruction Set Computer (CISC) architecture rather than a RISC design. In a CISC microprocessor the instruction set is very rich, and single instructions can carry out quite complex tasks. For instance, it's possible to copy an entire character string from one location to another in an Intel system with a single instruction. However, the availability of such a rich set of instructions has traditionally enforced some limitations on the design so that individual instructions may take many clock cycles to execute. This was particularly apparent in the 386 design with which it quite commonly took two to four clock cycles to execute an instruction. Intel's 486, Pentium, and Pentium Pro processors, by comparison, are nearly RISC-like in their performance.

All RISC designs can achieve throughputs as high as the clock rate, and some can use multiple instruction units and instruction reordering to achieve superscalar results, just as the Pentium and Pentium Pro can. A 333MHz Digital Alpha 21164 processor, for instance, by definition, will achieve *at least* 333 MIPS; with instruction reordering it actually can approach 500 MIPS.

Floating Point Performance

There is a second important figure of merit for CPU performance: Millions of Floating Point Operations Per Second (MFLOPS). Like the MIPS figure, MFLOPS refers to the number of simple floating point instructions (such as fetching a floating point operand into memory, performing a floating point multiplication or division, and comparing two floating point operands) that can be performed per second. The significance of this figure by comparison with the MIPS figure of merit is that for certain operations, especially in technical applications, the floating point figure becomes overwhelmingly important. This is also significant because a major weakness of Intel microprocessors prior to the Pentium chip was substantially lower floating point performance than integer performance. For example, a 100MHz Intel 486DX4 processor could achieve somewhere in the vicinity of 80 to 90 MIPS throughput while executing 32-bit code such as Windows NT. It was capable, however, of fewer than 40 MFLOPS because of the limitations of its floating point unit design.

RISC processors have historically been designed with significantly more efficient, better optimized floating point units that can achieve floating point execution speeds approaching (in some cases, exceeding) those of their integer execution speeds. For applications that are floating point intensive, such as Computer Aided Design/Computer Aided Engineering (CAD/CAE), scientific applications, and the like, this speed could be a significant advantage.

Figure A5.1 illustrates both integer and floating point performance for high-end NT-compatible CPUs that are currently available in shipping systems, based on manufacturer's data[1] for performance on the current state-of-the art SPEC95[2] benchmark. The SPEC95 benchmarks use arbitrary performance indices, rather than MIPS and MFLOPS. By way of comparison, an AST Bravo MST6200 system (based on Intel's 200MHz Pentium Pro) achieved 416 MIPS and 111 MFLOPS on a recent *WINDOWS Magazine* test.

As you can see, Intel's Pentium Pro, at 200MHz equals or betters the performance of Motorola and Mips RISC processors. Digital's Alpha, however, retains a significant advantage in floating point performance, though there are other factors to take into account before buying a RISC-based system, as we will discuss later in this appendix.

With an understanding of these figures of merit, we can now take a look at the alternatives available for Windows NT.

---

[1]   Taken directly from the vendors' Web sites:

http://www.intel.com

http://www.mips.com

http://www.digital.com

http://www.motorola.com

[2]   A product of the Standard Performance Evaluation Corporation, which maintains a database of SPECint and SPECfp results. For more information see the SPEC Web page at http://open.specbench.org.

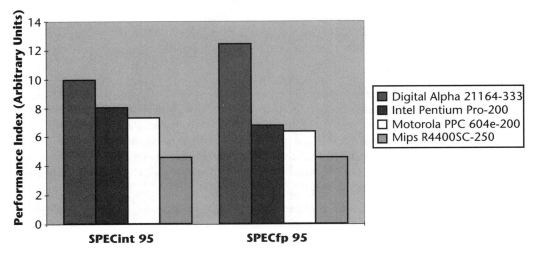

FIGURE A5.1 Performance comparison of CPU architectures. Current SPECint and SPECfp benchmark results claimed by manufacturers for their fastest NT-compatible processors.

The First Alternative: Classic Intel PC-Compatible Single-Processor Systems

Let's begin by looking at what is possible with the conventional architecture. Currently available Intel CPUs span performance ranges to over 400 MIPS and 100 MFLOPS in the 200MHz Intel Pentium Pro. This performance compares very favorably with that for individual RISC processors and competes quite effectively with the lower end of the symmetric multiprocessor machines.

Single-processor PC compatibles have a number of significant advantages as Windows NT platforms. The first of these of course is *price*. The Intel PC-compatible market is very much a commodity market—many manufacturers and assemblers provide machines in any given performance class. This competition tends to drive the price down. For example, the AST Pentium Pro/200 system mentioned earlier costs under $4,000 fully configured (and there are competing systems that cost less), while competing systems using RISC processors can and do cost thousands of dollars more.

There is also a tremendous infrastructure of peripheral devices, service, and support available for these machines, and don't overlook the fact that these are the *only* machines that will run *both* Windows NT *and* other operating systems like DOS, OS/2, or NetWare. An investment in such a machine, therefore, is safe. If Windows NT for any reason fails to live up to your expectations, you can replace it with another operating system.

Symmetric Multi-Processing

No feature of Windows NT has received more attention than Symmetric Multi-Processing (SMP). Press reports treat this, for all intents and purposes, like science fiction, referring to machines that can deliver mainframe-class performance. And indeed, the raw specifications can be quite impressive. More than two years ago, Sequent Computer Systems demonstrated Windows NT on a 30-processor SMP machine theoretically capable of somewhere in the vicinity of 1500 MIPS, which is still well beyond the performance of any single CPU system today. Yet, one should beware when reading mind-boggling benchmark numbers for SMP systems. Raw integer performance does not provide an adequate guide to overall system capabilities.

The Problem of Contention

The basic idea of a symmetric multiprocessing system is quite simple. A number of identical CPUs share the computer's memory and data busses. Each executes a copy of Windows NT's microkernel, and each can execute either kernel or application code at any given time. Under ideal conditions, this should provide N times the performance of a single processor (where N is the number of processors). Unfortunately, this *linear scaling* assumption breaks down whenever any two or more processes *contend* for a single resource.

Contention can occur when any two or more processors attempt to access a shared resource. A shared resource can be an I/O device such as the video display or a network card, or it can be a memory location in the system or a component of the operating system. For instance, although Windows NT can execute multiple copies of its microkernel, certain shared resources will be contended for by each copy. The most critical of these is the task-switching database that determines when each task in the system may be scheduled for execution. It should be obvious that only a single copy of that database can be maintained, so each processor will at various times have to access that database. When any one processor is accessing it, the other processors cannot. In the event that they attempt to, they will have to *spin lock* waiting on that database until the other processor or processors release it.

Designing an SMP architecture to minimize contention is something of an art form. It demands careful attention to the memory architecture of the system. Consider a four-way Pentium Pro SMP. Such a system is theoretically capable of four times the performance of a single Pentium Pro or on the order of 1600 MIPS.[3] Because all four processors can attempt to access memory simultaneously, to achieve full throughput it would be necessary for this system to have a memory architecture capable of supporting up to 1600 million memory fetches per second. Don't hold your breath!

This problem can be mitigated to some extent if large secondary cache memory is provided for each central processor. In most existing SMP designs it's typical to see each processor

---

3   Note the irony that a four-processor Pentium Pro system is now theoretically capable of outperforming the 30-processor Sequent demonstration system mentioned earlier. In just two years, the price of such power has fallen from millions of dollars to tens of thousands, and all indications are that over the next few years it will fall farther still!

buffered with 256KB of Level-2 cache—indeed, such a cache is built into the Pentium Pro.[4] Such a design is based on the assumption that most memory fetches can be satisfied by the cache. Contention then occurs only on a cache miss.

Unfortunately, that assumption doesn't always hold. No matter how much cache is provided for each individual CPU, at some point data must be written to main memory and from there, to disk or a network (for example, when a database query is *committed* to disk). At that point, contention appears. For example, during test procedures at *WINDOWS Magazine* in May of 1993, we experimented with an early two-processor machine based on the Intel Pentium CPU, and we saw very impressive performance from it. However, in an effort to determine the real-world performance of this system, we experimented with running multiple graphical applications simultaneously on it and got something of a shock. As additional graphical applications were added, we found that with both processors operating, beyond a certain number of instances of graphics applications running, the system would actually run more slowly with two processors than with one.

The reason for the slowdown turned out to be contention for the display as a shared resource. Consider two applications attempting to access the screen at the same time. Each issues operating system calls to its own copy of the Windows NT microkernel. One copy of the Windows NT microkernel then accesses the screen. The other spin locks waiting on the screen. The data rate is now limited to the performance of the video subsystem, and a multiprocessor actually pays a penalty in additional overhead (all those spin locks!) waiting on the video board (in this case, a slow Super-VGA display).

It's highly unlikely that this particular kind of situation will occur in practice. Systems designed for graphics-intensive use should have highly optimized graphic display subsystems that are unlikely to be fully loaded by their processors. But the point still holds: SMP is not a panacea.

SMP does produce very fast results on computationally intensive tasks where the maximum advantage can be taken of multiple simultaneous computations exploiting local cache memory. However, if a large percentage of the work requires fetching data from outside the processor caches or contends for external I/O, system performance can be expected to slow down dramatically.

Moreover, deriving maximum benefit from an SMP depends on having applications that are designed to exploit it. Consider the example illustrated in Figure A5.2.

In this case, a large software company was porting a popular client/server application to NT from another operating system. The other system supported threads (the basic programming construct used in SMP programming), but not SMP hardware. A first, direct port yielded an application that ran—slowly—on single-CPU NT systems, but crashed on SMP hardware (insufficient attention had been paid to shared resource synchronization issues). When those problems were addressed, the lower curve on Figure A5.2 resulted, which did not scale as additional users (and thus, additional threads) accessed the service.

---

4   In the earlier editions, we said, "We expect to see even larger caches become the norm in future systems." They have!

SMP Client-Server Application Performance
(All tests on 6xP5-90)

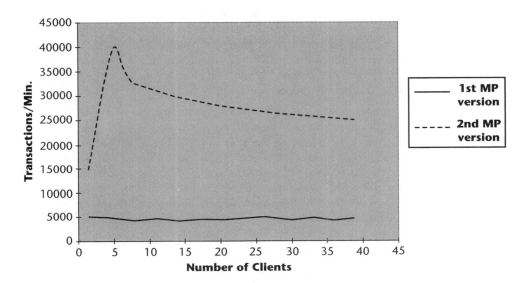

FIGURE A5.2 Multiprocessor contention. The benefit gained from a multi-processor system is *highly* dependent on the application's design. This chart illustrates the effect of internal changes to an early NT port of a popular network messaging server. The first version, bottlenecked on a shared resource, did not scale with additional users, regardless of the number of CPUs available. The second version did scale, but in a highly nonlinear manner as a direct result of using one thread per client. An ideal design would use a thread pool containing only as many threads as there are processors (in this case six). Theoretically, such a design would scale nearly linearly up to six clients and remain flat thereafter.

At this point, the programmers took a hard look at the design and discovered that they had a major contention problem. When they relieved that problem (by redesigning the service's I/O interface) the upper curve in figure A5.2 resulted.

Additional SMP Issues

The assumption that you will achieve four times the performance of any given application with a four-processor SMP machine is clearly naive. You *may* achieve four times the performance (more likely a bit less) *if* the application has been fully optimized for SMP use. The moral of this story: check out your applications thoroughly before buying an SMP to run them on!

Finally, consider cost. Which is more expensive: a single CPU RISC-based machine operating at 1500 MIPS or a three-processor Intel machine with three 500 MIPS processors? Thinking about this naively, one would assume that the three-processor Intel-based machine will give some advantage because, after all, one can indeed have three tasks executing at the same time. This logic is incorrect.

Regardless of a system's architecture, it has an upper limit, which is the total number of MIPS it can execute. If you have three 500 MIPS processors, the most computational work you can ever get done is 1500 MIPS. That identical figure can be achieved by a single-processor machine operating at 1500 MIPS. But the single-processor machine needs to have only a single cache. It will not require the additional system board complexity of a multiprocessor memory controller. It will almost certainly be cheaper. It will also be more reliable because, in general, the reliability of a system is inversely proportional to its parts count.

Therefore, use of an SMP system should never even be considered unless all possible single-CPU alternatives have been exhausted. There can be one exception to this rule. Some of the SMP designs offered for Windows NT are *scalable*. That is, you may purchase them with a single processor and then add more processors as your needs grow. This can be a very attractive approach, especially if you are uncertain of your ultimate needs, but expect them to grow over time. In such a case, a scalable SMP may be worth considering. However, you should carry out a cost analysis because you may find that the cost of upgrading your SMP system to add more processors exceeds the cost of replacing a single-processor system with a more powerful single-processor system when the time comes. If the cost is higher, there is no reason to use the SMP.

You should also very carefully examine the contention issue discussed earlier. Is the system supplied with enough network bandwidth to support the kind of loads you will see as you add multiple processor cards? There's no sense providing a system with an additional processor card when that processor will spend most of its time waiting for access to the network! In a desktop application, is the application principally bound by graphic speed? If a graphic card is in use in a system that is capable of only 100 million graphical operations per second, adding processors to push performance above 100 MIPS may not produce a significant performance improvement in graphic-intensive applications.

Another example (discussed in the November 1995 issue of WINDOWS Magazine[5]) is the following: While testing client/server database performance on single- and dual-CPU systems, we found *no* scaling initially. Investigation showed a bottleneck in disk performance that could be (and was) relieved when the database was distributed over two disk platters, at which point we found another bottleneck. The LAN in use (standard 10-base-T Ethernet, with a bandwidth of 10MB/sec) was 90% saturated with just one CPU in use. Adding a second CPU, therefore, resulted in only a 10% performance gain; to do better, we'd have had to change our wiring.

Evaluate these facts very carefully. For large-scale client/server use, particularly for mainframe replacement in downsizing applications, SMP may very well offer the best alternative, but be sure you understand the issues before you buy![6]

---

[5] "Hammering Out a Multiprocessor Strategy," p. 269.

[6] Many people are buying SMP who should not. We've seen performance monitor logs (see Chapter 5 for procedures to generate them yourself) from dual-processor Pentium-based servers used for departmental file-and-print sharing and Internet Web services. *Neither showed more than 10% CPU utilization on a steady-state basis*; both were clearly gross overkill for their current application.

Alternative Three: RISC

It's an odd coincidence that the acronym for Reduced Instruction Set Computing should sound "risky" to so many people. But RISC solutions do represent a risky alternative. The promise of the RISC approach is significantly higher performance from a given set of components. Traditionally, the absolute performance of Intel CPUs has been low. Processors in the 486 series offered about half the integer performance (measured in MIPS) as the clock rate (measured in MHz). You could expect about 50 MIPS from a 100MHz 486. Floating point performance of these processors tended to be even less—on the order of one-quarter the clock rate. This low performance could be compensated to a certain extent by *clock doubling,* in which the CPU runs internally at twice the external clock rate. For instance, in Intel's 486DX2-66 CPU, a 33MHz external clock was doubled internally to 66MHz. Because the 486 on the average requires two clock cycles to completely process an instruction,[7] the 66MHz internal clock is well matched to an effective throughput of 33 MIPS.

The problem with this approach is that access to external devices and memory has to be mediated at the external clock rate of 33MHz. Thus the chip cannot be serviced at any more than a 33 million memory fetch per-second rate. Because the chip generally accomplishes 33 million instructions per second, this tends to work out reasonably well, and the 486's 8KB on-chip cache provides sufficient buffer capacity to make up the difference. But it can become a problem at higher rates, as users of the 486DX4-100 (actually a clock-tripled 33MHz processor) are well aware.

As discussed earlier, RISC processors, by limiting the number of instructions and optimizing these instructions for speed, attempt to achieve an overall throughput of *at least one instruction per clock.* Thus a 500MHz RISC processor should, theoretically, achieve 500+ MIPS. The processors attempt to do the same thing for floating point instructions, although they are generally less successful with this. But the overall result has historically been about twice the performance available from an equivalent x86 chip at a given clock rate. That is, at a given clock rate in MHz, you could expect to see twice the performance from a RISC processor as from an otherwise equivalent 486. Because the cost of a computer tends to be governed by the number of components and the clock rate, particularly the clock rate at which memory is accessed, a computer that can accomplish twice as much as a given clock rate has an obvious advantage.

All things being equal, the world should long since have converted from Intel processors to one of the various RISC processors. Of course, this has not happened, and the reasons it hasn't have a lot to do with the "risky" nature of the alternatives.

No Single Standard

Although Intel is not viewed with love by vendors in the computer industry, the fact that a single company has dominated the PC microprocessor market for the last 10 years has a

---

7   Some individual instructions on the 486 can be executed in just one clock. Other instructions may take much longer. On the average, taking into account the limits of the 486 8KB on-chip primary cache, we believe two instructions per clock is approximately correct.

number of notable advantages. It's now possible to order a computer from hundreds of vendors—even by mail—and be reasonably certain it will execute the hundreds of PC-compatible applications on the market without being seriously concerned about the possibility that some applications will prove to be incompatible. The reason for this is that all these computers use the Intel family of microprocessors (or clones) and are thus inherently compatible.

No such compatibility exists in the RISC market. Indeed, Intel itself has made several different varieties of RISC chips, the *i*860 chip among them.[8] Other major players in the RISC business have at various times included Sun Microsystems, Data General Corporation, IBM, Hewlett-Packard, Fairchild, and virtually every maker of silicon in the United States (among other places).

This situation has produced what might be called a RISC anarchy. There are *dozens* of different RISC processors available today, all more or less incompatible and each running its own operating system. The operating systems have this in common: they are almost all *called* UNIX. The resemblance begins and ends right there. Microsoft, of course, hopes to change this. As we noted in Chapter 1, Windows NT was designed to be portable. Providing Windows NT for a new architecture requires only that the portable C-based NT source code be recompiled for that architecture and that a new Hardware Abstraction Layer be written for the architecture. However, it's worth noting that when one moves to RISC, one leaves behind all that vast legacy of compatibility. You cannot expect to run DOS, OS/2, SCO UNIX, or any other Intel-based operating system on a RISC machine. When you buy into RISC, you effectively lock yourself into Windows NT.

The 16-Bit Legacy Application Issue

Windows NT endeavors to overcome the problem of RISC anarchy in a second way. Beyond the portability of Windows NT itself to the new architecture, a high degree of legacy application support is provided for DOS and Windows applications.[9] Windows NT accomplishes this by providing a special version of Insignia Systems' *SoftPC* emulator optimized for each version of Windows NT. On RISC processors, Soft PC provides a software environment that appears to legacy programs as though it were in fact a PC.[10] The effectiveness of SoftPC is generally quite good. In the past, we routinely ran 16-bit versions of Visual Basic, Word for Windows, Microsoft Project, Microsoft Excel, and various other applications on a MIPS R4000 machine. All, for the most part, performed on the MIPS machine as happily as if they were running on the 486 machine on the other side of the office.

---

8   This was, in fact, the first CPU upon which NT was implemented.

9   Of course, NT also provides source-level support for POSIX 1.0 applications and OS/2 1.3 support. The former requires that applications be recompiled for a particular processor and thus avoids the aforementioned emulation penalty. The latter is available only on Intel x86-based systems.

10   In NT 3.*x* the emulation was at the Intel 286 (AT-compatible) level. NT 4.0 improves the emulation to the 486 level, but with about the same performance constraints.

Unfortunately, they did not perform as *fast* on the MIPS system as on a real 486. The way SoftPC works is to *translate* each Intel instruction in the legacy application that is executing and then *emulate* the function of that instruction with one or more RISC instructions. In a string copy this might be no more than one instruction per byte. But that is *eight times* less efficient than the 486 implementation. In general, our experience is that the Soft PC emulation on NT RISC machines tends to require an average of five RISC instructions per Intel instruction. Thus it has the effect of slowing down the machine by a factor of five, and our clock-doubled 100MHz R4000 machine thus ran no faster than a 20MHz 386SX. Today, we'd expect a 333MHz DEC Alpha to run 16-bit applications with performance equivalent to that of a 66MHz 486, for exactly the same reason.

In fairness, this is a slight oversimplification. The raw integer performance from a 333MHz RISC machine running a 16-bit Intel application may be equivalent to that from a 66MHz 486, but other performance parameters will be much higher. RISC systems generally have high-performance video and disk subsystems, but what was said in Chapter 5 and Appendix 6 about the throughput chain and bottlenecks applies: overall performance is governed by the *slowest* component in the system, and with a 5:1 instruction overhead, *any* RISC CPU becomes a bottleneck when running legacy code.

32-Bit Windows Applications: The Holy Grail

Of course running largely 16-bit applications on a 32-bit RISC machine is slightly ridiculous. Doing so effectively cuts the clock rate of the machine by a factor of five, so you've bought 486 performance at a Pentium Pro price. However, as soon as 32-bit applications *compiled for the machine* become available, the situation changes. RISC machines can deliver results as good as or better than those for a Pentium Pro, and the fastest RISC processors can approach the performance of a dual-Pentium Pro SMP system.[11]

The principal problem with 32-bit Windows applications is that they must be compiled separately for each CPU architecture for optimum performance. That's a great burden for software developers. It means that the developer of a Windows NT utility, for instance, cannot simply compile one (presumably Intel-based) Windows NT executable file and ship it blindly assuming that it will work on every machine in sight. If the application is properly designed, it will run on all *Intel* machines including SMP machines without modification. But to provide a version for a RISC platform the developer must compile it for that specific platform. To support another platform the developer must compile it again. An application developer wishing to cover the entire market then must, as of today, supply at least four separate executable versions of each application: one for each family (we've also seen cases in which multiple versions are supplied for a given family, as for example, providing a standard Intel build and a special version optimized for the Pentium).

Of course, no software developer will put in that extra effort unless it believes its product will sell enough copies to justify the effort—and thus we arrive at *the chicken-and-the-egg*

---

11 See for example, the feature on NT CAD platforms in the February 1996 issue of *WIN-DOWS Magazine*.

problem. Before developers will put much effort into RISC, they need to see a viable market, and before end users will buy RISC machines (creating that market) they need to see a broad range of applications. You can see the results in Figure A5.3.

Not surprisingly, relatively few software developers are willing to expend the effort to port their programs to a RISC platform when doing so will add only single-digit percentages to their market (to be fair, the percentages for NT Server are probably higher). Examination of Microsoft's InfoSource CD shows that only 30% of the 4,000 NT-based programs listed support Alpha; fewer still support the Mips[12] or PowerPC architecture.

That's how the situation stood until September 1996—then Microsoft changed the rules.

32-bit Intel Applications on Any RISC: WX86

As we went to press with the third edition, Microsoft had just presented an online preview of technology that allows RISC-based NT systems to run Win32 applications written for the Intel architecture—including Windows 95 applications. That technology is called WX86 (Win32 x86 emulation on RISC) and is implemented as an add-on service for RISC machines. It's currently downloadable from Microsoft's Web site,[13] but will likely be added to a future NT service pack, and in any case, it will ship with NT 5.0 (AKA "Cairo") as discussed in Chapter 12.

WX86, though developed internally by Microsoft, works in exactly the same way as Insignia Systems' Soft-PC: it translates Intel instructions (in this case, 32-bit instructions) into native RISC instructions on the fly. The process is somewhat simpler with 32-bit

Processor Architecture Share of NT Market (1995)

■ Intel x86 (93%)
■ Digital Alpha AxP21x64 (4.4%)
□ Mips R4x00 (2.2%)
■ Motorola PPC 6xx (0.4%)

FIGURE A5.3 NT Market share by processor architecture (1995). Intel-based systems account for well over 90% of the NT market. Source: Download counts of processor-specific NT software in CompuServe's WINNT forum.

---

12 Late-breaking news: In October 1996, Microsoft announced that further development of NT was being terminated for Mips-based systems, making NT 4.0 the last one to support the Mips R4x00 processor line.

13 The Web address at press time was http://www.microsoft.com/ntworkstation/x86.htm. Check our electronic update Webpage (discussed in the introduction) for current location.

instructions because there are no segments to load and unload, so a 32-bit emulator is potentially subject to less of a performance penalty than the 5:1 we've seen with NT's 16-bit emulator. However, early experience with WX86.EXE shows performance very similar to that of the existing 16-bit emulator.

We won't go into the details of how the WX86 preview is installed—that's bound to change as Microsoft updates the technology and makes it part of the operating system. It does have two special implications for RISC users: first, when WX86 is installed, it adds a *Force x86 Installation/Upgrade* check-box to the Add/Remove Programs item in Control Panel (see Figure A5.4). This is the primary method Microsoft recommends using to install Intel-based applications on a WX86-equipped RISC system (though our experience is that stand-alone Intel .EXE files can simply be executed as usual and will work). RISC users should also be aware that the WX86 preview takes up a substantial amount of disk space, which grows over time. A WINNT\SYSTEM32\WX86 directory contains Intel versions of system DLLs, and after brief use (among other things, installing MS Office 95) we observed this to grow to over 9MB.

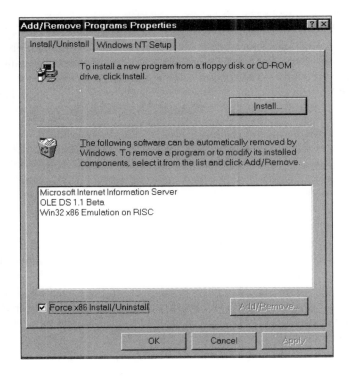

FIGURE A5.4 WX86: Add/remove programs. Microsoft's 32-bit x86 emulator for NT 4.0 RISC systems' (WX86) add-on provides a new check-box on the Add/Remove Programs wizard that allows you to force x86-mode setup. This is the only approved way to install 32-bit x86 (i.e., Windows 95) applications, though other methods may work.

Microsoft's WX86 isn't the only approach to getting Win95 applications to run on RISC. Indeed, Digital has been working on a competing technology for over two years, and may be on the verge of a breakthrough.

32-Bit Intel Applications on Alpha-RISC: FX!32

The great limitation of both Insignia Systems' Soft-PC and Microsoft's WX86 is that they translate applications on the fly. Consider an application that does one operation repetitively: the search or find function in any word processor, for example. A given set of instructions (load the next word or phrase into memory, check each byte against the target to see if it matches, continue) is executed over and over.

Now let's take an Intel program containing that function and run it on a RISC system using either Soft-PC (if it's a 16-bit program) or WX86 (if it's a 32-bit program). Every time that repetitive set of instructions is executed, each Intel instruction must be inspected and translated to an equivalent RISC instruction, *even though the same instructions are being issued over and over*. That's the root cause of the 5:1 penalty discussed earlier—emulation isn't done on a one-pass basis; it happens *continuously* as a program executes (Soft-PC uses a translation cache to minimize this, but the basic argument still applies).

There is another approach. An application can be completely translated from Intel to RISC instructions (a process known as *cross-compiling*), resulting in a native program that runs on the RISC architecture. This process has been common in the past on mainframe computers, but is rarely used on PCs because it's inherently inefficient. The resulting program is never as fast as one written specifically for the RISC architecture. It is, however, much more efficient than translating from one instruction set to another on the fly.

Digital's FX!32 technology is a cross-compiler for RISC systems running Intel's Alpha AXP-61*xxx* processors. Developed as an outgrowth of Digital's VAX cross-compiler technology, FX!32 works on a single-pass basis the first time non-native programs are loaded. On program load, translation occurs, resulting in a larger (typically by around 50%) native Alpha executable file with an execution penalty of around 2:1 or 3:1 rather than the 5:1 we've seen with Soft-PC and WX86.

Unfortunately, Digital has yet to make any preview or beta version of FX!32 widely available, let alone ship it.[14] There may be technical reasons for this (for example, applications that mix 16- and 32-bit modules can be easily handled with Soft-PC and WX86: just execute the 16-bit instructions on the former and the 32-bit instructions on the latter. How FX!32 would handle such a situation is unclear as this is written), and there are certainly legal ones. When an Intel executable runs on Soft-PC or WX86, it's unchanged—the emulator translates a few instructions at a time and immediately executes them, but no complete translation of the program ever exists. FX!32, however, creates a completely new program, whether on disk or in memory. That

---

14 Late-breaking development: Alpha-NT users can now download FX!32, free of charge, from Digital's Web site: http://www.service.digital.com/fx.32—and based on Digital's performance information, it works much, much, better than Microsoft's WX86.

typically isn't a problem in mainframe cross-compiling, in which the person running the cross-compiler owns all copyrights to the original program, but it may be a big problem if its done by an end user.

Digital has discussed an interesting strategy to avoid the legal issues with FX!32: running the cross-compiler only on program load and cross-compiling directly to memory. The new (RISC) version of an application then exists only in RAM, never on disk. That might be enough to satisfy the lawyers—it's too soon to say.

At any rate, those considering an Alpha RISC-based system would be well advised to keep an eye on Digital's Web site (http://www.digital.com) for more information.

Pentium/Pentium Pro: CISC Chips with RISC Performance

As if things were not already confusing enough, in 1993 Intel introduced its long-awaited Pentium chip, followed just two years later by the even more impressive Pentium Pro. The Pentium and Pentium Pro combine most of the generally accepted advanced features of RISC architectures with full x86 compatibility. In effect, they are RISC chips that happen to be x86 compatible. These chips appear to offer the best of all things. At a 200MHz external clock rate a Pentium Pro is capable of internal throughputs well over 400 MIPS. It has an eight-stage floating point pipeline that can achieve floating point execution rates of over 100 MFLOPS. It compares very favorably with the various RISC processors (as illustrated in Figure A5.1).

As members of Intel's x86 processor family, the Pentium and Pentium Pro don't suffer from the 16-bit emulation penalty.[15] Thus it would appear that those who are interested in RISC performance have an easy solution. Buy a Pentium Pro and get RISC performance without taking any "risks."

Again, matters are not so simple. First-generation Pentium chips suffered from high cost, high power consumption, and in rare cases, heating problems severe enough to cause system crashes. Intel solved these problems by 1994, only to have a floating-point math error surface that caused a major public relations flap. That problem was dealt with, too, and to date, no such problems have surfaced with the Pentium Pro (though controller chipsets for early Pentium Pro-based SMP systems exhibited contention problems—it seems that new processors cannot be introduced without some teething troubles).

Properly configured Pentium Pro-based systems can approach the performance of RISC systems for all but the most demanding applications—and generally at a much lower cost. In high-performance applications, SMP systems based on Pentium Pro processors can equal or beat equivalent RISC configurations (if necessary, by adding processors), albeit with all the SMP

---

15 The Pentium Pro is, however, more optimized for 32-bit than for 16-bit software, resulting in a curious situation: for users concerned mainly with legacy application compatibility, a fast Pentium may be a better choice! See, for example, the November 1995 issue of *WINDOWS Magazine*.

caveats mentioned above. And the Pentium Pro has one tremendous advantage over true RISC processors: it is *safe*. The widest possible range of software and peripherals is available for it: unlike with a RISC processor, you *can* run DOS, Windows 3.*x*, or even OS/2 on a Pentium Pro.

Which Alternative to Choose

Selecting a CPU architecture for Windows NT is a bottom-line decision that needs to be subject to a rigorous cost justification. *It is not a decision that should be made emotionally.* We have found several rules of thumb that may prove useful and developed a simple decision tree that can take you through the process of elimination, helping you make a rough decision about the types of system you should examine.

- Step One: Determine and *write down* your requirements.

- Step Two: Decide whether these requirements can be met by a conventional 386/486/Pentium/Pentium Pro-based PC-compatible system. (No cheating—this is not the time to worry about whether you have adequate growing room or whether this system will scale!) If you answered yes, stop here. The cost advantages of a PC-compatible, along with their known reliability and the huge supply of PC-compatible software, outweigh any other consideration. If you spend $2,000 or $3,000 today on a PC-compatible and you outgrow it, simply recycle that system to another application and upgrade to the next larger system.

- Step Three: Decide if 16-bit legacy application performance a major issue. If it is, don't bother with the RISC machines. Bear in mind that the RISC machines will always be a bad deal for 16-bit application support. It is true that higher-performance RISC machines will show higher 16-bit performance, but compare the $15,000 to $20,000 one pays for a RISC machine today with the few thousand dollars one pays for a PC-compatible. This same logic applies if you will run mainly Intel-based 32-bit code on a machine using Microsoft's WX86 or Digital's FX!32 technology.

- Step Four: If there is no other way to achieve acceptable performance, look at SMP. Because it is complex, SMP is expensive, but as mentioned earlier, SMP machines can deliver *thousands* of MIPS—performance that boggles the mind. There is no way (today) to achieve this performance with single processors.

One balancing thought: 16-bit applications are almost *never* run on servers. Therefore, it's worth noting that there is nothing to prevent you from running x86-based client systems on the LAN with a RISC-based server. And indeed, this combination can be cost effective. If 16-bit legacy application performance is a non-issue, take a close look at RISC. Why? Because dollar-per-MIPS RISC is always a better deal than SMP. The cost of any computer system is largely a function of the number of components in the system. Take the lid off the system and count the chips. You'll find you can get a very close correlation between the number of chips on the motherboard and the cost of the system. Indeed, the decreasing cost per performance of systems over the years is attributable to the fact that the density with which electronic components can be incorporated into a chip doubles approximately every 18 months.

If you've ever wondered why you never seem to get quite two years' use out of your system before it becomes obsolete, that's your answer. A single-processor RISC machine at any given performance level has approximately the same number of components as a single-processor classic x86 machine. The SMP machine, on the other hand, has to have a second processor, support chips to support that processor, cache RAM to support the second processor, and a more sophisticated memory controller architecture. Therefore, at a given performance level, the number of chips, and therefore the cost, increases. So if single-CPU Intel performance isn't enough and the 16-bit problem doesn't bother you, you need to look at RISC.

The only situation in which you should have any concern about RISC in a server environment is if you are concerned about application services rather than file and print services. If you are dependent on applications services or particularly interested in these services, it would be wise to check which platforms are supported before selecting a platform for your server. It would be an awful waste, for example, to burden a RISC-based server with the aforementioned 5:1 instruction penalty in order to run, say, an Intel version of a network database server. But again, for basic file and print services any RISC architecture is a good bet.

For More Information

Custer, Helen (1993), *Inside Windows NT.* Redmond, WA: Microsoft Press, ISBN: 1-55615-481-X. Good detail on how SMP and RISC systems are supported.

Patterson, David and John Hennessy (1988), *Computer Architecture—A Quantitative Approach.* San Mateo, CA: Morgan Kaufmann Publishers Inc., ISBN: 1-55880-069-8. Covers Amdahl's Law, which governs system performance in both single-processor and multiprocessor cases.

Van Zandt, John (1992), *Parallel Processing in Information Systems.* New York: John Wiley & Sons, Inc., ISBN: 0-471-54822-7. Good general work on multiprocessor systems.

Kane, Gerry and Joe Heinrich (1992), *MIPS RISC Architecture.* Englewood Cliffs, NJ: Prentice-Hall Inc., ISBN: 0-13-590472-2. Aside from details of the R4000/4400 architecture, Chapter 1 gives an outstanding overview of basic RISC theory and was extremely helpful in formulating this appendix.

Sites, Richard (1992), *Alpha Architecture Reference Manual.* Burlington, MA: Digital Press, ISBN: 1-55558-098-X. Not for the faint of heart, this is an engineering text on the Alpha CPU design. Interesting, but far too technical for general readers.

Appendix

Principles of Preventive Maintenance

6

Chapter 5 gives all the details available to us on the specific steps you can take to tune Windows NT system performance and correct faults when they happen, but a larger question is how to prevent the faults from happening in the first place. As we said in the opening to Chapter 5, the main approach to this is called preventive maintenance (or PM), and in this appendix we explore PM concepts in some detail.

In principle, computer *software* does not wear out (indeed, it tends to become *more* reliable with age), but hardware does. Computer software, in the main, doesn't wear out and should not normally require adjustment. Examination of one simple fact should show you that this nice theory breaks down when it's applied to a Windows NT network or any other network.

Why Does Software (and Hardware) Fail?

The probability of a piece of software malfunctioning is roughly proportional to the number of lines of code that make up that software, simply because the more code programmers write, the more likely they are to make a mistake. There's been a good deal written about Windows NT, much of it misinformation, but many writers seem to agree on one point: Windows NT 3.1 contained some *two million* lines of code. Would anyone care to bet that all two million lines of code were bug free? In fact, Microsoft released the first bug-fix disks just a few weeks after NT 3.1 shipped.

Even though the probability of failure of any single component, software or hardware, in a modern PC system may be infinitesimally small, that infinitesimal smallness has to be multiplied by the number of connections in a network. The basic microcomputer we know today can be described as a "state machine," a very large table that says when the input state is X, the output state is Y. Years ago, a state machine was the basic mechanism used to describe all sorts of interesting things ranging from simple switches to microprocessors. The state machine for a modern microprocessor is slightly large, the size of one's office perhaps. But the state machine that you'd need to describe a modern microprocessor, disk controller, video controller, several dozen megabytes of RAM, and the rest of a Windows NT PC would be *appallingly* large.[1]

It gets worse. Connect two of those machines on a network, and no one could write a state table that completely describes the resulting (very simple) network. The state of one machine may depend on the state of another. In a Windows NT network the size of each state machine is multiplied by the number of machines connected on the local segment, perhaps also by the state of the gateway that connects one segment to another, perhaps by the state of the server.

Such a system can't be described by the use of a state table. In a term borrowed from modern mathematics, such a system is, by definition, *chaotic*. It is describable only in probabilistic terms, but this doesn't mean the operational status of your network is a crap shoot! *You can load the dice*.

The way you can load the dice is to employ a technique that people in the insurance business have been using since time immemorial, *actuarial statistics*. Let's begin with one of the most overused terms in computing today, mean time between failure (MTBF). MTBF is the statistical number that's used to describe hardware reliability, and the MTBF numbers that are quoted are typically huge. It's not uncommon, for instance, to find a hard disk with an MTBF quoted at 30,000 hours. Because there are just 8,760 hours in a calendar year, it is not surprising that most people look at a 30,000-hour MTBF disk drive and assume that they don't have to worry about it for three years or so.

Such an attitude is naive. The MTBF refers to the *mean* time to failure—that is, the *average*. Although a disk drive may have a mean time to failure of 30,000 hours, it, in fact, may fail at 15,000 hours or it may run perfectly up to 45,000 hours. You can't make a precise prediction

---

1   If you write very small, it could be the size of the state of New York. Then again, given the permutations introduced by the state of the RAM, a Windows NT state table *might* be larger than the size of the known universe!

of exactly how long a disk drive will operate, but on average, it will operate for 30,000 hours. This becomes significant if you have an installation with a large number of disk drives. Let's say, for instance, that your organization bought 10 drives with a mean time to failure of 30,000 hours. Because each disk drive has a mean time to failure of over three years, the naive approach would be to assume you could run them all for three years and then buy 10 new disk drives. But let's look at the statistics.

With ten drives operating, the probability of failure is multiplied. It is now *10* chances in 30,000, or *one chance in 3,000 hours*. 3,000 is a good bit less than one year! So the probability that one of the 10 drives will fail within the first year is very high. The way you approach this problem is to buy insurance in the form of buying spare disk drives. If you have 10 of these drives, you can be reasonably certain that one will fail the first year. So don't buy 10, buy 11. Then you have the hardware in position and can respond as quickly as possible once the failure occurs.

The second thing you can do is monitor the performance of all 10 disk drives because disk drives, being electromechanical devices, very often will give some indication of failure before they fail completely. You may begin to notice a high error rate, low data transfer rate, continuing detection of soft errors, or any of a variety of signs that will give you early warning of an impending failure *if you take the time to look for the warning*.

Therefore, by keeping a maintenance history of all 10 disk drives and comparing them, you *may* be able to determine that a drive will fail before it does, but you can never be certain of predicting that, so you can't wait and buy a spare disk drive when the maintenance history begins to indicate that a drive failure is likely. You may get no warning at all, depending on the nature of the failure.

You also can't wait and assume that you will be able to transfer data from a drive onto a new disk drive after it has given indications that it will fail. For this reason it's essential to run backups of mission-critical information so that you're in a safe position, in the worst case. If the drive has failed without giving any prior indication, you're in a position to pop in a new disk drive and restore the backup data and lose no more than the last 24 hours of work or so. This consideration should be looked at very carefully when you are establishing the backup procedures for your organization. If you can't afford to lose 24 hours of work, do backups more frequently than once every 24 hours!

The Mathematics of Fault Prediction

As we've seen in the preceding section, probably the most critical number one deals with in setting up a maintenance system for Windows NT (or any other hardware/software environment) is the mean time between failures (MTBF). This number is generally part of the specifications for any hardware device. When you're quoted a price on a system, if you look closely at the specifications, you will see an MTBF listing. You will also see MTBF listings for disk drives, memory components, and so forth.

For software, of course, MTBFs are never stated because the software industry persists in a naive belief, first of all, that it can produce things that never fail and also, one suspects, that the software industry would be unwilling to publish its MTBF numbers because they are likely to be so poor. However, it is possible to achieve a statistically valid set of MTBF information over time simply by recording how frequently errors occur and building your own database. In any case, with MTBF information available to you, it becomes possible to get quite elaborate in predicting the availability of a system and making statistical predictions that you can use to determine when problems are likely to occur and then fix them before they do.

Availability and Reliability

Of course the goal of any system maintenance project should be to maintain the highest possible availability of the overall end-to-end system. Achieving a 100% availability is impossible, but you can get quite close to it if you pay sufficiently close attention to the reliability of individual components.

We begin with some definitions and simple mathematics to provide insight into what's happening. First is the reliability of a system. Assuming a constant failure rate, (that is, that on average failures occur at a fairly constant interval), it can be shown that the reliability over time will follow the equation:

$$\mathbf{r}(t) = e^{-\mathbf{a}t} \quad 2$$

where: $\mathbf{r}$ is the reliability at any given time, $\mathbf{t}$ is time the component has been in operation, and $\mathbf{a}$ is a constant characteristic of the component in question.

If you know these figures for the reliability, you can predict the mean time between failure (MTBF), which is equal to $1/\mathbf{a}$ (and you can get $\mathbf{a}$ if you have the MTBF: it's just $\mathbf{a} = 1/\text{MTBF}$). See Figure A6.1 for a graph of MTBF for a hypothetical hardware component.

This model is generally accurate for hardware components, but not for software, because hardware tends to wear out. After an initial burn-in period (which isn't covered by this equation), hardware will be at its most reliable when it is new, and then it wears out over a period of time at a generally constant rate. So reliability falls off with time, as shown by the equation.

The equation for software tends to be exactly the opposite. A new piece of software is apt to be buggy, but it will tend to become less buggy over time as bugs are found and fixed. There is no simple equation that can describe this model adequately for all cases. One that is widely used will have the unavailability over time go as:

$$u(t) = \mathbf{a}(1 - e^{-\mathbf{b}t/\mathbf{a}})$$

where $\mathbf{a}$ is the total number of defects, and $\mathbf{b}$ is a system-dependent constant.

The mean time between defects then is:

$$\text{MTBD} = (1/\mathbf{b})e\mathbf{a}^{t/\mathbf{b}}$$

---

2   This and other equations in this appendix are taken from *Introduction to Client/Server Systems* by Paul Renaud (details in "For More Information" at the end of this appendix). Although the author disagrees with Renaud's centralized approach to systems management, his book is very, very good!

Reliability of Hardware Components

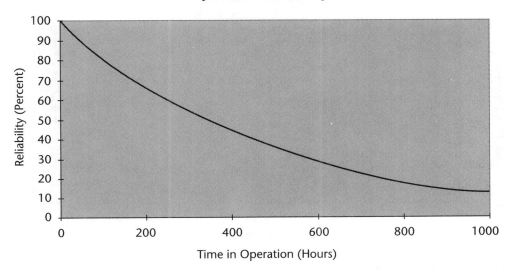

FIGURE A6.1 MTBF for hardware. Reliability of hardware components falls off over time after an initial burn-in period; thus, as components become old they are certain to fail.

Because a failure is, by definition, a defect, this equation also covers MTBF. The best way to find the *a* and *b* constants is by collecting data on a software system over time and then fitting the equation to the data. The fit will tend to improve with time as the amount of data increases. For instance, if you're running a piece of database software, the appropriate thing to do is to maintain a log of the bugs that are discovered in the software, the frequency with which they are discovered, and the time it takes to get a repair or a bug fix in place. It's then possible over time to fit the equation to the statistics. Please note that this equation will essentially start again when you upgrade to a new piece of software. New versions, although they will never be as unreliable as the first version,[3] will represent a new start to the equation, so the curve will not be a simple downward slope as one might expect. Figure A6.2 shows the MTBD for hypothetical software undergoing a major revision.

Similarly, the MTBF equation given earlier does not cover the burn-in period for hardware. For instance in our "buy 11 disk drives" example, you might burn in all 11 disk drives for some time before they're actually used. A general rule of thumb is that the burn-in period should be on the order of one-tenth of 1% of the total life of the drive. For a 30,000-hour MTBF disk drive, therefore, the burn-in period should be on the order of 30 hours. You can have a laboratory or maintenance shop set up with a test stand so that individual pieces of

---

3   Now you know where the expression *"never buy version one of anything"* comes from!

Reliability of Software

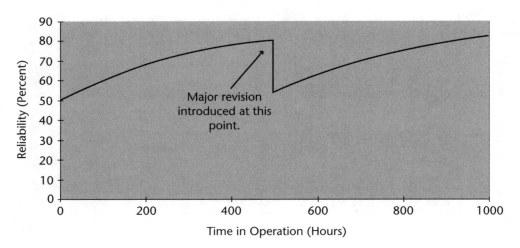

FIGURE A6.2 MTBD for software. In contrast to that for hardware, the reliability of software *improves* over time, except for temporary unreliability introduced by new versions.

equipment can be subjected to continuous testing. A relatively simple program written in BASIC that will cycle the disk drive continuously, writing data and reading it back, is sufficient. Then run it for a 30-hour burn-in period, and once this is complete (assuming that the disk hasn't had any problems), format the disk and store it. A disk can then be taken out and installed when required. The odds are quite high that any burn-in defects will be detected during the burn-in period. That is, the drive will fail, at which point you can conveniently send it back to the manufacturer for replacement, because this will happen within the warranty period.

Given that the MTBF (or MTBD) is known, the one remaining factor that affects availability is the Mean Time to Repair (MTTR). This will be the time that it takes to correct the defect by replacing a failed disk drive or finding and fixing a bug in the software (or providing a workaround, like reindexing a corrupted database, for instance). Given this number, the availability of any component is then given by:

`A = MTBF/(MTBF + MTTR)`

Components in Series

You can compute the availability of a system that depends on a number of components connected in series by multiplying the availability of the individual components. As an example, suppose that you have a network system that's used to back up data on three file servers. If we ignore the issue of software reliability, the availability of the total backup will be equal to:

$$a_{Total} = a_1 \times a_2 \times a_3 \times a_{BS} \times a_{Net}$$

where:

a_1, a_2, a_3 = Availability for file servers 1 through 3, respectively

a_{BS} = Availability of the backup system

a_{Net} = Availability of the network

If the backup system and file servers all have 99% availability, and the network has 90% availability, the total availability will be:

$$a_{Total} = .99 \times .99 \times .99 \times .99 \times .90 = .87$$

That is, the total reliability is just 87%. Notice that the governing factor is always the *least* reliable component, which will tend to reduce the reliability of the entire system, something that should be obvious from common sense in any case.

Redundancy

If you have a system with a certain number *n* of redundant components, and the operation of the system depends on the correct functioning of only one, the overall availability will be:

$$a_{Overall} = 1-((1-a_1) \times (1-a_2) \ . \ . \ . \ (1-a\mathbf{n}))$$

where **n** is the number of components in parallel.

Suppose, for example, that you have a server that contains two mirrored disk drives, each of which has an MTBF of 10,000 hours and a mean time to repair of two hours. Availability of each drive will be over 99.98%, but the availability of the mirrored pair will be:

$$a_{Overall} = 1-((1-.9998) \times (1-.9998)) = .9999999 \text{ or } 99.99999\%$$

The overall availability in this case is actually *higher* than the availability of any single component—exactly the opposite of the series case discussed above. This is the reason that the highest-reliability systems are achieved by the maximum use of redundant components. Indeed, in the ultimate case, in which one must deal with systems that cannot be permitted to crash, one will typically run actual backup servers and employ mechanisms like Windows NT Server's *directory replication*[4] feature to see that the data on one server is always duplicated on the second server.

What Do We Do with These Numbers?

As was covered in Chapter 4, Windows NT includes some extremely sophisticated built-in system performance-monitoring and event-logging features. We suggest that you maintain a continuous maintenance history on your system based on the information from the event log and the performance monitor. If you maintain this information over the life of your system, you can apply to it the mathematics we have just described, and you will find that you then know a great deal more about the system behavior than you would otherwise.

---

4   See Chapter 7 for details on replication.

For example, you can, on a regular basis, conduct some simple performance tests on a system. First, examine event logs to note whether there have been any disk errors. If there have been errors, enter them into a statistical log and have the cause of the errors investigated. If you graph these disk errors over time, you are likely to find that they will fit the hardware reliability equation given earlier. As these errors begin to arise, you'll see that the reliability is decreasing with time, and at some point it will become apparent to you that if this trend continues, the component will fail. This is the time to replace the disk drive—*before* it fails.

Similarly, you can maintain a record of overall system performance for a variety of components: the CPU, disks, network, and so on. This can be particularly valuable in two ways. First, just as with maintaining a record of information on the disk drive, it'll let you predict failures before they occur. The other important advantage is that the record can help you detect system bottlenecks and maximize throughput.

Predicting failures and detecting system bottlenecks becomes particularly important as networks grow. Initially, you may be able to simply stick network cards in PCs, link them together into an Ethernet, and assume that everything will work. But as the network becomes larger and larger, some inherent limitations of the hardware will start to show up. Ethernet has a maximum throughput (on conventional 10-base-2 or 10-base-T cabling) of 10 million bits per second. It should be obvious, for instance, that if you continue to add machines to an Ethernet segment, you will eventually find that you are trying to push more than 10 million bits down the wire each second. You can't do that. And you will find that your overall system performance will degrade because of something called *the queuing effect*.

The Queuing Effect and Performance Tuning

In any kind of a shared service environment (such as a network) multiple simultaneous requests for access to the service must be *queued;* that is, they are suspended while they await a response. Each request will then experience some delay before it can be responded to. The relationship between these factors is covered by the equation:

$$r = ns/t$$

where **r** is the response time, **ns** is the average number of requests competing for service, and **t** is the overall throughput (responses per second) of the service. Obviously, the response time increases as the number of requests increases.

This equation, for instance, governs the response time of a server with multiple clients competing for a response, say, from a database server with multiple clients attempting to access it simultaneously. Response time will increase as the load on the server increases. If simple queuing effects apply (actual queuing models can become quite complex, and although the mathematics involved are fascinating, they are far beyond the realm of this book), one can estimate the utilization of the system and the delay due to queuing according to a very simple model.

Utilization of the system will be governed by the equation:

$$U = r/x$$

where **r** is the rate of requests per second and **x** is the maximum throughput in transactions per second. Thus, if the number of requests per second is equal to the transactions per second, you have a utilization of 1.0 or 100%. The delay due to queuing will then be:

```
d=(U/x)/(1-U)
```

Total response time for the system will be the sum of the delay due to queuing plus the amount of time needed to process the request:

```
R = d + 1/x
```

The *perceived* throughput at any workstation will then be equal to **1/R** (that is, users will see the system as slow because they see a slow response), although the actual system throughput will always be equal to the arrival rate (**r**). As the system becomes fully loaded, each workstation will experience a slowdown and will perceive the system as being slow when—in fact—the system is working at full capacity. That by itself is the single most important implication of the overall queuing equation for our purposes.

It's also important to understand that queuing effects occur for networks just as they do for servers. In effect, you can treat the LAN or WAN in a system as being a sort of server from the point of view of queuing delays. And, again, bear in mind that the maximum throughput of an Ethernet is 10 million bits per second. It should be obvious that the perceived response degrades as the number of requests on the system begins to approach 10 million bits per second.

For example, if some number of clients on an NT-based LAN generate 50 packets per second over a 1,000,000-bit-per-second network, and the packets have a mean size of 8,192 bits (1KB, the standard packet size for NT's NetBEUI protocol), the throughput will be:

```
x = 1,000,000/8,192 or 122.1 packets per second
```

Utilization will be:

```
U=50 / 122.1 = .41 or 41%
```

Then **d** will be equal to six milliseconds, and perceived throughput will be 71 packets per second. The significance of this example is that although the total throughput that the network experiences is 122.1 packets per second, *perceived* throughput at any station is only 71 packets per second. This is key to understanding how low-data-rate lines in a WAN environment can become a bottleneck.

The Throughput Chain

Any network is inherently an end-to-end system. There is a "chain" of throughputs involved that extends from the client to the server. Consider a system in which each client CPU can process 1,000 transactions per second, the network interface cards can handle 1,000 packets per second, the LAN can carry 10,000 packets per second before saturating, routers can forward 5,000 packets per second, the WAN can handle 500 packets per second, and the server CPU can handle 5,000 transactions per second, but the server's only disk can perform just 50 I/O accesses per second. Then you have a chain extending from the client through the network interface to the LAN to the router to the WAN to the server to the disk, but the fastest that this overall system can work is only 50 transactions per second, assuming that a transaction requires one disk operation.

The server's disk drive is now the bottleneck for this system. If we upgrade the server's disk drive to something that can handle 3,000 I/O operations per second, the governing factor will be the next slowest link in the chain—the WAN that can only handle 500 packets per second. It's important in examining the operation of an end-to-end system to examine the throughput of each component, looking for the slowest one, which is called a *bottleneck*.

The issue of performance tuning then is simply to find and eliminate all bottlenecks (see the "Performance Tuning" section of Chapter 5).

For More Information

Renaud, Paul (1993), *Introduction to Client/Server Systems*. New York: John Wiley & Sons, Inc., ISBN: 0-471-57774-X. This is an *outstanding* text on maintenance and performance, as well as general LAN issues, in addition to providing good client/server coverage.

Jain, Raj (1991), *The Art of Computer Systems Performance Analysis*. New York: John Wiley & Sons, Inc., ISBN: 0-471-50336-3. A much deeper treatment of performance issues than Renaud's; Jain gets deep into queuing theory, simulation, and modeling.

Fortier, Paul (1992), *Handbook of LAN Technology, Second Edition*. New York: McGraw-Hill, Inc., ISBN: 0-07-021625-8. Good modeling and simulation coverage, along with excellent general coverage of LANs from an engineering perspective.

Index

X

Z